Disraeli

Disraeli

SARAH BRADFORD

STEIN AND DAY/*Publishers*/New York

First published in the United States of America in 1983

Copyright © 1982 by Sarah Bradford

All rights reserved, Stein and Day Incorporated

Printed in the United States of America

STEIN AND DAY / *Publishers*
Scarborough House
Briarcliff Manor, N.Y. 10510

Library of Congress Cataloging in Publication Data

Bradford, Sarah.
  Disraeli.

  Bibliography: p.
  Includes index.
  1. Disraeli, Benjamin, Earl of Beaconsfield, 1804-1881.   2. Great Britain — Politics
and government — 1837-1901.   3. Prime ministers — Great Britain — Biography.   I. Title.
DA564.B3B78 1983   941.081′092′4 [B]   82-42728
ISBN 0-8128-2899-2

For William

Contents

List of Illustrations   ix
Acknowledgements   xi
Introduction   xiii

1 The Byronic Youth   1
2 The First Fall   13
3 Eastern Odyssey   27
4 The First Steps   45
5 Dreams of Fair Women   59
6 Roundabouts and Swings   77
7 Mary Anne   95
8 A Rising Talent   111
9 Young England   128
10 Peel's Adversary   147
11 Emotional Undercurrents   161
12 The Mystery Man   177
13 The Jew and the Jockey   189
14 Public Affairs and Private Friendships   206
15 The Restless Fifties   222
16 A Time for Reflection   242
17 Disraeli v Gladstone   259
18 The Top of the Greasy Pole   274
19 Success and Sorrow   287
20 Power and the Affections   306
21 To the Elysian Fields   320
22 The Road to Berlin   335
23 The Last Defeat   354
24 The Twilight of Existence   375

Epilogue   391
Notes   395
Manuscript Sources   407
Bibliography   409
Index   417

Illustrations

Benjamin D'Israeli, artist unknown (*National Trust*)
Sarah D'Israeli by F. Ferrière (*National Trust*)
Isaac D'Israeli by J. Downman (*National Trust*)
Maria D'Israeli by J. Downman (*National Trust*)
Sarah D'Israeli by Daniel Maclise (*National Trust*)
Mary Anne Disraeli by Francis Rochard (*National Trust*)
Disraeli aged twenty-eight by C. Martin (*National Trust*)
Portrait of Disraeli by von Angeli (*By gracious permission of Her Majesty the Queen*)
George Smythe by Richard Buckner (*National Trust*)
Count d'Orsay by John Wood (*National Trust*)
Lord George Bentinck by Samuel Lane (*National Portrait Gallery*)
Lord John Manners, after Sir Francis Grant (*National Trust*)
Lord Lyndhurst by d'Orsay and Landseer (*National Trust*)
Edward Bulwer Lytton, after Daniel Maclise (*National Trust*)
Lord Henry Lennox; cartoon by Ape in *Vanity Fair*, 30 July 1870
    (*Mansell Collection*)
Anne, Countess of Chesterfield, after Landseer (*National Trust*)
Selina, Countess of Bradford, after Sir Francis Grant (*National Trust*)
Caroline Norton and Helen Blackwood by J. Swinton
    (*Marquess of Dufferin and Ava*)
Sir Francis and Lady Sykes by Daniel Maclise (*National Portrait Gallery*)
Montague Corry by von Angeli (*National Trust*)
Edward Stanley, 14th Earl of Derby, by F. R. Say (*National Portrait Gallery*)
The younger Edward Stanley, 15th Earl of Derby, by Samuel Laurence
    (*National Portrait Gallery*)
H. M. Queen Victoria, after von Angeli (*National Trust*)
Disraeli, cartoon by Singe in *Vanity Fair*, 6 February 1869 (*Mansell Collection*)
Gladstone, cartoon by Singe in *Vanity Fair*, 6 February 1869 (*Mansell Collection*)

Acknowledgements

No modern biographer of Disraeli can fail to acknowledge a major debt to the definitive works on the subject by Moneypenny and Buckle and by Robert Blake. I should also like to express my thanks to the editors of the Disraeli Project for allowing me the advantage of consulting in advance the first two volumes of the *Letters* (1982).

I owe a debt of gratitude to the following for their help and for permission to use archives and privately printed sources:

Her Majesty the Queen for her gracious permission to quote previously published material from the Royal Archive, the Marquess of Dufferin and Ava, the Marquess of Northampton, the Marquess of Salisbury, the Earl of Bradford, the Earl of Carnarvon, the Earl of Derby, the Lord Rothschild, the Princesse Jeanne-Marie de Broglie, the late Comtesse Corisande de Gramont, Mrs Barbara North and the Trustees of Hughenden Manor, the Trustees of the Broadlands Estate, Mr Paul Woudhuysen and the Syndics of the Fitzwilliam Museum, Mr I.G. Sparkes of the Wycombe Central Library, the staff of the British Library of Political and Economic Science, the staff of the Public Record Office of Northern Ireland, Mr Gordon Phillips of the Archives of *The Times*, Mr Douglas Matthews and the staff at the London Library, Professor John P. Matthews of the Disraeli Project, Dr Peter Gordon, Dr R.L. Davids, Mr R.P. Hook, Mr Christopher Falkus, Mr John Curtis, Mr John Gross, Miss Elizabeth Burke, Miss Julia Brown, and my husband, William Ward.

Introduction

On the day of Disraeli's death a colleague wrote of him, 'a large character has disappeared from the stage ... a man who will be a puzzle and a subject of wonder'. Yet, despite the multiplicity of the roles Disraeli played – novelist, professional politician, romantic lover, parliamentary duellist, country squire, royal courtier and, finally, elder statesman, there remains an integrity between the private life and the public career of this complex man. Knowledge of his private behaviour is as essential to an understanding of the man as is the interpretation of his political career. This book is an attempt to explore his inner life – his intricate relationships, private disasters, hopes and fears – and to relate this to his often enigmatic public face. I have relied upon contemporary letters, diaries and memoirs to give a picture of Disraeli as others saw him; but, above all, upon the essential source, Disraeli himself.

A considerable body of material, much of it relating to Disraeli's non-political career, has emerged since the publication of the official Life by Moneypenny and Buckle (6 vol, 1910–20) and Robert Blake's magisterial Disraeli (1966). Research by the Disraeli Project, engaged in the vital task of publishing a definitive edition of Disraeli's letters, has not only discovered many unpublished letters, but also the existence of a hitherto unknown novel written by Disraeli and his sister Sarah. An important letter by Disraeli to his sister has recently come to light indicating that contrary to previous belief, he did, on one occasion at least, deceive his wife. The strains in this apparently perfect marriage are further revealed in Disraeli's clandestine correspondence with his sister Sarah, letters which as yet remain unpublished from the major sources of Disraeli papers. The Dufferin Papers in the Public Record Office of Northern Ireland have produced evidence of an early romance with Helen Blackwood, and, thanks to the kindness of the Earl of Bradford, I have been able to examine Disraeli's letters to Lady Bradford, a considerable portion of which were expurgated from the edition of the Letters by the Marquess of Zetland (2 vol, 1920). Lastly, Professor J. R. Vincent has edited the journals of Lord Stanley, later fifteenth Earl of Derby, who was first Disraeli's protégé, then his colleague; these throw important new light on both his political actions and his private beliefs and behaviour.

I have referred to my subject throughout as 'Disraeli', the name by which he is best known, although in August 1876 he became Earl of Beaconsfield. Born D'Israeli, as a young man he quickly dropped the apostrophe.

Disraeli

1 *The Byronic Youth*

Benjamin Disraeli was born at half-past five on the morning of Friday 21 December 1804 at 6 King's Road, Bedford Row, now 22 Theobald's Road, in Bloomsbury. On the eighth day following, in accordance with Jewish custom, he was circumcised and his birth entered in the register of the synagogue of Bevis Marks to which his parents belonged.

Neither his ancestry nor his surroundings were as exotic as Disraeli would have liked; indeed in later life he romanticized the first and turned his back upon the second. Three months before his death he was to tell a friend, Lord Barrington, who questioned him on the subject: 'I was born in a set of chambers in the Adelphi – I may say in a library for all my father's rooms were full of books.'[1] It is doubtful whether Disraeli ever saw the set of chambers which he claimed as his birthplace; his father, Isaac D'Israeli, had lived there as a bachelor, before his marriage in February 1802, but moved in the spring of that year to 6 King's Road. This curious inaccuracy was typical of Disraeli, who was frequently (and deliberately) vague; his dislike of the commonplace would not allow him to accept the facts of his birth as being as middle class and undramatic as they really were.

Bloomsbury, where Disraeli was born and where he spent the first two decades of his life, was, much as it is now, an area of dignified, brick-fronted eighteenth-century houses, then largely inhabited by the professional classes, chiefly lawyers and men with interests in the City. For Disraeli's father, Isaac, whose absorbing passion was literary research, the great advantage of the area lay in its proximity to the British Museum; it was home ground for his wife, Maria, who had lived in Biliter Square before her marriage, while her near relations, the Basevis and Lindos, also lived in the district. It was genteel, quiet, stuffy and dull, far removed from the London of the aristocratic establishment which ruled England, the world of politics and fashion for which the young Disraeli was to yearn; and which he later was to enter and dominate. This world centred upon Mayfair and St James's, the great noble houses, Parliament and the clubs.

The central fact of Disraeli's birth and indeed of his whole life was his Jewishness; in the terms of early nineteenth-century England this meant political and social impotence, even isolation. Until the rise of the English house of Rothschild in the second quarter of the century, a Jew was barred by religion from entering the political establishment and by birth from entering Society. The way in which Disraeli was to come to terms with what was the principal obstacle to his advancement is vital to an understanding of his character and outlook. He was a man of middle-class birth and moderate means in a world in which aristocratic blood and money were the only things that counted. Yet he felt himself innately superior, an aristocrat by instinct; the only way in which he could face up to and enter the world of politics and power for which he longed and for which he felt himself destined was by glorying in his ancient lineage as a Jew. He was to describe his situation in one of his early novels, *Contarini Fleming*:

> Was then this mixed population of Saxons and Normans, among whom he had first seen the light, of purer blood than he? Oh no, he was descended in a direct line from one of the oldest races in the world, from that rigidly separate and unmixed Bedouin race who had developed a high civilization at a time when the inhabitants of England were going half-naked and eating acorns in their woods.[2]

Disraeli's Jewishness, instead of being a humiliating fact to be concealed, became something to be gloried in, an aristocracy of race far older, and therefore superior, to a mere territorial nobility going back less than a thousand years. But Disraeli, being the man he was, could not let well enough alone; he was a Jew and therefore a natural aristocrat – he must also be an aristocratic Jew, descended from the great Iberian families of the Sephardim. In 1849 in his foreword to an edition of his father's works, he claimed:

> My grandfather was an Italian descendant of one of those Hebrew families whom the Inquisition forced to emigrate from the Spanish Peninsula at the end of the fifteenth century, and who found refuge in the more tolerant territories of the Venetian republic [where] they flourished as merchants for more than two hundred years under the protection of the Lion of St Mark.

There was not a word of truth in this, as there was none in his further claim that, on reaching Venice in the fifteenth century, the family changed their name to D'Israeli, 'a name never borne before or since by any other family'. In fact the name Israeli (El Israeli) is not Italian but Arabic, commonly used in the East to denote Jewish origin, and in all probability the family emigrated from Turkey via Ancona to Cento in the district of Ferrara where there was a considerable Jewish community. Very little is known of the D'Israeli family beyond Disraeli's grandfather, also named Benjamin, who was born at Cento in 1730, the son of one Isaac Israeli, of whose position in life there is no record.

Benjamin D'Israeli emigrated to England at the age of seventeen, becoming established in 1757 as an importer of straw hats, alum, marble and other Italian goods. This business having failed, he later resumed operations both as a merchant and as a stock jobber, made a moderate fortune, was a member of the Committee which built the Stock Exchange of 1801, retired as a qualified member of the

Exchange two years later and died in 1816 leaving £35,000. Disraeli's paternal grandmother, Sarah Shiprut de Gabay, whom Benjamin the Elder married as his second wife in 1765, had better connections. Her father was a wealthy London merchant related to the great Jewish family of Villareal, while her mother was sister-in-law to the Rabbi of Venice, Simon Calimani.

Disraeli liked to represent his grandfather as living a gentlemanly life at his country house at Enfield, regaling his guests with exquisite dishes of macaroni and playing whist with the cultivated Sir Horace Mann. (This was almost certainly untrue since Benjamin the Elder took the Enfield house in 1780 and Sir Horace Mann who died in 1786 never left Florence in the last years of his life.) Enfield was given up in 1794 when Benjamin took a house at Woodford, where he tried his hand unsuccessfully as a gentleman farmer for three years. Benjamin the younger remembered his grandfather as a good-natured man 'who was in the habit of giving me presents when his wife was away'. He must have had an aptitude for business which, perhaps fortunately, he transmitted neither to his son nor to his grandson, and possibly some social ambition too, expressed in his attempts to break out of the traditional City-Jewish mould by leading the life of an English country gentleman at Enfield and Woodford. These experiments having failed, he returned to London where, after his retirement in 1803, he lived at Church Street, Stoke Newington, becoming known locally as 'Old Mr Israel'.

Such a designation cannot have pleased Benjamin's wife, Sarah Shiprut, whose frustrated social yearnings may have been chiefly responsible for the move from the City to Enfield. Sarah's proud, hard nature impressed itself on her grandson's memory more deeply than her husband's kindness did, for he over thirty years later remembered her as a 'demon' whose tyrannical nature equalled that of Catherine the Great of Russia. He could also write understandingly of her that she was not 'incapable of deep affection but [was] so mortified by her social position that she lived until eighty without indulging in a tender expression'.[3] She did not care to mix with Jews and could not mix with English Gentiles, and therefore lived out her life in frustration and bitterness. One cannot help feeling that the strong ambition and inner fibre which her grandson Benjamin possessed to such a notable degree may have been inherited from his fierce grandmother. Benjamin remembered his Sunday visits to her as a boy 'with horror' - 'no public conveyances, no kindness, no tea, no tips - nothing'. Her hardness was so notorious that when, on the occasion of a visit to the younger D'Israelis, she was seen to be unusually mellow, her daughter-in-law Maria correctly prophesied: 'Depend upon it - she is going to die.' She died in 1825, aged eighty-two, being, in her grandson's words, 'informally a Protestant' at her death.[4]

Her son, Isaac, Disraeli's father, born at 5 Great St Helen's on 11 May 1766, was quite unlike his ill-assorted parents. With 'a mind utterly unfitted for every species of business', he was, according to his son, a pale, pensive child who showed early signs of a rebellious poetical temperament. On one occasion he is said to have run away from home after a quarrel with his mother and to have been found lying morbidly on a tombstone in Hackney churchyard. Benjamin the Elder, who 'took it for granted that a boy in a passion wanted a toy or a guinea', then 'embraced him and gave him a pony'. He was sent to a private school at Enfield where he learned little but displayed literary tendencies which alarmed his parents who despatched him to stay with his father's agent in Amsterdam to study under a free-thinking tutor. Isaac returned even more inclined towards a literary career; his father threatened to send him to join a business in Bordeaux; he riposted by dashing off a poem against commerce. He later recalled his early clashes with his parents in a deeply-felt footnote to his novel *Vaurien*: 'Literary Jews must always be rare ... their most malignant and powerful enemies will be found among their domestic associates'. Defying his parents, he continued to write indifferent essays and verse until his father once again lost patience and sent him to study in Paris and to travel through the Rhineland, France and Italy from 1788–9.

Returning to England in 1789, Isaac produced his first and most lasting literary success, a volume of compilations entitled *The Curiosities of Literature*, published by John Murray I in 1791. The *Curiosities* earned him an immediate reputation and, by the time of his death in 1848, had run into at least thirteen editions. In the same year, 1791, his maternal grandmother Esther Shiprut died, leaving him enough money to be financially independent of his parents. At twenty-five Isaac had made a name for himself and could afford to devote himself to literature; unfortunately, although he was, as his son admitted, an indifferent poet and had little gift for fictional characterization, he still dreamed of making a reputation as an imaginative writer. His failure to do so led to a nervous breakdown from 1794–6 which curiously paralleled the breakdown of his son at almost the same age. He wrote verse, romances, Voltairean satire and novels, and it was not until 1811, after the failure of his last work of fiction, *Despotism*, that he finally admitted his lack of genius as a writer.

Isaac's literary career is chiefly interesting for the influence which it was to exert upon his son; until shortly before his death he was constantly either at work on a book or had one in the press and Benjamin was therefore brought up in a literary atmosphere. Like his father, Benjamin was to experiment with verse and Voltairean satire before finding his true form of expression in the political novel. Isaac wrote a scandalous social novel, *Flim-Flams*, in which contemporary figures were lampooned in extremely bad taste, a precursor of his son's more graceful *Vivian Grey*; while his last novel *Despotism*, with its melodramatic portrayal of the sinister European operations of the Jesuits, was to colour his son's conspiratorial view of the workings of international politics. Isaac's persistence in his literary career and his refusal to conform to the tradition that commerce was the only suitable way of life for a Jew provided not only the example, but also the background to his son's aspirations.

Isaac was a successful literary figure, but, it appears, not personally highly respected. His contemporaries found him faintly ridiculous; Robert Southey, who frequently dined with the D'Israelis when in London, was to write of him in 1822:

'An oddly-furnished head he has, and an odd sort of creature he is altogether; – thoroughly good-natured, the strangest mixture of information and ignorance, cleverness and folly.' Samuel Rogers, a doyen of the London social scene whose parties were more appreciated than his poetry, commented with more than a touch of envy: 'There is a man with only half an intellect; and yet he makes books that can't help living'. Another visitor, John Herman Merivale, found Isaac 'incredibly, almost ludicrously, dull in conversation, perpetually aiming at something like wit and attempting to tell a story, in which he uniformly fails in a manner burlesque enough for a stage character'.[5] It is strange to find such failings in the father of a man who was to be famous for his brilliant conversation; but Isaac differed from his son in many ways, both in appearance and character. He was fair-complexioned, with a round, cheerful face and a figure which quickly became corpulent, where his son was dramatically pale, sardonic in expression and always spare in figure. Isaac was fussy, short-tempered, and easily upset by small things, while Benjamin was to become famous for his self-control and public impassivity in the face of disaster.

Yet despite all the differences in character and temperament, Benjamin loved his father, and, as he later recorded, was greatly influenced by him, perhaps most of all because of what he called the 'poetical temperament' which he believed they shared. His mother, Maria Basevi, whom Isaac married in 1802, seems to have been in contrast a shadowy figure in his life. Maria was the daughter of Naphtali Basevi, a wealthy Jewish merchant of Biliter Square, Bloomsbury, who, like Benjamin D'Israeli the Elder, was a first generation Jewish immigrant of Italian origin, having emigrated from Verona and settled in London as a merchant in 1762. On her mother's side, however, she could boast of two or three generations of English and Jewish ancestors, and a prolific clan of relations, most of whom her son Benjamin was to despise or dislike.

The marriage of Isaac and Maria D'Israeli was, as their son described it, an 'excellent domestic match'. Maria was a pliant wife and a good housekeeper. As Isaac wrote with sublime selfishness to his friend, the collector Francis Douce, a year after their marriage, 'I have never yet found her desires interfere with my wishes, my pleasures are her pleasures, & my friends are her friends.'[6] Visitors to the D'Israeli household in Bloomsbury commented on the 'capital grub' to be had there, with such delights as 'asparagus, new potatoes, hot and cold desserts', and in later years Benjamin would send up from their country home at Bradenham to his aristocratic friends presents of his mother's dairy cheeses, home-cured hams, tongue and milk-fed pork, by which it will be seen that the D'Israeli family had no scruples about breaking Jewish dietary laws.

It is strange that, for a man like Disraeli, who adored women and depended upon them throughout his life, his relationship with his mother should have been relatively unimportant. He rarely corresponded with her when away from home and hardly mentioned her in his letters to his father and sister. While he was anguished at the death of his father, Maria's death seems to have made little impression on him, and, to his sister's chagrin, he made no mention of her in the affectionate and filial biographical sketch of his father with which he prefaced the commemorative edition of the *Curiosities of Literature* in 1849, although she had been dead only two years. She was 'an excellent domestic match' for Isaac and no more. Benjamin took her for granted; she provided his creature comforts and fussed over his health, but, with two younger sons to look after, she seems not to have been able to give him the undivided, adoring attention which he demanded from women. Benjamin required what he called 'sympathy' from women, and Maria, who was by no means intellectual, frequently ill, and absorbed by domestic cares, must have failed to satisfy his psychological needs, however well she may have ministered to his physical comforts. Disraeli's biographer, Robert Blake, has suggested that, since she failed him in this way, he sought a mother-figure in the other women in his life: his sister, his mistresses, and his wife, who were all, with one exception, older than he was. Certainly in Disraeli's early autobiographical novels, *Vivian Grey* and *Contarini Fleming*, fathers are portrayed as wise and loving, while mothers are somewhat unsympathetically represented. In *Contarini Fleming* in particular, the hero's stepmother is a stolid, unintellectual figure who is incapable of appreciating the dark, Byronic boy's passionate and poetic nature, lavishing her attention on his two uninteresting blond younger stepbrothers, who may well have symbolized Benjamin's own younger brothers, Ralph and James, both noticeably Anglo-Saxon in appearance. Maria, it seems, simply did not measure up to Disraeli's intellectual and romantic standards.

Benjamin found instead in his sister Sarah the intellectual companionship and supportive admiration he needed. Sarah, born on 29 December 1802, was almost exactly two years older than he, and resembled him in appearance, interests and quality of mind. Where the two younger brothers were fair and pink-complexioned, Sarah shared Benjamin's Jewish looks: his well-defined nose, dark hair and eyes, translucently pale, slightly olive skin. They were indeed more like twins than brother and sister in their passionate affection for each other which lasted all their lives. Sarah was a woman of strong character and intelligence who understood her brother as no one else did; and in return Benjamin, naturally secretive as he was, confided everything to her, as he did to no one else, not even his wife. Confined as she was to the domestic role expected of a woman of her time and station, Sarah found a vicarious outlet for her ability and energy in the career of her adored brother. As long as she lived she was to be, in his own words, his 'audience'.

Benjamin, Isaac, and Sarah formed a family triumvirate linked by intellectual sympathy. Benjamin's two surviving brothers (the second boy, Naphtali, having died in infancy) were considerably younger than he was, Ralph, born in 1809 being five years younger, and James, known as 'Jem', born in 1813, nearly ten years younger. Although Benjamin remained on friendly brotherly terms, more or less, with Ralph throughout most of his life, Ralph was essentially more pedestrian in talents and outlook than his brilliant elder brother, and never succeeded in scaling the social heights achieved by Benjamin, much as he would have liked to. James was of course far too young to be a companion to Benjamin and differed entirely from him in interests and intellect, being somewhat ill-educated despite attending Winchester, fond of horses, dogs and farming, and inclined to what Benjamin disgustedly termed 'low ties'.

It would, however, be wrong to think of the D'Israelis as a divided family; even such sophisticated visitors as the celebrated dandy Count d'Orsay were later to remark on the happy simplicity and 'patriarchal' atmosphere of their family life at Bradenham, the country house to which they moved in 1829. Despite Benjamin's later Byronic attitudes of being 'misunderstood', there is little doubt that during his childhood and early youth he was the focus of a comfortable and loving family. In the future, the quiet solidity of the family home was to provide a necessary haven to which he could retreat from the storms of an unexpectedly hostile world.

One may wonder when Benjamin first encountered that hostility; for him, as for most people, it was probably at school, and, no doubt, connected with his being a Jew. This is unlikely to have occurred during his first schooldays at Miss Roper's 'very high-class establishment' at Islington, which he attended at the age of six – more probably when he was a boarder at the Reverend John Potticary's 'academy' in Elliott Place, Blackheath. A schoolfellow of Benjamin's,[7] son of a Bloomsbury apothecary, remembered that he and another Jewish boy, Moses Saqui, 'stood back' during school prayers, and that they had weekly lessons in Hebrew; Benjamin must, even then, have been conscious of belonging to an alien minority. Other early school memories of Benjamin were of his kindness to younger boys, to whom he used to tell stories of robbers and caves, his fondness for acting – he once played Gratiano to Saqui's Shylock – and his precocious interest in public affairs. He subscribed to a newspaper, *Bell's Weekly Messenger*, and was the compiler and editor of what passed for the school paper which he sold on Saturdays at the price of a sheet of gingerbread.

At the age of thirteen, a change took place in Benjamin's life which was to have far-reaching consequences on his future career. On 31 July 1817 he was baptized a Christian, his father's intimate friend, Sharon Turner, on whose advice Isaac D'Israeli had taken this momentous step, standing as godfather. A complex combination of circumstances lay behind Isaac's decision; trouble had been brewing for some time at the Sephardi synagogue of Bevis Marks as a result of an ideological quarrel between the older members of the congregation (such as Benjamin D'Israeli the Elder) who upheld the old ghetto orthodoxy, and the proponents of the Mendelssohnian Reform movement which had spread from Germany, represented by the younger generation such as Isaac D'Israeli. In 1813, without consultation, Isaac was elected warden of the synagogue. He declined to serve, unwilling to take on anything which might interfere with his literary research, and out of sympathy with the ruling orthodox party at the synagogue. A row ensued and Isaac was fined £40, then a considerable sum, for his refusal.

Furious, he bided his time until the death of his father in 1816, when he terminated his connection with the synagogue, and although remaining a Reform Jew himself, had all his children baptized Christians. At the same time the family moved to the house at 6 Bloomsbury Square which was to be their home for the next ten years.

The simple ceremony of baptism changed the course of Benjamin's life. As a Christian he could now embark on the public career which remained closed to a practising Jew by the Test Acts. How far he was aware of this enlarged horizon is impossible to tell, but it is more than likely that Isaac should have explained to him the consequences of this change in religion, and it may be that the seed of his political ambition was sown at this moment when, for the first time, the possibility of a parliamentary future was opened to him. It was an age in which the power and prestige of Parliament were at their height; when politics was considered the only career for a gentleman, when parliamentary debates were eagerly followed (although often inaccurately reported) in the press, and membership of the House of Commons was considered the highest pinnacle to which a man could aspire. Outside that charmed circle of political power, nothing counted in the public eye, a fact of which the young Benjamin, as a regular newspaper reader, could hardly fail to be aware.

If Isaac D'Israeli, with his relaxed attitude towards Judaism, his connections with the London literary establishment, and, above all, his decision to have his children baptized as Christians, did much to orientate his son towards the mainstream of English life and Gentile society, his decision that Benjamin should be educated privately and not at public school, served, on the contrary, to isolate him from the experience of his contemporaries. Eton, Harrow, Winchester, Rugby and the other public schools formed the characters of English statesmen and administrators in the nineteenth century, who consequently moved from public school to university and to parliament as a homogeneous group, similar in birth, upbringing, education and outlook. Eton, above all, was the school for statesmen.

Benjamin bitterly resented the decision, for which, it appears, he blamed his mother. He had, he told a would-be biographer in 1860, been intended by his father for Winchester, and indeed both Ralph and James were later sent there. In his first autobiographical novel, *Vivian Grey*, the hero's mother could not be persuaded that public school was anything but a place where boys are roasted alive, 'and so with tears, taunts, and supplications, the point of private education was conceded.' This does not explain why Ralph and James, but not Benjamin, were sent to public school despite their mother's fears; Benjamin's delicate health and his obviously Jewish appearance may have had something to do with it.

His parents' decision may have been justified; but at all events the private school to which Benjamin was subsequently sent, Dr Cogan's, at Higham Hill, Walthamstow, was not a success, and in the summer of 1820 the sixteen-year-old Benjamin returned home. It seems that Benjamin detested Dr Cogan's, and was bored with the school's concentration on Greek and Latin grammar – 'Nothing was thought of there but the two dead languages,' he later recalled.[8] Judging by his accounts of school life in his autobiographical novels, his experiences at Cogan's were unhappy, and the only skills he learned there were how to defend himself with ready tongue and fists against the possibly anti-Semitic hostility of his school fellows. Benjamin acquired the art of self-defence early; he was a duellist by nature, and, while he no doubt got the best of the verbal fencing at Dr Cogan's, he also took boxing lessons when at home in London.

And so, after this brief, bruising encounter with the outside world, Benjamin spent two sheltered years studying with a private tutor in Buckinghamshire, his education supervised by his father. From fragments among the Hughenden Papers in Isaac D'Israeli's hand, it is clear that he took a close and guiding interest in his son's education, helping him with his Latin verse, Greek history, and grammar. Two notebooks record the progress of his studies in the summer and autumn of 1820, and his highly personal reactions to them; faced with the dreaded Greek metres, he wrote despairingly 'bewildered! lost! miserable work indeed'.[9] Even then, he attached great importance to style: 'Mitford's style [*History of Greece*, 1784-1810] is wretched, nay scarcely English,' he commented, 'a striking contrast to the cadenced periods of the Decline and Fall ...' He felt a keen sympathy for great men unjustly treated by their contemporaries, writing conventionally but prophetically, 'Genius has always possessed some jealous detractor to blast its character and sully its Fame.' Significantly, for the man whose devastating philippics against Peel were to make his name, his imagination was fired by Demosthenes' great speeches against Philip of Macedon. At seventeen, the signs of the future were already there; scribbled across the end-paper of the *Historical Almanac* for 1821 is a telling quotation from Petrarch: 'I desire to be known to posterity; if I cannot succeed, may I be known to my own age, or at least to my friends'.

Benjamin, self-absorbed, ranged through his father's library, seizing upon books which seemed to him to offer explanations or parallels to his own consciousness of his character and abilities, pointers towards what he felt might be his destiny. Was he destined to be a writer or a man of action, a poet-philospher or a statesman? Voltaire, whose style 'enchanted' him, seemed to offer the solution in *Zadig*; he could be both – 'A philospher and statesman, I moralised over the condition of man and the nature of government'.[10] He was profoundly influenced by his conversations with his father, and it may well have been Isaac, biographer and defender of Charles I, who imbued him with the romantic Toryism which coloured his political thinking – reverence for the Monarchy and the Church as ancient institutions of England, hatred of the Whig oligarchy which in 1688 had captured the monarchy and used it in the interests of its own class, equal detestation of Cromwell and parliamentary dictatorship. Disraeli was a Cavalier by nature.

In 1822, at eighteen Benjamin was eccentrically educated, widely read, with no experience of the outside world beyond what he had gleaned from books and

9

newspapers, and yet confident of his own genius – a perilous combination. He was now considered old enough to enter his father's social circle which, beyond Bloomsbury relations and neighbours, centred upon the publisher, John Murray II. At forty-four, John Murray, with a string of celebrated authors including Byron, Thomas Moore and Thomas Hope, was known as a prince among publishers, and entertained magnificently at his headquarters in Albemarle Street which Washington Irving described as 'a great resort of first-rate literary characters'. During Benjamin's childhood and youth the Murray and D'Israeli families were on intimate terms; Murray's father, John Murray I, had published Isaac's *Curiosities of Literature*, and Isaac had acted as the younger John Murray's literary adviser when he took over the business on his father's death and as his 'marriage trustee' when he married Anne Elliot. Apart from his bookselling business, Murray owned the influential Tory journal, the *Quarterly Review*, to which all the most eminent Conservative writers such as John Wilson Croker contributed. But for Benjamin his principal attraction was his role as the friend and publisher of Byron.

It was ten years since Byron had taken London by storm with *Childe Harold*, six since he had left England in a cloud of scandal over his separation from his wife and his sexual relations with his half-sister, Augusta Leigh, but even in exile he remained a charismatic figure of irresistible attraction for the romantic youth of his age. It is hardly surprising that Benjamin, impressionable as he was, should have taken Byron for his model, copying him in everything – appearance, attitudes, style and dress. Byron was extremely narcissistic about his beauty, taking purgatives to preserve his pallor, and even, it was rumoured, sleeping in curl-papers for the sake of his carefully-tousled locks. Disraeli was naturally pale, and probably had no need to go to such lengths, but was obsessively sensitive about his hair, writing anxiously to his mother and sister for advice as to how to stop it falling out, and wearing dyed and ringletted curls to the end of his life. Byron was elaborately dressed, with ruffled shirts, golden chains and rings on his fingers; young Benjamin slavishly copied him, to the amazement of staid Bloomsbury. Byron adopted an air of supercilious melancholy as his public face, and the pose of leaning upon one elbow, his cheek resting against his clenched hand in romantically pensive attitude; Benjamin did the same. Benjamin, unlike his idol, had no poetic talent, but he imitated his wonderful epistolary style: elegant, flowing, witty, often self-mocking, and his earlier letters are spattered with obviously Byronic phrases. Later in life, as dandyism was overtaken by more sober male fashions, Disraeli dropped the ruffles, the rings and the chains, but he kept the curls and the expression of melancholy which by then had become a habit, and he remained faithful to Byron. As he was to tell a sympathetic young woman some fifty years later, 'When one is young [one] chooses one's poet and abides by him'.[11]

Isaac D'Israeli also admired Byron, and was proud of the great man's praise of his *Curiosities of Literature*, expressed in an enthusiastic letter to John Murray, 'I don't know a living man's books I take up so often, or lay down more reluctantly, as Israeli's'. Yet he seems to have followed his own father's example in his absolute determination that Benjamin should not turn to literature as a career. 'The way of genius is rarely that of fortune or happiness', he wrote in that same year of 1822, 'and the father . . . dreads lest his son be found among that obscure multitude . . . who must expire at the barriers of mediocrity'. Benjamin therefore had some justification for his Byronic claim to being misunderstood; years later, he said that his father, although a very kind, gentle, amiable man, was 'without a particle of heart, with no real sympathy', the very last man, in fact, to have 'encouraged any dreams of authorship or of anything else'. He never dared show his father any of his early writings because 'he was very sarcastic & said things that were hard to hear'.[12]

And so the romantic Benjamin, dreaming of poetry and literature, found himself articled as a solicitor's clerk to a firm of City lawyers, Messrs Swain, Stevens, Maples, Pearse and Hunt, of Frederick's Place, Old Jewry. Frederick Maples, a senior partner in the firm, was apparently an old friend of Isaac D'Israeli, described by Benjamin as, 'rich, with a fine library, and one daughter'. It was part of Isaac's plan, which, according to his son he was 'very warm about', that Benjamin should be safely launched as a lawyer with a view to taking eventual possession, not only of Mr Maples' business, but of his library and his daughter as well. The best laid parental plans, however, often go astray, and Isaac's was to be no exception. Despite visits from Benjamin, gorgeously dressed in a black velvet suit with ruffles and black silk stockings with conspicuous red clocks, the young lady, as he later wrote, declared, 'You have too much genius for Frederick's Place; it will never do'.[13]

If Isaac D'Israeli seriously intended that Benjamin would eventually accustom himself to the dreary routine of a solicitor's office, he committed a cardinal error in taking him abroad in the summer of 1824. Perhaps inspired by an unusual burst of youthfulness, he wished to recreate his own experiences in the Low Countries and the Rhineland as a young man. Possibly he was persuaded into the project by Benjamin and his friend William Meredith, who seem to have been plotting some such adventure as early as December 1822, writing excitedly to each other of their dreams of 'plays, operas, cafés and vingt et un'. Meredith was a serious-minded, steady young man, a Bloomsbury neighbour, and heir to a rich uncle. The Meredith and D'Israeli families were on intimate terms, and Benjamin, William and Sarah were the closest of friends, William being steadfastly determined to marry Sarah, despite opposition from his uncle.

The three set off for the Continent in the last week of July 1824, leaving the remainder of the D'Israeli family installed for the summer at Worthing, where the Merediths were to join them. It was Benjamin's first trip abroad, and, to judge from his letters home, he was quite ecstatic, ogling pretty girls, talking French 'with a sangfroid perfectly inimitable', and gourmandizing on a 'pâté des [de] grenouilles quite sublime' at Brussels. 'My mother really must reform our table before we return,' he wrote impertinently.[14] They travelled through the Low

Countries to Spa, Cologne, Coblenz, Ems, Heidelberg and Frankfurt, the days given over to rigorous sightseeing, the evenings to cafés, or, when in fashionable watering-places such as Spa and Ems, to the casino, Benjamin boasting, 'I have become a most exquisite billiard player'. The two young men had heady encounters with Rhine wine; 'The governor [Isaac] allows us to debauch to the utmost and Hochsheim, Johannisberg, Rudesheim ... and a thousand other varieties are unsealed and floored with equal rapidity,' Benjamin informed Sarah.[15] Isaac's letters were naturally more sober in tone, many of them on a theme which was to become constant in the D'Israeli family – concern for Benjamin's health. 'I wish Ben's constitution was much stronger than it is,' he wrote anxiously to Maria, 'he often ails'.[16] One might conjecture that Benjamin's digestion, never strong, was upset by guzzling 'sublime' pâtés and over-indulgence in Rhine wine.

For the romantic Benjamin, indeed, the high point of the tour was their journey down the Rhine from Mainz, in what Isaac crossly described to Sarah as a 'rather dirty and disagreeable ... Batteau [sic]'. Benjamin, stimulated by the Gothic panorama of wooded crags and baronial castles, made no mention of the disagreeableness of the 'Batteau'. Later, he was to describe his journey down the Rhine as a turning-point in his life. 'I determined when descending those magical waters that I [would] not be a lawyer'.[17]

He returned to his clerk's stool in Frederick's Place, but not for long. Mr Maples advised Isaac that he 'had too much talent for a solicitor' and recommended he should try for the Bar. On 18 November 1824 he was enrolled as a student of Lincoln's Inn, and joined his uncle Nathaniel Basevi's chambers in Old Square, where he scandalized Basevi by arriving at the office with a copy of Spenser's *Faerie Queene* under his arm. Benjamin transferred for some months to the offices of Benjamin Austen, a neighbour and close family friend. Here too he manifested the seriousness of his attitude to a legal career by reading Chaucer during working hours. Benjamin Austen, more sympathetic towards literary ambitions than Nathaniel Basevi, advised Isaac that his son would never make a lawyer and should be allowed to devote himself to literature.

Literature, however, did not form a part of Benjamin's immediate plans; he was already contemplating a spectacular career in the great world. 'Even then I dreamed of politics ... I became pensive and restless, and before I was twenty I was obliged to terminate the dream of my father and his friend ... My father then made a feeble effort for Oxford, but the hour of adventure had arrived.'[18]

2　The First Fall

'In England,' Benjamin was to write just under two years later in *Vivian Grey* (1826), 'personal distinction is the only passport to the society of the great. Whether this distinction arise from fortune, family or talent is immaterial; but certain it is, to enter high society, a man must have either blood, a million, or a genius'.[1] He was burning to break out of the confines of Bloomsbury and Old Jewry into the world of fashion and politics that lay only a few miles to the west of the dull chambers in which he worked. He had no aristocratic connections to help him; as he later said, neither his father's family nor his fortune entitled him to mix in any society other than that of the 'middling classes'. Convinced as he may have been that he had genius, it was as yet unproven; to Benjamin, as to many others in those money-grabbing, speculating years of the early 1820s, the surest passport to society was to buy your way into it. '*Riches are Power*', he concluded.

For Benjamin, the frontier between dream and reality was always ill-defined; since he imagined himself rich and powerful he took steps to make that dream a reality. England during the years 1823 to 1825 witnessed a Stock Exchange boom fuelled by the speculating fever of thousands of small investors, and even before he was twenty Benjamin was speculating on the Market, buying and selling mining shares with a confidence that turned out to be as unjustified as it was precocious. According to his own account, he was led on by a certain Robert Messer who, acting as his broker, invested in Mexican, Colombian, Argentinian and Canadian mining stocks, either on his own or in a partnership with a fellow clerk at Swain Stevens, Thomas Mullett Evans, and later with John Murray.[2] A mysterious Thomas Jones was also involved, perhaps to the extent of lending Disraeli money to finance his speculations. Since on paper these sums ranged from £2,000 to £9,000, a considerable sum of money in those days, these operations would, without assistance, have been quite beyond Benjamin's means.

It was in the course of his duties as clerk at Swain Stevens that Benjamin met the man who he probably hoped would become his financial patron, J.D. Powles of J. & A. Powles & Co., of Freeman's Court, Cornhill. Powles had a dazzlingly successful record in floating mining companies; in January 1825 the £10 shares of one of the companies which he promoted, the Anglo-Mexican Mining Association, were already selling at £150. It was in connection with the drafting by Swain Stevens of the prospectus for yet another company, the Colombian Mining Association, that Disraeli first came into contact with Powles, who seems to have been favourably impressed by the young lawyer's abilities; at any rate he soon made use of him. Doubts as to the solidity of the mining companies promoted by Powles had been publicly raised by such establishment figures as Lord Eldon, John Cam Hobhouse, and Alexander Baring, and in an attempt to calm fears raised by these aspersions, Powles employed Disraeli to write three largely fraudulent pamphlets 'puffing' the solidity and profitability of his companies. Between the spring and summer of 1825, working on facts supplied by Powles, Benjamin wrote *An Enquiry into the Plans, Progress and Policy of the American Mining Companies, Lawyers and Legislators or Notes upon the American Mining Companies*, and *The Present State of Mexico*. Dazzled by Powles and by the prospects of the South American El Dorado which he hoped would bring him millions, Disraeli, who was always financially naive, was apparently unaware of the extent of the fraud perpetrated on the investing public by Powles – or of the fact that he was describing, in the most laudatory terms, mines and companies which existed only on paper.

The pamphlets were printed by John Murray, who over the past year had become literally infatuated with Benjamin's charm and talents. Their intimacy seems to have commenced in May 1824 when Benjamin with youthful confidence sent Murray the manuscript of his first work, a juvenile satire entitled *The Adventures of Mr. Aylmer Papillon*. Benjamin later had second thoughts about placing 'so crude a production' before the public, and, with a cheeky reference to Murray's burning of Byron's memoirs that month – 'as you have some small experience in burning MSS' – advised him to consign *Aylmer Papillon* to the flames. Murray, however, appears to have continued to have sufficient confidence in Benjamin's literary capacity to entrust him with the American edition of a life of Paul Jones to be published at the end of 1825. Murray indeed had conceived a very high opinion of Benjamin's character and abilities, as he was to write in a eulogistic letter of introduction to Sir Walter Scott's son-in-law, J.G. Lockhart, in the autumn of 1825:

> I may frankly say that I never met with a young man of greater promise. He is a good scholar, a hard student, a deep thinker, of great energy, equal perseverance, and indefatigable application, and a complete man of business. His knowledge of human nature, and the practical tendency of all his ideas, have often surprised me in a young man who has hardly passed his twentieth year.[3]

Benjamin was, indeed, not yet twenty-one; John Murray, at forty-five, was a shrewd cautious Scot, whom Byron had called the 'most timorous of God's publishers', and that Benjamin could win such encomiums from such a man at so early an age is a tribute to the spell which he could cast.

Perhaps the most remarkable proof both of Murray's confidence and the young

Disraeli's persuasiveness was Murray's involvement, through Benjamin, in speculation in shares in Powles' Anglo-Mexican Mining company. Benjamin, it appears from a letter he wrote to Murray on 31 January 1825, arranged for Murray to buy shares in this and in the Colombian Mining Association. By the end of March the two men were in partnership in the mining shares, with Murray holding two thirds and Benjamin one third. The initiative in this partnership appears to have been Benjamin's: 'I have therefore formed a partnership with you with proportionate interests according to the annexed paper', he wrote. '... I hope that this partnership is but the forerunner of mutual brilliancy of fortune'.[4]

It is not surprising that Murray should have had a personal interest in the publication of Benjamin's pamphlets 'puffing' the mining companies. He evidently believed Benjamin's claim that their publication would bring the partnership a quick and startling profit by causing a rise in the value of the shares which they had bought cheap in the crisis of confidence caused by Eldon's pronouncements. Benjamin himself was gripped with a speculative fever, investing £4,000 in a separate project with loans from Robert Messer and 'my uncle', presumably his mother's brother, George Basevi. A letter which he wrote to Messer in April 1825 demonstrates the extent to which he believed riches to be within his grasp:

> I possess a certain number of shares which are worth tho' at the lowest price they have yet sunk about 6000£ sterling, which I calculate at the end of this year will be worth 1200 – but 35 of which I calculate in the course of 5 years will be worth as many thousand.
>
> I have 4000£ invested in a speculation which I expect will produce me in the course of 8 mon[th]s 1000 a year.[5]

Benjamin clearly (and disastrously) believed the fraudulent claims put out by the mining companies, for he went on to hold out to Messer visions of enormous profits:

> When I tell you that one single mine which everybody in this kingdom believes to be inundated and to be incapable of producing under five years at the least is, altho' it has not been worked for 8 months – producing at the rate of £3000 net profit pr. week and that at the end of the first year of working ... it will give us a net profit at the least of 150,000, when I tell you moreover that this mine contains veins of immense and incalculable worth, which have only been discovered by our own surveyors and that it is their opinion that it alone may yield cent[100] pr. Ct. for our money, when I tell you I have seen the weekly accounts of profits and loss and every paper and memorandum connected with it's [sic] management, when I tell you that all our agents are writing home to us to buy them additional, no matter *at what price*. Can you call me too sanguine?

Benjamin's vision was already leaping beyond the acquisition of riches to a project which he hoped would bring him political influence and an entrée into the corridors of power: the founding of a new daily newspaper, which he described to Messer as 'the object of my highest ambition'. He saw himself as the entrepreneur between Murray, who had long dreamed of owning a newspaper, and Powles, who would be quick to see the propaganda advantages which such a project would bring to his commercial interests. Discussions began in May with Disraeli acting as the go-between, working up the enthusiasm of both publisher and financier, and three months later, on 3 August 1825, an agreement was signed at Albemarle Street by Murray, Powles and Disraeli, by which the three contracting parties agreed to establish a morning newspaper. One half of the capital was to be provided by Murray and one quarter each by Powles and Disraeli, and the newspaper was to be published by and under the management of Murray. The political tone was to be Conservative, like that of Murray's other prestigious publication, the *Quarterly Review*, and would support the liberal foreign policy promoted by Canning which had, in fact, by recognizing South American independence, opened the way for Powles' speculations. It was intended to rival the only other serious daily newspaper of the day, *The Times*, under its influential editor, Thomas Barnes.

For the twenty-year-old Benjamin, the signing of the agreement must have been the most glorious moment of his life hitherto. Presumably he was still looking to his mining investments to finance his share of the capital, or, characteristically, dismissed such a mundane consideration as being of small importance in comparison with the great goal. He must have congratulated himself upon the successful step he had taken in the art which he liked to describe as 'the management of men'; it was, after all, his persuasive charm and enthusiasm which were responsible for bringing together the financial magnate and the great publisher.

The intrigue, deception and betrayal of the next few months, however, were to provide him with a bitter example of the pitfalls awaiting those who aspire to the 'management of men'. In September 1825, armed with the laudatory letter of introduction from Murray quoted above, he travelled to Scotland on Murray's behalf to persuade Sir Walter Scott's son-in-law, J.G. Lockhart, to accept the editorship of the projected newspaper. As he journeyed north in the highest of spirits, picturing himself as the motive force in a vast enterprise of endless possibilities, the future Tory leader had his first glimpse of the English county aristocracy in all its glory, pouring into York to attend Quarter Sessions. The 'splendid sight' of the 'gorgeous equipages', the immaculate carriages with their liveried grooms, outriders, footmen and magnificent horses deeply impressed him; later in life, when he had had first-hand experience of the prejudice and narrow-mindedness of that same county nobility and gentry, he still gloried in the romantic panoply that surrounded them.

From Edinburgh, where he revelled in the 'various beauties' of a Scottish breakfast, particularly cold grouse and marmalade, he travelled to meet Lockhart at Chiefswood, on the edges of Scott's Abbotsford estate. J.G. Lockhart was ten years Benjamin's senior, a prickly, difficult Scot, partially deaf, shy to the point of appearing arrogant, with an almost fierce reserve and a habitually pensive, melancholy expression defined by his father-in-law as 'hidalgo airs'. Trained as a lawyer, Lockhart had had considerable experience of journalism, having been involved with John Wilson in the production of articles for *Blackwood's Magazine* under the pseudonym 'Christopher North'. Ironically, the sarcastic and personal nature of those articles had been the cause of Murray's earlier withdrawal from participation in *Blackwood's*. Lockhart, who had been expecting Isaac D'Israeli and had never heard of Benjamin, was taken aback by the youth and exotic appearance of Murray's emissary. By Benjamin's account, however, his reserve soon melted, and the next day, Sir Walter Scott having arrived from Abbotsford, the three men were closeted together after breakfast to discuss the project.

Benjamin, in his attempt to persuade such cautious men, presented his plan in the most grandiloquent terms. It was not, he told them, a question merely of the editorship of a newspaper, but of the representation of powerful political and commercial interests, and even, for Lockhart, a parliamentary seat for a Tory borough. As he wrote in a letter of melodramatic secrecy to Murray, referring to Lockhart as 'M' and Scott as 'the Chevalier', 'through Powles, all America and the Commercial Interest is at our back ... Wilmot H[orton], &c., not as mere under-secretary, but as our private friend, is most staunch ... the West India interest will pledge themselves ... such men and in such situations as Barrow, &c., &c., are *distinctly in our power*; and finally, ... he [Lockhart] is coming to London, not to be an Editor of a Newspaper, but the Directeur-General of an immense organ, and at the head of a band of high-bred gentlemen and important interests ...'[6] He assured Murray that he was already on the most intimate terms with both the Scott and Lockhart households, and would not leave Scotland until he could bring back Lockhart with him to London.

Benjamin was deceiving himself as to the enthusiasm felt by Lockhart and Scott both for himself and for the projected editorship. His self-congratulatory optimism would have been considerably dampened, had he known of a letter addressed to Lockhart by Murray's legal adviser, William Wright, which arrived even before he left Scotland. In this letter, Wright warned Lockhart to take what Disraeli said with a large pinch of salt. 'I believe he is a sensible clever young fellow', Wright wrote.

> His judgement, however, wants settling down. He has never had to struggle with a single difficulty, nor has been called on to act in any affairs in which his mind has been necessarily forced to decide and choose in difficult situations. At present his chief exertions as to matters of decision have been with regard to the selection of his food, his enjoyment, and his clothing, and though he is honest, and I take it wiser than his father, he is inexperienced and untried in the world, and of course though you may ... safely trust his integrity, you cannot prudently trust much to his judgement.[7]

Nor would Benjamin have been flattered by the opinion of him retailed by Scott to his friend the poet, William Stewart Rose, which showed scant respect for the D'Israelis, both father and son: 'Here has been a visitor of Lockhart's, a sprig of the rod of Aaron, young D'Israeli,' Scott wrote. 'In point of talents he reminded us of his father, for sayth Mungo's garland, "Crapaud pickanini, Crapaud himself," which means a young coxcomb is like the old one who got him.'

In fact, neither Scott nor Lockhart was anxious that Lockhart should abandon Edinburgh, where he had achieved a certain reputation as a lawyer, for London and the doubtful honour of becoming editor of a newspaper, a position then considered not quite gentlemanly. They were angling for a more prestigious post for Lockhart, the editorship of Murray's *Quarterly Review*, in which they were encouraged by Murray's legal adviser, Wright, who had himself put Lockhart's name forward to Murray. In the same letter of 3 October in which he told Lockhart to be wary of Disraeli, Wright did his utmost to undermine Disraeli's position: 'Whatever our friend D'Israeli may say or flourish on this subject, your accepting of the editorship of a newspaper would be *infra dig.*, and a losing of caste; but not so ... the accepting of the editorship of the *Quarterly Review*. ... An editor of a Review like the *Quarterly* is the office of a scholar and a gentleman; but that of a newspaper is *not.* ... And there is something in it (when D'Israeli has gilded and adorned it with his new notions as much as he can) that is repugnant to the feelings of a gentleman ...'

On receipt of this letter, Lockhart sat down to disabuse Murray of the impression, doubtless given him by Disraeli, that he might be willing to undertake the editorship of the newspaper; an intimation that was backed up by a firm letter on the same lines from Scott to Murray five days later. Murray, who was by nature indecisive and open to pressure, caved in, writing to Scott on 13 October, that 'to obviate any difficulties which have been urged,' he had 'proposed to Mr. Lockhart to come to London as the Editor of the Quarterly, also as adviser about the newspaper and about literary undertakings in general ...'[8] Thus, while Benjamin fondly imagined that he was at the centre of negotiations, matters were really being carried on behind his back by Wright, Lockhart, and to a lesser extent Scott, who pressured a vacillating Murray into offering them what they wanted.

Benjamin had failed in his primary object, that of persuading Lockhart to edit the newspaper which was his cherished dream. He was, however, too intelligent not to accept a *fait accompli*, and still hoped to involve Lockhart, with whom he now thought himself on intimate terms, in the setting-up of the newspaper. He was witness to the agreement, signed on 20 October in London, by which Lockhart was to edit the *Quarterly Review* for three years at £1,250 per annum, and probably present when John Murray agreed to pay Lockhart a further £1,500 or its equivalent in shares in the newspaper for 'hints and advice' and occasional articles. When Lockhart returned to Scotland after signing the agreement, Benjamin kept him informed of all his preparations for the launching of what he called 'the magnum opus'. He was indefatigable: finding a large house in Great George Street which was rented and fitted out as a printing office, employing his cousin George Basevi as architect for the planning of the offices and printing premises, and engaging foreign correspondents.

Meanwhile, a storm had broken out at Albemarle Street, where the wretched John Murray found himself beset by the great guns of the *Quarterly Review*, John Wilson Croker and Sir John Barrow among them, to whom word had leaked out of Murray's negotiations with Lockhart. Not only were they strongly opposed to Murray's involvement in the projected newspaper, but they regarded his appointment of Lockhart, without consulting them or the existing editor, J.T. Coleridge, as 'underhand'. They looked upon Lockhart himself with suspicion in view of his record at *Blackwood's*, and not only did they attempt to set Murray against Lockhart, but at the same time they tried to sow suspicion of Murray's sincerity in the minds of Scott and Lockhart. Beset on all sides, Murray immediately dispatched Disraeli to Abbotsford to persuade Scott to write an 'open' letter attesting to Lockhart's soundness and suitability, which he somewhat reluctantly did on 17 November. Disraeli unwisely exceeded his brief by telling Lockhart of the cabal working against him in London, and arrived back to a stormy reception from Murray. Young Disraeli, the infuriated publisher wrote to Scott, had totally mistaken the object of his mission, which was 'to tell *you alone* the apprehensions which had been expressed by the most valuable friends of the Quarterly Rev[iew] at the appointment of one who had been so long connected with Blackwood's Mag. but which could be instantly dissipated by the influence of yr. name ... Mr. L[ockhart] was not to have been told of it by any means ...'[9] The unfortunate editor of the *Quarterly*, Coleridge, generously let Murray off the hook by resigning on 19 November but the cabal continued to make trouble, with Croker writing to Lockhart on the same day, 'I think you will agree with me that there is something very odd in Mr. Murray's conduct to Mr. Coleridge and yourself ...'

Disraeli seems at first to have been surprised by this intrigue, and his experiences at this time may have given him the first reason for the distaste for literary men which he was to evince later in life. He wrote hastily to Lockhart justifying Murray: 'Had I any conception of the utter worthlessness of the intriguing, selfish and narrow-minded officials by whom he has been so long surrounded, I certainly would have refrained my sentiments, and have pitied the noble and generous-minded being who was subjected to such disgusting thraldom.'[10] At the same time he immediately set to work on Murray to counteract the doubts raised in his mind by the cabal both as to the suitability of Lockhart and the viability of the newspaper. His success proved that with his persuasive eloquence he was still capable of winding the older man round his little finger. On 23 November Murray sat down to write to Lockhart praising Disraeli's 'admirable' account of his talks with Lockhart and Scott in Scotland, and promising in emotional terms that 'after this, Heaven and Earth may pass away, but it cannot shake my opinion, and I am prepared to go on with you with every good feeling, and with every exertion of which my nature is capable.' Lockhart's plans for the *Review* were, he said, both noble and just, but his overall idea for the newspaper was 'magnificent, and very far beyond my previous conception.' He was convinced that success would be 'certain and instantaneous ... the public mind must capitulate at once.'[11]

Disraeli had succeeded in defeating the intrigues of the cabal, or, as he characteristically put it to Lockhart, in 'slaying the mighty Python of Humbug, whose vigorous and enormous folds were so fast and fatally encircling us ... you may now come to London in *triumph*.'[12] Happy in the conviction that he had managed to set things right once and for all, Benjamin continued his efforts for Lockhart and the newspaper, searching for a suitable house for Lockhart to rent and engaging still more foreign correspondents, sending Lockhart 'a sketch of our correspondence at *present established*'. It was an impressive, though somewhat vague list: 'All South America, All the Morea, All the Baltic, All the Levant, Smyrna, Constantinople, Greece, All the North American newspapers, and private intelligence from a family of distinction at Washington by every packet ...' Among the German correspondents was to be a Herr Maas, whose only qualification for the job seems to have lain in his being proprietor of the Trierscher Hof in Cologne where Benjamin had stayed on his tour of the Rhineland in 1824; others were to be recruited with the help of Mrs William Elliot, Murray's German sister-in-law. Many of the letters they had written had not been answered, Benjamin admitted ingenuously, 'but we do not anticipate the *slightest* doubt of their success.'[13]

Of all the letters that Disraeli wrote to Lockhart at this time, none illustrates his naivety and lack of knowledge of the world better than his delighted account of his engagement of Dr William Maginn as the newspaper's Paris correspondent. William Maginn, Ll. D, was a literary mercenary who, although but recently arrived from Cork, was already as well known for his proverbial drunkenness as for the profundity of his learning and the brilliance of his wit, both of which he frittered away on periodical writing. It would be hard to imagine a more unreliable and unsuitable candidate as Paris correspondent, and Disraeli's proud account of his negotiations with the Doctor simply reveal him as an inexperienced youth skilfully conned by the plausible Irishman.

Maginn set the pace at the interview by declaring that £300 to £350 a year would be the normal salary for the post, but that he could not possibly go to Paris for less than £500, meanwhile strengthening his bargaining position by pouring scorn on the whole project of setting up in competition with *The Times*. Disraeli riposted by giving Maginn, whom he floridly described as 'a very prosopopoeia of the public press', an outline of their intentions for the paper, which he no doubt pitched in the most grandiloquent terms. Maginn, now sure of his £500 per annum, feigned amazement. 'The Dr. started from his chair like Giovanni in the banquet scene and seemed as astounded – as attonitus – as Porsenna when Scaevola missed him. A new world seemed open to him, and this sneering scribe, this man of most experience, who had so smiled at our first mentioning of the business, ended by saying that as to the success of the affair doubt could not exist, and that a year could not elapse without our being the first paper going.'[14] Striving to impress Lockhart with classical allusion and high-flown language, Benjamin naively depicted the Irishman's reactions as being representative of the highest echelons of the press: 'Upon my faith, Lockhart, I consider this a most important interview, because really after all, it is becoming acquainted, as it were, with the private opinion of Barnes, etc.' For Maginn, a man who could wheedle a bottle of brandy out of a City undertaker on the pretext of arranging an expensive funeral for an imaginary wife, Benjamin must have been child's play.

By 21 December 1825, Disraeli's title for the newspaper, *The Representative*, had already been chosen; it was to be his last contribution to the enterprise. In that fatal month of December all his soaring plans of fame, riches and power, all his carefully laid schemes for *The Representative*, his courting of Lockhart, Murray and Powles came crashing about his ears. On 17 December, four days before Benjamin's twenty-first birthday, the mining bubble finally burst; all over England banks closed their doors; Benajmin and hundreds of small investors like him were ruined. Disaster had been looming for some weeks before the crash came; Macaulay, whose family bank was involved in the general bankruptcy, wrote to his brother Henry on 12 December of 'a perfect reign of terror . . . going on around us . . . all is confusion and dismay in the City and has been so for a week or more'. A thick fog accentuated the atmosphere of impending disaster: 'This gloom in the heaven on the first day of so important a week seems to me to portend terrible events in the commercial world,' he wrote.[15] Terrible events indeed; the *Annual Register* for 1825 named no fewer than seventy-three London and country banks that failed or suspended payments in the panic of that December. For Benjamin, who had incurred debts that he could not possibly pay for shares that were now worthless, December 1825 marked the beginning of a trail of financial troubles that was to follow him into middle life.

The immediate result of the crash was, of course, that neither Benjamin nor Powles could put up his share of the capital for *The Representative*, now on the eve of production. Powles, moreover, having used Benjamin, now cast him aside, even leaving him to pay the debt of £150 owed to Murray for printing the mining pamphlets. Murray too turned against his former protégé; a similar situation depicted in *Vivian Grey* the following year was probably based on Benjamin's experiences with Murray at this nadir of his fortunes: 'He raved! he stamped! he blasphemed! but the whole of his abuse was levelled against his former "monstrous clever" young friend; of whose character he had so often boasted that his own was the prototype, but who was now an adventurer – a swindler – a scoundrel – a liar – a base, deluding, flattering, fawning villain etc., etc.'[16] Lockhart too, turned his back on Benjamin, and their relationship soon degenerated into downright hostility.

Meanwhile Murray went ahead on his own with the production of *The Representative*, despite the warnings of the literary Cassandras of the *Quarterly*. The first number appeared on 25 January 1826 and quickly justified their predictions; nonentity succeeded nonentity as editor and in the words of S.C. Hall who had been recruited to the paper by Benjamin himself, 'Dr. Maginn was better at borrowing money than at writing articles . . . Editor there was literally none, from the beginning to the end. The first number supplied conclusive evidence of the utter ignorance of editorial tact on the part of the person entrusted with the duty . . . and the reputation of the new journal fell below zero in twenty-four hours

...' Within a week John Murray had taken to his bed, ill with chagrin, and not only to his bed, if Lockhart's wife Sophia is to be believed: 'All would do well but the worst is when alarmed he [John Murray] takes to his bottle at night which makes a perfect coward of him the following day.' [17] *The Representative* ceased publication on 29 July after only six months' existence, with a loss to Murray of £26,000.

Benjamin, thwarted in his attempts to achieve power through riches, turned to another project which he hoped would not only make his name, but afford him the exquisite pleasure of revenge upon Murray and the intriguing officials who surrounded him. He never forgot an injury; once, on being asked which passion gave the most lasting pleasure, he replied 'Revenge. A man will enjoy that when even Avarice has ceased to please',[18] and in his books and in his parliamentary speeches he would use the pointed rapier of his ridicule to prick those who had wounded him. Murray and his circle were to be the first of a long line of enemies to receive this treatment.

Disraeli seems to have embarked on the new project, a society novel, even before the Murray débâcle, in the late autumn of 1825, while staying with his family at Hyde Heath House, near Amersham, which they had rented for the season from Robert Plumer Ward. In that same year, 1825, Ward had published the book of the season, *Tremaine*, a society novel of the genre known as 'silver fork' fiction which pandered to the public taste for aping the manners of the aristocracy, being shamelessly based on social and political figures of the day. The success of *Tremaine* undoubtedly inspired Disraeli as to the form his first novel should take, and he was eagerly encouraged in this idea by a new friend and patroness, a woman who had been closely connected with the publication of *Tremaine*, Sara Austen.

Sara Austen, the first in a series of women of whom Disraeli made use to advance his career, was a neighbour of the D'Israelis in Bloomsbury, living at 33 Guilford Street, off Bloomsbury Square. Twelve years older than Benjamin, beautiful, talented, and childless, she was the wife of Benjamin Austen, in whose chambers Disraeli had been briefly employed, and, despite her relatively modest social origin (she was the daughter of a successful miller named Rickett of Oundle in Northamptonshire), she had considerable social pretensions. She prided herself on her literary and artistic salon, which included such figures as Henry Crabb Robinson, Turner, Eastlake and Maclise, and of course, Plumer Ward, a client of Austen's, who had negotiated the anonymous publication of *Tremaine* with the most successful commercial publisher of the day, Henry Colburn.

No doubt Sara promised to persuade Colburn to publish Benjamin's novel, and to act as intermediary with him to preserve the author's anonymity, as her husband had done for Plumer Ward. Benjamin sent her the first draft of the book in February 1826, and her reactions were ecstatic. 'I am quite delighted with your MS. & enter into the spirit of the book entirely', she wrote to him on 25 February. 'I will be faithful to your secret, & can undertake to manage it exactly in accordance to your wishes ... The moment I have yr. permission & instructions, I will write to C[olburn] ...' She was, it appears, more than a little in love with the handsome young man who had so flatteringly confided in her. 'You have the entree *whenever you like to come at all hours*', she wrote daringly, adding a coquettish note that she was sending 'this very *unladylike* paper' with instructions for the servant who was to deliver it to say it was from her husband, and signing herself 'Yr. sincere friend & Ally.' [19]

From then on Benjamin and Sara, carried away by mutual enthusiasm and, no doubt, flirtation, worked together on the novel, with Sara copying out the drafts to be sent to Colburn. Neither of the eager collaborators was in fact qualified, as Plumer Ward had been, either by birth or experience to write a novel based on the manners of high society, nor did Sara, despite her social pretensions, have the sense to make Benjamin excise some of the sillier passages from the book, in which Benjamin fancied himself to cut the figure of a dandy exquisite, but only succeeded in appearing ridiculous, or, in contemporary terms 'a puppy'. Nor do they seem to have realized the risks Benjamin was running in basing the theme of the novel, which was to be called by the name of the hero, Vivian Grey, so obviously upon the recent story of *The Representative*, with the figure of Murray both clearly recognizable and cruelly lampooned. In the novel, Murray was to appear as the Marquess of Carabas, a stupid and drunken nobleman who is manoeuvred by the silver-tongued young hero, Vivian Grey, into the formation of a new political party, which is later destroyed by intrigue, Vivian himself being then socially ruined.

By mid-March the complete manuscript of *Vivian Grey* was in the hands of Colburn at New Burlington Street. Colburn, a bustling little man, reputed to be an illegitimate son of Lord Lansdowne, did not enjoy the prestigious publishing reputation of John Murray, but he had a good commercial eye for a book, and was an expert in the art of 'puffery', or working up public interest in a book through his two journals, *The Literary Gazette*, which he owned in partnership with Longman, and the *New Monthly Magazine*. As the publication date for *Vivian Grey* drew nearer hints were dropped in their columns of the imminent appearance of a daring novel of a satirical nature 'a sort of Don Juan in prose', written by 'a talented young man of high life', the hero being 'acquainted with every fashionable and political character of the day.' Colburn maintained the fiction after the publication of the book on 22 April, telling the journalist Cyrus Redding, 'I have a capital book out, *Vivian Grey*, the authorship is a great secret – a man of high fashion – very high – keeps the first society.' Redding replied spitefully that he thought the characters imaginary, which piqued Colburn.

The fashionable world did not agree with Redding; the identification of the personages characterized in the novel became a society sport. *Vivian Grey* was an immediate success, widely read and much talked about. It was racy, readable, superficial and at times witty; altogether a precociously skilful book for a young man of twenty-one who had no first-hand knowledge of the world he described.

It was also, in the opening chapters, clearly autobiographical; Vivian's father being modelled on Isaac D'Israeli, and Vivian himself on Benjamin. It is amusing to see how Benjamin pictured himself at nineteen in comparison with the gauche youths of his age: 'Vivian Grey was a graceful, lively lad, with just enough of dandyism to preserve him from committing gaucheries, and with a devil of a tongue.' Vivian had considerable success with women – 'the only rival to be feared by a man of spirit is a clever boy', while, doubtless with Sara Austen in mind, he wrote, 'there is no fascination so irresistible to a boy as the smile of a married woman'. But the most interesting of the biographical details is Vivian's early discovery that politics was the goal for which his soul had unconsciously been yearning, and in that sense *Vivian Grey* could be said to have been Disraeli's first political novel. 'The want, the indefinable want, which he had so constantly experienced, was at last supplied; the grand object on which to bring his mind to bear and work was at last provided. He paced his chamber in an agitated spirit, and panted for the Senate.'[20] Almost ten years later, when Benjamin was desperately but unsuccessfully trying to get into Parliament, he was to note in his private diary, 'In *Vivian Grey* I have portrayed my active and real ambition.'

Robert Plumer Ward, writing to Sara Austen on 16 May just three weeks after the publication of *Vivian Grey*, testified to the *succès de scandale* which the book was obtaining in high society circles. Public men and fine ladies admired the skilful satire of their snobbish, superficial, money-worshipping counterparts, but they also resented it. 'It certainly frightens a great many people, who expect to be shown up,' Ward warned, 'and you must really be careful of discovering the author.'[21] In fact, rumours that the author of *Vivian Grey* was not, as he claimed, a man of fashion, started soon after publication, when Jerdan in the *Literary Gazette* pointed out that the author must be a literary rather than a society man: 'The class of the author was a little betrayed by his recurrence to topics about which the mere man of fashion knows nothing and cares less', he wrote perceptively. By June, Disraeli's name was being mentioned everywhere as the author, and Colburn's rival publications pursued him with malignancy, holding him up to public ridicule. In July *Blackwood's* denounced him in a sentence which must have cut him to the quick: *Vivian Grey*, it declared, had been written by 'an obscure person for whom nobody cares a straw.'

Benjamin recorded his appalled reaction to this damning dismissal by 'the great critical journal of the north of Europe', in a heartfelt passage in a later novel, *Contarini Fleming* (1832):

> With what horror, with what blank despair, with what supreme, appalling astonishment, did I find myself, for the first time in my life, a subject of the most reckless, the most malignant, and the most adroit ridicule. I was sacrificed, I was scalped ... all my eloquence, and all my fancy, and all the strong expression of my secret feelings! these ushers of the court of Apollo fairly laughed me off Parnassus, and held me up to public scorn ... The criticism fell from my hand. A film floated over my vision; my knees trembled. I felt that sickness of heart, that we experience in our first serious scrape. I was ridiculous. It was time to die.[22]

His 'first serious scrape', Benjamin called it, and it was serious indeed in its effect on his life and reputation. Not only had he been made an object of ridicule and been exposed as a pretentious young puppy who should not be taken seriously, but he had made himself influential enemies among the English literary establishment, not least those of the *Quarterly Review* who could not sympathize with the lampooning of Murray, and saw themselves or their friends publicly caricatured by a dandified twenty-one-year-old Jew, the son of a man for whom they had little respect. Benjamin's involvement with a satirical weekly, *The Star Chamber*, further increased the dislike with which they regarded him. This short-lived publication was ostensibly owned and edited by Peter Hall, a Cambridge friend of William Meredith's, and Meredith, Sara Austen and Benjamin had a hand in it. It ran to only nine issues between 19 April and 7 June 1826, the period immediately preceding-and following the publication of *Vivian Grey* and indeed included a key to the characters in Benjamin's novel. Benjamin contributed, or certainly inspired, at least two satirical articles in *The Star Chamber*, one of which, *The Dunciad of Today*, again recklessly attacked Murray and his cronies.

For John Murray himself, mortified by the failure of *The Representative*, Benjamin's caricature of him as the Marquess of Carabas was the last straw. His understandable denunciations of Benjamin caused a rupture between the Murray and D'Israeli families, since Isaac and Maria, with more loyalty than sense, rushed to their son's defence. Incredibly, they seem to have failed to see the parallels between Murray and Carabas, and attributed Murray's resentment to the failure of the newspaper. It was all Murray's own fault, Maria D'Israeli told him roundly, and Benjamin should not have been blamed, for 'tho' a clever boy he was no prodigy, and I must say I believe the failure of the Representative lay much more with the Proprietor and his Editor than it ever did with my son.' Murray, she told him, should not be 'going about blasting the character' of Benjamin simply because he [Murray] had 'formed in his imagination a *perfect being* and expected impossibilities and found him on trial a mere mortal and a very very young man ...'[23] Benjamin's godfather, Sharon Turner, stepped in to mediate when, in October, the row threatened to become public, and Murray wrote him a dignified letter of explanation, denying that his anger against Benjamin arose in the smallest degree from the money he had lost 'by yielding to [his] unrelenting excitement and importunity.' Benjamin, he said, had received from him 'nothing but the most unbounded confidence and parental attachment, my fault was in having loved not wisely but too well.' The motive for his resentment, he said, lay in that 'outrageous breach of confidence and of every tie which binds man to man in social life in the publication of *Vivian Grey*'.[24]

'Never was anything so imprudent', Benjamin was to write six years later of *Vivian Grey*; indeed the scandal of its publication was to weigh him down for many years. 'The hour of adventure' had ended in total disaster. He had failed in business, accumulating debts which he had no hope of paying, and which were still to haunt him over twenty years later. In the place of fame he had achieved not only notoriety but ridicule, and earned himself powerful enemies among the London literary establishment. Aged only twenty-one Benjamin, tortured by frustrated ambition and a deep sense of failure, slid helplessly into a state of mental anguish and nervous depression. Six years later, when the worst was over, he was to write in *Contarini Fleming* of his feelings at this time:

> They know not, they cannot tell, the cold, dull world: they cannot even remotely conceive the agony of doubt and despair which is the doom of youthful genius. To sigh for fame in obscurity is like sighing in a dungeon for light ... But to feel the strong necessity of fame, and to be conscious that without intellectual excellence life must be insupportable, to feel all this with no simultaneous faith in your own power, these are moments of despondency for which no immortality can compensate.[25]

3 Eastern Odyssey

The four years following the disasters of 1825-6 were for Benjamin a long and painful expiation of his fall from grace, a period of mental and physical illness with brief periods of respite, which was to last until his departure for the East in 1830.

Anguished at his rejection by society in the summer of 1826, Benjamin immediately fell ill. Sara Austen was solicitous, her notes displaying a mixture of anxiety and flirtatiousness, beseeching him to have a care for his health and to come round to her house 'to lie on the sofa & eat boiled lamb & be quiet as you please'.[1] Together, they planned a tour to Italy which they hoped would restore both Benjamin's health and his peace of mind. Sara's husband, Benjamin Austen, who seems to have been almost as infatuated with the young Disraeli as his wife, lent him money to pay for the trip, and early in August the three of them set off from Dover, where the D'Israeli family were taking the sea air.

Leaving England seems to have had an immediately therapeutic effect upon Benjamin, who, by the time they reached Paris, was, as he wrote to Sarah, 'a thousand times better'. Sara Austen, whose letters to the D'Israelis tended to be ingratiating and insincere, also wrote, 'My dear friend, I would give the world at this moment to be transported to Dover for indeed I am most anxious to hear how you all are, particularly dear Mrs. D'Israeli.'[2] Sarah D'Israeli, her letters to her brother breathing her passionate affection – 'you know how much my happiness depends upon yours' – retailed to him in return the details of their contrastingly mundane life. Isaac took daily walks on the pier, their mother was as usual unwell, and spent most of her time despondently on the beach watching ships pass, and the two boys grumbled that Dover was an excessively quiet place, but not, she added thankfully, as much as they did at Worthing, and not nearly as much as they did at Hyde. Ralph was being extremely amiable and reasonable, but Jem was 'so dreadfully impudent that the sooner he is off the better'.[3]

By 21 August, they had reached Switzerland, with Benjamin in a romantic reverie at the sight of the Alps, heightened when they reached Lake Geneva by his sense of following in the footsteps of Byron. He interrogated Byron's boatman,

Maurice, 'v. handsome and v. vain, made so by being the pet of the English', and was rewarded by an amusingly disloyal tale of Byron writing for $2\frac{1}{2}$ hours in the dungeon at Chillon by lighted torches, then tipping the gendarme a napoleon with specific instructions to Maurice to tell the man Byron gave it to him. Benjamin, whose penchant for self-advertisement was at least as strong as Byron's, commented, 'most ludicrously ostentatious'.[4] He re-lived the poet's experiences on the lake, hiring Maurice to take him and Austen out in his boat all night. The unromantic solicitor, made drowsy by the quantities of burgundy they had consumed, slept, wrapped in Benjamin's cloak, while Benjamin shared a bottle of brandy with Maurice and revelled in his own sensations. For Benjamin, the experience was 'my heart's content', as, exalted by alcohol, he watched the lightning shimmering above the lake, taking strength, perhaps, from the thought that Byron too had been persecuted and misunderstood by the society which he had outraged.

Crossing the Alps by the Simplon pass, they visited the Italian Lakes, and were shocked by the 'universally indelicate' frescoes of the Villa d'Este. At Milan, Benjamin was tormented by insects but impressed by the number of dandies he saw there, retailing details of the niceties of their leader, Count Cicogna, to his father, while at Venice he enjoyed the splendours of the Hotel Danieli, with its marble floors, satin chairs and ceilings painted by 'Tintoretto and his scholars' as much as any of the artistic treasures. He did not emulate Byron by swimming the Grand Canal, but at Ferrara he visited Tasso's cell, where his hero, with vain-glorious vandalism, had scratched his name upon the wall. From Ferrara, they followed the usual tourist route to Florence, Pisa, Lucca, Genoa and Turin; at Florence Benjamin shone among the English community, making such a favourable impression on a Mr Brown that he was invited to spend the winter there at the Villa Capponi in Arcetri.

Back in London in October, Benjamin, revived by the stimulus of travel and new sensations, was writing again, the second part of *Vivian Grey*, which he had begun while abroad. Part II was intended to expunge the impression made by Part I, and to present to the world a reformed Vivian Grey, purified and having found his true self through experience. The idea for the theme of the sequel undoubtedly came from one of his favourite books, Goethe's *Wilhelm Meister*, which had been published in translation by Carlyle the previous year, Vivian Grey being made to tread much the same path as Goethe's hero. In the opening chapter Benjamin made a plea for understanding, as much for himself as for Vivian, as a youth of great talents 'whose mind had been corrupted as the minds of many of our youth had been, by the artificial age in which he lived'. It is doubtful whether anyone listened; the book was duller than its predecessor, lacking the conviction and sparkle of Part I, and Benjamin himself seems to have tired of his hero, killing him off abruptly at the end. One good result, however, did emerge from the sequel, for Colburn paid him £500 for it as compared with £300 for Part I. With this he was able to repay Powles' debt of £150 to Murray.

'My son's life within the last year and a half, with a very slight exception, has been a blank in his existence', Isaac was to write sadly to a friend in January 1829.[5] Benjamin himself was probably recalling these 'blank' years when he later described Isaac's similar experience in 1786, as 'that mysterious illness to which the youth of men of sensibility and especially literary men, is especially subject – a failing of nervous energy ... The symptoms, physical and moral, are most distressing: lassitude and despondency.' His physical symptoms, probably psychosomatic, were diagnosed by one doctor as 'chronic inflammation of the membranes of the brain', and most of the remarks made about Benjamin at this time indicate that the illness was primarily mental. While William Meredith wrote to him in December 1828 of 'the alarming news about your head spread by Mrs. Austen and Dr. Arbuthnot,' members of the literary set who were acquainted with his father hinted maliciously that at one point 'his mind gave way'. And so Benjamin led a secluded, wretched life, often lying in darkened rooms, apparently drugged with digitalis, moving with his family from London to the country houses which they rented, or to Lyme Regis, of which Isaac was particularly fond.

From hints in later letters it would appear that Benjamin and his family believed that his mental illness would prevent him from marrying. His only sexual stimulus, and one which was almost certainly frustrated, was the 'smile of a married woman', Sara Austen. The Austens were constantly with the D'Israelis, frequently sharing summer houses with them, and it would appear from a distracted note by Sara among the Hughenden Papers that she was certainly in love with Benjamin. It is unlikely, however, given the close quarters in which the two families lived, that their relationship could have progressed beyond secret meetings and anguished notes. There is evidence that they carried on a clandestine correspondence; a letter of Sara's, written from Lichfield where she was staying, was addressed to Benjamin not at Bloomsbury Square but at her own house in Guilford Street, which suggests that she intended to keep knowledge of their correspondence a secret from his family.

Sara's letter was written in early April 1828, a period of remission for Benjamin, when, as he wrote to his godfather, Sharon Turner, he hoped that he was 'slowly recovering from one of those tremendous disorganisations which happen to all men at some period of their lives & which are perhaps equally necessary for the formation of both body & constitution.' He was not, in fact, yet fully recovered; the sense of failure and incapacity stemming from his nervous breakdown was still upon him: 'Whether I shall ever do anything which may mark me out from the crowd I know not', he wrote to Turner. 'I am one of those to whom moderate reputation can give no pleasure & who in all probability am incapable of achieving a great one.'[6]

As his creative energy returned, he began work on another book, *The Voyage of Captain Popanilla*, which was to be his last literary collaboration with Sara Austen. Disraeli was a fast writer. *Popanilla*, which he began about mid-April, was published, again by Colburn, on 3 June 1828. It was a lively, sometimes silly, satire, owing something to Peacock and Swift, but principally to Voltaire, recounting the experiences of a 'Candide' figure, Captain Popanilla, in 'Vraibleusia', obviously contemporary London. It was primarily a tract against Benthamite utilitarianism, a theme to which Disraeli was to remain faithful throughout his political life. It also, however, ironically for the future leader of the Tory Party, attacked such Conservative targets as the Agricultural Interest, the Corn Laws, the Duke of Wellington, the Colonial System, the Aristocracy, and the London Clubs. *Popanilla* was an amplification of his earlier abortive satire, *Aylmer Papillon*, most of which Murray, on Disraeli's advice, had consigned to the flames. It was dedicated to Plumer Ward, who flatteringly compared it with the productions of Swift and Voltaire; but, although it ran to a second edition in 1829 illustrated by Daniel Maclise, who was later to play a painful part in Disraeli's life, nobody took much notice of it.

Exhausted by the effort of writing *Popanilla*, and, perhaps, discouraged by its lack of success, Benjamin fell ill again, a prolonged fit of depression which lasted, more or less continuously, for some two years. In the summer of 1829, the D'Israeli family left 6 Bloomsbury Square for good and moved to Bradenham House in Buckinghamshire, their principal reason for the move being, Isaac D'Israeli told Southey, 'the precarious health of several members of my family' – presumably meaning Maria and Benjamin.

From then on Benjamin looked on Bradenham as home and adopted Buckinghamshire as his native county. Indeed the move seems to have done him good; in the autumn of 1829 his spirits began to revive. Once again, he was full of ideas; he was working on two serious novels, which were to be *Alroy* and *Contarini Fleming*. He was tempted by dreams of Parliament, and wrote to Benjamin Austen asking him for help in negotiating the purchase of an estate at Stockton, which would give him the property qualification then necessary for a parliamentary candidate. Austen was willing, but the Stockton plan proved to be yet another of Benjamin's castles in the air; Isaac was unlikely to finance it. 'The Governor is fairly frightened' by the agricultural distress in his county, Benjamin informed Austen, 'Stockton is no go'. Benjamin may have contemplated the immunity from arrest for debt conferred by membership of Parliament as an escape route from the creditors who were so pressing him that he hardly dared venture to London.

At the same time, he had evolved another more important plan, suggested perhaps by Byron's solution to a similar situation in 1809. This was to leave England for a protracted tour of the Mediterranean and the Near East, escaping his creditors, collecting background material for his novels, and restoring his health at the same time. It is clear that Byron was in the forefront of his mind at this time; writing to Austen whom he considered his closest friend and confidant, he deliberately copied Byronic phrases. 'You are my sheet anchor & the most valuable of friends', he told Austen, using Byron's terminology for his friend and banker, Douglas Kinnaird; and, referring to his projected tour, a quotation from *The Corsair*, Canto III, 'The fact is I am "spellbound within the clustering

Cyclades" and go I must', ending with an impudent and revealing postscript: 'By the bye, I advise you to take care of my letters, for if I become half as famous as I intend to be, you may sell them for ten guineas a piece to the Keepsake for 1840: that being the price, on dit, at which that delicate creature D[ouglas] K[innaird] furnishes a Byronic epistle to the Annuals.'[7]

But how was the trip to be financed? Isaac 'fairly knocked [the idea] on the head' when it was broached to him; there was nothing for it, Benjamin concluded but to write a potboiler novel: 'I fear I must *hack* for it', he told Austen. 'A literary prostitute I have never been, tho' born in an age of general prostitution ... My mind however is still a virgin, but the mystical flower, I fear, must even be plucked – Colburn I suppose will be the bawd. Tempting Mother Colburn!'[8]

The result of Benjamin's 'hacking' was another society novel, *The Young Duke*, written during this winter of 1829-30, and sold to Colburn for £500 in March 1830. 'What does Ben know of Dukes?' Isaac is said to have remarked on hearing of the project. The answer was of course nothing; Benjamin's young hero, the handsome, blond, intelligent, fabulously rich Duke of St James, bore a far closer resemblance to the type of figure Benjamin would have liked to be than he did to any real-life young English aristocrat. Written in a dashing, sparkling style, *The Young Duke* is an entertaining book, yet even in this 'hack' work Disraeli returned to the *Vivian Grey* theme of the brilliant youth corrupted by an artificial society; the hero, in this case, being redeemed through love for a pure woman. Nor could he resist the interpolation of deeply-felt autobiographical comment, another public plea for understanding:

> Mind is a fine thing, I won't deny it, and mine was once as full of pride and hope as an infant empire. But where are now my deeds and aspirations, and where the fame I dreamed of when a boy? I find the world just slipping through my fingers, and cannot grasp the jewel ere it falls ...
>
> My life has been a blunder and a blank, and all ends by my adding one more slight ghost to the shadowy reality of fatal precocity! ... My punishment is no caprice or tyranny. I brought it on myself.

The experience, he says, has led him to discover his own soul: 'I have that within me, which man can neither give nor take away, which can throw a light on the darkest passages of life, and draw from a discordant world, a melody divine.'[9]

Significantly, the subtitle of *The Young Duke*, 'A Moral Tale, Though Gay', was taken from Byron's *Don Juan*, and Benjamin, as can be seen from the quotations above, was here at his most Byronic, throwing down the gauntlet to a cynical world which had turned against the young rebel who had exposed its corruption. From the heights of poetic self-knowledge, he looked down with pity upon his critics, the literary establishment, 'A qualm comes over me, when for a moment, I call to mind their little jealousies and their minute hatreds, their wretched plans, and miserable purposes; their envy, their ignorance, and their malice.'[10] This was the real Disraeli, the duellist; unrepentant, challenging the world.

Disraeli initially thought highly of the book, the first which he had written without the help of Sara Austen; so much so that he sent the manuscript for criticism to Edward Lytton Bulwer (who later changed his name to Bulwer Lytton), author of the best-selling society novel of the decade, *Pelham*, published in 1828. Bulwer, just over a year older than Benjamin, had much in common with him, and indeed the two were destined to become intimate friends two years later when Benjamin returned from the East. He too was a dandy novelist, intelligent, sensitive, vain and foppish; like Benjamin he was loathed by the London literary set, indeed Benjamin's enemy, Lockhart, wrote of *Pelham* to Scott that it was 'writ by a Mr. Bulwer, a Norfolk squire and a horrid puppy'. Later he was to refer to Benjamin as 'Ben Disraeli – the Jew scamp'. Apart from dandyism and literary success, Bulwer attracted Benjamin as a past lover of Byron's mistress, Lady Caroline Lamb.

Bulwer's reaction was favourable, but cautious; warning Benjamin to take out 'the flippancies', he characteristically advised him to 'give matured attention to the Duke's *dress* – I confess I think the blonde edgings too bold – these are the things that make enemies'.[11] Encouraged, perhaps, by Bulwer's not unfavourable comments, and perhaps worried by Colburn's financial difficulties, which had obliged him to take on Bentley as a partner and defer the publication of *The Young Duke* for a year, Benjamin then had the audacity to approach John Murray. Murray's response to his request for an interview was stiff and in the third person, declining to see him and suggesting he simply deliver his manuscript. Benjamin was stung into hauteur in his reply, but, on further reflection decided against sending it to Murray. 'The work is one which, I daresay, w[oul]d neither disgrace you to publish, nor me to write, but it is not the kind of production which should recommence our connection, or be introduced to the world by the publisher of Byron', he wrote on 27 May.[12] Indeed, that he should have thought, after all that had passed, of submitting to Murray a book that contained yet another attack on Murray's literary friends, displays the astounding effrontery of which Disraeli was capable.

Effrontery was indeed a prominent characteristic of Benjamin at this time. Relieved from the menaces of his most pressing creditors by a loan of £50 from the ever-faithful Austen, he, according to Meredith, paraded down Regent Street at its most crowded hour, gaudily dressed in blue surtout, military light blue trousers, black stockings with red stripes and red shoes. He was delighted at the sensation he caused, boasting to William Meredith, 'The people quite made way for me as I passed. It was like the opening of the Red Sea, which I now perfectly believe from experience. Even well-dressed people stopped to look at me!' 'I should think so!' Meredith commented.[13]

Austen does not seem to have been disturbed that Benjamin must have been increasing his debts to unfortunate tailors to fit himself out in such peacock finery, for he gave him a letter of credit for £500 addressed to bankers at Malta, Smyrna and Constantinople, to finance his tour to the East. Perhaps he was grateful for Benjamin's helpfulness in smoothing out a quarrel which had arisen between the

Austens and the D'Israelis over the breaking off of an engagement between Benjamin's first cousin, Benjamin Lindo, and Sara Austen's sister, Louisa Rickett, apparently at Sara's instigation. Maria D'Israeli took her nephew's part, refusing to dine with the Austens on the ground that it would be 'a *marked* disrespect to him', writing resentfully to Sara that her own Benjamin had left home unexpectedly, but 'I dare say you know more of him than I do.' Benjamin, profoundly and exclusively interested in himself, and bored by such domestic dissensions, was quite unmoved by his cousin's discomfiture. Ben Lindo's accusations of 'undue influence' having been exerted over Louisa to break off the engagement, only proved, he said, that 'he had not succeeded in securing her affections, which shows a great want of *gumption*'. He for one, was not prepared to quarrel with his benefactor for his cousin's wounded pride, and did what he could to help Austen smooth things down. 'I hope the feelings between the families will not now change,' he wrote.[14]

Benjamin, absorbed by the prospect of his imminent departure for the East, did not for one moment contemplate settling his financial affairs before he left, although he does seem to have felt slight qualms as far as Thomas Evans, his former fellow clerk and speculator, was concerned. Their principal creditor on the transaction of 1824-5 was Robert Messer, whom Benjamin, in a letter to Evans, blamed for seducing 'our inexperienced youth' to financial ruin. Benjamin himself was not prepared to do anything about Messer's claims, and the onus of paying him off seems to have fallen upon Evans, now a respectable Bristol solicitor, and perhaps better placed to do so. Benjamin had not written to Evans for the past two years, even though he still owed him money on their transactions. Now, on the eve of departure, perhaps with a tinge of guilt, relieved by the knowledge that he would soon be beyond reach, he sat down to write to him, assuring him of his regret at leaving England without settling his 'distracted affairs', and of his continued 'friendship, interest and respect'. As soon as he could afford it, he promised, Evans would be first in line for the satisfaction of his debts. 'Sooner or later the power will be mine', he wrote, '... for there is something within me which in spite of all the dicta of the faculty [of medicine?] & in the face of the prostrate state in which I lie, that whispers to me I shall yet weather this fearful storm & that a more prosperous career may yet open to me'.[15]

It was typical of Benjamin's extreme egotism that he should have expected poor Evans to find this promise reassuring, and not to feel annoyance and betrayal at the prospect of his departure on an extravagant tour to the East without paying his debts. To Benjamin, the saving of himself for posterity and his destiny was of more importance than his financial obligations to Evans, a high line which he was to take with a long line of creditors, including Austen who had made his grand tour to the East possible.

Disraeli's tour to the East was to be the formative experience of his life, colouring his subsequent career – both literary and political. It was also a maturing process through which the Benjamin of 1830, nervous, outwardly flashy, inwardly unsure of himself or of what direction his career should take, afraid that he might remain an invalid for life, would be transformed into the young Disraeli of 1832, still dandified in manner and appearance, but with sufficient inner confidence to face the world of fashion and politics. In just over a year, between May 1830 and October 1831, he was to visit Gibraltar, Southern Spain, Malta, Corfu, Albania, Greece, Turkey, the Holy Land and Egypt. He would encounter such diverse personages as English governors and their ladies, Spanish bandits, ferocious Turkish beys, Italian philosophers and Egyptian prostitutes. He would experience all-night drinking sessions in the fastnesses of an Albanian caravanserai, the romantic contemplation of the ruins of ancient civilizations from Athens to Thebes, the mystical joy of visiting the land of his forefathers and meditating on Jerusalem, and the sensual pleasures of smoking *kif* in Cairo.

The letters which Disraeli sent to his family, to the Austens, and to Bulwer Lytton during his travels were some of the longest and most descriptive he ever wrote. He intended them to be kept and used in place of a journal as source material for the two novels, *Alroy* and *Contarini Fleming*, which were to be completed on his return home; whole paragraphs were to be quarried from them, sometimes word for word. They present his experiences, embellished as a theatrical panorama, a gorgeous backdrop, with himself an exotic figure in centre stage.

Benjamin left London by steamer for Falmouth on 28 May 1830, with William Meredith, recently officially engaged to Sarah, as his travelling companion. A week later they sailed on the mail packet for Gibraltar, arriving on the Rock at the end of June. They had letters of introduction to the Governor, Sir George Don, whom Benjamin described as 'a very fine old gentleman ... almost regal in his manner', and his wife, 'though very old, without exception one of the most agreeable personages that I ever met ... though excessively infirm, her eye is so brilliant and so full of *moquerie* that you quite forget her wrinkles'.[16] According to Meredith, Benjamin rapidly succeeded in impressing the august Sir George with his lectures on morals and politics, and his acute lady with the brilliance of his conversation, and the two young men were soon frequent guests at Government House. Benjamin delighted in the grandeur and formality of Sir George's entourage, the 'elegant and recherché' repasts, and the Governor's summer drink, 'half champagne and half lemonade'. Even a sightseeing expedition to some caves near the Dons' summer residence was conducted with gubernatorial pomp, with Sir George riding in a carriage preceded by two grooms on Barbary horses, and accompanied by a walking footman and an outrider. On reaching the caves, Sir George donned an enormous plumed cocked-hat, 'because', Benjamin commented, 'the hero will never be seen in public in undress, although we were in a solitary cave looking over the ocean, and inhabited only by monkeys'.

The Governor advised them to visit the wild Sierra de Ronda in Spain, even lending them Brunet, his *cazador* (huntsman) for the expedition. Brunet's colourful history and talents excited Benjamin's admiration. 'What a man!' he exclaimed, 'Born in Italy of French parents, he has visited, as the captain of a privateer, all countries of the Mediterranean ... as valet to Lord Hood, he was in England, and has even been at Guinea. After fourteen years cruising he was taken by the Algerines, and was in various parts of Barbary for five or six years. ...'[17] Although fifty years old, Brunet was 'light as a butterfly and gay as a bird', speaking every language but English, a great shot and an exquisite cook. Accompanied by this paragon and by a local guide, Benjamin and William, mounted on Andalusian ponies, roamed the Sierra de Ronda for a week, often spending eight hours in the saddle. They risked a night at Castellar, 'the very haunt of the banditti', Benjamin wrote dramatically, describing the Sierra as 'a land entirely of robbers and smugglers ... who commit no personal violence but lay you on the ground and clean out your pockets. If you have less than sixteen dollars they shoot you'.[18]

Sarah replied on receiving these reports that the family at Bradenham 'quite tremble at your exertions'. Previously they had heard no news and Benjamin's mother 'with her facility in auguring evil, is quite sure you are very ill.' Benjamin's ill-health runs like a theme through these early letters of the tour, haunting him even in the delightful Sierra de Ronda. To Isaac he wrote of 'the great enemy', the strange sensations in his head; 'had it not been for the great enemy I should have given myself up entirely to the magic of the life; but that spoiled all. It is not worse; sometimes I think it lighter about the head, but the palpitation about the heart greatly increases'. He went on to utter a cry of absolute despair: 'Never have I been better; but what use is this when the end of all existence is debarred me? I say no more upon this melancholy subject, by which I am ever and infinitely depressed, and often most so when the world least imagines it'.[19] What did he mean by 'the end of all existence'? Not literature, because he had already proved he could write in the intervals of his illness, nor was it politics, since Austen, writing about this time of the general election in England precipitated by the death of George IV, expressed regret that Benjamin, being abroad, would not be able to take part in the campaign. One can only conjecture that he meant marriage, from which he felt himself 'debarred' by his uncertain mental health.

As if aware of the uselessness of complaining, Benjamin immediately switched to a lighter tone, a dandy again:

> Tell my mother that as it is the fashion of this place ... not to wear waistcoats in the morning, her new studs come into play, and maintain my reputation of being a great judge of costume, to the admiration and envy of many subalterns. I have also the fame of being the first who ever passed the Straits with two canes, a morning and an evening cane. I change my cane as the gun fires ... It is wonderful the effect these magical wands produce. I owe to them even more attention than to being the supposed author of – what is it? – I forget![20]

His recurrent fear of baldness appeared again; the prospect being so awful that he must adopt a half-joking, half-serious manner:

> I am sorry to say my hair is coming off, just at the moment it had attained the highest

perfection, and was universally mistaken for a wig, so that I am obliged to let the women pull it to satisfy their curiosity. Let me know what my mother thinks. There are no wigs here that I c[oul]d wear. Pomade and all that is quite a delusion. Somebody recommends me cocoa-nut oil, which I c[oul]d get here; but suppose it turns it grey or blue or green![21]

'We mourn over your locks', Sarah replied sympathetically. 'Mamma advises you to try Cocoa-Nut or anything. I am sure Smith could send you a wig.'[22]

Their experiences in the Sierra de Ronda having whetted their appetites for Spain, Benjamin and William abandoned their plan to go on to Malta for the present, and doubled back to Cadiz, Byron's 'perfect Cythera', for a tour of Andalusia. It was already late July, but despite the heat they visited Seville, sailed up the Guadalquivir and then rode on to Cordova. Benjamin's reactions were those of the conventional travelogue: 'Cadiz ... white houses and the green jalousies sparkle in the sun. Figaro is in every street; Rosina is in every balcony'. From Granada he treated his mother to a patronizing discourse on Spanish women, 'these Espagnolas are nevertheless very interesting personages' whose only fault, apart from their sallow complexions, was a tendency to run early to fat, but he forgave them everything for their soft little hands and the graceful language of their fans. He sent her a receipt for an 'olio ... the most agreeable dish in the world ... my father would delight in it.'[23] The 'agreeable dish' turned out to be an indigestible mixture of boiled meat and sausage, vegetables and fruits, drowned in tomato sauce, a highly unsuitable diet, one would have thought, for an elderly gentleman.

The sun and the 'calm voluptuousness' of Spanish life suited him, he told his mother; his general health had never been better, but mentally he was not recovered. 'The moment I attempt to meditate ... or in any way to call the greater powers of intellect into operation, that moment I feel a lost man. The palpitation in my heart and head increases in violence, an indescribable feeling of idiocy comes over me, and for hours I am plunged in a state of the darkest despair.'[24] Maria, ignoring all talk of 'Espagnolas' and 'olios', sent an anguished reply, saying that Ben's letter 'gave me great pain to me the news of your returning health will be the greatest [news]'.

At Granada Benjamin, with his empathy for the East and his fantasies of Spanish ancestry, felt himself at home. He was carried away by the Islamic splendours of the Alhambra: 'The Saracenic architecture is the most inventive and fanciful, but at the same time the most fitting and the most delicate that can be conceived', he wrote to Isaac. Wandering through the halls and courtyards, his imagination was fired with brilliant scenes of the past, almost as if he had lived it. Indeed, Benjamin's Oriental appearance and his theatrical manner as he pictured himself living in the time of the Caliphs convinced their guide that he was a Moor, as Meredith recorded:

The old lady who showed us over the Alhambra, talkative and intelligent, would have it that Benjamin D. was a Moor, many of whom come to visit this palace, which they say will yet be theirs again. His southern aspect, the style in which he paced the gorgeous apartments, and sat himself in the seat of the Abencerrages, quite deceived her; she repeated the question a dozen times, and would not be convinced to the contrary. His parting speech, 'Es mi casa'. 'This is my palace [sic]' quite confirmed her suspicions.[25]

'Oh! Wonderful Spain! Think of this romantic land covered with Moorish ruins and full of Murillo!' Benjamin apostrophized from Gibraltar, recalling the two aspects of Spain that had really moved him. His artistic taste was indeed conventional – Murillo's madonnas appealed to him so much that he later had a copy of one hanging in his London dining-room. From Gibraltar, they sailed to Malta, arriving there on 19 August, and, after an unpleasant week spent in the regulation quarantine in the Lazaretto, launched themselves on the pleasures of garrison life.

At Malta, Benjamin made a new friend, James Clay, a companion much more to his taste than the sober Meredith, whose principal advantage to the impractical Benjamin had been his efficiency in dealing with the mundane details of travel, which Benjamin found 'a bore'. Clay, a year younger than Benjamin, was rich, exceedingly handsome, a great card-player who later wrote an authoritative book on whist, a sportsman and womanizer; he had been at Winchester at the same time as Benjamin's brother Ralph, and the D'Israeli family knew him, and disapproved of him. Benjamin, whose sexual experience and knowledge of the world were both limited and largely vicarious, was obviously fascinated by the dashing Clay, and as the tour wore on, his references to Meredith in his letters became ever rarer, while Clay's name was seldom absent. The D'Israeli family were alarmed; they 'had a horror of him and dreaded his influence over D.', Disraeli's legal adviser, Philip Rose, later noted. 'I am sure', Sarah wrote meaningly to her brother, 'James Clay must be very much improved for you to make such a friend of him.'

The two of them spent their days playing billiards and cards, racing and smoking with the young officers of the garrison, with whom Clay made himself very popular, while Benjamin, it would appear for good reason, was heartily detested. This was the account of his own behaviour Benjamin sent to his father:

> To govern men [a favourite and revealing phrase], you must either excel them in their accomplishments, or despise them. Clay does one, I do the other, and we are equally popular. Affectation tells here even better than wit. Yesterday at the racket court, sitting in the gallery among strangers, the ball entered and lightly struck me and fell at my feet. I picked it up, and observing a young rifleman excessively stiff, I humbly requested him to forward its passage into the court, as I really had never thrown a ball in my life. This incident has been the general subject of conversation at all the messes to-day![26]

Disraeli's boast of being 'equally popular' had a pathetic ring; he was an outsider among the pink-cheeked, public school young officers and seemingly had no idea of the disgust and hostility which his behaviour would arouse. Clay's version of their time in Malta, later retailed to Sir William Gregory, had the ring of truth. 'It would not have been possible to have found a more agreeable, unaffected companion when they were by themselves; but when they got into society, his [Disraeli's] coxcombry was intolerable ... He made himself so hateful to the officers' messes that, while they welcomed Clay, they ceased to invite "that damned bumptious Jew boy".'[27] Disraeli's 'coxcombry' was, as he later admitted in his diary, the reaction of insecurity in the face of the Anglo-Saxon tribe, of which this was his strongest experience hitherto. According to one contemporary, Disraeli never overcame the feeling of being 'not quite up to the mark' in social matters, and that he was being criticized by his interlocutors. It was this feeling, perhaps, that expressed itself in the wistful worship of Eton in his later books.

The subalterns' reaction of distaste, did, of course, reach him, although he would not admit it, taking his revenge upon them by contemptuous references in his letters home. Comparing the two officers, George Liddell and Edmund Pery, who were friendly to him, with the rest of the tribe, he wrote: 'They are both men of the world and g[oo]d company, forming a remarkable [contrast] to all their brother officers for sooth to [tell] a visit to Gibraltar and Malta ... has quite opened my eyes to [the] real life and character of a milita[ire]. By heavens! I believe these fellows are boys until they are majors, and sometimes d[on't] even stop then.'[28]

Benjamin's public reaction to this hostility was, characteristically, challenging. He showed off; dining at a regimental mess in Andalusian dress, and paying calls, according to Meredith 'in his majo jacket, white trousers, and a sash of all the colours of the rainbow; in this wonderful costume he paraded all round Valetta, followed by one-half of the population of the place, and, as he said, putting a complete stop to all business. He, of course, included the Governor and Lady Emily in his round, to their no small astonishment.' The Governor, Sir Frederick Ponsonby, being a brother of Lady Caroline Lamb, can have been no stranger to exhibitionist behaviour. At any rate, although he had the reputation of being 'a very nonchalant personage, and exceedingly exclusive in his conduct to his subjects', Disraeli amused him so much that he rolled about on the sofa, Benjamin told Isaac 'from his rissible [sic] convulsions.'

To his brother Ralph, he boasted of his prowess at smoking, picturing himself sitting in an easy chair with a Turkish pipe six feet long with an amber mouthpiece and a porcelain bowl. Friends had presented him not only with this, but with a meerschaum and a green Dresden china pipe set in silver. He wrote: 'What if I tell you that I [h]ave not only become a smoker, but the greatest smoker in [M]alta. The fact is I find it relieve my head'.[29]

Clay, he told Ralph, had in true 'milord' style hired a fifty-five-ton yacht, with the sadly unpoetical name of *Susan*: 'a bore; but as we can't alter it, we have painted it out.' Clay's greatest *coup* in Benjamin's eyes was the acquisition of a former servant of Byron's, a huge Venetian named Giovanni Battista Falcieri, known as 'Tita'. Tita, from being Byron's gondolier, became his personal servant, and was with him at Missolonghi; after Byron's death, he continued fighting for the Greek cause at the head of a regiment of Albanians, ending up after the war at Malta in a state of poverty. For Disraeli, who had embarked on this tour in Byron's footsteps, the finding of Byron's servant must have seemed strangely significant. 'Byron died in his arms, and his mustachios touch the earth,' he told Ralph.

In the third week of September, Benjamin and William left Malta as paying passengers on Clay's yacht, Benjamin having acquired the costume of a Greek pirate. 'You should see me ... A blood red shirt with silver studs as big as shillings, an immense scarf or girdle full of pistols and daggers, a red cap, red slippers, blue broad striped jacket and trousers. Excessively wicked!'[30]

Their destination was, again in Byron's footsteps, Albania. Benjamin had conceived a plan, extraordinary in so devoted an admirer of the hero of Missolonghi, of volunteering for the Turkish army fighting the Albanian rebels. Disraeli aped Byron's dress, style and attitudes, but not, it would seem, his political views. Perhaps influenced by his father, he looked upon the French Revolution and its ideals as a dangerous and fanatical error; he was never to have any sympathy with nationalist causes or indeed rebels anywhere. His reactions were always highly personal and idiosyncratic, even illogical; the Turks appealed to his Oriental imagination, their rebellious subjects, the Greeks, did not. He was undeterred when, on arriving at Corfu, they discovered that the war had petered out into a savage mopping-up operation by the Turks. 'I shall turn my intended campaign into a visit of congratulation to headquarters', he told Austen.

And so Clay, Meredith, Disraeli and Tita set off into the interior of Albania on a journey which included a night of wild drinking with a young Turkish Bey, graphically described in a letter to Isaac:

> The wine was not bad, but if it had been poison we must drink it; it was such a compliment for a Moslemin; we quaffed it in rivers. The Bey called for the brandy – we drank it all – the room turned round, the wild attendants who sat at our feet seemed dancing in strange and fantastic whirls, the Bey shook hands with me; he shouted English – I Greek. 'Very Good' he had caught up from us. 'Kalo, kalo' was my rejoinder. He roared; I smacked him on the back. I remember no more.[31]

At Yanina Benjamin had audience with the redoubtable Grand Vizier, Reschid Pasha, in an enormous Hall built by the Pasha to house the largest Gobelin carpet ever made, once in Versailles, which he had bought during the French Revolution. Squatting on a corner of the large divan was a 'little ferocious-looking, shrivelled, care-worn man, plainly dressed, with a brow covered with wrinkles', the Grand Vizier, 'who' the Austrian consul observed to Disraeli 'has destroyed in the course of the last three months, *not* in war, upwards of four thousand of my acquaintance'. Benjamin, according to his own account, 'bowed with all the nonchalance of St. James's Street' and seated himself on the divan 'with the self-possession of a morning call'. The Pasha was clearly too busy to spend much time on three young Englishmen and the interview was speedily concluded, but Benjamin was enchanted by his reception, as he wrote later to Austen: 'For a week I was in a scene equal to anything in the arabian nights – such processions, such dresses, such corteges [sic] of horsemen, such caravans of camels. Then the delight of being made much of by a man who was daily decapitating half the Province.'[32] He conceived a strong admiration and liking for the Turks and the Turkish way of life, a prejudice that was to colour his view of the Eastern Question nearly fifty years later: 'I am quite a Turk, wear a Turban, smoke a pipe six feet long, and squat on a divan ... in fact I find the habits of this calm and luxurious people entirely agree with my own preconceived opinions of propriety and enjoyment, and I detest the Greeks more than ever'.

Wrapped up in this exciting Oriental world, Disraeli did not notice, or at least did not mention, the sufferings of the Albanian Christian population under the Grand Vizier's reprisals; 'the delight of being made much of by a man who was daily decapitating half the Province', his flippant aside to Austen foreshadowing his reaction, years later, to the Bulgarian Atrocities which he would fail to see in terms of human tragedy, as he would also fail to perceive that Gladstone's passionate condemnation of the massacres would be the view of the vast majority of Englishmen. The righteous compassion of liberal do-gooders had no part in Disraeli's make-up.

He did not emerge from the savage Asian fantasy of Albania until the contemplation of Olympus at dusk, touched by the rays of the setting sun, reminded him that he was in Europe. 'When I gaze upon this scene, I remember the barbaric splendor, and turbulent existence I have just quitted with disgust ...', he wrote, adding again that cryptic despairing phrase: 'I recur to the feelings in the indulgence of which I can alone find happiness, and from which an inexorable destiny seems resolved to shut me out ...'.[33] After Olympus they sailed through the Ionian sea, spending a week at Navarino, thence to Nauplia, Corinth, Argos, Mycenae, arriving at Piraeus on 24 November. At Athens they were fortunate enough to be able to visit the Acropolis which had been closed for the past nine years, and although evidence of the late siege lay all around them and every house in the city was roofless, Disraeli wrote enthusiastically to Sara Austen: 'Nothing has more completely realized all that I imagined and all that I could have wished than Athens'. The memory of Athens soon faded when Benjamin saw Constantinople at sunset, a sight, he told Isaac, which 'baffles all description ... an immense mass of buildings, cupolas, cypress groves and minarets. I feel an excitement which I thought was long dead.'[34]

At Constantinople, Disraeli was entertained by the genial pro-Turk British Ambassador, Sir Robert Gordon, a first cousin of Byron. Benjamin spent some six weeks at Constantinople, revelling in the luxurious strangeness of Turkish life, lounging daily in the shop of 'Mustapha the Imperial perfumer', attending masked balls and Embassy dinners. As he wrote to Bulwer on 27 December:

> I confess to you that my Turkish prejudices are very much confirmed by my residence in Turkey. The life of this people greatly accords with my taste which is naturally somewhat indolent and melancholy.... To repose on voluptuous ottomans and smoke superb pipes, daily to indulge in the luxury of a bath which requires half a dozen attendants for its perfection; to court the air in a carved caique, by shores which are a perpetual scene, and to find no exertion greater than a canter on a barb is I think, a far more sensible life than all the bustle of clubs, all the boring of saloons [salons].[35]

It is probable that Benjamin did not limit his enjoyments to baths, Turkish pipes, and embassy parties; it is very likely that, under Clay's expert auspices, he had his first sexual initiation in the brothels of Constantinople. Benjamin was probably, until then, a virgin; his sexual drive does not seem to have been very strong, indeed previously on the tour there were only a few facetious references to women – 'a beauty which threatened to endanger your brother's peace of mind' etc. But by the time he reached London again he had venereal disease, contracted either at Constantinople or at Cairo.

In January Benjamin and Clay set sail for Smyrna, Meredith, probably disapproving of their Turkish debaucheries, having left them two weeks earlier to make his way there overland. From Smyrna they sailed via Cyprus to Jaffa, once again parting from Meredith who was determined upon an expedition to what Benjamin termed 'the unseen relics of some unheard-of cock and bull city'. From Jaffa they rode inland towards Benjamin's goal, Jerusalem. He was, he told Sarah, 'thunderstruck' at the sight: 'I saw before me apparently a gorgeous city. Nothing can be conceived more wild and terrible and barren than the surrounding scenery, dark, stony and severe, but the ground is thrown about in such picturesque undulations, that the mind [is] full of the sublime, not the beautiful, and rich and waving woods and sparkling cultivation wo[ul]d be misplaced'.[36]

Clay and Disraeli, lodged in a house belonging to the great Franciscan monastery of San Salvador, spent a week, described by Benjamin 'as the most delightful in all our travels' in Jerusalem, sightseeing, receiving various ecclesiastical dignitaries, and dining on the roof of their house by moonlight. Benjamin was deeply impressed by Jerusalem and the land of his fathers, on which he was to dwell at length in his novels, *Alroy*, *Contarini Fleming* and *Tancred*, drawing on his impressions of that brief week in the early spring of 1831. He wrote few letters while there, and one may conjecture that he was already at work on *Alroy*, or taking notes for it.

From Jerusalem Disraeli and Clay travelled to Egypt, reaching Alexandria on 12 March 1831. From Alexandria they proceeded up the Nile 'for seven hundred miles to the very confines of Nubia' spending a week at Thebes where they were fortunate enough to have the guidance of Mr (later Sir) Gardner Wilkinson, an expert in the study of hieroglyphics 'who can read you the side of an obelisk or the front of a pylon as we would the last number of the *Quarterly*'. By the end of May he was back in Cairo to receive family congratulations for *The Young Duke*, which Colburn, with a very poor sense of timing, had chosen to bring out, together with Isaac's *Commentaries on the Life and Reign of Charles I*, on the very day that Parliament was dissolved, when no one was thinking or talking of anything but Reform. But Benjamin, his mind upon more serious literary projects, was nonchalant, 'I don't care a jot about the Y[oung] D[uke]. I never staked any fame on it. It may take its chance.'[37]

At Cairo Benjamin was living in a world far removed from that of the fashionable novel. While Meredith explored the Upper Nile and Clay and Tita spent the days shooting and swimming in the Delta, making themselves ill in consequence,

Benjamin passed his time with a new and fascinating friend, Paul Emile Botta. Botta, the son of an Italian historian living in Paris, was a year younger than Benjamin, a brilliant, adventurous man who later became a distinguished archaeologist. Disraeli wrote that he was one of the three men from whose conversation he had derived most benefit, describing him, thinly disguised as Count Marigny in *Contarini Fleming* as 'a sceptic and an absolute materialist, yet influenced by noble views, for he had devoted his life to science, and was now ... about to penetrate into the interior of Africa by Sennaar'. From Botta's letters to Benjamin, it appears that they spent long nights communing together at the house of an Englishman called Galloway, lounging on divans with legs outstretched, smoking *kif*, drinking Turkish coffee and talking of 'the Old Story, these poor injured great men, or against Cant and Superstition.' 'My mind made a jump in these high discourses,' Benjamin later recorded, and it seems that, in conversation with this brilliant, tortured young man who often sought to ease his mental pain with drugs, he achieved a plane of communication which he had not experienced before. Botta, as well as smoking *kif*, was addicted to opium, spending his days 'in racing and nights enjoying the delights of opium, that great soother of pains.' 'My soul,' he wrote to Benjamin, 'if I have one, is as sick as ever. I am always tired of myself, disgusted with the world where nothing is certain but misery and longing without any hope after what cannot be obtained, the word of that great secret of Creation and existence'.[38] Their conversations were not always on the high plane of the meaning of existence, for a letter which Botta wrote to Benjamin from Sennaar in the summer of 1832 described in a tone of black comedy and graphic detail the savage process of infibulation, and the advantages, from the male point of view, of vaginal cloture.[39]

Finally, in June, as Disraeli and Clay were planning to leave Cairo, Meredith arrived from his solitary tour of Upper Egypt. They postponed their departure to give Meredith the chance to enjoy Cairo, a fatal decision; ten days before they intended to leave, he went down with smallpox. He was, however, thought to be in no danger, and Clay went off to Alexandria to see about a passage, leaving Benjamin with the patient who was attended by an Italian doctor from the hospital, Dr Gaettani. At 5 pm on 19 July, Benjamin was conversing with Botta in a room adjacent to Meredith's, when Meredith's servant came rushing in crying that his master had fainted. The two men ran to his room where he was lying, apparently lifeless. At first Disraeli refused to believe he was dead; it was not until Botta opened a vein to prove it that the dreadful truth dawned upon him.

Benjamin's thoughts were all for his sister who he knew would be utterly crushed by this blow. Her marriage to William, after the ten-year courtship, had been certain; now, at almost thirty, it was unlikely that she would find another husband. She seems to have had a premonition that something was wrong, for on 1 August, when William had already been dead for over ten days, she wrote to Benjamin: 'We should be more satisfied could we hear that you & William are well for in these days of universal plague we know not what we fear, and fancy all sorts of evils'. After a 'night of horror' during which Botta sat up with him 'as I cd. not sleep and dared not be alone ... my anguish was overpowering', he sat down to the dreadful task of writing the letters that were to bring intelligence of William's death to both families. Drafts in Benjamin's hand, which begin in a formal script and swiftly degenerate into a despairing scrawl testify to the difficulty he found in shaping the form the terrible news was to take. The first letter was to his father, headed 'READ THIS ALONE'. It began, 'If you were not a great philosopher as well as a good man, I do not think that I could communicate to you the terrible intelligence which is now to be imparted by this trembling pen ... Our William is lost to us'. 'Our innocent lamb is stricken', he continued. 'Save her, save her ... I wish to live only for my sister. I think of her all day and all night'.[40] It is not difficult to imagine with what a heavy heart he wrote to Sarah, 'Ere you open this page, our beloved father will have imparted to you with all the tenderness of parental love the terrible intelligence'. There was only one solution in the midst of this great grief; they must live for each other:

> Live then, my heart's treasure, for one who has ever loved you with a surpassing love, and who would cheerfully have yielded his own existence to have saved you the bitterness of this. Yes, my beloved! be my genius, my solace, my companion, my joy! We will never part, and if I cannot be to you all of our lost friend, at least we will feel that Life can never be a blank while illumined by the pure and perfect love of a sister and a brother....[41]

Benjamin had described all too accurately what was to be the future pattern of Sarah's life; as for himself, it was not in his nature to 'live only' for someone else.

Abandoning his plans to wander slowly with Clay back through Italy and France, Benjamin decided to make his way home as quickly as possible, sailing from Alexandria to Malta, and, after a tedious sojourn in quarantine, he boarded H.M.S. *Hermes* for England. In a long letter to his father, written on board ship off Cape St Vincent on 17 October, he revealed his plans and hopes for the future. He had abandoned his dream of marriage which a year ago he had described as 'the end of existence'; 'The [fata]l event [Meredith's death] has entirely changed [my chara]cter, or rather forced me to recur to my original one. I wish no more to increase the circle of domestic sympathies, since they lead to such misery – I will cherish what remain – threefold.'[42] One may surmise that Meredith's death might not have been the only reason why Benjamin's desire to marry became less pressing: his sexual experiences with women in the East had shown him that there was an alternative to marriage as a means of sexual fulfilment. There was also an immediate physical obstacle to marriage; he had venereal disease, as Clay wrote to him from Venice: 'Between us we have contrived to stumble on all the thorns with which (as Mr Dickens the porter at Winchester was wont poetically to observe) Venus guards her roses; for while you were cursing the greater evils, I contrived to secure the minor, viz. a glut from over-exertion and crabs.'[43]

Despite venereal disease and the horror of Meredith's death, Benjamin felt himself reborn as a result of his experiences. His general health was better, he was full of creative energy, and longing to get home to start his life again despite the sad welcome which must await him. He was writing furiously, at work on a book which he hoped would startle the literary establishment, probably *Contarini Fleming*. 'I have some of the right stuff ready for them,' he wrote to Isaac, 'but shall probably let a year at least pass before I publish. I am at last going to attack them in good earnest. I think you will agree that I have at length knocked the nail on the head ... Whatever may be the result I shall at least unburthen my mind, which is absolutely necessary, whatever is to be my future occupation.'[44]

Benjamin had not made up his mind whether he was destined for literature or for politics. But as he approached the shores of an England in the throes of the agitation over the Reform Bill, he could not resist the temptation to throw his hat into the parliamentary arena. 'If the Reform Bill pass,' he told his father, 'I intend to offer myself for Wycomb[e].'

4 *The First Steps*

Disraeli arrived back in England on the day Parliament was prorogued after the House of Lords' rejection of the Second Reform Bill on 8 October 1831. The wit, Sydney Smith, compared the peers' last-ditch resistance to reform with Mrs Partington's efforts to keep the Atlantic out of her cottage with a mop, and indeed the aristocratic citadel of political power was being shaken to its foundations by an irresistible tide of public opinion in favour of parliamentary reform.

Benjamin was to make his first attempts to enter the political citadel in the year following his return from the East, but, for the moment, he could only be a bystander in the great political struggle. Indeed his immediate prospects on returning to the grey realities of England were depressing. It rained incessantly on his arrival at Falmouth so that he caught a bad cold and was forced to lie up at Exeter for two days and took almost a week to reach London, where he spent a few days summoning up the courage to face the bereaved Sarah at Bradenham. There is no account of the meeting between brother and sister, but it must have been heart-rending for Benjamin. Wet autumn days at Bradenham, the gloom cast over the family circle by Sarah's bereavement, the alarming reports of serious riots in favour of Reform all over the country and of a new cholera epidemic, coupled perhaps with anxiety over his venereal disease, soon depressed Benjamin's volatile spirits. 'The times are damnable', he wrote to Austen, and his account to Clay of the circumstances of his return, including the mercury treatment he was undergoing, was so depressing that Clay replied condoling with him for 'having lost the first rush on London ... tho' by your gloomy account London now seems hardly worth a rush'.[1]

The capital, however, was Benjamin's goal and he did not spend long moping at Bradenham. By the second week in November he had taken the first step towards climbing the social ladder, taking lodgings at 15 Pall Mall East, St James's, the 'right' part of town. He soon found himself engaged in a dramatic hunt for Henry Stanley, son of the thirteenth Earl of Derby, whom he had met on the packet travelling to England and who had since disappeared in scandalous circumstances. After a friendly, fraternal letter from Benjamin to the young

Stanley had been opened by his anxious father at Knowsley, Benjamin found himself 'surrounded by Stanleys, all day long, full of despair, making researches and following clues'. Benjamin, aided by a Colonel Long of the Guards, made 'some very extraordinary discoveries and you cannot imagine what curious characters I am obliged to see'. All this, he wrote, prevented his coming down to Bradenham, 'I think you will agree with me that it will be neither kind nor judicious to desert them'.[2] No doubt the heartbroken but loyal Sarah agreed that it would not be 'judicious' to desert the family of one of the greatest magnates in England; her brother was zealous in his efforts to ingratiate himself, tracing Stanley's trail 'to the new exclusive [gaming] Hell in St James' St.', where, 'after a mixture of diplomacy & courage, which I trust were worthy of Mr. Pelham, or any other hero of these volumes post 8vo', he forced the owner, the sinister Mr Bond, to make 'strange and sad disclosures. Nothing can be done now but to call in the aid of the Police'.[3] Benjamin's efforts do not seem to have brought him any reward or social favour; the wretched Henry's brother, Edward Stanley, who was later to be Disraeli's leader and colleague, seems to have blamed Benjamin for his brother's disgrace, and Benjamin's relations with the great Lancashire family were not to be close for another twenty years.

In fact, Benjamin's first attempts to launch himself into society were a failure. He was determined to join a club of standing, not only for the advantages of companionship and reasonably priced food and drink which they provided, but for the social affirmation conferred by membership. His feverish attempts to gain admission to clubs at this stage of his career contrast strangely with his professed dislike of them in the years of success, when almost all of them were open to him. The Benjamin of the 1830s, still in search of identity, yearned to be part of society, however dull; his repeated rejection symbolized his failure to gain acceptance by the solid core of the English establishment who disliked and distrusted him both as a Jew and as the author of *Vivian Grey*. Bulwer warned him, while promising to lobby for his election to the Athenaeum, that he was unlikely to succeed since 'the Ninnies' suspected he would 'clap them into a Book'.[4]

Certain clubs were beyond his reach; membership of the ultra-Tory, ultra-aristocratic Whites' Club, which, with the Garter, was one of the two things, he wrote later, an Englishman could not command, was out of the question for a man of his birth and standing, as was membership of Brooks's, supported by the core of the old Whig aristocracy. Crockford's, the smart club of the 1830s which was essentially a gaming club for the dandies and bloods who played for the highest stakes, with its superb cellar and food presided over by the great Ude, the first to introduce French cooking to England, was also inaccessible. Benjamin, therefore, aimed at the Travellers' to which he thought his journeys entitled him, and the Athenaeum, a club for literary men, of which his father was already a member. Despite the efforts of his family and any friend he could lobby, he failed at both, and it was not until 1833 when he was at last making some social progress that he managed to join a short-lived club, the Albion.

By installing himself in St James's, Benjamin had symbolically turned his back on Bloomsbury and the Austens, but he had not, as yet, the entrée to fashionable society, the world of the nobility and landed gentry which revolved round Parliament and the great London houses of Mayfair and St James's. As a lonely young man in London with few connections, it was, therefore, only too easy for him to fall into the clutches of a dubious couple, Dr George Buckley Bolton and his wife Clara and their circle. Bolton was a rich, successful doctor, with a house in fashionable King Street, St James's. His wife was a vulgarly attractive woman, used, as a more worldly-wise Benjamin noted later, as a 'decoy duck' to attract wealthy clients and to bring the fringes of the smart set to his house. Benjamin had become acquainted with them at Bradenham in the autumn of 1829, when they had made a prolonged stay there to give him medical treatment, and may have begun a flirtation with Clara Bolton then, for the fastidious Sarah certainly disapproved of her. Benjamin's relations with Clara quickly became intimate; by the summer of 1832 she was his mistress, and, according to Disraeli's later legal adviser, Sir Philip Rose, known by his family to be so.

Clara Bolton, a vulgar, pretentious snob liked to think of herself as a society hostess. 'Tonight I have a Soirée of about 20 think of that', she wrote to Benjamin, 'Baron Ralmont, D'Haussez & Haber ... Ellis, Hictons, Gores, Hills, a regular mob we are *as you know* not a formal set and do not sit in rows – and I never amuse people give them nothing to do & nothing to eat and yet they come'.[5] The inexperienced Benjamin was amused, comparing the raffish, cosmopolitan Bolton evenings with the dull dinners given by D'Israeli relations and friends, all of which took place outside the fashionable pale. He wrote to Sarah of dining with acquaintances of the Disraelis: 'So many guests all equally awkward, so many servants of different heights & so many dishes & courses and sauces & such regular boredom'. Benjamin summed up such evenings in one dismissive phrase: 'cold coffee and colder women'.[6] By the end of the summer he was to write proprietorially of Clara's soirées, boasting: 'At Mrs. Bolton's we always command if necessary an evening reunion. Marcus Hill and Charley Gore etc ... We all agree it's better than a club'.[7]

Among the people whom Benjamin met on his frequent visits to the Boltons was a mysterious figure, the Baron de Haber, whom he described to Sarah in a letter of 14 November as 'a nobleman spy, as I conceive, in the interest here of Charles 10 [the late King of France], but who moves in the first circles & is altog[ethe]r one of the most remarkable men I have ever met'. By the next day when he met the Baron again, dining with Captain Angerstein of the Guards, another protégé of Mrs Bolton, he was referring to him as 'my friend, the Baron, most original, wonderful ...' The Baron, a financier of German Jewish origin based at The Hague, was indeed involved with the reactionary party supporting the deposed Charles x of France. The aura of international intrigue and capitalist schemes which surrounded him was calculated to appeal to Benjamin, who loved mystery and a melodramatic view of international politics. Over the next few years he was to involve himself in several intrigues with Haber, none of which were to do him any good.

The truth was that Benjamin was still very much on the fringes of society, although he had become acquainted with a brace of lords, and his name-dropping impressed his family. 'There is no calling on Ben without finding him engaged with Lords', Isaac wrote proudly to Sarah on 19 May 1832. 'I have just escaped by sliding through his bedroom from Lord Strangford & the other day from Lord Eliot – & had he not cut his lip shaving he was to have dined with Lord Stanley at Coll [sic]. Long's . . . he dines on Wednesday to meet Peele [sic]'.

Disraeli wrote to Sarah describing this first meeting with Sir Robert Peel, the Conservative leader whose parliamentary career he was to help to destroy a decade later:

> Yesterday I dined at Eliot's – a male party consisting of eight. I sat between Peel and Herries, but cannot tell you the names of the other guests, altho' they were all members of one or other House . . . Peel was most gracious. He is a very great man indeed, and they all seem afraid of him . . . I can easily conceive that he co[ul]d be very disagreeable, but yesterday he was in a most condescending mood and unbent with becoming haughtiness. I reminded him by my dignified familiarity both that he was Ex-minister and I a present Radical.[8]

Eliot's version of the first encounter between the Tory leader and the political aspirant was somewhat different. Appreciating Disraeli's abilities and his Tory sympathies, he had invited him to dinner with the deliberate intention of enabling him to impress Peel; no easy task, as he admitted, because Peel was never easily approachable or, as Eliot put it, 'You could not go up to him in the stables' with certainty. Disraeli, probably from nervousness, did not recommend himself when, hoping to flatter him, he asked Sir Robert to lend him some papers to illustrate a work he was writing. Peel apparently seems to have taken an 'intuitive dislike to him', for he 'buried his chin in his neckcloth' and did not speak a word to Disraeli during the remainder of the meal.[9] It was hardly an auspicious beginning.

For the moment, therefore, lacking any support from the political establishment, Benjamin fell back on his indefatigable helper, Clara Bolton, to aid him in furthering his career. He seems to have believed that she had some political influence, and in March wrote a guileful letter to Sarah asking her to invite Mrs Bolton to Bradenham on the grounds that she could be of use to him: 'I sh[oul]d like Mrs. Bolton to be asked to Bradenham for many reasons, first because I don't think it possible for her to come 2ndly because she is of great service to me & I know she would highly prize the attention & 3rdly because if she did come she would not bore you & you w[oul]d rather like her. She is so very much improved', adding a pleading postscript, 'If you do not *disapprove* of Mrs. B. it wo[ul]d be well for you to write to her. I much wish to pay her attention'.[10] In fact Mrs Bolton was an inveterate intriguer who could not resist meddling in other people's lives, attempting to stage-manage the political and amatory affairs of her circle.

Acutely materialistic as she was, 'Madame', as Benjamin referred to her, saw clearly that her young lover had little chance of climbing either the social or political ladder without one essential attribute – money. Resolved to keep Benjamin tied to her, she determined he should marry a rich wife of her own choosing, while at the same time she planned to solve the financial problems of another protégé, Angerstein of the Guards, by marrying him to Sarah D'Israeli. 'My head is a complete novel', she wrote to Benjamin, 'my characters yourself & M[argaret] T[rotter], then Angerstein ... his father pays all his debts if he would but take unto himself a wife.'[11] Margaret Trotter was a close friend of the Boltons, an unclaimed treasure with some capital, and both the doctor and his wife worked hard to ensnare Benjamin as a husband for her. Benjamin himself, wary of their machinations, does not seem to have been attracted by their candidate, nor was her money enough to compensate for the loss of his freedom, as he wrote in a frank letter to Sarah, describing his first glimpse of Miss Trotter. 'I perceived a Diana-Vernon-looking personage gallopping [sic] thro' St James Sq., on a bay charger followed by a groom on a grey cob whose tail swept the ground. She stopped at Bolton's as I quitted the door. I suspected it was the fair Margaret, & the next day the puffer General called on me & informed me that the lady's heart was equally prophetic, but as I understand by anõr & more accurate source that the lady has *down* only £20,000, why I am in no hurry'.[12] Bolton's attempts to lure Benjamin to Miss Trotter's house in Grosvenor Square were described by the intended victim as 'supremely ludicrous'. 'Everyday he calls & fetches away a pipe or a dagger to show Mrs. B. & always lets out when he returns that they have been to Grosvenor Sq.,' he told Sarah. Clara Bolton backed up her husband, although her description of her friend was hardly calculated to throw the prospective lover into transports '... she is a splendid wreck & now in great misery ... I have much to tell you & show you about her when you come to town – no one thing could reconcile me more to this world of ill nature than to see her your wife – all her feelings are thrown back and she with all her brilliant qualities & splendid fortune there she is a lone solitary creature.'[13]

Benjamin, however, declined the charitable undertaking of saving the 'splendid wreck' from her lonely misery, as too he seems to have resisted family pressure in favour of a marriage with one of William Meredith's two sisters, Georgina and Ellen, now, since their uncle's and their brother's death, considerable heiresses. In February 1832, Isaac indicated his wishes that either Benjamin or Ralph or both should marry into the Meredith family in a typically obfuscatory note: 'There is a *subject* I have often wished to have opened myself to you – perhaps some hints have been dropped by me, & I cannot doubt that either yourself or Ralph must be aware of my notions. Such an opportunity will never again recur – & happy shall I feel if Time ... also may bring "some healing on its wings".'[14] Benjamin, briefly, seems to have been tempted, as would appear from some coy remarks in a letter to Sarah, 'a certain youth in whom we take an interest has been mentioned more than once by a certain damsel ... I think there is every hope, & if they once are down at Bradenham ...'[15] while a week later he writes optimistically, 'I don't think that Hope, or anyone is more in the field than myself, but Ralph has no chance unless they come down to Bradenham'. Whether the candidates were the Meredith sisters or no, the rumour that Benjamin might be contemplating marriage to someone who did not bear her imprimatur, evoked a frantic, ill-punctuated missive from Clara: 'Pray do not wed one of them you must have a brilliant star like yourself Keep your heart quiet. I do not like *those girls from what I hear the person* who told me made use of these words they are half city half [illegible] half clever half fools ... do not fall in love I am nervous about you', adding an anxious injunction not to show her letter to Sarah, 'the dear little thing'.[16] Clara's advice that he should only marry 'a brilliant star like yourself', may have touched a responsive chord in Benjamin; at any rate he seems to have abandoned the Meredith project, only to revive it, disastrously, a year later.

The Misses Trotter and Meredith may indeed have appeared somewhat drab and middle-class in Benjamin's eyes, compared with the sparkling people he now met through Edward Bulwer Lytton, with whom he had become particularly friendly since his return to London in November 1831. Their intimacy, it appears, even extended to visiting brothels together – 'We shall meet at the Naughty House on the 8th', Bulwer had written to him that winter. Bulwer was living in an exquisitely appointed house, 36 Hertford Street, with his wife, Rosina, an unbalanced, penniless, Irish beauty whom he had married for love, to the disgust of his domineering mother, who had instantly cut off his allowance. Rosina, daughter of a feckless, drunken father, whom she despised, and a fierce, revolutionary mother with whom she quarrelled, had, strangely enough, been a protégée of Caroline Lamb, Bulwer's former mistress. Despite her beauty, her manners were unsympathetic; a fellow Irishwoman, the writer Lady Morgan described her as 'insolent and unamiable'. In fact the Bulwers Lytton were an ill-assorted couple. Rosina was shallow, demanding, incapable of love except for her dogs, and later became a hysterical drunkard; while Bulwer was selfish, spoiled and vain. Disraeli later wrote that he was one of the three vainest men who had ever lived, and by his own admission had 'little or no tenderness in his nature', but he was at the same time highly intelligent and sensitive. The marriage was soon to reveal itself a disaster, a vindictive, running battle which darkened both their lives, while the quarrel that arose between Bulwer and Benjamin's future wife over the separation of Bulwer and Rosina would virtually end the two men's friendship.

All this, however, was in the future, in the spring of 1832 when Benjamin became a regular guest at the Lytton Bulwers' parties. Bulwer's taste in dress and decoration was dandified and luxurious, and his soirées sparkled with wit – unlike the inarticulate gatherings of the high 'ton' of English society which he mocked in his books. The poet Tom Moore, friend and biographer of Byron, a society pet who went everywhere and knew everybody, was impressed, recording in his diary for 1 April 1832: 'Mrs. Lytton Bulwer's assembly ... such a collection as is seldom brought together'. The guests included Byron's half sister, Augusta Leigh, William Godwin, an Indian prince – and Disraeli. Moore remembered having met Benjamin as a very young man at Murray's, 'I have heard of you, as everybody has', he told the delighted Disraeli. On another evening there was a heady mixture of literary women, known as 'blues': Lady Morgan, who noted in her diary that Disraeli shuffled about with his cane looking like Hamlet, Mrs Catherine Gore, most successful of the 'silver-fork' novelists, and the tragic poetess, Letitia Eliza-beth Landon ('L.E.L.') whom Benjamin disdainfully avoided because of her suburban appearance, 'the very personification of Brompton – pink satin dress and white satin shoes, red cheeks, snub nose, and hair à la Sappho', he retailed to Sarah. There was also the darkly beautiful Caroline Norton, poetess and novelist, who was to introduce Benjamin into the Sheridan circle, and two other people who were soon to become important in his life: Alfred, Count d'Orsay, known as 'le beau d'Orsay', undisputed leader of the dandy set, later to become Benjamin's closest friend, and the woman who was to become his wife, Mary Anne Wyndham Lewis, then the wife of a wealthy Welsh coal-owner.

Benjamin told Sarah that Mrs Wyndham Lewis 'particularly desired' to be introduced to him, describing her as 'a pretty little woman, a flirt and a rattle; indeed gifted with a volubility I should think unequalled. She told me that she liked "silent, melancholy men". I answered "that I had no doubt of it".'[17] Rosina Bulwer, who later came to hate Benjamin as a friend of her estranged husband, recalled that he was anything but impressed by Mary Anne; when asked to take her down to dinner he drawled, 'Oh! anything rather than that insufferable woman. But Allah is great', and putting his thumbs in the armholes of his waistcoat, a favourite attitude of his, walked up to offer her his arm.

To those who disliked Benjamin, and they were not a few, his affectation was intolerable. Rosina was to draw a malicious portrait of the young Disraeli in her novel *Very Successful*, published in 1856, where he featured as Mr Jericho Jabber, the '*Jew*-d'esprit' with elaborate black ringlets who, when discoursing on the dancing of the ancient peoples or some such subject, would end by drawing the handkerchief he was flourishing in his right hand across his left, and if someone mocked him, would resort to 'his favourite attitude of sticking his thumbs in the armhole of his waistcoat and uttering his usual Caucasian truism of "God is great", ostentatiously admiring the ceiling'. Disraeli's clothes were deliberately designed to cause remark, and in this he was eminently successful. He had not the taste of d'Orsay, whose clothes, according to such witnesses as Jane Carlyle, were breathtakingly beautiful, but not, as Benjamin's were, ostentatious. Benjamin would appear in a black velvet suit, lined with white satin, gorgeously embroi-dered waistcoats, his breast a medley of gold chains, rings on his fingers, and, attached to his wrist by a tasselled cord, one of the canes that had astounded Gibraltar. On one occasion his fondness for velvet occasioned a cruel joke by Samuel Rogers, the society-loving poet, whose cadaverous appearance earned him the nickname 'the Dug-up Dandy'. Rosina recalled that she was seated beside Rogers in the drawing room when Disraeli, who had been lounging nonchalantly in a cane-seated chair, crossed the room 'with his coat-tails as usual over each arm leaving his dark green velvet adorables with the chair marks on them clearly visible.

Rogers: Who is that?

Rosina: Oh! young Disraeli, the Jew.

Rogers: Rather the wandering Jew, with the brand of *Cane* on him.'[18]

Benjamin, she says, hearing their laughter, turned round and glanced scornfully at them, but he noted in his diary:

'Rogers hates me. I can hardly believe, as he gives out, that V[ivian] G[rey] is ye cause. Considering his age, I endeavoured to conciliate him, but it is impossible', adding with a characteristic note of defiance, 'I think I will give him cause to hate me'.[19]

Rogers, indeed, was one of the Murray circle, scornfully portrayed by Bulwer in *England and the English* (1833) as 'the Albemarle Clique', a set of old literary has-beens. 'Some few years ago, there was the Authors' *clique* of Albemarle Street, a circle of gentlemen who professed to weigh out to each man his modicum of fame; they praised each other – were *the* literary class and thought Stewart Rose a greater man than Wordsworth – peace be with them – they are no more – and fame no longer hangs from the nostrils of Samuel Rogers...'

Bulwer, like Disraeli, was hated by most of literary London; like Disraeli he had produced successful society novels at an early age, although he was a more prolific writer and had enjoyed greater commercial success. Lockhart, whose comment on Bulwer has been quoted above, seems to have disliked both of them equally, a feeling echoed by his circle of friends, which included Thackeray and Benjamin's erstwhile colleague on *The Representative*, Dr William Maginn. Maginn was by now the editor of *Fraser's Magazine*, a periodical that first appeared in 1830 and reflected Maginn's aggressive criticism, his extreme Toryism and fondness for satire. Among the young staff at *Fraser's* was Thackeray, whom Maginn set on to bait Bulwer, the latter in November 1831 having become editor of Colburn's *New Monthly Magazine*. A running battle ensued between the *New Monthly*, to which Benjamin was also a contributor, and *Fraser's*, with occasional yelpings from *The Age*, a scandal-mongering publication run by Maginn's friend and collaborator, the disreputable Charles Molloy Westmacott, whose blackmailing activities led to his carrying a loaded crop to protect himself. From 1830 to 1838 Bulwer and Disraeli were persecuted by this pack for their dandyism, self-advertisement, and suspected radicalism. To this generally bad press was added the more heavyweight enmity of the *Quarterly Review*, of its editor Lockhart and of the Albemarle clique who were its principal contributors. Both Bulwer and Benjamin smarted under its slights. In December 1832 Benjamin wrote a furious letter to Lockhart in which he accused him of having deliberately and maliciously misquoted *The Young Duke* in the last issue, thus holding him up to ridicule. 'Sir, I have long been aware of the hostile influence (to use no harsher term) which you have exercised on my literary career ...', he began, going on to speak of 'those ... sneers for which I have often been indebted to you'. He considered replying to Lockhart in the rival

Whig periodical, the *Edinburgh Review*, but Lockhart made a gracious apology and the subject was dropped. Enmity remained, however, to the extent that Lockhart was later to refer to *Coningsby* as 'a blackguard novel written by that Jew scamp Ben Disraeli'. It is hardly surprising, therefore, that Benjamin should have avoided the society of literary men, or that he should have reserved especial venom for them, cruelly lampooning such antagonists as Croker and Thackeray in his novels. As in the case of Samuel Rogers, their enmity was not to go unpunished. He would give them cause to hate him.

Benjamin still hoped to silence his critics by proving himself as a serious writer. By 1832 both he and Bulwer had abandoned the frivolous 'silver-fork' genre with which they had made their literary débuts, as unsuited to the spirit of the revolutionary Age of Reform, and by February of that year Benjamin, having completed a six week course of mercury for his venereal disease and working 'like a tiger' as he put it to Austen, had finished the novel that he hoped would 'knock them [his literary critics] on the head'. With a sublime disregard for the past, he sent the manuscript to Murray, hoping that the publisher's professional sense would overcome his personal resentment. Murray forwarded it to Lockhart to read, who replied equivocally: 'I can't say what is to be done with this book. To me, knowing whose it is, it is full of interest; but the affectations and absurdities are such that I can't but think that it would disgust others more than the life and brilliance of many of the descriptions would please them.' Having received a more enthusiastic report from another reader, Henry Hart Milman, who described it as 'very wild, very extravagant, very German, very poetical', Murray agreed to publish it, and the book appeared in May 1832, entitled *Contarini Fleming, A Psychological Autobiography*.

Contarini, to Benjamin's intense disappointment, was not a success with the public, making a profit of only £18 each to author and publisher. It was, as Milman, had said, 'very German', and, like Part II of *Vivian Grey*, owed a great deal to Goethe's *Wilhelm Meister*, and was intended, as the sub-title indicated, to chronicle Disraeli's psychological pilgrimage towards self-realization. As such, it had scant interest for the general public; it was not as easily readable as *Vivian Grey* or *The Young Duke*, and the latter half of the book was not much more than a travelogue taken from Benjamin's letters home on his tour to the East. For the self-obsessed Benjamin, *Contarini* was part of 'the secret history of my feelings' containing some of his most deeply-felt experiences: his schooldays, his realization of his alienness from the Anglo-Saxons who surrounded him, and the bitter shame of his humiliation over *Vivian Grey*. For him it was primarily the exploration of what he, like Byron, felt to be his 'dual nature': his poetic feeling and his hankering for the career of a man of action. *Contarini* was intended to prove, which it eminently failed to do, that Benjamin was a true poet, but he was blind to its failings, writing defiantly in his diary 'I shall always consider the *Psychological Romance* [the title he had originally intended for *Contarini*] as the perfection of English prose and a chef d'oeuvre'. But although he liked to think of himself as a poetic talent, Benjamin showed himself willing to change direction, making Contarini declare, in a revealing passage, that he is 'cured of any predisposition that ... I once conceived I possessed for literary invention ... my ambition is great. I do not think that I should find life tolerable, unless I were in an eminent position, and conscious that I deserved it. Fame, although not posthumous fame, is ... necessary to my felicity. In a word, I wish to devote myself to affairs.'

It was a public declaration of intent; Benjamin was preparing to take the first active step along what was to be for him the uphill road to parliament, putting himself forward for his local borough, High Wycombe.

If the Third Reform Bill should pass, as it seemed inevitable that it would, an election at Wycombe would be held not under the old closed corporation franchise, which offered no prospect whatever to a political newcomer outside the party system, but under the new wider franchise, which might give him a chance, however minimal. Since February the D'Israeli family at Bradenham had been doing what they could to improve Benjamin's electoral prospects, sweetening local politicians with jars of his choicest tobacco and invitations to dinner. In March Isaac bought a small farm at Hambledon, thus becoming a landed proprietor in the county and providing Benjamin with the property qualification necessary for a parliamentary candidate.

Meanwhile Benjamin, having handed over the manuscript of *Contarini* to Murray in February, fondly imagined himself to be furthering his cause by writing another book, which he hoped would establish him in the public eye as a political thinker and a man with influential contacts. He appears to have been lured into this project by the sinister Haber and other reactionary supporters of Charles x who were part of the Bolton circle, including the Baron d'Haussez, a Minister in the French government overthrown by the revolt of July 1830. Although Benjamin deluded himself into thinking that the project was to his own advantage, he was being used by Haber for his own ends, much as he had been manipulated by Powles in the affair of the mining pamphlets.

Carried away by the heady atmosphere of international intrigue, he wrote excitedly to Sarah on 20 February:

> I have got before me all the Cabinet Papers of Charles the 10th, all the dispatches of the Dutch Ambassador, & a secret correspondence with the most eminent opposition member in France – all from Haber & Baron D'Haussez one of the Ex-Ministers. Such secrets! I am writing a book which will electrify all Europe. I am perfectly uncontrolled &, if I have time enough, I hope to produce something which will not only ensure my election, but produce me a political reputation, which is the foundation of everything, second to none.[20]

Even Isaac, not known for his judgement, was alarmed at this euphoria, warning, 'Beware, my dear, of secret agents, beware of forgeries and delusions', wise advice which his son chose to ignore. He went ahead with the 'Haberian volume' as he called it, and it was published by John Murray in April under the title *England and France; or, A Cure for the Ministerial Gallomania*, with an ironical dedication to the Whig Prime Minister, Earl Grey, as ' the most eminent Gallomaniac of the day'. Written from a John Bullish, eminently Tory standpoint, it was a sustained 300 page attack upon the policy of the Grey government in allying itself with the liberal regime of Louis Philippe.

The *Gallomania*, far from electrifying Europe and establishing its author's reputation, only succeeded in creating confusion as to his political views. His putative political supporters at Wycombe were certainly taken aback, as a concerned Sarah anxiously informed him. 'You can imagine the astonishment and consternation of old and young Wycombe,' she told him. 'Huffam [Disraeli's agent] is in a great fright that you are going to betray him by proving yourself a Tory after he has for so many months sworn to all Wycombites that you were not one.'[21] Benjamin had only himself to blame for this, and indeed the confusion in his own mind as to the political line he should adopt seems to have been equally great. Although the theme of the book was pre-eminently Tory and anti-liberal, and so logically should have been anti-Reform, he absolutely refused to allow Croker, who, to his dismay was commissioned by Murray to check the proofs, to insert phrases hostile to Reform. 'It is quite impossible that anything adverse to the general measure of Reform can issue from my pen or from anything to which I contribute', he firmly informed Murray.

Benjamin's motive for refusing to take up the Tory anti-Reform stance was clear; no parliamentary candidate putting himself up for election for the first time on an anti-Reform platform would stand the slightest chance of being elected under the open constituency franchise to be constituted under the forthcoming Reform Bill. This said, Benjamin remained in a quandary as to the political colours he should adopt. 'Toryism is worn out, & I cannot condescend to be a Whig', he declared to Austen. He had no official connection with either party; his early sympathies, influenced by Isaac and the Murray circle, were Conservative; no one who had sympathized as he had with the despotic proceedings of the Turkish Empire could have been liberal by instinct. Of the two parties, the Tories were the least socially exclusive, prepared to accept men of talent such as Canning, Peel and Lyndhurst, who were not of the high nobility, while the Whigs despised their own erratic genius, Brougham, for purely snobbish reasons. But Toryism, as Disraeli said, was, for the moment, a worn-out creed, and, moreover, as he must have privately admitted to himself, his first encounter with Peel had been anything but successful. There was more than one reason why he would not 'condescend to be a Whig'. The two sitting members for High Wycombe, Sir Thomas Baring and Robert Smith, were Whigs; and even without his unwise attack on the Whig leader, Lord Grey, in the *Gallomania*, the Whigs – the most aristocratic of tribes – would never have accepted him. His only real political connection was Bulwer, who had been elected as a pro-Reform candidate for St Ives in 1831. Bulwer did what he could for his friend, trying hard, but in vain, to persuade the Whigs to accept Disraeli as their candidate for Wycombe when Sir Thomas Baring resigned; but the most he could do for Benjamin was to obtain letters of recommendation for him from his Radical connections, Joseph Hume and Daniel O'Connell. And so Benjamin, in default of any encouragement from either of the major parties, had little alternative but to present himself to High Wycombe as a Radical. Yet, as he later claimed, his political committee consisted of as many Tories as Radicals, and his original plan had been, as revealed in the letter written by Sarah at this time, 'the ... regenerating of [Whig] Wycombe and turning them all unconsciously into Tories'.[22]

This view of Benjamin's real opinions is borne out by Clara Bolton's letters to Benjamin. 'I hate to hear *you* called a radical ... Thou art thyself', she wrote, having taken it upon herself to defend him at London parties. 'I told them your object was not to preserve old things or to recast them into new shapes, but to remove them entirely away, & that it was [as] easy for a radical without infringing his integrity, to unite with the Tories, who admit of no change, as for him to unite with the Whigs, who are for *all change*', she added confusingly.[23] Not surprisingly, since the Radicals normally acted with the Whigs, her audience 'stared in chorus'. The Boltons threw themselves behind Benjamin's parliamentary candidature, the doctor standing surety to the tune of £2,500 for a bond given by Benjamin to a Thomas Mash to prevent any danger of the candidate's being arrested for debt, and arranging for his 'triumphal entry' into Wycombe. Clara, apart from acting as Benjamin's spy and political adviser, 'worked her fingers to the bone' making artificial flowers and favours in Benjamin's colours of pink and white to be distributed to his supporters, and even a pink and white collar for Sarah's dog, Pop.

In the event, Benjamin was unlucky; Baring's resignation took place in the first week of June before the Reform Bill became law, and the resulting by-election was the last to be held under the old unreformed franchise, confined to the Corporation and Burgesses of Wycombe. The new Whig candidate, Colonel Grey, a son of the Prime Minister, arrived, according to Benjamin, with a hired mob and band. After parading the town with his hirelings he made a brief stammering speech from his carriage, whereupon Benjamin seized his opportunity:

> Feeling it was the crisis, I jumped up on the Portico of the Red Lion & gave it them for an hour & ¼ - I can give you no idea of effect', he wrote proudly to Sara Austen, 'I made them all mad - A great many absolutely *cried* - I never made so many friends in my life, or converted so many enemies - All the women are on my side - & wear my colours, pink & white ... The Colonel returned to town in the evening, absolutely astounded out of his presence of mind, *on dit* never to appear again.

'If he come,' he added pugnaciously, 'I am prepared for him.'[24]

According to one account, Benjamin, using the lion on the portico as a prop, declared, pointing to the head, that when the poll was counted he would be 'there', and, indicating the tail, his opponent 'there'. Presenting himself as a man of the people, he declared that he had 'not a drop of Plantagenet blood in his veins'. It was good rousing stuff, and the crowd seems to have forgiven Benjamin his outrageously dandified appearance, his ringlets and his ruffles, but they were not the electors, and of the 32 votes, Grey obtained 20 and Disraeli 12. Pugnacious even in defeat, Benjamin, in his speech after the declaration of the poll, defied the Whigs in such strong terms as to provoke a challenge to a duel from a local Whig peer, Lord Nugent. Disappointingly for Benjamin, who would have revelled in the publicity this would have excited, the affair was amicably settled, with Clara Bolton's other protégé, Captain Angerstein, acting as his second. Predictably, Benjamin's first assault on the political citadel had ended in failure, but for him it had been a stimulating experience; he had succeeded in getting himself talked about, a primary objective, and he had identified his political enemies, the Whigs.

The Wycombe by-election was merely a preliminary round in the more serious battle – the General Election – which was to take place in December that year. Benjamin put himself forward once again as a Radical independent, despite his innate Tory sympathies. He seems to have decided that the primary objective was to get into Parliament first, then join whichever major party suited him, or would have him, later. Radical attitudes, which frightened the bourgeois, suited Benjamin, always out to shock. Indeed they had a certain attraction for those who did not fit into the common mould: men like Bulwer and Clay, who stayed at Bradenham in October, and stood surety for yet another bond of Benjamin's to Mash for £1,000 to finance election expenses. The genuineness of Disraeli's attachment to some of the Radical political beliefs, particularly the ballot and triennial parliament, which he put forward as his electoral platform, may perhaps be doubted. Clara Bolton, on being asked why Disraeli supported the ballot, declared that he was 'v. wise not to quibble at such minor things as a ball[ot] or scraps of paper and that you have very powerful extraordinary notions about extraordinary things'.

One of these 'extraordinary notions' was that he could stand upon a Radical platform that included Tory planks; his defence of the Corn Laws, for instance, sacred cow of the arch-Tory agricultural interest. There were sound political reasons behind this; the local Tories, aware of the hopelessness of putting up a candidate under their own colours, were prepared to support Benjamin in his attempt to defeat the hated Whigs; indeed his political agent, Nash, was also the agent of the ultra-Tory local magnate, Lord Chandos. Disraeli's critics regarded this combination of opposites as evidence of his political opportunism, which to a large extent it was, but Benjamin was always capable of making a virtue of necessity; he was later to incorporate the idea of a Tory-Radical alliance into his political strategy.

Disraeli was defeated, but under the new wider franchise he succeeded in obtaining a respectable number of votes from the newly-extended electorate; when the poll count was declared on 12 December, the figures were: Robert Smith 179, Colonel Grey 140, Disraeli 119. It was to be his last appearance on the hustings as an independent Radical. At Wycombe in the winter of 1832, the signs for the future were already there: the concept of Tory democracy which was to be such a powerful image for the party in years to come; the concern for 'the condition of the people', coupled with a defence of the Corn Laws and a bid for the support of the Tory agricultural interest; and, perhaps most important, hatred for the exclusivity of the Whig social caste which he was later to describe in a favourite phrase as 'the Venetian oligarchy'.

After Wycombe, Benjamin made two more abortive attempts to stand for Parliament: at Aylesbury, where he hoped to put himself up for one of the two county seats beside Lord Chandos, but prudently withdrew when a second official Conservative candidate declared himself; and at Marylebone in the spring of 1833, when he put out a Radical electoral address but in the end did not stand. In the Marylebone address he developed the theme of the Tory-Radical alliance, which he had begun at Wycombe. Both sections, he said, should merge 'under the dignified title of a National Party'. The address ended in true Disraelian style:

> Let us not forget also an influence too much underrated in this age of bustling mediocrity – the influence of individual character. Great spirits may yet arise to guide the groaning helm through the world of troubled waters; spirits whose proud destiny it may still be at the same time to maintain the glory of the Empire and to secure the happiness of the People!

Imperial glory and social welfare: two themes for the future leader of the Tory party which were, for all Disraeli's vision, to prove mutually incompatible. Benjamin had no doubt that he was to be this 'great spirit'; he felt it his destiny to lead; for the immediate future, however, politics having proved an expensive failure, he was to turn to other avenues of fulfilment – to literature and to love.

5 Dreams of Fair Women

'O reader dear! do pray a look here, and you will spy the curly hair and forehead fair, and nose so high and gleaming eye of Benjamin Dis-ra-e-li, the wondrous boy who wrote *Alroy*, in rhyme and prose, only to show, how long ago victorious Judah's lion banner rose ...'. Thus Maginn apostrophized Benjamin in *Fraser's Magazine* for May 1833, in a witty parody of Benjamin's overheated prose style in the *Wondrous Tale of Alroy*, published in March of that year. With the article appeared a pen and ink portrait by Maclise of Benjamin with poetic curls and dreamy expression, leaning on his elbow in Byronic pose, with one of his long Turkish pipes thrown carelessly upon the sofa behind him. The Byronic effect was so striking that Tita, who was now part of the household at Bradenham, thought it was an unskilful likeness of his former master. At twenty-eight Benjamin, like Byron, had achieved notoriety – which is often conducive to social success, particularly with women. In January, he and Bulwer, visiting Bath, were 'quite mobbed' at a public ball; for Benjamin, the year 1833 was to be one of amorous achievement.

The *Wondrous Tale of Alroy* increased his reputation as a strange, romantic figure. It was the last book in his personal trilogy, 'the secret history of my feelings'; it was also the first Jewish historical novel. As such it was an odd book to be published by a man determined to make his way in English aristocratic society, showing him, as it did, glorifying in his Jewishness. It was, in fact, Benjamin's answer to the challenge posed by that Anglo-Saxon society in which such a premium was placed on aristocratic blood; he would not merely be the equal of these English peers, he must be more aristocratic than they were, belonging as he did to a race more ancient than theirs. The hero David Alroy, with whom Benjamin clearly identified, uses a key phrase when he declares that he has 'a deep conviction of superior race', a conviction that would enable Benjamin to endure the aristocratic contempt and anti-Semitic hostility which confronted him throughout most of his long career.

The book, Disraeli noted later, portrayed his 'ideal ambition'; he did not elucidate what that ambition might be. The novel was conceived in 1829, the year in which, following the emancipation of the Catholics, an attempt was made to gain the same rights for Jews, and published in 1833 when the idea was again mooted; one might, therefore, surmise that the idea of Jewish emancipation was the inspiration for the book. In one passage, Alroy (a twelfth century Jewish Prince) declares 'I would fain be a prince without my fetters', and dreams of leading his people to Jerusalem. Later Disraeli was to play a part in the parliamentary struggle for Jewish emancipation, and to reveal, in private conversation, strong Zionist feeling.

Alroy was a seminal book in the evolution of Benjamin's most deeply-felt personal credo. It was stylistically his worst novel. Benjamin believed that he was initiating a 'literary revolution', forming a new style 'founded in some degree on Arabian prose',[1] but the effect, in many passages, was ludicrous rather than poetic. *Alroy* was dedicated to Sarah, personified as the hero's sister, Miriam, and was intended as a celebration of 'the pure and perfect love of a brother and a sister'; interestingly, it was also the only one of Disraeli's novels in which a woman (the Caliph's beautiful daughter, Schirene) was presented as an overtly sexual object and her relationship with the hero based upon strong physical attraction. The language was erotic; Schirene's pet gazelle 'presses her soft and idle hand' with 'a warm voluptuous lip' at which the excited girl burst out, '... thy lips are softer than the swan ... but his [Alroy's] breathed passion, when they pressed'.

Alroy ran into two editions that year, read, one might imagine, chiefly by women to whom the combination of historical romance and suppressed eroticism greatly appealed. It certainly earned him the admiration of the beautiful Sheridan sisters with whom he became very intimate in the spring and early summer of 1833. The three sisters were the granddaughters of Richard Brinsley Sheridan and inherited from him their beauty, intelligence and reckless wit. Caroline Norton, the eldest, a raven-haired, Grecian beauty who was also a poetess and novelist, held court at her house in Storey's Gate, attended by her even more beautiful younger sisters, both of whom had made brilliant marriages: Helen, then Mrs Price Blackwood, later becoming Marchioness of Dufferin, and Georgiana, then Lady Seymour, becoming Duchess of Somerset. Poor Caroline, in contrast, was married to the detestable George Norton, with whom she was totally incompatible; their stormy marriage was to end in separation and a *cause célèbre* in which Norton accused his wife of 'criminal conversation' with Lord Melbourne.

Benjamin's initiation into the Sheridan circle came on 13 February when he dined with the Nortons at Storey's Gate, meeting Helen Blackwood, whom he described to Sarah as

> ... very handsome and very Sheridanic. She told me she was nothing. 'You see Georgy's the beauty [Lady Seymour] and Carry's the wit [Mrs Norton], and I ought to be the good one, but then I am not.' I must say I liked her exceedingly; besides, she knows all my works by heart, and spouts whole pages of 'V.G.' and 'C.F.' and the 'Y.D.' ... My greatest admirer is old Mrs. Sheridan, the authoress of *Carwell*, who, by the bye, is very young and pretty ... The truth is the whole family have a very proper idea of my merits ...[2]

Benjamin was soon on the friendliest of terms with them all, but he was more than a little in love with the adorable Helen Blackwood, whom he nicknamed 'Sunny Day' in contrast to her dark sister Caroline whom he called 'Starry Night' in a poem which he wrote for them. He sent Helen his own rough proofs of *Alroy* so that she should be the first to read it, even before his own family, promising to send her the first bound copy 'wherein I will venture to inscribe thy fair & adored name!'³ Helen's letters in return, sometimes signed 'Schirene' and addressing Benjamin as 'Contarini' or the 'Caliph' were teasing and tantalizing, skating gaily over his suppressed passion. Benjamin, as always when he was in love, could be touchy, difficult, over-dramatic and quick to take offence at imagined slights. He wrote:

> I am overwhelmed with a deep, a terrific, & an invincible melancholy. (I see, as usual, you laugh – some day or other you will find that all this is not affectation) – your continued absence, the conviction that if even in town, I could only by wretched fits & starts, enjoy your inspiring presence, fill me with uncontrollable sadness. I feel that the only & the last chance of felicity is forever lost. Enough of this, as I cannot bear being ridiculed.⁴

If Helen responded to his passion, her surviving letters to him do not show it; instead, she rallied him on being 'very *grumpose* indeed', telling him roundly, 'I offer you no consolation on the subject of your vexation, Mr. Contarini, because you have as many aspects as the Moon . . .'⁵

Politics, Disraeli feared, would divide them; the Sheridans were committed Whigs, and Mrs Sheridan and Caroline certainly suspected that he intended to become 'a nasty Tory', even during the period when he was announcing plans to stand for Marylebone as a Radical. Although in one letter he denied that he would turn Tory, in another it appeared that he was certainly contemplating such an eventuality. '. . . I have a melancholy presentiment that horrible politics will ultimately, if not very soon, dissolve that agreeable acquaintance which has been the consolation of my life', adding in an interesting sentence which seems to indicate that he would have stood for parliament as a Whig if they had been prepared to accept him, 'We met a year too late – but it is useless to regret, & now impossible to do anything else.'⁶

It was not politics that was to end their relationship, but Benjamin's involvement with another woman. Helen Blackwood was virtuous, but her husband was abroad on naval service, and Benjamin later dropped hints that he thought she might have yielded in the end. A year later, when he had a passionate mistress, he regretted the abrupt termination of his friendship with the Sheridans. Helen, he thought, might forgive him if he gave up the other woman: 'Methinks that fair Helen wd. be merciful if – but never, never!'⁷ Nearly half a century later, only a few months before his death, gazing into the fire, he reminisced to a friend about the days with the Sheridans at Storey's Gate, and of 'the wit and humour that then flowed, more copiously by far than the claret. Lady Dufferin was his chief admiration, more beautiful than her beautiful sisters. "Dreams! dreams! dreams!" he murmured'.[8]

When he was not haunting Storey's Gate in the hope of a glimpse of the fair Helen, Benjamin was making steady social progress through the drawing-rooms of those titled hostesses who were prepared to accept wit and talent as a passport to their parties in default of wealth and rank. Lady Holland, the high-priestess of the Whigs, was beyond his reach, but he was soon a frequent guest at Lady Charleville's house in Cavendish Square, or at Lady Cork's in New Burlington Street. With Irish titles and moderate fortunes, both ladies were regarded as being only in the second rank of society, far below such tribal queens as Lady Jersey and Lady Salisbury, but 'Corky' as the Countess of Cork and Orrery was affectionately known, was a character in her own right. Aged nearly ninety and an intimate of Dr Johnson in her youth, she was still tireless in her pursuit of amusement. Tiny and stout, with a loud voice and forthright speech, always ready to ridicule herself or anyone else, she had outraged society during the Reform Bill agitation by, in her rival Lady Charleville's words, 'playing égalité', hanging flags outside her windows inscribed 'The Bill, the true Bill, and down with the Rich!' She owned a macaw whose party trick was drawing out, clipping and smoking a cigar, and who had once had the temerity to make, in his mistress's words, 'a bit of an assault on George the Fourth's stocking'. Disraeli, who must have appreciated her eighteenth-century attitudes and racy talk, was to make her the model for Lady Bellair in his novel *Henrietta Temple*.

Amid flirtations with the Sheridans and parties at Lady Cork's it is hardly surprising that Benjamin forgot his old friends, the Austens, whom he had now come to regard as importunate bores, despite, or perhaps because of, still owing them money. In February Sarah, who shared his view of them, wrote that the Austens were 'V. irate against' him as they had invited him to dinner and even waited dinner for him '& you never appeared or apologised!'

Benjamin may have been ungrateful to the Austens, but he was a dutiful son, and frequently responded to calls for help from Bradenham to solve problems arising from quarrelsome servants or villainous horse-copers. Benjamin had sent Tita to join the Bradenham household in July the previous year, and the advent of this exotic personage had caused endless domestic jealousy and intrigue. 'Mamma will be glad to see you as soon as you can', Sarah wrote to her brother on 25 February, 'as she is as usual in a fuss about the domestics.' A few weeks later it was Isaac's turn to bother Benjamin; their cook, Adams, who quarrelled with Tita, had sunk into childishness and a replacement was required. 'It is too bad of the Governor to torment you about cooks,' Sarah sympathized, but nonetheless instructed Benjamin to send candidates for interviews to their aunt Olivia Trevor at 55 Gower Street. Young Jem D'Israeli was in charge of the livestock at Bradenham and was frequently cheated by unscrupulous horse-dealers; Benjamin was then called in and Jem felt slighted by his elder brother's lack of appreciation. Ben has not knowledge enough properly to appreciate the wonderful things I have done for his mare', he complained in his childish scrawl, 'he will never thoroughly feel all that he owes me'.[9]

Benjamin may not have minded being tormented about cooks, but constant parental injunctions to reform his way of life did indeed, in Helen Blackwood's words, make him 'grumpose'. '... has "Papa" been tormenting you?' she wrote, 'I ask anxiously, as I know your habit of visiting on your Town friends, all Paternal Iniquities.'[10] 'Papa' wrote to Helen herself complaining of Benjamin's 'vast number of odd acquaintances. He has been in a series of scrapes ever since he was fourteen',[11] he grumbled. The burden of the parental injunction seems to have been that his son should marry and settle down; Benjamin was still on the hunt for an heiress, keeping his sister posted as to his every move.

He considered Lady Charlotte Bertie, daughter of the Earl of Lindsey, whom he met at the opera, and whom he seems to have impressed, for Charlotte confided in her journal: 'The younger Disraeli was in the box ... He is wild, enthusiastic, and very poetical. The brilliancy of my companion infected me, and we ran on about poetry and Venice and Baghdad and Damascus ... nothing could compensate him for an obscure youth – not even glorious old age.' Half-jesting, he wrote to Sarah, 'By the bye, how would you like Lady Z – [Charlotte Bertie] for a sister-in-law, very clever, £25,000 and domestic?' Sarah was alarmed that he might be selling himself too cheaply and hastened to find out about Lady Charlotte – 'Beware! Oh beware,' she warned Benjamin, 'of 25,000 which belongs to a young lady who can spend the greatest part of it on herself & who will expect from you sooner or later three times that sum. Remember what improvident blood more than half fills her veins. Are you sure there is even that? Mrs. Austen says her mother wanted to make a match between her & Plumer Ward, which if true makes the money doubtful.'[12] Sarah need not have worried; despite all the poetical talk, both Benjamin and Charlotte were distinctly practical when it came to matrimony. Charlotte, although far from improvident herself, had in fact little money and an unhappy family background from which she was determined to escape to security. She was to marry Sir Josiah John Guest, a rich ironmaster many years her senior, partner to Mary Anne Wyndham Lewis's husband in the Dowlais iron works, to build Canford and become one of the century's great collectors of porcelain and fans. She was to translate the *Mabionogion*.

Sarah's own candidate for Benjamin's hand, and doubtless Isaac and Maria's too, was the remaining Meredith sister, Ellen, Georgina having married early in May. At the end of that month, Benjamin made an offer to Ellen which to his surprise and mortification was rejected. Ellen and her mother, with some justification, accused him of being insincere in his professions of affection; Sarah rushed in to try and save the situation: 'I think the game *is still yours* if you should ever be inclined & with an honest right to take your own time, for Mrs. M wishes her to marry ... I like E. all the better for being difficult ... If she be sincere for love of me save her from Clay ... PRAY BURN THIS INSTANTLY.'[13]

Benjamin did not burn his sister's letter, nor did he take her advice; he was wounded and unforgiving, and justified his cold behaviour to the Merediths (with which Sarah reproached him) on the grounds that Ellen had played a heartless game with him, deliberately leading him on to humiliate him while flirting with another man. 'As for Ellen, enough has passed between her & [Thomas] Salmon with regard to myself in my presence, tho' of course supposed by them unperceived, to justify a much more icy temperament than I have thought fit to assume,' he replied haughtily. The Merediths had accused him of offering marriage without love. 'As for love', he retorted; 'all my friends who married for love and beauty either beat their wives or live apart from them ... I may commit many follies in life, but I never intend to marry for "love", which I am sure is a guarantee of infelicity ... So this affair ends.'[14]

Benjamin's pride was hurt by Ellen Meredith's rejection of him, but that he should have offered for her at all was an act of extreme cynicism, prompted, perhaps, by his sister's pressure. Not only had he been carrying on an *amitié amoureuse* with Helen Blackwood, but he had already met the woman who was prepared to give him what the fair Helen would not – a passionate physical relationship.

Henrietta Sykes was the daughter of a Norfolk squire, Henry Villebois of Marham, a partner in the brewing firm of Truman and Hanbury. In 1821 she had married Sir Francis Sykes, a wealthy baronet descended from an East India nabob, and a man of considerable property who owned a Palladian country house, Basildon Park, a house in Upper Grosvenor Street and a yacht. Henrietta was a sensuous beauty, with dark hair, large eyes, pouting lips, well-rounded shoulders and bosom. She was gregarious and by no means an intellectual, determinedly refusing to attend the 'blue' parties given by her husband's aunt, Lady Cork. Her husband, Sir Francis, was an odd mixture of talent and eccentricity, an agreeable but weak character, who loved the traditional gentleman's sports of fishing and shooting, but detested England, preferring to escape abroad on his yacht. His health was poor, the result of his having had scarlet fever as a child, and he spent much of the year moving from spa to spa on the Continent in search of cures, a convenient fact which allowed Henrietta and Benjamin to indulge their passion for each other. Henrietta too was good-natured and agreeable, but if there was no malice in her, there was also not much sense, and in her love affair with Benjamin she threw caution to the winds. For Benjamin, now nearly thirty, it was at last an opportunity to live the recklessly romantic part that he had imagined for himself in *Alroy* and *Contarini*.

By June, if not before, the pair were lovers; Benjamin, unable to resist the temptation to show off his beautiful, titled mistress, took her down to Bradenham in the absence of Sir Francis in the second week of June. Sarah was very nervous at the prospect of entertaining a society lady. 'Lady Sykes will die of ennui, for how can we amuse her of an evening ... & the long mornings too. She will hate us ...' she wrote anxiously to her brother. But Henrietta, deeply in love, was gracious; at Bradenham she had the opportunity to be alone with her lover away from the inquisitive eyes of London society, 'that white couch, & the walks,' she sighed nostalgically when they were parted. In London she visited him at his rooms in 35 Duke Street, revelling in being 'snugly placed by him on the comfortable couch sipping coffee & kisses at the same time'. They went to the opera together, using the innocent Charlotte Bertie as cover. All seemed well until, in late June or early July, a familiar but now inimical figure reappeared on the scene: Clara Bolton.

From November, the date of her last letter to Benjamin, until April, Clara Bolton had been staying at The Hague without her husband; a stay possibly not entirely unconnected with Baron Haber who was based there. To Sarah D'Israeli's great annoyance, Clara, to calm the scandalous tongues of the British community, had been parading her friendship with the D'Israelis as evidence of her respectability. 'Amongst her other rhodomontade,' Sarah wrote angrily to Benjamin, 'she has said that she has a Sunday school supported entirely at her expense, & another in conjunction with the D'Israelis'. The chaplain at The Hague, suspicious of Clara's pious declarations, had written to enquire through the vicar at Bradenham, whether there was any foundation for her stories. Sarah refused to lend her respectability: 'I wrote to him in reply that I knew nothing whatever about her', she told Benjamin tartly.[15]

Benjamin, it seems, had dropped the Boltons much as he had the Austens in his climb up the social ladder. At any rate, both Clara and her husband to whom she had returned, were by now hostile to him, and determined to stir up trouble for him in the Sykes household. Sir Francis Sykes, rich and obsessed with his health, was the ideal victim for the doctor and his wife, who haunted the Sykes house, poisoning his mind against Benjamin. Clara, full of resentment at her former lover, had, by the end of July, become Sir Francis' mistress.

Benjamin and Henrietta were soon aware of what was going on and afraid of the damage the intriguing couple could cause. 'Dearest,' Henrietta scribbled in a hasty note written as she was dressing, 'Will you go & call on those horrors of Boltons – *They* are your enemies here . . . Get out of them what Baron Haber really said after you left the dining room. Even the most abject have a sting to wound, & you must put a stop to much that is muttered about you – ask Bolton firmly if he is your friend or not, the way to make him so is to consult him about your health, & I wish you to do so, taking especial care not to swallow any of his drugs.'[16]

At the end of July Sir Francis departed for Scotland and the grouse moors; Benjamin lingered on in London until the 15th August, when he could no longer defer his departure for Bradenham. Henrietta moped in bed, brooding on past happiness and writing letters to her lover, which although addressing him as her 'Child' and signing herself 'Your Mother' were anything but maternal: '12 o'clock Thursday night. It is the night Dearest the night that we used to pass so happily together . . . the returning to *our* House and seeing the solitary chair and knife and fork and the bright fire blazing, as if from cheerfulness spoke more forcibly to me than any language could do.'[17] Benjamin's letters have disappeared, probably destroyed, but Henrietta's remain among the Hughenden papers, a testimony to her breathless passion: '*Love me*, my Soul *love me* and be assured that the measure of my idolatry for you is full to the brim. Every breath I draw is yours, even *now* your kisses live on my lips and face and I feel the passion of your embrace.'[18]

Henrietta's reveries were soon to be disagreeably interrupted; on 17 August, two days after Benjamin's departure, both her two sisters and Clara Bolton called, evidently on a mission of espionage. Henrietta did not see them, and Clara evidently suspected that Benjamin was still there. She must have sent a message to that effect to Sir Francis, for a few days later he appeared at the house like a bolt from the blue, furiously questioning his wife as to her behaviour in his absence. Henrietta dashed off a warning letter to Benjamin: 'There is a storm brewing over our devoted heads ... Francis is off to dine at Mrs. Bolton's he had been there ere I saw him. He asked if I had seen you every day, I said for an hour or two – he forbid [sic] my ever doing so again. I said there was no probability as you were off for six months – evidently he suspected that I shld. refuse giving the promise & then he would have an excuse for a fracas. I shall be calm for so much is at stake.'[19] Mrs Bolton, she suspected, had recalled him, 'she is at the bottom of this'. Henrietta tried to remain calm and exert her influence over her husband, but the threat of social ostracism was hanging over her should he make an open scandal of the affair.

Luck was with her as she resolved to fight back and have a confrontation with her husband's mistress. Arriving at the Boltons' house, she found Sir Francis' carriage at the door, and, walking into the drawing-room unannounced, surprised the pair tête-à-tête. Delightedly if ungrammatically she described the scene to Benjamin:

> Fancy their consternation. I really thought Francis would have fainted. Lady S. stiff as a poker and perfectly cool: 'Mrs. Bolton I have called upon you in consequence of a scene to which I am perfectly aware I owe entirely to you, and I am here to have an understanding ... [You and] Sir F. are aware of my more than intimacy with Disraeli. It has suited all parties to be a great deal together, not certainly from the intimacy of the ladies, for I have never expressed a friendship for you. I have never been even commonly lady-like in my conduct to you and when Disraeli and I Francis and you formed to [two] distinct parties, and it can be *proved* that we did. Consequently in Sir Francis' absence there was no change in me, and should he leave London to-morrow your doors I *would never* enter ... but I will give Francis the sanction of my presence on the strict condition of his not again violating by unjust and ungenerous threats ties which he himself has sanctioned and which both himself and yourself *know* have been necessary to carry on your own game.[20]

Clara then revealed the depths of her resentment against Benjamin, claiming that the man she had defended over nine years of friendship was a 'heartless wretch' and producing as evidence letters from him (which unfortunately have disappeared) 'vowing undying, unspeakable, obligation'. She hit back at Henrietta, telling her that she had heard from good authority that no one would visit her next year because of her affair with Benjamin, warning her bitterly '. . . he will leave you, he has left you. I know him well, he is everywhere despised.' But Clara was on weak ground; she and Sir Francis had been caught red-handed, and, as far as Henrietta was concerned, the game was up. According to Henrietta, both 'Madame' and Sir Francis cried and begged her to be 'merciful', and the evening ended with all three parties dining together at the Sykes' house. Henrietta kept her side of the bargain by agreeing to chaperon her husband and Clara on a trip to Paris, and, after a brief farewell to Benjamin who had come up from Bradenham on 28 August, the following day she accompanied them abroad. She was an unwilling duenna, giving vent to her feelings in letters to Benjamin: 'I *hate* Mrs. B. I think her a positive devil & plays dreadfully on the feelings & sense of my husband' she wrote from Paris on 9 September. The couple even dared to make denigrating remarks about Benjamin in her presence, making fun of his habit of walking with a stoop, 'they said walking behind you you looked quite aged. I was quite in a rage', she wrote indignantly from Rouen, *en route* for home.

Benjamin's reactions to the sexual comedy being enacted by the curious three-some are, in the absence of his letters, unrecorded. What evidence we do have of his feelings at the time from the fragmentary document known as 'the Mutilated Diary' which he began on 1 September, suggests that his characteristic absorption with himself and his career had come to the fore, and that Henrietta, despite his passion for her, had been pushed to the back of his mind. His one reference to her is cautious, half-doubting the enduring quality of his feelings for her: 'one incident has indeed made this year the happiest of my life. How long will these feelings last? They have stood a great test [? the Sykes–Bolton scene], & now absence perhaps the most fatal of all'. These were hardly the passionate sentiments to be expected of a bereaved lover; and indeed, Henrietta then fades from the scene giving way to the central figure, Benjamin himself, as he ponders over his past life and the lessons to be drawn from it for the future. 'My life has not been a happy one,' he wrote. 'Nature has given me an awful ambition and fiery passions. My life has been a struggle, with moments of rapture – a storm with dashes of moonlight. Love, Poetry'. Here two lines are obliterated; he talks of achieving 'the difficult undertaking', he has no doubt of success, 'but the result will probably be fatal to my life'. This was almost certainly a reference to his parliamentary ambitions; a later passage reads, 'I could rule the House of Commons altho' there would be a great prejudice against me at first. It is the most jealous assembly in the world.' He did not underestimate the difficulties ahead. 'The character of our English society, the consequence of our aristocratic institutions renders a career difficult.' His self-confidence was supreme, 'I have an unerring instinct. I can read characters at a glance; few men can deceive me. My mind is a continental mind. It is a revolutionary mind. I am only truly great in action.' He was determined to fulfil his ambition, defy his critics, and astonish the world: 'My career will probably be more energetic than ever, & the world will wonder at my ambition

... I struggle from Pride, they shall not say that I have failed.' Although he had not yet learned patience or self-control, he saw the importance of reserve: 'I make it a rule now never to throw myself open to men', he wrote; this was the beginning of that self-controlled public impassivity that later led him to be caricatured as a sphinx.

The last entry in the Diary for 1833 read: 'Oct. 21st 1833. Seven weeks and not a line in my book!' Recent research by the Disraeli Project has uncovered what Disraeli was doing in those seven weeks at Bradenham; he was writing, in collaboration with Sarah, a political novel based upon his previous year's experience of the elections at Wycombe, to be published in March 1834 under the title *A Year at Hartlebury*. By the time he left Bradenham in November, he had already written almost one volume of the book which Sarah was to complete. His sister was the heroine of the novel; the hero was Aubrey Bohun, an idealized version of Benjamin, a much-travelled man of great wealth and talent, who stands for the Whig borough of Fanchester as a Radical with Tory support. Bohun, significantly, was no democrat: 'It is the fashion now "to go along with the people", but I think the people ought to be led, ought to have ideas given them by those whom nature and education have qualified to govern states and regulate the conduct of mankind', Benjamin wrote. Like Benjamin, Bohun hated the Whigs, considering them 'tyrants' and 'a party of political swindlers'. Unlike Benjamin, however, Bohun won his election, going on to make the most successful maiden speech ever heard in the House of Commons. *Hartlebury*, the first manifestation of Disraeli's talent for political fiction, was published under the pseudonyms, 'Cherry' and 'Fair Star', its real authorship remaining unknown until its rediscovery in an American library in 1979. Sarah insisted on appending what she herself described as 'a curious little preface' to the novel, which would seem to intimate that since the death of Meredith she looked upon Benjamin as a surrogate husband, or more correctly perhaps, herself as a surrogate wife: 'Our honeymoon being over, we have amused ourselves during the autumn by writing a novel. All we hope is that the Public will deem our literary union as felicitous as we find our personal one.'

Sarah was the constant in Benjamin's life, but he was still in love with Henrietta. The Sykes ménage in Upper Grosvenor Street continued to be haunted by the presence of both the Boltons. Henrietta's letters to Benjamin during October are full of references to the 'damnable Boltons', although she appears to have escaped for a rare rendezvous with her lover in his rooms in Duke Street, occupied in his absence at Bradenham by Ralph Disraeli. Although she was having no trouble with Sir Francis – 'the fracas did good not anything now but praise', she wrote to Benjamin, the Villebois family were relentless in their disapproval of her connection with him. A distraught Henrietta wrote to Benjamin on 11 October:

I cannot wait for your brother's departure as I have much to tell you which has sent me to the verge of madness. I received a letter from my Sister on the part of my Father telling me that when last in London he had passed you & I without speaking, that he intended to pursue that course of conduct until my intimacy with you ceased. [He said]

Francis' conduct was every thing unprincipled & Mrs. Bolton no fit companion for either of us. In fact that extreme *fear* for the consequences, & wretchedness, had almost broken his heart & he was ill, & it only remained for me to continue my present dishonourable flirtation to send him to the grave but he trusted to my making the sacrifice for all our sakes more particularly for yours & so on. I wrote back to say how little I had seen of you that I was AGONISED by his displeasure but as long as Sir Francis allowed me your society I should enjoy it etc. etc.[21]

By 20 October, Henrietta was with Sir Francis at Southend, where they had rented Porter's Grange, which she described to Benjamin as 'a very pleasant House ... a nondescript between a French chateau & an English farm house'. Even here the damnable Boltons were in attendance, and Clara could not resist torturing Henrietta by suggestions that she might go to Bradenham 'to see her dear friends'. The thought of the harm which Clara's sly insinuations might cause in the Disraeli family circle threw Henrietta into a panic:

What's to be done? for She has impudence for anything – Mr. Hamond ... as good as told me that Madame was 'an untruth from beginning to end' & hinted that Monsieur B[olton] was artful – Gods [sic] knows whats [sic] to become of us for I turn cold when I think of them ...[22]

It seems that both the Boltons continued full of malevolence towards Benjamin, their former protégé, and that they held the threat of scandal over Henrietta's head to keep her humble and in line with their wishes. Although Sir Francis by his own behaviour and tacit permission condoned her liaison with Disraeli, the age was one of double standards and, should he be persuaded to make a public issue of his wife's affair, she would be socially ruined. Henrietta, despite her reckless passion, was a prey to terrors in her Bolton-haunted isolation at Southend, suspecting that Bolton had been dropping hints about her affair to Charles Westmacott, editor of the notorious scandal sheet, the *Age*. 'Bolton has been introduced to that wretch Westmacott', she wrote nervously to Benjamin, ' – what did he [Westmacott] mean by mentioning your name in last Sunday's age [sic]? Bolton talked mysteriously & said he knew all about it.'[23] Her only consolation was the prospect of Benjamin's visit the following month: 'I think beloved Amin you will like the quiet of this place the greatest drawback will be the damnable Boltons, they poison even my sweetest source of enjoyment'.

Early in November, Benjamin and Henrietta were reunited at Southend in a curious house party consisting of themselves, Sir Francis and the Boltons. Benjamin had his own suite of two rooms where, inspired by love, he set to work on an epic poem which he was convinced would be his masterpiece. Apparently, perhaps because he felt guilty, he had not told Sarah where he was going or any details beyond that he was not going to spend the accustomed winter months with her. Poor Sarah, missing her beloved brother, discovered his whereabouts from Ralph and Jem, and wrote sadly to him on 12 November in a letter addressed to the post office at Southend: 'My dearest, why have you forgotten me ... Will you come back next Saturday?', and, again the next day, 'My dearest love, No letter again this morning. After you left me so unhappy I was sure you would not have failed to have kept your promise of writing to me if there was not something amiss. Pray send me a single line. We are so dull here.'[24] It was not until 14 November that she received a letter from the errant Benjamin revealing that he was staying with the Sykes, in which he attempted to console her by telling her that 'The muse has favoured me much', and that Sir Francis is painting his portrait as a present for Isaac.

It would appear that at this stage the Disraeli family were unhappy and suspicious of his affair with Henrietta, and it is possible that an anguished letter from Isaac to Benjamin written on 25 September 1833 relates to some scene between them on the subject which had led to Benjamin's precipitate departure from Bradenham:

> Believe me, my dearest son, that I who can sympathise with all your feelings – and your Errors – have still most at heart our combined happiness – I am but too deeply sensible – how this has been risked! how much must be repaired! it is a work well worthy of Ourselves, should we discover how to set about it. It ceaselessly occupies my thoughts.[25]

Henrietta, it seems, was unhappily aware of their feelings, writing on Christmas Eve to Benjamin at Bradenham: 'How sincerely I wish it was my fate to be loved by them but alas that cannot be – I love them tho', for I should feel as they do – try & make the good Papa not hate me.'[26]

Within a month Benjamin was back at Bradenham, and apparently appalled by the quantity of his debts; so much so that, with supreme effrontery, he applied once again to Austen for help, claiming that he was so preoccupied by 'an unconquerable desire to produce something great & lasting' that he could not be interrupted by 'the cruelty of having my power of creation marred at such a moment'. Not surprisingly, the much-tried solicitor penned a dignified refusal, unable to resist an embittered dig: 'You say in yours "you appeal to me as a friend often tried but never found wanting". I am sorry to say, my dear Disraeli, that you have tried me too often, & more so to add that I have felt for some time past that your Recollections of it ceased with the necessity.'[27] At the same time Benjamin, probably hoping to flatter Sara Austen into softening up her husband, wrote to her describing the concept of his *Revolutionary Epick*, whose theme was to be the embodiment of the spirit of the age, 'the Revolutionary Principle', indirectly comparing his production with those of Homer, Virgil, Dante and Milton. Surprisingly Sara seems immediately to have forgiven him his past neglect, for she wrote back sympathetically: 'To me also does the conception of your Poem appear to be SUBLIME', regretting 'the petty annoyances' which were disturbing the serenity of his mind. Since one of the petty annoyances was a debt of £300 still owing to Austen, Benjamin wrote his erstwhile friend the most affectionate letter, promising to repay him as soon as he received anything from a publisher, and swearing undying loyalty and gratitude to the Austens: 'No conduct on my part can ever repay you & Mrs. Austen for your fidelity to me – Believe me that there is not a person in the world who, if it came to the trial, wo[ul]d. more cheerfully hazard everything he valued for your united service'.[28] The Austens believed him, against their previous experience, and, after an amicable visit paid by Benjamin to Guilford Street late in December Austen gave him a draft for the £1,200 he had originally asked for, at only 2½ per cent interest for the year.

While Benjamin was at Bradenham, working on his poem and wheedling money out of the Austens, Henrietta was still at Southend, plagued by the presence of 'those damnable Boltons', annoyed every minute, she told him by 'the coarse vulgarity of the one the hypocrisy the low cunning of the other'. Mrs Bolton was always splendidly dressed, financed, Henrietta suspected, by Sir Francis, and full of rancour against the Disraelis. 'She tells me your father is an admirable compiler but as an original genius no one can consider him & you are extravagant in your writing', she retailed, but somehow she managed to keep her temper. They moved to London for Christmas, where Henrietta solaced her loneliness by playing the wife to the absent Benjamin in his Duke Street lodgings:

> Last evening I amused myself turning over all your Duke St. wardrobe – washing the brushes etc. & I felt a gush of tenderness even for the old slippers ... I shall send your Hat to be altered against your arrival in Town – & be not angry the 2 that were in D. St. I have sent to be *put in form*, & will take them with me – you have LOTS ... of shoes & boots – so do not send any more from Bradenham.[29]

Like all Disraeli's women, Henrietta was solicitous about his hair: 'I must now inquire after his raven locks ... is he duly careful of all his Mother's playthings & pets?', and his jewellery, advising him to bring all his rings and chains with him when he came up from Bradenham. She looked forward to the happy future after Christmas at Southend, where he was to finish the *Revolutionary Epick*, 'that is to be the glory of his life as well as mine'.

Benjamin returned to Southend in January 1834 to put the finishing touches to his epic; it was to be read to a select public at a dinner given for the occasion by the Austens on the sixteenth. Among the guests was the Austens' seventeen-year-old nephew, Henry Austen Layard, later to be famous as the discoverer of Nineveh. Years later he was to record his impression of Benjamin's grand recital:

> Standing with his back to the fire, he proceeded in his usual grandiloquent style and with his usual solemn gesture to ask why, as the heroic age had produced its Homer, the Augustan era its Virgil, the Renaissance its Dante, the Reformation its Milton, should not the Revolutionary Epoch, in which we live, produce its representative Poet? The scene was not to be forgotten by those who witnessed it. There was something irresistibly comic in the young man dressed in the fantastic, coxcombical costume he then affected – velvet coat of an original cut thrown wide open, and ruffles to its sleeves, shirt collars turned down in Byronic fashion, an elaborately embroidered waistcoat whence issued voluminous folds of frill, and shoes adorned with red rosettes – his black hair pomatumed and elaborately curled, and his person redolent of perfume – announcing himself as the Homer or Dante of the age! After he had left the room, a gentleman [Samuel Warren] who excelled as a mimic, assuming the attitude and voice of the poet, declaimed an

impromptu burlesque of the opening lines, which caused infinite merriment to those present ...[30]

Benjamin may not have been aware of the mirth that his recital aroused in the Austens' guests, but he was discouraged by the apathetic public reaction to his great work. The *Epick*, a high-flown, declamatory account of the career of Byron's idol, Napoleon, in Italy and the conflict between the spirits of feudalism and federalism, was a complete failure. Benjamin, who had defiantly promised in his preface to the poem that if it did not succeed, he would 'hurl his Lyre, without a pang, into Limbo', never attempted to express himself in poetry again.

Despite the failure of the *Epick*, the summer of 1834 was to be for Benjamin a period of social progress and private happiness. In the spring Sir Francis left for a prolonged tour of the Continent; on 7 March Benjamin accompanied him to Harwich and the two men were on the friendliest of terms. The baleful figures of the Boltons were no longer there to poison the atmosphere; Sir Francis seems to have become disillusioned with them, now referring to his erstwhile friends as 'those dreadful people in King Street'. Dr Bolton, he said, was 'a double-faced villain', while his feelings for Clara were now those of 'disgust'. And so, as Sir Francis put it, in an obscure 'war of fiddle, diddle, *riddle*' the Boltons passed out of Benjamin's life for ever. There was to be only one further mention of Clara in his correspondence; on 3 December 1839 Sarah wrote to him, 'I see Mrs. Bolton is dead at Havre'.

With Sir Francis off the scene and the trouble-making Boltons in disgrace, Benjamin and Henrietta continued their affair with reckless openness. After Easter Benjamin moved to lodgings at 31a Park Street to be near Henrietta at 34 Upper Grosvenor Street, and the two were to all intents living together, making no attempt to hide their love. In March Benjamin sent Bulwer a copy of the *Epick* accompanied by a confession of his love for Henrietta. Bulwer, who had just returned from a disastrous tour of Italy, was on the worst possible terms with Rosina and wrote gloomily that he rejoiced in Disraeli's happiness but '... alas it cannot endure ... I see into the Future & know that no Earthly Love can withstand CUSTOM!' Benjamin ignored his friend's glum prognostications; life seemed to him idyllic, 'a season of unparalleled success and gaiety', he was to write in his diary, 'What a happy or rather amusing society Henrietta & myself commanded this year. What delicious little suppers after the opera!'

Benjamin, however, was not always with Henrietta; in the early summer of 1834 he was introduced by Bulwer to the brilliant circle centring upon Lady Blessington and Count d'Orsay at Seamore Place. Marguerite, Countess of Blessington, was not received in society; men of talent flocked to her house for brilliant conversation and exquisite food, but women, for fear of damaging their reputations, could not. Scandal hung like a cloud over Lady Blessington, for reasons connected with her strange past, as well as her present mode of life.

Born Sally Power in Tipperary in 1789, she had an unhappy childhood and was sold for the first time into marriage with a Mr Farmer at the age of fifteen.

She left him and returned to her drunken father's household, only to escape her sordid surroundings by eloping to live with a Captain Jenkins in Hampshire. In 1816 Jenkins sold her for £10,000 to the rich and eccentric Lord Blessington, whose wife she became on the death of her first husband, Farmer, changing her name from Sally to the more refined Marguerite. In 1821, Alfred, Count d'Orsay, a young Frenchman of extreme beauty, charm and taste, then aged just twenty, came into the Blessingtons' lives, never to leave them again. For eight years the trio lived, mainly in Italy, in a strange *ménage à trois*; the world was convinced that d'Orsay was Lady Blessington's lover, but her husband was equally infatuated with him, to the extent of marrying his daughter by a previous marriage, Harriet Gardiner, to d'Orsay in 1828. Blessington died in Paris in 1829; the following year his widow, with d'Orsay and his young bride, moved to London, and settled in Seamore Place, among scandalous rumour which reached fever pitch when Harriet d'Orsay abruptly quitted the household in 1831.

If Marguerite was hurt by her social ostracism, she was too proud to show it. Her response to the closed doors of London society was to make her house a centre of wit and intellect that would far outshine the other 'blue' hostesses. A visiting American, N.P. Willis, said of her parties that they were 'the only attempt at a republic of letters in the world of this great, envious & gifted metropolis.' Marguerite Blessington, aided by the exquisite taste of d'Orsay, made her surroundings as luxurious as possible; her octagonal dining-room was lined with mirrors, and the magnificent library where she held her receptions, had floor to ceiling mirrors alternating with bookcases, and long windows overlooking the trees of Hyde Park. Here, as described by Willis, she would receive her guests, herself carefully posed in a yellow satin *fauteuil*, 'a delicate white hand blazing with diamonds arranged artistically on the spine of the book, reading by a magnificent lamp suspended from the ceiling' and surrounded by sumptuous sofas and ottomans, interspersed with busts and Sèvres tables.[31]

But the foundations of all this magnificence were precarious; Blessington had left her relatively badly off, with the tenuous income from one of his Irish estates, the bulk of his money having been bequeathed to his daughter and to the wildly extravagant d'Orsay. She worked furiously to supplement her income by writing bad novels and by editing a fashionable social annual, *The Book of Beauty*, pestering her literary friends for contributions. Marguerite's opulent beauty was over-ripe; she wore an odd bandage-like muslin headdress to support her sagging chin and cheeks; but she was an excellent listener and her conversational powers were as brilliant as ever.

Alfred d'Orsay, reputed by the world, almost certainly untruly, to be Marguerite's lover, was the centre of the Blessington circle. Born in 1801 and thus three years older than Disraeli, he was the son of a Bonapartist general and an illegitimate daughter of the Duke of Württemberg; the duke's mistress, d'Orsay's grandmother, was a fascinating adventuress who later married a fabulously wealthy 'nabob' and, as Madame Craufurd, ruled Parisian society. Alfred and his sister Ida, were therefore brought up in surroundings of the utmost luxury, the perfect setting for a man of d'Orsay's tastes. There were many witnesses to d'Orsay's good looks and perfection of dress, from the social chronicles of Captain Gronow to the unlikely pen of Jane Carlyle. Gronow described him as rather above six feet in height with a figure fine enough to serve as a model for a classical statue.

> His neck was long, his shoulders broad, and his waist narrow, and though he was, perhaps, somewhat underlimbed, nothing could surpass the beauty of his feet and ankles. His dark chestnut hair hung naturally in long waving curls; his forehead was high and wide, his features regular, and his complexion glowed with radiant health. His eyes were large and of a light hazel colour, he had full lips and very white teeth, but a little apart; which sometimes gave to the generally amiable expression of his countenance a rather cruel sneering look, such as one sees in the heads of some of the old Roman emperors.[32]

Carlyle described him to his brother, as 'the Phoebus Apollo of dandyism ... with an adornment unsurpassable on this planet', but was surprised to find intellect and wit beneath the beautiful exterior, 'a rather substantial fellow at bottom, by no means without insight, without fun, and a sarcasm rather striking out of such a porcelain figure.'[33]

For nine years from 1832 to 1841, while dandyism still ruled the social scene before the onset of the austere forties, d'Orsay was the unquestioned leader of London's gilded youth. His white greatcoats, blue satin cravats, even his sky-blue cabriolet were slavishly copied. For d'Orsay, despite his perfumed baths and his ostentatious gold dressing-case (which accompanied him everywhere and was so heavy that two men were required to carry it) was popular with men, from the crusty Carlyle to the young bloods of Crockford's, the gaming house in St James's Street which was the temple of the 'swells'. He was, as Gronow recorded, 'thoroughly manly' in his tastes and habits: a reckless horseman in the hunting field, a member of the exclusive Coventry Club which determined the rules of the turf and the ring, and one of the highest gamblers at 'Crocky's'. His undisputed sway over the fashionable world was summed up by a contemporary, Bernal Osborne, in the *Chaunt of Achilles*:

> O'er play, o'er dress extends his wide domain
> And Crockford trembles when he calls a main.

This was the man who was to become Benjamin's mentor and his closest friend over the next few years. As he was proudly to record in his diary that autumn 'I have become this year very popular with the dandies. D'Orsay took a fancy to me, and they take their tone from him. Lady Blessington is their muse, and she declared violently in my favour. I am as popular with the first-rate men as I am hated by the second-rate'.

D'Orsay and Lady Blessington did what they could to favour Benjamin's social and political career. In July, d'Orsay's sister-in-law, Lady Tankerville, obtained for him a subscription for Almack's, the rigidly exclusive place of assembly for

London society, male and female. Even d'Orsay's influence, however, was not enough to get him into Crockford's until 1840 (in the summer of 1834 Benjamin told Sarah 'he was sure to be blackballed'); but at some point he did succeed in making him a member of the Coventry Club.

His ambition undimmed by his electoral defeats, Parliament, however, remained Benjamin's primary goal. Early that summer, at a dinner at Caroline Norton's, with whom he had become reconciled, he told a surprised Lord Melbourne that he intended one day to become Prime Minister. Melbourne was shocked out of his usual urbanity. 'No chance of that in our time', he replied firmly. 'It is all arranged and settled. Nobody can compete with Stanley [Edward Stanley, brother of Benjamin's unfortunate acquaintance, Henry]. If you are going to enter politics and mean to stick to it, I dare say you will do very well, for you have ability and enterprise; and if you are careful how you steer, no doubt you will get into some port at last. But you must put all these foolish notions out of your head: they won't do at all.' Melbourne's implication, too brutal to be expressed directly, was that the office of Prime Minister in the foreseeable future was the preserve of men like Stanley, heir to the thirteenth Earl of Derby, not of Jewish novelists of moderate fortune.

Disraeli never forgot Melbourne's discouraging dictum; years later, when he had achieved all that he had ever dreamed of, it would amuse him to recall the conversation word for word.[34] Such an opinion from such a man might have dispirited the average young political aspirant, but it would have been characteristic of Benjamin to be even more determined to prove Lord Melbourne wrong. In June he contemplated furthering his career by attempting to attach himself, with Lady Blessington's help, to a man who appeared to be a rising star in the political firmament: Grey's son-in-law, the Earl of Durham, known as 'Radical Jack'. Distrusted by his Whig colleagues for his radical views and uncompromising temper, Durham had resigned from the Ministry in March the previous year, but with widespread popular support for him, it was generally considered, as Disraeli wrote to Sarah on 4 June, that 'the Whigs cannot exist as a party without taking in Lord Durham'.

On that same day, 4 June, Lady Blessington arranged a dinner party at which Benjamin was to impress Durham with his intelligence and promise. Among the guests was the egregious chronicler, Willis, who recorded his impressions of the occasion for publication. The dinner began quietly, and had it not been for d'Orsay, sparkling as usual, the first half of the meal would have passed in what Willis characterized as 'the usual English fashion of earnest silence'. Lady Blessington, with perfect timing, then gave Benjamin his chance to shine, with 'an appeal to his opinion on a subject he well understood'. Benjamin responded quickly; according to Willis:

> he burst at once, without preface, into that fiery vein of eloquence which, hearing many times after, and always with new delight, has stamped Disraeli in my mind as the most wonderful talker I have ever had the fortune to meet. He is anything but a declaimer

... If he catches himself in a rhetorical sentence, he mocks at it in the next breath. He is satirical, contemptuous, pathetic, humorous, everything in a moment. Add to this that Disraeli's is the most intellectual face in England – pale, regular, and overshadowed with the most luxuriant masses of raven-black hair, and you will scarcely wonder that meeting him for the first time Lord Durham was impressed.

Durham was indeed impressed, so much so that he went to the length of calling upon Benjamin on 18 June, 'the first day he has been in town since we met', Benjamin told Sarah proudly. Unfortunately, he was not at home, but he wrote optimistically about his political prospects, 'I am also right in politics as well as in society, being now backed by a very powerful party, and I think the winning one.' Although there seems to have been no concrete foundation for his extravagant claims to political support, he was, from the evidence of his letters, nonetheless climbing with some success in society. He could not help retailing with delight an interview between Lady Cork and old Lord Carrington, the neighbouring Tory magnate in Buckinghamshire. Carrington told Lady Cork that he thought the young Disraeli a very extraordinary sort of person and 'a great agitator'. Lady Cork, whose admiration for Benjamin extended to expending 17 shillings on crimson velvet to have the *Revolutionary Epick* bound by her maid, riposted that Disraeli was 'the best *ton* [the smart set] in London!', that no party was a success without him: 'Lady Lonsdale w[oul]d give her head and shoulders for him', adding contemptuously 'He w[oul]d not dine at y[ou]r house if you were to ask him. He does not care for people because they are lords: he must have fashion, or beauty, or wit, or something: and you are a very good sort of person but nothing more.'[35]

Old Lady Cork's partisanship must be taken with a pinch of salt; but Benjamin's letters of the summer of 1834 are a roll-call of noble names – Lady Salisbury, Lady Tavistock, Lord Hertford *et al*. River parties, dinner parties, receptions and evenings at the opera or the ballet were all very enjoyable, but hardly of much value in winning Benjamin the longed-for seat in Parliament. In mid-July, however, when the social season was nearing its close, Benjamin at last met the man who was to become his political patron: John Singleton Copley, 1st Baron Lyndhurst.

6 Roundabouts and Swings

Lord Lyndhurst was sixty-two when Disraeli met him in 1834, a self-made man and a highly successful lawyer. Born in Boston, he was the son of the celebrated American portrait painter, also called John Singleton Copley. Since his arrival in England in 1775 he had risen steadily in the legal profession becoming First Baron of the Exchequer and Lord Chancellor in the brief Wellington administration of 1827. His politics were High Tory; indeed with his great debating ability and acute mind, he was one of the ringleaders of the House of Lords' opposition to Reform and the Whig government of Earl Grey. He was a tall, handsome man, powerfully built with a majestic forehead and deepset piercing eyes, 'the countenance', Disraeli wrote, 'of a high-bred falcon'.[1] He was gregarious, good-humoured, kind-hearted and cynical, his main deficiencies, in Disraeli's view, being 'a want of high purpose & some sensual attributes'. Although Lyndhurst, a widower with three daughters and an unmarried sister, was a devoted family man, he had had a raffish past and a record of liaisons with women of easy virtue. Indeed he was notoriously susceptible to women and not given to purely sentimental relationships. Once, when asked by Lady Tankerville whether he believed in 'platonic friendship', he replied, 'After, but not before'.

This then, was the man to whom Henrietta introduced Benjamin in July 1834, and indeed the three of them were later to become involved in a dubious relationship that was to do serious damage to Benjamin's reputation. The two found an instant *rapport*, and both Henrietta and Benjamin saw in Lyndhurst a political patron whose influence might at last obtain for him a parliamentary seat. Henrietta was to work on Lyndhurst in Benjamin's favour; neither of the lovers seemed then to contemplate what might be the outcome should Lyndhurst, being the man he was, demand his quid pro quo.

The 'season of unparalleled success and gaiety' ended sadly for Benjamin and Henrietta; they were still passionately in love, but debts and the threat of social ostracism hung over them. They were both extravagant and careless about money and the summer had been expensive; worries about their finances and the scandal their affair was causing, added to the sadness of their annual end of season parting.

'Dearest we are not happy because we are not rich'. Henrietta wrote. 'This want of money is a heavy blackness wh. presses us to the earth.'[2] She was terrified what Sir Francis would say when he found out the extent of her extravagance; worse still he had intimated that he might come home in December. Moreover, she was under constant siege both from Sir Francis' aunt, Lady Cork, and her Villebois sisters, who warned her that no one would visit her next season if she continued her relationship with Benjamin.

And so, when Disraeli left London at the beginning of August for Bradenham where he intended to work upon the novel, *Henrietta Temple*, which was to be not only a celebration of their love but also, they hoped, a solution to their financial situation, Henrietta, fearful of facing her family at Marham, accepted an invitation from Lyndhurst to stay at St Leonards. Benjamin apparently was jealous, for Henrietta hastened to reassure him that Lyndhurst was there with his family: '*Everything* you say I *will mark*, & be assured I will be as prudish as an old maid of 70 – Ld L goes to the Hotel ... he treats me as if he valued my society, but never glances at love & seriously I do not think he cares for anything beyond killing reflection.'[3] Nevertheless, she was already becoming indebted to her protector, despite what she described as her 'cavalier' treatment of him; Lyndhurst paid for everything, and in October she agreed to accompany him and his family abroad. 'I can rule him in everything and where women are concerned never was there a greater fool', she boasted to Benjamin. By the end of the tour, Henrietta considered that she could twist Lyndhurst round her little finger. 'Ld. Lyndhurst arrived in town last night', she reported to Benjamin in October. 'I can make him do as I like so whatever arrangement you think best tell me & I will perform it. Ld. Lyndhurst is anxious you should be in the House'.[4]

Benjamin, who for the past two months had been ill at Bradenham where he had been laid up on a sofa with 'a great pain in the legs and extraordinary languor' and had suffered a fainting fit, was instantly restored to health by the prospect Henrietta held out to him. He hurried up to London at the end of October to take advantage of the situation, and was rewarded by long confidential conversations with Lyndhurst on the state of politics. It was Lyndhurst's opinion, he told Benjamin, that 'the end of Whiggism was at hand'.[5]

Since the early summer of 1834 the Whig government had been riven by a series of shocks; in May two of the abler members of the Cabinet, Edward Stanley and Sir James Graham, had resigned over Lord John Russell's proposal to appropriate the revenues of the Irish Anglican Church for secular purposes; in June the Prime Minister, Grey, defeated by his supposed ally, Daniel O'Connell, on the Irish Coercion Bill, resigned, to be replaced by the languid Lord Melbourne. In the first week of November, Melbourne lost the services of his able Leader in the Commons, Viscount Althorp, elevated to the House of Lords on the death of his father, Earl Spencer. On November 14, the King, William iv, whose hatred of the Whigs was notorious, refusing to contemplate the left-wing Lord John Russell as Leader of the Commons, dismissed the Government and sent for

Wellington. While Peel travelled back from Rome to take up the reins as Prime Minister, Wellington and Lyndhurst formed a caretaker government. The King's action would inevitably precipitate a general election, but until Peel arrived back in London, nothing definite could be decided.

Despite his friendship with Lyndhurst, and the fact that the two of them had been involved with such ultra-Tories as Lord Chandos in a scheme to bring down Melbourne which had been too extreme even for Wellington to stomach, Benjamin hesitated until the last minute before throwing in his lot with the Tories. It is hardly surprising that he should have been accused of political opportunism when, after intriguing with such men as Lyndhurst and Chandos, he wrote to the Radical Whig, Durham, asking him to persuade one of his radical friends, Hobhouse, to stand down at Aylesbury in his favour, and promising Durham in return to exercise his almost non-existent 'local influence'. Nor would Lyndhurst have been pleased had he known of the contempt with which his young protégé referred to the Tories in his letter to 'Radical Jack'.

Durham was friendly but non-committal; Lyndhurst, however, now in a powerful position as Lord Chancellor in Peel's government, and pressured by Henrietta, did what he could to help. He persuaded Wellington to write to the Tory election committee recommending that Disraeli be found a seat, and lobbied the local Tory magnate, Lord Carrington, whose poor opinion of Benjamin as 'a very extraordinary young man' and 'a great agitator' has already been noted. Benjamin was still undecided. He wrote to Sarah as late as 8 December, 'It is impossible to say how things will go: but at present I have not thought it proper to write to Durham.' Even Lyndhurst's powers of persuasion failed to convince the Tory establishment that the young Jewish Radical would be a suitable Tory candidate. Charles Fulke Greville's acid comments on a proposal made to him by Lyndhurst expressed the general view of the elasticity of Benjamin's political principles:

> The Chancellor [Lyndhurst] called on me yesterday about getting young Disraeli into Parliament [through the influence of Lord George Bentinck, Greville's cousin] for Lynn. I had told him George wanted a good man to assist in turning out William Lennox, and he suggested the above-named gentleman whom he called a friend of Chandos. His political principles must, however, be in abeyance, for he said that Durham was doing all he could to get him by the offer of a seat and so forth; if therefore he is undecided and wavering between Chandos and Durham, he must be a mighty impartial personage. I don't think such a man will do, though just such as Lyndhurst would be connected with.[6]

Lord George Bentinck, who twelve years later was to be Disraeli's closest colleague and friend, absolutely refused to help; 'Disraeli he won't hear of', Greville commented.

By mid-December Benjamin had no alternative but to stand for Wycombe, the third time as a Radical, although Lyndhurst managed to cajole £500 out of central Conservative funds for him, there being no official Tory candidate. Disraeli's election address, however, which he published under the title, *The Crisis Examined*, was independent rather than Radical in tone, chiefly dedicated to attacking the Whig claim to the country's eternal gratitude for having passed the Reform Bill, and ridiculing their trouble-ridden Cabinets – Melbourne being compared in a comical passage with a famous trick circus rider, Mr Ducrow. Once again, his opponents were Smith and Grey and once again, when the poll was declared on 7 January, he came bottom, the figures being Smith, 289; Grey, 147; Disraeli, 128.

It was his last appearance as an independent; three months later in April 1835, after the defeat of the Peel government, he was sent down to Taunton as official Conservative candidate to oppose Henry Labouchere, Master of the Mint in Melbourne's second administration. The Taunton by-election was Disraeli's first real step up the political ladder; for the first time he was fighting an election as candidate for a major political party, backed by party funds and endorsed by the Conservative election manager, F.R. Bonham, as 'a gentleman for whom all the Conservative Party are most anxious to obtain a seat in the House of Commons.'

One may indeed wonder how Benjamin, within three months of his third appearance on the hustings as a Radical, succeeded in convincing such shrewd politicians as Bonham, Peel's right-hand man, that he was a trustworthy Conservative candidate. In fact, the hand of Lyndhurst – and of Henrietta – was behind his candidature; early in April Henrietta told Benjamin that she was pressing Lyndhurst to get up a subscription for him at the Carlton Club, hub of the Tory electoral machine, and that Lyndhurst had written to Bonham on his behalf.

No doubt Lyndhurst had persuaded Bonham of the soundness of Disraeli's political principles, but Benjamin still needed to convince the electorate and his critics that in changing his party colours he had not changed his basic views. Characteristically, his mode of defence was to attack; nor did he at Taunton, any more than he had at Wycombe, make any concessions to provincial prejudice, addressing the amazed crowd 'very showily attired in a dark bottle-green frock-coat, a waistcoat of the most extravagant pattern, the front of which was covered with glittering chains, and in fancy-pattern pantaloons.'[7] With his glossy black ringlets carefully combed away from his right temple to fall in luxuriant clusters over his left cheek, and a Byronic half-smile, half-sneer playing on his lips, Benjamin told the electors that his political stance had never changed: 'Gentlemen, here is my consistency. I have always opposed with my utmost energy the party of which my honourable opponent is a distinguished member'. He had advocated the Radical principles of triennial parliaments and the ballot only to break the dictatorial power of the Whig oligarchy; now, he said, somewhat ingenuously, the balance of the parties being restored, such measures were no longer necessary. He then launched a swingeing attack upon the Whigs and their alliance with the Irish leader, O'Connell, as a cynical compact with a man whom they despised, effected solely for the purpose of keeping themselves in power. His language was violent – 'the Whigs had seized the bloody hand of O'Connell'– describing the Whigs as 'that weak aristocratic power in the state who could only obtain power by leaguing themselves with one whom they had denounced as a traitor.'

Garbled newspaper reports of Disraeli's speech reached O'Connell in Dublin. His response showed that he was at least Benjamin's equal in outrageous invective. He was enraged, he said, that a man who had once sought his political help (for the first Wycombe election) as a Radical, now had the impudence to denounce him as a 'traitor' in order to curry favour with his new Tory friends. Benjamin was a 'reptile', possessing 'all the necessary requisites of perfidy, selfishness, depravity, want of principle &c.,' to make such a change of allegiance possible. He was the worst possible type of Jew, O'Connell continued, 'He has just the qualities of the impenitent thief on the cross, and I verily believe, if Mr. Disraeli's family herald were to be examined and his genealogy traced, the same personage would be discovered to be the heir at law of the exalted individual to whom I allude'.

This was just the kind of public cut and thrust which Benjamin revelled in: he lost no time in sending a challenge to O'Connell's son, Morgan, through an open letter in *The Times*, and when this was sensibly refused, he assailed O'Connell and the Whigs in a lengthy letter to the same newspaper, firing off another aggressive public missive to Morgan O'Connell, praying that either he or some other member of the family 'may attempt to avenge the inextinguishable hatred with which I shall pursue his existence'. No duel took place; Benjamin was arrested on the orders of a magistrate friendly to the O'Connells and bound over to keep the peace, but he was highly delighted with the whole affair which, at the very least, had brought him notoriety. 'Row with O'Connell in which I greatly distinguished myself', he wrote with satisfaction in his diary for the year.

Benjamin was convinced that he would win a seat in the next general election, when he would be able to meet O'Connell face to face in Parliament, 'We shall meet at Philippi' he warned him. With the Melbourne government only recently returned to power, however, a general election in the near future was unlikely. Benjamin meanwhile was determined to keep himself in the public eye until the occasion should arise, and, with Lyndhurst's help and encouragement, launched himself on a new career as Tory publicist and political journalist, belabouring the Whigs and O'Connell in print as he had assailed them from the hustings.

Unfortunately, Lyndhurst's influence on Benjamin's political career was to be not entirely propitious. Lyndhurst and his ally, Lord Chandos, with whom Benjamin had also been involved, belonged to the ultra-Tory right wing of the party, pledged to diehard opposition to any reforming measure which the Whigs might put forward. They were distrusted by the real power in the Conservative party, Peel, who, since the publication of his Tamworth Manifesto in 1835, had been attempting to rebuild the party on more progressive lines and to rescue it from the political dead-end in which it had found itself after 1832.

Benjamin's anonymous début as Lyndhurst's hack came in late August 1835 when he wrote fourteen leading articles in the *Morning Post*, supporting Lyndhurst and the Tory peers in their opposition to the Municipal Corporations Bill. The measure was one of necessary reform, drawn up by the Radical Joseph Parkes and his committee, and designed to remove the corrupt influence of 'the lord of the manor' in the election of municipal corporations by establishing household suffrage. Lyndhurst and his fellow peers saw it as a purely partisan measure, an attempt to replace Tory electoral influence in the boroughs with that of the Whigs and their Radical allies. In a series of pitched battles they amended the Commons' Bill out of all recognition, leading Melbourne to issue a public warning of the dangers of a collision between peers and people. Disraeli's articles, supporting the peers and attacking the Commons' claim to represent the people, were liberally spattered with personal invective, Melbourne being referred to as 'Manchester-massacre Melbourne ... Prime Minister by the grace or disgrace of Daniel O'Connell', and the attorney-general who had had the temerity to attack Lyndhurst being compared with an orang-utang.

Amidst the invective there were some telling points; Disraeli was perfectly correct in asserting that the Whigs were being forced into radical measures because they needed the support of the Irish and the Radicals to keep themselves in power. It was also undeniable that the Commons' claim to represent the people under the limited franchise of 1832 was a fallacy. '... the Commons form a class in the state, privileged, irresponsible and hereditary, like the Peers', he declared. It is doubtful whether Disraeli really believed in parliamentary democracy, his vision of the representative function in the English constitution being more nearly allied to the idea of a corporate state. Here, not for the first time, he played on one of his strongest political themes, the claim of the Conservative party to be the 'national party', with a long roll-call of the interests they represented – the King, the Peers, the gentlemen, the yeomanry, 'the universal peasantry of England', the services, the professions, the Church, Universities, magistrates, merchants, and 'a large body in every town, agricultural, commercial, even manufacturing'. 'What constitutes a people', he demanded rhetorically, 'if these do not afford the elements of a great and glorious nation?'

Disraeli further expanded these views in his first, and last, political treatise, written in the autumn of 1835 and published in December of that year. Entitled *A Vindication of the English constitution in a letter to a noble and learned Lord*, it was addressed to Lyndhurst and is worth examining as the only sustained exposition of Disraeli's political thought and attitudes, attitudes which he never significantly changed. Its principal theme was the validity of the Conservative party as the 'national' party, pledged to defend the institutions of England, the Monarchy, the Church and the People, and it represented the Whigs, 'that Venetian oligarchy', as a selfish faction whose claim to represent the people was manifestly false.

Interestingly, in the light of his future role as leader of the Tory party and author of *Coningsby*, Disraeli here described the English aristocracy as:

a class of individuals ... noble from the generosity of their nature, the inspiration of their lineage, and the refinement of their education; a class of individuals who, instead of meanly submitting to fiscal immunities, support upon their broad and cultivated lands all the burthens of the State; men who have conquered by land and sea, who have distinguished themselves in every honourable profession, and acquired fame in every department of learning ... science and art; who support the poor instead of plundering them, and respect the court which they do not fear; friends alike to liberty and order, who execute justice and maintain truth – the gentlemen of England.

This was an exaggerated picture of the English aristocracy of the time, but not an entirely untrue one.[8] The darker side of this was represented by the ferocious Game Laws and the iniquitous penal system but in the absence of a centralized administrative system, the English landed class played their part conscientiously in the administration of local justice and charitable relief until the late 1880s. Disraeli was to cling tenaciously to this view of the role of the English aristocracy as the natural leaders of the people to the end of his life, despite his personal experience of the individual stupidity, selfishness and prejudice of 'the gentlemen of England'.

The *Vindication* expressed other characteristically Disraelian themes: his hatred of abstract political theory as a basis for the shaping of political institutions, and the validity of Benthamite Utilitarianism ('the greatest happiness of the greatest possible number') in particular, which he had attacked with especial venom in *Popanilla*. 'The blended influence of nature and fortune', he declared, formed individual character; ' 'tis the same with nations.' His conception of a democracy was highly individual, being defined as 'the country where the legislative and even the executive office may be constitutionally obtained by every subject in the land'. Any country where a man like Benjamin Disraeli, without power or connections, could become Prime Minister was certainly 'a democracy of the noblest character'.

In a long, highly subjective passage, Disraeli identified himself with the maverick Tory thinker of the early eighteenth century, Henry St John, Lord Bolingbroke, author of *The Patriot King*. His description of Bolingbroke's career was clearly based on his own political experience:

> Opposed to the Whigs from principle, for an oligarchy is hostile to genius, and recoiling from the Tory tenets, which his unprejudiced and vigorous mind taught him at the same time to dread and to condemn, Lord Bolingbroke, at the outset of his career, incurred the common-place imputation of insincerity and inconsistency, because ... he maintained that vigilant and meditative independence which is the privilege of an original and determined spirit.

Bolingbroke, like Disraeli, contemplated the formation of a new party, but discarded the idea as impractical. Forced to choose between the Whigs and the Tories, he opted for the latter, but through his writings preached a new brand of Toryism, eradicating its most odious prejudices and clearly developing 'its essential and permanent character'. Bolingbroke, the *Vindication* concluded, thus 'laid the foundation for the future accession of the Tory party to power'. This personal parallel did not escape Disraeli's friends; Lord Eliot, on reading the Bolingbroke passages, 'could not help thinking that if opportunities were not withheld you may become what he might have been.'

The *Vindication* was a highly personal and subjective book; it had little to do with logic or with accepted political theory. It was to be characteristic of Disraeli's idiosyncratic approach to his own actions, both political and personal; if he instinctively felt something to be right or necessary then he would evolve a justification for it. Convinced of his own genius and of his destiny as Prime Minister he had the romantic idea that nothing that he did to achieve that end could be dishonourable or mean.

Indeed, Benjamin was in extremely aggressive mood, flying to his own defence when his honour was touched upon. Having been accused by the Radical Charles Buller, writing in *The Globe*, of political inconsistency and of having personally solicited help from both Hume and O'Connell at Wycombe, his prolonged and vituperative correspondence on the subject through the letter columns of *The Times* achieved a new low in gutter invective. He declared in that newspaper on 8 January 1836:

> It is not then my passion for notoriety that has induced me to tweak the editor of the Globe by the nose, and to inflict sundry kicks upon the baser part of his base body; to make him eat dirt, and his own words, fouler than any filth; but because I wished to show the world what a miserable scarecrow, what a mere thing, stuffed with straw and rubbish, is the *soi-disant* director of public opinion and official organ of Whig politics.

Within a few days of this parting shot in the campaign against *The Globe* and its allies, Disraeli was again assailing the Whigs in the columns of *The Times*, with the active encouragement of Lyndhurst and of its editor, Thomas Barnes, to whom Lyndhurst had introduced him. In a series of nineteen open letters using the pseudonym 'Runnymede' written between 18 January and 15 May 1836 to coincide with the sitting of Parliament, Disraeli lampooned the government with a rapier-like wit, delicately skewering his ministerial victims like so many butterflies. The nonchalant Melbourne was described as 'sauntering over the destinies of a nation, and lounging away the glory of an empire', while Palmerston, known for his boudoir exploits and fondness for rouging, was apostrophized as 'the Lord Fanny of diplomacy, cajoling France with an airy compliment, and menacing Russia with a perfumed cane!' Most notorious was his depiction of a repentant Earl Grey, author of the Reform Bill, as a 'worn-out Machiavel, wringing his helpless hands over his hearth in remorseful despair and looking up with a sigh at his scowling ancestors'.

Not all the attacks were in the best of taste, as for instance the portrayal of Disraeli's principal enemy O'Connell: 'Towering above all, and resting on a lurid shrine bedewed with blood and encircled with flame, with distended jaws and colossal tail, is the grim figure of the O'Connell crocodile'. There would undoubtedly have been more of this sort of thing had it not been for the restraining influence of Barnes, whose early letters to Disraeli on the subject of *Runnymede* pleaded for caution. Barnes excised some of the more outrageous gibes, such as a reference to Melbourne's supposed affair with Caroline Norton; Benjamin's description of Caroline as 'a very substantial Siren whose fleshly attractions are supposed to be as agreeable to Lord M. as the last patent easy-chair', was, in view of his past friendship with her, neither gallant nor kind. By the end of May, however, when the *Letters of Runnymede* were the talk of the town, Barnes was forced to admit that the game might be worth the candle. 'You have a most surprising disdain for the law of libel,' he wrote to Benjamin: 'but I do not object to considerable risk when the stake is worth playing for.'[9]

In striking contrast to the abuse heaped upon the Whig Ministers, the letter addressed to Peel was couched in the most fulsomely flattering language: 'In your chivalry is our only hope. Clad in the panoply of your splendid talents and your spotless character ... rescue THE NATION', Benjamin apostrophized his leader. When the *Runnymede Letters* were published in July together with a summary of the *Vindication* under the title *Whigs and Whiggism*, Benjamin dedicated the volume to Peel. He had already sent an early copy of the *Vindication* to Peel, of whom he was clearly distinctly nervous, with, as he told Sarah 'a cold, dry note', and had been gratified to hear that Peel had not only read it but was 'surprised that a familiar and apparently exhausted topic could be treated with so much of original force of argument and novelty of illustration'. 'Lyndhurst thinks this is *much*, considering the writer', an exhilarated Benjamin reported to Sarah. He was well aware of the necessity of ingratiating himself with Peel, who, as future Prime Minister, would be the arbiter of his political destiny, and he seems to have felt, mistakenly as it turned out, that he was making progress in that direction. 'Established my character as a great political writer', he noted immodestly in his diary, 'Resume my acquaintance with Peel. My influence greatly increases from the perfect confidence of L[yndhurst] and my success as a political writer'. Indeed, political affirmation seemed now within his reach; in March 1836 he had been elected to the Conservative holy of holies, the Carlton Club.

Socially too, Disraeli felt that he was making considerable strides. At a costume ball the previous summer which was 'the talk of the season' he had been introduced by his friend Lord Castlereagh to his stepmother, Frances Anne, Marchioness of Londonderry. The Marchioness represented Cleopatra 'in a dress literally embroidered with emeralds and diamonds from top to toe', Disraeli told Sarah, adding cruelly, 'It looked like armour, and she like a rhinoceros'.[10] It was the beginning of an intimate, albeit on Disraeli's part somewhat servile, friendship between himself and the haughty Frances Anne, which, with a brief interruption when the Marchioness dropped him on the occasion of his marriage, was to continue in a close correspondence until her death in 1865. Being taken up by the Londonderrys was a considerable social *coup*, for although they were universally disliked for their pride and ostentation ('their united Vanity and Selfishness amounts almost to madness', one critic wrote[11]), everyone who was anyone went to their magnificent entertainments. Disraeli quickly became one of their intimates and was invited to dine at Rosebank, their summer villa at Fulham, which he described to Sarah as 'the prettiest baby-house in the world ... all green paint, white chintz, & looking-glass',[12] where Lady Londonderry, in the manner of

Marie Antoinette, sat in pseudo-rustic splendour in her conservatory, dispensing tea from a wealth of gold and silver pots.

At the beginning of 1836, therefore, the signs seemed promising. Benjamin had high hopes of obtaining from James Halse, a local Tory mine-owner, the nomination for the safe seat of St Ives, then, when that failed he was off in hot pursuit of another, this time at Lewes. He was not, however, to achieve the longed-for object until over a year later; in the intervening twelve months he was to pay the price of political patronage and social success with the break-up of his affair with Henrietta and a severe financial crisis.

Benjamin's private reputation was being severely damaged by widespread speculation as to the nature of the relationships between himself, Henrietta and Lyndhurst. Even such close friends as Bulwer believed that Benjamin was sharing Henrietta's favours with Lyndhurst in return for his political support; while two visits paid by the threesome to Bradenham in July and September the previous year had shocked Buckinghamshire society. In October, a reluctant Sir Francis Sykes, bombarded by Henrietta's family with accounts of the scandal surrounding her and the extent of her debts, returned to England from Venice to a rented villa in Richmond. Though annoyed by his wife's debts, he continued to be perfectly complaisant as far as Benjamin's relationship with Henrietta was concerned, even apparently regarding him as an ally who would do his best to control her. In December, either for the sake of appearance or from economy, Benjamin moved from Park Street to Long's Hotel in New Bond Street, but he continued to use Henrietta to pressure Lyndhurst on his behalf. On 22 December he wrote to his mother deferring an invitation to Bradenham for Henrietta: 'I am very sorry . . . but it is important for me that she should not leave town until the Election [Wycombe]'; while in April, as we have seen, Henrietta's influence with Lyndhurst had been instrumental in obtaining official Conservative backing for him at Taunton.

Benjamin must have known what the world was saying about him; but one wonders what his private feelings were, and how he justified to himself the fact that he was cynically using a woman whom he had passionately loved in order to obtain favours for himself. One can only speculate that either he closed his eyes to the quid pro quo, or accepted it as a necessary part of the great plan of getting himself into Parliament. His own family, too innocent perhaps to realize the full implications of the triangle, seem not to have disapproved; Sarah's letters during the winter 1835-6 were full of references to Henrietta and Lyndhurst, and at Christmas she sent them both presents of 'cocoa sweetmeats'.

From the time of the Taunton election in April 1835, the tone of Henrietta's letters had become distinctly less passionate, but, through the summer of 1836, despite the erratic comings and goings of Sir Francis, the tripartite relationship continued, with Benjamin, Henrietta and Lyndhurst spending Whitsun together at Bradenham. In mid-August, Benjamin, Lyndhurst and his family went down to Basildon Park to stay with Henrietta, Benjamin still evidently acting as Lyndhurst's political collaborator and preparing fair copies of his patron's speeches for the press. On 21 August, the two men went down to Basildon again, on what Benjamin described to Sarah as a visit of charity, 'for Sir Francis has returned with a train of savage men ... three or four foreign servants, & all his hangers-on & toadys – Dreadful. He is quite mad & tossed up a ducat not knowing what to do with himself, whether he should go to Aix la Chapelle or return home. It unfortunately came down heads & here he is – ill, I think dying & very frenzied.'[13] Henrietta, he told Sarah, would be staying at Basildon until 1 September, and intended to ask the D'Israeli family over when Lyndhurst was there. 'We', he wrote proprietorially, 'hope to find you all there as I think it will be an amusing change.'

It was to be the last time he would write proprietorially about Henrietta and her possessions. In mid-September he returned to Bradenham to finish his novel, *Henrietta Temple*, and to escape his most pressing creditors. Indeed, Benjamin's debts seemed about to overwhelm him; to the debts of his early years of speculation and the money he owed Austen (who continued, in vain, to address him for repayment), had been added the cost of cutting a dash with Henrietta in society, for such items as a cabriolet [carriage] with which to impress his dandy friends, bills to wine merchants, tailors, hosiers and livery stables, which, if they had been settled at all had been paid for by further sums borrowed from moneylenders at outrageous terms of interest. Added to this was the cost of raising money for his election expenses. At one point it seems certain that he ended up in a sponging-house, and was only rescued by d'Orsay from the threat of a debtor's prison, a scene which he graphically described in *Henrietta Temple*. Early in the year he had become involved once again with Haber, this time in speculations on French railways and other projects which apparently included 'Swedish turnips' and 'Naples biscuits'; from which he confidently expected to make at least £1,000. But despite two visits to Haber in The Hague, he was doomed to disappointment – as usual with Disraelian dreams of making money, the railways, turnips and biscuits vanished into thin air. By July he was under daily threat of arrest at the instigation of the moneylender, Thomas Mash, from whom he had borrowed considerable sums to finance the Wycombe elections. 'Peel has asked me to dine with a party of the late Government at the Carlton', he wrote to his new friend, the solicitor William Pyne, on 21 July, 'Is it safe? I fear not.'[14] Indeed, he was already borrowing money from Pyne, who seems to have been seduced by Benjamin's charm into following in Austen's footsteps. Benjamin's utter financial irresponsibility and eternal optimism was demonstrated in a letter he wrote to Pyne on 30 May 1836:

> On Saturday the *Carlton Chronicle* a new weekly journal under the highest patronage will be started. I have been offered & have provisionally accepted *half the proprietorship*, which, how[eve]r will require £500. This speculation ... may turn out & quickly *a considerable property*. The affair has been so sudden that I have not had time to consult you. I have little resources except the £200 which are in fact yours, but I think I could scrape enough tog[ethe]r.[15]

Nothing came of that project either; in July Isaac, whom Benjamin informed of his financial failures and of his intention to write a pot-boiler novel to recoup them, wrote anxiously: 'How will the Fictionist assort with the Politician?' It was a question which his son was not prepared to discuss; he had begun *Henrietta Temple* three years earlier, and now he must finish the book as soon as possible. He had agreed with the 'bawd' Colburn to bring out the novel in November, and a further pot-boiler, which was to be *Venetia*, the following January. And so, leaving Henrietta alone, the erratic Sir Francis being once again abroad, he retired to Bradenham to work furiously on his novel. He must have been glad to take refuge in his work, for the atmosphere at Bradenham was gloomy. Isaac's temper, exacerbated by his son's financial problems, can hardly have been improved by the consciousness of his failing sight. 'I shall never live to turn a whiter page in the volume of my fate', he had written to Benjamin the previous December, ' – a darker one is preparing'.[16] To make matters worse, in February 1836 Sarah's last hopes of marriage had been extinguished. She had formed an attachment for a friend of Ralph's, John Eyton, which to some extent had consoled her for Benjamin's frequent absences and his preoccupation with his career and Henrietta, and for the failure of her own literary experiments. But on 21 February Isaac had written to Benjamin informing him of Eyton's death; he said Eyton had been 'a possible contingency of happiness for our Angel – her last & secret hope wh. supported her through her disappointments.'[17]

Amidst the prevailing dullness, Benjamin found light relief in corresponding with Pyne about his debts, their mutual speculations in the City, and the stimulating question of evading arrest by his creditors. Benjamin felt not the least sense of guilt about his debts; they were all part of the image of a gentleman dandy in the mode of his heroes, Byron and d'Orsay; in fact, he rather enjoyed them. As he was later to write in *Tancred*, 'Fakredeen was fond of his debts; they were the source indeed of his only excitement, and he was grateful to them for their stirring powers'. Ironically, just at the moment when he was liable at any time to be arrested for debt, he had been, through the influence of Lyndhurst and Chandos, appointed JP for the county, and entitled therefore to dispense justice from the bench at the local Quarter Sessions. Indeed it was only in the unavoidable pursuance of his magisterial duties that he ventured out in daylight as he lived in constant fear of being 'nabbed' by his creditors. Mash in particular seems to have been a threat on the eve of a great county Conservative dinner where Benjamin was to give a toast to the House of Lords before 'the Lord Lieutenant, the High Sheriff, four peers, two privy councillors, eight baronets and fifty fellow magistrates', a thousand guests in all. 'I trust there is no danger of my being nabbed by Mash', he wrote to Pyne on 5 December, 'as this would be a fatal contretemps, inasmuch, in all probability, I am addressing my future constituents.'[18]

Henrietta Temple was published on 1 December; on the 10th, the day after the county banquet, Benjamin went up to London. Some time within the following week he made the shattering discovery that Henrietta had taken another lover,

Daniel Maclise, a big, handsome Scots-Irishman, who was one of the most fashionable portrait painters of the day. Maclise, in fact, had been working on a portrait of Henrietta since April; the proximity of artist and sitter, coupled with Benjamin's prolonged absence in the autumn, probably being responsible for the affair. Benjamin's pride must have been doubly hurt by the fact that Maclise was an old friend, having executed his portrait for *Fraser's* three years previously, as well as sketches of both Isaac and Sarah. Benjamin's biographers have hitherto followed his statement in his diary that he 'parted for ever from Henrietta' in the autumn of 1836, but he was always notoriously inaccurate about dates, and there is no indication whatever from his light-hearted letters to his friends, or indeed from the novel that he was then finishing, that anything was wrong, until on 19 December he wrote a moving letter to d'Orsay, confessing his misery and its cause:

Carlton [Club] Sunday   *Confidential*   [19 December 1836]

My dear D'Orsay,

You will have thought my conduct very strange, but I am sure your goodness will have put the most charitable construction on it. I will now confess to you what I can confess to no other person, that I am overwhelmed with some domestic vexations which it is out of the power even of your friendship to soothe. Your quick but delicate mind will make you comprehend what I cannot venture to express.

As a man of the world, you will perhaps laugh at me & think me very silly for being the slave of such feelings, when perhaps I ought to congratulate myself that an intimacy which must have, I suppose, sooner or later concluded, has terminated in a manner which may cost my heart a pang but certainly not my conscience. But it is in vain to reason with those who feel. In calmer moments, I may be of your opinion; at present I am wretched.

I have been nowhere, since I was in London & seen no one, except Bulwer. It seemed to me that some suspicions were lurking in his mind. I could not hear a person spoken lightly of to whom I am indebted for the happiest years of my life & whom I have ever found a faithful friend, therefore I spoke of her in that way that I have entirely misled him.

I have not spirit at the moment to venture to call ... Try to say something to Lady B[lessington] to account for my strange conduct. These pangs, like everything human will, I suppose pass away nevertheless they are sharp.

Yrs. ever my dear D'Orsay, Dis[19]

Deeply wounded, Benjamin retreated to Bradenham for Christmas, arriving, he told Pyne in a letter written on Boxing Day, just in time, for the road to the house was now blocked with snow drifts 'as high as a man's breast'. Bradenham seemed a peaceful refuge after the lonely week of wretchedness in London. 'I assure you', he told Pyne, 'when I reached the old hall, and found the beech blocks crackling and blazing, I felt no common sentiments of gratitude to that kind friend whose never tired zeal allowed me to reach my house, and is some consolation for the plague of women, the wear and tear of politics, and the dunning of creditors'.[20] It was an unhappy ending to a year which had begun so full of hope.

Benjamin was too proud to tell his family what had happened, nor did Henrietta, naturally under the circumstances, enlighten Sir Francis. There remained the question of how Lyndhurst might react. Benjamin and his friend Lady Blessington feared that the affair might cause a breach with Lyndhurst and that Henrietta might try to influence him to Benjamin's detriment. Benjamin clearly wrote immediately to Lyndhurst, perhaps putting his side of the case, for Lady Blessington wrote to him on 26 December that she was glad to hear he had written 'and that you will never permit *anything* to make a division between him & you, as nothing could have a worse appearance before the public, or be more likely to give rise to reports injurious to you both.'[21] In the event Benjamin had nothing to fear; as he wrote to d'Orsay, he received a 'most affectionate letter' from Lyndhurst. 'All is right, nothing could be better as far as he is concerned, & I should think my letter of today to him will lay all doubts if any remain as to her [Henrietta's] influence.'[22] He need not have worried. Lyndhurst, who was engaged on a successful courtship in Paris of Miss Goldsmith, whom he later married, was no longer interested in Henrietta.

But Henrietta had not yet passed out of Benjamin's life for ever. Just over six months later, in July 1837, Sir Francis found his wife and Maclise in bed together, and instituted public proceedings against Maclise for 'criminal conversation'. In his fury against his wife, Sir Francis did not hesitate to rake up the past, necessarily involving Disraeli, who was accused, among other offences of squandering Sir Francis' money without his authorization. From Bradenham at the end of August, Benjamin appealed to d'Orsay to help clear his name of the scandalous gossip that was circulating as to his use of Sir Francis' money. He had, he said, laid open all the necessary documents in a statement to a lawyer, adding, 'I need not assure you that throughout this wretched business my only object has been to assist Lady S.'[23]

Benjamin, throughout his life, was admirably loyal to the people he really cared for and, despite the traumatic ending to their affair, he did not desert Henrietta in her time of trouble. All his romantic feelings and memories of past happiness were reawakened by the news of Henrietta's plight, and he seems to have written offering to visit her, for Henrietta replied, in her last letter to him:

'I am sorry you are ill, & regret that I should have awakened feelings of bygone years. As for me I am not as thought, & whatever may be my present sufferings I have brought them on myself & no one can judge more harshly of my conduct for the last 2 months than I ... I thank God no one can reproach me of anything but romantic folly ... I cannot think for I am distracted & feel as if there were no resting place on earth for me. If you do come we had better walk somewhere'.[24]

There is no record of their meeting, if it did take place. Henrietta deserved his pity, for she was now irretrievably socially ruined. Ironically, her fall – in July 1837 – occurred just as his career was rising, for in that month he was finally elected to parliament as MP for Maidstone. She died, three years after her husband, on 15 May 1846, the exact day on which Disraeli delivered his most brilliant philippic against Peel, the speech that made his career.

Benjamin was sustained at this painful period of his life by the friendship of d'Orsay, Lady Blessington and Bulwer. In 1836 Lady Blessington had moved from Seamore Place to Gore House in what was then 'out of town', now the site of the Albert Hall. This was a splendid country house, with grounds large enough to accommodate her two cherished cows and d'Orsay's aviary which in Bulwer's words, contained the 'best-dressed birds in all Ornithology ... The very pigeons have trousers down to their claws and the habit of looking over their left shoulder.'[25] Disraeli spent most of January and February staying with d'Orsay in his 'cottage orné' next to Gore House. He was working on *Venetia* surrounded, according to his letters to Sarah, by the most luxurious comforts despite the impenetrable London fog outside. 'No life can be more easy & agreeable than Mirabel's [d'Orsay's] & the adjoining establishment. Everything is perfectly appointed & conducted with such admirable taste & finish in all details. We dine with Miladi tête à trois. Déjeuner à la fourchette at $\frac{1}{2}$ past one; before that tea & admirable pipes & my own room which has every luxury of writing materials'.[26] d'Orsay's friendship, described by Benjamin as 'the magic sympathy of a joyous temperament', was the perfect antidote to his own melancholic nature. His philosophy, as described by Disraeli in *Henrietta Temple* where he appeared as Count Mirabel, consisted principally in never being bored or depressed. 'Life is too short for such bêtises', Mirabel declared, 'Existence is a pleasure, and the greatest. The world cannot rob us of that; and if it is better to live than to die, it is better to live in a good humour than a bad one.' His recipe for happiness was simple, and selfish: 'Feel slightly, think little, never plan, never brood. Everything depends upon the circulation; take care of it. Take the world as you find it; enjoy everything. *Vive la bagatelle!*'[27]

In February the trio were joined by Bulwer, 'the only literary man whom I do not abominate or despise', Benjamin told Lady Blessington. Bulwer, although he had never liked Henrietta, could sympathize with Benjamin, for he too was now living alone, having formally separated from Rosina the previous year. Both Bulwer and Lady Blessington provided Benjamin with background information for the characters of Byron and Shelley who were to be the heroes of *Venetia*, and in which, naturally, Lady Caroline Lamb appeared, and by mid-February the book was finished.

But Benjamin's troubles were by no means over; on 16 February he had a serious fainting fit outside the George Inn at Aylesbury where he was helping Chandos in the election of the Tory candidate, Harcourt. Sarah described it to d'Orsay as an 'epileptic attack', but there is no evidence that Disraeli suffered from epilepsy, and it was more likely to have been caused, as *The Times* reported, by over-exertion and fatigue. Benjamin, 'very shattered and disfigured by the violence of the fall,' was put to bed and bled with leeches, but the most serious consequence of the incident was to bring his creditors, convinced he was dying, once again upon his head.

From his correspondence with Pyne it appears that matters were even worse than they had been the previous December; early in March he was threatened with arrest by two separate creditors, a Mr Collins, and a Mr Davis, a wine merchant. Isaac D'Israeli, at a hint from Lady Blessington, came to the rescue and the danger was temporarily averted, but the atmosphere in the family was far from pleasant. '*Jaw succeeds jaw with never-ending row, Jaw* and *row* in school dialect being a paternal lecture', he told d'Orsay who had written congratulating him on having made a clean breast of it to his father.[28] 'Your lively and brilliant imagination makes you build castles in Spain', d'Orsay warned him. 'All that is very well and good for the *Wonderful Tales of Alroy* but for the material life in England the positive beats the imaginary.'[29] 'I quite agree with you about imagination', Benjamin replied, 'the possession of wh. I deem the greatest curse that can befall a human being. However,' he added hopefully, 'I am yet young enough to turn into a man of business & a screw.'

Benjamin of course had not told his father the whole truth, and late in March the threat from Davis became a real one, bringing not only a writ for Benjamin's arrest but Mr Davis Junior in person to Wycombe to 'nab' him. Benjamin was truly appalled at the effect his public arrest in his own local town might have upon his father and family. 'I really believe he wd. never forgive me' he wrote to Pyne, 'Indeed I do not think my family cd. hold up their heads under the infliction. They are so simple & unused so utterly to anything of the kind.'[30] Fortunately the sheriff's officer was a partisan of Benjamin's, and managed to fend off Davis by getting a surprised Jem, who was in Wycombe for market day, to sign a bond on his brother's behalf. Worse still, Benjamin had involved d'Orsay in his troubles; on 10 April d'Orsay wrote him an understandably hurt letter saying that there was a writ out against him for a bond of Benjamin's to a moneylender named Houlditch. Benjamin was guilty and appealing, 'Pray, my dear, dear d'Orsay, do not quarrel with me', he wrote, 'for if you do, I shall feel very much like a chilly person when a cloud steals over the sun.'[31] Peace-offerings in the form of dairy-fed pork and 'an experimental tongue' for Lady Blessington and special tobacco for d'Orsay were sent up from Bradenham, but Benjamin himself steered clear of Gore House. He had mistaken his man; d'Orsay's fastidious pride was offended by the presents. Benjamin did him an injustice, he said, in supposing that he could only approach his friend for forgiveness bearing gifts like some Oriental pasha. Benjamin excused himself for not calling by pleading a multiplicity of business to attend to and a 'v. gouty and grumpy' father to placate. Isaac was in town, too unwell to go out and very demanding, sitting at home 'reading the Pickwick papers & bullying his sons'.

No doubt the coolness with d'Orsay did not last long, and some financial miracle seems to have occurred, for there is no more mention of creditors. In May *Venetia* appeared, dedicated to Lyndhurst with a wistful reference to 'happier hours'. Based on the lives of Byron and Shelley, it was the least autobiographical of Disraeli's novels, and, from the dedication, it would appear that he had originally intended it as a serious work, an attempt to 'shadow forth ... two of the most renowned and refined spirits that have adorned our latter days'. In the actual composition, however, he seems to have treated it as a quick pot-boiler, and, although Byron, who appears as Herbert, and Shelley, as Cadurcis, indulge in several pseudo-intellectual conversations artificially inserted into the narrative, Disraeli seems quickly to have tired of them, polishing off the poetic pair in a sailing accident based on the drowning of Shelley off Lerici. There is, however, one clear bitter reference to Henrietta and her malignant attempts to set Lyndhurst against him:

As for women, as for the mistresses of our hearts, who has not learned that the links of passion are as fragile as they are glittering; and that the bosom on which we have reposed with idolatry all our secret sorrows and sanguine hopes, eventually becomes the very heart that exults in our misery and baffles our welfare?[32]

Despite the fact that it was better written than *Henrietta Temple*, *Venetia* failed to justify Colburn's confidence in promising £600 for the book. Benjamin seems not to have been much concerned, writing airily to Sara Austen in reply to her letter of congratulation that he had not had time to look the book over or even to read a single review, ' I hope she will make her way'. Both *Venetia* and Lyndhurst now belonged to the past; his political prospects appeared to be approaching a point where he would no longer need his former patron.

In May he was the leading spirit of the Carlton election committee canvassing for a Radical turned Tory, Sir Francis Burdett, as candidate for Westminster. According to his diary, Benjamin was personally responsible for the success of the candidate, having organized 'the youth of the Carlton, including all the nobility, fashion and influence of our party to canvas'. Disraeli admired Sir Francis whom he described as 'the greatest gentleman I ever knew', frequently dining at his house, where he met Sir Francis' daughter, Angela, later as Angela Burdett-Coutts to become one of the richest women in England and a great friend, even perhaps a matrimonial prospect of Disraeli's.

Within just over a month the political excitement generated by the Westminster election was superseded by the news that the King was dying, as Disraeli put it, 'like an old lion'. At half-past two on the morning of 20 June 1837 he died, to be succeeded by the eighteen-year-old Princess Victoria. For Disraeli and for Britain a new era was about to begin.

Benjamin accompanied Lyndhurst to Victoria's first meeting with her Privy Councillors that same morning. Waiting in the ante-room, he was not present when the diminutive young Queen, simply dressed in black, read out the Declaration in a clear, silvery voice, and blushingly received the homage of her Councillors, but Lyndhurst described the scene to him as they returned from Kensington Palace and he committed it to memory, to be reproduced eight years later in *Sybil*. His thoughts as he drove home on that splendid June morning were concerned with his own future rather than that of the young woman who was later to play such an important role in his life. The death of the sovereign was by law followed by an immediate general election, and Benjamin looked forward with confidence to success with the help of a new political patron – and patroness.

Disraeli's new political partner was Wyndham Lewis, MP for Maidstone, husband of the woman whom he had once called 'insufferable ... a rattle and a flirt', but who had since become a close friend. Tony Wyndham Lewis, generally known as 'Wyndham', was a Welsh squire aged fifty-nine, owner of a magnificent house at Grosvenor Gate, Park Lane and of holdings in ironworks at Dowlais which brought him an income of some £11,000 a year. Wyndham's money was to be of inestimable help to the penniless Benjamin in a constituency where the electors were notorious for being, in Greville's words, 'universally corrupt', and the cost of a vote could be anything from £5 to £50 each. Wyndham, it appears, was prepared to advance his young colleague money for his election expenses.

The two candidates set off for Maidstone on the evening of 30 June; Benjamin, fearful of being 'nabbed' by his creditors before he could escape from their clutches into the privileged recesses of Westminster, was delighted to find on his arrival that the Maidstone Sheriff's Officer was a staunch Conservative. He had hoped that the election would be uncontested (and therefore inexpensive) but at the last moment a Radical candidate, Colonel Perronet Thompson, came forward to oppose them and the campaign became fiercely vituperative. There were the usual Jewish gibes to contend with, cries of 'Shylock' and 'old clothes', but Benjamin was used to them and delivered, as he told Sarah, 'the best speech I ever made' on his by now established theme of support for the constitution, the Church and the agricultural interest, with a blistering attack on the unpopular New Poor Law introduced by the Whigs in 1834. Wyndham Lewis was impressed: 'Disraeli was on his legs more than an hour; he is a splendid orator and astonished the people,' he reported to Mary Anne. The result was a triumphant victory for the two Conservatives; when the poll closed on 27 July the figures were: Wyndham Lewis 706, Disraeli 616, Thompson 412; Benjamin was a Member of Parliament at last.

Mary Anne Wyndham Lewis, reporting the result to her brother, John Viney Evans, predicted a dazzling future for her husband's young colleague. 'Mark what I say', she wrote, 'Mark what I prophesy, Mr. Disraeli will in a very few years be one of the greatest men of his day ... They call him my Parliamentary protégé'.[33] Mary Anne's prophecy would be fulfilled, even beyond her wildest expectations, but not 'in a very few years'. At thirty-two Benjamin had achieved his first goal, becoming a Member of Parliament, but perhaps he subconsciously sensed that there was to be a long, bitter road ahead, as he was to note in his diary later that year: 'I am now as one leaving a secure haven for an unknown sea'. The waves of that sea were to be higher and the voyage longer than he could have predicted in 1837, the first year of the Victorian age, and the opening of Disraeli's new career.

7 Mary Anne

Queen Victoria opened her first Parliament on 20 November 1837. It was Disraeli's first view of the sovereign with whom he was later to enjoy a unique relationship, and his first experience of the assembled majesty of the Lords and Commons. It was, as he told Sarah, 'the most remarkable day of my life'.

The House of Commons in Disraeli's first Parliament sat, not in the splendid Gothic chamber designed by Sir Charles Barry which would not be completed for over a decade, but in the old House of Lords which had survived the fire that destroyed the Commons in October 1834. But if the surroundings were temporary, the men who sat there constituted an impressive array of talent and personality; many of them were to dominate English political life over the next four decades. Indeed the Commons of 1837 included (with the exception of the Prime Minister, Melbourne, and Aberdeen, who were in the Lords) every Premier until Salisbury's first administration in 1885.

On the Treasury bench sat two future Prime Ministers: the then foreign Secretary, Lord Palmerston, whose artificially pink cheeks and jaunty whiskers seemed to advertise the fact that, although over fifty, he intended to be there for a good few years yet, and the small alert figure of Lord John Russell, then Home Secretary and Leader of the House of Commons. On the Opposition front bench sat the Conservative leader, Sir Robert Peel, who at forty-nine was in his political prime, and whose supreme parliamentary skills seemed to ensure his dominance of the House for many years to come. Beside him was Lord Stanley, described by Melbourne as 'a young eagle' in appearance, the future fourteenth Earl of Derby and Prime Minister in the first administration in which Disraeli was to hold office. Also on the opposition benches sat the man who was to be Disraeli's great opponent, William Ewart Gladstone, whose aquiline features, dark hair and piercing eyes made him a striking figure. At twenty-seven he was almost exactly five years younger than Disraeli, but despite his bourgeois background (he was the son of a rich Liverpool merchant), Eton, Christ Church and his own towering abilities had ensured him a parliamentary seat for the past five years and junior office in Peel's brief administration of 1835.

Apart from the two front benches, the dominant personality was the man upon whom Disraeli had poured so much vituperation, Daniel O'Connell, leader of the Catholic Irish and bugbear of the English gentry. O'Connell, then aged fifty-two, the son of a small land-owning family from County Kerry, was typically Irish in appearance, with fresh complexion, blue eyes and curly brown hair, and gifted with a Celtic eloquence. As the man whose defiance of the British Government had led to Catholic Emancipation in 1829, he was still unquestioned leader of his 'tail' of Catholic Irish members and their Radical allies, upon whose support Melbourne's tottering Government depended for its existence in the face of the ever-growing strength of Peel's Conservative Party. This was the man whom Disraeli in 1835 had challenged to meet him at Philippi.

The House of Commons in 1837 was still a club for the English landed classes, 'the club of clubs' some people called it. Most of the members were either related or knew each other from childhood, school or university, and indeed, behaved as though the House were a school debating club, lounging on the benches eating fruit or cracking nuts provided by Bellamy, keeper of the members' dining-room, always known as 'Bellamy's'. The dining room, presided over by Bellamy and his butler, Nicholas, immortalized by Dickens in *Boz*, provided solid food – chops, steaks, veal and pork-pies, the last being so famous that Pitt's dying words were 'I think I could eat one of Bellamy's pork-pies.' Disraeli, with his strong sense of history, was enchanted to find the waiter serving him was the man who had carried the pork-pie to Putney only to find Pitt already dead. Bellamy, Nicholas, the fierce 'Jane' who kept the stillroom and the equally haughty waitresses who served the drinks, were staunch Tories, looking down with scorn upon the impoverished Irish and metropolitan members who, instead of indulging in Bellamy's famous port and claret, drank as much tea and free table beer as they could and went back to their lodgings for whisky.[1]

It was in this essentially club atmosphere that Benjamin rose to make his maiden speech late on the night of 7 December, making the fatal mistake of treating the House as a theatre. He had decided that he would make a 'smashing' speech on the model of his *Hartlebury* hero, disregarding the wise advice of 'old fools' and 'young fools' who counselled caution. It was typical of Disraeli to take the bold course, and to keep his promise of meeting O'Connell at Philippi by choosing to follow him as speaker on the highly provocative subject of the Irish election returns. His speech was over-elaborate and delivered in an affected style; by tradition the House was lenient towards new members making their maiden speeches, but Disraeli, as usual, went too far and paid the penalty. Not unnaturally he was heartily loathed by O'Connell and many of the Radicals, and as his attacks upon O'Connell and the Irish became more violent so did the noise-level from the Irish-Radical benches, 'hisses, groans, hoots, cat-calls, drumming with the feet, loud conversation, and imitation of animals', almost drowning what he was saying. Unfortunately, the parts of his speech which were audible above the uproar, and particularly the elaborate peroration which he had carefully prepared, brought down upon him the laughter of his political friends. He became inextricably entangled in classical allusions while his audience dissolved into mirth; Peel, according to one eyewitness, 'quite screamed with laughter'. But Disraeli with his customary courage fought back: 'I have begun several things many times, and I have often succeeded at the last – though many predicted that I must fail', he told them, ending with the famous ringing challenge, 'I sit down now, but the time must come when you will hear me.'

'A début should be dull,' was the comment of O'Connell's lieutenant, Richard Lalor Sheil, himself a noted orator, on Disraeli's tumultuous reception. With considerable magnanimity the Irishman, invited by Bulwer to dine the following evening to meet Disraeli, went out of his way to comfort the despondent younger man, giving him sound advice on how to succeed in the House of Commons. Sheil told him to 'get rid of your genius for a session', to speak often to show that he was not cowed, but shortly and quietly and try to be dull. By boring the House with fact and figures he would make them 'sigh for the wit and eloquence, which they all know are in you; they will encourage you to pour them forth, and then you will have the ear of the House and be a favourite'. Disraeli, in his letters home, put a brave face on the disaster, but his family read the newspaper reports and were not deceived. 'I am always fearful that theatrical graces will not do for the English Commons', Isaac wrote sadly. 'Whether any display of that nature you may have indulged in, I know not.'[2] Following Sheil's advice, Disraeli spoke again, tersely and well, on the Copyright Bill on 18 December, but for him only a spectacular parliamentary triumph would erase the humiliating memory of his disastrous début.

Genius alone, Disraeli must have concluded from this initial experience, was not enough; to acquire influence he needed the social standing that only money could buy. At thirty-four it was high time that he should fulfil his family's wishes and his own by marrying a rich wife. There were, however, no heiresses on Benjamin's horizon for whom he might successfully apply; as a Jew of doubtful reputation and no personal fortune he could by no stretch of the imagination be regarded as a good catch by the matrons who controlled the marriage market. He must follow his friend d'Orsay's advice: 'You will not make love! You will not intrigue! You have your seat: do not risk anything! If a widow, then marry!'[3]

On 14 March 1838 Benjamin's prospects changed dramatically when Tony Wyndham Lewis died suddenly of a heart attack while writing letters in his wife's dressing-room at Grosvenor Gate. Benjamin reported the event in an unsentimental note to Pyne: 'To complete my vexations, my colleague has fallen down in a fit and died.' In fact, far from 'increasing his vexations', Wyndham Lewis' death had provided him with the perfect solution to his problems by leaving a rich widow with whom Benjamin's relations were already intimate.

Mary Anne Wyndham Lewis was forty-six in the spring of 1838, twelve years older than Benjamin to whom she appears never to have admitted her real age, telling him that she was four years younger than she in fact was. Like Benjamin, she was vague and given to romanticizing her early life, telling people that her parents had made a runaway match, that her father was a naval captain, and that at one time she had worked as a milliner's apprentice. In fact no evidence to support the millinery story has ever come to light; her father John Evans was a naval lieutenant not a captain, the son of a well-to-do farmer, respectably married to her mother, Eleanor Viney, who was relatively well-connected in Wiltshire and Gloucestershire and brought him a reasonable dowry. Mary Anne herself was born in her paternal grandparents' farmhouse, Sowdons, in the village of Brampford Speke near Exeter on 11 November 1792, a year before her father died on active service towards the end of 1793. Her mother married again, an obscure personage named Thomas Yate and was widowed for a second time. Mary Anne had an adored, feckless elder brother, John Viney Evans, who took up an army career. In 1815 she made a brilliant match to Wyndham Lewis, who was twelve years older than she was, and when he died in 1838 after twenty-three years of marriage, she was left with a life interest in his entire real and personal estate, which with her Gloucestershire property amounted to some £5,000 a year, the splendid house at Grosvenor Gate and the magnificent collection of jewels given her by Wyndham.

On the face of it, it was not a romantic choice for Benjamin to make. Mary Anne was, as he described her, 'a pretty little woman', with a good complexion, a well-proportioned figure, sparkle and vivacity. But, despite her girlish manner, a Rothschild daughter found her 'very much older than the man to whom she was about to give the unquestioning devotion of her life; quite elderly, in fact for the post she was about to fill'. When told of their engagement the girls' reaction was: 'What that old woman and our brilliant friend? Impossible!'[4] She was ill-educated and not at all intellectual, as she herself cheerfully admitted; Disraeli was later to say of her, 'Mary Anne never can remember which came first, the Greeks or the Romans'. She was slightly vulgar with, like Benjamin, an ostentatious taste in clothes, and had more than a little of the social climber about her. As Disraeli had said, she was a 'rattle', who chattered on about anything that came into her head and, in later life when her eccentricities became more marked, she was an easy target for the great ladies of English society who regarded her as a figure of fun.

Yet Mary Anne had great human qualities; both her husbands, the one twelve years older than she was, the other twelve years younger, were devoted to her. For the people who knew her well, like the Rothschilds, 'one could smile at her absurdities and love her all the same'.[5] She had a natural gaiety and spontaneity which made the perfect foil for Disraeli's melancholic, reserved temperament. She was courageous to the point of gallantry; once, when accompanying Disraeli to Westminster, the footman accidentally crushed her hand in the carriage door and she forbore to make a sound of pain in case Benjamin might be upset before a major speech. On another occasion, when she bruised her face in a fall *en route* for Hatfield, she asked her hostess to put her at a distance from Benjamin at dinner so that, short-sighted as he was, he might not see what had happened to her. She was generous to her friends; she once gave the tragic poetess, Letitia Landon, a diamond ring, saying gently that she need not keep it, thus tactfully implying that as far as she was concerned, Miss Landon might sell it to raise money for herself. With all her superficial silliness, Mary Anne was a good *bourgeoise*, a careful, perhaps too careful housekeeper with excellent judgement. The hopelessly impractical Benjamin was to rely on her absolutely for all that aspect of his life, even trusting her judgement to the point of consulting her before taking critical political steps or on points in his novels.

Some of her faults were his also; both of them, with their passion for youth, refused to grow old gracefully, she wearing white lace and pink satin at the age of fifty-five, he dyeing his hair to conceal grey and wearing stays beneath his frock-coat. Nor can Disraeli be acquitted of social climbing; he may have felt naturally more at home in aristocratic circles and his success may have been due to his personal qualities rather than sycophancy, but his courtship of great ladies like Lady Londonderry and Lady Jersey can hardly be regarded in any other light. Since he had always preferred older women, Mary Anne's age mattered to him not at all (a Russian ambassador was to remark of him that 'all his women were grandmothers'), nor did her comparative lack of education. With the exception of Sara Austen, whom he had used and then discarded, he had never really liked intellectual women, nor, for that matter, with the exception of Bulwer, intellectual men. Perhaps because he found companionship and equality of mind in his sister Sarah, he needed other women for their softer qualities. He wanted maternal cherishing and demanded total devotion, both of which Mary Anne provided to a superlative degree. Possibly because she too was an outsider in the social circles in which they moved, she could understand him better than any of the fine ladies could.

Disraeli was always sensible of the debt he owed her for her financial and emotional support in his career. He never showed that her social absurdities embarrassed him, nor would he allow anyone to slight her; on one occasion when a Tory nobleman with whom they were staying upset Mary Anne by teasing her, he left the house the next day. The famous story that, when asked what his feeling for 'that old woman' could be, he replied 'gratitude', does not ring true; he was sincerely devoted to her. To the end of her life when she resembled a painted idol rather than a woman, he played out his fantasy role of lover with her, kissing her hand and kneeling to her even in front of his friends and writing her romantic little notes. The key to their successful relationship was one of Disraeli's favourite words, 'sympathy' – 'Marriage is the greatest earthly happiness, when founded on complete sympathy,' he was to say.[6]

At the time of Wyndham's death, however, the future partnership between Benjamin and Mary Anne was far from inevitable. Mary Anne, although temperamentally cold, was, as Benjamin had diagnosed on first meeting her, an incorrigible flirt. At forty-six, with her physical attractions lessening and her need for male reassurance consequently increasing, she was more of a coquette than ever. Benjamin had flirted with her when they first met, as a gallant note from him addressing her as '*la belle du monde*' and signed 'your true knight, Raymond de Toulouse', attests; at the time of the Maidstone election she was referring to him as her 'parliamentary protégé', and, after a visit which she paid to Bradenham in the New Year of 1838, their correspondence had taken on a note of intimate friendship. Benjamin, however, was far from being alone in the field; Mary Anne had other fortune-hunting suitors, among them George Beauclerk, of Ardglass, County Down, a year older than Benjamin and a notorious chaser of heiresses, and Augustus Fitzhardinge Berkeley, an old love of Mary Anne's from the days before her marriage to Wyndham. Mary Anne seems to have kept them all guessing until she finally made up her mind; indeed as late as November 1838 she and Berkeley were meeting alone, and she did not give him his marching orders until after Christmas, when he riposted with a wounded letter apostrophizing her with quotations from Hamlet: 'He who can best play the Fool to amuse the present hour becomes for that hour the God of your idolatry. Continue to play your fantastic tricks . . . "To a Nunnery, go" – you know the rest.'[7]

Berkeley, however, seems to have suspected from the first that Benjamin might be the favourite, writing jealously to Mary Anne only a month after Wyndham's death, 'the babbling world already gives you to the Tory novelist'. Disraeli proceeded cautiously at first; perhaps he could not quite bring himself openly to pursue her for her money, and his letters to the recently-widowed Mary Anne were correct, friendly, supportive, almost elder-brotherly in their advice. There were cautious hints of cosy intimacy; writing from Bradenham on 17 April 1838 to Mary Anne who was staying at Bristol, he contrasted the grey tedium of the country with the delights of Grosvenor Gate, 'a sea-coal fire . . . to say nothing of all the concomitant delights of cozy luncheons and confidential chat.'[8] Two days later, Isaac's illness gave rise to a stronger suggestion of a permanent relationship:

My father's health gives me the *greatest possible uneasiness* – Altho' an eldest son it seems to me that I could scarcely survive his loss. The first wish of my life has ever been that after all his kindness to me, and all the anxiety wh. I have cost him, he shd. live to see me settled & steady & successful to his heart's content.

Mary Anne's letters in return were wretched, incoherent, demanding and slightly hysterical. Everyone around her was odious, even her adored brother John seemed not to love her any more. There was a strong note of possessiveness and jealousy in her tone as she wrote, 'I do not know where to turn for love', then, changing from the pathetic to the waspish, 'I am glad you spend so much time with Lady Londonderry, because the more you go there or to any other married lady, the less likely you are to think of marrying yourself . . . I hate married men. I would much sooner you were dead. Selfish, yes I am.'[9] Disraeli defended himself sharply: 'I do not know what you mean by passing "so much" of my time with Lady Londonderry. I do not pass any more time with her than with Lady anybody else'.

Mary Anne was back in London in time for the Queen's Coronation on 28 June 1838, a brilliant week of which Disraeli sent back colourful accounts to Sarah. The town was teeming with distinguished foreigners who were being universally fleeced by the natives – from Lord and Lady Chesterfield who 'had the audacity to ask £5000 for the loan of their house' down to the most miserable hoteliers. Lord Francis Egerton told Disraeli that he had visited 'a brace of Italian princes' in one such establishment, 'never in the dirtiest *locanda* of the Levant ... had he visited a more filthy place; but they seemed to enjoy it, and are visible every night with their brilliant uniforms and sparkling stars, as if their carriage at break of dawn were not changed into a pumpkin.'[10] D'Orsay gave a party, which Disraeli attended, for such exotic figures as Count Esterhazy, the Duke of Ossuna and the Hungarian Count Zichy who dazzled everyone with his jewelled jackets, one of diamonds the other of turquoises. Later in the week, probably to Mary Anne's annoyance, Disraeli was one of 150 privileged guests at a magnificent banquet at Holdernesse House given by Lady Londonderry.

At first Disraeli, who had no court dress, had intended not to go to the Coronation, telling Sarah that 'to get up very early ... to sit dressed like a flunkey in the Abbey for seven or eight hours, and to listen to a sermon by the Bishop of London can be no great enjoyment.' In the end he could not resist the temptation, and with Ralph's help somehow acquired the appropriate suit by the morning of the ceremony, and was in his place in the abbey to see Victoria crowned. He particularly admired the grace and precision with which the young queen performed her part. Others unhappily lacked such grace: 'Melbourne looked very awkward and uncouth with his coronet cocked over his nose, his robes under his feet, and holding the great sword of state like a butcher': Lyndhurst, instead of backing away after performing his act of homage, turned his back on the Queen, and the same manoeuvre was altogether too much for the aged Lord Rolle, who lost his balance and fell down the steps of the throne while Lord Ward was seen after the ceremony with robes awry and coronet askew drinking champagne out of a pewter pot. Coronation commemorative medals were scattered among the congregation which led to an undignified scramble for them on the abbey floor. Disraeli, younger and more agile than many of the distinguished figures present, succeeded in securing one and presented it, not to the ever-faithful Sarah, but to Mary Anne.

By the end of July, Disraeli had convinced himself not only that he should marry Mary Anne, but that he was deeply in love with her. Despite the declaration he had made to Sarah five years before that he would never marry for love, his own romantic nature would not allow him a merely materialistic marriage. Just as he had closed his eyes to the cynical implications of the relationship between himself, Lyndhurst and Henrietta, so now, as he set out to marry for entirely practical reasons, he convinced himself that Mary Anne was indeed the love of his life. What had begun as a feigned romance ended in passionate feeling, which became stronger as the cool-headed Mary Anne refused to commit herself absolutely to him. When he went down to Maidstone to deal with constituency affairs, he wore a locket she had given him with the ribbon shortened 'so that it rests upon my heart', and experienced a lover's 'secret joy' whenever her name was mentioned. Separated from her during August, he wrote from Bradenham that he found the family conversation 'insipid after all that bright play of fancy & affection which welcomes me daily with such vivacious sweetness'.[11]

Mary Anne was with him at Bradenham in September, and at moments when they were apart, Benjamin wrote her romantic little notes whose 'mother and child' images were reminiscent of his correspondence with Henrietta: 'How is his darling? and when will she come & see her child? He is up in the little room'. When she left early in October, he was wretched; unable to resist self-dramatization he wrote to her of his love, 'Alas! Alas! mine I fear will be wild & turbulent. May it not terminate in a fatal cataract.' 'Remember!'[12] he added mysteriously, signing the letter with the rectangular symbol, apparently symbolizing a kiss, which they now both used when writing to each other.

Love had once more awakened in him the vein of poetry. As his passion for Henrietta had inspired *The Revolutionary Epick*, so his love for Mary Anne was the muse for a tragedy in verse, *The Tragedy of Count Alarcos*, based on a Spanish tale of star-crossed lovers. By mid-October he was working unceasingly and enthusiastically at the play, rising early, working from nine to two, with a brief interval for breakfast at eleven. By two o'clock he was exhausted, 'beyond two I cannot write, & pass the day as well as I can; reading a play, sauntering when it is genial as today . . . & ever thinking of my sweet love', he told Mary Anne. Thinking of his love and writing verses to her in the twilight could bring tears to his eyes; one sheet of paper was blotched as if by tears, 'I send you the mystical mark but my hand trembles as I sketch it, my lips grow pale . . .'[13]

Mary Anne's replies were fond, but in a far less passionate vein, and it seems she clearly had the upper hand in the relationship. He was her 'eagle' and her 'child', she was 'his little dove'. 'Think of me only as the *comfort & joy* of your life', she wrote in an apparent attempt to lower the despondent lover's temperature. Disraeli was wracked by jealousy, rightly suspecting that she continued to see other suitors while in London, among them Berkeley, a Mr Stapleton and Captain Neil. 'Fortunate Berkeley, thrice happy Stapleton', Disraeli wrote miserably, but was temporarily solaced by a visit from Mary Anne in mid-November.

On 20 November he was in London himself, this time to appear before the Court of Queen's Bench as a result of yet another of his fierce public quarrels. Following the election of Mr Fector as Wyndham Lewis's successor at Maidstone the previous summer, an election petition had been lodged against him alleging bribery. In the course of the hearing the plaintiff's lawyer, Austin, had implied that Disraeli too was guilty of bribery at his election, and, which was far more damaging, that he had failed to pay. Disraeli's reaction was characteristic; following the pattern established in the O'Connell row, he fired off a letter to *The Times* on 5 June 1838, with insulting references to the petition lawyer, Mr Austin, which were clearly intended to provoke him to a duel. Austin, however, preferred to use the weapons provided by the law, lodging a complaint of criminal information against him, and on 22 November Disraeli appeared in court to answer the charge. It was just the sort of public occasion that he relished, and his speech, though accepted as 'an ample apology' by the Court, was rather a defiant repetition of what he had said in his letter to *The Times*. It was widely reported in the press, and Disraeli returned to Wycombe, 'by a new engine called the North Star ... at the rate of 36 miles an hour', thoroughly pleased with himself and delighted at having created another public sensation.

For Disraeli in love, triumphant feelings were of short duration; after a visit by Mary Anne to Bradenham before Christmas he was again desolate, and not even a chance visit by d'Orsay who was staying with Lord and Lady Carrington at Wycombe Abbey succeeded in cheering him up. The good-natured d'Orsay enticed Disraeli over to the Abbey so that he could make friends with the local Tory magnate and his smart guests. This apparently was a success. 'They were all delighted with you at Wycombe', d'Orsay wrote. 'Wherefore you were right & have put again your destiny in my hands, I hope you will continue so'.[14] D'Orsay came over to Bradenham for the night on 27 December to give his friend the benefit of his worldly advice on how to proceed with his affair with Mary Anne. Somewhat ungratefully Disraeli wrote to Mary Anne that he was so lovesick that he was actually glad to see d'Orsay go, but d'Orsay seems to have been happy with the results of his visit. 'Follow my advice,' he told Disraeli firmly, 'and you will always find yourself alright.'[15]

Disraeli was indeed in need of advice; he was mishandling the affair, pressing Mary Anne too hard, inventing quarrels, being passionate, touchy, and, to use his own phrase, turning pleasure into a bore. He was uncertain as to the outcome of their relationship, suspecting that she might let him down in the end. Furious with hurt pride because he had not heard from her, he had written on 23 December:

> You told me once you required a year to study a character; our year has nearly elapsed, and your meditations may have dissatisfied you with mine. What my feelings may be if I find that I am doomed ever to waste my affections, and that a blight is ever to fall on a heart which nature intended to be the shrine of sensibility, it matters not. At present I will believe that my fate is indissolubly bound up with yours, until your voice or your conduct assures me that all this time I have laboured under a miserable delusion.[16]

He was, in fact, the most egotistical lover, totally wrapped up in his own sensations, and all this pressure, coupled with the suspicion that his basic motivation may still have been mercenary, may well have caused Mary Anne to hesitate before committing herself irrevocably to him.

She still led him on; the prospect of her visit, accompanied by her mother, to Bradenham in the New Year, evoked a letter from Disraeli breathing physical passion:

> I am mad with love. My passion is frenzy. The prospect of an immediate meeting

overwhelms and entrances me. I pass my nights & days in scenes of strange & fascinating rapture ... take care to have your hand *ungloved* when you arrive, so that you may stand by me & I may hold & clasp & feel your soft delicious hand as I help your mother out of the carriage; now mind this or I shall be insane with disappointment.[17]

This would seem to indicate that their physical relationship had not progressed very far as yet. It is possible that at this time Mary Anne may have succumbed to Disraeli's physical passion, for his letters to her immediately after her visit appear to have been written in a dreamily satisfied state, 'The happiest of New Years; and, indeed, I hope and believe it will be the happiest of our lives ...'[18] Later in January he was still happily in love, ' 'Tis twilight after a lovely day, but I have no dark thoughts. All my motions are soft and glowing as the sky. Sweetest and dearest of women, our united loves shall flow like two rivers; as gentle and as clear'.

Such serenity with Disraeli could not last long; they were soon quarrelling again. Mary Anne may have given herself to him, may have sworn that she loved him exclusively, but she had not, it seems, yet firmly committed herself to marrying him. Their quarrelling grew fiercer, with Disraeli accusing Mary Anne of trifling with his affections, while she counter-attacked accusing his friends (by whom she undoubtedly meant Bulwer who disliked her for taking Rosina's part in their separation) of setting him against her, and, more seriously of his wanting to marry her only for her money. She charged him too with having failed to repay the loan she made him to pay for the expenses of the Austin case. Even d'Orsay began to be worried by his friend's lack of progress towards matrimony, when, probably towards the end of January, he received a letter from Disraeli announcing that he had finished *Alarcos*. He replied, 'My good D'Is, When I read in the beginning of your letter, The Tragedy is finished, I thought that you were married ... How is it that you leave her in London by herself ... how are your affairs going in that quarter?'[19]

Disraeli did not intend to leave her any longer in London by herself. Early in February he came up to London with the dual purpose of arranging for the publication or performance of his tragedy and of settling the Mary Anne affair once and for all. There were several reasons why it had become imperative that she should be brought to a final decision; firstly, the anniversary of her widowhood fell on 7 March and the conventional year of mourning would soon elapse, and secondly, and, in Disraeli's eyes, still more importantly, Parliament was to meet on 5 February and the London season was therefore about to begin. It was vital for his self-respect that he should appear in the fierce light of that small world not as the rich widow's gigolo, but as her future husband. Mary Anne must not be allowed to prevaricate further.

Disraeli, therefore, sat down to write her a long letter which was intended as an ultimatum. It was frank, bitter and did not spare her feelings. He began:

As a woman of the world, which you are thoroughly, you ought not, you cannot be, unacquainted with the difference that subsists between our relative positions. The continuance of the present state of affairs cd. only render you disreputable; me it wd. render infamous. There is only one construction which Society, & justly, puts upon a connection between a woman who is supposed to be rich & a man whom she avowedly loves & does not marry. In England especially there is no stigma more damning ...

He openly admitted that when he made his first advances to her he was 'influenced by no romantic feelings'. His father wished him to marry, and indeed implied that it was a condition of his leaving him his property. As far as his own motives were concerned, 'I myself, about to commence a practical career, wished for the solace of a home, & shrunk from all the torturing passions of intrigue.' He had not been, he confessed, blind to the worldly advantages of marrying her, but, he said, with an oblique reference perhaps to the Meredith affair, had already proved 'that my heart was not to be purchased'. 'I found you in sorrow & that heart was touched,' he told her, going on to give a very clear exposition of what he was looking for in his wife: 'one whom I cd. look upon with pride as the partner of my life, who cd. sympathise with all my projects & feelings, console me in moments of depression, share my hour of triumph, & work with me for our honor & happiness.'

As far as her personal jointure was concerned, it had turned out to be far less than most people, including himself, had imagined, and had he been 'a mere adventurer' he would have abandoned her on discovering this; but, he said 'I felt that my heart was inextricably engaged to you, & but for that I wd. have terminated our acquaintance. From that moment I devoted to you all the passion of my being. Alas! It has been poured out upon the sand.' He had not, he said, discussed the question of repayment of the loan with her from a sense of delicacy, and a perception (which was to turn out to be absolutely correct) that money questions would lead to trouble between them. 'As time progressed I perceived in your character & in mine own certain qualities, wh: convinced me that if I wished to preserve that profound & unpolluted affection wh: subsisted between us *money* must never be introduced.' It was a perspicacious remark; Disraeli's cavalier attitude towards money, what d'Orsay called his 'scrapes' and 'plasterings-over', contrasting as it did with Mary Anne's bourgeois regard for it, was to cause endless rows in the future.

Then in two wounding concluding paragraphs, much of which his official biographer, Moneypenny, discreetly omitted to print, he accused her of being a heartless flirt:

Upon your general conduct to me I make no comment. It is now useless. I will not upbraid you, I will only blame myself. All warned me: public and private – all were eager to save me from the perdition into which I have fallen. Coxcomb to suppose that you wd. conduct yourself to me in a manner different to that in which you have behaved to fifty others!

... And for the gratification of your vanity, for the amusement of ten months, for the diversion of your seclusion, could you find the heart to do this? Was there no ignoble prey at hand that you must degrade a bird of heaven? Why not have let your Captain

Neil have been the minion of your gamesome hours witht. humiliating & debasing me. Nature never intended me for a toy or a dupe. But you have struck deep. You have done that which my enemies have yet failed to do: you have broken my spirit.

His peroration was unconsciously reminiscent of the words used in a similar situation by his unsuccessful rival, Augustus Fitzhardinge Berkeley only a few weeks before:

Farewell. I will not affect to wish you happiness for it is not in your nature to obtain it. For a few years you may flutter in some frivolous circle. But the time will come when you will sigh for any heart that could be fond and despair of one that can be faithful. Then will be the penal hour of retribution; then you will recall to your memory the passionate heart that you have forfeited, and the genius you have betrayed. D.[20]

This remarkable document goes a long way towards explaining why Disraeli was bound to succeed in life. Few men are blessed with the intense belief in themselves that enabled him to write this letter, with its references to 'a bird of heaven' and 'genius'. Indeed his pride was cut to the quick and his vision of himself immeasurably wounded that he should publicly be put in the same category as Mary Anne's other suitors, 'your Captain Neil', Beauclerk and Berkeley. He had an almost Latin regard for his honour, a point on which, largely through his own fault and his inability to see himself as others saw him, he was so frequently wounded. High-flown, proud and passionate, without a hint of pleading or self-abasement, such a document was calculated to bring any woman to heel, and it was none the less masterly for being sincerely felt.

The effect on Mary Anne was electric. She surrendered unconditionally: 'For God's sake come to me. I will answer all you wish. I never desired you to leave the house, implied or thought a word about money ... I have not been a widow a year. I often feel the impropriety of my present position ... I am devoted to you.'[21]

With one bold stroke, Disraeli had triumphed; the prize was his. Under the circumstances the failure of the tragedy which his love had inspired seemed of less importance. With a recommendation from d'Orsay, he sent the manuscript of *Alarcos* to W. C. Macready, the shrewd actor-manager and friend of Dickens and Bulwer, with a view to his producing the tragedy at Drury Lane. Macready did not think much of it; an entry in his diary for 26 March reads: 'Coming home, I finished the perusal of Disraeli's play, which will never come to any good', and on 31 March he wrote to Disraeli politely refusing it.[22] Rejected by Macready, Disraeli fell back again upon Colburn, and it was published in May with a dedication to the rich young aristocrat, Lord Francis Egerton. It was not well received at the time, although later produced on stage in 1868 and 1879 for reasons which were probably more closely connected with the celebrity of the author than the merit of the play.

Meanwhile at Grosvenor Gate the advent of Disraeli as Mary Anne's future husband was equally ill-received by her family. He was definitely sleeping with Mary Anne by this time, and not too careful about concealing the fact, sometimes leaving a watch or a ring behind which had to be hurriedly retrieved before the

. servants should discover it. Mary Anne's mother, Mrs Yate, disapproved of his presence on moral grounds. Her brother John, who was passionately fond of his sister, referring to her as 'Little Whizzy' or 'Angel Mother', and upon whom he depended financially, was frantically jealous. Disraeli seems to have been amused rather than otherwise by the family upheavals to which his presence gave rise, as he wrote to Sarah, from whom he concealed nothing:

> The broils betw[ee]n mother, brother & dau[ghte]r rage so terribly & continuously that I hardly know what it will end in, I cannot venture to ask Ralph [D'Israeli] in the present state of affairs; as I suppose my constant presence tho' not confessed, is at the bottom of it on their side; for they begin [the quarrels] – I of course never open my mouth, & am always scrupulously polite: but what avails the utmost frigidity of civilisation against a brother in hysterics, & a mother who menaces with a prayer-book!

That day they were to dine with the Scropes, a well-born family whose connection with Mary Anne made Disraeli very proud. Years later, recommending a member of the family for a dormant peerage, he was to write 'his blood is the best in England'. He wrote wickedly to Sarah of Scrope that 'the old sinner has only asked myself & *"not John"*. The mother is frenzied.'[23]

The detested John was not destined to trouble Disraeli much longer as a rival for Mary Anne's affections or for the contents of her purse. He died suddenly at Grosvenor Gate on 2 July 1858.

With his domestic future assured, Disraeli could concentrate upon politics, which in the early summer of 1839 offered interesting prospects for his party. The Conservatives were at their strongest in parliament and country since the Reform Bill; the Whigs were at their weakest, and the Melbourne government, dependent upon O'Connell and the Radicals for its parliamentary majority and upon the goodwill of the Leader of the Opposition to keep itself in office, was staggering towards inevitable demise. Although Peel, in view of the rising Chartist agitation in the country, forbore to bring the Government down, the Whigs precipitated their own fall by bringing in a bill to suspend the constitution of Jamaica in favour of direct rule by the governor and council. The severity of the measure offended the government's Radical supporters, but, despite Peel's efforts to delay the bill, the Cabinet resolved to press ahead with it; nine of their supporters voted against them in the division on 6 May, and their majority had sunk to only five. Melbourne, weary of two sessions of cliff-hanging manoeuvres, seized the opportunity to go and resigned office the following day, advising the Queen to send for Wellington. Wellington recommended Peel, who accepted office as Prime Minister for his second, and, as it turned out, his briefest, administration.

Prospects looked bright for Peel and the Conservatives when affairs took an unexpected and ludicrous turn in the 'Bedchamber Crisis.' The twenty-year-old Queen, suspicious of Peel and devoted to Melbourne, refused to allow the Whig Ladies of her Bedchamber, all Melbourne appointees, to be replaced by Conservatives. Melbourne, protective of the Queen and misled by her as to the extent of Peel's demands, supported her in her refusal. Peel insisted, the Queen remained adamant, and Peel gave up the seals of office only two days after he had received them.

Disraeli did not hesitate to throw himself into the fray. 'Peel is out and given up the Government in consequence of Whig intrigues about the household', he wrote in a hasty note to Mary Anne, adding that he had not the slightest doubt that the Queen would be obliged to surrender, and that he was writing something which Lyndhurst thought might be 'of service to them and myself'. The 'something' was an open letter to the Queen, published in *The Times* on 13 May and signed 'Laelius', in which Disraeli lectured his sovereign upon the constitution, and the dangers of employing ladies opposed to the policies of her Government:

> You are a Queen; but you are a human being and a woman ... You will find yourself with the rapidity of enchantment the centre and puppet of a Camarilla, and Victoria, in the eyes of those Englishmen who once yielded to her in their devotion, will be reduced to the level of Madrid and Lisbon.

It is doubtful whether the Queen or anyone else paid much attention to this effusion; while political London agonized over the royal storm in a tea-cup, the misery of the English working classes was put before Parliament in the form of the People's Charter. The Charter's six points, which included universal suffrage and the ballot, were considered by the political establishment to be revolutionary and utterly unthinkable, and, when the expected revolution of the Chartists did not accompany the presentation of the Charter, almost no one in Parliament was prepared to take it seriously.

Disraeli, however, sympathized with certain aspects of Chartism, if not its political demands. Much working-class anger was directed against the new Poor Law of 1834, which had substituted the administration of centrally appointed Boards of Guardians and Inspectors for the local autonomy of parish and magistrate, and the dreaded workhouse system stigmatized by Dickens in *Oliver Twist* for the old methods of outdoor relief that had been in operation since the days of Elizabeth. Disraeli was opposed to centralization throughout his life, regarding it as destructive of the old traditions of England, and as a magistrate he was well acquainted with the facts of the situation. He determined to make a great speech in the debate on the Poor Law and Chartism which, he told Mary Anne, would be 'the last great blaze of the season'.

In the event, however, he was wrong. Although the speech he delivered in the debate on 12 July was, as he told Sarah 'capital', and reported in the *Morning Herald* which devoted a leader to it as 'a speech of very considerable talent', it was made to a thin House. The Tories, Disraeli said, stayed away 'thinking Chartism would only be a squabble between Whigs and Radicals', while Peel had only come down to the House to speak on the Penny Postage, a subject which seemed to him to be of more moment than Chartism. Disraeli appears to have been among the few politicians who perceived that, although Chartism as a movement was destined to be ephemeral, the issues it raised were not. Disraeli's approach was not the outraged humanitarianism of Dickens; this was his first encounter with the problem of 'the condition of England', the great social and political question of the future, later defined by Disraeli as 'two nations', the rich and the poor.

The parliamentary session closed in August, and at 10.30 on the morning of the twenty-seventh Disraeli and Mary Anne were married at the fashionable church of St George's, Hanover Square. The ceremony was simple and private. Mary Anne who 'blazed in a travelling costume of exotic brilliancy', Disraeli told his mother, was given away by her distinguished relative, William Scrope. Lyndhurst, as best man, played his part with dignity and grace, despite a mishap *en route* to the church with Disraeli when one of the carriage horses had been 'seized with the staggers'. Mary Anne was graceful and composed, but Disraeli was so nervous that he was about to put the wedding ring on the wrong finger until corrected by his bride. The couple left the church in their new carriage, a wedding present to the bride from Isaac, attended by their own servants in the personal livery of silver, brown and gold that Disraeli and Mary Anne had chosen, to spend the first days of their honeymoon at Tunbridge Wells.

At Bradenham the wedding was celebrated with a grand dinner and dance for the household, 'dancing and feasting alternately for 12 hours' Sarah wrote to her brother on 29 August. There seems to be no explanation as to why none of Disraeli's family attended the wedding; it was certainly not because they disapproved. Perhaps Sarah may have felt secretly jealous, knowing that there would now always be another woman in her brother's life who must inevitably usurp the position that had been hers. Isaac, however, was thoroughly delighted to see his son settled at last, and quite captivated by his daughter-in-law's girlish manners and playful ways. Addressing him as her 'only dear Papa' she wrote to him describing the first days of their honeymoon in a style that can only be called arch:

> I wish you could see your happy children – we simplify life – first to talk – to eat – to drink – to sleep – love and be loved ... Dizzy is so lost in astonishment at finding himself a husband that the first time he had to introduce me to some of his friends he called me Mrs. Wyndham Lewis! – and at the ceremony he was going to put the ring on the wrong finger! Is not his conduct most atrocious, considering we all know him to be so great a character, that naughty man![24]

The 'happy children' left Tunbridge Wells after a few days of incessant rain and travelled to the Continent, visiting Baden-Baden, which Mary Anne thought 'not much better than Cheltenham – public dinners, balls, promenades, pumps, music and gambling', and driving on through the Black Forest to Munich. The Bavarian capital suited Disraeli's rococo tastes: 'Since Pericles no one has done so much for the arts as the King of Bavaria', he wrote to Sarah, describing Ludwig as 'a poet, which accounts for Munich, for a poet on a throne can realise his dreams.' They arrived in Paris in the first week of November, staying at the Hotel de l'Europe in the Rue de Rivoli to be welcomed by their friend Henry Bulwer, Lytton's brother, who was Minister at the British Embassy. Mary Anne, of course, went shopping and looked, according to her fond husband's description, like 'Madame de Pompadour in her new costumes'.

They returned to Grosvenor Gate at the end of November to find 'perpetual fog' and bad news about Isaac's eyesight. Some doctors diagnosed the trouble as cataracts, others attributed it to congestion of the blood vessels of the head due to too much indulgence in food and drink; Isaac, Benjamin told Sarah, 'appears to be known at the A[thenaeum] as the gentleman who drinks so much soda water and sherry'. Whichever diagnosis was right, there seems to have been no cure; Isaac gradually lost his sight, although he continued to work on his books with the devoted Sarah as his amanuensis.

Despite such worries, Disraeli was content, having at last found a permanent refuge from the hostile world. As he had written to Mary Anne some six weeks before their marriage: 'whatever occurs afterwards will I am sure never shake my soul, as I shall always have the refuge of your sweet heart in sorrow & disappointment & yr. quick & accurate sense to guide me in prosperity & triumph.'[25]

8   A Rising Talent

Disraeli had been right to take account of the Chartists. For although they were to be ephemeral as a political force, it was their underlying challenge – that Parliament should respond to the 'condition of England' – that was to dominate events in the 1840s.

Disraeli shared the Chartists' antagonism towards what he called 'the monarchy of the middle class' created by the Reform Bill, hostile alike to the poor and to the landed interest, and to the New Poor Law of 1834, which he saw as a further assault on traditional England.

In his defence of the Chartists he must have appeared distinctly Radical to the majority of the landed classes with whom he was to identify himself, who regarded the Chartists as dangerous revolutionaries. He was one of only five MPs to protest against the harsh treatment of the Chartist leaders in June 1840:

> He was not ashamed to say, that he wished more sympathy had been shown on both sides towards the Chartists . . . the time would come when Chartists would discover that in a country so aristocratic as England, even treason to be successful must be patrician. When Wat Tyler failed, Henry Bolingbroke changed a dynasty, and although Jack Straw was hanged, a Lord John Straw might become a Secretary of State.

Members laughed at this jibe against the Radical-Whig, Lord John Russell, but nonetheless the speech must to them have had an egalitarian ring.

Nor was he consistent on all aspects of 'individualism'; while believing, as he told Parliament, that 'the individual should be strong and the government weak', on the great issue of free trade versus protection he was at one with his party, believing that state intervention should continue to support of the landed interest through the Corn Laws. He was opposed to the principles of political economy – free trade and the unrestricted operation of market forces – fathered by Adam Smith and promoted in evangelical fashion by Richard Cobden and the Anti-Corn Law League. Disraeli not only had a hatred of the doctrinaire in politics, but he was motivated also by an instinctive hostility to what he saw as the selfish and materialistic policies of the middle class.

It was easy perhaps for Disraeli, totally unconnected as he was with industry and capital, to pledge himself to the defence of the traditional landed interest, and indeed the poor, against the encroachments of the middle class. Taking sides on such questions was, however, inherently more difficult for Peel, as the son of a cotton-mill owner, who had become himself a land-owner and was now head of an aristocratic party whose power was based upon the land. Tall, handsome and thoroughly 'gentlemanly' in appearance, Peel still spoke with a touch of a Lancashire accent, and, although supremely at his ease in Parliament, was frigid and shy in general society. He was widely admired and respected for his great abilities, but, since his abrupt volte-face over Catholic Emancipation in 1829, not regarded as totally trustworthy. Instinctively he was at odds with the traditional attitudes of the majority of his party, since he believed in progressive centralization and was increasingly attracted by the principles of political economy. Significantly, in the opening parliamentary session of 1841, Peel and Disraeli found themselves on different sides, with Peel supporting the government against an amendment to the Poor Law proposed by Disraeli and seconded by the Radical, Wakley.

In the spring of 1841 Peel was the unquestioned leader of a strong Conservative Party, united in what it stood for – for Protection and against Free Trade, and for the maintenance of the Corn Laws. In contrast, the Whig majority was made up of a hotch-potch of conflicting sections – free-trading reformist Whigs like Lord John Russell, moderate Whigs like Melbourne who secretly sympathized with the Tory position on the Corn Laws, the Radicals and the Irish. Moderate opinion in the country disliked the Government's dependence upon the Radicals and the Irish, and blamed it for the Chartist disorders of the previous year. As the Conservative election manager Bonham reported to Peel at the end of 1840, the strength of the Conservative party in the country was such that from their point of view an election could not come too soon. The government soon proved him right by losing four successive by-elections in 1841; on 18 May they were defeated in the Commons over a free-trade measure for reducing the duties on foreign sugar, and on 5 June they lost by one vote on a motion of no-confidence moved by Peel. Parliament was dissolved; a general election announced, with the Whigs going to the country with the slogan of 'cheap bread' – that is, the dismantling of the Corn Laws.

By the time Parliament rose to face the general election, Disraeli, who had long since decided to part company with his expensively-corrupt constituents at Maidstone, had successfully negotiated for the Conservative nomination to another borough, Shrewsbury, with the help of the local magnate, Lord Forester of Willey Park. Disraeli and Mary Ann hurried to Shrewsbury in the second week of June to begin canvassing from eight in the morning until sunset. Mary Anne was of particular help in persuading the tradesmen, as a note from Disraeli's election committee shows: 'John Legh thinks Mrs. Disraeli had better call upon Mr. Gough Butcher of Pride Hill tomorrow morning ... The son Mr. John Gough Junr. who lives with his father *rules all* & he is a little queer at present, being in a bad neighbourhood ... The son is famous for Shrewsbury Brawn when in season.'

Mary Anne's canvass seems to have met with only partial success, for the paper is annotated 'Gough got out the way the son won't promise as yet.'[1]

It was a struggle in which no holds were barred. Printed posters appeared on the walls of Shrewsbury giving a list of judgements for debt against Disraeli in the courts of Queen's Bench, Common Pleas and Exchequer to the sum of £22,036. 2s. 11d, concluding, 'In the list are included the names of unhappy Tailors, Hosiers, Upholsterers, Jew Money Lenders (for this Child of Israel was not satisfied with merely spoiling the Egyptians) Spunging Housekeepers, &, in short, persons of every denomination who were foolish enough to trust him', while the anonymous author charged him with seeking a place in Parliament in order to avoid the debtors' prison.[2] Immediately, on 24 June, Disraeli posted off an urgent letter to Pyne, worrying that judgements in at least three of the cases might not have been satisfied and entered up. The next day, however, he put a brave face on it and issued a broadsheet condemning the charges as 'UTTERLY FALSE', and claiming somewhat ingenuously that some recent judgements against him had been incurred because of standing security for 'a noble friend' [presumably d'Orsay].[3] 'An Elector' replied impertinently that Disraeli, far from being a man of 'Ample Independence' as his broadsheet claimed, in fact owed a further £6,842.[4]

At Shrewsbury, as at Taunton, anti-Semitism came into play. Disraeli's speech on nomination day was marred by incessant shouts of 'Jew' and 'Judas', portions of a pig being held up on a stick and advanced as close as possible to his nose, with cries of 'Bring a bit of pork for the Jew', all of which, it is reported, he endured with perfect good temper. His election address enunciated three points; the maintenance of the constitution, the interests of the poor, and the liberties of the people, while he derided the Whig election cry of 'cheap bread', and castigated the late government for clinging to office against the wishes of the people.

Defiantly, Disraeli had the crest that he had adopted, the Castle of Castile, emblazoned on his banners, with the motto *Forti nihil difficile* – 'Nothing is difficult to the brave', which hostile papers translated as 'The impudence of some men sticks at nothing'. On polling day, 29 June, his supporters were on the streets by 6.30 am; their procession of respectable electors and tradesmen of the town, with a band and a plethora of blue banners, contrasting favourably in the opinion of the *Shropshire Conservative* with that of the Radicals, composed of 'poor Factory Children' and hired miners, who were stigmatized as 'ragged boys and drunken men', who could only afford one green and white banner and two symbolic loaves of 'cheap bread', the largest of which was so badly made that it fell to pieces.

At the declaration the following day, the two Conservative candidates topped the poll: Tomline with 793 votes and Disraeli with 787, trailed by Sir Love Parry and Mr Temple with 604 and 579 votes respectively. The successful candidates then mounted a carriage drawn by six greys and decorated with blue and white rosettes, and, accompanied by two bands, banners and flags, proceeded through the town, followed by eight hundred gentlemen, to the Lion Inn, where a

'Gorgeous Triumphal Arch' embellished the street, and Mary Anne and other Conservative ladies appeared at the windows to throw flowers into the carriage. At the dinner that followed, the *Shropshire Conservative* reported, Disraeli was received 'with such deafening cheers, it was full five minutes before the applause ceased sufficiently for him to speak'. He concentrated on the role of the Conservatives as defenders of the constitution, with a great eulogy of Peel as the founder of the party, attacked the Poor Law and the centralization of administration, and returned to his theme of Tory self-help, '. . . the national character could not have been formed if people had done nothing for themselves & always appealed to authority for advice.' His triumphant speech was followed by resounding cheers for 'the Duke [Wellington] and Mrs Disraeli'. Mary Anne herself, whose energetic canvassing and skilfully applied flattery had contributed to her husband's success, dashed off a note in her curious cuneiform handwriting to the one amongst Disraeli's close friends whom she really liked: 'VICTORY dear Count Dorsay a perfect triumph, we are all so happy here'.[5]

As if to underline the Conservative victory, in the midst of the celebrations at the Lion, the 'Wonder Coach' arrived with the news that Lord John Russell 'had been rejected by the citizens of London'. Throughout England the Conservatives demonstrated their strength in the counties and the smaller boroughs such as Shrewsbury, where the major issue had been, as Disraeli had divined, the defence of the constitution and the Church against the Whigs' dangerous Irish Radical allies. As the pro-Conservative *Times* trumpeted in a leader on 27 July: 'No other nation has ever witnessed the spectacle, now exhibited by Great Britain to the admiration of the world, of a triumphant reaction of sound public opinion against the progress of a partially-successful democratic movement'. The Conservative Whip, Sir Thomas Fremantle, counted the Conservatives as having 367 seats, the Opposition 289, giving them a majority of 78. The most important result of the 1841 election from the political viewpoint was that, for the first time in recent English history, the government would enjoy the support of a single-party majority.

For Sir Robert Peel, the acknowledged leader, it was the high point of a successful career. When, on 3 September, having formally dislodged the Whigs from power (the Melbourne government having resigned on 30 August), he kissed the hand of a stiff young queen still suffering from the loss of her adored Melbourne, he deservedly enjoyed a personal supremacy and parliamentary power such as no politician had held since the days of Pitt. For Disraeli, the Shrewsbury triumph and the enjoyable sensation of belonging to a party firmly in power were followed by a period of nervous anxiety and bitter disappointment. At thirty-six, with unbounded confidence in himself, looking forward to the dawn of a new career, he expected office and did not get it.

In the circumstances, it is hard to see why he entertained such expectations, and one can only surmise that his normally acute judgement deserted him. It seems always to have been hard for him to realize the effect some of his actions had upon others. He refused to acknowledge the fact that in so far as Peel considered him at all, he rather disliked him, and that he himself had sometimes evinced a half-unconscious animus against Peel. Although he had voted dutifully with his leader on most occasions since 1837, he had differed from him on how much support should be given to the Whigs in their more moderate and liberal measures such as the recent Poor Law Amendment. Moreover, such political connections as he had were with the ultra-Tory section of the party which Peel distrusted and despised, with Lyndhurst and the Duke of Buckingham and Chandos, 'the Farmer's Friend', whom Peel had included in his Cabinet simply in order to control the right wing. The men whom Peel trusted and consulted – Bonham, Graham, Goulburn and Stanley – scarcely knew him, while Stanley, according to Monckton Milnes, positively disliked him, blaming him unjustly for the Henry Stanley incident eleven years earlier. As recently as August Disraeli had been unwisely involved in an attempt by the more rabid spirits of the Carlton to oust the Liberal Speaker of the House, Shaw Lefevre, whom Peel and the leading men of the party had decided should not be opposed. Stanley, Arbuthnot and Bonham all believed Disraeli to be the author of an impertinent letter addressed to Peel on the subject in *The Times*, signed with the pseudonym Psittacus, and while Disraeli specifically denied this in a letter to Peel of 17 August, his previous record in such affairs did not add conviction to his disclaimer. Years later when the question of his having expected and sought office in 1841 came up again, he was to tell the House of Commons that he was encouraged by a member of Peel's Cabinet, but Disraeli was never a stickler for accuracy, and there is no mention whatever of such a justification in his letters reporting his disappointment to his family at this time. It is possible that Lyndhurst may unwittingly have given him some reason to hope for preferment, but if he did so, it is strange that Disraeli should not have mentioned it to Sarah.

Whether justified or not, Disraeli, mortified and feeling himself to have been publicly humiliated, sat down on 5 September to write a letter to Peel that was neither wise nor tasteful. 'I am not going to trouble you with claims similar to those with which you must be wearied', he wrote, going on to do just that, following up with a most personal and almost pathetic appeal:

> I have had to struggle against a storm of political hate and malice which few men ever experienced, from the moment, at the instigation of a member of your Cabinet, I enrolled myself under your banner, and I have only been sustained under these trials by the conviction that the day would come when the foremost man of this country would publicly testify that he had some respect for my ability and my character.[6]

The previous night Mary Anne had written her own anguished appeal on her husband's behalf to the Prime Minister. Disraeli's biographer Moneypenny says that she did so without her husband's knowledge, but the similarity of both their references to four expensive election contests indicates that they must have previously discussed it. Mary Anne went even further than Disraeli in heaping responsibility for her husband's career upon the unfortunate Peel: 'He has gone further than most to make your opponents his personal enemies ... He has stood four most expensive elections since 1834 ... Literature he has abandoned for politics. Do not destroy all his hopes, and make him feel his life has been a mistake'. Her final paragraph might have served as a model for one of the political place-seekers whom Disraeli was so wittily to caricature in his political novels: 'My I venture to name my own humble but enthusiastic exertions in times gone by for the party, or rather for your own splendid self? They will tell you at Maidstone that more than £40,000 was spent through my influence only.'[7]

One may imagine the expression of weary distaste with which Peel, whose dislike of the exercise of patronage was notorious, received these effusions. Besieged as he was by applications for preferment, he clearly had not time to read them properly, and indeed picked angrily upon a phrase in Disraeli's letter, misinterpreting it. 'I must in the first place observe that no member of the Cabinet which I have formed ever received from me the slightest authority to make to you the communication to which you refer', he began haughtily, ending reasonably that he hoped that when applicants for office considered the number of claims upon him arising not only from his tenure of office in 1835, but also from 'new party combinations' by which he meant Stanley and the converted Whigs, they might understand 'how perfectly insufficient are the means at my disposal to meet the wishes that are conveyed to me by men whose co-operation I should be proud to have, and whose qualification and pretensions for office I do not contest.'[8]

Disraeli hastened to assure Peel that he had 'entirely misconceived my meaning is supposing that I intended even to intimate that a promise of official promotion had ever been made to me, at any time, by any member of your Cabinet.'[9] He conveniently neglected to make a copy of these letters which he no doubt preferred to forget; he may have made drafts but if he did there is no trace of them, and five years later, at a time of great parliamentary stress, he was to refer again to 'the instigation of a member of your Cabinet'. Peel, on the other hand, kept the letters and, with his prodigious memory for detail, did not forget them.

'All is over', Disraeli wrote to Sarah, conveying the news of the débâcle to his expectant family at Bradenham, '& the crash would be overwhelming were it not for the heroic virtues of Mary Anne whose ineffable sweetness & unwearied devotion never for a moment slacken.'[10] Wounded in his private hopes and, as he saw it, his public image, Disraeli retired in mid-September with Mary Anne to Caen in Normandy to recoup his forces for the new parliamentary session.

As the new Parliament opened in 1842, Disraeli felt himself at sea, 'utterly isolated' as he told Mary Anne, 'a solitary animal', in search of allies and a policy to put forward.[11] The great issue before Peel's first Parliament concerned what remedies should be adopted to alleviate the widespread distress of the working population of England, distress which during the winter of 1841–2 had reached such proportions as to force Parliament to open its eyes to the problem. Four bad harvests and a trade depression had exacerbated the misery of a population that had doubled over the last fifty years and was increasing at the rate of a fifth each decade. By March 1842, out of a population of some 16,000,000, over 1,000,000 were receiving poor relief, while in places like Paisley, a third of the population were on relief. In Leeds it was calculated that 20,000 people out of a population of about 150,000 were living on an average income of $11\frac{1}{4}$ pence a week. In the words of Thomas Hood's 'Song of the Shirt', bread was dear and flesh and blood were cheap.

Opinions differed both as to the causes of the distress and to the remedies for it. Richard Cobden, leader of the Anti-Corn Law League, who had entered Parliament as member for Stockport in August 1841, blamed the action of the Corn Laws, which, by imposing protective duties on the import of foreign corn, ensured that prices remained high. He argued that repeal would not only result in cheap bread for the poor, but also in a revival of trade by opening wider markets for British goods in exchange for the much increased volume of foreign corn that would be imported. This in turn would benefit the British working class by creating a higher, steadier demand for labour and consequently increased and more regular wages. The Chartists advocated the Charter, and blamed unrestrained capitalism for the distress of the working classes, fearing that the extension of commerce would only serve to 'make the rich richer and the poor poorer', and that a reduction in the price of food would only be used as an excuse by factory owners to reduce their workers' wages. This view was shared by many on the Tory side, who also blamed the operation of the Poor Law and the introduction of machinery for the miserable condition of the working classes. The humanitarian solution proposed by Lord Ashley, later Earl of Shaftesbury, and the working-class members of the Short Time Committee, was to limit the hours of labour and to prevent the exploitation of women and children in mines and factories, measures opposed by the political economists and manufacturers, as being fetters upon commerce and the operation of a free market. In the midst of all these conflicting opinions, Peel chose a middle course, adjusting the sliding scale upon which the Corn Laws operated, reducing a number of tariffs to stimulate trade, and balancing the budget by the re-introduction of income tax.

In view of the critical situation in the country Disraeli's failure to take sides in the opening stage of the question seems curious, and, given his previously declared sympathy with the Chartists and his open attacks upon the Poor Law, the only initiative he did take – a proposal for the reform of English consular establishments – notably irrelevant to the main issues. While Parliament discussed with vigour and passion Charles Villiers' annual motion for the repeal of the Corn Laws, Disraeli took no part, watching as he put it 'like a cat after a mouse' for the chance to put himself down to introduce his motion, then staying away from the House preparing his speech at Grosvenor Gate on a rigorous diet of roast mutton, wine or port and water, and doses of ammonia.

At five o'clock on the afternoon of 8 March, Disraeli rose from his place behind Peel to deliver his carefully prepared consular speech. His nervousness, and, a symptom of his isolation, his dependence on Mary Anne, was illustrated by the hasty note he scribbled to her before he rose '... in a few minutes the eventful affair will commence. The remembrance of your love & the joy of being the companion of your life supports me under what after all is a somewhat queer affair – opening at 5 o'clock a question in the H of Commons – all cold & frigid & faint ... But I love you. D'. It was indeed a queer affair; Disraeli's argument that England's representation abroad was ineffective, which was always to be a favourite subject with him, and that consular and diplomatic services should be amalgamated, was received with cold discouragement by Peel, who remarked that he saw no reason for such a change and that he hoped Disraeli would not feel it necessary to press for a division on the subject, but that if he did, he, Peel, would feel obliged to cast his vote against him.

This douche of cold water was the reverse of what Disraeli had hoped to receive from Peel and his mortification was only relieved by the chance of a thrust at Palmerston, whom he had attacked in his speech for corruptly appointing incompetent political adherents to consular posts while Foreign Secretary in the late Government. Palmerston, insouciant as always, was incautious enough to make a hit below the belt, referring to Disraeli's disappointed desire for office: 'The hon. Gentleman had indeed affirmed the general principle, that political adherents ought to be rewarded by appointment, and he regretted to observe an exception to that rule in the person of the hon. Gentleman himself', adding sarcastically that he hoped by the end of the Session to see Disraeli rewarded. Experienced debater as he was, Palmerston had yet to discover the duelling qualities of the young MP for Shrewsbury; rising impromptu, Disraeli thanked 'the noble Viscount' for his good wishes, which, as Palmerston was such an expert in the art of getting and retaining office, must be considered auspicious. 'The noble Viscount was a consummate master of the subject; & if the noble Viscount would only impart him the secret by which he had himself contrived to retain office during several successive administrations, the present debate would certainly not be without result.' For Palmerston, the Tory turned Whig, the thrust, delivered in a sarcastic drawl, was unanswerable, and for the House, unaccustomed to see Palmerston caught out in debate, the effect was electrifying. At supper at Crockford's afterwards, even the dandy 'swells' congratulated him on having, in Eliot's words, been one of the few men to 'have broken lances with Palmerston and ridden away in triumph'. Few of them perhaps realized that they had witnessed the début of one of the greatest masters of the art of cut and thrust that Parliament would ever know.

Disraeli's duel with Palmerston brought him the congratulations not only of the Crockford 'ton', but the admiration of a small band of aristocratic young Conservative MPs who had just entered Parliament, the men for whom he coined a phrase 'Young England'. Overestimating, perhaps, the effect of his speech, he seems to have been encouraged by their reaction to feel that his isolation was about to come to an end. '... All young England, the new members etc., were deeply impressed,' he told Mary Anne, writing, somewhat prematurely on 11

March, 'I already find myself leader of a party'. At dinner with an old friend, Henry Baillie, he was delighted to meet the brilliant dilettante George Sydney Smythe, son of an old acquaintance, Lord Strangford, and, although fifteen years younger than Disraeli, destined to become one of his greatest friends and the model for the 'Young England' hero in *Coningsby*. Smythe pleased him unutterably by remarking on his new manner of speaking in the House, saying that the conversational style was the most difficult to sustain and admiring Disraeli, who had attempted it for the first time, for being already 'so great a master' of it.[12]

But although the success of his speech of 8 March may have laid the foundations for the formation of Young England later that year, Disraeli can hardly have failed to take note of, and to resent, the coldness of Peel's reaction. This seems to have convinced him of the wisdom of playing safe, and throughout the session he voted dutifully with his leader, making no attempt to take part in discussions of the social and economic questions of the day. On 2 May, a friend of d'Orsay's and Disraeli's, Tom Duncombe, Radical MP for Finsbury, presented the National Petition of the Chartist Convention, moving that the petitioners be heard at the bar of the House; Peel rejected the motion, and Disraeli said nothing. He did not speak on Ashley's motion on the report of the commission on the employment of women and children in mines and collieries which revealed the dreadful conditions under which the weak and exploited suffered; nor did he have anything to say when the powers of the Poor Law Commissioners that he had so forthrightly opposed were renewed for five years. The one occasion on which he did speak in May was indicative of the line he had decided to take when (ironically enough in view of his future action against Peel) he defended his leader from opposition charges of inconsistency in his attitude to Free Trade and tariff reductions.

Peel indeed seems to have been the key to Disraeli's political quiescence that session, which is otherwise inexplicable. Disraeli had already perceived clearly enough that, real though the misery of the working classes undoubtedly was, the 'condition of England question' was the battleground over which an ideological power struggle was being fought, and the welfare of the workers was merely incidental. That battle was the confrontation between the industrial North and the agricultural South, the thrusting assault of the newly-rich capitalist middle class upon the landed aristocratic citadel of political power, which had begun with the Reform Bill and which would be waged over the following decades of the nineteenth century. Disraeli had already taken up his stand, and he would never change, but it remained to be seen what line Peel would take. In 1841 Disraeli still hoped for office, which meant that he must win the approval of Peel; there was no alternative for as yet he had no power base from which to challenge him.

Indeed if Disraeli's political situation during the first part of 1842 was somewhat ambiguous as he sought for a policy and friends in parliament, his financial position was rocky in the extreme, and he would have welcomed the extra money to be gained by office. In fact the anonymous 'Elector' at Shrewsbury (whom Disraeli suspected to be a local Whig solicitor, William Yardley), was not far wide of the mark when he claimed that Disraeli owed nearly £29,000 in 1841, at least from the evidence of judgments entered against him. His financial adviser Pyne appears to have been 'done up' by the winter of 1841, and he fell into the hands of a new usurer, a Mr Ford, who promised to lend him money to cover his more pressing debts in return for an introduction to the wealthy Mary Anne. Indeed, before Christmas of 1841 the situation had become so dangerous for Disraeli that he was forced to confess at least part of his position to Mary Anne, who loyally came to the rescue. Ford agreed to lend the Disraelis £5,000 in anticipation of a charge on Mary Anne's life estate, and in March 1842, with or without Mary Anne's knowledge, a further £2,781 on the security of the contents of the house at Grosvenor Gate.[13] The list of Disraeli's creditors was a long one, as was the number of his friends whom he had entangled in his financial affairs, the complexity of which, on the evidence that remains, seems unfathomable. Among those who had stood surety for Disraeli's bonds to various moneylenders were Bolton and James Clay in the thirties, and, in the late thirties and early forties, d'Orsay and another close friend, Lord Exmouth. As a typical example, Exmouth's involvement with Disraeli had begun in 1838 when he stood surety for £3,500 borrowed from Charles Waller, and a further sum from Thomas Ward in two separate indentures dated 26 May, as a result of which judgements were made against him the following year. Undeterred by this, Exmouth again stood surety for Disraeli's borrowing of £5,000 from William Lovell on 23 September 1840, while in December 1842 Ford was to bring a successful action for debt against both Exmouth and Disraeli to the tune of £10,000. Disraeli's indebtedness to his friend continued until after Exmouth's death, when on 27 April 1876, Disraeli paid the Exmouth estate £4,000.[14]

Disraeli's debts were a part of his bachelor days, of the dashing, carelessly extravagant way of life which he and such friends as d'Orsay and Exmouth had enjoyed, owing money to hatters, tailors, hosiers and various moneylenders to finance it. But the advent of the hungry forties, that 'frigid period' as Disraeli called it, was to spell the end for such feckless friends as Exmouth and d'Orsay, glittering butterflies of the thirties who could not survive the new cold climate and were driven abroad to escape their creditors. By the end of 1841 d'Orsay was, in the contemporary phrase, 'done up', immured within the walls of Gore House between sunrise and sunset to escape arrest for debt, and, when he did visit his clubs after dark, unable to find credit to live high as he had done before. He passed his time painting, drawing and sculpting portraits of his friends, but his life as leader of the 'ton' was over, and in December 1843 he fled precipitately to Paris.

Disraeli owed his survival to Mary Anne, and was grateful. On 13 August 1842 he set out his gratitude in a letter to be given to his father in the event of his predeceasing him.

> At this date, after a life of constant struggle, I find myself commencing an era of worldly prosperity & material satisfaction. I am entirely indebted for this position and this state

of mind, doubly appreciated by one whose state of mind has hitherto been so much the reverse, to the unexampled devotion of my beloved wife, to whom I am indebted not only for those worldly accidents which make life desirable, but for that peace of mind & consequent physical health which render it even delicious. Since our marriage, it should be distinctly known ... that she has defrayed either for those parliamentary contests so indispensable to my career, or for debts incurred before our union, no less than thirteen thousand pounds ... & is prepared to grapple with claims & incumbrances to an amount not inferior ... [15]

Mary Anne had helped, but could not cure, the chronic indebtedness that was to haunt him over the next two decades, and which, to avoid 'domestic storms' he endeavoured to keep a secret from her.

Nonetheless in August 1842 Disraeli felt that a new era was beginning for him; six months ago he had written of being 'utterly isolated', a 'solitary animal'. As old friends like d'Orsay and Bulwer, who had lost his seat at the last election and whose friendship with Disraeli, owing to Mary Anne's hostility had virtually ended, left his life, so Disraeli felt that he had made new ones. These new friends, who in Disraeli's visionary mind were already a party of the future – 'Young England' – were a small band of idealistic young aristocrats who had been at Eton and Cambridge together, and had entered Parliament for the first time at the election of 1841. Their leader was that George Sydney Smythe who had praised Disraeli's consular speech at Henry Baillie's dinner party. Described by his contemporaries as ' the sun of our existence' at Cambridge, Smythe was twenty-four when Disraeli met him: handsome, heartless, witty and cynical; Disraeli who heard him speak for the first time in February, had described him to Mary Anne as making 'an elaborate speech ... unprincipled as his little agreeable self'. Contemporaries predicted a great future for Smythe, but he was destined to fritter away his talents and to be, in the words of a friend, Lord Lyttelton, 'a splendid failure'. Disraeli was fascinated by Smythe, and remained so until his death at the age of only forty-one; he was to be the unlikely model not only for the high-principled hero of *Coningsby*, but for characters far more closely resembling his real self: the unscrupulous Emir Fakredeen in *Tancred*, and the imaginative, exuberant dilettante Waldershare in Disraeli's last novel, *Endymion*. Disraeli's private reminiscences were full of Smythe's 'bon mots' which he admiringly recorded, and it is not difficult to see why Smythe appealed to him; Sir William Gregory, recalling Smythe's brilliant conversation over the famous dry champagne at the Carlton, wrote of his 'strange paradoxes, his fierce attacks on the conventionalities, and his scorn of the men whom we regarded as the Olympian gods of the party to which we belonged'.[16] Smythe himself wrote to Disraeli shortly before his death: 'I once heard that you had said of me that I was the one man who had never bored you.' This was the first of a series of friendships between Disraeli and far younger men.

The second member of the group, also destined to be a lifelong friend, was Lord John Manners, second son of the fifth Duke of Rutland. Also twenty-four, handsome, clever and high-minded, Manners, as the son of a Duke, already a member of White's, and installed in chambers in Albany, could hardly have been closer to

Disraeli's aristocratic ideal. The third and less brilliant member of the group was Alexander Baillie-Cochrane, known as 'Kok', who, unlike his friends Smythe and Manners, was impervious to Disraeli's fascination and regarded him with a hard-headed suspicion and distrust. The ideals that united the group were a romantic Toryism and a belief that the only hope for the future lay in a new paternalistic feudalism, an alliance between the working classes and a responsible idealistic aristocracy against the hard-hearted materialism of the manufacturers. Both Smythe and Manners were deeply influenced by the religious attitudes of Pusey and the Oxford Movement, and a nostalgia for the medieval Church; 'nothing but monastic institutions can Christianise Manchester', Manners once wrote, and his recipe for the happiness of the industrial poor has been described as 'a curious mixture of public baths, public open spaces and Church festivals'. While Disraeli regarded Manners' nostalgia for monasteries and maypoles as a lovable eccentricity, he was to find his own inspiration in the wider ideals of Young England.

Disraeli's boast to Mary Anne on 11 March 1842, 'I already find myself the leader of a party chiefly of the youth and new members', was certainly premature; but the sympathetic reaction of the younger men seems to have sown the seeds of a plan for a new political combination in his mind. It seems to have been Disraeli who made the first approaches to Smythe and Manners, since Manners recorded in his diary for July: 'D'Israeli wishes us to form a party with certain general principles . . . He says even six men acting so together would have great weight.'[17] By the end of the session, there was still no formal agreement on parliamentary co-operation, but in Disraeli's mind he already had a party, and he now also had a plan. It was a project that appealed to him far more than the issues that had been agitating the last session of what he disdainfully termed 'the political economy Parliament'; he would personally promote an alliance with France. He had already taken the first steps in that direction in a series of foreign policy speeches in July.

As the beautiful summer of 1842 wore into the heat of July and August the violence of the language used by the alienated people outside Westminster increased. So far the anger of the working classes, the Chartists and the Anti-Corn Law Leaguers had been confined to their newspapers and public speeches, but no one could predict whether or when it might spill over into physical violence. The turbulence outside was felt within Parliament, as the House of Commons anxiously debated 'the Distress of the Country'. In the course of these fiery debates, Disraeli pursued his own unemotional independent course, speaking only twice, both times on foreign policy. 'To the mismanagement of our foreign affairs must be attributed infinitely more of evil than to our own Corn-Laws', he told the House on 1 July, attacking Palmerston's 'gunboat' diplomacy and refusal to proceed with a commercial treaty with France as chiefly responsible for the recession in Britain's foreign trade. In a highly-charged debate three weeks later he played the same theme; while a passionate Tom Duncombe berated the House for having done nothing to alleviate the general distress, and other speakers denounced the Corn Laws in no uncertain terms, Disraeli again blamed Palmerston's 'anti-national diplomacy', praised Peel's tariff reductions as 'steps in the right direction', and hoped that the Government's future policy would be directed towards commercial treaties with European powers.

It was a theme that Cobden himself was later to develop, but in the troubled summer of 1842 Palmerston's past misdemeanours and future commercial treaties seemed to have little relevance. It was Disraeli's weakness as well as his strength as a statesman that he was able to view current events with detachment, an Olympian and unemotional stance which could lead him to miscalculate the public temper, as he was later so notably to do at the time of the Bulgarian Atrocities agitation. He was bored by the debates of the 'political economy Parliament', the detail and the statistics, believing that what he himself called his 'revolutionary mind' was better suited to range a higher plane, to ponder the destinies of peoples and the control of continents. As he had written a decade before in *Contarini Fleming*: 'Foreign policy opened a dazzling vista of splendid incident. It was enchanting to be acquainted with the secrets of European Cabinets, and to control or influence their fortunes.' And so, at a time when *The Times* was reporting in horrifying detail the death of a child from starvation in a workhouse at Ringmer, and the brutal labour conditions of women and children in the mines was brought to light in the report of a parliamentary committee, and people, including the Home Secretary, Sir James Graham, feared imminent social revolution, Disraeli upbraided Lord Palmerston for riding roughshod over the rights of distant peoples and called for a commercial treaty with France.

Almost forty years later, Disraeli still considered this passage of his life important enough to be featured in his last novel *Endymion*, when the sophisticated heroine, Lady Montfort, advises the young hero and aspiring politician to go to Paris. 'This', said Lady Montfort one day to Endymion,

> is a political economy Parliament, both sides alike thinking of the price of corn and all that. Finance and commerce are everybody's subjects, and are most convenient to make speeches about for men who cannot speak French and who have had no education. Real politics are the possession and distribution of power. I want to see you give your mind to foreign affairs ... There is nothing like personal knowledge of the individuals who control the high affairs ... Paris is now the capital of diplomacy.[18]

It was a wonderfully impudent paragraph; Disraeli had no real gift for economics but, on the other hand, his French was notoriously bad all his life. According to his own account, he had, since March, been keeping 'a sort of diary of affairs and thoughts in French', which, he said 'I write now with great ease and some elegance', but judging by later comments on his poor linguistic ability, one may doubt whether he progressed very far. It was perhaps no coincidence that the letter in which he reported to Mary Anne that he was practising French was dated 15 March, only four days after he had written that he was the leader of a party of the youth of England; the two ideas were intimately connected. Disraeli proposed to use the projected alliance between England and France as a bridge by which he might be able to pass to a position of greater influence in English politics. He wanted to impress the Young Englanders whom he planned to meet in Paris with the extent of his influence in foreign affairs, and at the same time to present them to the French king as a party of which he was already leader.

Disraeli and Mary Anne arrived in Paris in mid-September to stay once again at the Hotel de l'Europe where they had spent their honeymoon. They had several useful contacts in Paris and Disraeli intended to use them to the full – to enter influential political circles and, above all, to obtain an introduction to the king, Louis Philippe. Through d'Orsay's sister, Ida, Duchesse de Gramont, they had the entrée to aristocratic French society while Lyndhurst's father-in-law, Lewis Goldsmith, was an influential financier who knew all the bankers and politicians; lastly, there was Henry Bulwer at the Embassy under Lord Cowley.

Disraeli was flattered by the attentions of society hostesses like the Comtesse de Castellane and men of intellect such as Thiers, but his principal object was to meet the king, the obstacle to an official introduction by the English Ambassador being that the court was in mourning for the death of the king's son, the Duc d'Orléans. Here Henry Bulwer was of help, introducing them to the English wife of the king's aide-de-camp, General Baudrand, to whom Disraeli wrote expressing his great desire to meet the king, with a heavy hint that such a meeting might be to his Majesty's advantage:

> I had wished to have enjoyed that favor because, before I quitted Paris, I desired to lay before his Majesty some facts respecting the state of parties & the disposition of power in our Parliament, the importance of which I think cannot be exaggerated; which in truth cannot be entrusted either to French Ministers or to English Ambassadors; but which, if properly appreciated, might have exercised an important & immediate influence on the lasting policy of the two countries.[19]

For Louis Philippe, who was an avid reader of *The Times* and deeply interested in English affairs, the bait of inside knowledge proffered by a member of the ruling majority in the English Parliament was not to be dismissed. Disraeli followed up this enticing prologue with a document which he knew the king would find irresistible, to be handed to him in confidence by General Baudrand. Entitled 'Very confidential note on the means of restoring the understanding between France and England', it represented one of the most curious documents ever drawn up by an English Member of Parliament for perusal by a foreign Head of State.

In the opening paragraph of the memorandum, Disraeli introduced himself as 'one who has observed with deep attention the characters and circumstances in France which exercise an influence on the relations between the two countries'. While this may have been true, the following passage in which he described himself as having 'that knowledge of the actors and motives of the political world of England which years of thought and action and intimate intercourse with the chiefs of parties can alone give', was, in a man of thirty-eight who had barely been five years in Parliament, patently unfounded. He concluded with the somewhat surprising observation that there was no historical basis for hostility between England and France, and that all that was required to make the relationship run smoothly was that the ruling class in England should be 'instructed' to change their John Bull attitudes towards France, and wounded French sensibilities soothed by changing the hostile tone of the English press.

This, Disraeli proposed, should be effected by forming a parliamentary lobby to put pressure on Peel in the Commons and to work upon public opinion through the national and provincial press. Now, he urged the king, was the moment to launch such a campaign, since Peel's 'apparent majority' of ninety was vulnerable in that it included forty to sixty 'agricultural malcontents' who frequently abstained from debates. 'It is obvious, therefore,' he declared, 'that another section of Conservative members, full of youth and energy and constant in their seats, must exercise an irresistible control over the tone of the Minister', and while supporting his domestic policies, 'may dictate the character of his foreign [policy].' Not only was such a party in existence, but, he intimated, he was in a position to control it: 'A gentleman has already been solicited to place himself at the head of a Parliamentary party which there is every reason to believe would adopt the views on the Foreign Policy of England referred to, a party of the youth of England, influenced by the noblest views and partaking nothing of a Parliamentary intrigue'.

There followed a very curious passage which could be interpreted as a request for financial support: 'It is right to state that it is calculated that the leadership of a Parliamentary party in England involves an extra expenditure of a very great amount. This circumstance is mentioned only to show that no one would heedlessly contemplate such a contingency'.

It is perfectly clear that he intended the king to understand that he was 'the gentleman' in question, and that he hesitated to accept such a financial onus, hinting delicately that royal encouragement might tip the scale towards acceptance. Should he do so, this leader would, on the first day of the opening session of Parliament, give notice of a motion inviting the House to consider 'on the earliest occasion' the state of Anglo-French relations, while a simultaneous campaign should be organized in the press to promote an Anglo-French *entente*.

Disraeli no doubt sincerely believed that an Anglo-French alliance was in England's interest. As a Jew, an alien Englishman, he did not share the historical prejudices of his compatriots; an internationalist in his attitude he was never to understand and always to underestimate the forces of nationalism. Nonetheless, however lofty his ideals may have been, he was in effect offering to become a parliamentary agent in the French interest, whether paid or unpaid. The end, to Disraeli, justified the means; amidst all the practical suggestions in the memorandum, a characteristically messianic phrase may reveal his underlying motivation: 'It is with machinery of this description that the ideas of a single man ... soon become the voice of a nation'. This was the authentic voice of Disraeli the dreamer.[20]

Louis Philippe rose to the bait; although there is no evidence as to whether or not he responded to the veiled request for financial subvention, the King received Disraeli for lengthy private conversations, and invited him to intimate royal dinners where no foreigner or indeed anyone outside the court and the royal family was present. All this royal attention went to Disraeli's head; his reverence for monarchy as an institution and his belief in the power of an individual to guide the destinies of nations leading him to invest the prosaic figure of Louis Philippe with the divine aura of kingship. His admiration for this intelligent though scarcely divine sovereign carried him to ludicrous lengths, later expressed in the words of Sidonia, the Jewish philosopher-financier in *Coningsby*:

> I have a creed of mine own that the great characters of antiquity are at rare epochs reproduced for our wonder, or our guidance. Nature, wearied with mediocrity, pours the warm metal into an heroic mould. When circumstances at length placed me in the presence of the King of France, I recognised, ULYSSES![21]

Unfortunately for Disraeli's prognostications, less than four years after these words were written the distinctly un-Homeric figure of Louis Philippe was indeed to be on his travels as an exile after the revolution of 1848.

Meanwhile, the members of Disraeli's 'party of the youth of England' observed his euphoric state of mind and the glittering circles in which he moved with baffled amusement. As Alexander Baillie-Cochrane wrote to John Manners on 3 December:

> Disraeli's salons rival Law's under the Regent. Guizot, Thiers, Molé, Decazes and God wots how many *dei minores* are found in his antechamber, while the great man himself is closeted with Louis Philippe at St. Cloud, and already pictures himself the founder of some new dynasty with his Manfred love-locks stamped on the current coin of the realm.[22]

Baillie-Cochrane had some reason to be nervous of Disraeli's intentions, since he and Smythe had entered into an informal compact with Disraeli in Paris in mid-October, subject to Manner's approval, '*to sit together, and to vote together, the majority deciding*', as Smythe wrote to Manners on 19 October. If Disraeli failed to cast his spell over Cochrane, he certainly succeeded in impressing Smythe, who continued:

> *Most private.* Dizzy has much more parliamentary power than I had any notion of. The two Hodgsons are his, and Quintin Dick. He has a great hold on Walter [proprietor of *The Times*], and "The Times". Henry Hope (who will come in soon) is entirely in his hands ... You understand? We four vote, and these men are to be played upon, and won, and wooed, for the sense in which we esoterics may have decided. I am now going to write to Henry Baillie, to try him first, by proposing that he should *sit with us*. We can judge, by seeing how this will take, how far he can be admitted into our counsels.[23]

The term 'esoteric', with its unmistakably Disraelian ring, caught Manners' imagination, for it was as such that he described the party thus formed in his journal, noting with satisfaction that it would be of 'no particular principles – but a hotch-potch, each surrendering his own to the majority'. Here indeed was the rub, clearly recognized by Smythe, who was preoccupied with avoiding conflict between Disraeli and Cochrane. 'I have already nicknamed us the Diz-Union', he wrote to Manners on 22 October, 'in two several letters to Dizzy and Kok to warn them against the dangers of dissidence, obstinately persevered in, and above all things, of war against one another's *amour propre*'.[24] Distrust of Disraeli's character, motives and principles was one of the chief obstacles to the formation of the 'esoteric party'. Cochrane feared the predominance of Disraeli, and would have preferred to see the party confined to himself, Smythe and Manners. 'Kok does not know him well', Smythe told Manners, 'and sometimes dreads his jokes, and is jealous of his throwing us over.' Even Smythe could not be absolutely certain that Cochrane's suspicions were without foundation, for he continued, 'even if he did, it is always better to *be in a position* to be thrown over, than to be *nothing at all*.'[25]

Even John Manners' trusting nature shared the general English reaction to Disraeli's enigmatic character; on first meeting him at dinner in February 1841, he had noted 'Disraeli spoke well, almost too well', while in mid-1843 after six months of parliamentary co-operation with him he was still uneasy as to his sincerity. 'Could I only satisfy myself', he confided to his journal, 'that d'Israeli believed all that he said, I should be more happy: his historical views are quite mine, but does he believe them?'[26] Smythe himself, for all his enthusiasm for the alliance, was well aware of the shady nature of Disraeli's public reputation, and the dangers of contamination from it, writing to Manners, '... to be of power, or fame, or even office, we cannot ... be too much *liés* with Disraeli'. Beresford Hope, brother of the millionaire Henry Hope, on being approached by Manners to join the 'esoterics' replied forthrightly, 'The co-operation of such men as D'Israeli, though he may be clever, will not be of permanent good to any one, as he has not character to support'.[27]

It would be amusing to speculate on what the reaction of the 'esoterics' would have been, had they been aware of the contents of Disraeli's memorandum to Louis Philippe, or conversely, that of the king, had he known of the wary attitude of the 'party of the youth of England' towards their 'leader'. Disraeli, however, seems to have succeeded in bamboozling both, as, with his mind full of plans that he described to the king as 'vast ... but not visionary', he prepared to return to London in January 1843.

9   Young England

Disraeli, dreaming of 'great movements' and 'vast combinations', returned in January 1843 to the hard realities of an England distracted by domestic distress and disorder. Once again the omens were not auspicious for discussions of foreign policy. With the mass turn-outs in Lancashire in August, violence in the great industrial towns in which two policemen were killed, and the menacing language proffered at public meetings by Anti-Corn Law Leaguers and Chartists alike, the year that had just passed seemed to most Englishmen to have been the most dangerous period of civil unrest since the Reform riots, while the shameful facts of degradation and distress among the working people had been widely publicized in newspapers and parliamentary reports. In Ireland, O'Connell, now aided and abetted by a group of young Irish nationalists, proclaimed 1843 the Year of Repeal; while the assassination of Peel's secretary Drummond, almost certainly in mistake for the Prime Minister himself, in Whitehall on 20 January shortly before the opening of Parliament on 2 February, became a symbol of the perilous state of the country.

Within the House, Free Trade and the 'Distress of the Country' were not unnaturally the main topics of debate. Broadly speaking, the battle lines were drawn up by class interest, with the landed aristocracy on the one side, the middle class and the interests of capital on the other. Peel and the more liberal-minded Conservatives stood in the middle as unpopular referees, whom both sides at times attacked, the ammunition being statistics on trade and employment, wages and poor relief. Among the protagonists for the League was Richard Cobden, one of the most lucid and eloquent speakers in the House, and on the agricultural side, Walter Busfield Ferrand, a Tory squire and MP for Knaresborough, an intemperate speaker and rabid hater of the mill-owners and the Poor Law, who was frequently to act with Disraeli and Young England. Cobden accused Peel of being personally responsible for 'the lamentable and dangerous state of the country', by refusing to listen to the advice of the manufacturers urging the total abolition of the Corn Laws. Ferrand attributed the industrial misery to 'the greed, avarice and tyranny' of the capitalists, and accused the League of using the wretchedness of the masses for their own selfish and mercenary ends, while charging Peel with reversing his public pledge to maintain the Corn Laws inviolate by acting on Free Trade principles. Peel, assailed by both Free Traders and Protectionists and hampered by a continuing budget deficit, had temporarily abandoned his forward economic policy and, in his uncomfortable situation seemed, as Disraeli told Sarah in one of his favourite alliterative phrases, 'feeble and frigid'.

Disraeli, testing the political temperature at the Carlton, found 'general grumbling' against Peel's government; he should not have overestimated it. A perceptible gulf was beginning to open between the Conservative leader and his followers, but this was largely due to faults in Peel's style of leadership. Neglecting to flatter them, or even to inform them of his intentions, he was a distant, some thought tyrannical leader, confiding only in his trusted lieutenants. Yet, however much the agriculturalists may have disliked Peel's high-handed treatment of them, whatever suspicions they may have subconsciously entertained of his attachment to Protectionist principles, he was still indisputably their leader, and not even the most fervent agriculturalist contemplated more than sporadic rebellion against his orders. As Knatchbull-Hugessen, a protectionist member of Peel's cabinet noted in his diary: 'I never in my time saw a Minister who possessed more absolute power in the House of Commons than Peel.' Within a few years Disraeli was to succeed in toppling that supremacy and rousing the grumbling squires to mutiny.

Sitting, as had been agreed in Paris, with Smythe, Manners and Cochrane, Disraeli entered the parliamentary fray on 14 February. True to his preconceived plan he declared that commercial treaties were the remedy for trade distress, inquired why the Government had not proceeded with the projected treaty with France, and urged that full discussions should take place between the Parliaments of England and France. 'A commercial treaty with France would do more for the town of Sheffield than both the Americas', he said, proceeding to lecture a House distracted by domestic issues on Eastern markets and the evil results of Palmerston's policies. From Paris Baudrand, to whom he sent cuttings of his speech to be shown to the king, applauded him, and the French were even more delighted when Disraeli came to grips with Palmerston, their *bête noire*, in the debate on the Washington Treaty on 22 March. All this showed, Baudrand wrote on 5 April, 'how justified was the confidence that the King has shown in the loyalty of your sentiments and the firmness of your convictions.' On 24 and 28 April Disraeli fulfilled a pledge he had made to the French when he harried the government over Russian interference in the Turkish province of Serbia. The House of Commons was tired of Disraelian disquisitions on foreign affairs, and he received short shrift for his attempts to enlighten them on the subject of Serbia: 'If the House would permit him, he would explain the circumstances on which his inquiry was founded ... (cries of "No", "no").'[1] Peel coldly declined to discuss the question, and Disraeli perforce swallowed the snub, but it rankled, fuelling a cutting attack he was later to make on the same subject later in the session.

Disraeli was sensible enough not to persist in his pro-French lobbying for the time being in the face of these repeated rebuffs. Accepting that free trade must be the issue of the day, in a speech to his constituents at Shrewsbury on 9 May, he made a strong bid for the support of the squirearchy. The speech, which was widely reported in the press, clearly defined his position on the Corn Laws, and threw down the gauntlet to Cobden and the League. 'The preponderance of the landed interest has made England,' he told his audience:

> it is an immense element of political power and stability ... And this, gentlemen, is the reason why you have seen an outcry raised against your Corn Laws. Your Corn Laws are merely the outwork of a great system fixed and established upon your territorial property, and the only object the Leaguers have in making themselves masters of the outwork is that they may easily overcome the citadel.

Any attempt to change that system by government, he warned prophetically, would provoke 'great party convulsion'. The speech may have been intended as a warning to Peel of the dangers to party unity of any attempt upon the Corn Laws; more importantly it was designed to present Disraeli to the public eye as the spokesman of the agricultural interest against Cobden, who had held a much publicized Anti-Corn Law meeting in the Drury Lane Theatre shortly before. Cobden's Anti-Corn Law campaign was a brilliant example of what could be achieved by extra-Parliamentary tactics, and it was a lesson not lost upon Disraeli. The Shrewsbury speech was the platform from which Disraeli intended to launch an appeal to public opinion outside Parliament, which would not only counteract the small weight attached to his opinions within the walls of Westminster but would add to his status there. It was the first shot in what was to be an escalating propaganda campaign.

The creation of the myth of 'Young England' towards the latter end of the summer of 1843 is a tribute to Disraeli's outstanding talents as a publicist, to the striking force of his ideas and to his masterly means of expressing them. Despite Baudrand's congratulations to Disraeli in April on his party's having taken on substance, there is no evidence that the 'esoterics' had made much impression in the House before mid-summer. Indeed the principal parliamentary action in the early part of the session had been carried on by Disraeli's friend, John Walter II, proprietor of *The Times* and MP for Nottingham, combining with W.B. Ferrand to attack the Poor Law.

John Walter II not only owned, but also controlled *The Times*, as the former editor Thomas Barnes had died in May 1841 and the great J.T. Delane, his successor, was then only twenty-three and had not yet risen to the absolute predominance which he later attained. Indeed, the previous autumn Disraeli, Smythe and Cochrane had considered offering Walter the 'nominal leadership' of their group, which they regarded as 'a small sacrifice' in return for 'a certain control' over *The Times* reporting, since they were sure that they could always overrule Walter if necessary.

Walter's house, Bearwood, was the meeting-place for the group in mid-July, and it seems to have been here that parliamentary action between them for the rest of the session was organized. Walter certainly took it seriously enough to refer to it as 'the New Party'. His daughter Catherine, more interested in personalities than politics, wrote with the cruel candour of youth that Mr and Mrs Disraeli were a very strange couple, Mary Anne 'the greatest curiosity I ever met', and 'D'Issy . . . the oddest being I ever saw.'[2] It certainly must have appeared an odd group, the exotic Jewish-looking Disraeli with his three half-admiring, half-wary friends, Smythe, Manners and Cochrane all of a younger generation. Beyond these three, Disraeli could count on the support of Walter's ally, Ferrand, a somewhat doubtful accession since he was generally regarded as a Tory wild man; of his friend the millionaire Henry Hope; Augustus Stafford O'Brien, MP for Northampton, a contemporary and friend of Smythe and Manners; and, among the older generation, Henry Baillie. The egregious 'Dicky' Monckton Milnes, literary son of a Yorkshire squire, always eager to take up the latest trend, but anxious to support Peel and get himself a peerage, might also sometimes be called upon.

To an experienced observer such a collection of youthful romantics must have seemed a precarious foundation from which to launch an attack on the parliamentary supremacy of Peel. Disraeli's young followers, moreover, were not quite sure of either his motives or his principles. Disraeli shared their romantic Toryism but he was uninterested in the practicalities of Manners' and Ferrand's schemes for public holidays and allotments for the poor. Their conception of a revived feudalism was for him essentially a pretty notion, useful as a symbol of the 'territorial constitution' of England in which he really believed. He was attracted by their idea of the role of the Church as a revivifying force against the spiritual degradation of materialism, but not by the 'Romanising' tendencies of the Oxford Movement which had so deeply influenced them. As Smythe wrote to Manners, 'Dizzy's attachment to moderate Oxfordism is something like Bonaparte's to moderate Mahomedanism'.[3] In Disraeli the visionary was always mixed with the practical politician; he was that rare combination of a man with a genius for the ideal and with an instinct for the pragmatic. He was a myth-creator and a spell-binder who believed in the power of his incantations. He created the myth of Young England and used it to the full to put forward his view of English politics. On a personal level he was attracted by the youth of Manners and his friends and by the aristocratic aura of Eton and Cambridge which surrounded them, enjoying their company and basking in their admiration. It was all great fun.

For Disraeli in the midsummer of 1843, the support of *The Times* and a 'party of the youth of England', however small, was enough to decide him upon a course of sustained opposition to Peel and to the path which the party leadership appeared to be taking. As a practical politician he sensed that the all-powerful Peel administration had, in mid-session, become unaccountably unpopular. As another Conservative MP Lord Ashley noted in his diary for 8 June:

How and by what means, from what Cause, or what influence have the Ministry so declined in public and private estimation? that it is so shown by the papers ... by the joy of the Opposition, by the dejection of friends; by the looks ... and the language of the Government themselves – their numbers are undiminished, and yet they carry nothing; they have committed no leading palpable folly; and yet no one confides in their wisdom; no great and manifest crime; and yet who animates himself by conviction of their honesty? all is doubt, uncertainty, vain wishes and disappointed hopes; much anger and discontent, personally and collectively, with present men, & yet an unwillingness to change them ...[4]

Disraeli chose his ground for attack carefully and well; it was to be on the third reading of the Irish Arms Bill on 9 August, a law and order measure which, being at the same time both coercive and cautious, was generally unpopular. It was his first crossing of swords with Peel in a duel that was to be to the death. In a speech that had more than an undertone of personal hostility he charged Peel with political inconsistency, in that having come to power by defeating the Whigs in 1841 on their Irish Bill, he had subsequently abandoned the two Irish policies (the reform of municipal corporations and registration of voters) that he had then pledged himself to pursue. Disraeli argued that since Peel had abandoned the principles upon which he had come to power, being now convinced they were erroneous, he had thus dissolved the bonds of party that obliged his supporters to follow him on specific issues. It was the deadly germ of an idea which he was to hammer home in speech after speech over the next three years; its acceptance by the bulk of the Tory party in the end would lead to the destruction of Peel. Supported by Smythe, Disraeli told the House that he regarded the Government's 'do-nothing policy as not Conservative'; pointing to the vacuum in the leadership, he could not resist one of his favourite messianic phrases; the times, he said, required 'a great man to have recourse to great remedial measures'.

Peel turned upon Smythe and Disraeli with that hauteur which, as Disraeli rightly said, he reserved for his own supporters, challenging them to have the honesty to oppose him with their votes as well as their speeches, before making a counterattack upon Disraeli in a particularly sneering and sarcastic vein. Peel regarded Disraeli as a mischief-maker and a disappointed opportunist and their duels reflected that conviction. 'The hon. Gentleman, the member for Shrewsbury', he said, '... with his strong opinion as to what ought to be the principle which should govern the administration of Irish affairs ... has, in past time, made greater sacrifices to party connexion than any Member of this House'. Disraeli's unfortunate messianic phrase was a heaven-sent opportunity for a 'hit' which a debater of Peel's calibre would not let slip:

Some great man, it seems, is expected to arise with some vast and comprehensive measure, and I was in hopes that I should find from the nature of the measure proposed by the hon. Gentleman, some indication of the coming man by whom such great results are to be achieved; but, considering that the hon. Gentleman has come to no other conclusion with respect to the Arms Bill, than that on the whole it is better to give no vote at all, I am afraid I cannot infer that he is the man who is to realise this vision of a great statesman.[5]

This was a foretaste of the hits Disraeli could expect to receive in crossing swords with the foremost parliamentarian of the age, but he liked nothing better than a worthy adversary and, far from being discouraged, renewed his attack on 15 August. The government's foreign policy with respect to the East, he said, 'made them ... the laughing-stock of Europe; and, as to their domestic situation, was there anyone who could deny, that, in returning to their counties, they would not meet dissatisfaction and distress?'

This open rebellion was too much for Viscount Sandon, a loyal supporter of Peel, who rose to make an apoplectic attack: 'He did not think that it was seemly on the part of Younger Members of that House, to rise up behind her Majesty's Ministers whom they pretended to support, and not only express a difference of opinion, but to heap the grossest terms of contumely and opprobrium on those whom they affected to support'.[6] Sharp exchanges between Disraeli and Sandon followed, with Disraeli denying he had used any such terms and a spluttering Sandon unable to recall specific instances. Smythe joined in the fray and a lively parliamentary fracas ensued, with the Young Englanders defended by such un-likely members of the Opposition as the Radical Joseph Hume and Lord Palmerston. From outside the walls of Parliament, John Walter's *Times* berated Sandon for his attempt to 'bully and cow' Young England, declaring that the Prime Minister should not be considered beyond criticism by his own party and that it was not for the public good that any rising talent should be silenced and kept down.

It had been a thoroughly satisfactory session for Disraeli and his fellow musket-eers; not only had they succeeded in publicly discomfiting Peel in Parliament, but they had made a great noise in doing so, a noise quite out of proportion to their numbers or real importance. 'Young England' was talked of everywhere. As the Opposition newspaper, the *Morning Chronicle* trumpeted on 28 August, four days after Parliament had risen, the Government was 'now so humbled and so changed that Young England drives its mystic chariot, with Disraeli and his ambiguous comrades on the car, over the prostrate spirit of the Ministry'.

As far as Peel and his inner circle were concerned, however, Disraeli was now a marked man, a dangerous maverick who should be expelled from the fold, as the Home Secretary, Sir James Graham, wrote to Disraeli's old enemy, John Wilson Croker, a week after the Sandon affair:

With respect to Young England, the puppets are moved by Disraeli, who is the ablest man among them: I consider him unprincipled and disappointed, and in despair he has tried the effect of bullying. I think with you that they [Manners, Smythe & Co.] will return to the crib after prancing, capering and snorting; but a crack or two of the whip may hasten and insure their return. Disraeli alone is mischievous; and with him I have no desire to keep terms. It would be better for the party if he were driven into the ranks of our open enemies.[7]

A few months later Disraeli, with a sublime unawareness of the effects of his own conduct, had the surprising effrontery to ask first Stanley, and then Graham, for a post for his brother James. Graham refused the request but sent it on to Peel whose reply was expressive of the contempt with which he regarded Disraeli:

> I am very glad that Mr. Disraeli has asked for an office for his brother. It is a good thing when such a man puts his shabbiness on record. He asked me for office himself, and I was not surprised that being refused he became independent and a patriot. But to ask favours after his conduct last session is too bad. However, it is a bridle in his mouth![8]

Graham may have been right in surmising that Disraeli intended to force the government to 'buy him off' by giving him office; certainly he had not yet admitted to himself the extent of his subconscious animus against Peel, nor had he probably, despite the odds against it, entirely given up hopes of a post in the Conservative administration. But elated by the initial success of Young England, he had no intention of suspending action when Parliament rose at the end of August; he was now aiming for a wider audience beyond the walls of Westminster.

He had conceived the idea of writing a trilogy, in which he would examine the political, social and religious condition of England, publicizing his ideas and those of Young England in this most palatable way. The first two books of the trilogy – *Coningsby*, published in May 1844 and *Sybil*, which appeared in May 1845 – were fired by the political and social conditions of the 1840s, the third, *Tancred*, published after a two year interval in 1847, although purporting to be an examination of the Church of England, evolved into an exposition of Disraeli's highly personal views of race and the Jewish tradition.

Coningsby, dedicated to Henry Hope and begun at his house, the Deepdene, near Dorking, where Disraeli was staying in September, was the first English political novel. In it Disraeli combined the two themes, politics and society, at which he as a writer was most adept. Disraeli's proclaimed intention was to call public attention to the state of the political parties; their origin, history and present position. The book was a vehicle for the ideas of political and constitutional history and the nature of the Conservative and Whig parties that he had first expounded in the *Vindication*. As such it was not only an attack on Whig 'exclusiveness', but more importantly, presented Peelite Conservatism as having lost sight of the original 'national' ideals of the old Tory party, of Bolingbroke and the younger Pitt. It was also a blatant piece of propaganda in presenting the real-life members of Young England, thinly disguised as characters in the novel, as the rising generation in whose idealism the hope for the future was to lie. 'In an age of political infidelity, of mean passions, and petty thoughts,' Disraeli was to write later in *Sybil*, 'I would have impressed upon the rising race not to despair, but to seek a right understanding of the history of their country and in the energies of heroic youth, the elements of national welfare.'

As representatives of that 'heroic youth', the witty, cynical, sexually adventurous George Smythe appears in the unlikely guise of the priggish, idealistic hero, Harry Coningsby; while John Manners is Lord Henry Sidney and Cochrane is Lord Buckhurst. Coningsby, the mouthpiece of Young England, asks the pertinent question – what is Conservatism? In a famous passage in the fifth chapter of Book II Disraeli claims that present day Conservatism, as established in Peel's famous Tamworth Manifesto of 1835, is little better than watered-down Whiggism:

> The Tamworth Manifesto was an attempt to construct a party without principles: its basis therefore was necessarily Latitudinarianism: and its inevitable consequence has been Political Infidelity ... There was indeed a considerable shouting about what they called Conservative principles; but the awkward question naturally arose, what will you conserve? The prerogatives of the Crown, provided they are not exercised; the independence of the House of Lords, provided it is not asserted; the Ecclesiastical estate, provided it is regulated by a commission of laymen. Everything, in short that is established, as long as it is a phrase and not a fact ... Conservatism discards Prescription, shrinks from Principle, disavows Progress; having rejected all respect for Antiquity, it offers no redress for the Present, and makes no preparation for the Future.[9]

Coningsby's recipe for the 'Future' is characteristically vague, as he tells his irritated and astonished grandfather, Lord Monmouth:

> ... to establish great principles which may maintain the realm and secure the happiness of the people. Let me see authority once more honoured; a solemn reverence again the habit of our lives; let me see property acknowledging, as in the old days of faith, that labour is his twin brother, and that the essence of all tenure is the performance of duty...

'Fantastical puerilities', was Lord Monmouth's dry comment.[10]

The real hero of the book, however, is not the cardboard Anglo-Saxon aristocrat, Harry Coningsby, but the mysterious, omniscient Semite, Sidonia; half-Disraeli, half-Rothschild, a great financier and a philosopher, much-travelled, passionless, a truly international man without a country. He produces another Disraelian recipe for political happiness; the advantages of what he calls 'pure Monarchy' over 'the imperfect vicariate of representative government'. 'In an enlightened age', Sidonia tells Coningsby, 'the Monarch on the throne, free from the vulgar prejudice and the corrupt interests of the subject, becomes again divine.' As an idea it was neither original nor practical, but interesting in that it expressed both Disraeli's reverence for the idea of monarchy and his lack of belief in representative government.

Coningsby suffers from the literary faults common to the whole trilogy: banality of plot, an awkward conjunction of lectures on political history and fictional scenes of society and romance, and woodenness of the hero and heroine. Indeed only the figures taken from real life are well drawn; the superbly portrayed arrogant old aristocrat Lord Monmouth [Lord Hertford], for instance, and his factotum, Rigby – a portrait of Croker. Perhaps the least felicitous of all the chapters describes Eton, that temple of English aristocratic youth, which the young Disraeli/Vivian Grey had yearned for and the mature Disraeli regarded with mystery and awe. Disraeli took a great deal of trouble to get things right, even enlisting the help of Smythe's former tutor, W.G. Cookesley, but to the ears of Old Etonians there were details that did not ring true. Sir William Fraser,

Disraeli's biographer, said that Eton boys voted the conversations 'absurd', while Lyttelton, one of the Smythe-Manners circle, had 'grave doubts' as to whether boys would ever have had goose for breakfast. Despite these faults, *Coningsby* remains one of the wittiest and most readable of Disraeli's novels; its social and political vignettes alone would put Disraeli in the first rank as a novelist.

The same cannot be said of the second book of the trilogy entitled *Sybil or the Two Nations*, dedicated to Mary Anne as 'The most severe of critics, but a perfect wife!' *Sybil* is a less readable, less skilful but more powerful book than *Coningsby*, its faults as glaring as its virtues. The plot is feeble, the principal characters flat and unconvincing and the working class dialogue even more clumsy and artificial than the conversation of the Eton boys in *Coningsby*; but the book contains powerful concepts and passages which have echoed through subsequent history. The theme of the book is the striking contrast between the gilded life of the rich in England and the misery and degradation of the working classes. These are the 'two nations' of the title, described in one of the most famous passages in English literature:

> Two nations; between whom there is no intercourse and no sympathy; who are as ignorant of each other's habits, thought and feelings, as if they were dwellers in different zones, or inhabitants of different planets; who are formed by different breeding, are fed by a different food, are ordered by different manners, and are not governed by the same laws ... THE RICH AND THE POOR.[11]

Disraeli wrote the book for political motives and his material for the descriptions of the degraded life of the poor was secondhand, garnered from parliamentary reports and published letters, but he can be forgiven much for being able to write a passage of such striking truth, as true in many ways of today as it was of the 1840s.

In another equally bold passage, he condemned the greedy materialism of the age:

> ... since the passing of the Reform Act the altar of Mammon has blazed with triple worship. To acquire, to accumulate, to plunder each other by virtue of philosophic phrases, to propose a Utopia to consist only of WEALTH and TOIL, this has been the breathless business of enfranchised England for the last twelve years, until we are startled from our voracious strife by the wail of intolerable serfage.[12]

Disraeli offered no specific remedies for this drastic situation beyond the beneficent action of a revivified Toryism in closing the gulf between rich and poor, a theme to which he was to return in the last decade of his political life. 'Toryism', he predicted, 'will yet rise ... to bring back strength to the Crown, liberty to the subject, and to announce that power has only one duty: to secure the social welfare of the PEOPLE.' The whole book is a passionate plea for idealism to replace materialism as the motive force in political life; and as such there is little reason to doubt its sincerity. Disraeli was supremely ambitious, but never materialistic. The concluding pages of *Sybil* were couched in the high-flown language of an incantation, ending with a ringing appeal to youth which is among the most quoted passages of all his works:

We live in an age when to be young and to be indifferent can no longer be synonymous. We must prepare for the coming hour. The claims of the Future are represented by the suffering millions; and the Youth of a Nation are the trustees of Posterity.[13]

In the first two volumes of the trilogy Disraeli was staking his claim to be the ideologist of the Conservative party of the future, the guardian of the true spirit of Toryism; his underlying theme was an attack upon the soullessness of Peelite Conservatism. He was already, consciously or not, set on a collision course with Peel, and during the next two years was to struggle with Peel for the body and soul of the Conservative party, first with the support of Young England, later fighting alone.

The opening of the apparently unequal contest in the session of 1844 went badly for Disraeli; Peel was now in a far stronger position than he had been at the beginning of the previous year. Trade and industry were looking up, the 1843 harvest had been a good one, there was a net surplus of £1.4 million on the budget, and in Ireland the firm line taken by the Government with the ageing O'Connell had succeeded in bringing him to heel. Even before Parliament opened Disraeli received a shock. Peel, in keeping with Graham's expressed desire to drive Disraeli out of the party, deliberately refrained from sending him the customary circular summons to attend the meeting of Parliament. Disraeli sent his leader a pained but defiant letter, defending himself on the grounds that his criticism of the government had been no more severe than that of other Conservatives, particularly on its agricultural policy. 'I am bound to say that I look upon the fact of not having received your summons, coupled with the ostentatious manner in which it has been bruited about, as a painful personal procedure, which the past by no means authorised'.[14] Peel replied that Disraeli's past opposition had indeed led him to believe that he would not be justified in sending him the party summons, ending on a coolly ironical note: 'It gives me, however, great satisfaction to infer from your letter – as I trust I am justified in inferring – that my impressions were mistaken and my scruples unnecessary.'[15] The tone was courteous, but the underlying threat unmistakable; if Disraeli persisted in his previous course Peel would cast him into political limbo.

The threat seems to have shocked Disraeli, temporarily, into submission. In the first great debate of the session, an Opposition motion of censure on the Irish administration, he supported the government in an able speech, defining the Irish problem in a passage that was later to be quoted against him as: 'a starving population, an absentee aristocracy, and an alien Church, and in addition the weakest executive in the world'. Peel publicly congratulated him, and his sister, Mrs Dawson, once a friend of Mary Anne's, wrote to her urging her to tell Disraeli to offer Peel his hand: 'They are both reserved men and one must make the first advance; the other would accept it gladly.'

There was to be no reconciliation. In May *Coningsby* came out, to be received with rapture by Young England. 'I am so dazzled, bewildered, tipsy with admiration, the most passionate and wild!' Smythe wrote to Disraeli, and the book was generally well received, although literary enemies like Carlyle and Thackeray enjoyed lampooning the anachronistic affectations of Young England. Its appearance emboldened Disraeli to take up an ideological stand against Peel, supporting Lord Ashley in an attempt to reduce women and children's statutory working hours from twelve to ten. On the one hand Cobden, the political economists and the manufacturers believed that a reduction in hours would be disastrous to industry, and would only lead to a similar reduction in the hours worked by men; while on the other the non-coal-owning agricultural interest were always glad of a chance to tilt at the industrialists. Peel was not an inhumane man, but his acceptance in this case of the manufacturers' arguments that to reduce the hours of labour further would damage the ability of British industry to compete in world markets, indicated a shift of direction in his opinions. Manners put the case for the agriculturalists in a moving speech; the rejection of Ashley's Ten Hours Amendment, was, he said, tantamount to 'affirming in the face of all Europe – that the whole secret of our vast manufacturing power lay in the one hour before sunrise, and in the one hour after sunset which we snatched from the poor people of England!'[16]

Disraeli did not speak, leaving Manners, Cochrane and Ferrand to support Ashley but he voted for the Amendment and against the Government Bill in the subsequent division on 13 May. Liberals, Whigs and Radicals naturally voted against the bill, but when the Young Englanders were joined by such Tory stalwarts as Sir Robert Inglis and Colonel Sibthorp to defeat the Conservative government, the significance of the combination was not lost on Disraeli.

Peel acted swiftly and fiercely to put down the rebellion; bringing in a new bill after Easter he forced the deserters to rescind their vote by making the issue the survival of the government. He repeated these strong-arm tactics a month later, when faced with a protectionist revolt over the government bill to amend the sugar duties, a measure which the protectionists regarded as one more step towards Free Trade. Peel's reaction was hard and uncompromising; he told the Cabinet that a government which could not carry its measures should resign, making it known to the party at large that he would consider a further defeat on the issue as a matter of resignation. Even such a committed Peelite as Gladstone considered this tactic to be 'a great error'.

Disraeli was by now determined not only to oppose but to unseat Peel, even at the cost of putting the Whigs into power, and, on Sunday 16 June, on the eve of what was to be the decisive debate on the sugar duties, he made approaches to the Whig leaders with a view to engineering Peel's defeat. The occasion was a grand party given by Disraeli's friend, Baron Lionel de Rothschild. It included the Opposition leader, Lord John Russell, and other prominent Whig politicians, among them John Cam Hobhouse, who suspected from Disraeli's conversation that the party had been deliberately designed by Baron Lionel de Rothschild to bring Disraeli together with the Whig leaders at this critical week-end.

In conversation with Hobhouse Disraeli, speaking 'with that sort of confidence which sometimes belongs to men of genius, and sometimes to very impudent pretenders', told him that he believed that if the Whigs played their cards well, the government would be defeated by five o'clock the next day. Hoping that Hobhouse would retail this conversation to his colleagues, Disraeli declared that Russell was 'one of the very few men in the House of Commons who had a *strong* will and was fit to govern', and that 'Peel had completely failed to keep together his party and must *go*, if not now at least very speedily.'[17]

It was a curious error of judgement prompted by over-confidence; Disraeli underestimated Peel's hold over his party and overestimated the Whigs' desire for office at any price. As a liberal Whig, Russell could hardly have committed himself to combine with protectionists against a Free Trade measure, and in any case did not consider his party in a fit state to take over government. Meanwhile, Peel's party came crawling to heel; at a meeting at the Carlton on the day of the debate, a humble and placatory resolution was passed, with only Disraeli, Ferrand and a few others dissenting, affirming the party's determination to afford Ministers 'a general and cordial support'.

It was a blow to Disraeli's hopes, but he did not retreat from the stand he had taken, and the hectoring tone adopted by Peel towards his followers in the debate was to give him an opportunity to make a telling point against the Prime Minister. Peel accused those of his supporters who had voted against him on the previous occasion of conspirng with the opposition, threatening that if they did not rescind their vote and support him now the Government would resign.

Following Lord John Russell who warned members that a second surrender to Peel would 'exhibit yourselves to the country as a most degraded and slavish assembly', Disraeli rose to press home the point in one of his most slashing and effective attacks upon Peel. Speaking in a low, calm but distinct voice, he employed his most effective weapon against Peel – mockery. Taunting the Prime Minister with the inconsistency between his previously declared opposition to slavery and his present support of cheap (i.e. slave-grown) sugar, he went on: 'But it seems that the right hon. Baronet's horror of slavery tends to every place except the Benches behind him. There the gang is still assembled, and there the thong of the whip still sounds'.[18] At this the House erupted. Hobhouse reported that there was 'a tremendous cheer' not only from the Opposition benches, but from many Government supporters, while 'Peel, Stanley, and Graham sat in most painful silence and submission to the rebuke ... I never saw them look so wretched.'[19]

Elated by the effect of his speech, Disraeli was once more betrayed into over-confidence, telling Hobhouse before the division that 'all the Ministerialists who voted [against Peel] ... on Friday would be staunch, and that Peel would be beaten.'[20] As before, he had underestimated both the loyalty and the self-interest of the majority of the party, who were not prepared to turn out Peel – whom they still regarded as their only leader – in favour of the Whigs. In the division on Monday night the government majority was a reasonable twenty-two, including thirty-five Conservatives, absent from the previous division, who now cast their votes for the government. It was, however, a Pyrrhic victory for Peel; in riding roughshod over the feelings and opinions of his supporters, and twice forcing them to rescind their vote, he had caused a deep and festering wound in party loyalty of which Disraeli was later to make full use.

Disraeli's all-out opposition to Peel was to lead to the break-up of Young England. Both Smythe and Manners were under parental pressure to separate themselves from Disraeli and conform to the Peel line; indeed Smythe, deeply in debt and anxious for a place, was particularly vulnerable, and had voted with the Government on Ashley's Ten Hours amendment. Disraeli's attack on Peel was two-pronged; an attempt to drive a wedge between the protectionist majority of the party and their leader in Parliament, and to make an idealistic Young England appeal to the country at large. The session of 1844 was to be the last in which Young England acted together as a party; Smythe and Manners were to refuse to follow Disraeli's lead against the Maynooth Bill in 1845 voting in accordance with their religious views, and in 1846 Smythe was to take junior office under Peel.

But in the autumn of 1844, they were still united; this was to be both the apogee and the swansong of Young England. In July Disraeli, as author of *Coningsby*, had been invited to chair a literary meeting of the Manchester Athenaeum in October. The Athenaeum was an institution for the self-improvement of working men, and, alive to the propaganda potential of such an occasion, he had eagerly accepted, describing it to Sarah as a 'coup'. Both the Duke of Rutland and Lord Strangford – who no doubt shared their friend the King of Hanover's opinion that such institutions only served to 'make the lower orders too big for their boots' – were extremely nervous at the prospect of their sons appearing in public at such a place together with the distrusted Disraeli. As the Duke wrote to Lord Strangford:

> It is grievous that two young men such as John and Mr. Smythe should be led by one of whose integrity of purpose I have an opinion similar to your own, though I can judge only by his public character. The admirable character of our sons only makes them the more assailable by the arts of a designing person.[21]

In the event the speeches made at Manchester by the trio were high-flown but politically innocuous. Predictably, they stressed the marriage of industry and intellect and the benefits of knowledge, described by Disraeli as 'the mystic ladder in the patriarch's dream. Its base rests upon the primeval earth – its crest is lost in the shadowy splendour of the empyrean'. All this was hardly revolutionary, as the Duke wrote with relief to Strangford, '... not a syllable of party feeling or politics was uttered even by the arch-president'. The next public occasion for Young England was to be more controversial, as the group proceeded to Bingley in Yorkshire to join John Walter and Ferrand at a grand dinner to celebrate 'the introduction of the Allotment System and Old English Pastimes'. Manners, as the author of a pamphlet entitled 'A Plea for National Holy-Days' was to preside, while Ferrand told Disraeli optimistically that such measures would be an antidote to Chartism for the working classes.

Disraeli's own attitude to such paternalistic projects had been expressed in a gentle jibe at Manners in *Coningsby*: 'Henry thinks ... that the people are to be fed by dancing round a May-pole'. His speech at Bingley was to be a synthesis of the themes of both *Coningsby* and *Sybil*, a last celebration of the myth of Young England, whose aims he explained:

> We want in the first place to impress upon society that there is such a thing as duty ...
> If that principle of duty had not been lost sight of for the last fifty years, you would never
> have heard of the classes into which England is divided ... We want to put an end to
> that political and social exclusiveness which we believe to be the bane of this country.

The Bingley speech goes far to explain the bewilderment and distrust with which Disraeli was viewed by the English establishment; to him it was an argument for the natural alliance between a responsible aristocracy and the labouring classes, but to the English aristocracy a call for an end to political and social exclusiveness pointed to revolution and democracy. It is hardly surprising that Manners, whose ducal family epitomized the attitudes of the ruling class, should have reported to Disraeli at the end of October: 'some of the gentry are not best pleased with our movement.' The beginning of the end for Young England as a party was signalled by a letter which he wrote to Disraeli from Belvoir in mid-November. He had, he said, refused an invitation to a 'Young England' meeting at Wakefield, firstly because the Duke disapproved of political meetings outside his own territory, and secondly because there was 'no object but to laud Young England, and we by sanctioning it would at once separate ourselves as a distinct political party, which I for one am not prepared to do'.[22]

One may wonder how much Disraeli really cared about this implied warning that Young England would not be prepared blindly to follow him wherever he might go. He had already used them to the full both as a source of ideas and to provide him with a public image. *Coningsby* for which they had provided the inspiration was already published, and *Sybil* was in the course of completion. Young England had had its day, and the issues of the next session were to be narrowed to the simple question of Protection versus Free Trade. Manners was not alone in thinking that Disraeli might be aiming at the formation of a separate political party; a certain D.D. Jameson, who appears to have been on terms of some intimacy with Disraeli, wrote to him on 2 November referring mysteriously to the great sums of money Disraeli would need 'to work your new political party', and hinting at combining with 'some of the heaviest men in the Country' to make a 'hit on the Stock Exchange' to finance it. Disraeli, however, would have none of it, writing to his new financial confidant and adviser, William Wright, that he did not like 'Jameson's business.' He was realist enough to know that there could be no real political future for him outside the two major parties.

While the ducal splendours of Belvoir were as yet closed to him, Disraeli and Mary Anne had their first introduction to the Queen and Prince Albert at Stowe, home of Disraeli's early political friend, the Duke of Buckingham. The party was grand but uncomfortable as Mary Anne described it to Sarah, and they were forced to wait over an hour in an unheated vestibule before being presented to the royal couple. 'Fancy, dear shivering Dizzy', she wrote, 'and cross-looking Mary Anne, in black velvet, hanging sleeves looped up with knots of blue and diamond buttons. Head-dress, blue velvet bows and diamonds'. After the Queen had retired 'all became joy and triumph to us'; Peel shook hands with them and talked cordially for some time and the Duke offered Mary Anne his arm:

> taking me all through the gorgeous splendid scene, through the supper room and back again, down the middle and up again – all making way for us, the Queen and your delighted Mary Anne being the only ladies so distinguished. After this I retired to a sofa, with the Duchess, who told me that her Majesty had pointed Dizzy out, saying '*There's* Mr. Disraeli.' Do you call all this nothing?[23]

In a later letter she could not help recurring to the Stowe visit and 'its brilliant success; her Majesty, Peel, Aberdeen and all equally distinguishing us by their courtesy.' The reality behind the courteous façade was somewhat different; Peel's feelings towards Disraeli were anything but cordial, while the Queen thoroughly disapproved of him and of his conduct towards her Prime Minister the previous session which she had described to her uncle Leopold, King of Belgium, as 'the recklessness of a handful of foolish half-"Puseyite", half "Young England" people'.[24]

The simulated courtesies of Stowe were soon forgotten as Parliament reopened on 4 February 1845. This session saw the escalation of Disraeli's campaign against Peel into open hostility and to a point at which he parted from his two closest lieutenants, Smythe and Manners. There were to be no more appeals to Young England, rather a sustained personal assault upon Peel as Disraeli voiced the feelings and suspicions of a party that felt betrayed and abandoned by its leader. Disraeli's political instinct in going for Peel personally and on the ground on which he chose to fight him was unerring; as Greville was to note in his diary: 'The truth is that the Government is Peel, that Peel is a Reformer and more of a Whig than a Tory'.[25] As Peel's convictions moved ever closer to the powerfully-voiced views of Cobden, Disraeli ensured that the Conservative party should recognize the extent of their leader's betrayal.

The first skirmish took place on 20 February on a comparatively minor issue – the opening of the Radical Tom Duncombe's letters by the Post Office on warrant from the Home Office. The relative unimportance of the question only served to highlight the bitterness of the exchanges between Disraeli and Peel. Disraeli unwisely handed Peel a stick with which to beat him by making the unfounded assertion that Peel's lieutenant Bonham had been involved in a treasonable plot in 1802; this Peel was able crushingly to refute, thus forcing Disraeli to a public apology. Disraeli had accused him of 'simulating warmth' in his speech, an accusation that Peel turned against him:

> Notwithstanding the provocation of the hon Gentleman, I will not deal so harshly with him as he has dealt with me. He undertakes to assure the House that my vehemence was all pretended, and warmth all simulated, I on the contrary, will do him entire justice; I do believe that his bitterness was not simulated, but that it was entirely sincere.

Perhaps carried away, he continued ironically that Disraeli had a perfect right to support a motion hostile to the government, but not to say that he did it in a friendly spirit, ending with a quotation that was to prove a double-edged weapon:

> Give me the avowed, erect and manly foe;
> Firm I can meet, perhaps turn the blow;
> But of all plagues, good Heaven, thy wrath can send,
> Save, O save me, from a candid friend.[26]

Disraeli, undone by his *faux pas* over Bonham, could have been said to have lost the round. He sat down, but bided his time for revenge. A week later, on 28 February, rising to second Duncombe's motion for the examination of the Post Office official concerned, he was at his most deadly. With some justice he accused Peel of tyrannizing over his party, and refusing to brook any form of opposition from them, reminding him that a great many of his supporters had been elected to support measures very different from those proposed by the government. As if echoing Greville's words, he continued: 'I was sent to swell a Tory majority – to support a Tory Ministry. Whether a Tory Ministry exists or not I do not intend to decide; but I am bound to believe that the Tory majority still remains, and therefore I do not think that it is the majority that should cross the House but only the Ministry'. He underlined his point in a famous phrase: 'The right hon. Gentleman caught the Whigs bathing, and walked away with their clothes. He has left them in full enjoyment of their liberal position, and he is himself a strict conservative of their garments'.[27]

Disraeli had Peel on the hip; becoming ever more deadly as he approached his peroration, he proceeded to cut him down with his own weapon – Canning's verses on 'a candid friend' – thus obliquely reminding the House that it was Peel himself who had deserted Canning in 1827. The passage was a masterpiece of sarcastic fencing, beginning deceptively quietly with a quick hit here and there, advising Peel to stick to quotation rather than obloquy as the safer weapon. He complimented Peel on his masterly use of the art of quotation, masterly because 'he seldom quotes a passage that has not previously received the meed of Parliamentary approbation', and because he is aware of the electrical effect that the quotation of a great name can produce:

> Canning for example. That is a name never to be mentioned, I am sure, in the House of Commons without emotion. We all admire his genius; we all, at least most of us, deplore his untimely end; and we all sympathize with him in his fierce struggle with supreme prejudice and sublime mediocrity – with inveterate foes, and with 'candid friends'. The right hon. Gentleman may be sure that a quotation from such an authority will always tell. Some lines, for example, on friendship, written by Mr. Canning, and quoted by the right hon. Gentleman! The theme – the poet – the speaker – what a felicitous combination.

This was a new style of oratory and one which Peel found unanswerable.

The bulk of the Conservative party, restive and suspicious though they might be, did not greatly care whether the Home Office opened letters or not; it was quite a different matter when their sacrosanct Corn Laws were threatened. In March Cobden made a great speech in which he pointed out that the Corn Laws were in practice of no real benefit to the agricultural interest, and warned the 'gentry of England' that if they stood in the way of repeal and progress they were doomed to extinction. This speech marked the final turning-point in Peel's conversion to the cause of repeal; crumpling up his notes for the speech he had intended to make, he told Sidney Herbert who sat next to him, '*You* must answer this, for I cannot.' Herbert followed with a maladroit speech in which he used an unfortunate phrase about 'whining for protection' which roused the agriculturalists to fury. Their reaction was to put forward a hostile motion moved by the Protectionist MP, William Miles.

Disraeli seized the occasion of this protectionist revolt to make one of his most telling attacks upon Peel. He charged Peel with having courted the country gentlemen when in opposition, only to turn his back on them when in power:

> There is no doubt a difference in the right hon. Gentleman's demeanour as Leader of the Opposition and as Minister of the Crown ... It was a great thing to hear the right hon. Gentleman say, 'I would sooner be the leader of the Gentlemen of England than possess the confidence of Sovereigns' ... We don't hear much of 'the Gentlemen of England' now. But what of that? They have the pleasures of memory – the charms of reminiscences. They were his first love, and though he may not kneel to them now as in the hour of passion, still they can recall the past; and nothing is more useless and unwise than these scenes of crimination and reproach, for, when the beloved object has ceased to charm, it is vain to appeal to the feelings.

Peel, he said, had met their reproaches with arrogant silence and haughty frigidity: 'he sends down his valet [Sidney Herbert] who says in the genteelest manner, "we can have no whining here" ... And that, Sir', he continued, 'is exactly the case of the great agricultural interest – that beauty which everybody wooed and one deluded ... Protection seems to be in about the same condition that Protestantism was in 1828.'

This was a clever reference to Peel's notorious volte-face over Catholic Emancipation, and it was not the end of this damaging attack. If they were to have free trade, Disraeli said, then he would prefer such measures to be initiated by Cobden 'than by one, who through skilful Parliamentary manoeuvres has tampered with the generous confidence of a great people and of a great party'. He ended with a direct challenge to Peel: 'Dissolve, if you please, the Parliament you have betrayed, and appeal to the people, who, I believe, mistrust you. For me there remains this at least – the opportunity of expressing thus publicly my belief that a Conservative Government is an Organised Hypocrisy.'[28]

The House rang with shouts of laughter and Opposition cheers, but the speech had little effect on the division, Miles' motion being supported by only eighty votes. The Conservative party were sullen, but not yet prepared to desert the man whom they still regarded as indispensable. Disraeli's sallies evoked laughter but no support; nonetheless, his attacks upon Peel, widely reported in *The Times*, would affect public opinion outside Parliament, as Monckton Milnes recognized. 'His Philippics of late have been capital, most artistic and *telling*', he wrote to his friend C. J. MacCarthy on 26 March. 'It is the fashion to say he only injures himself by them, and this may be true for the moment; but he must take a long *range*, and twenty such speeches must tell in the country.'[29]

Peel had warned his party in no uncertain terms that he would do what he thought was right, whether they liked it or not, and on 3 April he brought in the Maynooth Bill which he knew would be objectionable to the ultra-Protestant section of his party. It was in essence an innocuous measure, increasing the annual Government grant to the Catholic seminary at Maynooth from £8,000 to £30,000 a year, and was designed as a gesture of conciliation towards the Irish Catholics in general and the Irish priesthood, who were suspected of fomenting sedition, in particular. Given the religious passions and prejudices of the time, however, it was bound to be a controversial measure. The Carlton rang with cries of 'No Popery', and Gladstone resigned from the Government for reasons so convoluted that hardly anyone understood them. Disraeli, after hearing his speech of explanation wrote to Sarah, 'Gladstone may have an avenir but I hardly think it.'

Disraeli's speech in the debate on 11 April was absolutely unequivocal; he was not interested in the intrinsic rights or wrongs of the bill or in the religious passions it aroused. The main thrust of his speech, which Hobhouse described as 'most bitter ... and so contrived as to wound him [Peel] in the most sensitive and assailable points of his charater', was that Peel was once again guilty of a dishonest volte-face, having brought down the Whigs on a 'No Popery' cry, and that he was proceeding against the will and without the consent of his party. The issue as he saw it concerned not Irish seminaries but English party government. Peel was tending increasingly to regard himself as a Minister of the Crown independent of party, abandoning the principles upon which his party had been elected. As Disraeli told the House in a much-quoted passage:

> Something has risen up in this country as fatal in the political world as it has been in the landed world of Ireland – we have a great Parliamentary middleman. It is well known what a middleman is; he is a man who bamboozles one party, and plunders the other, till, having obtained a position to which he is not entitled, he cries out, 'Let us have no party questions, but fixity of tenure'.[30]

The speech, according to Greville, was loudly cheered in the House 'and well bepraised out of it by Whig and Tory papers and all the Haters of Peel, who now compose a large majority of the world'. For Peel, the experience of hearing himself thus attacked was galling. Hobhouse, who was sitting opposite, noted that he hung his head down, changed colour and drew his hat over his eyes, while Graham beside him sat mute with a fixed grin, eyeing the opposition leaders to see their reaction. The Whig front bench, who supported Peel on Maynooth, behaved well, said Hobhouse, but Palmerston, Russell and George Grey could not refrain from whispering 'It is all true'.

The Maynooth affair offered one minor crumb of consolation to Peel: the refusal of Young England to follow their leader. Manners and Smythe, linked as they had been in their formative years to the Oxford Movement, could not sink to any anti-Catholic cry. Accepting the measure for what it was, a genuine, if cautious attempt to conciliate the Irish, they were bound to support it. In his winding-up speech on the sixth night of the debate, Peel singled out the prodigal sons, Manners and Smythe, praising Smythe's 'ability and eloquence' and predicting great future eminence for Manners. Ironically, by the time *Sybil* was published the following month, Young England, the myth which had been its inspiration, had virtually ceased to exist.

Peel won his majority on Maynooth, a considerable one. Although generally unpopular, he seemed invincible; Disraeli's 'philippics' had pierced his armour, but they had not unhorsed him. As Disraeli and Mary Anne left England for the Continent at the end of the session, Peel seemed to be as firmly in the saddle as ever. Greville, an experienced political commentator, summed up the political scene at the end of the 1845 session thus:

> The Session of Parliament has ended, leaving Peel quite as powerful, or more so, than he was at the beginning of it. Everybody says affairs are in a strange state, but nobody foresees, and few seem to desire any change. The world seems weary of what was called politics, there is not a spark of party spirit visible. The Whigs see no prospect of coming into office, or making a Government that would be able to stand ... On the other hand, everything like enthusiasm for Peel is extinguished; the Tories hate, fear, but do not dare oppose him. If the Whigs cannot see any alternative, the Tories can see still less and odious as Peel's conduct is to them, and alarming as his principles are, they still think they are better off, and on the whole less in danger with him than with any other Ministry that could be formed. He has completely succeeded in getting the Court on his side ... Everybody expects that he means to go on, and in the end knock the Corn Laws on the head, and endow the R.C. Church; but nobody knows how or when he will do these things.[31]

10 Peel's Adversary

Disraeli was in Paris when on 4 December 1845 *The Times* leaked the news that Peel had indeed resolved to 'knock the Corn Laws on the head'; two days later, faced with bitter opposition from Lord Stanley and others in the Cabinet, he went down to Windsor to offer his resignation. Excitement in the French capital at the news was almost as intense as it was in London. Disraeli wrote frantically to John Manners asking for concrete information, while, in his capacity as interpreter of the English political scene to the French monarchy, he was summoned to Saint-Cloud by Louis Philippe. To the king's enquiries about Gladstone, who, it was rumoured, would lead the Conservative party in the place of Peel, Disraeli replied that 'he was quite equal to Peel, with the advantage of youth'.

Privately, Disraeli seems to have come to the premature conclusion that Peel was finished. Moreover, in a curious letter to Palmerston written on 14 December, he implied that he himself had been responsible for Peel's fall: '... the great object of my political life is now achieved', he told Palmerston.[1] Convinced that the Whigs would form a government and that Palmerston, who was greatly distrusted by the French, would again become Foreign Secretary, Disraeli was reverting to his old role of French lobbyist. Somewhat impertinently he offered Palmerston his assistance in making a pro-French declaration at the meeting of Parliament; Palmerston forwarded this strange missive to his brother-in-law, Lord Beauvale, who commented: 'What a curious fellow to want to rehearse a scene with you to reassure Louis Philippe'.[2]

Nothing came of Disraeli's approaches to Palmerston; by 20 December, Lord John Russell having failed to form a Government, Peel was back in office, with the announced intention of repealing the Corn Laws in the forthcoming session of Parliament. Once again, Disraeli had underestimated Peel's hold upon his party; even the deaf old Duke of Wellington loyally toed the Peelite line, grumbling 'Rotten potatoes have done it all; they put Peel in his damned fright.'

The Duke was right, but only half right; the famine in Ireland which loomed after the failure of the potato crop in October 1845 merely precipitated a decision that had been maturing in Peel's mind since the previous session. Peel had come to accept Cobden's argument that the steadily-increasing population of England demanded more imported food, that wages would not fall if prices fell, and that in these circumstances the Corn Laws were not only no longer necessary to protect English farmers from foreign competition, but were actively harmful in preventing the importation of sufficient grain to satisfy the growing demand.

In theory and in practice Cobden and Peel were right; unfortunately for himself Peel, in using the urgency of the Irish potato famine as a pretext for immediate repeal without recourse to a dissolution of Parliament to endorse his great volte-face, chose a false position from which to launch. As the protectionists were able to point out, the real consequence of the failure of the potato crop was that the Irish peasant had no money with which to buy food anyway, and, moreover, Ireland continued to export grain to England throughout the famine years. In any case there was a compromise course open to Peel; he could have suspended the operation of the Corn Laws by Order in Council, achieving the immediate effect he desired and avoiding a headlong collision with his party. Peel had come to power in 1841 pledged to maintain the Corn Laws; having decided to reverse that pledge he should either, as he attempted to do, have left it to Lord John Russell, who had declared himself favourable to repeal; or, when that failed, he should have dissolved Parliament and gone to the country on the question.

Peel chose neither the compromise nor the wise constitutional course; he was convinced that the Corn Laws should be repealed immediately, and that he was the only man who could do it. Moreover, as Gladstone later testified, he believed he could carry repeal without breaking up his party; 'But he meant at all hazards to carry it', Gladstone added.[3] Peel was affected by the hubris that can follow in the wake of too much power; having taken office in 1841 with the largest single party majority in English political history, he had succeeded in forcing through progressive measures against the deeply-felt principles and prejudices of his party by riding roughshod over them. He had an understandable contempt for the political intelligence of the Tory squires who made up the bulk of his party: 'As heads see', he wrote to Sir Henry Hardinge, 'and tails are blind, I think heads are the best judges as to the course to be taken.'[4] He was coming ever closer to seeing himself as a leader ruling in the overall national interest without regard to party or parliamentary responsibility. Disraeli clearly saw this tendency in Peel as he wrote to Manners in a passage spiced with malice:

> He is so vain that he wants to figure in history as the settler of all the great questions; but a Parliamentary constitution is not favourable to such ambitions: things must be done by parties, not by persons using parties as tools – especially men without imagination or any inspiring qualities, or who, rather, offer you duplicity instead of inspiration.[5]

There is no doubt that by this time Disraeli truly hated Peel, seeing him as the arch-enemy. All his life he had talked obsessively about 'enemies' as if he somehow needed them to spark his brilliance and his will to overcome. Members of the House were shocked by the bitterness underlying his 'philippics' against Peel, as Lord Ashley was to note in his diary later that session: 'D'Israeli must have taken a vow of hatred to Sir R. Peel; no ordinary condition of mind wd. lead to such ferocity.'[6] Monckton Milnes preferred to see in it the emergence of racial characteristics: 'Disraeli has no Christian sentimentalities about him; none of your forgiveness of injuries; he is a son of the old jealous implacable Jehovah'.[7]

Hitherto Disraeli had fought Peel almost alone; the decision to repeal the Corn Laws was to end his political isolation and to bring him a friend who hated Peel as much, perhaps even more, than he did. Lord George Bentinck, second son of the Duke of Portland, was typical of his age and class. Handsome, imperious, devoted to hunting and the turf, he had, in his own words 'sat in eight parliaments without having taken part in any great debate'. As a silent MP for eighteen years, he had been first a follower of Canning, who married his aunt, then of Stanley, with whom he seceded from the Whigs to the Conservatives, becoming a staunch supporter of Peel. He was a man of vehement temper, of violent hates and prejudices, and many enemies, including his cousin the diarist Greville with whom he had bitterly and irrevocably quarrelled. He was an unrelenting enemy but a loyal friend, who was to stand by Disraeli through thick and thin, and who, despite his defects of temper, had many good qualities: a natural capacity for leadership, and a clear grasp of economic facts and statistics which enabled him to grapple with the complexities of Free Trade controversy. Loyal as he was he had refused to believe, even as late as December 1845, that Peel intended to repeal the Corn Laws; when the truth dawned upon him, he felt a fierce sense of betrayal. 'I keep horses in five counties, and they tell me I shall save some £1,500 a year by free trade', he is reputed to have said, 'but I don't care for that; what I cannot bear is being sold.' This was, indeed, the general view among the landed classes on both sides of Peel's conduct, expressed by the ageing Melbourne at dinner with the Queen at Windsor when he burst out 'Ma'am, it is a damned dishonest act.'

The partnership of Disraeli, the political maverick, with Bentinck, the representative of the aristocracy, was to be a vital factor in the drama of the next six months, in which Peel broke up the Conservative Party that he had created and was himself destroyed. Five years before, Monckton Milnes had written prophetically to Guizot that 'Peel has now got so strong a grip of the aristocracy that he must either drag them along with him in his advance or perish in the attempt'. Disraeli began the apparently unequal contest alone, the gadfly adversary of the man whom England regarded as the supreme leader of the country; backed by Bentinck, he became the spokesman of the bulk of the Conservative Party, leaving their former idol, Peel, broken and deserted.

This outcome, however, was far from being a foregone conclusion when Parliament assembled on 22 January 1846. The general opinion in the country houses that Christmas had been, as Disraeli was later to describe in his biography of Bentinck, that Peel would drag his reluctant party along behind him as he had in the two previous sessions; the only organized body hostile to repeal being the extra-parliamentary Central Agricultural Protection Society headed by the Duke of Richmond, of which neither Bentinck nor Disraeli was a member. The Tory squires came up to London sullen and apprehensive but not yet defiant, waiting to see what their leader would say; among them was Bentinck who, according to Disraeli, sat in the House 'with a stern look and a glittering eye, watching the treasury bench as an eagle would its quarry'.[8]

There was dead silence as the Prime Minister rose to make his speech. Peel spoke for two hours, explaining that the process of his conversion to repeal had been going on over the last two years, stimulated by the success of his free trade tariff policies, whose benefits he enumerated at length, and declaring that the autumn failure of the Irish potato crop had convinced him that the time had come to open the ports to foreign grain. In a deliberate attempt to lower the temperature of the debate, he wearied the squires with a battery of statistics: 'lucid narratives of the price of flax and wool, some dissertation on domestic lard, the contract price for salt beef for the navy, and the importation of foreign cattle'. It was, as Disraeli later described it, the tactic of an unrivalled Parliamentarian:

> When a senate after a long interval and the occurrence of startling transactions assembles if not to impeach, at least to denounce, a minister, and then are gravely anointed with domestic lard, and invited to a speculation on the price of salt pork, an air of littleness is irresistibly infused into the affair.[9]

Having beaten the bewildered squires into submission with statistics, Peel, proceeded to defy them, in a ringing peroration which even Disraeli admitted to be 'in his best style', reserving to himself the right to act in what he saw to be the public interest:

> I will not, Sir, undertake to direct the course of the vessel by the observations which have been taken in 1842. I will reserve to myself the marking out of that course; and I must, for the public interest, claim for myself the unfettered power of judging of those measures which I conceive will be better for the country to propose. Sir, I do not wish to be Minister of England; but while I have the honour of holding that office, I am determined to hold it upon no servile tenure. I will only hold that office upon the condition of being unshackled by any other obligations than those of consulting the public interests, and of providing for the public safety.[10]

The Tory benches sat silent and stunned under this tirade from their leader; their cheers were to be reserved for Disraeli, who, in his own words 'changed the frigid silence of this senate into excitement and tumult.' Leaping to his feet after a polite but rambling speech by Lord John Russell, he launched into what Greville termed 'an hour of gibes and bitterness', an out and out attack on Peel himself, accusing him of personal ambition and betrayal of the party system of government, making no reference whatsoever to Peel's carefully explained principles or to the facts and figures upon which he had rested his advocacy of free trade.

It was a dashing, clever and at times extremely funny attack; using the simile of Peel as the nurse who murdered the infant in his charge, Protection, Disraeli delivered his 'hit' in a low, monotonous but striking voice:

Ours was a fine child. Who can forget how its nurse dandled it, fondled it? (Loud laughter) What a charming babe! Delicious little thing! so thriving! (Loud laughter) Did you ever see such a beauty for its years? This was the tone, the innocent prattle; and then the nurse, in a fit of patriotic frenzy, dashes its brains out (Loud laughter), and comes down to give master and mistress an account of this terrible murder. The nurse, too, a person of a very orderly demeanour, not given to drink, and never showing any emotion, except of late, when kicking against protection.[11]

It must indeed have been galling for Peel, who had just delivered what was for him one of the most serious and important speeches of his life, to find himself thus wittily mocked by a man whom he despised, and, what was worse, to see his once-devoted followers rolling in their seats with laughter at the man's sallies, delivered in that calm though curiously effective manner. Disraeli's jibes were damaging. A great statesman, he said, is one who represents a great idea, not a man who never originates one but who is:

a watcher of the atmosphere, a man who, as he says, takes his observations, and when he finds the wind in a certain quarter trims to suit it. Such a man may be a powerful Minister, but he is no more a great statesman than the man who gets up behind a carriage is a great whip (Tremendous cheering and laughter). Certainly both are disciples of progress. Perhaps both may get a good place (More laughter).

Disraeli put it to the House that the issue was not so much one of protection versus free trade, but of parliamentary integrity and the validity of the party system. Peel, he said, had appealed to posterity to judge him over the heads of his supporters. But, he went on:

Posterity is a most limited assembly ... I advise ... that we all – whatever may be our opinions about free trade – oppose the introduction of free politics. Let men stand by the principles by which they rise, right or wrong ... Do not, then, because you see a great personage giving up his opinions – do not cheer him on, do not give so ready a reward to political tergiversation. Above all, maintain the line of demarcation between parties, for it is only by maintaining the independence of party that you can maintain the integrity of public men, and the power and influence of Parliament itself!

Disraeli's speech, wrote Greville, was 'wonderfully fluent ... his cleverness great' and it was 'vehemently cheered by the Tories'. Disraeli had given voice to their feeling of betrayal; the Protectionists would remain silent no longer. The debate was wound up by that colourful High Tory figure, Colonel Sibthorp, in a ferociously anti-Peel speech in which he summarized the change in the feelings of the party towards their leader. He was not surprised, he said, at this final deception on the part of Peel, who had already deceived them once on the question of Emancipation; he was only surprised that the 'right hon. Baronet had not gone before this, and joined the ignominious band of Corn-Law Leaguers'. His peroration expressed the revolution that had taken place in the Tory party: 'He had once said in this House, that the right hon. Baronet was the only man to save the country; but he now distinctly asserted, that if there was one man more likely than another to destroy the country, it was the right hon. Baronet.'[12]

The Tories cheered Disraeli, but they remained wary of him. Warned by their newspaper, *The Standard*, against associating with him, and encouraged by hints from the Duke of Wellington that Peel intended to compensate the agricultural interest for the weakening of protection, the majority decided to sit, uncomfortably, on the fence and await the unveiling of Peel's plan on 27 January.

The House of Commons was crowded on Monday night when Peel rose to make a protracted, deliberately tedious speech. Disraeli could only applaud the Prime Minister's parliamentary skill:

> This remarkable man, who in private life was constrained and often awkward, who could never address a public meeting or make an after-dinner speech without being ill at ease, generally saying something stilted or even a little ridiculous, in the senate was the readiest, easiest, most flexible and adroit of men.

He admired the manner in which Peel anaesthetized the anxious squires before delivering the fatal blow:

> And to-night the manner in which he proceeded to deal with the duties on candles and soap, while all were thinking of the duties on something else; the bland and conciliatory air with which he announced the reduction of the impost on boot-fronts and shoe leather; the intrepid plausibility with which he entered into a dissertation on the duties of foreign brandy and foreign sugar; while visions of deserted villages and reduced rentals were torturing his neighbours, were all characteristic of his command over himself and those whom he addressed.[13]

At length, after more than two hours of this, the Tories learned the worse – the repeal of the Corn Laws was to become total within three years, with a sliding scale of duty in the interim. The much discussed compensatory measures consisted of no more than a certain amount of local taxation relief to which the squires already considered themselves entitled, and some high farming schemes to improve agriculture in which they were not much interested. A feeling of blank disappointment, Disraeli said, spread along the Tory benches; Greville, analysing opinion at the Travellers' Club after the debate, wrote that 'the Protectionists were generally angry and discontented, none reconciled, and some who had cherished visions of better things very indignant.'

The indignation of the squirearchy provided Disraeli and Bentinck, together with the more active members like William Miles and Augustus Stafford O'Brien, with the initiative to organize concerted parliamentary opposition to Peel. At a meeting of the London Protection Society to which all Members of Parliament were invited, a parliamentary committee was set up to liaise between protectionist members of both parties. Managers were appointed to act as whips to secure the attendance of protectionist members at debates, and to look after by-elections that were then taking place as Peelite Conservatives resigned their seats to seek re-election on the repeal platform. The form of a Protectionist amendment to the Government Bill was agreed upon, to be moved by Miles and seconded by a respected county member, Sir William Heathcote. It was at this meeting that Bentinck first took an active part in organizing opposition to Peel's measure;

his tactics were to protract the coming debates on the Corn Laws for as long as possible in order to delay the measure, demonstrate the strength of the opposition to it and gain time so that protectionist members elected in the by-elections should have time to take their seats and swell the opposition to Peel.

The strength and organization of the Protectionists was a well-kept secret; Greville reporting on 8 February, the eve of the debate, that their anger had given way to despondency and that Peel was in high spirits. The contempt with which Peel continued to regard the mass of his party contributed to his confidence. The proceedings of 9 February when Miles moved the Protectionist amendment came as an unpleasant shock to Peel and indeed as a surprise to everybody outside the organization. It became clear that Peel was faced with a determined and organized insurrection of his party, and that to carry his measure he would have to rely on a combination of loyal Conservatives, Whigs and Free Traders. On 11 February, Peel despondently told the Queen that the Conservative Party would not survive, while Greville noted in his diary the next day: 'Nobody now doubts that the question will be carried, and that Peel will go out soon after.'

Disraeli, Greville sneered, was the Protectionists' 'great Hero'; for the first time he experienced the sensation of having a real party behind him. Organized with untiring effort by Bentinck, Disraeli and Stafford O'Brien, the Protectionists succeeded in protracting the debate on the first reading of the Corn Bill through February. Disraeli contributed a long speech full of statistics, intended, according to Greville to 'exhibit his powers in the grave line', in which he failed signally, being easily shot down by Sir George Clark who 'made a very complete exposure of the fallacy of his arguments and the inaccuracy of his facts'.[14] He coached Bentinck, who had a weak voice and no confidence in his oratorical abilities into making his first major speech, which even Greville, who hated Bentinck, admitted was 'a very remarkable performance, exhibit[ing] great power of mind, extraordinary self-possession and clearness'. Disraeli was a member of the party committee on parliamentary strategy, and was frequently to be found at the Carlton explaining complicated tactics to bewildered squires. 'Pray continue to be at the Carlton about three', Stafford O'Brien wrote to him on 23 February, 'the squires cannot in the least comprehend our schemes of voting and there may be some hideous confusion to-night.' Although the Government carried the first division on the Corn Bill by a majority of 97, the Protectionist hard core was already reckoned to number some 100 members, and by mid-March they had achieved the outward semblance of a party. They had elected two Whips, William Beresford and Charles Newdegate, and Bentinck was to be their leader, in close touch with Stanley in the Lords.

Bentinck and Disraeli had become not only political allies, but firm friends, in close correspondence with each other and acting in concert in Parliament in March where the Protectionists harried Peel on every issue, Bentinck leading and Disraeli seconding. Greville was shocked by the bitterness of the Protectionists against Peel and their insulting behaviour towards him. 'No Prime Minister', he wrote on 29 March, 'was ever treated as Peel was by them.' The state of parties was curious, he said, with the Whigs 'guarding' Peel until he should have carried repeal, when they would turn upon him at the first opportunity. As for the Protectionists: 'They do not care what happens so long as they can break up this Government; they do not care how publick business can be carried on, or by whom, whether a strong or a weak Government can be formed. Revenge is their sole object.' Peel, he added, 'holds office for the sole purpose of carrying *the* Bill.'[15] Indeed the missionary zeal with which Peel pressed on his measure, as if bent upon self-destruction, worried moderate supporters like Monckton Milnes, who told McCarthy on 16 May that he had lost confidence in Peel's prudence and management of men, looking upon him 'with a sort of compassion for his reckless honesty, a quality of all others disagreeable in a political leader'.[16]

Disraeli and Bentinck were pitiless; in the final clash over the Corn Bill on 15 May, Disraeli delivered perhaps his most brilliant and damaging philippic against Peel. He began by speaking against the Corn Bill, skilfully rehearsing what Hobhouse called 'the old arguments' in favour of protection; but the sting of the speech was in the tail, twenty minutes of sustained invective against Peel which, according to Hobhouse, 'was very powerful indeed, and produced a great effect in all parts of the House. Peel looked miserable, and his brother Jonathan more wretched still ... even Macaulay told me he thought ... the speech the best Disraeli ever made'.[17] Greville, watching the scene in horrified amazement, wrote that Disraeli 'hacked and mangled Peel with the most unsparing severity, and positively tortured his victim.' Lord Ponsonby, congratulating Disraeli afterwards, talked of his having 'crucified' Peel.

It was by all accounts an extraordinary scene: the livid gaslights hissing in the silent, crowded chamber; Disraeli's slight figure standing up directly behind his victim; his face with its usual pallor and the dark curl hanging low on his forehead; his delivery impassive; his stance motionless except for his habit of drawing his handkerchief out of his pocket when he was about to make a 'hit'. According to eyewitnesses, the 'hits' were many and deadly, producing an effect which is difficult to reconstruct from the flat pages of *Hansard*. In a stinging conclusion Disraeli charged Peel with political plagiarism:

> ... when I examine the career of this Minister, which has now filled a great space in the Parliamentary history of this country, I find that between thirty and forty years, from the days of Mr. Horner to the days of the hon. Member for Stockport [Cobden], that right hon. Gentleman has traded on the ideas and intelligence of others. (Loud cheering). His life has been one great appropriation clause. (Shouts of laughter and cheers). He is a burglar of others' intellect ... from the days of the Conqueror to the termination of the last reign, there is no statesman who has committed larceny on so great a scale.[18]

When Disraeli sat down, the roof of the chamber rang with Protectionist cheers, so prolonged that Russell who followed him was unable to speak for some time because of the noise. When Peel got up to defend himself, the Protectionists 'screamed and hooted at him in the most brutal manner', assailing him with 'shouts of derision and gestures of contempt'. Such treatment, Greville said, in a House of Commons where for years he had been an object of deference and respect, nearly overcame him. For a minute or more he was obliged to stop, his voice choked, and his eyes full of tears, before faltering out, 'The honourable Gentlemen have succeeded . . .', and, after a further pause, 'I was going to observe . . .'.[19] The non-Protectionist members were appalled at the spectacle, Hobhouse remarking that he had never seen Peel '*beat*' before, while Greville called it 'a miserable and degrading spectacle', comparing it with the hunting-field: 'They hunt him like a fox, and they are eager to run him down and kill him in the open.'

For Disraeli, the cheers of his party ringing in his ears, it was a moment of triumph, wiping out for ever the memory of the humiliation of his maiden speech almost a decade ago. There was, too, the pleasure of savouring his revenge, of publicly humiliating the man who had treated him with contempt. As he sat impassive among the wildly cheering Tories, Disraeli must have thought that Peel's extinction, 'the great object of my political life', was near.

The wounded Prime Minister did, however, have one weapon with which to strike back at his tormentor – Disraeli's application for office in 1841. If Disraeli, he said, after reviewing all the years of his public career, had in 1841 entertained the opinion of Peel which he now professed, why then was he prepared not only to support him but even to join him in office? 'It is still more surprising that he should have been ready, as I think he was, to unite his fortunes with mine in office, thus implying the strongest proof which any public man can give of confidence in the honour and integrity of a Minister of the Crown.'[20]

Disraeli, taken by surprise, was horror-struck, lost his head and lied in a stumbling, obscure, repetitive denial of having ever applied for office; '. . . I can assure the House nothing of the kind ever occurred. I never shall – it is totally foreign to my nature – make any application for any place'. He had lied before on this same point, publicly affirming to his Shrewsbury constituents in August 1844 that he had never asked Peel for a place; now, in Parliament, a far more dangerous forum, he lied again. As Peel's biographer, Professor Gash, points out, it was a compound lie; not only had he applied for office himself in 1841 but also for his brother in 1843. Why did Disraeli take the risk of being shown up as a liar? Lying to his constituents in far-off Shrewsbury was one thing, lying in the House of Commons quite another. There can hardly be any question but that he knew that Peel had him; his awkward denial shows that his conscience was far from clear. One can only surmise that it was a panic reaction; Peel's accusation fell like a bolt from the blue, boding disaster in the midst of triumph. He could not afford to be held up as a political opportunist in that place and at that time; and so he lied, taking the chance that Peel was relying on memory alone and had no concrete evidence to prove his allegation. It seems that he was lucky, and that Peel did not have the letter with him at the time. Professor Gash scouts previous assertions that Peel had it beside him in his bag, and Lord Rosebery in his *Life* of Peel records Peel as searching among his papers for the letter late into the night after the debate. The letter was among Peel's papers, and he eventually succeeded in finding it, for at some unspecified date he showed it to Lord Lincoln. Disraeli's luck held, but his denials and obscure references to there having been 'some communication, not at all of the nature which the House perhaps supposes, between the right hon. Gentleman and me' made an unfavourable impression. 'Disraeli had better not have spoken', Hobhouse commented.

Peel was not yet finished; in the division which followed, 327 voted for the Corn Bill, 229 against; but an analysis of the votes showed how tenuous the Prime Minister's hold upon his party had become. Of those Conservatives who voted in the division 106 supported Peel, but 222 voted against him. The Peelite whip John Young reported that, including those who paired in favour of the Bill or were absent for unavoidable reasons, the Prime Minister's support among his own party stood at 117, while the Protectionists who opposed him, including 5 who deliberately absented themselves, numbered 234. Hobhouse marvelled that the great Protection Parliament had actually passed the repeal of the Corn Laws: 'No living soul could have done this but Peel!' Peel had succeeded in forcing the measure through, but at the cost of his political credibility. As Lord Ashley wrote in his diary:

> This Statesman's career is without precedent in the history of Politicians – he has begun by opposing, & ended by carrying (not simply supporting) every great question of the day. He denounced 'party' that he might set up 'Peelism', he led the Tories & followed the Whigs.[21]

It was now apparent that Peel governed by grace of the Whigs, and indeed the Protectionists hoped that Whig Lords of Protectionist sympathies would join the Tory peers led by Stanley in a last ditch stand against the Corn Law Bill when it reached the Lords. All hopes of such a juncture were however dispelled by the Lansdowne House meeting on 23 May where the Whig Lords, who, in Palmerston's words, were 'all unanimous against the Bill', bowed to pressure from Russell to support it. The battle for the Corn Laws was over; a few days later the Bill passed its second reading in the Lords by a majority of 47.

The Protectionists had lost, but they were bent on revenge upon the man whom Bentinck in his letters to Disraeli referred to as 'the Arch-Traitor'. Now that repeal had become a certainty, Bentinck, Disraeli and Stanley had only one object; they no longer wanted a dissolution (which being called by Peel would have left him still in control of the Conservative Party), nor did they wish to face the country in the divided state of their party. They wanted to excise Peel, whom Stanley, once Peel's 'right arm', now regarded as a more dangerous liberal than Lord John Russell, to cut him out from the body of the party which they would then reunite. The issue they chose for their final attack was one that Disraeli had suggested, but which had been rejected, as early as 31 March – the periodically-renewed Irish Coercion Bill. Peel had made the tactical error of introducing the Bill as an emergency law and order measure before Easter, when the majority of Conservatives including Bentinck but not Disraeli, had voted for it, and then deferred its reintroduction until 8 June, thus destroying any argument for its urgency. Even so, it was risky ground on which to oppose Peel, for, although Disraeli and Bentinck could count on the Young Ireland Repealers, Smith O'Brien and his colleagues to vote against it, it was by no means certain how many Protectionists would bring themselves to vote against a law and order measure for Ireland. Bentinck told Disraeli on 5 June that they must make the issue one of confidence in the government and not a discussion of the Irish question, hoping thus to focus the discontent of the Tories upon it, and to attract the crucial votes of the Whigs upon whom Peel must depend. Fortunately for the two allies, although they did not know it, the very next day the Whigs held a meeting at Russell's house and pledged themselves to oppose the Coercion Bill as soon as the Corn Law repeal had safely passed the Lords. Peel was doomed.

In the event, Bentinck mishandled the debate, giving Peel a chance to turn the tables upon him. In blunt and intemperate language he insulted Peel and his supporters, whom he described as 'his forty paid janissaries and some seventy other renegades'. He accused Peel of being 'base, dishonest, incoherent and treacherous', alleging as an example of his base conduct that Peel had 'chased and hunted an illustrious relative of mine [Canning] to death.' While moderate men like Greville were 'disgusted' by the 'coarseness and virulence' of Bentinck's attack – 'that *blackguard* Lord G.B.' Ashley called him – the Protectionists cheered him to the rafters. Peel bore the onslaught quietly but when he rose later to speak about some trifling matter he was so upset he could scarcely speak. Peel's defence and Bentinck's charges against him occupied the interest of the House over subsequent days to the exclusion of the Irish Bill. Disraeli, using material supplied by Bentinck, returned to the charge with another bitter philippic; but unfortunately for the two friends, Bentinck's allegations were based on a misreported speech of Peel's, and on 19 June, Peel was able to produce documentary evidence to show that the allegations were unfounded, successfully vindicating his honour, and, in Greville's words, 'crushing G.B. and D'Israeli'. Bentinck rose to renew his charges, 'in a fury that his well-known expression revealed to me' wrote his ex-racing partner, Greville, 'with the dogged obstinacy which super-eminently distinguished him, and a no less characteristick want of tact and judgement, against all the sympathies of the House.' Peel's dignity contrasted favourably with Bentinck's violence, as Greville recorded: 'this affair has been of great service to Peel, and sheds something of lustre over his last days ... Nothing', he added with malicious delight, 'could be more miserable than the figure which the choice pair, G.B. and Disraeli, cut: and they got pretty well lectured from different sides of the House.'[22]

Peel's last days were long drawn out; the Irish debate proceeded on 22 June, and was adjourned until Thursday 25 June when the Corn Bill passed its final reading in the Lords, thus precipitating the long-awaited division in the Commons. Suitably the last speech of the night was Cobden's, delivered almost on a valedictory note, thanking Peel on behalf of the working classes, 'for the unwearied perseverance, the unswerving firmness, and the great ability with which he has during the last six months conducted one of the most magnificent reforms ever carried, in any country, through the House of Commons'.

Cobden's speech must have been gratifying to Peel, but it can hardly have helped him in the eyes of his party. If there had been any undecided Protectionist votes before the division, they would have been swung against Peel by this eulogy to a Conservative Prime Minister by the man whom they regarded as the arch-enemy of their class. It was a galling reminder that their leader had chosen to follow Cobden; that the League had won, and they had lost. There was only one man whom the squires could blame for their defeat, and they punished him in the division lobbies that night. Even though they knew that defeat for Peel would mean handing power to the Whigs, 69 Protectionists voted against the Bill and 74 abstained. The gentlemen of England, 'the men of metal and large-acred squires' as Disraeli was to describe them, joined with Whigs, Irish and Leaguers to defeat their former leader. Ashley, burning with righteous indignation, thought it just retribution for Peel's desertion of his own party: 'Those whom he had hoped to conciliate, not a Whig or a "Leaguer" to whose principles & for whose applause, he had sacrificed his own consistency, voted in his behalf! All the Whigs against him! Cobden against him! Bright against him!'[23]

Peel, in Disraeli's words, was a general without an army. The next day he resigned and the Queen sent for Lord John Russell. The Conservative party was irrevocably split and would be out of power for a generation.

On Monday 29 June Peel made his resignation speech to a crowded House. Defiant to the last, he delivered what Disraeli described as 'a remarkable speech ... of glorification and pique', reviewing the achievements of his administration, fulsomely praising Cobden, whose name, he said, must be associated with the success of his free trade measures, ending with a ringing peroration in which he celebrated Cobden's picture of him as the hero of the working classes:

> I shall leave a name execrated by every monopolist who maintains Protection for his own individual benefit, but it may be that I shall leave a name sometimes remembered with expressions of goodwill in the abodes of those whose lot it is to labour and to earn their daily bread by the sweat of their brows, when they shall recruit their exhausted strength with abundant and untaxed food, the sweeter because no longer leavened with a sense of injustice.[24]

Peel's words were to be engraved on wood and stone throughout the industrial towns of England during the nineteenth century, but in Parliament the speech caused deep offence. As Greville wrote, 'his unnecessary panegyrick of Cobden, his allusion to selfish monopolists, and his clap-trap about cheap bread in the peroration, exasperated to the last degree his former friends and adherents, were unpalatable to those he has kept, [and] were condemned by all parties indiscriminately.'[25] The speech and its reception symbolized the gulf which had opened between Peel and his fellow Parliamentarians.

History has tended to oversimplify the conflict over the Corn Laws, with Peel on the side of progress, the 'selfish monopolists' and 'large-acred squires' on that of reaction. There is a good deal to be said for this view, and it was one which Cobden himself propounded; but it was not that of the contemporary political class. To them Peel, in twice reversing his position on two great issues of the day, Catholic Emancipation and the Corn Laws, was guilty of betraying his party and the principles upon which he had come to power. It was this view, which concerned not economics but party principle, that Disraeli hammered home so successfully and it was this same general feeling among parliamentarians of both sides that was primarily responsible for Peel's fall.

Peel's fall had the elements of tragedy; if his methods were unwise, his motives were unimpeachable. He believed that he was saving the aristocracy from the consequences of their own selfishness, that in repealing the Corn Laws he was not only alleviating working-class distress, but removing a widespread sense of injustice that could lead to revolution. He chose to follow Cobden's way not only because he had, in Disraeli's words, 'a dangerous sympathy with the creations of others', but because he was by nature attracted to the principles of political economy. He could have adopted other ways which might have alleviated the sense of injustice and yet not split his party. He could have reformed the Poor Law, the target of working-class and Tory hatred alike, but he did not, because it was based upon the principles of economy that he believed to be right. He could have realized the ideas of Lord Ashley and the Short Time Committee in reducing the hours of labour in mines and factories, but he did not, because the theories of political economy were against it. In the words of one authority: 'He cared a great deal, he saw so much so clearly, and yet at some points he was shut in by political economy as if by a fog.'[26]

There was more than a touch of hubris in Peel's last two years in power; he did see himself, as Disraeli maliciously divined, as 'the settler of great questions' without reference to party ties, as he proclaimed in his opening speech of the session of 1846. Thinking along these lines and elated by previous successes in forcing his party to vote against their principles, he believed that he could carry the repeal of the Corn Laws without breaking up his party. As Ashley wrote in his diary on 22 May after hearing Disraeli's great philippic against Peel:

No one believes that Peel could have foreseen the tenth part of the sensation that has been caused by his political conduct. I cannot conceive that the notion crossed his imagination. He calculated, & despised, an expression of feeling; a small band of dissidents, a large band of turncoats, a week's debate, a large majority, triumph & commendations, & the total oblivion of the whole matter.[27]

That the outcome of the Corn Law affair should have been very different from that envisaged by Peel was to a very considerable extent due to the part played by Disraeli. Not only did he point out with extreme clarity the political principles involved, but his mocking attacks showed that Peel was vulnerable, dissipating the aura of fear and awe with which he had been hitherto surrounded. Disraeli himself thought that his extra-parliamentary campaign through the novels and the propagation of the myth of Young England was also largely responsible. Writing excitedly to Mary Anne from the Carlton with the news of Peel's resignation, he said: 'The Ministry has resigned. All "Coningsby" & "Young England" the general exclamation here. Everyone says they were fairly written down'.[28]

Disraeli's campaign both within and without Parliament against the 'organized hypocrisy' of Peelite Conservatism, his appeals to public opinion through his novels and through the Press, his manipulation of the myth of Young England, and, above all, his brilliant philippics helped tip the scales against Peel. One must, however, wonder how much he would have achieved had it not been for his partnership with Bentinck. The friendship and support of Bentinck, impeccably aristocratic, rich, popular, a great 'swell' who spent £9,000 a year on betting and racing, made Disraeli a viable ally in the eyes of the squirearchy who had hitherto steered clear of him. The curious combination of great aristocrat and Jewish genius was a powerful force in the destruction of Peel.

Disraeli's motives for his vendetta against Peel are, as usual, difficult to analyse. He hated Peel and rationalized his hatred by injecting it with political principle. Personal antipathy and disappointment at not being given office certainly played their part; it was also a question of Disraeli's political survival. As long as Peel was in control of the Conservative party, there could be no future in it for Disraeli. It does not, however, necessarily follow that, because there were elements of personal bitterness and political opportunism in Disraeli's campaign against Peel, his opposition was cynical and insincere. There is little ground for thinking that he did not himself believe what he wrote and said; he had always been an opponent of liberal economics as a determining factor in policy, and, partly from romantic instinct, an advocate of what he called 'the territorial constitution of England'. If one accepts this, then the central attitude of Peel's government offended against every canon of Disraeli's political belief, and certainly against the concept that he shared with the majority of his party, that a Conservative government represented the landed interest, which, to Disraeli, formed an integral part of the constitution of England.

The fall of Peel made Disraeli's political career possible. The main obstacle to his future advancement was removed. For the first time, he found himself among the leading members of a serious political party, and, through Bentinck, in touch with the English ruling class as represented by the great magnate, Lord Stanley. Moreover, with the exception of Stanley, all the men of ability in the Conservative party – Graham, Gladstone, Aberdeen, Sidney Herbert and Lincoln – had followed Peel into the political wilderness; they were now 'Peelites', divorced from the bulk of the Conservative party, and the bitterness accompanying the split over the Corn Laws made it unlikely that, in the foreseeable future at least, they would return to the fold. With his friend Bentinck as leader of the Protectionists, and himself the only man of outstanding ability in their ranks, Disraeli could look forward to receiving, eventually, his reward.

11 Emotional Undercurrents

'The most severe of critics – but a perfect Wife!', thus Disraeli eulogized Mary Anne in the dedication of *Sybil*; but behind the façade of the apparently perfect marriage lay tensions of which very few people were aware. For twenty years from his marriage until Sarah's death in 1859, Disraeli walked an emotional tightrope between his sister and his wife.

Mary Anne was devoted but also demanding, jealous, possessive, temperamentally inclined to hysterical rows and a mental state verging on instability. As early as September 1843 Smythe, writing from the Deepdene where the Disraelis were guests of Henry Hope, reported to Manners that he hardly saw Disraeli 'as he is engrossed in the twofold occupations of conciliating his "Proserpine" [Mary Anne] and converting his host to Young England'.[1] Some eight years later, in January 1851, Stanley's son the Hon. E. H. Stanley noted in his diary after a visit to Hughenden that one of Disraeli's most amiable characteristics was the gratitude which he never ceased to evince towards Mary Anne, 'to whom he owes much of his success, but whose claims upon him in return are neither slight, nor easy to satisfy.'[2]

Given Mary Anne's possessive nature, it is hardly surprising that she should have been violently jealous of Sarah, whose steadfast hold upon her brother's affections and role as his sole confidante were not lessened by his marriage. Sarah was the one person in Disraeli's life whom he never deceived, to whom he revealed all his secrets, not only of the periodic financial crises that he endeavoured to keep from Mary Anne, but of other, more dangerous escapades.

In November 1839, within two months of his return from his honeymoon, Disraeli began a clandestine correspondence with Sarah, writing to her and receiving letters from her through the medium of the Carlton Club where they would be safe from Mary Anne's jealous, prying eyes. It was disloyal to his wife, but he was determined to fulfil the pledge he had made to Sarah at the time of Meredith's death, and he knew that his sister, in the domestic tedium of Bradenham, lived only for him and, vicariously through him, in the pageant of London life that he presented to her in his letters. Most of the correspondence which survives is harmless enough; gossip about mutual friends, reports of his social progress – 'I have asked nearly sixty MP's to dine with me & 40 have come ... There is scarcely any one of station in the House or society that I have not paid this attention to.'[3] The style is reminiscent of his dandified days in the thirties: 'Venice too vulgar with Monckton Milnes writing sonnets in every gondola & making every bridge a bridge of sighs. I breakfasted with him today & he really was divine. ... such a stream of humor, fancy, philosophy & quotations – in every language.'[4] He reports the courtship of the heiress Angela Burdett-Coutts by his friend Walpole, known as 'the Pole', describing him as 'more elegant, fantastical & interesting than ever & talks of changing his name, retiring to Parma or Cremona or some city equally decaying and unvisited'. Not all his letters were to be so innocuous, but the fact that he should have thought it necessary to conceal correspondence as innocent as that quoted above, shows how much he feared the intensity of his wife's jealousy. He took great pains not to arouse Mary Anne's suspicions, telling Sarah to write officially sometimes to Grosvenor Gate: 'Write now & again to Gro[svenor] Gate. *Charles* [?a servant] our friend, will be absent four days he says.'[5]

With such domestic tensions, it is hardly surprising that a serious family row should have erupted towards the end of 1841; it was patched up, with Disraeli promising Mary Anne to cease any correspondence with Sarah, and practically to stop communicating with Bradenham at all. He did not entirely keep his promise, as is evident from a letter which he wrote to Sarah on 29 January 1842, complaining of a 'trick' played upon him by his former financial adviser, Pyne. Mary Anne, however, seems not to have suspected this, and relations between Grosvenor Gate and Bradenham were restored to the extent that Mary Anne went down to the D'Israelis early in 1842 to nurse her mother who had suffered an attack there. Disraeli, left behind at Grosvenor Gate, wrote her lovesick letters, talking of his streaming eyes at the memory of their last embrace, and of his sadness at entering her boudoir and finding 'my bird flown'. 'I can think of nothing but her infinite tenderness, & how cold & wretched all is with[ou]t her, who is indeed my only real companion, & joy & blessing.' He often, he told her, spoke her name, and, musing on her charming qualities, broke out into involuntary exclamations of love. He was indeed the bereaved lover: 'my widowed bed ... this was worse than all.'[6]

Just over a week later the fond husband's uxorious musings were rudely interrupted by news of another domestic scene at Bradenham. A fierce row had broken out because Sarah had been forwarding letters addressed to Disraeli to Grosvenor Gate without first showing them to Mary Anne. All Mary Anne's latent jealousy of her sister-in-law was rekindled, and she now once again suspected that Disraeli was carrying on a secret correspondence with her. She fired off a violent letter of complaint to her husband (which has not survived), as is evident from his pained, defensive reply:

I have just rec'd your letter wh. fills me with the greatest astonishment & affliction – I was not at all aware of the nature or circumstances of the case you mention, or that my sister had taken any part in the affair. I was vexed & mortified that after all that had past, anything similar shd. occur again. I never gave orders that my letters shd. be sent from Bradenham, & indeed never expected to receive any there. I did not write to my sister for two reasons, because I was not ware that she was particularly mixed up in the business, as I inferred in haste & total absence of interest with wh. I viewed the matter at first, that it was others who had done this – & 2ndly because as correspondence betw. her & myself had entirely ceased, it is to me by no means agreeable to resume it, so that since you have been at Bradenham, & especially during the first days when you were unable to write, & she addressed me entirely, as it were by your direction, I have confined myself merely on one or two occasions to a few barren lines of thanks, & requests that they wd. take gt. care of you.

After yr. letter of today I have thought proper to write to her as I view the matter in exactly the same light as yrself ... tho' I cannot suppose, or will not suppose for the sake of peace – that she or any others cd. act except from general inadvertence, & a total want of appreciation of the relations that subsist between us.

With regard to the general expression of yr. letter, I will only say it makes me very unhappy. I perceive that nothing can remove the perverted view in wh. you choose to consider my relations with my family. My correspondence, almost my cordial intercourse, with them has ceased; & as for Bradenham I can truly say, that after all that has occurred there, I never go there but with disgust & apprehension.[7]

One cannot but feel sorry for Disraeli, torn between his family and his wife: 'I perceive nothing can remove the perverted view in wh. you choose to consider my relations with my family'; this was indeed a heartfelt cry. It seems he took Mary Anne's part; she was his wife and he loved her, moreover, the discovery that her husband's letters were being forwarded without her knowledge was a just cause for annoyance even if not for the violence of her reaction. There was an additional reason why he should wish to be on good terms with her at that point, for this was the time of his financial imbroglio with Ford, when he was, as we have seen, depending on her assistance to carry him through. It was also the time of his greatest political isolation, when he was most in need of her sympathy and support.

At any rate, he apparently ceased correspondence with Sarah until June when good relations were restored, with Sarah sending up presents of poultry and vegetables, and Jem, calling at Grosvenor Gate, being cordially received by Mary Anne. It was at the end of that summer, in August 1842, that Disraeli wrote the letter to his father declaring that he owed his serenity of mind entirely to the support, financial and otherwise, of Mary Anne. The ensuing period was one of domestic serenity with Disraeli, happy at the success of Young England, writing *Coningsby* in his 'old writing-room' next to Sarah's at Bradenham, and sending Mary Anne affectionate little notes: 'My dearest, I feel a great desire for a cigar but will not smoke one unless you approve'. 'Dearest, I wish you wd. come up & talk a little over a point, if you are not particularly engaged'. 'How does my darling do? What are her little plans?' 'My dearest, it is impossible to get on better – I have already written ten pages, and have never stopped. Send me $\frac{1}{2}$ a glass of wine & a crust of bread'.

All seems to have been well until the hectic summer of 1845, when Disraeli was not only finishing *Sybil* but also composing and delivering his philippics against Peel. As he wrote to Sarah on May Day: 'I have never been through such a four months, and hope never again. What with the House of Commons, which was itself quite enough for one man, and writing 600 pages, I thought sometimes my head must turn.' Moreover, his parliamentary performances, Young England, and *Coningsby* had made him a celebrity and the Disraelis were ascending the social scale rapidly. They were invited everywhere, even to great Whig houses where they had not previously set foot, like Lansdowne House: 'a palace – nothing can be conceived more splendid or more courteous than the son of Shelburne', Disraeli wrote glowingly to Sarah. 'On Tuesday a gigantic ball at Lady Salisbury's', he continued, '& yesterday a colossal fete at Ashburnham House. Tonight ano[the]r invitation and an assembly at Lady Palmerston's. M. A. suddenly finds herself floating in the highest circles & much feted. She is of course delighted. Lady Jersey [a byword for snobbish arrogance] who meets us everywhere, in a stupor of malice and astonishment.' Even the awesome Lady Londonderry unbent, Disraeli having taken the first step towards resuming his friendship with her, broken off on his marriage, by sending her a copy of *Sybil*. Since the Londonderrys were proprietors of coal mines in County Durham, one may wonder with what pleasure the haughty Frances Anne may have perused the passages condemning conditions in the mines, but she replied to the author's overture with a polite note, and at Ashburnham House she was, as Disraeli reported to Sarah, 'most friendly to me & suff[icient]ly courteous to M. A.'[8]

But the strain of high society combined with acting as her husband's secretary reduced Mary Anne to a state of nervous exhaustion. As she once breathlessly told the young Lord Rosebery: 'I have no time, I have so many books and pamphlets to read and see if his name is in any of them. And then I have everything to manage, and write his stupid letters'.[9] Agitated secret reports were sent from the Carlton to Bradenham; Disraeli had been unsuccessfully attempting to persuade Colburn to publish another novel of Sarah's, and, apparently involved in yet another financial crisis, he was afraid that Mary Anne would insist on leaving town before he had settled his affairs.

> M.A., exhausted by work, is proceeding with her packing, with now almost fatal rapidity, for unless things rapidly mend (wh: after all, they generally do) it will be quite impossible for me to go; & I know not what excuse to make for my staying in town & for many other things. But I hope the best tho' daily disappointed. As it is, it is quite out of my power to be away: or even to avoid calling at this club where really I have no decent excuse to be. M.A. seems surprised.[10]

On September 6 he wrote what he called a 'public despatch', having told Mary Anne he would write to Sarah from the Carlton, but the contents were certainly not 'public', since, apart from reporting Mary Anne's 'low and shattered' state, he promised to sneak out of Grosvenor Gate early on Monday to write Sarah a 'private despatch with all my instructions etc'.[11] Mary Anne had authorized him to ask Sarah to forward their letters while they were away, but there were to be secret 'supplementary instructions' on this subject also. Sarah, he warned, had better answer this 'by return of post to *Grovr. Gate.*' In a letter written two days later, it seems that his financial worries at least were presently in abeyance, for, after saying that the financial future looks more promising than he can remember it, he goes on: 'I think it *quite impossible* that any unpleasant letters can arrive – You must howr. use your discretion.' Once again his loyalties were torn; Mary Anne was insisting on leaving London before his family arrived there, 'I need not say how many pangs it costs me to leave London without seeing you all – but there is no alternative. I can keep M.A. here no longer.'[12]

Mary Anne was certainly in a curious state, and her eccentric behaviour at this time astonished her friend, Baroness Lionel de Rothschild, who wrote a description of an interview with Mary Anne, 'our excellent and eccentric friend', so graphic that it is worth quoting at length. Mary Anne, she said, called on her without warning one evening, and threw herself into her arms, breathless and in a state of high excitement:

'I am quite out of breath, my dear, I have been running so fast, we have no horses, no carriage, no servants, we are going abroad, I have been so busy correcting proof-sheets, the publishers are so tiresome, we ought to have gone a month ago; I should have called upon you long ere now, I have been so nervous, so excited, so agitated, poor Dis has been sitting up the whole night writing; I want to speak to you on business, pray send the darling children away' &c.. &c., for it would, without exaggeration, take more than ten pages to put down conscientiously all the lady's words, not noting exclamations and gestures and tears ... I had never seen her in such a state of excitement before, and all I could do was to gasp out – 'Has anything happened?'

Mrs. Disraeli heaved a deep sigh and said: 'This is a farewell visit, I may never see you again – life is so uncertain ... Disi and I may be blown up on the railroad or in the steamer, there is not a human body that loves me in this world, and besides my adored husband I care for no one on earth, but *I* love your glorious race, I am rich, I am prosperous, I think it right to entertain serious thoughts, to look calmly on one's end, &c., &c.'

Mrs. Disraeli's conversation is not exactly remarkable for clearness of thought, precision of language, or for a proper concatenation of images, ideas and phrases, nevertheless, I had always been able to understand her meaning ... I tried to calm and quiet my visitor who, after having enumerated her goods and chattels to me, took a paper out of her pocket saying: 'This is my Will and you must read it, show it to the dear Baron, and take care of it for me.' I answered that she must be aware of my feelings, that I should ever be truly grateful for such a proof of confidence, but could not accept such a great responsibility. 'But you must listen,' said the inexorable lady: she opened the paper and read aloud:

'In the event of my beloved Husband preceding me to the grave, I leave and bequeath to Evelina de Rothschild [Baroness Lionel's daughter, aged six] all my personal property.'

'I leave you to picture to yourself my amazement and embarrassment,' Baroness Lionel wrote. 'Mrs. Disraeli rose and would hear no answer, no objection. "I love the Jews – I have attached myself to your children and she is my favourite, she shall, she must, wear the butterfly." Away rushed the testatrix leaving the testament in my unworthy hands', Baroness Lionel added wryly.

The Baroness spent a restless night, with pictures of dreadful accidents to the Disraelis alternating with visions of her daughter weighed down by Mary Anne's jewels, her emerald tiara and diamond butterfly. The next morning, she said, she had a hasty breakfast and then 'walked in a hurry to the abode of genius and his wife, to whom I returned the Will. There was a scene, a very disagreeable one.'[13] In view of scenes such as these, it is hardly surprising that there should have been rumours of Mary Anne's mental instability. In 1868, Lord Clarendon (who disliked the Disraelis) went so far when dining with the Queen as to make a joke 'about Mrs. Disraeli's men[tal] illness'; Victoria would not comment, merely saying repressively that 'Mr. Disraeli was a very good husband.'[14]

Mary Anne's exclamation 'I love your glorious race ... I love the Jews', was almost certainly inspired by the fact that her husband had begun to write his second novel on a Jewish theme, *Tancred*, which was to be the third volume of the trilogy. It is, however, indicative of her attitude to Disraeli's family, and to Sarah in particular, that she had clearly not considered bequeathing her jewels to her.

The Disraelis left London for the Continent shortly after the Rothschild 'scene', and drove to the French town of Cassel, where they took a house and settled down to a life of intimate seclusion. It was, as Disraeli wrote to Sarah on 17 September, 'an extremely savage place'. Few of the inhabitants spoke French, since the poorer classes spoke only Flemish; there was no library, no bookseller's shop, and no English or French newspaper to be had. With a Flemish cook to prepare such dishes as pigeons stewed with cloves, eggs and onions in a red brown sauce, Disraeli disciplined himself to a spartan regime, getting up at half-past five in the morning, and going to bed by nine, and in consequence, as he told Sarah, writing very regularly and making excellent progress on *Tancred*. The novel, however, was not, as Disraeli had intended, to be published the following year; at the end of November, with Mary Anne's health and nerves restored by two months of uneventful seclusion, the Disraelis left for Paris, where they were to receive the stunning news that Peel had decided to repeal the Corn Laws. Disraeli the novelist would have to give way to Disraeli the 'Peel-smasher'.[15]

Mary Anne seems to have recovered her balance and Disraeli continued his secret correspondence with Sarah, confiding to her, but concealing from his wife, the ever-present complexities of his financial affairs. Sarah's own domestic world was, however, changing. On 21 April 1847 Maria D'Israeli died, quietly and apparently unexpectedly, aged 71. Disraeli was in London, and received the news in a hurried note from Jem: '½ past 2 o'clock. Our dear mother has just departed. Sa bears up under this sudden calamity, but we must break it to our father, I wish you would come down it were only for a few hours, as he suffered most severely this day'.[16] Clearly Jem envisaged the possibility that Disraeli, absorbed in his own activities, might not wish to interrupt them because of their mother's death, but that concern for their father would bring him down to Bradenham. Indeed, the death of the mother who had been incapable of sufficiently appreciating his genius probably had little effect upon Disraeli, although a month before her death she finally came round to admitting her son had talent. In March, after Disraeli had made a speech in a debate on the annexation of Cracow, Sarah passed on their mother's reaction: 'Mama at last confesses that she never before thought Dis was equal to Mr. Pitt'.[17]

No doubt Disraeli hurried down to Bradenham to support Sarah in comforting their bereaved father, but his thoughts were concentrated on Buckinghamshire for reasons quite unconnected with his family. He was about to effect the transition from a lowly landless borough member to the more gentlemanly status of member for the county of Buckinghamshire and squire of a Buckinghamshire estate. Given the state of his finances, the first step was easier to achieve than the second; although even then it was only after two months of anxiety, intrigue and assiduous canvassing that he succeeded in being elected as one of the two Protectionist members for the county in the General Election of June 1847. It was, nonetheless, a considerable advance; as a county member Disraeli would in future be spared the hurly-burly and expense attendant upon borough elections. As his Buckinghamshire colleague, Caledon Du Pré, was to remark years later to Disraeli's biographer, Sir William Fraser: 'Do you think that Disraeli would have been Prime Minister if he had been fighting Boroughs all his life?' As a JP and a member for the county, Disraeli was on the way to achieving his dream of becoming part of the English landed establishment.

Ownership of a country estate in Buckinghamshire had long been Disraeli's aim. In 1837 he had contemplated, without any serious financial foundation, buying Chequers Court, and in 1842 Exmouth had lent him £10,000 at 3½% to purchase the Addington estate, but the sale had fallen through. Now the Hughenden estate was up for sale, its owner, 'Daddy' Norris, friend of the D'Israelis and the model for Mr Melville in *Hartlebury*, having died in the autumn of 1845 leaving no male heir. Disraeli had made plans to buy Hughenden in December 1846, the negotiations and the raising of funds to be carried on by Philip Rose, a local man with a partnership in a firm of London solicitors. Correspondence with Rose, who was privy to Disraeli's financial secrets (including the private bank account which he kept secret from Mary Anne), was carried on through the usual medium of the Carlton, and the negotiations for Hughenden were long drawn-out. Disraeli wrote optimistically to Rose on 24 March 1847: 'It is quite true that I have purchased Hughenden, or rather that my father has purchased it, but for me',[18] but the sale was not to be completed until September 1848, when George Bentinck and his brothers came to the rescue with a loan of £25,000.

Disraeli had been contemplating the likelihood of Isaac's death since August 1847, when he wrote to Rose from Bradenham that 'if anything happens here to place ample funds at our disposal', it would be as well to pay off the moneylenders,

Hume and Houlditch, to avoid a scandal. Nevertheless, when his father's death took place five months later on 19 January 1848, he was shattered. Isaac was eighty-one, blind, gouty, and totally dependent on the devoted Sarah to read to him and act as his amanuensis, but he had retained his interest in history and literature to the end. He was contemplating publishing three of his manuscripts under the title 'A Fragment of a History of Literature', and, when seized with his fatal attack, was, according to his son, listening to Sarah reading from a life of Lord Hardwicke and 'revelling' in an extraordinary interview between Hardwicke and George II. 'My only consolation for the death of my father is his life', Disraeli wrote sadly to John Manners. He had been devoted to Isaac, despite his absurdities, quick temper and his lack of sympathy for his son's youthful aspirations. He had been deeply influenced by him in his youth and grateful for the paternal pride with which Isaac had greeted his later successes. He had always had the assurance that, whatever others might think of him, he had an appreciative audience in his father and sister. Now only 'Sa' was left.

Disraeli was his father's principal heir and sole executor, the personal property being valued for probate at just under £11,000, of which one third each went to Benjamin and Sarah, one sixth each to Ralph and James. Benjamin as the eldest son was to inherit the real property, although there is unfortunately no record of how much that represented. Isaac bequeathed his collection of prints – he was one of the first connoisseurs to appreciate Blake – to 'my beloved daughter-in-law, Mary Anne Disraeli', and Benjamin made a selection from his father's books for his own library at Hughenden, mainly history and philosophy; the remainder, the 'belles lettres' collection, were to be sold at Sotheby's in March the following year for £418.2.6.

And so, even as Disraeli was becoming squire of Hughenden, the family home at Bradenham was to be broken up. The rented house was too large for Sarah and James on their own, Ralph being established in chambers in London. Disraeli managed to arrange a comfortable sinecure for Byron's old servant Tita, who had married Maria D'Israeli's maid, as a messenger at the India Office.

Sarah's future could not be settled so easily; at forty-six, still a spinster and unlikely to marry, she was condemned by Victorian convention to play no active part in life. Her attempts at a literary career having failed, her occupation would be to act as editor, in Benjamin's name, of a commemorative edition of Isaac's most popular work, the *Curiosities*, published at Christmas that year, and later to expurgate her brother's worst 'puppyisms' from his early books, *Vivian Grey* and *The Young Duke*, for the collected edition of his novels in 1853. With her father and mother dead, Sarah would now, more than ever, live only for Benjamin.

There was the question of where she should go; neither of her unmarried brothers seems to have wished to set up house with her, nor she with them. Ralph lived a happy bachelor existence in London, while Jem had always been difficult to get on with, good-hearted perhaps, but sometimes impertinent, rude and sulky towards his elder sister and brothers. Sarah planned to take a house in Hastings.

Benjamin disapproved: 'It is too triste for you – it's a melancholy residence – & watering-places, vagabond & rantipole & tawdry – I hate them.'[19] Jem's plans too were a source of annoyance: 'I cannot say that I am sorry the arrangements about Hughenden farm failed, as I never for a moment contemplated anything of the kind ... I am sorry James does not go to Bradm. [Bradenham home farm] as I think it the best thing on the whole. He continually writes me insulting letters wh: add to the many annoyances I labor under', Benjamin wrote irritably to Sarah on 30 April 1849.[20] Doubtless he did not wish to contemplate having the tetchy Jem farming on his doorstep at Hughenden, preferring him to remain further away at Bradenham. Jem himself, having written his brother a 'very offensive letter about the House [Bradenham]', followed it up with another hostile missive, 'saying I have acted "sneakenly". I don't mind the abuse but I do the spelling', Benjamin wearily told Sarah. A year later, James was installed at a place called Small-Dean, where Disraeli visited him, but he continued to add to his elder brother's annoyances to the end of his life.

The year 1849 was to be the stormiest period of Disraeli's private life. Not only was he in deep financial trouble, harried by his early creditors, Robert Messer and Thomas Jones, but relations with Mary Anne were reaching breaking-point. Recently discovered evidence in the form of a hitherto-unknown letter to Sarah indicates that he was deceiving his wife in other ways than concealment of his financial dealings and his correspondence with his sister. On 18 July 1849 Sarah received an agitated message from her brother which, as it is previously unpublished, is here quoted in full:

Carlton Club 18 July 1849

My dear Sa,

The storm wh: has, more or less, been brewing in my sky for the last 12 months burst rather suddenly yesterday, & at present I am residing at an hotel, leaving Grosvenor Gate to its mistress. An accès of jealousy brought affairs to a crisis & I found all my private locks forced – but instead of love letters, there were only lawyers bills & pecuniary documents – Had I not been taken unawares, I shd. have secured these papers, wh: may produce some mischief – but I hope not.

My case is very clear, tho' between ourselves it might have been otherwise – There is only one point in wh: I felt a little embarrassed, & used yr. name to carry me thro'.

I said I was going out of town last Thursday to Bucks Assizes – but I did not, & Meyer Rothschild unintentionally let the cat out of the bag.

I have replied that I went out of town to see you & that after the last rows, I was resolved that yr. name shd. never be mentioned by me to her again – & that the 'deceit' as she calls it, is the necessary consequence of her violent temper & scenes, wh: I will bear no more – So remember this – LAST THURSDAY.

I don't know how it will all end: I shall not give up a jot, whatever tides. I am rather confused & shaky of course, having had a bad night in a strange bed, without my usual conveniences, so pardon this rough epistle, & believe me yr. affec. brother

D.[21]

This curious letter was not included by Ralph Disraeli in his heavily expurgated edition of Benjamin's letters to his sister; somehow it escaped the destruction of incriminating or potentially scandalous material after Disraeli's death, possibly because it had been among Sarah's papers. It is the first, and only, evidence we have of a serious rift between Disraeli and Mary Anne; unfortunately it raises more questions than it answers. Had it not been for one phrase, one might dismiss the episode as referring to one of the recurrent jealous rows over Sarah, or over a concealed financial crisis. No doubt these factors played their part in the upheaval, but they do not seem to have been, on this occasion, the primary cause.

'My case is very clear, *tho' between ourselves it might have been otherwise* [my italics]' Disraeli wrote, admitting that he had lied in saying he was going out of town that Thursday to Bucks Assizes, and that, to save himself when Meyer Rothschild let slip that he had not done so, he had lied again, using Sarah to protect himself. One can exclude financial motives for this mysterious absence, since Disraeli says that her discovery of his secret pecuniary documents 'may produce some mischief – but I hope may not'. One can only surmise that it may have been a sexual escapade, but if so, with whom? There has never been a breath of sexual scandal concerning Disraeli after his marriage; Mary Anne's possessive love seems to have enveloped him to the exclusion of anyone else. Yet the absence of other surviving documentary evidence does not necessarily exclude the possibility that an adventure or adventures did take place at this time.

Disraeli was in his forty-fifth year, an age at which many men feel the need to prove themselves sexually at the onset of middle age; Mary Anne was approaching fifty-seven. No evidence has come to light as to who Disraeli's partner in the affair may have been, male or female. Over three years later Lady de Rothschild, an observant but by no means prurient witness, recorded that 'the Duchess of Somerset [the beautiful Georgiana Sheridan of Disraeli's youth] was desperately in love with him'.[22] But that was 1853, and does not necessarily mean that she was having an affair with him in 1849. It could have been a bachelor escapade with, say, George Smythe, or with one of the young men whom Disraeli increasingly attached to himself. In the present absence of any further evidence, one can only say that Disraeli certainly deceived his wife, and for a reason that was apparently neither financial, political, nor fraternal.

The affair was smoothed over somehow, but the period 1849–51 was to be one of emotional and political turbulence for Disraeli, struggling with an obstinate and suspicious party on the one hand and a jealous wife on the other, with the ever-present threat of financial disaster looming in the background. At one point his creditors seem to have threatened a scandal that would force him out of politics but, as usual with Disraeli, 'something turned up' and he escaped. Relations with Mary Anne were equally precarious; after the 'storm' of July, Disraeli dreaded going to Hughenden with her, although by early September the domestic scene appeared much less dangerous. 'Your letters, & none of mine now, are ever looked at,' he wrote to Sarah on 7 September. 'You may therefore write pretty freely – tho' not, of course, with the absolute safety of Carlton Club.'[23] It was, however, but a temporary lull; Mary Anne's jealous curiosity was soon alive again, and within a week he was having to lie in wait for the post in order to abstract Sarah's letters from the bag before Mary Anne could pounce on them, as he told Sarah on 16 September. 'In these cursed days of progress, Wyc. [ombe] has two posts & your letters arrive in the middle of the day sometimes ... as long as letters come only in the morning, all must be right – but I might be absent when mid-day letters arrive & then – '[24]

Sarah's letters in return were strangely reticent on the subject on Mary Anne, with no hostile references to her, nor any comments on her odd behaviour. Two hypotheses may be advanced in explanation; many of her letters are still missing, some lost, others destroyed, perhaps by Disraeli himself as a precaution against Mary Anne's jealous inquisitiveness. On the other hand, loyal and self-sacrificing as she was, she may have wished not to hurt her brother by putting any additional strain upon his divided loyalties, and she may simply have preferred to carry on her secret life with him without reference to his wife, as if Mary Anne did not exist. She was now living in lonely seclusion at Hastings, her correspondence with Disraeli the only joy of her existence. 'My dearest', she wrote to him at the Carlton on 16 August, 'I cannot thank you enough for your letters for I have not words to convey the value they are to me'.[25] When her 'year of banishment' was over, she intended to look for a house in Putney or Richmond, near a railway station so that he might easily visit her: 'I long to be in your atmosphere again.' He was ever-present in her mind as she pictured his daily movements. 'Yesterday', she wrote to him on 27 March 1850, 'about the time I thought of you as setting forth, the wind went completely round to the west & the sun shone ... I hope it was the same with you.'[26]

Disraeli's correspondence with Sarah was fond, but self-centred, much of it taken up with complaints about his health. Every autumn when he returned to Hughenden he suffered what he called an 'equinoctial attack at the fall of the leaf', while his letters from the autumn of 1849 until early 1852 complained constantly of recurrent trouble with his gums. Sarah recommended leeching, but even this unpleasant treatment did no good; he found his sufferings frequently absorbing to the exclusion of everything else. Even in late January 1852, on the eve of office, he wrote:

> It seems to me that I pass my life in remedies for that disorder of the gums of wh: I have often complained to you, and wh: greatly dispirits me. I have tried three dentists and have consulted surgeons & am going again to Rogers today. With everything at stake it absorbs me, & I think of nothing else & do nothing else but watch the progress of the complaint or try to baffle it. I fancy it affects my enunciation and & influences the tone of my voice. [The letter ended with the customary cautionary note] Don't mention my complaints in any letter addressed here.[27]

Rows and jealousies continued intermittently; the autumn and winter of 1849 being particularly difficult. Disraeli was bored and nervous in the strained atmosphere of Hughenden, tête-à-tête with a suspicious and emotional Mary Anne.

On 4 November he wrote to Sarah that they were to spend two days staying with the Chetwodes, then on for one day with Lowndes Stone, 'both dreadful bores but anything is better than Hughenden. I meditate decamping privately on Monday to town'.[28] And on the same day he laid his plans for 'decamping', writing to Rose, '*I wish you wd. write me a line to say that you want me in town about the twelfth inst. on business*'.[29] By Christmas it was no better. Disraeli had a cold, felt 'altogether paralysed' and unable to write a word of the Preface to his father's works. Mary Anne had a cold and a fever, which cannot have improved her temper; she was enraged because Ralph had failed to answer a note from her inviting him to Hughenden, and a wider storm was simmering in the background, possibly not unconnected with the July episode. Disraeli wrote wearily to Sarah; 'She never mentioned to me, that Ralph had called. I knew she was very angry with him, because he did not answer her note inviting him to Hughenden – but I was in hopes that this had been forgotten in the greater domestic ebullition.'[30]

In the summer of 1850 Sarah moved to Ailsa Park Villas, Twickenham, to be within closer reach of her beloved brother, missing him sadly when he left London in August for Hughenden. Lonely as she was, she was still not invited there, and at Christmas 1850 had to be content with the company of Ralph and James, while the Disraelis spent yet another disagreeable Christmas together at Hughenden. It was not until the autumn of 1851 that Mary Anne felt sufficiently softened towards her sister-in-law to invite her to Hughenden, but if Sarah was now *persona grata*, James D'Israeli was not. A quarrel, for reasons which have yet to be explained, had broken out between Mary Anne and Jem which lasted from mid-summer of that year until November, causing Disraeli much vexation. A letter which he wrote to Sarah from the Carlton on 1 August is indicative of the careful path which he had to tread between his wife and his family:

M.A. proposed this morning to dine with you on Sunday, if you were 'alone' but 'supposed you wd. not be' – She did not mean Ralph, but of course Jem – this led to one of our frequent rows upon the subject & I sd. that I shd. not write, or attempt to ascertain. Howr. on second thoughts, I deemed it best, as our time is numbered, to let you know, because it is just possible tho' very unlikely, that you might not expect Jem, tho' I wd. not for the world, even if you cd., that you should prevent his coming . . . If, as I quite anticipate you are so circumstanced that it wd. not be *advisable* for her to come, it is not impossible that I may come with Ralph but not as certain as I wd. wish for reasons wh: I will not dwell on now.[31]

The Jem affair continued through the autumn of 1851; poor Disraeli, trying to finish his biography of Lord George Bentinck which was to be published at the end of the year, found his work constantly interrupted with 'endless rows on the infernal subject' with Mary Anne. Moreover she was unwell and therefore making demands on his time when he had hoped to be 'entirely engrossed' with his biography. There was little of sympathy or affection for Mary Anne in her affliction in Disraeli's letters to Sarah at this time, rather a note of weary complaint:

M.A. came down here with what she considered a strain or sprain in her foot wh: she never mentioned to me in town (tho' I now learn she has had it some time) & cannot walk ten yards. It does not get better, & sometimes, tho' I can hardly intimate it, I think 'tis the gout. However it completely knocks up her principal resources, & terribly taxes me.[32]

A gouty Mary Anne must have been even more difficult than usual; possibly she did not like such signs of age being made public, for Disraeli warned Sarah, 'Don't allude any more to M.A.'s sprain; let her assume that I have told you it has recovered – wh: it has not'.

As if all this were not enough, Jem turned upon his harassed brother also, accusing him of not having done enough to help him in the world, and in particular for not getting him made a magistrate, which, said James, was perfectly within his power to do. Disraeli was obliged to tell him the embarrassing truth, which was that he had indeed asked the Lord Lieutenant of Bucks to make James a magistrate, and had had the mortification of being refused, on the grounds that James, who was running Bradenham farm, was a tradesman and therefore disqualified from being a magistrate. Disraeli justified himself to Sarah in a long defensive letter, his mind ranging back over a decade of mortifying efforts to help his brother. 'I have asked favours for James from Ld. Stanley, Sir Jas. Graham, Ld. John Russell, & the Ld. Lt. & always unsuccessfully. I regret that I moved in any of these instances – it was against my judgement, but I allowed, as I often do, feeling to guide me.'

One can only feel sympathy for Disraeli when one remembers Peel's scornful comment on his application on James's behalf in 1842 – 'just the sort of thing one would expect from such a man'. Disraeli was well aware of the obloquy that too eager pressing of his family's claims to advancement could bring upon him; moreover, his brothers were not men of any exceptional talent. Jem in particular had disqualified himself from claims to social advancement. 'The position of James is very disagreeable,' Disraeli told Sarah, 'but he has mainly himself to blame for it, as every man has'. Looking through his papers with regard 122to Jem, he recalled that he had first recommended that James should be a manufacturer, and then, when that fell through, a civil engineer, adding with some exasperation:

When he was his own master he might have got out of the hole in wh: he was & looked about him. He should have visited, as I told him, the U. States (& more lately) Ireland, to both of wh: I offered to give him great introd[uctio]ns but he was involved by low ties.[33]

Exactly what the nature of the 'low ties' was to which Disraeli referred we have no means of knowing. Six years later, after the death of his wife, Isabella Cave, James became involved with a Mrs Barrett who apparently acted as his housekeeper, and had at least one illegitimate daughter by her; while on his death in 1868, Disraeli received a blackmailing letter from a woman who claimed to have been dismissed from service with Augusta Leigh because of an affair with James.

All things considered, Benjamin was a good enough brother to James with whom he can have had very little in common; he later obtained first a County Court Treasurership and then a Commissionership of Excise for James, who late in life became something of a collector with a fine taste in wine. But 'Jem' at thirty-eight was still a black sheep, with a taste for small-scale farming and 'low ties'; his ill-spelt letters are evidence enough that he could hardly have been considered suitable company to mix with the Disraelis' grand friends at Grosvenor Gate. It was, therefore, somewhat ingenuous of Disraeli to excuse himself to Sarah for not doing more to better James socially on the grounds that there was no society in Bucks. 'It is impossible', he wrote, 'for me to advance his social position here – Even if there were not the domestic war, wh: I wd. entirely disregard, if I cd. do him good, there is no society here – we live in profound solitude, as everybody does.'

To Disraeli's great relief, the domestic war came to an end, and, on 7 November he was able to report to Sarah, 'You will be glad to hear that James and M.A. have at last, after having cost me much disquietude, made up their affairs very well – and now the talk is of a great family party at Xmas – '.[34] There was, of course, no great family Christmas party at Hughenden in that year of 1851 or in any other year, but at least things were now peaceful enough for him to concentrate on his biography of Bentinck, at which, he told Sarah, he was working night and day. Circumstances were looking up for James Disraeli too. He had abandoned his pretensions to being a JP and returned to farming and was, despite complaints of agricultural distress, making £400–£500 clear profit.

It would, however, be unfair to overstress this darker, private side of the perfect marriage; the Disraelis themselves, playing out their fantasy of two lovers, glossed over it. One famous story gives the key to their relationship; Disraeli, after the triumphant passage of the 1867 Reform Bill, left the celebrations at the Carlton to return to Mary Anne waiting for him with a Fortnum & Mason pie and a bottle of champagne. 'My dear,' he told her, 'you are more like a mistress than a wife'.[35] That was how they liked to see themselves – as lover and mistress rather than oddly matched couple of ageing younger man and a wife on the threshold of old age. It was typical of Disraeli to reject a more normal prosaic relationship; a woman was an object of romance and gallantry, therefore his marriage must be a constant romance. Possibly the pedestrian, domestic image of his mother haunted him; at all events he lavished compliments and attention on Mary Anne even in public, as a slightly shocked Lord Ronald Gower was to remark at Hughenden a month before Mary Anne's death, 'He often caresses her even before the servants'. The Irish MP Sir William Gregory, no admirer of Mary Anne whom he described as 'a most repulsive woman, flat, angular, underbred, with a harsh grating voice', said that George Smythe and the other young men who surrounded Disraeli irreverently called her 'Marianne' and found Disraeli's ostentatious gallantry towards her ludicrous. One evening, on coming up from dinner, he knelt before her, and covered both her hands with kisses, saying 'in the most lackadaisical manner, "Is there anything I can do for my dear little wife?"'[36]

Gregory, while admitting that Mary Anne was by no means a fool, was one of the many who noted that she was constantly saying stupid things, 'most frequently about him [Disraeli] which tended to make him ridiculous; as for instance, when the conversation turned on some man's complexion – "Ah", said she, "I wish you could only see Dizzy in his bath, then you would know what a white skin is."' If Mary Anne embarrassed him, Disraeli never showed it; Constance de Rothschild remembered meeting them at Ashridge when Mary Anne was

> getting old and not at her best, going to sleep after dinner in the drawing-room and waking up rather cross, and asking all manner of random questions. The younger members of the party rather made fun of the gallant old lady, and of her queer wig, so often awry, her flame-coloured dresses, her vain attempts at a somewhat youthful appearance; but her husband never seemed cognisant of such a state of things, and preserved his sphinx-like immutability of countenance, and his gracious, half-protective, half-deferential manner to his wife.[37]

Loyalty, gratitude, and a brave defiance of the outside world may all have played their part in Disraeli's public treatment of his wife, but his private letters to her, when not complaining about his own health, were also full of lavish compliments. Thanking her for her notes to him when they were both ill in separate rooms at Grosvenor Gate, he compared them to 'the productions of Horace Walpole or Madame de Sévigné', a hyperbolic description of Mary Anne's breathless disjointed prose style. It is not surprising that Mary Anne should have told Lord Rosebery that, although she had many people who called themselves her friends, 'I have no friend like him'.

Disraeli indeed, in young Stanley's words, 'owed her much'; her money and the fine house at Grosvenor Gate enabled him to keep up the position in society necessary to his political career. The house was big enough for the Disraelis to entertain at least sixty to dinner, an important factor when Disraeli became Leader of his party and was expected to dine them at his own house. Even Sir William Gregory admitted that the Disraelis' dinners were 'good and amusing', the guests being almost all connected with the political world, and the dinner furnished by a caterer at a guinea a head.

Grosvenor Gate, although a fine large house in a superb situation overlooking Hyde Park, was certainly not distinguished by an exquisite taste in furnishing or decoration. Sir William Fraser, who knew Disraeli in the middle and late years of his life, described him as having 'no taste', his house being furnished in a thoroughly conventional or 'upholsterer's' manner. The dining room on the ground floor had drab brown curtains and 'a bad copy of a well known Murillo' on its walls; the furnishings of the salons on the first floor were of yellow damask; and Disraeli's sanctum on the second floor was hung with pale blue poplin. There were, Sir William noted, about the house, 'none of the small articles of beauty which indicate refinement on the part of the householder'.[38]

The same could be said of Hughenden, which the Disraelis finally acquired in September 1848, moving in in mid-November. Before Disraeli came into the legacy that was largely to solve his financial problems in 1862, Hughenden was a plain, simple stucco manor house, set in a fine position on a hill above High Wycombe with beautiful views of rolling beechwoods and a common nearby covered with ancient juniper trees. Even when, in 1862–3, Mary Anne and her architect encased it in battlemented brick, it was never grand, nor filled with exquisite *objets d'art*. Disraeli had no ancestral portraits to hang on the walls; instead he formed a collection of portraits of his friends, and his idols Byron and Pitt. The objects were mementoes, like a cherished bust of Bentinck by d'Orsay, presentation plaques, and, unusually, an alabaster model of one of Mary Anne's small, shapely feet. Indeed, the only valuable objects that the Disraelis owned were Mary Anne's jewels. Disraeli was fascinated by jewels – the great ladies in his novels and letters glitter with diamonds – and at Hughenden he would carefully lay his wife's pearls out on the terrace to be warmed by the sun. Otherwise the only objects which Disraeli loved were books; he liked to work in his library, watching the sunlight playing over their spines, and to run his fingers over them. At first the library contained books on theology, the classics and history, a third of which came from Isaac D'Israeli's collection. Later in life, after Mary Anne's death, he was to collect rare books, particularly of the Italian Renaissance, his favourite period.

'I have a passion for books and trees', Disraeli later wrote in his *Reminiscences*; indeed his love for planting and conserving trees was as great as Gladstone's love of cutting them down. Whenever he came down to Hughenden, he would spend the first week 'sauntering about my park & examining all the trees', often carrying a small axe to cut away ivy from their trunks. He liked talking to woodmen; 'their conversation is most interesting . . . Nature whispers to them many of her secrets', he wrote. 'A forest is monotonous only to the ignorant. It is a life of ceaseless variety.' Disraeli's concern for his woods was carried beyond his own lifetime; in his will he specifically stated that no trees on the estate should be cut down.

Possession of Hughenden enabled Disraeli to identify himself with the 'territorial Constitution of England' in which he so passionately believed, as a gentleman of what he liked to call his 'native county' of Buckinghamshire. It was to be his refuge from the strain of assuming the leadership of a party of hostile squires.

12   The Mystery Man

Disraeli the 'Peel-smasher', the man who had overthrown the great Conservative Prime Minister, was an object of intense interest to the public, fascinated by the unlikely spectacle of a Jewish novelist among the leading members of a party of Tory squires. Although he had abandoned the rings, chains and exotic canes of his dandy days in favour of a more sober manner of dress, he still wore his hair in ringlets, and had recently adopted the small tuft of hair on the chin, known as an 'imperial', a French fashion which intensified his 'foreign' appearance. Disraeli was, and looked, completely different from his fellow-MPs, a difference accentuated by the deliberate air of mystery and aloofness that he affected in the House of Commons.

Fraser's Magazine for February 1847 devoted a long study to a description of Disraeli in Parliament. The author, George Henry Francis, admitted he found the task lamentably difficult, devoting several pages to an attempt to describe his subject's 'intangible manner'. 'The first impression', he said, as Disraeli 'with clothes shaped, apparently with too much care for effect, and those long flakes of curling black hair that can hardly be distinguished from the ringlets of a woman,' walked hastily, with a seft-absorbed air and a quick, short, shuffling gait towards his seat, was 'that of an effeminate, nay almost emasculated affectation. There seems to be a dandyism, not merely of the body but of the mind also.' Disraeli, he continued, walked with an habitual stoop, eyes cast down: 'See him where you will, he glides past you noiselessly, without apparently being conscious of the existence of externals, and more like the shadow than the substance of a man.' He seemed, said Francis, like one possessed by a monomania, and who has no natural relations with the realities of life. 'When he is speaking he equally shrouds himself in his own intellectual atmosphere', concentrating not upon his audience but upon the ideas he was enunciating and speaking with downcast eyes. If one of his friends attempted to break in upon his concentration with a suggestion 'the chances are that he will not notice him at all, or, if he does, it will be with a gesture of impatience, or with something like a snarl.'

Disraeli never relaxed in the House of Commons. He was never to be seen gazing round or lolling back in his seat as the other members did; he sat 'with his head rigid, his body contracted, his arms closely pinned to his side, as though he were an automaton'; looking, said Francis, 'like one of those stone figures of ancient Egypt that embody the idea of motionless quiescence for ever.' Disraeli's face was an expressionless, almost vacuous mask:

> The face is often abandoned to an expression, or rather a no-expression, that almost amounts to fatuity. The countenance seems to 'hang' . . . the forehead hangs (although the eye-brows are raised): the eyes hang, the mouth hangs, the chin hangs. The head hangs downward on the chest, the shoulders hang, and the whole body stoops.

Even when he was speaking his manner was odd and peculiar to himself; it would, Francis said, hardly be tolerated in anyone else being 'so careless, supercilious, indifferent to the trouble of pleasing':

> His action, where he has any, is ungraceful; nay, what is worse, it is studiously careless – even offensively so. With his supercilious expression of countenance, slightly dashed with pomposity, and a dilettanti [sic] affectation, he stands with his hands on his hips, or his thumbs in the arm-holes of his waistcoat, while there is a slight, very slight, gyration of his body, such as you will see ball-room exquisites adopt when they condescend to a flirtation. And then, with voice low-toned and slightly drawling, without emphasis, except when he strings himself up for his 'points', his words are not so much delivered as that they flow from his mouth, as if it were really too much trouble for so clever, so intellectual, in a word so literary a man to speak at all.

Disraeli never laughed at his own 'hits'; while those around him were convulsed with laughter, he stood there cool, impassive, waiting for quiet. 'The moment the shouts and confusion have subsided, the same calm, low, monotonous voice is heard still pouring forth his ideas, while he is preparing to launch another sarcasm, hissing hot, into the soul of his victim.'

Francis' remark on the dandyism of mind and body about Disraeli was an acute one; there was more than an echo here of the affected exquisite of the thirties. Deliberate carelessness, nonchalance, superciliousness, were all part of the dandy manner, as was the refusal to display emotion in public. Even in society the 'fiery eloquence' of the brilliant conversationalist described by Willis at Lady Blessington's, was rarely seen. There were occasions, his friend Lady Dorothy Nevill wrote, when he would hardly utter a word, and would 'assume an air which instinctively caused people not to attempt to rouse him from what appeared almost a lethargy'.[1] Only when a subject which particularly interested him was raised, or when he was in the company of his most intimate friends, would his charm and brilliance come to life. 'He does not talk much,' Sir John Hobhouse noted in his diary when the Disraelis spent Christmas of 1848 with him at Erlestoke, 'and what he says is given in set phrases and with hesitation, as he speaks in Parliament'. He was even more surprised by his guest's manner of saying goodbye. Disraeli, mindful of the fact that Hobhouse had been Byron's greatest friend, could not resist the Byronic touch: 'Disraeli took leave of me in a set speech, quoting Byron's lines, "Farewell". He had gone upstairs as he said, without taking leave, to avoid the pain of parting!'[2]

Disraeli had adopted this mask of iron reserve as self-defence for a temperament that was neither unfeeling or naturally phlegmatic. Intimates testified to the extremes of feeling he experienced, not in office when the sense of power sustained him, but in opposition, when one day he would appear elated and excited by events, the next totally cast down. An autobiographical line in *Tancred* was to give the motive behind the public mask: Disraeli wrote of 'the reserve which ever controlled him, unless under the influence of great excitement, a reserve which was the result of pride and not of caution.' It was the natural reaction of a proud man to a hostile world; he had revealed all too much of himself in his youth, done and said things which had held him up to public ridicule, and he had learned his lesson. 'I make it a rule now never to throw myself open to men', he had written in the Mutilated Diary in 1833. Dorothy Nevill, writing on Disraeli's conviction that he was unpopular, said that his early experiences of the House of Commons and the hostile reception of his first speech had made a deep and long-abiding impression on his mind. It would indeed have been strange had it been otherwise. Disraeli would not let the world see how much it had hurt him; he was determined to master his hostile environment.

That year Disraeli was to increase the mystification and suspicion with which he was regarded by the English political establishment by two public declarations of his belief in the historical and religious importance of the Jewish race. In the third novel of the triology, *Tancred* (published in March 1847), and in the Commons in December, in a great speech pleading the cause of Jewish emancipation, he came to terms with the anomalies of his position as a Christian and a Jew in a manner which many were to find both offensive and incomprehensible. For Disraeli, however, faced with an acute problem of identity, the views formulated in *Tancred* and repeated in Parliament represented the solution for which he had been searching since the genesis of *Alroy* almost eighteen years earlier.

Tancred, which Disraeli began in 1845, the year in which Peel's Jewish Disabilities Bill had opened every municipal office to the Jews (membership of Parliament still remaining closed to them), was Disraeli's favourite among his novels. It had originally been conceived as part of the Young England plan, an examination of the state of the English Church as an instrument of moral regeneration, but evolved into an exposition of the debt of gratitude which European civilization, and the English Church in particular, owed to the Jews as the founders of their religious faith. It was the expression of all his most deeply-felt convictions, combining his feeling for Palestine and the East and his theory of the superiority of the Jewish race with the revolt of the romantic against progress and scientific materialism. 'Our lot is cast in a material age. They never dream of angels. All their existence is concentrated in steamboats and railways', Disraeli wrote in a passage which presaged his famous anti-Darwinian remark at Oxford seventeen years later – 'My Lord, I am on the side of the angels'. Disraeli was always on 'the side of the angels', and never more so than in this curious, mystical and, finally, profoundly unsatisfactory book.

Once again Disraeli's hero, Tancred de Montacute, is young, rich and noble, heir to the Duke of Bellamont. Serious and deeply religious, Tancred, disappointed by the failure of the 'mitred nullities' of the Anglican Church to satisfy his spiritual needs, conceives the idea of a pilgrimage to Jerusalem in search of redemption. He is encouraged in this project by Sidonia, a thinly disguised London Rothschild, whose City office, Sequin Court, and select dinner parties are minutely described. Sidonia talks to Tancred of 'the spiritual hold which Asia has always had upon the North', recommending him to contact Lara, prior of the Convent of Terra Santa in Jerusalem, who is a descendant of an aristocratic Spanish Sephardic family and a *nuevo cristiano*, or converted Jew. He compares Lara's knowledge of the Old (Jewish) faith with the New (Christian) learning of the English Church in a manner extremely derogatory to the Anglican bishops, while introducing the main theme of the book: 'You see, he is master of the old as well as the new learning; this is very important; they often explain each other. Your bishops here know nothing about these things. How can they? A few centuries back they were tattooed savages'.[3]

This was hardly a tactful way of putting his argument to his English readers; but when Disraeli gets Tancred to the East, his statements become even odder and, to his Victorian Gentile audience, more offensive. Tancred visits Jerusalem and establishes himself in Syria where he meets the youthful Emir Fakredeen, modelled on George Smythe, who appears here more like his 'unprincipled little self' than as the high-minded Coningsby. He meets and falls in love with a beautiful Jewess named Eva, whom Disraeli uses as the mouthpiece for his main message. 'Half Christendom worships a Jewess', Eva tells Tancred, 'and the other half a Jew. Now let me ask you. Which do you think should be the superior race, the worshipped or the worshippers?' Disraeli goes even further, for not only do Christians owe a debt of gratitude to the Jews as the forerunners of their religion, but if the Jews had not crucified Christ there would have been no Christianity. He aims his arguments at a specifically British audience: 'Vast as is the obligation of the whole human family to the Hebrew race, there is no portion of the modern population indebted to them as the British people'.

As the book progresses Disraeli's arguments become even more mystical and confusing. He introduces an odd supernatural figure, the Angel of Arabia, who accords Tancred a visionary interview on Mount Sinai. The Angel, in Disraelian fashion, blames the sickness of human society on the atheistic influence of the French Revolution, proffering as a vague panacea for these ills 'the sublime and solacing doctrine of theocratic equality' of which he gives an equally vague explanation: 'the equality of man can only be accomplished by the sovereignty of God ... the longing for fraternity can never be satisfied but under the sway of a common father.' The Angel gives no practical advice as to how this is to be achieved, and Tancred's plans are scarcely more specific: 'We wish to conquer the world with angels at our head, in order that we may establish the happiness of man by a divine dominion, and, crushing the political atheism that is now desolating existence, utterly extinguish the grovelling tyranny of self-government.'⁴

This is Disraeli at his most confusing, and confused; all that clearly emerges is that the Angel, Tancred and the author are anti-Progress. In a famous passage which was to rouse *The Times* to fury, Disraeli declares:

> And yet some flat-nosed Frank, full of bustle and puffed up with self-conceit (a race spawned perhaps in the morasses of some Northern forest hardly yet cleared) talks of Progress! Progress to what, and from where? Amid empires shrivelled into deserts, amid the wrecks of great cities, a single column or obelisk of which nations import for the prime ornament of their mud-built capitals, amid arts forgotten, commerce annihilated, fragmentary literatures, and by populations destroyed, the European talks of progress, because by an ingenious application of some scientific acquirements, he has established a society which has mistaken comfort for civilisation.⁵

Tancred's cure for the 'fever of progress' is to 'work out a great religious truth on the Persian and Mesopotamian plains', and by revivifying Asia to regenerate Europe.

Disraeli, carried away by the onrush of his feelings and wild ideas, simply backs away when faced with the necessity of producing some solution to Tancred's vague plans for revivifying Europe. Eva prepares the reader for failure and anticlimax – 'perhaps all this time we have been dreaming over an unattainable end, and the only source of deception is our own imagination', she tells Tancred, a remark which could well be applied to the author. Disraeli had conceived the love between Eva and Tancred as a symbol of his most important message, the synthesis between Judaism and Christianity; but in the end he finds even this impossible to carry through. He rescues Tancred – and the reader – with the arrival of Tancred's parents, and the book ends flatly: 'The Duke and Duchess of Bellamont had arrived at Jerusalem'.

Not surprisingly, the world greeted *Tancred* with suspicion and bewilderment. *The Times*, which had welcomed the appearance of the two preceding volumes of the trilogy, wrote a largely hostile and condemnatory review on 2 April, indignantly rejecting the argument that contemporary society was rotten.

> 'We will not regard our active and progressive nation, intent as it is today upon the happiness of its people and the intellectual advancement of mankind, as used up, corrupt and selfish'.

It reproved Disraeli for writing a novel with a message: 'It is a bastard kind of writing – that of fiction "with a purpose", a form which might have been justified by "the fearful purpose" of Sybil but is certainly not so in this case by the "unsubstantial" aim of "converting the whole world back to Judaism".' The reviewer ridiculed this notion by pointing out the anxiety of contemporary Jewry to approximate itself ever more nearly to Gentile society, with particular reference to the Rothschilds:

> Whilst Mr. Disraeli eloquently discourses of a speedy return to Jerusalem, Sidonia buys

a noble estate in Bucks, and Sidonia's first cousin is high-sheriff of the county. So anxious, indeed, are the Hebrews generally to return to the Holy Land as a distinct race, that they petition Parliament for all the privileges of British citizens ... During the last ten years the Western Jew has travelled faster and farther from Jerusalem that he journeyed during ten centuries before.

In a sentence that only serves to reveal its underlying bias, *The Times* angrily rejected Disraeli's charges of English anti-Semitism, and also his romantic picture of a Whitechapel Jewish family celebrating their traditional feasts. 'Mr. Disraeli knows more of the Sidonias than of the Ikys and Abys of the brotherhood', the newspaper commented tartly. *Punch's* first mention of the book was frankly hostile and anti-Semitic with a cartoon accompanied by jibes of the 'old clo[thes]man' kind, while a further issue printed a parody by Thackeray entitled 'Codlingsby. by B. de Shrewsbury Esq.', which amusingly lampooned the whole trilogy.

Disraeli was not deterred by the public reaction to *Tancred*; he was to repeat his arguments in the debate on Jewish Disabilities on 16 December. The background to the bill was the election, in August that year, of Disraeli's friend, Baron Lionel de Rothschild, as Liberal candidate for the City of London. As a Jew, Baron Lionel had felt unable to take the oath requiring a member of Parliament to swear 'on the true faith of a Christian' and was therefore debarred from taking his seat. To remedy the situation, Lord John Russell announced at the opening of the winter sesssion his intention of bringing in a bill proposing the admission of Jews to Parliament. Disraeli was clearly placed in a very awkward position, with Stanley and the majority of the Protectionists bitterly opposed to the Bill, but, with his usual courage he intended to stand out against them and proclaim his support for Jewish emancipation. Loyally George Bentinck prepared to stand by him, dreading the consequences, as he wrote to John Manners:

This Jew Question is a terrible annoyance. I never saw anything like the prejudice which exists against them. For my part I don't think it matters two straws whether they are in or out of Parliament ... but I don't like letting Disraeli vote by himself apart from the party: otherwise I might give in to the prejudices of the multitude ... I am just starting for London, and I feel like a condemned felon going to Botany Bay ....[6]

The debate on the Jewish Disabilities Bill began on 16 December, with Russell arguing for the abolition of the disputed oath, on the grounds that religious opinions should not be a bar to the enjoyment of civil liberties which were the right of every Englishman. In the ensuing debate Whigs, Radicals and Liberal Conservatives followed the Russell line, while the Protectionists defended the exclusively Christian character of the British legislature.

Sir Robert Inglis, archetypal Tory and member for Oxford, led the opposition to the bill which he called 'an unmixed evil', with a very anti-Jewish speech. These civil privileges, he said, which were not enjoyed by Englishmen who did not possess the property qualifications necessary for a member of Parliament, the Bill proposed to give to 'some thirty or forty thousand strangers'. For some, whose very names and titles prove them to be un-English. For those who, as I believe, can never be English.' He declared:

> Two centuries ago there was not one single Jew in this realm of England . . . they came in drop by drop, preserving their own inherent and insoluble character. Did we invite them? – did they come in for our convenience? – did they not come in for their own? . . . can they ever, as true Jews, be amalgamated with us? . . .[7]

Inglis was joined in opposition by the humanitarian but deeply religious Lord Ashley, who was offended by the implication of the Bill that religion had nothing to do with politics and passionately defended the Christian nature of Parliament:

> He could not comprehend how Christianity could govern their legislation if a large proportion of the Members of the Legislature were persons who not only doubted, but whose very distinctive existence depended upon the continued, the conscientious, and persevering denial of the name of Christ and the precepts of the great Author of Christianity.

Pursuing this line of argument to its logical conclusion, he enquired thunderously of John Russell:

> . . . perhaps his noble Friend intended to admit everybody. Some years ago they stood out for a Protestant Parliament. They were perfectly right in doing so, but they were beaten. They now stood out for a Christian Parliament. They would next have to stand out for a white Parliament; and perhaps they would have a final struggle for a male Parliament . . .

According to the principle admitted by the Bill, he said, not only would Jews be admitted to Parliament, 'but Mussulmans, Hindoos, and men of every form of faith under the sun in the British dominions (Conservative cheers).'[8]

Later in the debate, Disraeli, the focus of attention, rose to speak. It was a strange occasion for him, Jewish by blood and Christian by religion, and, as Robert Blake has perceptively pointed out, the difficulties of the intermediary position in which he stood were indicated by the use of the words 'them' of the Jews and 'you' of the House of Commons. He had foreseen that the argument would publicly turn on the religious question, whatever the undercurrent of private anti-Semitism. His argument, therefore, aimed at removing Christian scruples by pointing out that Judaism and Christianity were practically synonymous, that Judaism was the foundation of Christianity.

'The Jews', Disraeli began, 'are persons who acknowledge the same God as the Christian people of this realm. They acknowledge the same divine revelations as yourselves'. No doubt many of the listening squires did not greatly like the idea of their Anglican faith being equated with that of 'the Ikys and Abys', but worse was to come. They should be grateful, Disraeli told them because, 'They [the Jews] are, humanly speaking, the authors of your religion. They are unquestionably those to whom you are indebted for no inconsiderable portion of your known religion, and for the whole of your divine knowledge'. At this point the first outraged cries of 'Oh!' broke out, but Disraeli only warmed to his theme. 'Every Gentleman here', he told the astonished House, 'does profess the Jewish religion, and believes in Moses and the Prophets', a statement that provoked a chorus of angry cries.

'Where is your Christianity, if you do not believe in their Judaism?' Disraeli asked them. He went on:

> On every sacred day, you read to the people the exploits of Jewish heroes, the proofs of Jewish devotion, the brilliant annals of past Jewish magnificence. The Christian Church has covered every kingdom with sacred buildings, and over every altar ... we find the tables of the Jewish law. Every Sunday – every Lord's day – if you wish to express feelings of praise and thanksgiving to the Most High, or if you wish to find expressions of solace in grief, you find both in the words of the Jewish poets.

No doubt most of Disraeli's hearers thought he was going much too far, and stirred uncomfortably in their seats. When, however, he prepared to launch into yet another paragraph on the same theme, '... every man in the early ages of the Church, by whose power, or zeal, or genius, the Christian faith was propagated, was a Jew', the dissidents in the House lost patience and shouted him down. 'Interruption' Hansard noted flatly.

At this, Disraeli too lost his patience. He rounded on his tormentors, telling them in so many words that much of their concern for the safeguarding of Christianity was humbug, and that the real reason for their opposition to admitting the Jews was pure anti-Semitic prejudice:

> If one could suppose that the arguments we have heard ... are the only arguments that influence the decision of this question, it would be impossible to conceive what is the reason of the Jews not being admitted to full participation in the rights and duties of a Christian legislature. In exact proportion to your faith ought to be your wish to do this great act of national justice ... But you are influenced by the darkest superstitions of the darkest ages that ever existed in this country. It is this feeling that has been kept out of this debate; indeed that has been kept secret in yourselves ... and that is unknowingly influencing you.

He ended defiantly:

> I, whatever may be the consequences – must speak what I feel. I cannot sit in this House with any misconception of my opinion on the subject. Whatever may be the consequences on the seat I hold ... I cannot, for one, give a vote which is not in deference to what I believe to be the true principles of religion. Yes, it is as a Christian that I will not take upon me the awful responsibility of excluding from the Legislature those who are of the religion in the bosom of which my Lord and Saviour was born.[9]

The debate was adjourned to the following evening when a division was taken. The figures were Ayes 233, Noes 186, the majority for the motion 67, with Whigs, Radicals and Liberals such as Gladstone voting in favour, the Protectionists opposing it almost to a man and watching with hostile eyes as their nominal leaders, Disraeli and Bentinck, voted with the majority for the Bill, which was subsequently defeated in the Lords. Measures for Jewish emancipation were to be introduced with almost monotonous regularity in 1849, 1850, 1851, 1853, 1856, and 1857 until, in the late summer of 1858, a compromise was reached by which each House should have the power to adopt the form of oath it wished. Lionel de Rothschild finally took his seat in the Commons as Liberal member for the City on 26 July 1858.

Disraeli had made his stand, a courageous one for a man who aspired to the leadership of the Protectionist party – a party which had revealed the depths of its opposition to the cause which he upheld, and indeed, the anti-Semitism which in most cases underlay it. He did not repeat it, remaining silent in most of the subsequent debates on the subject and twice voting against a Disabilities Bill on constitutional or parliamentary grounds. His silence drew down upon him the abuse of the Jewish advocates of emancipation and the taunts of Lord John Russell and *The Times*, accusing him of submitting his beliefs to the demands of party. Disraeli defended his 'silent vote' in a reply to Russell on 5 August 1850:

> Sir, if I thought that anything which I could say would have tended to accomplish an object dear to my heart as to my convictions, my vote would not have been a silent one. But, inasmuch as I believe that my opinions on the subject are not shared by one single member of the House, I thought that it was not inconsistent, both with good sense and good taste, that, after having once unequivocally expressed the grounds on which my vote was given, I should have taken refuge in a silence, which, at least, could not offend the opinions or the prejudices of any hon. gentleman on either side.

He reiterated that his views were, however, unchanged, claiming defiantly:

> Although I have no wish at any time to dilate on feelings or views which may not be prevalent or popular in this House, I will never relinquish them; and even now, shrinking as I do from offending the feelings of any one, I will still express my hopes that full and complete justice will speedily be done to the descendants of a race which you acknowledge to be sacred, and the professors of a religion which you admit to be divine.[10]

Disraeli was convinced that repeated airings of his unpopular views on the subject would be counter-productive, a view which, given the storm which his 1847 speech had aroused, was almost certainly correct. His friends the Rothschilds, however, accused him of being lukewarm in the cause of emancipation. Lady de Rothschild was disgusted at his silence in the debate of 1849, noting in her journal:

> Lord John [Russell] made a very clear, earnest speech, and Mr. Gladstone delivered a fine, silvery-toned one in our favour. Seven oppositionists attacked it [the Bill], but not very brilliantly and *Dis* was silent. Mrs. Disi was right when she spoke of the changes that Friendships undergo, last year he was our warmest champion and now![11]

Even in the last stages of the battle in the summer of 1858, when victory was in sight, the Rothschilds could not be sure of him. On 16 July Lionel wrote to his wife that he had pressed Disraeli 'that we were very anxious to have the royal assent this year, but you know what a humbug he is. He talked of what is customary without promising anything ... Mrs. Dizzy dined at Meyer's and told them the old story again, saying how much Dizzy had done for us and how angry he was once because we would not believe it'.[12]

Disraeli was not, as the Rothschilds suspected, lukewarm in the cause of Jewish emancipation but, as a practical politician and, by 1849, the official leader of the Conservative party in the Commons, he was anxious to avoid a confrontation between the emancipationists and the legislature. He no doubt foresaw that emancipation must eventually come to pass and he thought that the Jews in pressing too hard were doing their cause no good; indeed on one occasion, in August 1850, he told them roundly to be grateful for what they had already achieved and that they had no cause to complain of the British legislature. He saw the danger in admitting the traditional implication that to be pro-Jewish was to be anti-Christian, and, as leader of the Protectionist party he knew that if the measure was to pass, the hackles of Christian prejudice must not be raised against it. His solution, for both personal and practical reasons, was to stress the historical link between Judaism and Christianity.

But Disraeli's feelings for the Jewish race and his attitudes towards the Jewish religion were not one and the same; between himself and English Jewry there was a gulf bridged only by what Lady de Rothschild called 'his strange Tancredian strain'. He was not interested in the plight of the Jews in England, the majority of whom lived in conditions of poverty and degradation, nor apparently was he roused, as, say Gladstone would have been had he been in the same position, by the notorious cases of anti-Semitic persecution in Syria, Russia and even Italy during the forties. As Constance de Rothschild recorded, 'he believed more in the compelling power of a common ancestry than in that of a common faith. He said to me, as he has said over and over again in his novels, "All is race, not religion – remember that".'[13]

But Disraeli was a romantic Zionist; in *Tancred* he talked of 'those days of political justice when Jerusalem belonged to the Jews'. Four years later, when the young Stanley visited him at Hughenden, Disraeli spoke to him at length and 'with great apparent earnestness' on the subject of restoring the Jews to Palestine. Stanley, whose phrase 'apparent earnestness' shows the difficulty he found in believing that Disraeli had any deep feelings, was taken aback, particularly as Disraeli outlined his plans for the Jewish recolonization of Palestine while standing out in the open on a cold January day. 'Though usually very sensitive to influences of weather, he seemed to forget the thermometer in the earnestness with which, halting to enforce his views the better, and standing by the side of a plantation, he explained the details of his plan.' It was, Stanley recorded in his journal, 'the only instance in which he ever appeared to me to show signs of any higher emotion'. Suspiciously Stanley wondered whether this was one of Disraeli's deliberate mystifications, particularly since in the ensuing four years he never took any practical step towards the realization of his dream, but concluded that there could be no possible purpose in wishing to hoodwink his listener, and that, in this instance at least, Disraeli was sincere.[14]

The Times indeed was right when it surmised in its review of *Tancred* that Disraeli knew more about the Sidonias of English Jewry than about its Ikys and Abys. Since their marriage he and Mary Anne had become increasingly intimate with the Rothschilds of their generation - Lionel, Meyer and Anthony and their families. The first dinner they had attended as a married couple after their honeymoon had been an all-Jewish gathering at Mrs Montefiore's - Rothschilds, Montefiores, Alberts, Disraelis - 'Not a Christian name there', as Disraeli wrote to Sarah, 'but Mary Anne bore it like a philosopher.' Mary Anne not only bore it like a philosopher, but, as is evident from the scene with Baroness Lionel, embraced it all with passionate enthusiasm. The Rothschild ladies were among her most intimate friends, particularly the high-minded and serious Lady de Rothschild, born Montefiore, wife of Sir Anthony. On busy political nights when Disraeli could not leave the House of Commons 'Mrs. Dizzy' would spend the evening with Lady de Rothschild and her two daughters, indulging in the delights of 'high tea'.

Indeed it would seem that although the Rothschilds admired Disraeli's genius, they were sometimes wary of him, preferring the more straightforward Mary Anne despite her eccentric behaviour. Lady de Rothschild wrote of Mary Anne in 1848: 'Mrs. Disi was amusing and quick in her observations. In her constant smile there is perhaps a want of sincerity, but her enthusiasm is truthful and genuine, her heart is really kind and her talents of no ordinary description.' Mary Anne, she said, had 'penetration', a capacity for reading people, and good powers of observation. 'Strange', she commented, 'that she should be so blind to her own absurdities, however, notwithstanding them all, I like her, for she has a warm, true heart.'[15] Her attitude to Disraeli himself was more guarded. On 11 January 1853, less than a month after he left office as Chancellor after the defeat of his Budget, she noted at a dinner party that he was still downcast, commenting: 'Had Disraeli ever wished to carry out any great principle, or to bring forward some truly useful measures, he would not be so cast down; he would feel that in or out of office he had high and noble duties to perform and that his talents need never be unused - but his own elevation having been his only aim, he now has nothing to sweeten the bitter cup of ill success.'[16] Her husband's doubts as to the sincerity of Disraeli's attachment to the cause of emancipation have already been noted.

Nonetheless, despite suspicion of his sincerity, the Rothschilds liked and ad-mired Disraeli and their friendship was mutually useful. While on foreign affairs Disraeli doubtless made use of the exceptional intelligence service linking the London house of Rothschild with the branches in Paris, Frankfurt, Vienna and Naples. One may suppose that in return he supplied Baron Lionel with informa-tion that might be of interest. Although on different sides politically, they colla-borated on questions of mutual interest, the most famous instance being the Suez Canal purchase in 1875. Socially they saw a good deal of each other, in London, at Baron Lionel's sumptuous house Gunnersbury at Acton, and in Buckingham-shire where, between 1850 and 1880, the Rothschild family virtually bought up the Vale of Aylesbury, owning some 30,000 acres there by the end of the century. Meyer de Rothschild began the movement, acquiring Mentmore in 1851, to be followed by Anthony at Aston Clinton in 1853, then later by the next generation – Ferdinand at Waddesdon, Alice at Eythrope, Alfred at Halton, Leopold at Wing, and Nathaniel at Tring.

Disraeli liked and admired the Rothschilds, but he could still distance himself from them, referring to them and the great 'cousinhood' of Montefiores and Goldsmids as 'the Hebrew aristocracy'. Nor was he above gentle mockery of their love for lords. After the rejection of yet another Disabilities Bill by the House of Lords, Disraeli, who had sent on a present of venison from the Duke of Richmond, wrote to Sarah on 1 August 1851:

> Our establishment being on the point of breaking up I thought I had made a happy hit & sent it to Madame Rothschild (as we have dined there so often & they never with us) it never striking me for an instant that it was an unclean meat, wh: I fear it is. Howr. as I mentioned the donor, & they love Lords, notwithst[anding]. they throw out their Bill, I think they will swallow it.[17]

Disraeli's attitude to the Jews was paradoxical; identifying himself passionately with the genius of their race, he could still scoff at their orthodox traditions. Disraeli, Tory squire of Hughenden, saw himself as an Englishman.

13 *The Jew and the Jockey*

The immediate result of the row over the Jewish Disabilities Bill, described by Disraeli in a letter to Manners as 'the Hebrew explosion', was the resignation of Bentinck as Leader of the Protectionists on 26 December 1847. The resignation took place in circumstances of particular bitterness. It was prompted by a letter to Bentinck written by the Protectionist chief whip, the bigoted ultra-Protestant Irishman, William Beresford, expressing the dissatisfaction of the party with his leadership and threatening to secede from him if he did not resign. For Bentinck, who, in order to devote himself to leading the party, had sold his cherished stud in the autumn of 1846, only to see his former horse win the Derby six months later, and who had worked himself into a state of ill-health, his party's ingratitude was deeply wounding. As he told Manners: 'It is not merely what I have done or spent for them: but during these two years, I have shaken my constitution and shortened my days.'[1] It was a prophetic statement; within less than a year Bentinck was dead.

Despite Bentinck's resignation and the absolute dearth of talent in the Protectionist ranks, Disraeli was not yet to succeed him in the leadership. Stanley and a majority of the party were hostile to him, and a malicious campaign was waged against him by the whips, Beresford and Newdegate, aided and abetted by the journalist Samuel Phillips (a converted Jew whom Bentinck referred to as 'that circumcised renegade') through the columns of the *Morning Herald*. 'It seems they detest D'Israeli, the only man of talent', Greville commented on the leaderless Protectionists on 7 January. Bentinck suggested John Manners' elder brother, Lord Granby, as a figurehead supported by himself and Disraeli. As the son of a duke, a devoted Protectionist and Protestant, Granby was acceptable to the party, but, as Greville sneered, he was stupid and unimaginative:

> Except his high birth he has not a single qualification for the post; he is tall, good-looking, civil and good-humoured, if these are qualifications, but he is heavy, dull and ignorant, without ability or knowledge, destitute of ideas to express and of the art of expressing them if he had any; and yet this great party can find no better man.[2]

There was, of course, a better man, but at the meeting at Stanley's house in St

James's Square on 9 February at which Granby was elected, Disraeli's name was not even mentioned. Lord Malmesbury, a leading Protectionist peer, noted in his diary:

> There can be no doubt that there is a very strong feeling among Conservatives in the House of Commons against him. They are puzzled and alarmed by his mysterious manner, which has much of the foreigner about it, and are incapable of understanding and appreciating the great abilities which certainly underlie, and as it were are concealed by this mask.[3]

Granby, however, was not stupid enough to overrate his abilities and resigned the leadership only three days later, recommending his friends to 'consult George Bentinck and Disraeli'; there the matter rested, with the party leaderless and in confusion for the session of 1848. Bentinck, never one to let injustice lie, wrote to Stanley denouncing the party for their ungrateful treatment of Disraeli, whom he somewhat inaccurately described as 'earning by his writings £6,000 or £7,000 every two years or so' when not disturbed by the party's cries for his help. Stanley and Bentinck, once the greatest of friends, had quarrelled bitterly at a dinner at the Carlton the previous year and this letter can hardly have improved relations. Stanley, Bentinck said, had 'at the most generous interpretation', played the part of a Pontius Pilate in not dissociating himself from Phillips and the *Morning Herald* attacks upon Disraeli. 'I tell you,' he wrote, 'none of all this could have happened, had you played a generous part.'[4]

Disraeli, who had never experienced such loyalty in public life before, must have been grateful for Bentinck's bulldog defence of him, and the two collaborated in attacking Russell's government through the session of 1848, with Bentinck bellowing and thumping as usual, while Disraeli made Cobden 'writhe' as Peel had under his sarcasms.

It was to be their last parliamentary collaboration. On 21 September George Bentinck died, apparently of a heart attack, while walking alone from Welbeck to Thoresby to stay with Lord Manners. Disraeli received the news at Wynyard where he and Mary Anne were staying with the Londonderrys; a fellow guest recalled that his face underwent such a change that he thought he was going to die himself. It was indeed a severe loss; Bentinck had been a true friend and ally, and Disraeli had returned his affection. Even Monckton Milnes while saying cattily that Disraeli had 'made good use of his [George Bentinck's] ducality', admitted that he had been genuinely fond of him. Bentinck's valet Gardiner wrote to Disraeli as 'the bosom friend and daily Companion' of his late master, whom he pathetically described as 'the best friend I ever had'; and his brother, Lord Henry, told Disraeli: 'he had no secrets from you'. Ralph D'Israeli wrote to Mary Anne: 'How much dear Diz has suffered: but this is far, far beyond all', which considering that their father had died that same year is perhaps the strongest testimony of all to the bond that had existed between the two men.

The general opinion was that Bentinck had worked himself to death. Disraeli, on his return to London, found a six-page letter written by Bentinck an hour before he set off on his 'fatal walk'. It was a long, considered discussion of the issues likely to be raised the next session, 'full', Disraeli wrote sadly to Manners, 'of his accustomed vigour and keen interest in existence'. Manners replied that Bentinck had been 'as much destroyed by Parliament as ever soldier was by bayonet or bullet'. Manners and Disraeli had been the two men closest to him, as Manners wrote five days after his death:

> Until to-day I have really not had the heart to write a line to any one on this awful, well-nigh incredible loss, and now my thoughts turn first to you, who of all his friends most truly appreciated him, and who will most bitterly and truly mourn over this appalling calamity ... it was no ordinary tie of political or social friendship that bound us together, and to no one but you would I say so much.[5]

Disraeli replied in the same strain, 'I can't allow your letter to pass unrecognised, though I am quite incapable of dwelling upon its subject. I can neither offer, nor receive, consolation'.[6] In true Victorian fashion, Disraeli kept a lock of hair and the pen with which Bentinck had written his last letter as mementoes of his friend, and, using papers supplied by the family, was to write a hagiographical biography of Bentinck's brief political life, published three years later.

George Bentinck was buried a week later in the family vault in Marylebone, described by Disraeli as 'a small building in a dingy street, now a chapel of ease', on a dark, cold, drizzling autumn day. His death produced, as is often the case, a revulsion of public feeling in his favour. Even Greville devoted several pages to an obituary of his late enemy and cousin in which he strove to be objective:

> Notwithstanding his arrogance and violence, his constant quarrels and the intolerable language he indulged in, he was popular in the House of Commons, and liked more or less wherever he went. He was extremely good-looking and particularly distinguished and high-bred; then he was gay, agreeable, obliging, and good-natured, charming with those he liked, and by whom he was not thwarted and opposed. His undaunted courage and the confident, haughty audacity with which he attacked or stood up against all opponents, being afraid of no man, inspired a general sentiment of admiration and respect.[7]

Not all George Bentinck's former enemies were so generous. The Duke of Bedford wrote disgustedly: 'The nonsense that is written and spoken about G.B. surpasses anything I ever recollect.' Disraeli, who knew all too well what had been written and said about Bentinck in his lifetime, told Sarah he had met Exmouth in tears in the street – 'so I suppose it is the fashion to praise him', he wrote bitterly.

Bentinck's death was of as much service to Disraeli, perhaps even more, than his life had been. Disraeli was without a political patron, but he was also now unquestionably the first candidate for the leadership, as Malmesbury noted in his diary: 'No one but Disraeli can fill his place ... It [G.B.'s death] will leave Disraeli without a rival, and enable him to show the great genius he undoubtedly possesses without any comparisons.' Gratitude to the dead leader, perhaps not unmixed with guilt at the treatment to which he had been subjected, caused an emotional groundswell in Disraeli's favour among leading Protectionists. The Duke of Newcastle wrote eulogizing Bentinck and exhorted Disraeli to 'promote with your now well-known ability the ... cause of our country.' Henry Bentinck, Lord George's brother, who with his elder brother, Lord Titchfield, had agreed to carry on the £25,000 loan for Hughenden, even proposed to give up hunting and devote himself to politics in support of Disraeli. Disraeli's own strategy in the campaign for the leadership would be to let his supporters make the running while he worked behind the scenes, making contacts through quiet dinners and providential meetings in clubs. He took pains to allay Protestant suspicions by ostentatiously cultivating such ecclesiastical figures as Samuel Wilberforce, Bishop of Oxford; and he acquired a new and surprising ally in Samuel Phillips, the journalist who had attacked him so bitterly the previous year, but who was now prepared to work his contacts with the right-wing Protestant Protectionists of the National Club on Disraeli's behalf.

One powerful man, however, stood in his way. Edward Stanley, later 14th Earl of Derby, was to play an important part in Disraeli's political life over the next twenty years. Although only five years older than Disraeli, he seemed to belong to a different political generation – that of Peel, Palmerston, Grey and Melbourne – having been an MP since 1820 when he was only twenty-one. As a young man he had followed his family's Whig tradition and had been a member of Grey's Reform Cabinet as Chief Secretary for Ireland. He had resigned from Melbourne's Government in 1835 and joined Peel in 1841, seceding from him over the Corn Law Repeal at the end of 1845. He even dressed in what Sir William Fraser called a 'conspicuously old-fashioned manner', in green frock coat, canary yellow cashmere waistcoat and light coloured cloth trousers with a curious slit at the ankle, huge neckcloth and high pointed shirt collar. His fine features had led Melbourne to describe him as a 'young eagle', and he had an equally fine brain (he won a Latin verse prize while at Oxford, and later was to occupy himself translating Homer). He was the best speaker in the House of Lords and had a cutting wit which could make him both feared and resented. 'Gladstone's jokes', he once said, 'are no laughing matter'. Above all, he was a great sporting peer; his friend and colleague, Malmesbury, described him as 'the keenest sportsman I ever knew', and his great love was the turf, to which politics came a poor second. He was never happier than at Newmarket, where Greville, who disliked him, has left a graphic description of his behaviour:

> If any of his vociferous disciples and admirers, if some grave Members of either H. of Parliament, or any distinguished foreigner who knew nothing of Lord Stanley but what he saw, heard or read of him could have suddenly found themselves in the betting room at Newmarket ... and seen Stanley there, I think they would have been in a pretty state of astonishment. There he was in the midst of a crowd of blacklegs, betters, and loose characters of every description, in uproarious spirits, chaffing, rowing and shouting with laughter and joking. His amusement was to lay Ld. Glasgow a wager that he did not sneeze in a given time, for which purpose he took pinch after pinch of snuff, while Stanley jeered him and quizzed him with such noise that he drew the whole mob around him to partake in the coarse merriment he excited.

He was, said Greville, 'utterly regardless of appearances, and not caring what anybody might think of the Minister and Statesman so long as he could have his fun.'[8] Stanley's arrogance could be wounding; when later someone pointed out that Greville, who was Clerk of the Council, had not attended one meeting of the Privy Council since Stanley (then Lord Derby) became Premier, he replied. 'Is that the case? I had not observed it: when I order coals to be put on the fire, I do not notice whether it be John or Thomas who does it.'

Stanley, who as 14th Earl of Derby would be head of one of the oldest and richest aristocratic families in England with vast territorial interests in Lancashire and an income estimated at between £60,000 and £100,000 a year, could have little in common with Disraeli, and indeed his feelings about him were no secret. 'I know Disraeli has the feeling that I dislike him' Stanley confessed to the Earl of Wilton, 'I certainly have no personal prepossession in his favour.' Despite this undercurrent of dislike and distrust between the two men who were known familiarly in the Carlton Club as 'the Jew and the Jockey', Stanley was to be Prime Minister and Disraeli his Chancellor of the Exchequer three times over the next twenty years.

Stanley's motives in opposing Disraeli's candidature for the leadership were not entirely personal; he was anxious to reunite the party and lure the Peelites back into the Conservative fold, but, as he told one of Disraeli's supporters, Disraeli was 'the most powerful repellent we could offer to any repentant or hesitating Peelites.' Alerted to Disraeli's intentions by an article in the *Morning Chronicle* of 16 December 1848 pressing his claims, Stanley took immediate steps to counter him. Having tried and failed to recruit Granby once again, he decided upon the elderly plodder, E.H. Herries, and wrote Disraeli a singularly insensitive letter inviting him to withdraw on the grounds of his general unpopularity. 'Believing as I do,' he wrote, 'that, from whatever cause, your formal establishment in the post of Leader would not meet with a general and cheerful popularity on the part of those with whom you are acting', he invited him to place his talents at the service of Herries.[9]

Stanley had misjudged his man; Disraeli was prepared to act as the champion of the aristocracy, but not as its tool; moreover, with the support of Henry Bentinck and an influential body of squires, he was in a stronger position than Stanley knew. Bentinck's death, he replied to Stanley, had freed him from personal ties to politics, and, he said, he was no longer prepared to sacrifice 'interesting pursuits, health, and a happy hearth for a political career, which can bring one little fame, and, even if successful in a vulgar sense, would bear me a reward which I now little appreciate'; furthermore, he politely threatened to act as an independent.[10]

Disraeli was playing a clever game, maintaining an aloof public stance, while in private he was burning with ambition and excitement, the centre of a web of intrigue to advance his cause. While Henry Bentinck organized the squires, Disraeli was in contact with Samuel Phillips: 'Phillips has just gone, having set immense machinery to work', he wrote to Mary Anne at Hughenden on 7 January. He went to lobby Delane, editor of *The Times*, with a view to articles in the newspaper which 'done with discreet thunder, might do the business'. He was anxious but confident: 'They say Peel will never get over my appointment', he wrote to Mary Anne with gleeful malice on 20 January. As the Protectionists came up from the shires to prepare for the meeting of Parliament, support for him was growing, with even the ultra-Protestant National Club, possibly due to the intrigues of Phillips, declaring their support. Stanley was under pressure: prompted by Henry Bentinck, the Duke of Richmond wrote a 'strong letter' to him on Disraeli's behalf, while at an informal congress at Burleigh in the last week of January both Stanley's candidate, Herries, and Lord Exeter's candidate, Granby, declined the leadership. Disraeli remained at Grosvenor Gate, revelling in the atmosphere of political intrigue, his letters to Mary Anne redolent of mystery and excitement: 'I must write in initials and even that is dangerous', he told her. Everything would hinge on his meeting with Stanley, who was expected up in London at the end of January. Disraeli wrote anxiously to Mary Anne on 24 January asking her to come up to London 'to talk over affairs together, before I can see him'.

The meeting took place on 31 January 1849. Disraeli, who had been hoping Stanley would capitulate, was disagreeably surprised when Stanley proposed that the leadership should be a triumvirate of himself, Granby and Herries. He refused, and when Stanley reminded him of his offer the previous year to act with Bentinck under Granby, he reacted bitterly:

> It is quite true that I acceded to such an arrangement when acting in union, and on terms of equality with, Lord George Bentinck: but I am Disraeli the adventurer and I will not acquiesce in a position which will enable the party to make use of me in debate, and then throw me aside.[11]

'I am Disraeli the adventurer'; it was a wounded and yet defiant taunt to fling at the man who must have seemed to represent the entrenched, prejudiced opposition to him. He followed it up by telling Stanley that he would take no part in party arrangements, would give them support but as an independent, speak only when it suited him, and that he wished to retire and if possible devote at least part of his time to literature.

Stanley handled him with tact and skill, revealing all the qualities of a first-class chairman, pointing out the realities of the situation and the advantages to Disraeli of the compromise:

> I would not apply to you any such terms as you have applied to yourself, but this I will say, that certain feelings exist, call them prejudices if you will, that will make many of our friends desire, in the man who is to lead them, a degree of station and influence which circumstances have not as yet enabled you to acquire: and if I were speaking to an ambitious man, and speaking for your interest alone, I tell you fairly, I could suggest no proposal which I think you would gain more by accepting. You escape the envy which attaches to a post of solitary and supreme command; you are associated with two men, neither of whom in point of abilities can stand in your way for a moment.

Granby, he pointed out, had already shown he had no ambition to lead, while Herries was an old man, and would not long be on the political stage.

Disraeli was realist enough to take Stanley's point; as he wrote in a hasty note to Mary Anne: 'I should, or rather must, be the real leader', and, without formally withdrawing his refusal, simply accepted Stanley's invitation to the first meeting with Herries and Granville as part of the Committee of Three. It was nonetheless a humiliating experience, in which pride had perforce to give way to ambition; as Samuel Phillips later pointed out, he was being sandwiched between two pieces of 'very *stale* bread – Herries and Granby' to make him fit for squeamish throats to swallow. In 1860, only eleven years later, Disraeli was to give two versions of the leadership affair, both of which ignored the existence of the Committee of Three. According to the first, he was invited by the party through Sir John Yarde Buller and William Miles, to take the lead; while the second version, given to Miles himself, not unnaturally omitted this tale, representing Stanley as having written to him asking him 'to undertake, under certain conditions, the management of our party'. Everybody saw through the fiction of the Committee of Three, Lord Aberdeen remarking with a grim smile that it was like the triumvirate before Napoleon's coup of 18 Brumaire – 'Sieyès, Roger Ducos, and Napoleon Bonaparte.' By February Disraeli, taking a somewhat rose-coloured view of the situation, could write to Sarah, 'After much struggling, I am fairly the leader'.

But was he? Disraeli was too intelligent not to be aware that the party which he nominally led regarded him as a hired mercenary whose services might be dispensed with when and if someone more acceptable to them might appear. He knew, as he admitted to Stafford O'Brien early in February, that 'some of the party distrusted and some abhorred him', and, O'Brien told Manners, he 'conceived the aristocracy was merely using him as a tool'. There was no-one within the ranks of the parliamentary party upon whom he could truly rely, his one friend, John Manners, having lost his seat at Newark in 1847. The party chief, Stanley, kept him at arm's length, and what party organization there was, which should have been within the province of the leader in the Commons, was run by Stanley and the Whip, Beresford, both of whom disliked and distrusted him.

The great Conservative party of 1841–6 no longer existed; the electoral organization so carefully built up by Peel and Bonham had been fractured by the split of 1846, and the former executive talent of the party, headed by Peel, was now divorced from it and acting in support of the Russell government. Its identity even was no longer certain; only the previous year a furious quarrel had broken out between Stanley and Bentinck as to whether the party should, as Stanley wished, be known as 'Conservative'. 'I know nothing of *this* "Conservative Party"', Bentinck had written in a typically violent letter to Stanley. 'I gave my adherence to the "Protectionist Party" and to no other ... the term "Conservative" was repudiated "as a byword of reproach" ... justly branded as such by Disraeli, I acknowledge nothing in the "Conservative Party" but an "Organised Hypocrisy".'[12] Disraeli himself, having denounced 'Conservatism' in that famous phrase, could not easily revert to it; only gradually did the party cease to be called 'Protectionist', becoming 'Derbyite' when Stanley became Earl of Derby in 1851 and only later reverting to 'Conservative'.

The term 'Protectionist' symbolized Disraeli's dilemma. The party in the years following 1846 was committed to a defeated cause, as it had been after 1832 before Peel led it out of the political wilderness. Disraeli's task, therefore, when he became leader in 1849 was the same as Peel's had been in 1835 when he issued the Tamworth Manifesto: to give the party an electoral future by weaning it from its entrenched attachment to a lost cause. Bentinck was dead and Free Trade a reality; liberated by his friend's death from personal loyalty to Protection, Disraeli set out with courage and determination over the years 1849-52 to educate his party into the acceptance of reality. It was a course fraught with danger to himself, taken against the fixed opinions of Stanley and the body of the party, even of friends like Manners, and against an undercurrent of rumbling discontent with his leadership. His task, as he later put it to Lady Dorothy Nevill, was 'to drag an omnibus full of country gentlemen uphill'.

Disraeli not only had to drag the 'omnibus of country gentlemen uphill', he had to fill it with more and better passengers if his party were to have a serious political future. Surveying the scene in 1849 Disraeli saw the future of his party in occupying the middle ground. He wanted to attract the moderate Whigs whose class interests were identical with those of the Conservative landed gentry and aristocracy into a common defensive bond against the radical 'democratizing' tendencies of such men as Lord John Russell, Cobden and Bright. It was for this reason that he was to make repeated attempts to lure Palmerston, a man, he said 'whose tendencies were Conservative' to join Lord Derby. It was Palmerston's refusal to fall into this Disraelian trap, and, above all, his long and anti-progressive premiership which was to frustrate Disraeli's goal of a fusion of moderates until after Palmerston's death in 1865.

One factor was in Disraeli's favour: the aristocratic fear of revolution was revivified by the events of 1848, when thrones and empires toppled and mobs fought soldiers in the streets. The French monarchy collapsed in four confused days between 21 and 25 February 1848, and a month later there was a revolution in Germany and risings at Vienna and Milan with the whole Austro-Hungarian Empire in turmoil. As Disraeli put it in a letter to Lady Londonderry: 'The King of France in a Surrey villa, Metternich in a Hanover Square hotel, and the Prince of Prussia at Lady Palmerston's ... Kings and princes are turned off as we turn away servants – worse, without a character.'[13] Even Queen Victoria trembled as on 10 April of that year Chartism had its last dying blaze, with a mass meeting of 20,000 people on Kennington Common followed by the presentation of a petition to Westminster, supposedly signed by six million people. The affair was a fiasco. The mass meeting melted peacefully away and the petition turned out to be signed by less than two million instead of six and, as Greville put it 'of those there were no end of fictitious names [including Queen Victoria and Mr. Punch], together with ... every species of ribaldry, indecency and impertinence.'

Chartism faded away and reaction was quickly to set in in Europe, but 1848 reinforced the feeling among the English aristocracy that their bastions were being eroded by an encroaching tide of Liberalism. They had seen Peel as their saviour, but he had then betrayed them by letting the enemy in at the gates. The Peelite leaders were tarred with the same brush, while many of the aristocracy came increasingly to feel that, with the progress of democracy – which they equated with mob rule – they could no longer afford the high Whig opinions of Lord John Russell, the constant advocate of liberal measures. Disraeli saw the world in the same terms. He had not changed his views since he had analysed the situation in the thirties in the *Vindication;* he believed in the aristocratic order and was determined to be its champion, whether the aristocrats would or no. Dorothy Nevill wrote of him:

> My own impression is that he was deeply attached to the traditions of government by aristocracy, the romantic side of which appealed to his imagination and nature. At heart I think he feared the eventual triumph of a sort of mob rule, the coming of which it was ever his object to delay.[14]

John Manners already saw him in that role. He wrote to Lady Bradford (who was to be the last love of Disraeli's life) early in 1849, pleading for understanding for his friend: 'He ... only requires to have confidence shown in him to fight successfully the great battle of order against ceaseless change. If the Aristocracy choose to turn the cold shoulder on their ablest champion, the blame and penalty will be theirs.'[15] Unfortunately for Disraeli, that is precisely what the aristocracy were to do for most of his political life, until his last premiership in 1874. Lady Bradford's reply to Manners is interesting, not only in the light of her future relations with Disraeli but as expressive of the view of him taken by her class: 'I admire his wonderful and brilliant powers, but somehow he is a man I cannot respect ... Perhaps it is his countenance I don't like.' Disraeli's political difficulty through the early fifties and sixties was that having struggled to rid the party of Protection he then found Palmerston occupying the position of champion of the establishment.

One refugee of 1848 was to have a deep personal influence upon Disraeli; in May Metternich arrived in London. Aged seventy-five, his long reign over the councils of Europe was over. Foreign Minister of the Austro-Hungarian Empire for almost forty years from 1809–48, he had known the Europe of the French Revolution, witnessed the rise and fall of Napoleon, and dominated the Congress of Vienna after Waterloo. He had done more than any man to stem the tide of revolution, restore and maintain the old order of Europe. Disraeli met Metternich through Lord Londonderry on 17 May, and the two men were soon on intimate terms. There was an instant rapport between their political views. As Metternich wrote gleefully to Disraeli on 2 October applauding the process of reaction: '*Fraternity* is broken on the barricades; nationality [nationalism] has entered into liquidation ... in Italy [and] ... in Germany ... There remains only *progress*; it is strongly discredited by its most cruel enemy, by the misery which spreads about it.'[16]

Disraeli accepted the conspiracy theory of European politics, believing that revolutions were created by a network of secret societies at war 'against Property and the Semitic revelation'. He utterly discounted nationalism as a force – a serious defect it might be said in a statesman of the latter half of the nineteenth century in Europe. His veneration for Metternich reinforced the anti-revolutionary attitudes instilled in him so long ago by Isaac D'Israeli. Metternich returned his admiration; there was, in Disraeli's words, an 'irresistible sympathy' between them.

Disraeli began his campaign to save what Metternich had quaintly suggested should be called the party of 'conservation' immediately after the session of 1849. Unfortunately for his plans, the years 1849–52 were the worst for British agriculture since 1815, and the farmers, forced to sell reduced crops at low European prices, not unnaturally blamed Free Trade and the repeal of the Corn Laws. As Greville wrote that summer: 'The protectionists are gone mad with the notion of reaction in the country against Free Trade.' Disraeli, casting desperately about for a panacea to distract the agriculturalists from their obsession with a return to Protection, hit upon a somewhat hare-brained scheme for equalizing the land tax and creating a sinking fund to finance cheap loans to farmers. This scheme, put forward at a speech at Aylesbury in mid-September without consulting Stanley or even mentioning a return to import duties, immediately involved him in a 'scrape' with Stanley, who wrote furiously from Ireland demanding a public recantation and despatched Beresford to Hughenden to see what Disraeli was up to. Disraeli appears to have charmed Beresford, who reported to Stanley that he was living very quietly and working very hard at Hughenden, reading up all the Blue Books of the past session. 'He attributes Peel's great power and effect in the House to having always had Blue Books by heart', Beresford wrote. Disraeli he said, struck him as 'very zealous in the cause, and as feeling himself completely embarked now with us and I do trust that he is fully compromised and will remain true'.[17]

Disraeli made his recantation in a speech at Castle Hedingham in Essex, a process that he found distasteful, as he told Mary Anne: 'When a man is in a scrape, as I am, one must not complain of annoyances and sacrifices: but I have paid dear for the misconceptions of the Aylesbury meeting.' Within a short time of the Hedingham penitence, however, he was involved in a furious row with the rabid right wing of the Protectionist party, in the form of the National Association for the Protection of British Industry and Capital, described by Disraeli to an associate as 'the very rump I wished to put an end to.'[18] The Association, headed by a Limehouse businessman, G.F. Young, proposed petitioning the Crown for a dissolution of Parliament with a view to returning a majority pledged to restore the Corn Laws.

Disraeli was appalled; the use of such a weapon for such a purpose would only serve to show the Protectionists up as the deluded reactionaries they were. In a public letter to Young he lectured him upon the folly of such a course; there was no evidence that the country at large wanted an election on the isssue. In a passage which was a public statement of intent as far as Protection was concerned he renounced any idea of restoring the Corn Laws: '... unless the agricultural constituencies ... are prevented from running amuck against the financial system of this country, which, out of suffering and sheer spite and vexation, it is not unnatural that they should do, it is all over with England as a great monarchy.'

Once again, Disraeli's temerity in apparently pronouncing publicly against Protection brought down upon him the wrath of his chief, egged on by Beresford. Stanley's rebuke only served to underline the gulf between the party chief and his lieutenant on the question: 'I am firmly convinced that the public mind is beginning to be impressed with the conviction that Free Trade has proved a delusion,' he wrote. Once again Disraeli thought it prudent to make at least a partial recantation, this time at Aylesbury, where he paid lip service to the general principle of Protection, while again putting forward his alternative of a sinking fund supported by import duties. 'A shabby concern', he wrote disgustedly of the meeting to Sarah.

The row was again patched up, and after a cold and disagreeable Christmas at Hughenden, Disraeli, with Mary Anne, paid two courtesy visits to the Duke of Rutland at Belvoir and the Marquess of Exeter at Burghley, temples of Protection. Disraeli liked the glamour as much as he disliked the conversation and the sport. At Belvoir they lived in the State Apartments, deliciously warm and brilliantly illuminated at night. A military band played throughout dinner, announced to the tune of 'The Roast Beef of Old England', and all the gentlemen wore the colours of the Belvoir hunt in the evening. It was much the same amid the ancestral splendours of Burghley, where five hundred birds a day were slaughtered in the 'battues'. For Disraeli, insensible to the delights of shooting five hundred birds a day, still less to hearing of them afterwards, the tedium was dreadful. As Mary Anne once told Sir William Fraser: 'Whenever we go to a country house, the same thing happens: Disraeli is not only bored, and has constant ennui, but he takes on eating as a resource: he eats at breakfast, luncheon and dinner: the result is, by the end of the third day he becomes dreadfully bilious; and we have to come away.' Disraeli himself once described country-house visiting as 'a succession of meals relieved by the dresses of the ladies.'

On the morning of 3 July 1850, all political questions were eclipsed by the death of Peel, after a fall from his horse three days before. The House was adjourned as a mark of respect with Gladstone being unable to speak for tears and two members sobbing out loud.[19] Disraeli's private reaction to the death of his great adversary, witnessed by young Edward Stanley, was honest and characteristic. He made no parade of regret, said Stanley, but seemed bewildered by the suddenness of the event, and the prospect which it offered of new combinations, speculating on the possibility of some of the Peelites now joining the party. 'What an event!' he exclaimed, in the intervals of pacing the room discussing a new scheme to wean the farmers from Protection. Now, he told Stanley, was the favourable moment definitely to abandon protective duties as a policy. Stanley wisely told him that although he personally agreed with him, 'the mere suggestion of such a course would raise a mutiny in the camp' recommending him to leave it alone.[20] Disraeli was quite wrong in thinking that Peel's death would soften the Protectionists' feeling towards Free Trade. While people all over England mourned Peel's passing, the Protectionists were unforgiving towards the man whom they regarded as a traitor to his class. Peel, apparently, was unable to bear pain, and his behaviour during the three days before his death led one Protectionist Duke to exclaim in Stanley's hearing, 'Well, he lived a coward, and he has died one.'

Curiously insensitive as he sometimes was to the effects of his own actions upon others, Disraeli liked to think not only that Peel had forgiven him but had even come to appreciate him. He cherished the story that Gladstone had recounted in the Carlton: 'Peel died at peace with all mankind; even with Disraeli. The last thing he did was to cheer Disraeli. It was not a very loud cheer, but it *was* a cheer; it was distinct. I sat next to him.'[21] Indeed, latterly Peel had made some rather heavy-handed attempts to be cordial to Disraeli in his speeches, in a manner that had caused some amusement; but privately he had always regarded him with a cold dislike and there is no real evidence that he forgave the man who had ruined his career. The tone of his private papers remained hostile to the end, and, according to a late memoir by Gladstone, Peel who sat only a few places away from Disraeli on the Opposition front bench, absolutely disliked being 'in Disraeli's neighbourhood' and any idea of co-operating with him in any way. Disraeli as the victor was in a position to be magnanimous, and his portrait of Peel in the *Life of Lord George Bentinck* was generally considered to be fair, objective and in many ways the best that had been written. One may well conjecture, however, that, had the positions been reversed, his feelings would have been different. Lord Esher was to record that Disraeli once told him that when a man had injured him in some way he wrote his name down on a piece of paper and put it in a drawer, 'and something usually happened to him'.

Peel's death improved the Conservative party's prospects of office; it was unlikely that his policy of out and out support for Russell's government in order to keep the Protectionists out would be continued by the Peelites. Indeed in that same session of 1850 both Aberdeen and Gladstone had co-operated with the Protectionists against the government, and on 27 June Russell had.written to the Queen that 'Mr. Gladstone makes no secret of his wish to join Lord Stanley in forming an Administration'. But however much it might have helped the party, the accession of Peelite men of talent, so ardently desired by Stanley, represented a threat to Disraeli's position within it. The Peelites hated him for his treatment of Peel, and he could not be sure of the loyalty either of Lord Stanley or his party. It was true that his absence during a bout of influenza early in the session had impressed upon the party, even Beresford, that they needed him, as Graham, no friend to Disraeli, wrote to Londonderry: 'The Protectionists cannot do without him.' But if other leaders, equally able and more acceptable might appear, the position might well be different. Gladstone, for instance, younger than Disraeli, a man of acknowledged ability and previous experience of office, could represent a threat. The two men were already wary of each other. Gladstone, while admiring Disraeli's brilliance as a debater, wrote to his wife that he distrusted his sincerity – 'never, last night or at any other time, would I go to him for conviction'; while Disraeli told young Stanley that he 'distrusted Gladstone, whose professions of friendship he thought officious and over-acted'. Until the Peelites joined the Coalition Government of Lord Aberdeen in 1852, Disraeli could never be absolutely sure that Stanley might not offer him up as a sacrifice for party unity once the Free Trade/Protection issue was resolved. His hope of retaining the leadership lay in continuing to make himself indispensable; above all he hoped for office which would, he said, give himself and his party 'status'.

Office seemed within his grasp early in the session of 1851, when Russell, having just managed to squeeze his controversial Ecclesiastical Titles Bill through the Commons, was defeated on a radical motion for the equalization of the county and borough franchise. He resigned, advising the Queen to send for Lord Stanley. Stanley, suspecting it was a ploy by Russell to show up the weakness of the Protectionists, refused, advising the Queen to try for a Whig–Peelite administration. When this fell through he had no alternative but to try to form a Protectionist government. The omens were not good; Stanley strongly sensed the hostility of the Queen and Prince Albert, ardent supporters of Peel, to the Protectionists as a whole and to Disraeli in particular. A year earlier Greville had reported that the Queen had 'a horror of Disraeli', and, on this occasion, according to Disraeli's *Reminiscences*, she made herself quite plain to Stanley on the subject, 'I do not approve of Mr. Disraeli', she told him. 'I do not approve of his conduct to Sir Robert Peel'. Stanley himself recorded that she was furious with Disraeli for using her name in the previous day's debate in the Commons, and that she would only agree (and then with the greatest reluctance) to his inclusion, on Stanley's representation that it would be impossible to form an administration without him. Her last words were, 'Remember you make yourself responsible for him'.[22]

The results of Stanley's efforts to form an administration showed all too clearly, as Russell had hoped, the inability of the Protectionists to form a credible alternative to the Whig government. Nobody believed they would succeed, no one wanted to be involved in their failure, and every man of talent rejected Stanley's overtures. Gladstone escaped from Stanley's house with a feeling of relief that the offer of office had included a pledge to restore the Corn Laws. 'If he had put protection in abeyance, I might have had a most difficult question to decide', he told Albert, 'whereas now I had no question at all.'

The same lack of belief in their prospects was strikingly demonstrated by the Protectionist candidates themselves, summoned to Stanley's house on 27 February. Disraeli, concealed in Stanley's dressing-room, heard two candidates refuse Stanley's offers; 'Henry Corry', he later recorded, 'had not absolutely fainted, but had turned very pale' and had declined an offer which, as Stanley said, he was quite unworthy to receive. Stanley told his son that he had been taken aback at 'the absurd vanity and self-confidence of some of the least capable' of his party. 'It is bad enough', he said, 'to have to deal with mere sticks instead of men: but when these sticks fancy themselves great Ministers, what can one do?'[23]

The scene at the general meeting that afternoon, as described by Disraeli, was pure comedy. The proposed President of the Board of Trade, J.W. Henley, a survivor of previous Conservative administrations, sat 'with the countenance of an ill-conditioned Poor Law Guardian censured for some act of harshness. His black eyebrows, which met, deeply knit, his crabbed countenance doubly morose', while the other intended arm of the administration's financial policy, Herries, designated for the Exchequer, was equally apprehensive, foreseeing only difficulties; both men were apparently terrified by the prospect of having to fight the battle of revising Free Trade against Whig and Peelite financial experts in the Commons. Herries, Malmesbury recorded in his diary, 'looked like an old doctor who has just killed a patient, and Henley like the undertaker who was to bury him'.[24]

Stanley took Disraeli aside. 'This will never do', he told him, and, ignoring Disraeli's pleas not to give up, announced that he would not attempt to form an administration. Beresford 'frantically rushed foward', telling Stanley that 'there were several men, he knew, waiting at the Carlton expecting to be sent for'. Stanley inquired impatiently 'Who was at the Carlton', and on receiving Beresford's reply exclaimed 'Pshaw! These are not names I can put before the Queen. The thing is finished.' Beresford, said Disraeli, 'looked like a man who had lost his all at roulette', but while the 'mere sticks' at the Carlton grumbled at their lost prospects of office, Stanley himself felt a deep sense of relief. 'I have little to gain by office,' he told his son Edward, 'and everything to lose: they have nothing to lose, and much to gain.'[25]

For Disraeli, who could not afford to take such a patrician view, and whose firmness alone had pushed Lord Stanley into going as far as he did, it was a bitter blow. Edward Stanley, calling on him the following day, found him in very low spirits. He had, apparently, counted on success and felt the disappointment keenly, saying that he would retire from public life and return to literature 'leaving those who had brought him and themselves into this trouble to find their own way out'. This was a regular refrain of Disraeli's when things were going wrong politically, and Stanley did not take it seriously, but 'the ludicrous catastrophe' had thrown him into one of his moods of despair, and he told Stanley gloomily: 'There was a fatality about his own career – he had turned out two successive administrations, but it was fated that he should never himself succeed.'[26] While the Duke of Wellington consoled Stanley by saying that the Whigs were 'in the mud', Disraeli thought that the affair had embarrassingly and publicly revealed the weakness of his party: 'The Whigs might be in the mud', he wrote, 'but it was clear to me, that another party was not in a more clean predicament'.

In May, he and Stanley, deep in political discussion at Syon House, inadvertently wandered into a swamp by the river; 'a bad omen, as all agreed,' his son, young Stanley commented.

Deeply depressed, Disraeli returned to Hughenden towards the end of August 1851 to finish his biography of Bentinck as best he could, distracted by the demands of a gouty Mary Anne and the quarrel between her and Jem. The book was finally finished on 6 December at Grosvenor Gate, and published by Colburn that month, with a dedication to Lord Henry Bentinck. Disraeli had found it very hard going. Biography was not his literary forte, and he must have found it awkward to write a eulogy of the hero of Protection at the very time when he was attempting to persuade his party to abandon the cause for which that hero had fought. Subtitled 'A Political Biography', it was certainly more political than biographical and Bentinck, described as an ENGLISH WORTHY, appears as a marble statue in a public hall rather than a man of flesh and blood. Parliament, rather than Bentinck, came alive in its pages; the power and dramatic vividness with which Disraeli presented the Corn Law debates astounded even Greville.

The most famous chapter of the book, Chapter XXIV, which John Manners described as 'unjustifiable' and Greville as 'amusing and I like it for its courage', was wholly extraneous to the subject of the book. In it he propounded his racial theories, not only repeating the contentions of his 1847 speech on Jewish Disabilities and many of the phrases and sentiments of *Tancred* but making even more extravagant claims for his people: 'We hesitate not to say that there is no race at this present ... that so much delights, and fascinates, and elevates, and ennobles Europe, as the Jewish'. In *Bentinck*, however, he gets on to far more dangerous ground, which would hold a sinister significance for twentieth-century Europe. The doctrine of the equality of man, he declared, was pernicious because it was destructive of racial purity:

> The natural equality of man now in vogue, and taking the form of cosmopolitan fraternity, is a principle which, were it possible to act on it, would deteriorate the great races and destroy all the genius of the world. What would be the consequence on the great Anglo-Saxon republic, for example, were its citizens to secede from their sound principle of reserve, and mingle with their negro and coloured populations? In the course of time they would become so deteriorated that their states would probably be reconquered and regained by the aborigines whom they have expelled and who then would be their superiors.

How, one wonders, would Disraeli have reacted, had he been able to foresee that theories such as these would be used as grounds for genocide of the very race which, for him, had been their inspiration?

Any sensation that the publication of *Bentinck* might have caused was, however, eclipsed by two startling events in Paris and London that December. On 2 December, Disraeli's old acquaintance of Gore House days, Louis Napoleon Bonaparte, seized the government of France, arrested his chief opponents, dissolved the National Assembly and the Council of State, and declared Paris in a state of siege. In London Palmerston, whose independent actions as Foreign Secretary had already enraged the Queen and Prince Albert and embarrassed Lord John Russell, intimated his approval of Louis Napoleon's *coup d'état* to the French Ambassador, Count Walewski, without consulting the Queen or the Prime Minister, or bothering to inform the British ambassador in Paris, Lord Normanby, that he had done so. This was too much even for Lord John Russell, who had put up with a good deal from Palmerston, mainly because he feared that his loss would break up the Government and lead to his joining the Protectionists. On 23 December Palmerston was officially dismissed, to the delight of the Queen who wrote to her uncle, King Leopold of Belgium: 'My dearest Uncle, I have the greatest pleasure in announcing to you a piece of news which I know will give you as much satisfaction and relief as it does to us, and will do the *whole* of the world. *Lord Palmerston is no longer Foreign Secretary!*'[27]

Disraeli was immediately alive to the prospect that the 'Palmerston *coup*', as he put it to Sarah, might break up the Government, and his expectations were justified when, on 20 February 1852, Russell was defeated on an amendment to his Militia Bill put by a vengeful Palmerston. Russell resigned the next day, and the reluctant Queen sent for Stanley, now, since the death of his father the previous April, Earl of Derby. Disraeli, seeing the prospect of his long-term plan for the seduction of Palmerston coming to fruition, immediately wrote to Derby, who was shooting with the Duke of Beaufort at Badminton, offering to give up his place as Leader of the Commons to Palmerston. Derby replied that he would 'never forget the generous self-sacrifice', but Palmerston, whose sights were now set upon becoming Prime Minister, declined, ostensibly on the grounds of opposition to the reintroduction of Protection.

Malmesbury, visiting Disraeli on the morning of Russell's resignation, found him 'in a state of delight at the idea of coming into office. He said he "felt just like a young girl going to her first ball" constantly repeating "Now we have got a *status*".'[28] At forty-seven, after almost fifteen years in Parliament, Disraeli was in office at last.

Just as a door was opening upon a new life for Disraeli, another was closing on the past; among the many letters of congratulation he received was one from the dying d'Orsay. The splendours of Gore House had vanished for ever; in May 1849 its contents were sold at auction and Lady Blessington, ruined by the bankruptcy of her publisher Heath and the failure of her Irish jointure, left for Paris to join d'Orsay. A month later she died of a heart attack, aged fifty-eight. D'Orsay had been shattered, so much so that he had been unable to write to Disraeli until six months had passed, and when he did, on 7 January 1850, his letter was heart-breaking:

> I ought to have answered your first letter sooner, but the truth is, that you were too much our friend, for me to write to you without entering upon that great calamity. I have not yet the power, to believe that it is not a frightful dream, and time has not the slightest effect upon me ... my misfortune is to have the most extraordinary recollections

and visions of everything . . . I find myself transported at [sic] Gore House in every room, picking up even a pin at her feet, judge therefore, if a nature like mine can easily find a remedy by time. You will understand me, few can . . .[29]

D'Orsay's letter of congratulation to Disraeli was written on his death-bed; shattered in mind and body, he died of cancer of the spine in August 1852, having lived to see two of his friends of Gore House days, Louis Napoleon and Disraeli, reach the highest rungs of worldly success.

14 Public Affairs and Private Friendships

Queen Victoria's opinion of her new Government was unflattering; Lord Derby, she said, had taken office with 'a very sorry Cabinet. I believe, however', she wrote to her Uncle Leopold, 'that it is quite necessary they should have a trial, and then have done with it.'[1] The deaf old Duke of Wellington involuntarily coined a name for the new Ministry; cupping his hand to his ear as the names of the unknown Ministers were retailed to him, he muttered testily, 'Who? Who?'

The ingredients were much the same as for the abortive attempt of 1851 – Derby as First Lord of the Treasury, Malmesbury as Foreign Secretary, with young Edward Stanley as Under Secretary, Spencer Walpole at the Home Office, Herries at the Board of Trade, Henley at the Board of Control, Sir John Pakington, a dapper country gentleman, at the Colonial Office, while John Manners, who had returned to Parliament in 1850, was at the Ministry of Works, and a new friend of Disraeli's, Lord Henry Lennox, became a Lord of the Treasury. 'Jem' was rewarded with a Treasurership at £700 a year.

Disraeli's appointment as Chancellor of the Exchequer was greeted with incredulous disapproval. Disraeli himself had his doubts as, given his precarious private finances, he well might; but when he demurred, Derby had replied airily: 'You know as much as Mr. Canning did. They give you the figures'. 'Disraeli could not have been worse placed than at the Exchequer', a surprised Gladstone wrote to his wife on 23 February, and on the same day Lord Ashley predicted 'Dizzy's' downfall: 'Dizzy Chancellor of the Exchequer! Alas, poor man, he has in his day insulted and tortured many: now they will insult & torture him; &, for him, he is as odious to those who sit behind, as to those who sit in front of the Minister. But will not the House & the Kingdom regard him as an Adventurer?'[2] Even Lord Derby, who, after all had been responsible for the appointment, could not resist a biblical joke on the subject: 'The mess will be great', he said, 'but Benjamin's mess will be five times as great as the others!'

Disraeli was determined that there should be no 'mess' as far as he was concerned, and to prove to his enemies that he was capable of handling finance. He was equally determined that not even lip-service should be paid to the fallen idol of Protection, and his speech introducing his interim Budget on 30 April, praising the effects of free trade, delighted the Opposition and dismayed his supporters. It was, as Greville said, 'neither more nor less than a magnificent funeral oration upon Peel's policy ... it seems impossible that any sort of Protection in any shape can be attempted after it'. What pleased Greville enraged Derby, who despite having privately admitted on 22 March to the Queen and Prince Albert that Protection was finished, sat down to write a furious sixteen-page remonstrance to Disraeli:

> The silence of our friends & the rapturous and triumphant cheers with which the opposite side of the House greeted each successive illustration of the financial result of the remission of Taxes, & the advantage gained to the consumer ... must have shown you ... that you were making out a triumphant case for the Free Trade Policy which is the mainstay of our Opponents.[3]

This time, however, Disraeli did not recant, and while the squires grumbled, the political world in general thought he had acquitted himself well as Chancellor. Even Greville praised him:

> He has given undoubted proofs of his great ability, and showed how neatly he could handle such a subject as finance, with which he can never have been familiar; but having been well taught by his subalterns, and applying a mind naturally clear, ready and acute to the subject, he contrived to make himself fully master of it, and to produce to the House of Commons a financial statement the excellence of which was universally admitted and gained him great applause.[4]

Derby and Disraeli even succeeded in lessening the hostility of the Court towards them. 'A most talented, capable and courageous Prime Minister', the Queen wrote to Leopold on 9 March, while she was surprised and intrigued by the unusual style of the reports of the proceedings in the Commons sent her by Disraeli. 'Mr. Disraeli (*alias* Dizzy) writes very curious reports to me of the House of Commons ... much in the style of his books', she told her uncle. She was quite unused to official reports employing such phrases as 'the debate continued to languish ... with successive relays of mediocrity, until it yielded its last gasp in the arms of Mr. Slaney.' It was not the Queen, however, who ruled, but Prince Albert, whose influence over her was, as Derby wrote to Disraeli from Balmoral that autumn, 'boundless'. Disraeli had two long interviews with Albert in June, both of two hours' duration, and was impressed by him, describing him to Stanley as 'one of the best-educated men ... indeed over-educated, something of a pedant and a theorist, but a man of talent nevertheless'.[5] Stanley believed that Disraeli appeared to have 'acquired a certain degree of influence over Prince Albert's mind', but the Court remained wary of the Derbyites and uncertain as to their prospects of success. In June they tried to find a pretext to prevent Derby accompanying them to Ascot, on account, said Stanley, of 'a nervous dread of being implicated in any unpopularity which the government may incur'.[6]

The doubts of the Court as to the viability of the Derby Government were shared by the country at large; the results of the General Election in July of which both Derby and Disraeli had had high hopes were inconclusive and failed to give them a majority. They had no coherent policies to offer the electorate; no one was sure quite where they stood on the Free Trade question, and the elections were mismanaged by Beresford, one of whose agents was caught red-handed bribing electors at Derby. Moreover, a cynical attempt to win votes from Russell on a No Popery cry by issuing an anti-Catholic proclamation had resulted in riots at Stockport, and lost them any Irish, Radical or English Liberal support that they might have gained as a legacy of Russell's anti-Catholic Ecclesiastical Titles Bill.

Disappointed by the results of the Election, Disraeli began a desperate search for allies to strengthen the Government before the December session. Rebuffed by Palmerston, he sought to conciliate the Irish Catholic members, known as 'the Brigade', and reverse the effect of the No Popery proclamation (for which he himself had been as responsible as any) by a daring and typically Disraelian intrigue. Lytton's brother Henry Bulwer was sent to Rome that autumn on a secret mission to propose to the Pope that a permanent British legation should be established there, while in return the Pope was to have a lay representative in England. Given the rabidly Protestant temper of the majority of the Conservative party, it was a risky throw. Henry Lennox who had written from Scotland in mid-September that he was 'enchanted to hear of the Roman scheme looking healthy', and describing it as 'a magnificent idea', was terrified when he heard that rumours about Bulwer's mission were circulating at the Carlton late in October. 'Knowing the truth I *trembled*', he wrote to Disraeli. 'How I die to know what the Despatch was this morning & if we are safe, or whether that dirty Pope has betrayed us.'[7] Nothing came of the scheme, which was perhaps just as well, as it would undoubtedly have been quashed by Derby and would have brought down upon Disraeli's head the wrath of his party.

The principal topic of 1852, young Stanley wrote in his diary, was the hunting-down of the Protectionist government, and the particular game of the winter of 1852 would be the hunting-down of the Chancellor. Disraeli planned to meet his opponents head-on, and soon, before the elements of opposition to him could coalesce, by presenting his Budget before Christmas. Unfortunately for him, fears that Louis Napoleon, who had declared himself Emperor on 2 December, would emulate his uncle and invade England, caused a clamour for huge expenditure on defence, and destroyed Disraeli's plans to conciliate every interest by tax remissions. Disraeli's position was an unenviable one, with, behind him the suspicious Protectionists typified by the Duke of Richmond who had predicted that the Government would not last three weeks – 'I can see they are, damn them! at the old game of throwing over their principles!'[8] – and in front of him Russell and the Whigs, longing for office again, aided by the Peelites who had resolved to avenge their dead leader.

Indeed the omens at the outset of the session in which the crucial battle was to take place were not encouraging. The Duke of Wellington had died at Walmer in

September. On the day of his State Funeral at St Paul's Disraeli delivered the eulogy on behalf of the Government in the Commons; to the delight of his enemies it was discovered that a part of his speech had been borrowed from a similar oration by Thiers on the death of Marshal Gouvion Saint-Cyr. A storm of execration and accusations of plagiarism descended upon Disraeli's head, expressed with particular vindictiveness by the *Globe:* 'We have seen him [Disraeli] snatch a wreath of faded French artificial flowers for the pall of Wellington, with an audacity of larceny unsurpassed in Grub Street'. Disraeli's enemies in the literary set were especially venomous; on 22 November *The Times* berated them as a 'whole pack of jealous littérateurs', wondering whether it was worth their while 'to be flinging as much dirt as they can on the only littérateur who has ever yet succeeded in breaking that solid aristocratical phalanx which has hitherto monopolised the high offices of state'. Disraeli could only defend himself by saying, which was at least partly true, that he had been struck by the passage long ago, had written it down, and, coming upon it, had thought it was his own composition. The most likely explanation would seem to be that, pressed with business and faced with the necessity of delivering the oration, Disraeli had hurriedly searched through his notes for suitable material and had used the passage without remembering or, perhaps caring, where it had come from. It was a storm in a teacup, but Disraeli was greatly upset by it: 'I can bear a great reverse', he told Stanley, 'but these petty personal vexations throw one off one's balance.'

It was indeed a dangerous moment to be thrown off balance by 'petty vexations'. 23 November was the date set for the debate on Charles Villiers' resolution, the intention of which was to force the Protectionist Government not only to endorse Free Trade, which Disraeli was prepared to do, but further to declare that the 1846 Act repealing the Corn Laws was 'a wise, just and beneficial measure', which was completely unacceptable. If the Peelites joined the Whigs in supporting Villiers against the Government, the Derbyites would be beaten even before the Budget came on.

The ghost of Peel and the bitterness of 1846 hung over the debate on Villiers' motion. The majority of those who were there had sat there six years before watching Disraeli hunt down Peel. Now they saw him sitting on the Treasury bench, wearing Peel's free trade mantle. Disraeli himself must have been acutely aware of the anomalies of his position as he appealed to the new generation in the House to bury the worn-out quarrel over Free Trade and Protection: 'I appeal to the generous and the young . . . not [to] become the tools and victims of exhausted factions and obsolete politics.'

The debate was the Peelites' chance for revenge, and they enjoyed it to the full. Sidney Herbert, who had never forgiven Disraeli for calling him Peel's 'valet' in 1846, was particularly sneering: 'I acquit the Chancellor of the Exchequer as far as his own convictions are concerned, of the charge of having ever been a Protectionist. I never for one moment thought he believed in the least degree in Protection. I do not accuse him of having forgotten what he said or what he believed in those years; I only accuse him of having forgotten now what he then wished it to appear that he believed.' He slipped in an anti-Semitic jibe about the Jews making no converts, and conjured up the spectre of the injured Peel: 'I sat beside him when he was attacked by the foulest language, and accused of the meanest crimes.'[9] Gladstone, who followed him, ostensibly pleading for reconciliation, used some emotive language, of which the words 'Peel' and 'revenge' could be said to have summed up the entire debate.

The day was saved by a compromise amendment moved by Palmerston and supported by the Peelites, but the personal attacks made by the Peelites upon Disraeli made it clear to Derby that Conservative reunion could not be achieved without sacrificing his subordinate. This, to his credit, he was not prepared to do, even to the extent of resisting Court pressure to replace Disraeli with Gladstone. Albert, referring disparagingly to 'the laxity of the political consciences' exhibited by Palmerston and Disraeli, hankered after Gladstone: 'whatever his political crochets may be, he is a man of the strictest feelings of honour and the purest mind', he told Derby.[10] Derby, who, having made a cautious approach to Gladstone the previous day had received a typically delphic answer, firmly dissuaded the Queen and Prince telling them that Gladstone was 'quite unfit' to lead the party, with none of that 'decision, boldness, readiness and clearness necessary', and made it quite clear that 'he could not in honour sacrifice Mr. Disraeli, who had acted very straightforwardly to him as long as they had anything to do with each other, and who possessed the confidence of his followers. Mr. Disraeli had no idea of giving up the lead.'[11]

While Derby was being frustrated in his attempts to regain Gladstone & Co. by their refusal to 'swallow Dizzy',[12] Disraeli met with equal lack of success in a renewed effort to lure Palmerston into the fold. Encouraged by Palmerston's cooperative attitude over the Villiers' resolution, Disraeli decided to press it further. He wrote to Palmerston:

> As fate has decided that at various periods of our lives there should have existed between us relations of personal confidence I think it best to communicate with you at the present moment directly, & without reserve. I am confined to my house by a slight indisposition, but I should like very much to have some conversation with you, both on the subject of your letter of yesterday [re Villiers] & other matters respecting which you know my mind has long been on.

The letter is tersely annotated in Palmerston's hand: 'I went it was to ask me to join Lord Derby's Gov. I declined. I said I could not do so singly and the Peelites with whom I was acting shewed no disposition to approximation to the Gov.'[13] The Derbyite ship was clearly sinking, and Palmerston, supported by the Peelites, and about to become reconciled with his Whig colleagues, was not about to leap aboard. The Peelites, for their part, notably Gladstone and Newcastle, Stanley recorded, were so confident as to 'hint at a Govt of their own, and affect to believe that, Disraeli once removed, the Conservatives will transfer their support to them.'[14]

Benjamin D'Israeli (d. 1816), artist unknown   Sarah D'Israeli (d. 1825) by F. Ferrière, 1796

Isaac D'Israeli (1766–1848) and Maria D'Israeli (d. 1847) painted in 1805 by J. Downman

OPPOSITE:
ABOVE LEFT Sarah D'Israeli (1802–59) by Daniel Maclise, 1828
ABOVE RIGHT Mary Anne Disraeli (1792–1872) Miniature by Francis Rochard, 1829
BELOW Disraeli aged twenty-eight, by C. Martin
ABOVE:
Portrait of Disraeli by von Angeli, 1877

George Smythe (1818–57) by Richard
Buckner

Count d'Orsay (1801–52) aged forty, by
John Wood

Lord George Bentinck (1802–48) aged
thirty-four, by Samuel Lane

Lord John Manners (1818–1906), after
Sir Francis Grant

ABOVE LEFT Lord Lyndhurst (1772–1863)
by d'Orsay and Landseer
LEFT Edward Bulwer Lytton
(1803–73), after Daniel Maclise
ABOVE Lord Henry Lennox
(1821–86) The cartoon appeared in
Vanity Fair in 1870

Anne, Countess of Chesterfield (d. 1885), after Landseer

Selina, Countess of Bradford (d. 1894), after Sir Francis Grant

Caroline Norton (d. 1877) and Helen Blackwood, later Lady Dufferin (d. 1867) by J. Swinton

Sir Francis (1799–1843) and Lady Sykes (d. 1846), by Daniel Maclise

RIGHT Montague Corry
(1838–1903) by von Angeli
BELOW LEFT Edward Stanley,
14th Earl of Derby (1799–1869),
by F.R. Say
BELOW RIGHT The younger
Edward Stanley, 15th Earl of
Derby (1826–93), by Samuel
Laurence

LEFT The von Angeli portrait of
Queen Victoria presented to
Disraeli in 1876
BELOW Disraeli and Gladstone
(1809–98), as portrayed in
Vanity Fair, 1869

It was against this unpromising background that Disraeli rose on 3 December to introduce his Budget to a crowded House. He was ill, and spoke at too great length – five and a quarter hours – being at times almost overcome by weakness. It was, said Greville, 'tolerably well received', with one dangerous exception – Gladstone – who wrote to his wife that 'in a moral point of view it was not less disgusting and repulsive than the former one'.[15] His principal objection was to Disraeli's proposal to compensate the three major interests, agriculture, sugar and shipping for the abandonment of protection by the remission of certain duties. He proposed to pay for these compensations by lowering the income tax threshold, with a differentiation in favour of unearned income, and by extending the house tax to cover properties with a rateable value of £10 a year. This Gladstone justifiably saw as an attempt to buy off Conservative supporters at the expense of the less well-off sections of the population, and he was absolutely determined to oppose it.

In the week before the Budget debate was to commence on 10 December, Disraeli made desperate last-ditch attempts to gain votes, first from the Irish of 'the Brigade', then from Bright and the Radicals, offering to remodel the Budget in return. Both moves were frustrated by Derby who wrote him a letter such as Arnold of Rugby might have penned, telling him to stick to his guns and take his medicine like a man: 'We have staked our existence on our Budget *as a whole* ... You had better be defeated honestly in a fairly-fought field than escape under a cloud.'[16]

Ignoring his chief's advice, Disraeli made one more attempt to seduce Bright, the eloquent, passionate Quaker from Rochdale, Cobden's lieutenant, and the future protagonist of the Reform Movement. On the eve of the final debate, 15 December, Disraeli summoned Bright to Grosvenor Gate where, dressed in one of his exotic dressing-gowns, he received him in his private room at the top of the house. He was apparently frank with his visitor, referring to 'the infernal question of Protection' and 'those damned defences' which had wrecked his Budget, promising, in return for Bright's support or at least neutrality to remodel his financial scheme, hinting that in some future time there was no reason why a Conservative Government should not include both Cobden and Bright. The notion was so patently ludicrous that Bright burst out laughing. Disraeli, realizing that the game was up, relapsed into one of his rare fits of real frankness, revealing his feelings to Bright:

> No man knew what he had struggled against and overcome; he had been a Minister, and was now about to be beaten. He had always felt the insecurity of their position, and had not removed to Downing Street on that account. He would not keep office or try to cling to it if they could not have *power*, and it was clear they had not the numbers with them to enable them to go on, and it was doubtful if they could live to Easter if they now escaped.[17]

Disraeli's approach to Bright was the last reflex of a politician who refuses to admit defeat. Now, however, he did admit it, but he intended to go down fighting.

It was the end of the first Protectionist Government, but the beginning of the long-drawn-out combat between the two great parliamentary gladiators that was to last over the next three decades. Recognizing it as the first 'single combat', *The Times* dedicated a leader to comparing the styles of the two duellists. Admitting Disraeli's speech to have been 'clear, nervous, brilliant and epigrammatic', they condemned it for 'no less glaring faults in tone, temper and feeling ... invective pushed to the limits of virulence ... & a tone of studied and sardonic bitterness.' In contrast, the newspaper praised Gladstone's 'tone of moral superiority ... earnest sincerity ... his sense of decorum and propriety' and expressed the pious hope that Disraeli represented the stormy and indecorous past, and that debates in future would be carried on along Gladstonian lines.[22] The reporter failed to notice or omitted to mention that Gladstone was beside himself when he began his speech, choking with rage and excitement; while Gladstone frequently lost his temper in the House, his less decorous opponent was never seen to lose his. Gladstone's speech, however, was generally regarded as having defeated the Government, so much so that when a few days later, he imprudently ventured into the Carlton, some drunken Tories threatened to throw him out of the window.

The mighty clash between Gladstone and Disraeli in Parliament was followed by a petty private squabble between the two men over payment for the furnishings of 11 Downing Street, which Gladstone was to occupy as Chancellor in the Coalition Government, and Disraeli's refusal to hand over the Chancellor's robe which he had, in accordance with tradition, bought from his predecessor. The robe in question had once belonged to Disraeli's hero, Pitt, and he could not bear to hand it over to Gladstone; he was to wear it again during his two subsequent terms of office as Chancellor and kept it until the end of his life.

There were two consolatory factors to be salvaged for Disraeli from the wreck of December 1852: Protection was dead, and the Peelite threat to his leadership of the Conservative Party had disappeared. Derby had refused to sacrifice Disraeli to the Peelite demands, and he was now very bitter against them for having joined in a 'combination' to bring down a Conservative Government. Derby thought, and Disraeli agreed with him, that they had been motivated by 'jealousy and hatred' of Disraeli rather than by any general principle; in Derby's eyes they had behaved dishonourably, as he made clear in a bitter resignation speech in the House of Lords, and all hope of a reunion between the two sections was over. From now on the threat to Disraeli's leadership would come from within his own ranks.

Derby had committed himself to Disraeli, but still did not completely trust him, as his son noted in his diary at that time. The comment arose from a curious conversation between Derby and Prince Albert on the subject of Disraeli, in which Albert made it clear that although he admired Disraeli's talents, he believed him at heart to be a dangerous radical, even a revolutionary, 'not in his heart favourable to the existing order of things'. Derby defended Disraeli, arguing that he had 'better reason than anyone to be attached to our constitutional system since he has experienced how easily under it a man may rise', but the prince remained unconvinced. Disraeli, he said, had 'democratic tendencies', and, 'if that is the case, he may become one of the most dangerous men in Europe'. His views struck a chord in Derby; Stanley's private interpretation of the interview as reported to him by his father, was that Albert, 'wishing ill to both leaders, seeks to disunite them by prejudicing my Father's mind on a point on which it is very susceptible.'[23]

Apprised of the conversation by Derby, Disraeli hastened to woo the prince with what was by any standards an over-obsequious letter on leaving Downing Street. Expressing his 'grateful acknowledgements of the condescending kindness' shown him by Albert, he concluded:

> I may, perhaps, be permitted to say that the views which your Royal Highness has developed to me in confidential conversation have not fallen on an ungrateful soil. I shall ever remember with interest and admiration the princely mind in the princely person, and shall at all times be prepared to prove to your Royal Highness my devotion.[24]

It was an unpromising beginning for the man who was to become Victoria's favourite Prime Minister.

Freed from the burden of his responsibilities, Derby retired to Knowsley with a light heart, to vent his feelings about the Peelites on the local rabbit population. 'Ha!' he would cry, as a rabbit crossed the ride, 'there goes Gladstone; hope I haven't missed him. There, do you see that big fellow? That's Graham. He'll be none the worse for a few pellets in his ribs.'[25] Disraeli had no such resources to console him for the loss of office; as his old friend Lyndhurst told Stanley at the time, 'There was never a man so absorbed in one idea: I don't think he will like retirement and a Sabine farm, eh?'

There were compensations, however. Disraeli, distrusted as he was by the political establishment, was becoming a hero to the younger generation. At Oxford in 1853 where he received a DCL he was rapturously received by the undergraduates, who cheered him to the echo as, pale and nervous, he walked up to receive his honorary degree. They waited in the rain to escort him after the traditional gaudy banquet through Tom Quad, with enthusiastic shouts of 'Dizzy'.

In private life too, his friends and disciples were much younger than he was, a generation younger even than Smythe and Manners who were still his intimate friends. In 1849 he had acquired a political disciple in Derby's son, Edward Henry Stanley, then aged only twenty-three and fresh down from Cambridge where he had been a member of the Apostles. Stanley was quite unlike his father, to whom he was nonetheless devoted, and found the sporting life at Knowsley uncongenial. He was a shy, introverted, serious young man; another of Disraeli's young friends, Henry Lennox, dubbed him 'Young Morose'. He was liberal-minded, but with fatal character defects of caution, lack of self-confidence, indecision and stubbornness which were to ruin his career and his long friendship with Disraeli.

Stanley entered Parliament as member for King's Lynn, George Bentinck's old seat, on 23 March 1849. He had his first serious political conversation with Disraeli on 2 April, and by May he was a frequent visitor at Grosvenor Gate. Politically, he was far closer to Disraeli than to his father, or indeed to the majority of the Conservative Party to whom he felt bound by filial loyalty rather than conviction. Indeed his close friendship and collaboration with Disraeli over such issues as dropping Protection increased Derby's jealousy of Disraeli. Greville wrote maliciously of Derby's 'mortification at seeing his son devoted to him', and, on one occasion in 1855, when Stanley arrived unexpectedly at Knowsley to break the news that Palmerston had offered him a post, his father's reaction was: 'What the devil brings you here, Edward? Are you going to be married or has Disraeli cut his throat?'[26] From 1849 until 1855 when Stanley came under influences hostile to Disraeli, he was Disraeli's devoted disciple and political collaborator. In 1855, he rewrote his diary, including references to Disraeli which were at best equivocal and sometimes derogatory, but the tone of his private letters of the period was very different; friendly, eager, sometimes almost hero-worshipping. On 17 January 1854, Samuel Phillips, whose gift for invective was positively Disraelian, ridiculed Disraeli's influence over Stanley in an article in *The Times*:

> Everybody calls to mind a picture of Hogarth's, in which a young woman is represented as having just arrived in London by the country waggon. As she alights at the inn door a questionable-looking beldame accosts her. This is the first step in the downward progress of a pure mind. It is reported that Mr. Disraeli has, in similar fashion, welcomed with smiles the arrival of the heir of the house of Derby from the University of Cambridge.

Disraeli's relationship with Stanley was essentially intellectual, that of master and disciple, patron and protégé. Stanley was intelligent, unprejudiced and well-connected, exactly the type of young man whom Disraeli hoped to attract to the ranks of his party, and, amid the hostility which he had to encounter, the young man's admiration was both flattering and welcome. The same cannot be said of his far more intimate friendship with another young man at this time, Lord Henry Lennox, into which there entered a distinctly flirtatious note.

Lord Henry Charles Lennox, third son of the fifth Duke of Richmond and MP for Chichester since 1848, was just thirty in 1851 when their friendship began. He was an intriguing, rash, bright, amusing and not very sensible young man whom nobody took very seriously. 'I would never call H.L. a statesman', young Stanley wrote to Disraeli. By early 1852 when Disraeli had become Chancellor and Lennox been given a post in the administration, their friendship was on an intimate level, as is apparent from Lennox's letters to Disraeli, written in a graceful, flamboyant hand which was very much like Disraeli's own. 'Need I say', he wrote on 15 July, 'that I am quite effete without good news without the Chancellor!! and without Champagne Cup !!! – I go on Saturday to Hatfield ... How I wish you had accepted to do the same – ',[27] and, three days later, 'Thanks, a thousand thanks for your charming letter ... I dine at Hatfield tonight, but shall be down here tomorrow at 11.30. Till then Farewell! My dearest D! How could you suppose I should *not be dull* without you'. Disraeli's letters in return were evidently sometimes querulous, petulant and demanding as they had been at the time of his courtship of Mary Anne, as can be deduced from Lennox's replies. Writing of the possibility of seeing Disraeli passing through London *en route* for Osborne, Lennox assured him: 'I *shall* NOW be sorry to see you! & *you* shall you be glad, once more to meet your as ever most sincerely Henry Lennox'. An undated letter of the period reads; 'My dearest D., I am aghast at your letter. Our Friendship dissolved. God Forbid. I shall not NOW leave London', and in late August, while reading *Coningsby* on the train to Scotland, he wrote, 'I am so determined, that you shall not write a second letter like your last, that, at the risk of it's [sic] being quite illegible, I have commenced an Epistle, in the Railway Carriage!'

A selection of Disraeli's letters to Lennox is printed in Moneypenny and Buckle, an occasional phrase revealing the extent of his affection for him. 'I am glad you are dull in my absence', he wrote from Hughenden on 18 July in answer to Lennox's letter of the fifteenth, 'I also feel lonely'.[28] Again from Hughenden he wrote on 7 August: 'It was very kind of you to write to me, and most delightful to me to hear from you ... Work absorbs, or should absorb one; nevertheless, I think very often of my young companion, and miss him sadly, for his presence to me is always a charm, and often a consolation'. Congratulating Lennox on his effort to find a clever young writer to 'puff' the Conservatives, he chided him, 'You, my beloved, are a little fresh in supposing that your Phoenix could choose his journal, and that the Daily News, incontinently, would permit him to uphold the great captain [Derby] and your graceless correspondent'. Later in August, probably in answer to Lennox's 'aghast' letter above, he wrote: 'Excuse my frankness, but I do not wish, too hastily, to look upon our friendship as the last of my illusions. I shall be in D[owning] S[treet] tomorrow by two o'clock. I apprehend my morning will be very much engaged, but I hope we may dine together, alone, at the Coventry.' On 25 August Lennox, shooting with his father at Gordon Castle in Scotland, appealed to him, 'Write to me, dearest D., When you have time! a *nice*, kind affectionate letter; amusing! it *must* be – '. Disraeli replied on 1 September: 'I cannot let another day close without thanking you for your letter, but I am so tired that I can only tell you that I love you'.[30] He had no illusions about Lennox's intellectual stamina: 'Write to me very often, and tell me how you are. I am amused about *Coningsby*, and am rather surprised that you never read it before ... If you ever have inclination or power to read another book – for reading, I suspect, is not your forte – you must manage to read *Sybil*, and especially *Tancred*.'

Biographers of Disraeli have scouted the use of terms such as 'I can only say I love you', as quite normal in the context of Victorian male friendships, but Disraeli was not in the habit of using such terminology in his correspondence with men, not even in letters to his dearest friend, d'Orsay. That he should do so to a man seventeen years younger than himself, charming and amusing, but certainly not extraordinarily gifted, points to an affection verging on infatuation, at least during the first year of their friendship. Certainly Smythe was jealous and a trifle disgusted, writing to Manners on returning from a visit to Hughenden in the autumn of 1852: 'Puzzled I was ... to see how really and apart from all paradox, Diz is governed by H. Lennox. I see now how vain an ass I was in my Young England days, when I attributed to my intellect the favour, which I see accorded to his personal friendships only, for myself':[31] while in January 1853, Henry's younger brother, Lord Alexander, was reported as being 'intensely disgusted at his brother Henry's *engouement* for Disraeli'.[32]

The friendship with Lennox lasted over many years, though on a less intense level. Disraeli was loyal to the few people for whom he really cared, and remained so to Lennox, sometimes even at the risk of his public reputation, despite the latter's demands, jealousies, importunities and occasional desertions. Lennox, as a younger son who was without office since the Tories were almost always in Opposition, was, like Smythe, perennially in search of an heiress. 'There is but one thing left for me and that is to sell my rank and position for such a sum as will enable me to keep it up,' he wrote to Disraeli, to whom he was always turning for help and advice in his matrimonial projects.[33] Having failed to entrap a Spanish princess and a rich tradesman's daughter, he implored Disraeli to help him 'try it on with the eldest of Sir Anthony de Rothschild's daughters'. As late as 1868, he was still pursuing her, having, he hoped, overcome his parents' prejudice against Jews, but he never seems to have summoned up the courage to pounce upon his prey, and the Rothschilds regarded him as too old. It was hopeless, he lamented to Disraeli in 1863, 'It is always the same thing; either the lady has too little money or I am too old.'; he was to die unmarried in 1886. There were rows between them caused by Lennox's expectations of patronage, notably in 1858, when a sharp letter from Disraeli quickly brought Henry to heel: 'I have read your dear, kind letter again and again, & am so grateful for it: Remember my Dearest D., I am, henceforth, your own property, to do what you like with, my hopes & wishes are centred in but one thing; need I add that is your increasing success. – only let me be with, & by you'.[34]

Lennox was useful to Disraeli in minor ways. Like Sidonia, Disraeli maintained an informal intelligence network to keep him informed of what was going on in the social, political and diplomatic world. Lennox, as a Duke's son, had the entrée into Whig society; he frequently called on Greville, whom he irreverently called 'Groucher', and could bring Disraeli snippets of information and scandal from the other side of the political fence, and he had good contacts in Paris, increasingly the centre of European diplomacy in the fifties and sixties. Lennox busied himself there, forwarding Disraeli's intrigues against the governments first of Aberdeen and then of Palmerston, writing his chief such letters as these: 'If you could once get them [the Hollands], they would be invaluable. They are the most perfect schemers & "Intrigants" possible – *Just* the very people we want, anti-Aberdeen, pro-Palmerston, out of politics.'[35] He provided information for Disraeli's news-paper, *The Press*, founded in 1853, and apparently occasionally wrote for it; he was, in short, an active part of what might be termed the Disraelian underground.

All this, however, lay in the future; in 1852 the emotional nature of the relationship between the two men seemed uppermost. Mary Anne, it seems, was not satisfying Disraeli's emotional needs. She was after all with him at Hughenden when he wrote to Lennox, 'I am glad you are dull in my absence, I also feel lonely'. The latent homosexual element in Disraeli's friendships with younger men (not including Stanley) cannot be ignored in the case of Lennox, even if the relationship was almost certainly not physical.

Of Disraeli's close friends only two were his contemporaries, d'Orsay and Bulwer Lytton. Although they had been reconciled in 1850 when Disraeli and Mary Anne had visited Knebworth, the relationship between Disraeli and Lytton was no longer a close one. Despite the length of their acquaintance, they had not been true friends since the mid-thirties, and now regarded each other with mixed feelings. Disraeli was irritated by Lytton's more ridiculous facets, his vanity and his hypochondria, while Stanley has recorded what were probably Lytton's feelings towards Disraeli in return. 'There is in Lytton's mind a singular mixture of feelings towards Disraeli: he admires him, sneers at him, envies his position, yet cannot quite forget their long-standing intimacy, and the somewhat similar careers they have run. On the whole, his feelings of dislike prevail, and they are expressed with sufficient plainness.'[36]

With the exception, therefore, of d'Orsay and Lytton, all Disraeli's close friendships were with men younger than he was: Smythe, Manners, Henry Lygon, Viscount Elmley (later 4th Earl Beauchamp), who was two years younger than Smythe, Henry Lennox; later, from 1856–68 the sinister Ralph Earle, of whom Lennox was to be intensely jealous; and lastly, Montague Corry, who was to supersede Earle, and whom Disraeli, ageing and in love with Lady Bradford, would regard as a surrogate son. There were several common denominators among these friends: youth, wit, charm, good looks and good connections. They were all also, with the exception of Manners, lifelong bachelors. Indeed Manners, writing to Disraeli to announce his engagement to his first wife, Catherine Marlay, struck a curious note: 'I take this opportunity of communicating to you a piece of news which I fear may not be altogether agreeable to you – I marry Miss Marlay'.[37] Despite his unwavering loyalty to Disraeli, his two marriages, both to women whom Disraeli disliked, removed him from real intimacy, so that Disraeli could complain that Manners through being too uxorious had become bourgeois in his taste for food and 'vulgar women'. It would be unfair (while not dismissing it) to exaggerate the sexual element. Disraeli was in love with youth, its vitality, iconoclasm and lack of prejudice. Young in outlook himself, he needed the high spirits and levity of these young men to combat his natural melancholia, his tendency to be 'bored to extinction'.

D'Orsay, Disraeli's greatest friend, had died in 1852, George Smythe, whom Disraeli described to Elmley as 'one of the joys of my existence', was to die of consumption on 9 November 1857 aged only 39. Returning from Egypt in September where he had gone in vain search of health, he wrote to Manners describing himself as 'a bed-ridden Lovelace'. 'I have no stamina,' he wrote, 'my legs & arms are not larger than slate-pencils . . . Will you give me to November?' He was married on his deathbed; Disraeli wrote to a friend:

> I am afraid Strangford [Smythe had succeeded to his father's title] is very bad. A mysterious paragraph in the [Morning] Post announcing the postponement of his marriage with 'Miss Kincaird Lennox' in consequence of his illness. I apprehend, that he does not want to marry her unless he is sure of dying. He means the Coronet for a legacy. God grant he may be spared to us, and not mar a future with any sentimental ˙tomfoolery.[38]

Smythe had written his own bitter epitaph in a letter to his father years before: 'My life has been made up of two blunders: I am a failure, – and – I know it!' Disraeli sincerely mourned him; there had been a mutual fascination and attraction between them, although each had been aware of the other's faults. In his last surviving letter to Disraeli Smythe had written: 'You were of old the Cid and Captain of my boyish fanaticism and after that I was seduced to desert you (out of domestic reasons) I could never help feeling that you were the Cid and Captain of my every sympathy.'[39]

On his deathbed he gave Disraeli a cup of Derbyshire spar, which years later Disraeli showed to Sir William Fraser 'with much feeling' saying, 'It is not a great thing: but for a man to remember one at all at such a time is most gratifying.'

Smythe retained his fascination for Disraeli to the end of his life; a passage in his last novel, *Endymion*, in which Smythe features as Waldershare, was perhaps the best description of the friend whom he had lost over twenty years before:

> Waldershare was profligate, but sentimental; unprincipled, but romantic; the child of whims and the slave of imagination, so freakish and deceptive that it was always impossible to foretell his course. He was alike capable of sacrificing all his feelings to worldly considerations or of forfeiting the world for a visionary caprice.[40]

Smythe is generally credited with having asked Disraeli the cruel question of what his real feelings were towards 'that old woman', and one may wonder what Mary Anne's reactions were towards those young friends of her husband's who could follow him into that male political world of Westminster, Bellamy's, the Carlton and the Coventry from which she was excluded. 'When he is in office . . . I lose him altogether', she complained pathetically to Lord Rosebery, but office did not prevent Disraeli from seeing Henry Lennox, whose habit it became over the years to walk back with his chief from the House to Grosvenor Gate. Was Mary Anne jealous of her husband's young friends as she was of Sarah? It seems not, or, if she were, there is no evidence of it.

Disraeli continued his clandestine correspondence with Sarah while in office, her letters to him at 11 Downing Street being directed to him through his secretary, I.P. Courtenay. He also continued to conceal his financial straits from Mary Anne. Even as he took office as Chancellor, on 28 February 1852, Philip Rose had to lend him £1,500 to tide him over, while a fortnight later Hobhouse (now Lord Broughton) recorded in his diary that there were rumours that the new Chancellor was in great pecuniary difficulties, resuscitating the old, true story that whilst out of Parliament he had run the risk of being arrested. Disraeli's financial position was always the same; each year disaster loomed, and each year he managed somehow to wriggle out of trouble. Perennially optimistic he wrote to Sarah on 1 August 1851, '. . . as so many things have really turned up & always turned up when they were most wanted, the end will be as right as we all wish.'[41]

In the end something did turn up, in the unlikely form of a rich and eccentric elderly widow of Jewish extraction living in Torquay. Mrs Brydges Willyams was born a da Costa and, despite having married a colonel of Cornish militia, was, like Disraeli, obsessively proud of her race. According to a memorandum by Sir Philip Rose, she had written several admiring letters to Disraeli of which he, accustomed to receiving such missives, took no notice. Some time early in 1851, however, her advances took on a more concrete and attractive form. The substance of her letter, according to Rose's memory of it, was a request to Disraeli to act as her executor: 'I have often before addressed you in reference to your political speeches and your published works; but I now write to you upon a private subject. I am about to make my Will, and I have to ask, as a great favour, that you will oblige me by being one of the executors.' The bait came in the final sentence: 'I think it right to add that whoever are my executors will also be my residuary legatees, and that the interest they will take under my will, although not a considerable one, will, at all events, be substantial'.[42]

Both Disraeli and Rose agreed that this odd proposal from an unknown woman should be treated with caution, and he replied with a conditional acceptance, suggesting that he should visit her during the autumn recess. In August he sent her a copy of *Tancred*, which he described as 'a vindication, and I hope, a complete one, of the race from which we alike spring', and a copy of the recent edition of the *Curiosities of Literature* prefaced by his memoir of his father, in which, he told her, 'you will find the name of your family incidentally mentioned'. Encouraged, Mrs Brydges Willyams immediately wrote back suggesting that they should meet at the Great Exhibition, which she intended to visit that week, ending with the curious phrase, 'I should be delighted to meet you, and to pay my lawful debts; as to other debts, I must not soar to impossibilities'.[43] Possibly Disraeli was still not convinced of the lady's sanity or the seriousness of her intentions; he is said to have asked a fellow guest at Monckton Milnes' house, Fryston, 'Do you know a mad woman living at Torquay called Mrs Brydges Willyams?' In any case, he apparently left town before she arrived and did not meet her, nor did he visit her at Torquay in the autumn, but contented himself with sending her a copy of *Bentinck*, with a brief note, at the end of the year. Mrs Brydges Willyams persisted with the correspondence but Disraeli was too busy in 1852, his year of office, to make the promised visit, and it was not until mid-August 1853 that he and Mary Anne visited her at Torquay.

The visit was an overwhelming success; returning to London with a memorandum from Mrs Brydges Willyams about her will, Disraeli wrote gracefully to her from Hughenden: 'How often I recall, with charm, and often with consolation, the kindness which you have shown me, and the mysterious sympathy which now binds us together'.[44] It was the beginning of a relationship which lasted until Mrs Brydges Willyams' death ten years later, and which was to involve annual visits by the Disraelis to Torquay; the exchange of presents of flowers, fish, game and books; and long florid epistles by Disraeli, which, in their exaggerated gallantry and extravagant language, presaged his later letters to Queen Victoria – 'Where did you get the lobster which arrived for my *déjeuner* this morning? From the caves of Amphitrite? It was so fresh! Tasted of the sweetness – not the salt – of the ocean, and almost as creamy as your picturesque cheese'. Only Disraeli, one feels, could describe a cheese as 'picturesque'.[45]

It was somehow fitting that financial salvation should come to Disraeli not because of any business acumen, in which, despite his fond dreams of great *coups* on the stock market he was startlingly deficient, but because he was the author of *Tancred*.

15 The Restless Fifties

Disraeli – and the century – were approaching middle age; the years that followed his fall from office in December 1852 were, with the brief exception of the short-lived Derby-Disraeli Government of 1858-9, the most unsatisfactory of his career. After the fall of Peel it was unkindly remarked that Disraeli was like an anatomist without a body on which to operate; in the prosperous England of the fifties, after the clash between Free Trade and Protection in the forties and before the fierce battles over Reform in the latter half of the sixties, there were no major issues to raise the political temperature to the fever heat to which his talents were best suited. Faced with the apathy, even hostility, of Derby and his own party, Disraeli, in his single-minded pursuit of power, was in the position of a guerrilla leader, seeking issues and allies wherever he could find them, making lightning attacks on the Government that often left his own troops confused, and which earned him the reputation of a man without principle.

Perhaps the most perspicacious comment on Disraeli at this stage in his career was made by John Bright after their interview at Grosvenor Gate in December 1852. He wrote in his diary:

> This remarkable man is ambitious, most able, and without prejudices. He conceives it right to strive for a great career with such principles as are in vogue in his age and country – says the politics and principles to suit England must be of the 'English type', but having obtained power, would use it to found a great reputation on great services rendered to the country.[1]

Lord Malmesbury's view was less flattering, but more generally held; 'to get office', he told Stanley, 'he [Disraeli] would do anything and act with anyone'.[2]

Disraeli's objectives were threefold, to break-up the Coalition at all costs by acting with the Irish, Bright, and the Radicals to defeat them in the Commons; to detach Palmerston and the moderate Whigs from Russell and the Peelites using the internal jealousies within the Coalition; and to reorganize his party and present it as a viable alternative Government by giving it a more progressive, liberal image. In all these manoeuvres he was viewed with increasing suspicion by Derby and the party, whose political ideology, if such it can be called, was simply to 'impede progress'.[3] Hating the Radicals and distrusting the Whigs, Derby and his squires looked upon Disraeli's intrigues and his guerrilla tactics with disgust, and as he pursued his independent course, the gulf between himself and his party widened. While the squires looked on him with suspicion and distrust, he regarded them with contempt.

Derby, whose desire for power was at best spasmodic, remained distant at Knowsley and his house at St Leonards, seeing no one apart from his sporting companions and his racing trainer, John Scott. According to his son he was deeply disillusioned with politics, convinced he would never hold office again, and that the best policy for the Conservative opposition was 'to leave Ministers alone'. He was also in poor health, and frequently laid up with attacks of gout when he passed the time in translating the Iliad. He rarely saw Disraeli. 'Goodwood and the gout have prevented my seeing him of late', Disraeli wrote to Herries on 11 August 1853, on receiving notice of Herries' intended retirement, of which Derby had not bothered to inform him, complaining later that 'My despatches from Knowsley have only taken the form of haunches of venison'. When more serious despatches did arrive, the contents were not as agreeable; in June after Disraeli and his only ally, Stanley, had sided with Bright and the Radicals against the Government's India Bill, he received an admonitory letter: 'I cannot conceal from you,' Derby wrote, 'that there is reported to me a growing fear ... that you are gradually withdrawing yourself more and more from the Conservative portion of our supporters, and seeking alliances in quarters with which neither they nor I can recognise any bond of union.'[4]

He invited Disraeli to Knowsley for the first time in the second week of December 1853, but it was not a social invitation and Mary Anne was not included. The object of the meeting was, in Malmesbury's words, to make him 'ride to orders'. It was not a happy meeting; Malmesbury, who had been invited to put additional pressure on Disraeli, noted that Derby was visibly bored by Disraeli's arrival because it meant he would have to discuss politics. Disraeli, for his part, was lonely and in low spirits, describing Knowsley to Mary Anne as 'a wretched house'. He was lectured by the two peers on the 'necessity ... of taking a really Conservative line in and out of the House', and of the importance of seeing a great deal more of the members of his party, advice which Disraeli found singularly uncongenial and which he had no intention of following.

The bad relations between Disraeli and his party were not destined to improve. As early as February of that year Greville, after a conversation with the influential Conservative, Tom Baring, noted:

> It does not look as if the connexion between Dis. and the party could go on long. Their dread and distrust of him and his contempt of them render it difficult if not impossible. Pakington [the former Colonial Secretary] is already talked of as their Leader, and some think Disraeli wants to shake them off and trade on his own bottom, trusting to his great abilities to make his way to political power.[5]

Disraeli had no intention of bowing to the prejudices of the squires as he had in the humiliating affair of the leadership in 1849. He could afford to ignore their discontent with his leadership, knowing that Derby, however distrustful, was committed to him. A remark he made to Stanley after a January visit to Yorkshire that year revealed the deep gulf which separated him from his followers. 'He complained loudly', Stanley recorded in his diary

> of the apathy of the party: they could not be got to attend to business while the hunting season lasted: a sharp frost would make the difference of twenty men. They had a good natural ability ... taking them as a body: but wanted culture: they never read: their leisure was passed in field sports: the wretched school and university system was in fault: they learned nothing useful and did not understand the ideas of their own time.

If the hunting squires could not comprehend the ideas of their own time, Disraeli was determined to give the public the impression that they could, and to create an ideology for them whether they would or no. Early that year he conceived the idea of realizing an old dream, the setting-up of a progressive Conservative journal to counteract the reactionary attitudes of the two existing Tory papers, *The Herald* and *The Standard*. There were additional reasons for setting up a respectable Conservative journal; on circulation figures the bias of the metropolitan and provincial press in England and Scotland was almost 2–1 in favour of the Liberals, while *The Times*, the most influential newspaper in Europe, supported the Aberdeen Coalition.

Disraeli had talked of such a project since 1849, and had made several abortive attempts to buy or re-form existing journals, but now, possibly buoyed up by the prospect of capital from the cheap edition of his novels published by Bryce that year, he was determined to make it a reality, throwing himself into the scheme with all the ardour which he had devoted to the setting-up of *The Representative* nearly thirty years before. Stanley, who was his chief collaborator, said he had never seen him so much excited about anything since their conversation about Zionism at Hughenden in January 1851. At first Disraeli envisaged the new journal as a cross between *The Times* and *Punch*, but the more prudent Stanley persuaded him to drop the idea of satirical cartoons; it was then to be called *The Week*, but finally the title *The Press* was fixed upon. Disraeli appealed to his old friend Henry Hope for financial support, revealing his plans for the paper. It was, he said, to be a weekly journal 'of a somewhat peculiar character', and, 'though Tory, is of a very progressive and enlightened design'. In conversation with a prospective contributor, Kenealy, he outlined his purpose: 'The Coalition was to be attacked, and the true principles of the Tory party were to be put forward. The Tories were at present a great mass, but destitute of ideas, and *The Press* was to furnish them with these.'[6] Almost immediately he encountered the resistance of Derby, who had the Tory aristocrat's distaste for newspapers and journalists, and who persuaded the Duke of Northumberland, who had offered £2,000, to withdraw his support. When Stanley represented to his father that the existing Tory papers conveyed only the feelings of the lowest and least enlightened part of the party and that the more enlightened voice should make itself heard, Derby remained unimpressed. He thought its effect on the party would be divisive, which indeed it turned out to be, and, according to Stanley he 'expressed distrust of all the individuals engaged in the new design, not entirely excepting Disraeli.'

Disraeli was undeterred. Characteristically his visions of the success of his new paper rose higher and higher and he talked of a circulation of from 10,000 to 15,000, even of 'shaking the power of *The Times*'.[7] His predictions were wildly exaggerated. In the five years of its existence under Disraeli, the circulation of *The Press* was around 3,000, and its finances constantly in deficit, while, although serving Disraeli's purposes it hardly needs to be said that it in no way rivalled the influence of 'the Thunderer'. Funds were eventually raised, with Disraeli himself contributing £2,500, and the first number appeared on 7 May 1853 costing sixpence. It was a weekly journal, published on Saturdays, the editor being Samuel Lucas and the contributors mainly amateurs. Disraeli himself wrote ten of the first eleven leading articles, with Stanley contributing one third of the material of the first two volumes, while Lytton wrote a series of political letters under the pseudonym 'Manlius'.

The early theme of *The Press*, apart from attacking the Coalition, was to follow the Disraelian line of presenting Conservatism under Derby as the comfortable alternative to the Radicalism of Lord John Russell and Bright. This was intended as an appeal to the moderate Whigs, whose interests, like the Conservatives, were territorial. Disraeli's representation of Derby as a reformer was hardly believable: 'There are two men in England who occupy intelligible positions, and only two. They are both Liberals, both Reformers, and both Lancashire men; and these are Lord Derby and Mr. Bright ... Between these two intelligible systems the people of this country must, sooner or later, choose'. The paper was, over the years, to reflect the complex shifts in Disraeli's attitudes on different issues; when the Crimean War broke out, *The Press* fell in with the popular jingo line of supporting it, while blaming Aberdeen for allowing it to happen. In 1855 when Palmerston took office and Disraeli felt that the popularity of the war was helping keep him in power, *The Press* advocated peace, and its increasing pacifism was applauded by Bright but repudiated by the Conservative party.

Indeed Malmesbury, who referred to the paper as 'Disraeli's cursed Press', suspected him of using it to advance his own position to the disadvantage of the other leading Conservatives, notably Derby. He wrote in his diary for 26 April 1857:

> I can see that many believe Disraeli would like to place himself at the head of the Conservative party to the exclusion of Lord Derby. These suspicions are strengthened by the tone of his paper, 'The Press', which avoids mentioning the name of Lord Derby, or of anyone except Disraeli himself, whom it praises in the most fulsome manner.

The tributes of *The Press* to Disraeli could indeed be called fulsome; he had, the journal declared, on the question of both peace and war 'shown the energy of a patriot and the sagacity of a statesman'. Its report of a pre-session dinner given by Disraeli at Grosvenor Gate in February 1857 enthused: 'Never before did the banquet of any Opposition leader in the Lower House at the opening of the session exhibit such an array of names, representatives of rank and property, and associated with proud historical associations', asserting untruthfully that even Peel at the head of 'the gentlemen of England' had never met Parliament with a more united party.

Disraeli enjoyed journalism, indeed one cannot help feeling that had he not been a politician he would have been a journalist. He relished the opportunity *The Press* afforded him of firing a weekly salvo at the Coalition in support of his guerrilla campaigns against them at Westminster, and the means it provided for carrying on that campaign during the long silence of parliamentary vacations. His journalistic style as manifested in *The Press* leaders had not changed since *Runnymede* seventeen years before, and such passages as that in which he compared the Prime Minister, Lord Aberdeen's 'licentiously peevish manner' with 'the crabbed malice of a maundering witch', were hardly couched in the high Gladstonian tone recommended to him by *The Times* in 1852.

The Press was 'his' paper; its unprofitable financial affairs were handled by his adviser, Philip Rose, and when the leading articles were not written by himself or Stanley, they were executed by the editor under Disraeli's direction. Lucas was replaced by D. T. Coulton as editor in 1854, and T. E. Kebbel, a young Tory journalist who joined the staff of *The Press* in 1855, testified that Disraeli virtually wrote the leaders for Coulton who, when Parliament was sitting, would go down to the House as late as possible on Friday evenings, returning to the office in the Strand with a bundle of pencil notes dictated by Disraeli to be transformed into the first leader for the next day's issue.[8] Understandably Disraeli went to considerable lengths to conceal the extent of his connection with the paper. At the outset Lucas wrote to him reassuring him that 'No one will be able to say through me, "I know the originators and inspirers of this organ to be so-and-so", for I shall stand firmly and impenetrably between you and the public', and he conscientiously always destroyed Disraeli's copy himself.[9] No one was deceived, however, least of all Lord Aberdeen, the principal victim of Disraeli's attacks, who denounced *The Press* in the Lords as 'a publication which is supposed to enjoy great authority; at all events, from its malignity and misrepresentations, the origin of it is not perhaps very difficult to discover.'

Disraeli did not draw the line at outright lying to conceal his connection with the paper, telling Greville in the winter of 1855 that 'he now had nothing whatever to do with "The Press"'. However, a letter from Henry Lennox written in the autumn of 1857 at the time of the Stuttgart meeting between Napoleon III and the Tsar Alexander II, suggesting the use of some secret informant to provide material for the paper, certainly indicated that Disraeli was still very much in control of it. 'Why do you not write to the Mouse?' asked Lennox, 'He could tell us all the humbug, that went on at Stuttgard [sic] which would make a sensation in the P[ress].'[10] Disraeli had good reasons to distance himself publicly from the paper, increasingly the target of Tory hatred, but the likelihood was that he continued to exert influence over it until it was sold to Newdegate in May 1858.

Disraeli's public image suffered badly during these years; late in 1853 a venomous biography of him appeared in which every episode of his career from *The Representative* onwards was painted in the blackest possible light, the declared purpose of its anonymous author, believed to be T. MacKnight, being to counteract the corrupting influence of Disraeli on the younger generation through the example of his success and the circulation of the cheap edition of his novels. MacKnight's biography was so slanted as to defeat its own purpose, but it was followed by a far more damaging attack by Disraeli's former collaborator, Samuel Phillips, reviewing MacKnight in *The Times* of 17 January 1854. Phillips condemned the book, but then proceeded to do his own hatchet job on Disraeli in a bitter and masterly piece. He made the old charges of unmitigated self-interest and unprincipled opportunism, but made them cleverly:

> Benjamin Disraeli will stand before posterity as the great political infidel of his age – as one who believed in nothing but himself, who was earnest only in securing the dazzling objects of his ambition – sincere only in his all-engrossing anxiety to improve his own fortunes . . . say that Benjamin Disraeli is Genius without Conscience, and you have his character in three words.

Phillips' attack, reaching as it did the most influential breakfast tables in London, and indeed abroad, hurt Disraeli; some eight years later he was to write an angry note in his *Reminiscences*, 'Mr. P. was an impudent adventurer.' The charges were the more damaging because there was some truth in them; there was the echo here of Disraeli's bitter self-characterization to Derby in 1849: 'I am Disraeli the adventurer'. It would be interesting to know why Phillips, who had once been on assiduously friendly terms with Disraeli and in close correspondence with him, should have turned on him with such sustained hatred. Financial disappointment and the feeling that he had been insufficiently rewarded by Disraeli in office for his previous support may have been the cause of his rancour. He was in poor health with a large family to support, and his last surviving letters to Disraeli, dating from the autumn of 1852, were requests for favours for himself and his partners in various enterprises. They may have not been granted; hence Phillips' bitterness. Phillips died later that year, 1854; before he died he published two volumes of his pieces from *The Times*; curiously he did not reprint the article on Disraeli.

While Disraeli's career seemed to have taken a downward turn, Gladstone's star was in the ascendant. Since the clash over Disraeli's Budget in 1852, the rivalry between the two men had become public knowledge, and comparisons between their political and oratorical abilities were now frequently drawn, usually to Disraeli's disadvantage. Gladstone's performance as Chancellor greatly enhanced his reputation for financial expertise, marking him out as a future leader – 'a *man* equal to great political necessities, and fit to lead Parties and direct Governments,' Greville noted. He was, Greville said, the man whom Disraeli most feared as a parliamentary opponent, while the Saxon envoy, Vitzthum von Eckstaedt, called him the foremost speaker in the House. *The Times*, admittedly a prejudiced source, repeatedly contrasted Disraeli's abilities as a speaker unfavourably with those of Gladstone. While admitting that no one else had 'carried the art of making himself unpleasant to the same perfection as Mr. Disraeli', the newspaper thought that he was 'in imminent danger of becoming a member of the dreaded fraternity of bores ... Now that Peel is dead, he tortures the House of Commons with enormous harangues of $2\frac{1}{2}$ to 4 hours'. Gladstone, *The Times* continued, 'demolished him in a sentence'. Two young MPs, Stafford Northcote and Gathorne – Hardy, both future members of Disraeli's 1874 Cabinet, who, entering Parliament in 1855 had not seen the Disraeli of the Peel philippics, were both singularly unimpressed with his oratorical abilities.

Disraeli himself felt gloomy, isolated, and oppressed, as he complained to Lady Londonderry at the end of the 1854 session:

> I already feel, in the position which I now occupy, the want of sufficient fortune. There are a thousand things which ought to be done which are elements of power, and which I am obliged to decline doing, or to do at great sacrifice. Whether it be influence with the Press, or organisation throughout the country, everyone comes to me and everything is expected from me. Tho' so many notables and magnificoes belong to the party, there never was an aggregation of human beings, who exercised less social influence. They seem to disregard, or to despise, all modes and means of managing mankind. As for our Chief, we never see him. His House is always closed; he subscribes to nothing, tho' his fortune is very large; and expects, nevertheless, everything to be done. I have never yet been fairly backed in life. All the great personages I have known, even when what is called 'ambitious' ... have been unequal to a grand game. This has been my fate, and I never felt it more keenly than at the present moment, with a confederate always at Newmarket or Doncaster, when Europe, nay the world, is in the throes of immense changes, and all the elements of power at home in a state of dissolution.[11]

All Disraeli's hopes and intrigues during these years were thwarted; he seemed to lack that essential ingredient in every successful career – luck. Through all his secret intrigues with Palmerston he fondly imagined that he was using the older man for his own ends, underrating Palmerston's cunning and ambition; Palmerston, in fact, was using him. Disraeli's moods were mercurial, swinging from elation to depression with the course of events; in the early months of 1854 he had high hopes of effecting a juncture between Conservatives, 'old Whigs' and Palmerston, in opposition to Russell's Reform Bill, which, as Stanley remarked, was treated with absolute apathy by the working classes, but had thrown the Conservative classes into a paroxysm of alarm and fears of impending revolution.[12]

The signs were good for a Russell defeat; even before the introduction of the Reform Bill, Palmerston was reported as 'intriguing busily' against it, and on 10 February the Whig party in the House of Lords attacked the Government for bringing in an unnecessary Bill when war with Russia was imminent. Ten days after Russell introduced his Bill on 13 February, an excited Disraeli called Stanley to a special conference in the private room behind the Speaker's Chair. He was, said Stanley, 'in one of his sanguine moods, speaking of civilities received from the Queen and Prince, which he hopefully construed into proofs of political reconciliation'. He told Stanley that there had lately been a Whig meeting against the Reform Bill, and that he was in communication, directly or indirectly, with most of the leading Whigs. He thought a junction with them was quite possible, all depended upon Palmerston with whom Disraeli had been in touch, trying to pin him down. Palmerston once gained, he said, he felt sure of the rest; 'as to the lead [of the Commons], he was willing to give it up, P[almerston] being an old man, not capable of sustained exertion: the real power would always remain with himself'. Disraeli dreamed of a bright future with the defeat of the Coalition and the aged Palmerston as leader of the Conservative party in the Commons, the man who represented the great threat to his own future, Gladstone, would be forced to join the Radical minority. 'He exulted', Stanley said, 'in the notion of revenge on Gladstone and the Peelites, who would be driven to Manchester [i.e. into the arms of the political economists and Radicals] and must act under Bright. He even began to arrange offices'.[13]

Disraeli's optimism was, however, premature. On 28 March 1854, England declared war on Russia; eight days later Lord John Russell, shaken by a fit of hysterical crying, announced the abandonment of his Reform Bill. England had blundered into the Crimean War, and Disraeli's chances of a parliamentary *coup* were swept away by a wave of patriotic solidarity. His reaction, as reported by Malmesbury, was characteristic: 'Disraeli is furious with the war, which he thinks keeps the Government in.'

Disraeli's opinions about the Crimean War were mixed. While agreeing that Russian aggression towards Constantinople should be curbed, he thought war could have been avoided had Aberdeen taken a firm line with Russia, and considered the Crimean Expedition itself a disastrous mistake. 'We seem to have fallen into another Walcheren Expedition', he wrote to Mrs Brydges Willyams. Events seemed to be proving him right as, after the initial victories of the Alma and Inkerman, Sebastopol held out against the Anglo-French allies, and the terrible Crimean winter, official mismanagement and incompetence took its toll of the army. As casualty figures mounted and horror stories came flooding in from the Crimea, even *The Times*, shocked by the reports of its war correspondent, William Howard Russell, turned against the Government. Inspired by Disraeli, *The Press* added its voice to the rising chorus of public anger; it was only a question of time before retribution came upon the Coalition.

The Coalition Government fell early in 1855, defeated on Roebuck's motion for a Committee of Enquiry into the conduct of the war. Aberdeen went down to Windsor on 30 January to offer his resignation to the Queen and Prince who reluctantly agreed that there was 'nothing to be done' but to send for Derby. Disraeli was in a fever of excitement, pressing Derby to go ahead on his own if necessary. 'He must do it. I will make him do it', he told Malmesbury fiercely, '– if he does not I will break up his party'. Derby, however, was convinced he could not succeed without Palmerston, the hero of the English public, and the support of Gladstone and Sidney Herbert. Palmerston, for his part, saw the Premiership within his grasp, and was not tempted by Disraeli's offer to give up the Leadership, while Gladstone and Sidney Herbert, in Lennox's words, 'were determined not to sit in the Cabinet with the Peel-smasher'. Ambition dictated Palmerston's refusal; Gladstone was principally motivated by detestation of Disraeli, as he himself recorded: 'a sentiment of revulsion from Disraeli personally – a sentiment quite distinct from that of dislike, was alone sufficient to deter me absolutely from a merely personal and separate reunion with the Conservatives.' On 1 February Derby abandoned the attempt; Palmerston became Prime Minister, with Gladstone and Sidney Herbert in his Cabinet. Both Derby and Disraeli had seriously underestimated Palmerston's stamina and the extent of his ambition, Disraeli describing him as 'really an impostor, utterly exhausted, and, at the best only ginger beer and not champaign, and now only an old painted Pantaloon, very deaf, very blind, and with false teeth, which would fall out of his mouth . . . if he did not hesitate and halt in his talk.'[14] The 'old Pantaloon,' however, was to remain in power, with one brief interval, for the following decade.

Disraeli, reported by Malmesbury as being 'in a state of disgust beyond all control', told Derby some disagreeable home truths, but it was useless to remonstrate with a leader who, in Malmesbury's words, within a few days of throwing up the chance of being Prime Minister and telling the world that his party was unfit to govern, was out shooting wildfowl at Heron Court 'with enjoyment keener than any sixteen year old schoolboy'. In his bitter disappointment, Disraeli poured out his heart to Frances Anne Londonderry. 'Our chief has again bolted!' he wrote from the Carlton on 2 February. 'This is the third time that, in the course of six years, during which I have had the lead of the Opposition in the House of Commons, I have stormed the Treasury Benches: twice fruitlessly, and the third time with a tin kettle to my tail, which rendered the race almost hopeless. You cannot, therefore, be surprised that I am a little wearied of these barren victories, which like Alma, Inkerman and Balaclava, may be glorious, but are certainly nothing more.'[15]

Disraeli had every right to be furious with Derby. Even Gladstone sympathized with him in his disappointment; meeting him by chance in the lobby of the House of Lords, he impulsively put out his hand, which was, he recorded, 'very kindly received'. Disraeli was indeed in the depths of despair, telling Stanley that 'this failure was final'. Stanley gently reminded him that this was not the first time he had said this, and Disraeli, of course, had no intention of giving up the game. He was soon hard at work to topple Palmerston, combining with Bright, leader of the pacifist party, and Gladstone, who had resigned a few weeks after taking office, to attack the Government on every available issue. It was essentially a gadfly opposition which did Disraeli (particularly with his own party) no good, and Palmerston no harm. Palmerston was too clever for him, skilfully playing a John Bull role which ensured him majority support, as Derby ruefully admitted to Malmesbury:

> Since Pam came into office he has adroitly played his cards, so as to avoid, with one or two exceptions, making any attacks on our institutions, or affording much ground for

censure from a Conservative Opposition. In short, he has been a Conservative Minister working with Radical tools, and keeping up a show of Liberalism in his foreign policy which nine or ten of the House of Commons care nothing about.[16]

Disraeli, however, did care about foreign policy, and, despairing of English politics, towards the end of 1856 he returned to his old game of 1842 – using Paris to strengthen his position in London. On 25 November 1856, the writer Prosper Mérimée reported to his friend the Whig Lady Ashburton that Disraeli and Mary Anne had arrived in Paris: 'They are here to study the situation and to look for thunderbolts with which to pulverise you Whigs in the spring.'[17] Disraeli's primary aim was to drive a wedge between Napoleon III and Palmerston; the previous October, he had received private information through the ever-intriguing Henry Lennox that the French Emperor was upset by the treatment he had been receiving from the English press, and *The Times* in particular, and wished to contact some 'Conservative Powerful' with a view to remedying the situation. Through Lennox and his contact, the Duchess of Hamilton, a cousin of the Emperor, Disraeli sent a letter to be shown to Napoleon. It criticized the 'narrow-minded basis on which Lord Palmerston has rested the [Anglo-French] alliance', warned that Palmerston 'from ancient prejudices' would thwart the imperial aims; promised Conservative support in the next session; and, avowing his long-standing devotion to the alliance with France, concluded, 'With regard to the Emperor personally, there are many private as well as public reasons why I should wish to serve him.'[18]

Unfortunately for Disraeli, Napoleon III, perhaps because of their acquaintance of Gore House days, had a low opinion of his abilities as a statesman, and a correspondingly high opinion of Palmerston. Disraeli, Napoleon told Malmesbury, had 'not the head of a statesman, but . . . is, like all literary men . . . ignorant of the world, talking well, but nervous when the moment of action arises'. As a result, he kept Disraeli at arm's length, and, although he and Mary Anne were invited everywhere, Disraeli had still not achieved his object of a private interview with the Emperor over a month after his arrival. 'Nothing from the all-commanding mind definite', he complained to Lennox on 26 December, 'it is still brooding in its unfathomable recesses'. Apart from his personal opinion of Disraeli, Napoleon regarded the Tories as natural enemies of his schemes for re-drawing the map of Europe, the liberation of Italy in particular, and he was not prepared to seem to give countenance to Disraelian intrigues against Palmerston, whose liberal foreign policies offered him support. It was not until the end of January, on the eve of the Disraelis' departure for London, that he finally condescended to grant the desired interview and it was not, from Disraeli's point of view, a satisfactory one. He was unconvinced by Disraeli's claims as to the strength of Derby's party and the weakness of Palmerston. 'I saw the Emperor was quite sceptical as to my opinion', Disraeli recorded, 'and was entirely with Palmerston. His Majesty said to me: "Lord Derby has no men" '. When warned by Disraeli against throwing himself absolutely into the arms of Palmerston, Napoleon retorted that the Tories were 'his hereditary enemies'.[19]

Despite the Emperor's unco-operative attitude, however, Disraeli left Paris satisfied that he had found a 'thunderbolt' with which to pulverize Palmerston. The provider of this explosive material was a young secretary at the British Embassy, Ralph Anstruther Earle, who was destined to replace Henry Lennox as Disraeli's intimate confidant over the next twelve years. Earle, son of a Whig family of Liverpool, was only twenty when Disraeli met him in December 1856, a brilliant, ambitious, and treacherous young man with a Disraelian passion for secrecy and intrigue. He was violently anti-Palmerston and disloyal to his chief, Lord Cowley, even going so far as to press Disraeli to discredit him by representing him as 'Palmerston's bull-dog'. Naturally, he saw in Disraeli a chance to further his ambitions of a parliamentary career; while Disraeli, to whom the combination of youth, good looks and intelligence was irresistible, was fascinated by Earle. Their relationship soon became a close one, with Earle feeding Disraeli secret information from the British Embassy in a series of undercover letters signed 'X', and taking immense precautions to keep their correspondence undiscovered. Earle played the role of ardent young disciple to the hilt, assuring Disraeli of his 'affectionate devotion'.

The relationship between Disraeli, now 52, and Ralph Earle, over thirty years his junior, was a curious echo of his own friendship with John Murray in 1825, of Vivian Grey and the Marquess of Carabas. It is not difficult to imagine that he saw in the twenty-year-old Earle almost a reincarnation of his own precociously brilliant young self, which may explain his willingness to listen to the stream of advice which Earle poured forth in his almost daily letters, sometimes he even went so far as to incorporate Earle's phrases in his speeches. At times Earle in his eagerness and self-esteem overreached himself and annoyed his patron, even criticizing Disraeli's parliamentary tactics. 'When they [the Government] adopt our views we ought to approve their conduct – By adopting the opposite course, we do them little harm & forfeit our character for sincerity', he wrote.[20] Disraeli had received too much advice of that nature, and was clearly stung; Earle hastened to soothe him, 'I do not at all underrate the value of your Parliamentary experience but you should remark that the obscure spectator is sometimes right when the conspicuous actor is mistaken'. Ralph Earle wormed his way into Disraeli's confidence as even Henry Lennox, who became bitterly jealous of him, had not, probably because of his greater intellectual capacity. He was to receive his reward for his services as informer, becoming Disraeli's private secretary on his accession to office in 1858 and a Member of Parliament the following year. Ambitious, cynical and unscrupulous, he appealed to the less attractive side of Disraeli's nature, and was to exercise a malign influence over him in the following decade.

Meanwhile, Disraeli's other young man, Henry Lennox, on his usual round of country house visits, was busily engaged in what appears to have been a Disraelian intrigue against Derby. Derby, as Lennox reported from the Jerseys' house, Middleton, was completely absorbed in his pleasures, absolutely refusing to talk about politics:

As a Leader of a Party, he is more hopeless than ever!! Devoted to Whist, Billiards, Racing, Betting & making a fool of himself with either Ladies Emily Peel or Mary Yorke. Bulwer Lytton came to Bretby for three days & was in despair. Not one word could he extract from Derby about Public Affairs; nothing but the Odds and Tricks.

Lennox's somewhat feeble plot was designed to drive a wedge between Derby and his friend Malmesbury: 'I have primed Clementina Villiers, with whom Malmesbury is supposed to be in Love,' he went on, 'to tell M. that *Derby* is the bar to Conservative consolidation.'[21]

Indeed Disraeli seems secretly to have hoped that Derby, in ill-health and bored with politics, might retire in his favour. Over eighteen months before he had written mysteriously to Lady Londonderry of having received 'from the highest quarters' an intimation that 'if things take *their due course*, the next, and I hope, very lasting Tory government may be under a head, which I never contemplated.'[22] This extravagant hope was probably based on the vague 'civilities received from the Queen and Prince' of which he had told Stanley in February of that year (1854); and, in January 1856, a few days before the opening of the new session, he had visited Greville, the political sounding-board, for a conversation which he no doubt intended to be repeated in parliamentary circles. He told Greville that 'he had never stood so well with the *best* men of his party . . .' severely criticizing Derby, and talking of the best of the Conservatives being disposed 'to go with him rather than Derby'. He spoke to Greville 'of Derby and all the blunders he had made in spite of all the advice he had given and the remonstrances he had made to him . . . that Derby with all his great talents had no discretion, and suffered himself to be led and influenced by some of the weakest and least capable men of his party – Malmesbury in particular'.[23] The intrigue came to nothing; Disraeli was deluding himself as to the support he enjoyed among his followers, and he needed Derby as much as Derby needed him. Derby certainly recognized his need of Disraeli; replying to Malmesbury's complaints as to Disraeli's unpopularity with his party in December 1856, he told him firmly that he regretted it, 'but they could not do without him, even if there were anyone ready and able to take his place.'[24]

Disraeli had returned from Paris armed with what he thought to be an important secret weapon to be used against Palmerston. Earle's diligent burrowing in the Embassy files had unearthed evidence of a secret treaty of December 1854, by which, in return for Austria's support in the Crimean War, England and France had guaranteed the security of the Austrian possessions in Italy for as long as the war should last. Since Palmerston was notoriously anti-Austrian and warm in the cause of Italian liberty, Disraeli and Earle thought that disclosure of the treaty, skilfully exploited, could be used as a weapon to embarrass, if not to unseat him.

At his pre-session dinner at Grosvenor Gate, attended by some 50 MPs, Disraeli was noticed to be in a state of 'the highest exultation, alluding mysteriously to certain disclosures which he should make tomorrow', and saying in Stanley's hearing 'by this day fortnight we shall be in office'.[25] Disraeli went into action against Palmerston on the opening night of the session to the background of rumours that he was about to make some 'terrific revelations' and that Walewski, the French Foreign Minister, had 'told him all he knows against Lord Pam'.[26] After delivering a broadside against the Government's foreign policy in Europe, China and Persia, he brought out his secret treaty with a deadly flourish, rather as a conjuror might produce a rabbit out of a hat. Palmerston, jaunty as ever, totally denied the existence of such a treaty, calling it 'an entire romance', and, according to Malmesbury, Disraeli's revelations fell rather flat. Disraeli, however, was not to be put off, returning to the attack a week later, this time giving the date of the treaty's signature, 22 December 1854, only to be flatly contradicted again by Palmerston 'with great insolence of manner'. Disraeli, however, primed with daily communications from Earle in Paris, knew that he had rattled the government. On the day following the debate Earle reported anxious enquiries from the Foreign Secretary, Lord Clarendon, to Cowley, hopefully suggesting that the Franco-Austrian convention had not been officially communicated to the English government. Walewski, however, dashed Clarendon's hopes, telling Cowley that it had been official.

Typically, Palmerston brazened it out; two nights after he had contradicted Disraeli's assertions he came down to the House, and, according to Greville:

> In a very jaunty way said he must correct his former statement, and inform the House he had just discovered that the Convention *had been signed*. Great triumph on the part of D[israeli] who poured forth a rather violent invective. Then P. lost his temper and retorted that D. was trying to cover an ignominious retreat by vapouring etc ... This language, under the circumstances of the case, was very imprudent and very improper, and (unlike what he had ever experienced before) he sat down without a single cheer.

Disraeli and Earle had won, but in a House of Commons that cared little for foreign politics, their victory had no significant result. Palmerston continued to escape all Opposition attempts to embarrass him; in mid-February Disraeli and Gladstone mounted a concerted attack on the Budget, with Gladstone taking the leading part, but the landed interest, who loathed Gladstone for introducing the succession tax, refused to follow them, many of them abstaining or voting with the Government; Disraeli and Gladstone, supported by Cobden, Bright and the Radicals, were beaten by 80 votes.

Palmerston gained an even more signal victory in the case of the lorcha *Arrow*, when Derby co-operated with Cobden and the Peelites to attack yet another instance of Palmerston's gun-boat bullying of weaker nations. At Canton a mandarin had arrested the Chinese crew of the *Arrow*, which was flying the British flag although its right to do so was extremely dubious. The crew were released after British protests, but the Canton government refused to apologize and British gunboats bombarded the port. By way of riposte the Governor of Canton, Yeh, offered rewards for the heads of Englishmen and another furious bombardment ensued. Disraeli, who had not forgotten Palmerston's triumph in a similar case, that of Don Pacifico in June 1850, saw the danger of a frontal assault on Palmerston's strongest position, his bull-dog assertion of British power. Events proved his instinct right; Palmerston was defeated by a narrow majority in the Commons, but immediately appealed to the country on the issue and was triumphantly returned with a personal following of 370 out of a House of some 650. His opponents, including Cobden, Bright and many of the Peelites were swept away and, as Shaftesbury noted in his diary, the election turned on only one question: 'Were you, or were you not? are you, or are you not, for Palmerston?'

The election of 1857 had proved overwhelmingly that mid-Victorian England approved of Palmerston's bully-boy tactics towards Oriental nations, and the horror stories emanating from India as a result of the Mutiny which broke out in the summer only served to strengthen his position. Nobody listened when Disraeli blamed the insensitive and aggressive policy of the Government for uniting Hindus and Moslems against British rule in India. Still less did they listen when he argued against the spirit of revenge on the mutineers which was sweeping England. Disraeli discounted many of the reports from India. 'The accounts are too graphic', he told Mrs Brydges Willyams. 'The rows of ladies standing with their babies in their arms to be massacred, with the elder children clutching their robes – who that would tell these things could have escaped?' He was greatly amused by Lord Shaftesbury's public outrage over an utterly unfounded story that thirteen British ladies had arrived at Calcutta with their noses cut off and by the subsequent offer from a surgeon to provide them with artificial noses. Writing to the Committee for the Relief of Indian Sufferers the surgeon hoped, as the machinery was rather expensive, that the Committee would defray the cost of the springs. 'He then gave a tariff of prices', Disraeli told Mrs Brydges Willyams, 'and offered to supply noses for English ladies by the dozen, and, I believe, even by the gross'.[27] It was not the last time that he would stand against the current of opinion over atrocities, or be disgusted by the gut reaction of the British public. He was brave enough to make a stand to an assembly of farmers at Newport Pagnell on 30 September. 'I for one', he told them, 'protest against taking Nana Sahib as a model for the conduct of the British soldier. I protest against meeting atrocities by atrocities.'

Suddenly and unexpectedly, at the beginning of 1858, chinks appeared in Palmerston's armour; the invincible 'old Pantaloon' seemed to be weakening. The aged Premier, it was said, was always asleep in the House of Commons, where he endeavoured to conceal it by tipping his hat over his eyes; and in Cabinet where, according to the Foreign Secretary, Lord Clarendon, 'one half of them seems to be almost always asleep, the first to be off being Lansdowne, closely followed by Palmerston and Charles Wood'.[28] A powerful East India Company lobby was agitating against Palmerston's India Bill which proposed to transfer the administration of India from the Company to the government; but the most dangerous circumstance was of the kind that frequently destroys politicians – an offensive appointment. Palmerston, or rather Lady Palmerston who pressed the appointment, had offered a Cabinet post to Lord Clanricarde who, only three years before, had been involved in a scandal over the will of his married Irish mistress, by whom he had an illegitimate son. The Palmerstons, whose ideas of morality were those of the rakish thirties and not the sanctimonious fifties, had simply not realized the storm Clanricarde's appointment would raise. The aged Lord Brougham, visiting Lady Palmerston one morning in January with the Saxon ambassador, Count Vitzthum, told her that because of this appointment the Ministry was damned beforehand, while Vitzthum left with the impression that 'the only thing that was doubtful was whether they would fall on a home or foreign question'.

Ironically enough, Palmerston's fall was indirectly provoked by his ally and admirer, Napoleon III. An unsuccessful assassination attempt on the Emperor on 14 January 1858 by Orsini, an Italian refugee based in England and using bombs manufactured there, evoked angry French demands that England should make reparation. On 4 February Palmerston, jaunty as ever, announced that on 9 February he would bring in a Conspiracy Bill making it a felony to conspire to murder. In deference to a conciliatory despatch by Napoleon himself dissociating himself from anti-English declarations in the official *Moniteur*, Disraeli voted for the first reading, but in the interval the English press published the French foreign minister's peremptory demands to the British government, and public opinion gained the impression that Palmerston, the English bull-dog, had been cowed by the French into bringing in the bill. The Radicals Milner Gibson and Bright, who loathed Palmerston, moved an amendment amounting to a vote of censure; Derby and Disraeli saw their chance, and on 19 February the amendment was carried by 19 votes. Palmerston defended himself with unusual violence, as he usually did when he felt himself to be in the wrong, and even went so far as to shake his fist at the Radicals. Disraeli's face at this moment, Malmesbury recorded, 'was worth anything – a mixture of triumph and sarcasm that he could not repress'.

Palmerston resigned and the Queen sent for Derby; this time the 'Captain' did not bolt, and by the end of February the second Derby–Disraeli administration was formed. Disraeli was Chancellor of the Exchequer again. 'Behold me installed at the old place,' he wrote gleefully to Sarah, 'to the astonishment of the recent occupiers, not yet recovered from the stunning effect of the coup d'état'. There had been difficulties in forming the government; Lytton, offered the Colonial Office, had turned it down, hoping to blackmail Derby into making him a peer, but Disraeli persuaded Stanley to take the post instead. Stanley had in fact initially refused to join his father's government; since 1855 he had grown increasingly distant from Disraeli, and in principle more inclined to the Liberal than to the Conservative side. 'It draws tears from my eyes, and from your heart, I am sure, drops of blood', Disraeli wrote to Derby of Stanley's initial refusal, and hurried round to persuade the recalcitrant heir. His arguments in favour of Stanley's joining showed sound political instinct, if not lofty principle: Liberalism in the sense of a really progressive party as advocated by Bright & Co., he told Stanley, was 'impracticable for twenty years to come' and 'whatever was possible to be done in the meantime might be done as well by himself as by the Whigs'. Stanley's was persuaded, but Disraeli would have been mortified had he known that the disadvantages of joining the Government listed by Stanley in his diary included: 'Connection with Disraeli. Able as he is, this man will never command public confidence.'[29] Among Disraeli's other friends in the Government were Manners, again as Commissioner of Works, and Henry Lennox at the Admiralty; Ralph Earle was installed in 11 Downing Street as chief private secretary.

Disraeli, as ever, was sanguine, but the second Derby–Disraeli administration was destined to be merely a hiccough in the 'Pantaloon's' long reign. The cards were stacked against them from the outset, with a majority of three to two against them in the Commons, and (with the exception of Disraeli himself) all the stars of debate – Palmerston, Gladstone and Bright – on the Opposition benches. Indeed, they had only one card, and that was a negative one; the mutual suspicion and rivalry between Palmerston and his followers on the one hand, and Lord John Russell, the Peelites and the Radicals on the other. So long, therefore, as Derby and Disraeli did nothing objectionable and walked the moderate tightrope they had a chance of survival. Indeed Whig jealousies saved their only major proposal of the session, the India Bill, from disaster; it was unpopular, and Palmerston, expecting to return to power, was foiled by the intervention of Lord John Russell who enabled Disraeli to postpone the debate and modify his bill. Nonetheless, the Government was nearly upset by a political blunder by the President of the Board of Control; a vote of censure threatened, and had Ellenborough not retrieved his error by resigning, it would undoubtedly have been defeated.

Ellenborough's departure left his office vacant, and Disraeli attempted to detach the powerful voice of Gladstone from the Opposition by making him a personal appeal to join the Government. Disraeli may well have been genuine in his desire to neutralize Gladstone, but the phraseology which he employed, ostensibly to tempt him, suggested that the letter was without conviction.

> For more than eight years, instead of thrusting myself into the foremost place, I have been, at all times, actively prepared to make every sacrifice of self for the public good, which I have ever thought identical with your accepting office in a Conservative Government ... Don't you think the time has come when you might deign to be magnanimous?[30]

Since Disraeli proposed to retain both the leadership and the chancellorship, there was nothing in it for Gladstone; icily, he refused. He did, however, fall into a trap laid for him later by Disraeli and Lytton, who became Colonial Secretary (Stanley having replaced Ellenborough at the Board of Control). Lured by his passion for Homer, he accepted the post of Commissioner for the Ionian Islands, then a British protectorate agitating for union with Greece. 'If ... he fails, the failure will be his', Disraeli wrote with Machiavellian logic to Derby, 'if he succeeds, the credit will redound to the Government which selected him.'[31] Gladstone, mocked by *The Times* for allowing himself to be tricked by Disraeli into accepting a fifth-rate post in order to indulge his passion for classical scholar-ship, set sail in January 1859 armed with a plan of representative government for the islands. Unfortunately for Disraeli, the mission was a failure and all too soon his most dangerous enemy was back on the English political scene.

Trouble erupted in Disraeli's intimate circle that autumn when Henry Lennox objected to the promotion of James Disraeli to a Commissionership of Excise that he had wanted for his own brother, Lord March. Bitter words passed between the two friends, with Lennox, who needed Disraeli more than Disraeli needed him, eventually coming to heel with protestations of passionate devotion, but the reconciliation was only temporary, and in January Lennox resigned on the grounds of ill-health. Lennox's touchiness was almost certainly inspired by his intense jealousy of Earle, who was now indefatigable in Disraeli's service, em-ployed on every delicate mission, including patching-up a quarrel between Dis-raeli and Delane of *The Times*, acting as a channel of communication between Downing Street and Printing House Square, and, late in December 1858, going on a secret mission to Napoleon III.

The object of Earle's mission was twofold: firstly, to discover what intrigues Palmerston might have been up to as Napoleon's guest hunting at Compiègne in November, and secondly, to discover whether the Emperor, as was rumoured, seriously intended to go to war against Austria in the cause of Italian liberation. Disraeli, preparing his Budget for the next session, was seriously worried that warlike moves by France would result in increased demands for defence expendi-ture and torpedo his plans for 1858 as they had in 1852. Earle, therefore, was charged to give the Emperor to understand that Disraeli 'did not care what he did, provided he kept quiet until after the Budget',[32] a cynical message hardly calculated to appeal to a mind which Disraeli had himself described as 'as romantic as it is subtle ... fitful and moody, brooding over Italy'. Earle's report that the Emperor was indeed 'utterly absorbed' with Italy frightened Disraeli into sending a letter pressing Napoleon to make a public declaration that the expansion of the French navy involved no hostility towards England, with the bait that, if he did so, English public opinon would be prevented from supporting Austria over Italy.[33] Earle naively reported the Emperor as being impressed by this argument and Disraeli wrote excitedly to Derby, 'he [Napoleon] is meditating a great rhetorical *coup. This is a profound secret*'.[34] Unfortunately for Disraeli, Earle's mission had made very little impression on the Emperor; when the Chambers met, he made the vaguest of declarations and, in the words of Moneypenny and Buckle, 'believing that his projects would be furthered by the return of the Italophil Palmerston to office, sent Persigny back to London as Ambassador to intrigue for that result'. That Disraeli should employ a twenty-two year old on such an important mission is a testimony to his high opinion of Earle, if not his sagacity. The mission was a waste of time; Napoleon, having come to a secret agreement with Cavour at Plombières that summer, was only waiting for the opportunity to embark on the Italian war. Disraeli, by intriguing behind his Foreign Secretary's back, only succeeded in annoying Malmesbury who had undertaken his own diplomatic initiative, and creating an impression of Derbyite confusion in the Emperor's mind.

While the Emperor in Paris was preparing to convulse Europe, the English government, for purely opportunist motives, was preparing to take up the now-fashionable cause of Reform. Disraeli who, in his heart of hearts, was not convinced either of the virtue or the necessity of Reform, simply hoped that by poaching on the Whigs' liberal manor, they would settle the Conservative Party, as he told Derby, 'on its broad basis of popular respect'.[35] By 'popular' Disraeli meant middle-class; by no stretch of the imagination could his Bill be said to appeal to the working class. Rejecting the idea of a massive redistribution of seats on a numerical basis, he proposed the most convoluted qualifications for the borough franchise which would, in effect, limit it to the professional classes. It was a dangerous course; the Whigs considered it dishonest of the Conservatives to take up a cause they considered their own, while the more reactionary Conservatives had supported Derby under the impression that he would stand out against Reform. In Parliament Bright, with justification, ridiculed Disraeli's borough qualifications as 'fancy franchises', and Disraeli's attempts to make the Commons swallow this half measure as an alternative to Bright and democracy were unavailing. On 31 March Whigs and Radicals combined to throw out the Bill and the Government was defeated by 330 votes to 291.

Derby and Disraeli announced the dissolution of Parliament, hoping for an election victory which, in reality, they had done little to deserve. As Disraeli honestly admitted to Derby on the eve of the dissolution, 'every one knows that all we did would really have been done by our predecessors'.[36] In the event, the election, held in May, resulted in only minor gains of thirty seats, ten less than Disraeli's most pessimistic calculations. The Conservatives were still in a minority, and the possible reconciliation of the rival Whig factions headed by Palmerston and Russell loomed as an ever-present threat. Disraeli immediately attempted to avert the danger by an approach to Palmerston. If Palmerston would join Derby with twenty or thirty followers, he said, the Conservatives would have an absolute majority and Palmerston could then dictate foreign policy; while, on the domestic front, 'you could bring in your own Reform Bill, which . . . may be as conservative as you please'. He held out as a carrot the possibility that Derby might retire in favour of Palmerston, while brandishing the stick of John Russell as Prime Minister should he and the Radicals dislodge the Government.[37]

Palmerston sent him a brief, polite refusal. The old fox would not be caught in a Derbyite trap just as he scented events were turning in his favour; the fuse laid by his ally, Napoleon III, and Count Cavour at Plombières had finally caught fire. On 29 April, the day the English election campaign commenced, the Austrian army crossed the Piedmontese border; four days later Napoleon declared his intention of going to Piedmont's aid. The result of the Austrian attack was to revive latent English sympathies with Italian nationalism of which Palmerston was the acknowledged standard-bearer, and with it the suspicion that Derby and Disraeli were on the side of Austria.

The question of Italy reunited the warring Whig factions and attracted to them the support of Bright and the Radicals – and of Gladstone, always passionate in the cause of Italian liberty. On 6 June, the eve of the debate on the Address, a great meeting comprising all sections of the Opposition was held in Willis's Rooms, once the gilded salons of Almack's. The meeting, which has been called the birth of the modern Liberal party, boded danger for Derby and Disraeli. Palmerston and Russell agreed to serve under whichever of them should be sent for by the Queen, and it was unanimously resolved that the Government should be attacked on a motion of no-confidence. In Parliament, after three nights' debate, the final division came at 2.30 in the morning of 11 June. Despite a grand fighting speech by Disraeli the Government was defeated by a majority of 13, amid the cheers of the Opposition and of the French and Italian ambassadors waiting outside, with the Piedmontese envoy, d'Azeglio, throwing his hat in the air and himself into the arms of Jaucourt, the French attaché.

Malmesbury blamed Disraeli for the Government defeat; had the Blue Books containing the Foreign Office despatches been laid on the table, he said, the Government would not have been condemned for not preventing the war; Disraeli's excuse, according to Malmesbury being that 'he *had not read it*, and could not have fought it in debate'. Disraeli, when questioned by T.E. Kebbel on the affair, turned on him sharply; it was, said Kebbel, the only time he had ever seen him offended. 'Why, how could I produce them when they were not printed?' he retorted.[38] There may have been other reasons; when Malmesbury, 'in extremis' as the Saxon envoy put it, finally laid the Blue Books on the table of the House of Lords, study of the documents confirmed that the Foreign Secretary had indeed been incompetent. 'With a little more firmness and consistency he might perhaps have been able to prevent the war,' Vitzthum wrote.[39] Disraeli, who had a low opinion of Malmesbury's abilities, may have suspected this; the meeting at Willis's Rooms had made defeat on one issue or another certain, and he may well have preferred not to prolong the struggle uselessly on uncertain ground.

Disraeli did in fact blame Malmesbury; 'Malmesbury must go', he had written to Derby on the eve of defeat, but he also, characteristically, thought that Palmerston's intrigues with Napoleon III were at the bottom of it. He believed, he told Kebbel, that a secret understanding had been reached between Palmerston and the Emperor at Compiègne in November 1858, by which the latter undertook to time the outbreak of the war with Austria with the General Election in England, 'Lord Palmerston well knowing what a useful weapon it would place in the hands of the Opposition'.[40] There is no doubt that Palmerston did intrigue with the French against the Derby government; the Saxon envoy, Vitzthum, reported that the French ambassador Persigny 'continued to receive his instructions from Palmerston, and informed him of all that Lord Derby and Malmesbury confided to the French Ambassador'. Nonetheless, the story which Disraeli told Kebbel was in all probability a figment of his own over-heated imagination; he seems to have overlooked the fact that it was Austria, not France, which initiated the Italian war by invading Piedmont on the eve of the election campaign. Moreover the dissolution on 4 April was a surprise one, hardly something that could have been foreseen at Compiègne the previous November. That Disraeli could seriously have made such assertions illustrates his fondness for theories of international conspiracy.

Disraeli could, however, congratulate himself on one achievement: the astonishing fact that the Conservative Party had put forward, and been persuaded to vote for, a Reform Bill, a hopeful omen for the future. As Disraeli told the assembled party at a banquet at the Merchant Taylors' Hall on 16 July:

> I can truly say that, from the earliest moment when I gave my attention to public affairs, I have ever had it as one of my main objects to restore the power and repute of the great party to which we are proud to belong, and which I believe to be intimately bound up with the welfare and renown of this country ... I have always striven to assist in building it upon a broad and national basis, because I believed it to be a party peculiarly and essentially national.

This said, the prospects for the Party in the immediate future were bleak. Palmerston's government contained a wide spectrum of opinion and talent, a mixture of the Whig aristocracy represented by Russell, Earl Granville, the Dukes of Newcastle and Argyll, with two well-born Radicals, Milner Gibson and Charles Villiers – and Gladstone as Chancellor of the Exchequer. There was general surprise at Gladstone's acceptance of office under Palmerston, to whom his antipathy was well known. As his niece Lucy Lyttelton noted in her diary for 21 June 1859: 'Why, if he can swallow Pam, couldn't he swallow Dizzy, and in spite of him, go in under Lord Derby?' The reason was not hard to find; Gladstone, deeply ambitious, had not enjoyed his four years in the political wilderness since his resignation in 1855; moreover the leaders of the Liberal Party, Palmerston and Russell, were 75 and 68 respectively. Gladstone, at 50, should not have long to wait.

For Disraeli, five years older than Gladstone, the situation was not a pleasant one. A decade of struggle and intrigue had produced only two ephemeral administrations; his plans to lure the moderate Whigs and the disguised Tory, Palmerston, into the Conservative ranks had failed. As long as Palmerston, as firmly pledged as Lord Derby had been to impede domestic progress, remained in power, Conservative opposition would be impotent. At 75 Palmerston, hugely popular in the country and with a majority in Parliament, was in excellent health and spirits. For Disraeli, the immediate future would be a question of waiting for an old man to die.

16 A Time for Reflection

In December 1859 the most important link with Disraeli's youth abruptly snapped. Disraeli and Mary Anne, returning to London from a round of country house visiting, were stricken to find Sarah on her deathbed. As Disraeli wrote distractedly to Lady Londonderry on 12 December: 'We have returned to unspeakable sorrow – to the bedside of my only sister, our nearest and dearest relative, and who is soon, most unexpectedly and suddenly, to be lost to us.'

Sarah, who was fifty-seven, had probably suffered a stroke; clearly there had been previously no hint of a serious illness. Although Mary Anne had described her as 'very delicate' when she visited Hughenden in September that year, Sarah, unlike most Victorians, rarely complained of her health. Among the few late letters to her brother which have come to light, only two refer to her own indispositions. One, written from James Disraeli's house in Eaton Terrace on 2 September 1857, does mention recurring ill-health, 'this is now the third August I have been so very ill', she wrote, attributing it to the atmosphere of Twickenham in the 'obnoxious month'. The great heat of the late summer of 1859 must have fatally weakened her, but clearly the Disraelis had had no inkling of this as they went on their long country peregrinations in the late autumn.

Disraeli, like most people in the case of someone whom they truly love and upon whom they have always depended, seems never to have contemplated the possibility that Sarah might die before him. It was he, after all, who had always been the sickly member of the family, while Sarah, the strong one, was the ministering angel at family illnesses and deathbeds; now it was he who was helplessly watching his sister die. On 17 December he reported to Mary Anne, probably from Sarah's house at Twickenham, that she was 'sinking fast'. Two days later she was dead; Disraeli, shattered, wrote an emotional letter to Ralph:

> My dearest Ralph,
>   I have had a sleepless night, & so have you. Language cannot describe what this sudden, & by me never contemplated, catastrophe has produced on me. She was the harbor of refuge in all the storms of my life, & I had hoped she wd. have closed my eyes.[1]

Eight years later, on Disraeli's becoming Prime Minister for the first time, Philip Rose remarked to him, 'If only your sister had been alive to witness your triumph what happiness it would have given her.' He was slightly shocked when Disraeli replied, 'Ah, poor Sa! poor Sa! we've lost our audience, we've lost our audience'.[2] This apparently flippant, egotistic remark was a typical piece of Disraelian self-mockery. Sarah was indeed his first audience, to be followed by a succession of female confidantes – Mary Anne, Frances Anne Londonderry, Mrs Brydges Willyams, the Queen, Lady Bradford and Lady Chesterfield. She was, as Disraeli wrote sadly to John Manners, his 'first and ever-faithful friend', the most intelligent and the most trusted of all. He played scenes for her in his letters, but he did not posture; she was spared the rococo phrases all too often lavished on his later female correspondents. She alone knew all his secrets, of love, money and politics, things that he might conceal from Mary Anne or Philip Rose. She knew his faults but nonetheless adored him; she was mother, sister, friend and worshipper. She was the one woman close to him who possessed an intelligence equal to his own; he sought women, for their 'sympathy' rather than their intellectual power. Sarah and Benjamin's 'mystical affection' was celebrated by Disraeli in his novels, *Alroy, Tancred* and *Endymion*.

Sarah D'Israeli's life was a period tragedy. Doomed to perpetual spinsterhood by the early death of William Meredith, her second chance of marriage also blighted by death, she devoted her life to being, in Disraeli's words, 'the soul of a house and the angelic spirit of a family'. A woman of intelligence, strong character and intellectual aspirations, she was condemned to be the helpmate of a fussy, often ailing mother, the conscientious daughter and slave to a charming but demanding father, the trusted, relied-upon elder sister to three brothers. Her early efforts to achieve creative satisfaction writing in tandem with her brother faded as he went on to leave her behind; her frustrated love and ambition were concentrated upon Benjamin's career with an intensity which someone with less capacity for absorbing adulation might have found stifling. In one of the most poignant letters she ever wrote Disraeli she told him that his successful career was 'the only thing in my life that has never disappointed me'.[3]

Disraeli was to record his love for and gratitude to Sarah in his last completed novel, *Endymion*: 'The sister seemed to have the commanding spirit ... but if he were ruled by his sister, she was ever willing to be his slave, and to sacrifice every consideration to his caprice and his convenience'. The last paragraph of the book is dedicated to a scene between brother and sister as they meet in the former family home. Myra tells Endymion:

> What I came for, was to see our old nursery, where we lived so long together, and so fondly! ... All I have desired, all I have dreamed, have come to pass. Darling, beloved of my soul, by all our sorrows, by all our joys, in this scene of our childhood and bygone days, let me give you my last embrace.[4]

Sarah's death must have given him intimations of mortality, or, at the very least, of approaching old age. His fifty-fifth birthday fell two days later, on 21

December 1859; he was now well into middle age. Three years earlier, arriving in Paris in November 1856, he had met men who had been young and brilliant on his last visit in 1842, almost fifteen years before. He found them sadly changed, which forced him to ask himself the question 'Am I so altered?' He had been particularly shocked by the appearance of Alfred de Vigny 'who was supposed to be the prettiest poet not only in his verse but person in Paris', with 'a slender waist, long auburn locks shading his blooming & ingenuous cheek, & in dress picturesquely dandified'. Twenty years on de Vigny had become 'a corpulent, grey headed, oldish gentleman', and, with de Vigny's original image stamped on his memory, Disraeli was deeply and disagreeably impressed. 'Meeting people after an interval of twenty years', he wrote, 'is like people going out of one door of a room in youth, & returning, immediately after through another as old men'. His answer to the question whether he himself was so changed was reassuring: 'I don't think so. Certainly not in feeling'.[5]

He had long abandoned his dandyism in clothes, being now invariably dressed in a black frock-coat buttoned low, grey trousers, and a green or black neckerchief tied in a neat bow at his throat. But, unlike de Vigny, he had kept his figure, and, although later in life he wore stays which showed under the light stuff of his coat in summer, he was described at this time as being 'lithe and erect' and looking younger than his age.[6] His hair, of which he had always been obsessively careful, was never allowed to appear grey; Mary Anne dyed it black, cutting the cherished locks herself and collecting the discarded hair to be kept for posterity.

The pulse of politics had slowed, and with it the tenor of Disraeli's life. He was in reflective mood; his recollections of the past possibly prompted by a request for information from a prospective biographer, Francis Espinasse, to whom he replied in a lengthy letter on 27 March 1860, in which the inaccuracies were as revealing as the truth. He lied about his age, making himself a year younger than he was, and denied that he had been the cause of his father's rupture with Murray in 1826. He glossed over the humiliating struggle for the leadership in 1848–9, giving Espinasse the false impression that the party had officially offered him the sole leadership. There was certainly an unconscious irony in his concluding instruction to the would-be biographer, whom he was providing with such misleading details of his career; 'One shd. only record events, but it is desirable that they shd. be true'.[7]

Was Disraeli consciously trying to mislead Espinasse? He was notoriously inaccurate where dates were concerned, as the biographical jottings he made at the time show, but he himself wrote that he had 'a memory which never dims', and it is significant that the inaccuracies refer to episodes in his career which had hurt or humiliated him. The truth was inadmissible, he therefore blotted it out.

Over these years of reflection and semi-retirement, from 1860 to 1865, Disraeli made a series of biographical jottings which remained unpublished in their entirety until 1975. They were mainly vignettes and anecdotes of remarkable people he had known, from Louis Philippe to Bismarck. Disraeli recalled the eccentricities of dukes, the *faiblesses* of kings and politicians; Louis Philippe, proud of his prowess at carving ham; Lord Stanley's accent, 'a Lancashire patois'; and the parsimonious, fabulously rich Duke of Bedford climbing on to the card table after the guests had gone to bed to put out the candles in the chandelier. It was a private view of Disraeli's world, of Westminster and the aristocratic houses where politicians met, gossiped and intrigued, with no hackneyed reports of great events or banal reflections on the issues of the day. Nobody whom Disraeli did not know personally was allowed to intrude, and his subjects live with an immediacy achieved by few memorialists. The *Reminiscences* are intensely personal, written in a simple flowing style quite unlike the florid passages of his letters to Mrs Brydges Willyams. There are no gilded salons or glittering palaces, but a portrait gallery painted with a sympathetic but perceptive eye.

It is doubtful whether they were ever intended for publication; no nineteenth century publisher could have printed such records of royal conversations as Disraeli's with Prince Albert, containing the Prince's dicta on his fellow Europeans – 'the Italians were "a worn-out race"', or 'the French required to be "Licked" once every fifty years ... they were a little race & always beat in the long run'. Disraeli used these jottings as a repository for words, phrases or aphorisms that appealed to him, and as a quarry for stories of human frailty or seigneurial magnificence that he would use in his later novels. The anecdote of Lord Derby's daughter, Emily, for instance who, coming down to breakfast at Knowsley on her birthday, found a cheque from her father for £5,000 wrapped in her napkin reappears in *Endymion*. Many of Smythe's sayings were recorded:

> Smythe used to say 'Bulwer is dying of Dickens – & yet can't be without him. The moth & the candle. Just come up from Knebworth, Dickens & Co. acting in the Hall. Bulwer to give a piece of land to build cottages ... for scribblers. Fancies it makes the difference between his position & Dickens' – & dying all the time of jealousy & envy combined.

There were concise, cruel pen-portraits, 'Lord Houghton [Richard Monckton Milnes] was unfortunately short with a face like a Herculaneum masque, or a countenance cut out of an orange', interspersed with outbursts of real feeling: 'It was a melancholy day for human nature when that stupid Lord Anson, after beating about for three years, found himself again at Greenwich. The circumnavigation of our globe was accomplished, but the illimitable was annihilated & a fatal blow [dealt] to all imagination'.

The *Reminiscences* make entertaining reading, so much so that one wonders why Disraeli did not write another novel when he had the leisure to do so. His last novel, *Tancred*, had been published over a decade earlier; his next, *Lothair*, did not appear till 1870 – a period of over twenty years. He had, he told Lady Londonderry in 1857, lost all zest for fiction, and, in the opening paragraph of the dedication to the 1864 edition of the *Revolutionary Epick*, he seems to have abandoned the idea of ever writing again – 'As it has long been improbable that I should ever publish another work'. His mind, according to Stanley, was occupied during the fifties and early sixties by questions of a religious and philosophical nature, and he several times mentioned the curious project of writing a Life of Christ 'from a national point of view' – a singularly opaque phrase – but nothing came of it.[8] Disraeli himself never explained this fallow period; the lethargy that infected his political life until the death of Palmerston seems to have extended also into the creative sphere.

Another curious aspect of Disraeli as a writer is that, although living in the greatest age of the English novel, he rarely read the works of his contemporaries and when he did was not impressed. In September 1857 he confessed in a letter to Lady Londonderry, 'I wish, like you, I could console myself with reading novels ... but I have lost all zest for fiction, and have for many years. I have never read anything of Dickens, except an extract in a newspaper, and, therefore, I cannot help to decide on the merits of *Little Dorrit*.'[9] This dislike, it seems, did not extend to French novelists; while thinking nothing of George Eliot, he considered George Sand to be one of the great prose writers of the day and rated Balzac highly.[10] He was interested in contemporary thought and the growing confrontation between science and religion, reading Lyell's *Principles of Geology* and the controversial *Essays and Reviews*. He must also, although there is no documentary evidence of it, have read Darwin's *Origin of Species*.

He remained uninfluenced by the contemporary interest in realism; his novels, with the exception of *Sybil*, never changed either in style or content throughout his life. At the age of twenty-five he had yearned for, and finally succeeded in entering, the world of London political society; he remained in it until the day of his death. He saw the world outside in terms of issues or revolutions, or capitalists versus secret societies, but it was all a glittering chess-game played on a global board; the human squalor, tragedy and banality which lay beneath interested him not at all. When he was praised for his realism, as in the descriptions of the rural and urban poor in *Sybil*, his material came from other printed sources and brief visits to the industrial areas with Smythe or Ferrand. After *Sybil*, the working classes vanished from his novels, to be replaced by the society he knew, the world centred upon Westminster that he depicted with a wit and insight which made him unrivalled as a political novelist.

In the years up to 1862 there was no lack of financial stimulus to make Disraeli take up his pen and 'hack for it'. Although the shilling edition of his novels sold 300,000 copies in the year following its publication in 1853, and, he told Bright, another 100,000 copies would give him the equivalent of his salary as Chancellor of the Exchequer, in 1857 the eccentric Duke of Portland suddenly called in the Hughenden loan, and by 1862 his debts totalled around £60,000. But, as always with Disraeli, 'something turned up' in the form of a rich Conservative landowner. Andrew Montagu of Melton in Yorkshire offered to buy up his leader's debts, charging him a very low rate of interest instead of the heavy exactions of the moneylenders to whom he had previously had recourse. The negotiations were handled by Philip Rose, and Baron de Rothschild seems to have played a part in the affair. Disraeli's letters to Rose about 'the great affair' had the same tone of conspiratorial excitement with which he had always approached his financial dealings. The plan seems to have been for Rothschild to give or guarantee a loan. That it was not the first time he had done so is evident from a letter from Disraeli to Rose in December 1862: 'he likes to give to his friends, not lend', Disraeli wrote, 'as he never takes interest, from me, at least, it is a post obit without any return, & great risk – but he yielded to the urgency of the case, & the great result for me at stake.'[11] There was to be a second mortgage on Hughenden, '£35,000 to be raised by a charge of £800 p. annum, & after deducting the amount of the charge, the increase to the Income is £4,200'. Disraeli was anxious that the Baron and Montagu should meet and discuss the matter, but Rothschild, it appears, was wary of the affair. However, by a stroke of luck, the Disraelis, spending the Christmas fortnight at Torquay, discovered themselves to be in the same hotel as the Baron, upon whom Disraeli immediately went to work, reporting to Rose that he had succeeded in converting 'an unwilling into a zealous & even eager ally'.

Disraeli's financial luck continued to hold; in the autumn of 1863 Mrs Brydges Willyams died at Torquay, bringing him the long-awaited legacy. 'What has happened here is all that we cd. have wished', Disraeli told Rose on 17 November. 'My kind & faithful friend has never swerved from her purpose.'[12] The legacy amounted to some £40,000, and, with the Montagu-Rothschild arrangement, Disraeli at the age of fifty-nine was at the end of a long and tortuous road, free at last from a lifetime of financial worries. By 1866 he estimated that their joint income was nearly £9,000 of which only half was Mary Anne's. Rose had the quaint idea of advertising the Brydges Willyams legacy in the newspapers, in the hope of attracting like-minded rich widows – 'I wish you would consider whether some paragraph might not be advantageously put in the newspapers alluding to the bequest and the grounds for it. These things are catching and the great probability is that the example would be followed if properly made known'.[13] Mrs Brydges Willyams's body was brought back to Hughenden at her express request to be buried in what Disraeli intended to be the family vault inside the church. To his rage the vicar, Mr Chubbe, informed him that the Interment Act forbade burials inside the church, and he was therefore, as he wrote angrily to Rose, 'oblig'd by great exertions to have a vault made in the Church Yard, contrary to the wishes of the deceased, & where neither my wife nor myself will be buried, preferring even Kensal Green to anything so unprotected'.[14] In the end both he and Mary Anne were to be buried in the churchyard vault beside their benefactress.

The Disraelis spent these windfalls on Hughenden, Mary Anne supervising all the 'improvements'. With the help of her architect, E.B. Lamb, she transformed the plain three-storeyed eighteenth-century manor house into a more imposing – it could be said, pretentious – edifice of mid-Victorian Gothic red brick with battlements and a cloistered stable-yard. Stanley thought it a great improvement, and indeed the previous façade had been simple to the point of dullness, but another of Disraeli's younger friends, Lord Ronald Gower, perhaps spoilt by the glories of the family palace at Trentham, called it 'a curious bit of nondescript architecture'.[15] The interior too was gothicized, with a dark panelled hall and vestibule-porch lined with ferns. The drawing-room, which Lord Ronald somewhat unfairly described as 'a wonderfully hideous place', was, as it is today, 'very high with walls covered in green paper dotted with fleur de lys – great panelled high frames being the only relief'. Lord Ronald asked Disraeli why he did not have some pictures hung in these frames, particularly the large one over the fireplace; he replied that he had intended to have a portrait of Mary Anne there 'but she has never been done, except a miniature by Ross which I shall have copied'. Later, after Mary Anne's death, Disraeli commissioned a portrait of her by J.G. Middleton which hangs there today, a fanciful portrayal of a smooth-skinned, pink and white Mary Anne, looking as Disraeli liked to imagine her to have looked when they first met. Next to the drawing-room was the library, Disraeli's favourite place, with its handsome dark wood Gothic bookshelves, and, running along the front of the house, a broad terrace with a pergola and white geranium-filled Italian marble vases on which Disraeli's cherished peacocks perched.

During the sixties Disraeli extended the area of Hughenden to a compact estate of some 1,200 acres, and, although at the outset he had not been a popular landlord because he was poor where the previous owner, 'Daddy Norris', had been rich and easy-going, as soon as he could afford it, he spent all the rental of his cottages on their improvement.[16] Mary Anne was responsible for the planting of the grounds; clad in short skirt and gaiters, she spent hours out of doors supervising the creation of the 'walks' to which she gave fanciful names – 'Italy', 'My Lady's Walk', a 'Lover's Walk' and 'the German forest'. On a conspicuous hilltop site she raised an obelisk monument, designed by Lamb, to the memory of Isaac D'Israeli. One of Disraeli's favourite features was a lake, where he occasionally fished for trout, occupied by a pair of swans named Hero and Leander; Disraeli, Mary Anne told Kebbel, was very fond of birds.

Disraeli gave Hughenden and the county of Buckinghamshire a romantic past, particularly connecting them with the Civil War. Writing to his friend Lord Beauchamp on 9 June 1864, he described the renovation of Hughenden in characteristic terms: 'We have realised a romance we had talked of for many years, for we have restored the place to what it was before the civil wars & have made a garden of terraces in wh: cavaliers might have wandered with their lady-loves.'[17] Disraeli, said Kebbel, talked a good deal about the Civil War and his favourite theory that the Chiltern Hills had been the cradle of an aristocratic conspiracy to win back from the Stuarts the power the nobility had wielded under the Plantagenets. Kebbel, riding beside him in the carriage, could not help thinking that 'Mr. Disraeli, in his sugar-loaf hat and black cloak, resembled anything but a Cavalier.'[18]

Disraeli, however, a Cavalier at heart, was also certainly a courtier; and with the sudden early death of Prince Albert of typhoid on 14 December 1861, the most serious obstacle to his courtship of the Queen was removed. Albert, while admiring Disraeli's talents, had persisted, even at the end of the 1858-9 administration, in regarding him as a Radical. While Albert was alive, he ruled the Queen and she needed no one else; when he died, there was a vacuum in her life which Disraeli would come closer to filling than anyone with the exception of John Brown. Disraeli regretted the death of Albert, whose intellectual and political abilities he had admired; his tribute to the Prince, in conversation with the Saxon envoy, Vitzthum, revealed, not for the first time, his real, and un-English, feeling for the virtues of a strong monarchy. 'This German Prince', he said, 'has governed England for twenty-one years with a wisdom and energy such as none of our Kings have ever shown ... If he had outlived some of our "old stagers", he would have given us, while retaining all our constitutional guarantees, the blessings of absolute government.'[19]

Disraeli had none of the English aristocrat's distrust of absolute monarchy, typified by Lord Derby's political catechism, which began, 'A is for axe to chop off the King's head'. His public tribute to the Prince at the opening of the parliamentary session of 1862 was the most graceful, and probably the most sincerely felt, and much appreciated by the Queen, who sent him a grateful message of thanks. He in turn was gratified, later in the year, to hear that the Queen was in the habit of repeating to her entourage that 'Mr. Disraeli was the only person who appreciated the Prince ...' Indeed, the following year, he rather pathetically attributed to the Queen's increasing regard for him, an invitation to the wedding of the Prince of Wales and Princess Alexandra in March 1863, when in reality it had been issued to him as Leader of the Opposition at the instigation of Palmerston.

The places in St George's Chapel, Windsor, where the wedding was to take place were limited, and Disraeli revelled in the 'rage, envy and indignation of the great world' at his invitation. 'The Duchess of Marlborough', he gleefully recorded, 'went into hysterics at the sight of my wife ... and said it was really shameful after the reception the Duke had given the Prince of Wales at Blenheim; and as for the Duchess of Manchester, who had been Mistress of the Robes in Lord Derby's Administration, she positively passed me for the season without recognition.'[20]

For Disraeli, with his sense of history and love of royalty, it was a thrilling occasion. His description of it gushed like a social column, '... the glittering dresses, ... the magnificent music, the Queen in her widowed garments in her Gothic cabinet, all deeply interesting or effective'. Disraeli, not having seen the Queen since what he termed 'the catastrophe' and being near-sighted, ventured to observe her through his eye-glass. Unfortunately, H.M. caught him staring; 'I did not venture to use my glass again', he reported to Mrs Brydges Willyams, consoling himself with the thought that 'perhaps she was looking to see whether we were there, and triumphing a little in the decided manner in which she had testified "her gratitude" ...'. Although on the verge of sixty, Disraeli enjoyed it all enormously, the 'joyous festival' after the ceremony, even the confusion afterwards at Windsor station where the great ladies were mobbed to the imminent peril of their diamonds, and the crowded train where he had to sit on Mary Anne's lap.

The crowning glory of that year was a personal interview with his sovereign, when he had the honour of being invited to spend the night of 22 April at Windsor. His account of his stay and of the royal interview revealed his utter fascination with the mystique of royalty, with no hint of that criticism of the Queen's eccentric widowhood which featured in contemporary aristocratic accounts. If he was surprised to find that he was still expected to sign two visitor's books, one for the Queen and one for the late Prince – 'calling on a dead man', as Stanley put it – he made no mention of it, and reverently recorded the conversation of royalty, however banal. Disraeli was presented to the Princess of Wales and much impressed with her looks: 'Her face was delicate and refined; her features regular; her brow well moulded; her mouth beautiful; her hair good and her ears small. She was very thin. She had the accomplishment of being gracious without smiling. She had repose'.

Her English was not as fluent as he had expected and Disraeli, not knowing that she was slightly deaf, said that she appeared not to comprehend all that was said to her. On hearing that the royal couple were pleased with Marlborough House, where they awoke to the sound of birds singing in the garden, Disraeli, whose conversation with women tended to the floridly romantic, answered, 'I fear not nightingales, madam', and asked her what nightingales fed upon.

> While she was confessing her ignorance and her curiosity, the Prince came in, and she addressed the question to him, which he could not answer. I told them glow-worms; exactly the food nightingales should require. The Prince was interested by this, and exclaimed: 'Is that a fact, or is it a myth?'
>
> 'Quite a fact, sir; for my woodman is my authority, for we have a great many nightingales at Hughenden, and a great many glow-worms.'
>
> 'We have got one nightingale at Sandringham', said the Prince, smiling.[21]

The interview with the Queen took place the next day in Albert's special room, kept exactly as he had left it, decorated with his favourite objects, books and writing materials, and his accustomed chair, to which the Queen had attached a commemorative plaque. Disraeli was kept waiting for five minutes before the Queen appeared, dressed in mourning and, he had the impression, stouter than when he had last seen her. His account of the interview expressed the almost Oriental reverence he felt at meeting the Queen face to face, alone: 'I bowed deeply when she entered, and raised my head with unusual slowness, that I might have a moment for recovery. Her countenance was grave, but serene and kind, and she said, in a most musical voice: "It is some time since we met."' Disraeli, overcome, could only murmur a few words, until the Queen launched into a frank and animated discussion of public affairs which, he said, 'entirely removed the first embarrassment of the audience'. It was, he recorded with satisfaction, 'like an audience between a Sovereign and a Minister'.

Victoria's motive in granting the interview was, it appears, not only as a mark of favour for his appreciation of her beloved Albert, but to ensure that he would not by factious conduct displace Palmerston, once her *bête noire*, but to whom she had now not only become accustomed, but attached. 'She said', Disraeli recorded, 'she hoped no crisis would be brought about wantonly, for, in her forlorn condition, she hardly knew what she could do'. Disraeli reassured her that her comfort was a prime consideration and that he was convinced no action would be taken 'unless from commanding necessity'. The conversation then turned to Palmerston, the Queen saying anxiously, 'Lord Palmerston was grown very old', and Disraeli replying comfortingly, 'But his voice in debate, madam, is as loud as ever'. ' "Yes!" she exclaimed with animation. "And his handwriting! Did you ever see such handwriting? So very clear and strong! Nevertheless I see in him a great change, a very great change ..." ' The Queen then complimented Disraeli upon his recent appointment as Trustee of the British Museum and, after some more conversation, mainly in praise of Albert, she terminated the interview or, in Disraeli's words she 'with a graceful bow, vanished.'[22]

Disraeli returned to London in time for the debate that afternoon in the House of Commons on the question of a suitable memorial to the Prince. His speech was designed to please the Queen, and advocated a monument which 'should, as it were, represent the character of the Prince himself in the harmony of its proportions, in the beauty of its ornament, and in its enduring nature.' Its character, he said, should be worthy of the Prince, so that posterity might say, 'This is the type and testimony of a sublime life and a transcendent career, and thus they were recognised by a grateful and admiring people'. Afterwards Disraeli, concerned that the Queen should receive an accurate report of his speech, which had been recorded by second-string parliamentary reporters, wrote it out in his own hand and sent it to Windsor. The response was immediate; Victoria sent him a copy of the Prince's speeches in white morocco with a touching inscription in her own hand: 'To the Right Honourable Benjamin Disraeli. In recollection of the greatest and best of men from the beloved Prince's broken-hearted widow. Victoria R.' Disraeli hastened to transmit the news to Mrs Brydges Willyams: 'I think you will agree with me that this is the most remarkable inscription which a Sovereign ever placed in a volume graciously presented to a subject!' With it, he said, was a packet tied with black silk containing a letter showing how Disraeli's speech had touched Victoria's heart:

> The Queen cannot resist from expressing, personally, to Mr. Disraeli her deep gratification at the tribute he paid to her adored, beloved, and great husband. The perusal of it made her shed many tears, but it was very soothing to her broken heart to see such true appreciation of that spotless and unequalled character.

Disraeli responded with a letter which even his official biographer, Buckle, admitted to be a 'somewhat hyperbolic eulogium', touching upon what he described as 'a sacred theme', and recalling his acquaintance with Albert as 'one of the most satisfactory incidents of his life: full of refined and beautiful memories, and exercising, as he hopes, over his remaining existence, a soothing and exalting influence'. He compared the Prince with Sir Philip Sidney – 'The Prince is the only person whom Mr. Disraeli has ever known, who realized the Ideal ... There was in him an union of the manly grace and sublime simplicity, of chivalry with the intellectual splendour of the Attic Academe'. He comforted Victoria with the promise of immortal fame for her Prince, 'The writer of these lines is much mistaken if, as time advances, the thought and sentiment of a progressive age will not cluster round the Prince; his plans will become systems, his suggestions dogmas, and the name of Albert will be accepted as the master-type of a generation of profounder feeling and vaster range than that which he formed and guided with benignant power'.[23] This was indeed, as Disraeli himself once said, 'laying it on with a trowel',[24] but the mixture was not too thick for the Queen who forwarded it to the editor of the volume of the Prince's speeches, Arthur Helps, as 'the most striking and beautiful letter that Her Majesty has received'.

The doors of the Establishment were at last opening for Disraeli; in March 1863 Palmerston had invited him to become a Trustee of the British Museum, on account, as he gracefully put it, of his literary eminence as well as his parliamentary position. Two years later, he was elected to Grillion's, the select parliamentary dining club, and the following year to the Athenaeum, the club that had blackballed him thirty-four years earlier. These were signs of his advance, but Disraeli, who thirty years ago had struggled so hard to be accepted by the London club world, no longer cared. He hated all-male dinners and did not hesitate to express his feelings about Grillion's and its members, whom he described as 'a dozen prigs and bores ... whispering to their next-door neighbors over a bad dinner in a dingy room'. Much more to his taste were the festivities in honour of the marriage of the Prince of Wales to which he and Mary Anne were invited. With satisfaction he stressed the exclusiveness of these invitations; the Prince's Ball at Marlborough House was 'limited to 500 guests of the diplomacy and the *haute noblesse*', while at the dinner given by the Duke and Duchess of Northumberland, 'We dined sixty guests of the high nobility in a magnificent gallery ... far more splendid than the Galerie de Diane of the Tuileries. Such plate, such diamonds, so many Duchesses, and Knights of the Garter, were never before assembled together!'[25] 'Diamonds and duchesses' – Disraeli had entered the social paradise he had imagined in *The Young Duke* more than thirty years before.

Disraeli's serene ascent of the social ladder, however, was not mirrored in his political career. Discontent with his leadership among his party was more bitter, and more dangerous, in the period up to 1866 than it had been even in the fifties. Matters reached such a pitch that on 11 June 1860 Disraeli wrote to Sir William Miles threatening resignation, quoting from a Liberal journal to describe his leadership of the party, as one of 'chronic revolt and unceasing conspiracy'. The resignation was withdrawn but the discontent remained.

Among the chief Disraeli-haters was G. P. Bentinck, MP for Norfolk, known as 'Big Ben', a huge squire described by Disraeli as 'upwards of 6 feet 2 in. at least, with bandy legs, & the most inhuman face ever encountered ... really ... a caricature of a Gorilla.'[26] Disraeli discounted the hostility of the simian Bentinck, whom he had outmanoeuvred over the Reform Bill in 1859, but in that same year a far more dangerous threat had appeared, in the form of Lord Robert Cecil, later Viscount Cranborne, younger son of the Marquess of Salisbury. Cecil was a brilliant young High Tory whose intelligence and birth alone would have made him a formidable opponent to Disraeli's leadership, but he was also a good debater and a talented journalist. In April 1860 Cecil voiced the feelings of the party about their leader in a bitter article in the *Quarterly Review*, with particular reference to the 1859 Reform Bill which he held up as a betrayal of Conservative principle:

> To crush the Whigs by combining with the Radicals was the first and last maxim of Mr. Disraeli's tactics. He had never led the Conservatives to victory as Sir Robert Peel had led them. He had never procured the triumphant assertion of any Conservative principle or shielded from imminent ruin any ancient institution. But he had been a successful leader to this extent, that he had made any Government while he was in opposition next to an impossibility. His tactics were so various, so flexible, so shameless – the net by which his combinations were gathered in was so wide – he had so admirable a knack of enticing into the same lobby a happy family of proud old Tories and foaming Radicals, martial squires jealous of their country's honour, and manufacturers who had written it off their books as an unmarketable commodity – that so long as his party backed him, no Government was strong enough to hold out against his attacks.

The article caused a sensation, with Lord John Russell enquiring pointedly in the Commons 'who was now the leader of the Tories?', and *The Times*, always ready for a tilt at the squires, rushing to Disraeli's defence. Disraeli had shrugged off Tory discontent before, but this time he took it seriously. Early in the session of 1860 a large section of his party had refused to follow him, notably over the Budget debates which had developed into a series of contests between Disraeli and Gladstone in which, according to Greville, 'Gladstone signally defeated Disraeli'. Gladstone's success, he said, 'did not seem a matter of much grief to many of the Conservative party ... the hatred and distrust of Disraeli is greater than ever in the Conservative ranks'. A week later, Gladstone made another brilliant speech and obtained a great majority; many of the Conservatives voted with the Government, and, according to Greville, even more 'expressed satisfaction at the result being a defeat of Disraeli'.[27]

Disraeli's reaction was to behave in impeccably Conservative fashion during the latter half of the session of 1860, supporting Palmerston as the bulwark of the *status quo*, even if it meant, as it did in the case of the Paper Duties Bill, reversing his previous radical position. The Paper Duties were the last remaining of the three 'taxes on knowledge' preventing the establishment of a cheap popular press; in 1853 Disraeli had supported Bright on the repeal of the advertisement duty; now he connived with Derby and Palmerston to defeat Gladstone's proposed repeal of the Paper Duties. Bright berated him for 'being a party to the murder of the Cheap Press', but his Conservative stand earned him grudging approval from the rebel Cecil in a further *Quarterly* article in July. Disraeli, said Cecil, had shown no inclination 'to flinch from the assertion of Conservative principles', and appeared to have 'abandoned for ever the "unholy alliances" and the trimming tactics of which events had proved the hollowness and shame'. Grumbling and even revolt against Disraeli's leadership recurred in the following sessions, but Disraeli, in the years up to Palmerston's death, showed every sign of having turned his back on his Radical past.

In one respect Disraeli proved himself a true Conservative and pupil of Metternich; disapproving of Garibaldi and totally failing to share the popular enthusiasm for the cause of Italian unity, he supported the maintenance of the temporal power of the Pope, Pius IX, whom he quaintly described as 'an old man on a Semitic throne baffling the modern Attilas'.[28] In coming out for the Pope against Garibaldi, he hoped to win Roman Catholic votes for the Conservatives against Palmerston's pro-Italian attitudes, and, through Earle, he maintained friendly contacts with the Papal Court, and with the Pope's representative in England, Cardinal Wiseman. His attitude on the Italian question was also partly dictated by a natural distaste for revolutionaries, and when Garibaldi visited London in April 1864 he absolutely refused to meet him. While the London mob and the Whig duchesses alike worshipped at the feet of the Italian hero, Disraeli tried to present him to Stanley as a corrupt adventurer, 'denying that he had ever won a battle, asserting that his Neapolitan success was wholly due to bribery, that he bought off the officers opposed to him', and 'that his object in coming over was to collect a large fund'. 'Amusing at first,' Stanley commented, 'but his cynical affectation is apt to grow tedious'.[29]

While defending the Pope against Garibaldi Disraeli also emerged during the sixties as the unlikely champion of the Established Church, tilting against the Latitudinarians represented by Jowett and, more spectacularly, against Darwin. 'The maintenance of the Church is the great question of the age', he told Malmesbury in 1861. Stanley, always repelled by what he saw as Disraeli's cynical power-seeking, was shocked. 'How can I reconcile his open ridicule, in private, of all religions, with his preaching up of a new church-and-state agitation?' he wrote unhappily in his diary on 30 November 1861. '... How can I help seeing that glory and power, rather than the public good, have been his objects? He has at least the merit, in this last respect, of being no hypocrite'.[30]

Disraeli was quite incapable of seeing the heated religious controversies of the sixties in any but political terms. He saw the bishops and clergy of the Established Church as the natural allies of the Conservative party, and indeed, when he became Prime Minister, regarded church patronage as a means of advancing and rewarding political supporters. But, as usual, his motives were mixed; he genuinely regarded the Anglican Church as an ancient institution of England which it was the duty of the Conservative party to defend, and he had a natural antipathy to scientific theory as opposed to revelation. Inevitably, his defence of the Church was tinged with his favourite theory of Hebrew tradition – 'I look upon the Church as the only Jewish institution remaining', he wrote in his *Reminiscences*. His most famous declaration of faith was made in the Sheldonian Theatre at Oxford on 25 November 1864 when, standing beside the Bishop, Samuel Wilberforce, he ranged himself on the side of the Bible against Darwin's *Origin of Species*. 'The question is this – Is man an ape or an angel? My Lord, I am on the side of the angels.' To Disraeli, the defence of the Church was a part of the old fight against materialism which he had first undertaken in *Popanilla*, thirty-six years before. 'To those who have faith in the spiritual nature of man', he was to write in the General Preface to the novels at the end of the decade, 'the prospect is full of gloom ... what is styled Materialism is in the ascendant.' Strangely enough, in view of his public attitude, privately Disraeli predicted the victory of science over religion, telling Stanley in 1851, 'that the sentiment, or instinct of religion, would, by degrees, though slowly, vanish as knowledge became more widely spread'.[31]

The Sheldonian speech represented a rare burst of energy; at the beginning of the 1864 session Stanley noted with concern: 'D. seems to me either growing old or in weak health: he has lost his former vivacity, and sleeps much in his seat', while a year later he recorded that Disraeli's increasing apathy to public affairs was becoming a subject of general remark.[32] Disraeli's lethargy and increasingly conservative attitudes contrasted with his rival Gladstone's ferocious energy and ever-closer approximation to Bright and the Radicals. Reaching the age of fifty in December 1860, Gladstone wrote in his diary, 'I feel within me the rebellious unspoken word ... I will not be old. The horizon enlarges, the sky shifts around me. It is an age of shocks'.

Moderate opinion, both Whig and Conservative, had come to regard Gladstone as the likely author of 'shocks'. Suspicion grew that Gladstone was, in Greville's words, 'an audacious innovator because he has an insatiable desire for popularity, and in his notions of Government he is a far more sincere Republican than Bright.' Parliamentary success had gone to his head, making him arrogant, tactless and overbearing, turning his colleagues' distrust of him into loathing. The Whigs indeed, far more socially exclusive than the Tories, had never really accepted Gladstone, their view of him being summed up in the phrase 'Oxford on the surface, Liverpool underneath'. Emily Eden, an intelligent woman of impeccable Whig ancestry, who had tried to like Gladstone and failed, expressed the high aristocratic reaction to him in a letter to Clarendon:

> There is an element of parvenuism about him, as there was about Sir Robert Peel – something in his tone of voice, and his way of coming into a room, that is not aristocratic. In short, he is not frivolous enough for me. If he were soaked in boiling water, and rinsed until he were twisted into a rope, I do not suppose a drop of fun would ooze out.[33]

Among his Whig colleagues in the Cabinet, Gladstone felt isolated. Palmerston, regarding him as an enemy and a dangerous man who must be kept down, teased and bullied him. As Granville reported on 26 July 1860, 'Gladstone has been on the half-cock of resignation for two months ... Palmerston has tried him very hard ... and says that the only way to deal with him is to bully him a little'.[34]

Proud and passionate as he was, wounded by the Whigs' treatment of him and increasingly attracted by Bright, Gladstone began to move in the direction Disraeli had long predicted, towards Bright and the Radicals and away from the moderate Whigs. On 11 May 1864, without consulting Palmerston, he delivered a speech on Reform which was generally interpreted as a call for universal male suffrage. 'I venture to say', he declared to the Commons, 'that every man who is not presumably incapacitated by some consideration of personal unfitness or political danger, is morally entitled to come within the pale of the constitution.' Palmerston who, as he admitted to Clarendon, 'abhorred' the notion of lowering the franchise, and was 'determined to stand firm on the point of property as against numbers',[35] was outraged and delivered an immediate and stinging rebuke. Disraeli told the House that Gladstone was reviving the doctrine of Tom Paine, but Bright was delighted, telling his wife that Gladstone's speech opened a new era in the Reform question, indicating his future intentions, and predicted, correctly, that Gladstone would be 'more than ever the dread of the aristocratic mob of the West End of London'.[36] Clarendon circulated the story that one of Gladstone's doctors had predicted that he would die insane,[37] while Stanley, more objectively, commented that the general opinion was that 'he had broken with the old Whigs and placed himself at the head of the movement party'.[38]

While Disraeli, at the end of the session of 1864, was, Stanley noted, unusually gloomy about his political prospects, Gladstone was talking spiritedly of taking a new strong Liberal line on Reform, and launching himself on a new career as a demagogue. In a triumphant tour of the industrial towns he tasted for the first time the heady delights of public applause, as he noted in his diary for 14 October 1864: '– So ended in peace an exhausting, flattering, I hope not intoxicating circuit ... It is ... impossible not to love the people from whom such manifestations come ... Somewhat haunted by dreams of halls, and lines of people, and great assemblies'. Palmerston, venturing into the industrial north two months earlier, had received a very different reception. At Bradford, 30,000 working men stood in 'stony silence' outside the Town Hall where he was to speak, in protest against his refusal to receive a deputation asking for the vote. It was not the sort of reception the popular 'Pam' had been accustomed to, but was a portent of things to come.

As the session of 1865 opened the question uppermost in everyone's mind was how long Palmerston, now in his eighty-first year, would last. William White, doorkeeper of the House of Commons, described in his memoirs how, as Palmerston marched across the lobby, 'a hundred eyes examined him keenly ... for upon his shoulders rested the whole framework of our party arrangements'.[39] The general verdict seemed to be favourable; Disraeli was impressed to hear from the Speaker of the aged Prime Minister's gargantuan appetite at dinner, when Palmerston devoured:

two plates of turtle soup; he was then served very amply to a plate of cod & oyster sauce; he then took a pâté; afterwards he was helped to two very greasy-looking entrées; he then

despatched a plate of roast mutton; there then appeared before him, the largest, & ...
the hardest, slice of ham that ever figured on the table of a nobleman, yet it disappeared,
just in time for him to answer the enquiry of his butler 'Snipe, my Lord, or pheasant?'.
He instantly replied pheasant: thus completing his ninth dish of meat at that meal.[40]

Despite or perhaps because of, his capacity to enjoy such Rabelaisian meals as
this, Palmerston fell ill in April with what appears to have been prostate trouble
or a bladder complaint. The newspapers recorded his illness in a casual way, as if
it were nothing out of the ordinary, but Stanley heard that Dr Drage, who
attended him, said that it was 'the beginning of the end', although the end might
be protracted. Rumours gathered force that he would retire to the House of Lords,
leaving the leadership of the Commons to Gladstone, an outcome dreaded, but
regarded as inevitable by both Whigs and Tories. *The Times* was Gladstone's
declared enemy, said Stanley; the Tories loathed him, and his colleagues detested
him and said so openly, yet the general opinion was that 'he must lead, there is no
one who can compete with him'. Venomous gossip about him, much of it emanating from his Cabinet colleagues, was freely passed round society – reports of his
irritability and dictatorial manner, hints as to insanity in the Gladstone family,
and ridicule of his unsophisticated and eccentric behaviour in society. Palmerston,
however, showed no signs of retiring, and in July dissolved Parliament and called
a General Election. There was no real issue but Palmerston's popularity, and
Disraeli's attempt to make the defence of the Church a platform made no impression. The Conservatives lost 25 seats to Palmerston and were, in Derby's words,
'utterly rout[ed]' in Scotland, where, he said, 'the democratic spirit prevails'.[41]

For Disraeli, there was only one consolation in this defeat. Gladstone lost his
seat at Oxford to a young Conservative, Gathorne–Hardy. Gladstone was dismayed at this rejection, but the severance of his connection with the most conservative constituency in the country was to open up a new popular road for him, as
Palmerston had told Shaftesbury a few days before the election: 'Keep him in
Oxford and he is partially muzzled, but send him elsewhere and he will run wild'.
'Gladstone will soon have it all his own way', Palmerston warned, 'and whenever
he gets my place we shall have some strange doings'. Gladstone's success as a
popular orator at crowded meetings in the industrial towns where he was cam-
paigning for South Lancashire was widely reported; 'He has become,' Stanley
wrote in his diary for 26 June, 'the central figure in our politics and his importance
is far more likely to increase than diminish'.

Derby and Disraeli exchanged gloomy letters on the effects of the Conservative
losses. Derby thought there was no prospect of their taking office again even if
Palmerston died. Disraeli seems to have agreed, to the extent of proposing that
Derby should form a coalition with the moderate Whigs, and that he himself
should give up the leadership in the Commons to a Whig. Derby replied rejecting
the idea, with a tribute to Disraeli, 'I cannot forget that you & I have acted
together, with perfect cordiality, & I believe, mutual confidence, for more than
17 years'.[42] It was not strictly true; even at the beginning of 1865, Stanley, who

was in the best position to know, reported that they acted together with difficulty and that there was very little cordial feeling between them.[43]

The situation changed overnight with Palmerston's death on 18 October, two days before his eighty-first birthday. Stanley, visiting Disraeli at Hughenden shortly afterwards, found him transformed by the news, in good health and excellent spirits. It seemed, said Stanley, as if the 'prospect of renewed political life had excited him afresh, and that he had thrown off the lethargy which has been growing upon him for the last year or two'.[44] Palmerston's death meant Disraeli's political resurrection; as he wrote triumphantly, 'the truce of parties is over'. It was the end of an era; the great battle between Disraeli and Gladstone was about to begin.

17 Disraeli v Gladstone

Palmerston's death shattered the unnatural peace which had reigned in British politics over the last fifteen years, opening the way to renewed party struggle and a personal contest for power between Gladstone and Disraeli. Lord John Russell succeeded Palmerston as Prime Minister, but at seventy-six his tenure was destined to be brief, and the era of the Old Whigs who had governed England as if by divine right for nearly two centuries had come to an end. The future belonged to two men who were outsiders in terms of the traditional political establishment, who had risen by ability alone and who were regarded by their respective parties with distrust and even loathing.

The question of Reform, which Palmerston had skilfully kept submerged, now came to the fore. In the ensuing eighteen-month struggle over the issue Disraeli was to emerge the victor. Demonstrating supreme parliamentary and political skills, he was to force Gladstone on to the side of Bright and the Radicals, and, revealing the Old Whigs as a spent political force, to lead the Conservative party to a triumphant and unlikely victory as authors of the 1867 Reform Bill.

Disraeli's own attitude towards Reform was opportunist and purely partisan. Privately he had told Stanley as long ago as 1853 that he objected to reform, 'thinking that you could not find any point to stop at short of the absolute sovereignty of the people', and that what he most dreaded 'as fatal to the territorial principle' was the equalization of the representative areas – in other words, the principle of electoral districts.[1] Publicly, however, in keeping with his plan to present the Conservative party with a progressive image, he had always, as even Gladstone admitted, defended the party's right to initiate Reform. He had come of political age in the year of the 1832 Reform Bill which had endowed its authors, the Whigs, with political power for almost a decade, and he was determined that the experience should not be repeated by the Liberals in 1866. 'No matter how you modify the Bill', he told Stanley on 30 April 1866, 'it is still theirs, and not ours, and will give them the command of the boroughs for half-a-dozen years to come.' Moreover, in 1866 the Gladstone factor, always a touchstone in Disraeli's political calculations, was a prominent motive in determining his course of action.

Commenting on Disraeli's determination to defeat the Gladstone Reform Bill and turn out the Government at all costs, Stanley noted: 'It is after all natural and perhaps inevitable in his position he should feel as he does. To suppose that he can see Gladstone's success with pleasure would be absurd: and it is only human nature that he should look to a personal triumph over a rival [rather] than to the permanent effect of what he does on the party or principle which he represents.'[2]

At the outset of 1866 Gladstone, once again Chancellor of the Exchequer and now also Leader of the Commons, seemed in a strong position to carry the Bill. Disraeli's future looked less secure; there was a movement to replace the ailing Derby with Stanley, which would have put paid to any chances of Disraeli's becoming Prime Minister; and there was even a far-fetched plan put forward by Lady Salisbury for a Liberal–Conservative coalition led by Gladstone and Stanley. Disraeli, naturally, poured cold water on both proposals, describing the first to Earle as 'a fairytale', and writing to Stafford Northcote of the second:

> It won't do. W.E.G. and S. sound very well. One is a man of transcendent ability: the other, though not of transcendent ability has considerable power. But neither of them can deal with men. S. is a mere child in such matters. The other, though more experienced, is too impetuous and wanting in judgement to succeed as a leader.[3]

Events were to prove that Disraeli was not being entirely unfair in his judgement of Gladstone's failings as a leader. On 2 March 1866, ten days before Gladstone was to introduce the Reform Bill, Henry Lennox, whose social standing gave him access to high Whig circles, reported to Disraeli of their 'frantic hatred' of Gladstone; as early as January Disraeli had discovered incipient revolt among the Whigs which would obviate the need for any Conservative initiative against it. 'The other side will do the business', he told Stanley.

The 'other side' did indeed do the business, with Disraeli active behind the scenes, in touch with the rebel Whig leaders and mobilizing Conservative opposition to the Bill. The spearhead of the Whig revolt in Parliament was a man who was later to become one of Disraeli's most bitter enemies, Robert Lowe, the combative, sarcastic albino MP for Calne who concentrated all his intellectual brilliance and loathing of democracy against Gladstone and the Reform Bill. 'Mr. Lowe is the great reputation of the session', the *Spectator* wrote. 'No stranger goes there without looking for the white gleam, or rather flash, of his striking head, or listening anxiously for the cold, sardonic ring of his lucid voice, penetrating it [the House] with a shiver of half-mocking intelligence'. Supported by thirty or forty aristocratic rebels, dubbed the 'Adullamites' or 'the Cave' after Bright's simile comparing them with the men gathered round David in the Cave of Adullam, Lowe succeeded in destroying the Bill by raising the democratic spectre of which the aristocratic members were afraid, and by making Gladstone lose his temper and consequently his parliamentary tact. 'When angry', Stanley commented, 'he [Gladstone] becomes a radical'.

Taunted by Lowe and Disraeli, Gladstone conjured up extra-parliamentary forces, defying the House of Commons in a ringing but unwise speech. 'You connot fight against the future', he told them:

The great social forces which move onward in their might and majesty and which the tumult of your debates does not for a moment impede or disturb ... are against you ... the banner which we now carry in this fight ... soon again will float in the eye of Heaven, and it will be borne by the firm hands of the united people of the three kingdoms, perhaps not to an easy, but to a certain and to a not far distant victory.[4]

This was Gladstone the demagogue throwing the language of Bright in the face of the aristocratic House of Commons; the result was that the Government escaped defeat on the Opposition amendment by only five votes. 'I suppose Uncle William is wanting in tact', Gladstone's niece, Lady Frederick Cavendish, wrote in her journal, 'for there is treason through the camp, and the oddest combination and fermentation of parties against him'. 'Gladstone's extraordinary state of mental excitement', Stanley recorded, was the talk of the clubs, adding, 'most people agree that if the present strain on his mental faculties continues, he will give way.'[5]

Behind the scenes Disraeli worked upon these feelings, encouraging and indirectly organizing the Whig rebels in their opposition, and mobilizing his own supporters behind them. In the second week of June a meeting of rebel Whig-Liberal peers took place at Lord Lansdowne's House which was to prove fatal to Gladstone's bill. Disraeli had advance knowledge of the meeting, and, indeed, had helped to co-ordinate it, drawing up a list of anti-Government Whig peers whom Derby should persuade to attend. At the meeting it was agreed that Lord Dunkellin, Clanricarde's son, should propose an amendment hostile to the basic principle of the Bill, substituting rating for the rental franchise in the boroughs. Disraeli made sure that the rebels would be supported, writing to his followers to ensure their attendance and their vote. The emotive language which he used in these appeals is worth quoting in view of his own subsequent Reform Bill: 'If the Reform Bill passes', he wrote to the Hon. Henry Liddell,

> the aristocratic settlement of this country will receive a fatal blow from wh: it will not easily recover. Many of the Whigs, now, feel this, as keenly as we do, & Lord Dunkellin's motion for Monday, fatal to the Bill, will be carried if our friends are united ... It is our only chance of defeating a measure wh: will shatter both Whigs and Tories, & utterly destroy the present Conservative organisation.[6]

Having master-minded the opposition, Disraeli did not speak when the crucial debate took place on 18 June, leaving it to the Adullamites to put the motion against their own Government. Almost to a man the Whig 'Cave' voted for Dunkellin's amendment, and the Conservative country gentlemen turned out in strength against their bugbear, Gladstone. The Government was defeated by 315 votes to 304 amid great cheering and waving of hats from the Adullamites and the squires. The ministerial benches looked surprised; Gladstone, apparently unaware of having been secretly outmanoeuvred by Disraeli was, according to Stanley, 'not angry, but perplexed and disconcerted. I believe he had no idea of the result'. Stanley walked home from the House with an exultant Disraeli, turning in to the Carlton to celebrate the victory with champagne and mutual congratulations. It was nearly seven years to the day since Disraeli had been cast out into the political wilderness; he had defeated his great rival and office was now once again within his grasp.

Russell resigned on 26 June but, even as Disraeli seemed poised for success, a dangerous pitfall was revealed. The Adullamite Whigs, seeking their reward for the defeat of Gladstone, were aiming for a 'fusion' government with the Conservatives in which they would have the lion's share, with a Whig Prime Minister in the House of Lords and Stanley as Leader of the Commons. Such a combination would have spelt the end not only for Derby, but for Disraeli also, and, to make matters worse, Derby was in an undecided state of mind, described by his son as 'at one moment desponding, at another sanguine'. Disraeli was determined that at this critical point 'the Captain' should not bolt again; after all that had passed he now knew better than anyone how to handle him.

'You *must* take the Government', he wrote firmly to Derby on 25 June, two days after the Adullamite ultimatum. 'The honor of your house and the necessity of the country alike require it.' The Whig intrigue, he told him, was based on the hope that Derby would refuse office, that a Whig leader would then be sent for who would induce a section of the Conservatives to join his administration; the Conservative party would thus be broken up. 'There is only one course with the Queen: to kiss hands', he impressed upon him. 'Nothing can prevent your winning, if you grasp the helm.'[7] For three days Derby hesitated, but Disraeli's pressure and his own feelings of pique at the Whigs' presumption won the day and he agreed to form the third Derby–Disraeli administration. The incident underlined their mutual interdependence; over the following year as Derby's health worsened, he came to depend more and more upon his lieutenant, so much so that a member of the Cabinet complained that the Prime Minister never consulted anyone but Disraeli.[8]

Disraeli was once again Chancellor of the Exchequer, and the Cabinet included familiar figures such as Spencer Walpole at the Home Office, Pakington at the Admiralty, General Peel at the War Office, and John Manners at the Office of Works. However, Disraeli did manage to get Malmesbury 'kicked upstairs' from the Foreign Office to Lord Privy Seal, on the grounds of ill-health, and replaced him with Stanley. There were some new and able additions, notably the former Lord Robert Cecil, now Viscount Cranborne, as Indian Secretary; the Earl of Carnarvon as Colonial Secretary; Disraeli's protégé, Sir Stafford Northcote, once Gladstone's secretary, as President of the Board of Trade; and Gathorne–Hardy as President of the Poor Law Board.

Among the minor appointments was that of Ralph Earle as Secretary to the Poor Law Board under Gathorne–Hardy. Earle, a constant voice in Disraeli's ear over the decade since they had first met, had recently become ever more strident as anxious ambition pushed him to the edge of hysteria. He appears to have first aimed for a secretaryship at the Foreign Office and, to further his own ambition, had tried to push Disraeli into the Foreign Office himself, advising him not to undertake the Exchequer again. '*There is no opportunity of doing anything great in that*

Dept.,' he wrote to him on 1 July in a long, frantic letter in which punctuation and grammar alike were thrown to the winds. He threatened that Gladstone would try to 'sink the Ch. of the Exch. as much as possible', while tempting Disraeli with the prospect of a closer relationship with the Queen: 'Another advantage in your being Secretary of State is that you wd. sometimes be in attendance upon the Queen – & thus observed by the Country'. He seems to have been far from certain that Disraeli would do anything for him, and anxiously pressed his claims: 'the expectation *on both sides* that I shd. be included in Ld. D's arrangements, & *some* knowledge of the part wh: I have taken in recent affairs, that I feel I shd. be quite incapacitated for rendering any services in future, if I were discredited by being left out, on this occasion.'[9] Loyally Disraeli, on receipt of this letter, asked Stanley if he would take Earle on as his under-secretary, a proposal to which Stanley agreed, but either Disraeli or Earle seems to have changed his mind for it was eventually settled that he should have the post of parliamentary secretary to the Poor Law Board at a salary of £1,100 a year. Earle, apparently, was satisfied; 'I don't know how to thank you enough', he wrote to Disraeli, going on to make recommendations as to his successor as private secretary.

Disraeli ignored Earle's suggestions; he may, understandably, have become wearied by the young man's restless demands upon him, and he had already received an application for the post from another young man whom he had met and to whom he had been instantly attracted on a visit to Raby Castle the previous year. Montague Lowry Corry, generally known as Monty Corry, was twenty-eight when he met Disraeli. Like Disraeli's other young men he was good-looking and well-connected, his grandfather being the 2nd Earl of Belmore and his mother the daughter of the sixth Earl of Shaftesbury; he had been educated at Harrow, Trinity College, Cambridge, and the Bar. He was immensely sociable, charming and good-natured; Lord Salisbury described him as 'sympath-etically intelligent without being what people call "clever"'. Equally popular with men and with women, he was no intellectual; 'Art and nature are words that mean nothing to him,' commented Salisbury. His whole world revolved round his friends. His first meeting with Disraeli was characteristic; Disraeli came into a room one wet afternoon at Raby to find Corry amusing the girls of the house party by dancing and singing a comic song; Disraeli looked at him and went off without a word. Corry was dismayed, but that evening after dinner Disraeli came up to him and, putting his hand on his shoulder, said, 'I think you must be my impresario'. It was the beginning of a mutually affectionate relationship that was to last until Disraeli's death, and to which he was to pay tribute in his last novel, *Endymion*:

> The relations between a Minister and his secretary are, or at least should be, among the finest that can subsist between two individuals. Except the married state, there is none in which so great a confidence is involved, in which more forbearance ought to be exercised, or more sympathy ought to exist.

On 6 July 1866 the members of the third Derby–Disraeli Administration went down by train to Windsor to kiss hands and accept the seals of office. The omens,

Sir Stafford Northcote noted gloomily, were bad from the first; on the train going down Disraeli, sitting down without looking on what he thought would be a bench, sat on the floor instead, and, as they waited to be received by the Queen there was a violent thunderstorm, to be followed by another as they sat down to lunch afterwards, which whitened the terraces with hail like a snowstorm.

In London that month there were stronger portents of the future: on 2 July the leaders of the Reform League held a mass meeting in Trafalgar Square to protest against the 'killing' of Gladstone's Bill, and demanded manhood suffrage and the ballot. It was announced that on Monday 23 July processions from various parts of London would converge on Hyde Park, the preserve of the fashionable aristocracy, to hold a protest meeting in favour of Reform. The Government decided to close the park, but on the appointed day huge crowds of working men and some women arrived with bands playing and banners waving. At Marble Arch where the police, headed by their elderly chief, Sir Richard Mayne, stood behind the closed gates, a long section of the railings gave way under the pressure of the crowd who spilled into the park, trampling flower-beds and rooting up plants. Mary Anne, watching the crowds stream past from her vantage-point at Grosvenor Gate, was not in the least alarmed. Her concern, as usual, was for Disraeli to whom she sent messages telling him to look in his room at Westminster for his great coat as 'it has got quite cold', and despatching James the footman with a choice of boots and shoes for his master. Disraeli sent Monty Corry to look after her, and he reported back that Mary Anne wished him to know that the people in general seemed to be thoroughly enjoying themselves. 'I really believe she sympathises with them', he added.

Disraeli himself was not alarmed by the so-called 'Hyde Park Riots', but he suspected the Opposition of encouraging them with a view to upsetting the Government. Briefly, he was tempted to steal their thunder by slipping a quick Reform Bill through Parliament before the end of the session, an opportunist manoeuvre prompted by fear of Gladstone rather than the mobs. He put the proposal to Derby as 'my reflections this day on what Gladstone said yesterday', recommending it as a rapid solution to all their problems: 'It would cut the ground entirely from under Gladstone'.[10] Nothing, however, was done before the end of the session, but while Members of Parliament retired in August to the grouse moors or to Cowes, Bright stumped the towns of the industrial north in a series of great popular demonstrations for Reform.

Disraeli, in the rural surroundings of Hughenden, seems to have hoped that the Reform question would simply go away; but Derby at Knowsley in the heartland of Lancashire was better situated to feel the public pulse. It was he and not Disraeli who first came 'reluctantly' as he put it (in a letter to Disraeli of 16 September), to the conclusion that they would have 'to deal with the question of Reform'. Politely, Disraeli disagreed, 'Observation and reflection have not yet brought me to your conclusion as to the necessity of bringing in a Bill for Parliamentary Reform', he replied, and it was not until the end of the month that pressure from Derby and, indirectly, from the Queen, brought him round. Even then his approach was tentative in the extreme; he told Derby on 12 October that if they managed to proceed by resolutions only and avoid bringing in a Bill the next session 'we shall indeed be on velvet'.

The reasons for Disraeli's caution were not hard to find; for a Conservative minority Government to bring in a Reform Bill was a course fraught with danger. Reaction within the party ranks to the Reform Bill of 1859 had, as Cecil's attacks revealed, been extremely unfavourable. Moreover, Disraeli had rallied his supporters against Gladstone the previous year on the grounds that a Reform Bill would have been 'fatal to the territorial constitution of England'. The Liberals, headed by Gladstone, would be certain to contest the right of a Conservative Government to bring in a Reform Bill. All would in fact depend on whether the Conservative party would follow Derby and Disraeli, and, even more importantly since the Tories were in the minority, whether the Liberal Opposition would follow Gladstone.

And so Derby and Disraeli wavered, uncertain how to proceed; successive November Cabinets decided nothing, and it was not until some point between Christmas and the New Year of 1867 that Disraeli seems to have come to the conclusion that there was a general feeling in favour of settling the question that had bored and bedevilled the parliamentary scene for the past sixteen years. Monty Corry, gauging feeling in the country houses over the Christmas period reported to his chief on 2 January that he had been surprised at 'the unanimity with which all classes, in the provinces where I have been, desire a Reform Bill – from Lord Shaftesbury to the Shropshire rustic.'

The passing of the 1867 Reform Bill was to unfold as a complicated struggle between Gladstone and Disraeli for control of the majority in Parliament, a duel which could only be won by keeping control of their respective followers and detaching a sufficient number from the other side. It was a contest in which Disraeli's hope lay in apparently occupying the middle ground, thus driving Gladstone farther to the left than his followers would go. It was to involve a conflict between styles of leadership, in which Disraeli's subtle, flexible skills as a parliamentary manager triumphed, and in which Gladstone's faults of temper would lose him the game.

Initially the omens were not good for Disraeli. The Bill was to be based on household suffrage, a magic catch-phrase which, Gladstone later admitted, 'bowled us over'. It had the merit of being understandable, but was hardly revolutionary, being merely an extension of the old principle of property as the qualification for the franchise. Nonetheless the phrase alone was enough to ignite the hostility of the right-wing members of the Cabinet – Cranborne, Carnarvon, and Peel's brother, General Peel. As Disraeli commented to Derby on the General's reaction: 'on the phrase "household suffrage" his eye lights up with insanity'. Peel roundly told Disraeli that if the phrase remained, 'the whole of our back benches would rise up and leave us.' He threatened resignation but was persuaded by the Queen to stay, and Disraeli was optimistic when, on Saturday 23 February, his bases for the Bill were presented to the Cabinet. He wrote to Corry after the meeting: 'Cabinet unanimous for the great plan.' As so often, his hopes were premature; a distrustful Cranborne, examining the figures the next day, came to the conclusion that the franchise was to be lowered further than he was prepared to go. Furious, he sent Derby a letter of resignation, endorsed by his ally Carnarvon. Derby received it at 8.45 a.m. on Monday, the day on which the Reform Resolutions were to be debated. 'Utter ruin. What are we to do?' Derby wrote to Disraeli, summoning a Cabinet meeting at his house later that morning. Cranborne and Carnarvon, with Peel backing them up, absolutely refused to budge, and hastily a watered-down measure was decided upon. Disraeli, 'white as a sheet', Carnarvon reported, said that his Bill had been 'assassinated'.[11] It was a personal defeat for him and a victory for Cranborne, who, he knew, was motivated by a bitter personal hostility.

Disraeli, however, was seen to be in better spirits after the debate; he had decided to fight back. The uneasy reaction of his own Conservative benches during the debate and the united hostility of the Opposition told him that the Bill in its present form could not stand. Dining with Stanley at Bellamy's afterwards, he tested the feelings of key Conservatives, and had the satisfaction of being able to report to the Queen the next day that there was general anger against Cranborne's *coup* and a desire to return to the original plan. 'General Peel and Lord Cranborne', he told Victoria, 'have acted in complete ignorance and misapprehension of the real feeling of the country.' If Derby, his Prime Ministerial pride ruffled by Cranborne's insurrection, could be persuaded that a majority of the party would accept household suffrage, then Disraeli could still win. At a meeting on 28 February of 150 Conservative members a majority voted for a return to household suffrage if it should be necessary, as they put it in a phrase expressive of the party attitude to the question, 'as the best means of resisting further changes and obtaining a lasting settlement'. Backed by the pressure of the party, Disraeli emerged the victor at a Cabinet meeting on 2 March; a return to the original plan was decided upon and Cranborne, Carnarvon and Peel resigned.

Cranborne was, Disraeli knew, a dangerous opponent, but his numerical following was small, including, as usual, 'Big Ben' and Jem Lowther, kinsman of Lord Lonsdale, who went round the clubs saying that he would not know how to face his constituents if, 'having refused a bill last year from a good Christian, he were to accept it this year from a bad Jew'. Dislike of Disraeli, however, did not imply any desire to act with Gladstone; Cranborne wrote to his brother that, having escaped from the clutches of a 'rogue' he had no intention of falling into those of a 'lunatic'. Indeed, on the Tory side, the desire to 'extinguish Gladstone & Co.' was a strong motive in prompting them to follow Disraeli.

Given that the general feeling on both sides was that Reform was inevitable and a lasting settlement desirable, what might be called the Gladstone factor was an important consideration. In the closed atmosphere of nineteenth-century political society personal feelings counted for a good deal; Disraeli was not generally popular, either with his own party or with the Whigs, but he inspired dislike and distrust, not, as Gladstone did, fear. The feeling that Gladstone was dangerous and difficult to control was as strong among the Whigs as among the Tories. Even the Radicals, Gladstone's natural allies in the Liberal party, recognized this ungovernable quality in him, and accepted Reform at the hands of Disraeli because they believed him to be more flexible, and more vulnerable to pressure because of his minority position. As dislike of Disraeli had driven the Peelites to join the Whigs in 1852 and 1859, so fear of Gladstone pushed the Whig section of the Liberal party towards the Conservatives in 1867. This fear was exaggerated since Gladstone, although a passionate advocate of Reform, was essentially still a moderate, and had no intention of enfranchising the 'residuum', as Bright called the proletariat. But public agitation and the popular Reform press, in lauding Gladstone, advising him to distance himself from the Whigs, and reminding him that 'the unenfranchised millions' mattered more than 'the great aristocratic houses of Westminster, Sutherland, Bedford, Lansdowne and Derby', only served to reinforce the majority view of the Liberal leader as a public agitator and a demagogue. Even before Disraeli was due to introduce his Reform Bill on 18 March, he knew that at a meeting of 280 Liberals at Gladstone's house, some 35 to 40 Adullamite Whigs had told their leader bluntly that they would not back any move he might make with a view to turning out the Government. Subsequently the Adullamites sent Disraeli a confidential message that they would support his Bill provided he safeguarded the property principle by making personal payment of rates the basis for the franchise. Moreover, on 15 March a meeting of the Conservative party had assured him that the mass of his party would support the Bill.

With some confidence, therefore, Disraeli went ahead on 18 March to unveil a Bill which, although heralded with the ringing phrase 'household suffrage', was so hedged about with safeguards as to be exclusive enough to satisfy conservatives on both sides. In the boroughs he proposed to give the vote to every male householder who had occupied his house for two years, had been rated for poor law relief and had paid his own rates; in the counties it was to go to any man who had resided for a year in the county, owning or occupying property of a rateable value of £15 p.a.; while in both counties and boroughs 'fancy franchises', for example, being a teacher or member of a savings bank, conferred the vote. In the boroughs any householder paying 20 shillings a year in direct taxation was to be entitled to a second vote. The principal intent of the bill was insistence on personal payment of rates, designed to exclude the 'compound householders' – those tenants compounding with their landlord for rate payments – who formed a large section of the artisan class. Gladstone tore the bill to pieces in a very able speech, pointing out that it would enfranchise only 140,000 people, and not 240,000 as Disraeli claimed; he proposed instead to dispense with all restrictions, personal payment of rates, dual voting, fancy franchises etc., in favour of a £5 rating which would have confined the franchise to the upper working class.

Gladstone's party refused to follow him; at a meeting on 21 March at which he proposed to oppose the second reading of the bill, there was much scuffling and muttering among the Liberals, and Bright made matters worse by berating them for refusing to support their leader. The result was that the second reading of the bill passed unopposed, while a second attempt by Gladstone to subvert the Bill provoked another mutiny, known as the 'Tea-Room Revolt'. On 8 April, after a meeting in the tea-room of the House of Commons, 48 members, mostly Radicals, went in a body to inform Gladstone that they could not support his amendment, for fear of being 'made to appear in the eyes of their constituents, as having been opposed to ... and [not] fairly considering a bill which gave, ostensibly, that household suffrage which they had always advocated'.[12] Gladstone's opposition had the appearance of being dictated by mere party spirit, a charge which Disraeli skilfully made the most of in his speech in the debate on 12 April. The division which followed at 2 am on 13 April was a crushing defeat for Gladstone by 310 votes to 289; 47 Liberals deserted him to vote for the Government; only 6 Conservatives deserted Disraeli. 'A smash perhaps without example', Gladstone wrote bitterly in his diary, and in his mortification talked of relinquishing the leadership and retiring to the back benches. In contrast, the Carlton Club received their triumphant leader ecstatically; the dining-room rang with cheers as he entered, and Sir Matthew White Ridley proposed the suitably sporting toast: 'Here's the man who rode the race, who took the time, who kept the time, and who did the trick!' Declining pressing invitations to stay, Disraeli went home to Mary Anne and the famous Fortnum pie and champagne.

The vote of 13 April was crucial; Disraeli now knew that, with good management, he could win. Whig hatred of Gladstone and Radical fear of being seen to oppose a Bill proposing household suffrage had played into his hands. Gladstone had lost control of his party, while Disraeli knew he could count on his followers' support. Only six Conservatives had voted against him, but one name among them had given him personal pain: that of Ralph Earle.

The breach between Disraeli and Earle seems to have taken place a month earlier, when Earle sent a letter of resignation to his chief, Gathorne-Hardy. Hardy noted in his diary, 'I fancy his grievance is not Reform but some quarrel with Disraeli. Each is bitter against the other.' The quarrel seems to have arisen primarily out of Earle's jealousy at being supplanted in Disraeli's confidence and affection by Monty Corry; in February he had poured out his injured feelings to Philip Rose, accusing Disraeli of 'altered demeanour, of snubbing him before subordinates, and of excluding him, in spite of ten years of devotion, from his confidence'. Despite the fact that he was no longer Disraeli's private secretary, Earle had not given up his old habits, continuing to bombard him with suggestions as to Government policy and patronage, and, according to one authority, walking into the secretaries' room at Downing Street as if he still worked there until barred on Disraeli's orders.

There is no evidence as to when the final quarrel took place, or what was said, but both clearly felt a sense of bitterness and personal betrayal indicative of the depth of the relationship that had existed between them. Earle told Sir William Fraser, 'Disraeli and I have quarrelled ... the quarrel is absolutely hopeless: it can never be made up under any circumstances.' Disraeli certainly felt betrayed; writing to his friend Lord Beauchamp he referred to Earle's hostile speech and vote against him as 'the treason of Earle':

> The only black spot in this great business, and which I would not notice to anyone but yourself, is the treason of Earle! I have known him for ten years, and tho' warned from the first by the Cowleys, whom he treated as he has treated me, I utterly disregarded their intimations, and ascribed them all to prejudice and misapprehensions.
>
> I have worked for his welfare more earnestly than for my own, and do not believe that I ever, even in the most trying times, gave him a hasty or unkind word. I loaded him with favors, and among them introduced him to you. I am ashamed at my want of discrimination.[13]

Disraeli indeed had reason to blame himself for his want of discrimination, and he had, after all, encouraged Ralph Earle in his betrayal of Cowley. It was, in short, a case of the biter bit. Enough of Earle's correspondence with Disraeli remains to show that his cynical opportunism appealed to the least admirable traits in Disraeli's character. Disraeli's own letters to Earle were seen by his first biographers, Moneypenny and Buckle, but have since disappeared and were probably, because of their compromising nature, destroyed in 1917. Earle, in his resentment against Disraeli, had thrown away his political future; as Disraeli remarked to Lord Spencer, 'I am not so much surprised at Ralph's want of political morality, but I am surprised at his want of political sagacity.' Earle resigned his Maldon seat in 1868 and turned to finance; involved in transactions with a dubious financier, Baron Hirsch, he made himself a small fortune, and when he died at Soden in Nassau on 10 June 1879 he left £40,000 to his brother Charles. The whole Disraeli–Earle episode was an echo of Disraeli's relationship with John Murray, which had left Murray lamenting that he had 'loved not wisely but too well'.

Disraeli was hurt by Earle's 'treason', but Earle's place had already been filled by the devotion of the delightful Monty Corry, and Earle was soon forgotten in the elation of his victory over Gladstone. As Corry reported from Shropshire on Easter Sunday:

> Your name is in the mouth of every labourer, who, without knowing what 'Reform' means, or caring, hears that Mr – has won a great victory. I leave the blank as it is impossible to express the Protean variety which a name, revered and cherished by me, here assumes. My private opinion is that my aunt's carpenter, who 'hears say that Mr. Disraeli had laid Mr. Gladstone on his back' thinks that you really knocked that godly man down.[14]

Further 'knocks' were in store for Gladstone when Parliament reassembled after the Easter recess; the 'smash' of 12–13 April was followed on 9 May by an even more resounding defeat for the Opposition Leader, when 58 Liberals voted against him and for Disraeli in the aftermath of renewed public agitation. Three days earlier a great Reform meeting had been held in Hyde Park in defiance of a Government proclamation forbidding it; a display of force in the face of official weakness which damaged the government and caused the resignation of the Home Secretary, Walpole, who was replaced by Gathorne–Hardy. The cumulative effect of the Reform meeting, however, was to emphasize the necessity of passing a satisfactory Bill, and to reinforce fear of Gladstone. In his bitterness at the second smash on 9 May, Gladstone seems to have decided to heed the prayers of the popular press, and to make the Liberal Party in his own image, divesting himself of the hostile 'Old Whigs' whom he publicly attacked at a meeting of the Reform Union on 11 May. Disraeli, never one to pass up an opportunity of embarrassing his rival, contrived to do so in a cleverly oblique speech on 13 May. Referring to the Reform Union meeting he said: 'I regret very much that these spouters of stale sedition, these obsolete incendiaries, should have come forward to pay their homage to one who, wherever he may sit, must always be the pride and ornament of the House.' No one was fooled by the delicate compliment to Gladstone, who was thus, in the eyes of the House, tarred with the same brush as those 'obsolete incendiaries'.

Indeed, through the early summer months of 1867 as the Reform Bill went its wearisome way through Parliament, Disraeli demonstrated an absolute mastery of parliamentary skills such as he had not shown before, based not upon biting philippics, but on hard work and cool tactical skill. He sat hour after hour on the front bench, arms crossed, face expressionless, listening to interminable debates, taking the political temperature, watching for the first signs of a potentially dangerous attack. It was not, however, the triumphant progress of a forceful leader with a master plan to which he was determined to adhere, but rather a series of skilful tactical retreats, of which the most spectacular was his unilateral acceptance of Hodgkinson's amendment on 17 May. The amendment, by abolishing the practice of composition for the payment of rates, removed the principal safeguard of Disraeli's original Bill and virtually trebled the borough electorate. Gladstone, expecting that the Government must oppose it and anticipating at last a fight which he might win, pounded away at the Government for nearly an hour. Disraeli, who usually looked, in White's words, 'grim, impassive [and] impenetrable' when his rival was speaking, was seen to be looking 'unusually serene and pleased', lifting his downcast eyes every now and then, a slight smile flickering over his face. When he rose and announced quietly that the Government would not oppose the amendment, there was a gasp of astonishment. 'Think how we've been sold!' was the flabbergasted reaction of a member of the Whig Cave, 'We would not have Gladstone's Bill, and, by Jove, we have got one ten thousand times worse!'[15] In accepting the amendment on his own responsibility without previous consultation, Disraeli had cut the ground from under Gladstone, thrown over the Whigs of the Cave and demonstrated their impotence, and shown his complete mastery of his own party. Disraeli, writing to Gathorne–Hardy, excused his unilateral action on the grounds that the amendment had been a 'meditated coup' by Gladstone of which he had been secretly informed, and that he had acted 'to extinguish Gladstone & Co.' Disraeli may, as he told Hardy, have taken an instantaneous decision during the debate, but it is equally probable that he had made up his mind beforehand that it would be better to present his colleagues with a *fait accompli* than to risk a potentially explosive discussion in Cabinet. His action over Hodgkinson's amendment was as much of a *coup* over his colleagues and party as any which Gladstone might have been intending.

Even before the Reform Bill had passed through all its stages in the Commons, Disraeli introduced a Redistribution Bill, which, as in the case of the Reform Bill, he was driven to modify as it passed through Parliament. Nonetheless, in its final form the Bill tended to favour the Conservatives. Forty-five new seats were created by the removal of one member from boroughs of less than 10,000 inhabitants, twenty-five being allotted to the counties, and fifteen to the towns, while the large industrial cities, Liverpool, Manchester, Birmingham and Leeds gained a third member, and the University of London one. Moreover the re-drawing of electoral boundaries by a Commission packed with Conservatives effected the transference of artisan suburban voters from the counties to the boroughs, the object being that potentially Liberal votes would be attached to Liberal constituencies, while the counties remained undilutedly Conservative.

The Reform Bill finally became law on 15 August. Observers were surprised, even shocked, at the ease with which Disraeli had humiliated and outmanoeuvred his rival, completely reversing their respective positions of only eighteen months before. As Bishop Wilberforce wrote wonderingly: 'Disraeli has almost taught the House of Commons to ignore Gladstone'. Even Gladstone himself, Monckton Milnes said, appeared to be 'in awe of Dizzy's diabolical cleverness'. It is hardly surprising in the circumstances that his parliamentary manner should have degenerated, and that he often spoke 'with a kind of suppressed and bitter laugh, gesticulating with both arms and glaring from side to side'.[16] Even the small boys in the street mocked him with their riddle – 'Why is Gladstone like a telescope?' – 'Because Disraeli draws him out, looks through him, and shuts him up!'

The House of Commons door-keeper, William White, a Gladstone partisan, recognized that Disraeli had been single-handedly responsible for the passing of the Reform Bill. 'Alone he did it,' he wrote,'... and with what wonderful skill none but those who watched him from night to night can know ... for tact adroitness and skill the man that conquered all these difficulties has no superior and scarcely an equal in Parliamentary history.'[17]

Disraeli had not originally wanted a Reform Bill; he had certainly not envisaged the Bill in the form which it eventually took, giving, for the first time, the vote to the 'respectable' working class. It had been as Derby later admitted in a famous phrase, 'a leap in the dark'. Once he saw there was a chance of success, Disraeli had been determined to win, and, in the late summer of 1867, he and the

Conservative party relished the sweets of victory which they had not known since the fall of Peel. Disraeli had demonstrated the impotence not only of the opposition to him within his own party but also that of the Old Whigs, who had posed a threat to his leadership the previous summer. He had revealed them to be, as he had always claimed, a selfish, exclusive, aristocratic clique whose pretensions to be the rightful leaders of the people were mere 'humbug'. Disraeli was well aware of the implications of the passage of the Reform Bill for the Whigs, talking of 'the entombment of Whig principles' in his speech at Edinburgh that autumn. The Whigs were understandably gloomy and resentful, as Lord Dalhousie wrote to Halifax:

> Politics are disgusting to think of ... Derby has set himself to prove that dishonesty is the best policy, and he has succeeded ... The Reform Bill may be a leap in the dark to him; it is none to me. Where we lifted the sluices of democracy an inch, he and Dizzy have raised them a foot. My only hope is that they will be the first to be washed away in the flood.[18]

Others took the same view. Bagehot, writing in the *Economist* for 7 September 1867, regarded the Bill as the consequence of the slow honesty of the Tory party and the quick dishonesty of the Tory leader – 'fraud in a convenient place, and with singular ability'. Carlyle penned a furious denunciation of Disraeli and the Bill entitled *Shooting Niagara: and After*, in which the Bill is seen as a Gadarene leap into the rapids of democracy, the work of 'a superlative Hebrew Conjuror, spell-binding all the great Lords, great Parties, great Interests of England to his hand ... and leading them by the nose, like helpless, mesmerised somnambulant cattle'. Carlyle's violent language was, however, less damaging than a scathing attack delivered by Cranborne in the *Quarterly* that autumn in an article whose title spoke for itself – 'The Conservative Surrender' – which represented the Bill as a reckless and venal surrender of Conservative principles by politicians grasping at votes.

Disraeli hastened to put his own gloss on his victory, representing it as the realization of a plan, or, as he had put it to Beauchamp in April, 'the dream of my life ... re-establishing Toryism on a national foundation'. In a brilliant propaganda speech at Edinburgh that November he embroidered on his theme of the Conservatives as the 'national party', representing them as the proponents of orderly change in contrast to the reactionaries represented by the Whig *Edinburgh Review* and the Tory *Quarterly* which had both attacked the Bill. Using his most effective weapon, ridicule, he compared the two journals with rival coaching inns outdated by the railways:

> ... first-rate, first-class post houses which in old days, for half a century or so ... carried on a roaring trade. Then there comes some revolution or progress which no person can ever have contemplated. They find things are altered. They do not understand them, and instead of that intense competition and mutual vindictiveness which before distinguished them, they suddenly quite agree. The 'boots' of the 'Blue Boar' and the chambermaid of the 'Red Lion' embrace, and are quite accord in this – denouncing the infamy of railroads.[19]

He told his audience:

In a progressive country change is constant; and the great question is, not whether you should resist change which is inevitable, but whether the change should be carried out in deference to the manners, the customs, the laws, and the traditions of a people, or whether it should be carried out in deference to abstract principles, and arbitrary and general doctrines.

The Tories, flattered by this image of themselves, cheered the image-maker to the echo, or, as Clarendon caustically put it, 'the donkies [sic], conscious of the curriculum through which they had passed, were brought to cut capers of delight over the very thing they had always kicked against'.[20]

It was indeed a remarkable achievement, and 1867 opened a new era for the Conservative party. If the working classes failed immediately to show their gratitude, ejecting the Conservatives at the next General Election, the Tory working man was to be an electoral fact the next time the country went to the polls. Disraeli's omnibus of country gentlemen had reached the top of the hill.

18 The Top of the Greasy Pole

Disraeli had clearly established his claim to be Lord Derby's successor when the Prime Minister, increasingly incapacitated by gout, should be forced to resign. By the autumn of 1867 it was clear that Derby's departure could not be long delayed; the Queen of Holland, visiting Knowsley in September, found him 'like a candle burning out', pale as a corpse, and so weak that he had to be carried up and down stairs.[1] On 10 September Derby wrote to Disraeli warning him that if his attacks increased in frequency he would have to retire from public life; by the end of that month he was too ill even to hold a pen. Disraeli, in fact, was already virtual leader of the Government, and generally recognized to be so, as General Grey had written to the Queen on 7 May: 'Mr. D'Israeli is evidently the directing mind of the Ministry'.

Not least among his responsibilities was the delicate task of handling the Queen, a task regarded by most British statesmen as a major problem. Victoria was at the height of her unpopularity because of her refusal to show herself in public and because of the scandal of her relations with her personal servant John Brown; in smart circles where before she and Albert had been referred to as 'Eliza' and 'Joseph', she was now openly sneered at as 'Mrs John Brown'. Everyone knew of her morbid widowhood, of the sacred shrine in the Blue Room at Windsor in which Albert had died, kept unchanged but for the fresh flowers and wreaths laid upon the two beds in which he had spent his last restless illness. Victoria's obsession with death and its trappings was extreme even by the standards of the age, and her condition was exacerbated by her underlying fear of insanity stemming from her grandfather, George III. She was excitable and neurotic in some ways, and subject when anything upset her to violent fits of vomiting which her doctor, Sir William Jenner, regarded as a cathartic relief to tension; but she was not in the least mad. She was an intelligent, strong-minded woman in a position in which, alone, the pressure was almost intolerable. She needed sympathetic male devotion which she obtained from John Brown, and, in a more sophisticated form, from Disraeli.

The Queen frequently used Disraeli to put pressure on Stanley, whose cautious instincts inclined him to non-intervention in European affairs, a stance which exasperated her. 'The cold policy of non-interference', she told Disraeli, would bring on the calamity of renewed European war. 'Yet she fears that such may be the course which Lord Stanley, unless some pressure is exercised upon him, may be inclined to pursue'.[2] Disraeli, she urged, must oversee the conduct of 'our whole system of foreign policy'. Disraeli needed no pressing from the Queen to take an interest in foreign affairs, and agreed with her on the dangers of non-intervention. Moreover, he had the personal advantage of inside information on European affairs through his friends the Rothschilds, whose private intelligence system was the best in Europe. Stanley's diary for the late summer and autumn of 1867 contains several references to Disraeli's passing on to him intelligence from the Rothschilds; he seems not have resented Disraeli's interventions – there had been a rapprochement between the two men after the estrangement of the fifties.

While overseeing Stanley and the Foreign Office, Disraeli was also particularly occupied with the Home Office during the Fenian terror campaign of 1867-8. The Fenians were Irish nationalists dedicated to the ending of British rule in Ireland, with strong support in America among the immigrant Irish and anarchist links on the Continent. It was the old Irish story, but with a new element; for the first time the 'outrages' took place on English soil. On 18 September a police sergeant in charge of Fenian prisoners at Manchester was murdered, and on 13 December the Fenians blew up the wall of Clerkenwell prison, causing terrible casualties. There were rumours that a party of Fenians had set out from Canada to kidnap the Queen, while the Tsar of Russia told the French Ambassador in Moscow that Victoria and her family were to be the first terrorist victims among the crowned heads of Europe. Victoria, refusing to be panicked, was extremely irritated by restrictions on her personal freedom of movement and the constant police surveillance, and was delighted when this led to ridiculous mistakes, as at Osborne when policemen pounced on Prince Arthur.

Disraeli, and the Home Secretary, Gathorne-Hardy, took the Fenian threat seriously. The police force under its ageing chief, Sir Richard Mayne, was quite unsuited to combat a secret terrorist brotherhood; when Mayne first put a plain-clothes force on the street they were easily recognizable by their regulation police boots which they had neglected to change and were instantly surrounded by a cheerful hooting crowd. Disraeli had no confidence in Mayne; he and Hardy set up a detective department under a Colonel Feilding, making use of paid informers. Disraeli's close relationship with Feilding aroused Hardy's professional jealousy; be suspected that Disraeli was receiving information from the detectives which he himself was not being given. The Fenian affair indeed had the elements which most appealed to Disraeli – secret intelligence and international subversion – and he was to make use of his experiences in dealing with the Fenian conspiracy in his next novel, *Lothair*.

In the midst of the Fenian alarms, as Disraeli was preparing for the November session of Parliament, Mary Anne fell seriously ill. It was not the first attack, as would appear from a letter written by Gladstone to his wife on 7 July 1866: 'Disraeli and I were affectionate at the Mansion House last night. Poor fellow, he has been much tried about his wife's health'. The exertions of the Scottish tour early that month had exhausted her, and she was almost certainly already suffering from the cancer of the womb which was to kill her. For three days her condition was critical; early on the morning of 19 November, Disraeli was told to give up hope, but by late morning there was a change for the better and he was able to leave her side and take his place in Parliament. Gladstone, who was genuinely fond of Mary Anne, made a graceful and sympathetic allusion to her illness, and when Disraeli rose to answer there were tears in his eyes. 'For the first time since I have known him', Stanley recorded, '[he] was unable to speak audibly ... from emotion'. He was so touched by Gladstone's gesture that he sat down the next morning to write him an emotional letter of thanks: 'I was incapable yesterday of expressing to you how much I appreciate your considerate sympathy. My wife had always a strong personal regard for you, and being of a vivid and original character, she could comprehend and value your great gifts and qualities.'[3]

Mary Anne's illness and the responsibilities of carrying on the government in Derby's absence wore out Disraeli's strength, and, in late November when Mary Anne was still confined to her room, he too fell ill. Lying on his back in bed at Grosvenor Gate, he pencilled notes to his Cabinet colleagues, and to Corry, telling him that his illness was supposed to be sciatica, 'which frightens me ... James, my man, says his mother has the *sciatics*, and they last a year at least. But, though depressed,' he went on, 'I still have faith in my star. I think it would be a ridiculous conclusion of my career; and, after all ridicule settles nothing and nobody'.[4] He and Mary Anne, both unable to get out of bed to see the other, exchanged constant notes. Mary Anne's letters, bright, disjointed and full of social gossip retailed to her by Lady Dorothy Nevill or Baroness Meyer de Rothschild being described by her husband as 'the most amusing and charming ... I ever had. It beats Horace Walpole and Mme de Sévigné.'

Disraeli's notes were, characteristically, the more complaining – 'We have been separated four days and under the same roof! How very strange!' Mary Anne replied promising to sneak out of her room the next day to see him when no one was about. She agonized over his reports of sleepless nights and pain; 'I have been nearly a week in bed, and am much worse than when I took to it', he grumbled, 'I am so irritated at the blundering manner in which I have been treated'. He had some reason to grumble; Dr Gull, failing to recognize for several days that he was suffering from gout, made matters worse by prescribing doses of wine, brandy and James Disraeli's strongest old sherry. As he grew stronger Mary Anne, still herself confined to her room, continued to fuss, 'Pray put a strip of Flan[ne]l r[oun]d yr. waist it would not be seen Flan[ne]l drawers is not enough when you go out of yr. warm room',[5] imploring him not to tire himself by coming upstairs to see her. 'Dr Gull says yr. illness entirely proceeds from coming up & down so often the night I was so ill & agitation of mind combined'.[6] She tried to cheer him by retailing news from a Rothschild visitor, 'Mr. Gladstone spoke of you most highly & also of me – admired yr. great affection & love for me'.[7]

Mary Anne was the only personal link between Disraeli and Gladstone; their happy marriages were the only thing they had in common. She told Kebbel that Gladstone often used to drop in at Grosvenor Gate after having made a stinging attack on Disraeli in the House 'to show there was no malice'. Disraeli and Gladstone were magnanimous enough to recognize each other's great gifts and frequently did so in public, but after Mary Anne died their private dislike was to deepen into hatred.

Disraeli was well enough to attend to business for the coming session in January 1968; the same could not be said of Derby who was seriously ill at Knowsley. 'I'm in despair about the gout', Disraeli wrote to Stanley on 17 January, complaining that because of it the Cabinet had not yet been able to meet once. Within days he was summoned to Osborne; 'all that I could wish and hope for', he wrote cryptically to Mary Anne on 25 January. Monty Corry was more explicit, reporting that before his audience with the Queen, her secretary General Grey had informed Disraeli that 'the Queen intended to make him her First Minister on Lord D's resignation'. Disraeli, with his acute sense of the pattern of events, was much struck that Grey, his successful adversary in the Wycombe elections at the outset of his political career, should have been 'the bearer of such a message'. It was thirty-six years since he had first stepped on to the hustings at Wycombe, just over thirty since he had entered Parliament; now, after so many long years of patient and tenacious struggle against the odds, he was about to receive the supreme prize.

There were, however, still agonizing days of suspense to be endured; the Queen's decision had to be kept secret; Lord Derby had not yet resigned. Although 'lying here, like a useless log', as he described himself to Disraeli on 13 February, he still hoped to defer his decision to the end of the session. Understandably he was probably unwilling to admit that his active life was over and subconsciously he may still not have been prepared to hand over command to Disraeli of whom, despite their closer relations, he was still jealous. According to Lord Clarendon, admittedly not an unprejudiced witness as far as Disraeli was concerned, Derby, at the time of the Edinburgh meeting in November 1867 had 'congratulated himself on not having to assist at the banquet at Edinboro', where Dizzy was to be made all sorts of things'.[8]

On 16 February, however, Derby had a serious relapse which seemed to make further procrastination out of the question. Stanley was summoned to Knowsley, and on the 19th Derby wrote to Disraeli in confidence that he had definitely decided upon submitting his resignation to the Queen, with a graceful tribute to Disraeli's loyal past services. Disraeli replied, emotionally if somewhat disingenuously:

My dearest Lord,

I have not sufficient command of myself to express what I feel about what has happened, and after all, has happened so rapidly and so unexpectedly!

All I will say is that I never contemplated or desired it. I was entirely content with my position, and all that I aspired to was that, after a Government of tolerable length, and, at least, fair repute, my retirement from public affairs should have accompanied your own.[9]

This was, of course, graceful but untrue. Disraeli had been contemplating and desiring Derby's retirement for the past ten years; and by January 1866 his hopes of the succession had been concrete enough for Rose, in communication, apparently vainly, with the publishers Routledge, to be looking to 'the probability of events which may happen within the next two years [which will] greatly increase circulation'.[10]

Derby sent his letter of resignation to the Queen on 21 February; all seemed set for Disraeli's accession when there was another last-minute hitch. On 24 February an agitated Disraeli summoned Stanley and told him that Derby's letter to the Queen 'seemed to imply that he did not contemplate the immediate formation of a new Ministry under him', asking him to telegraph Knowsley for permission for Disraeli formally to accept the Queen's offer. Disraeli's anxiety was not allayed by a delphic cable from Derby, 'Glad there are no difficulties. Will write by post. Do nothing formal till you hear. A few days indispensable to me'. Derby, it transpired, wished to confer peerages upon a few chosen friends before retiring, and his feelings had been hurt by receiving only a few curt lines from the Queen on his resignation, 'without expressions of sympathy or regret', as his son put it. 'She seems to have told him he had better resign at once, in order to save her trouble.'[11]

And so it was not until 26 February 1868 that, Derby having finally stepped aside, Disraeli was able to write a fulsome letter of acceptance to the Queen:

'He can only offer his devotion', he wrote. 'It will be his delight to render the transaction of affairs as easy to your Majesty as possible ... he ventures to trust that, in the great affairs of state, your Majesty will deign not to withhold from him the benefit of your Majesty's guidance.' He continued:

Your Majesty's life has been passed in constant communication with great men, and the acknowledgement and management of important transactions. Even if your Majesty were not gifted with those great abilities, which all now acknowledge, this rare and choice experience must give your Majesty an advantage in judgment which few living persons, and probably no living prince, can rival.[12]

This was not the sort of language which Victoria had been accustomed to hear from her Prime Ministers, most of whom had been anxious that she should interfere as little as possible. It was hardly surprising, therefore, that when Disraeli hastened down to Osborne to kiss hands, she received him with 'a very radiant face'. True to his fantasy of Victoria as Spenser's 'Faerie Queene' and of himself in the role of a Raleigh or a Leicester, Disraeli knelt before her, and, taking her hand in both of his, said 'In loving loyalty and faith'.

Victoria was charmed; 'The present Man will do well,' she wrote to her eldest daughter, the Crown Princess of Prussia, rather as if she were referring to a butler, 'and will be particularly loyal and anxious to please me in every way. He is vy. peculiar, but vy. clever and sensible and vy. conciliatory.'[13] Disraeli himself might have been amused by her comment on his final accession to power: 'A proud thing,' she told the Crown Princess, 'for a Man "risen from the people" – to have obtained'.[14] Reactions to Disraeli's success were, as usual, mixed. 'A triumph of intellect & unscrupulousness', Bright wrote in his diary, while Lord Clarendon wrote to Lady Salisbury that it was 'rather good fun to see the Tory magnates scraping off the dirt they have heaped upon Dizzy for the last ten years, eating and affecting to like it.' He sneered, 'The Jew, who is "the most subtle beast in the field", has, like Job's tempter, ingratiated himself with the Missus and made her forget that, in the opinion of the Great and Good, he "had not one single element of a gentleman in his composition" '.[15]

Disraeli himself was unashamedly delighted; when John Manners called, Disraeli 'fairly embraced' him with more emotion than Manners had ever seen him show before, and when Dorothy Nevill congratulated him he said, 'It is all well and good now – I feel my position assured'. Publicly, however, his response to congratulation was cool and ironic: 'Yes,' he said, 'I have climbed to the top of the greasy pole'.

Disraeli was now truly leader of the aristocracy of England, chief of a Cabinet which included three dukes (Marlborough, Richmond and Buckingham) and two earls (Malmesbury and Mayo). It was essentially the same as Derby's, except that Disraeli had succeeded in ridding himself, not without an angry public row, of the Lord Chancellor, Chelmsford, and had given the Exchequer to a new man, Ward Hunt. Hunt was an enormous man, over six foot four in height and proportionately broad, described by Disraeli to the Queen in what must surely have been one of the most unusual ways of recommending a minister to a sovereign as, 'like St. Peter's, no one is at first aware of his dimensions. But he has the sagacity of the elephant, as well as the form.'

Disraeli entered the House of Commons for the first time as Prime Minister at exactly twenty minutes past four on the evening of Thursday 5 March to 'generous and hearty' Conservative cheers. It must have been an emotional moment for him, now the dominant figure on the scene of so many past struggles over the thirty years since his disastrous maiden speech. He may have been nervous for his first appearance as Premier was not a success. He began with a eulogy of Derby, which, an observer said, 'dragged heavily', and at times he stumbled, seeming at a loss for ideas and words. This obstacle cleared, he began to be slightly more, but not entirely, himself. He was described as being like a cat walking over broken glass, anxious not to antagonize the strong Liberal Opposition by proposing too limited and Conservative a policy, and at the same time not to frighten his own supporters with a too liberal-sounding one. 'Our domestic policy' he said, 'will be a liberal policy'. Loud cheers from the Opposition greeted this announcement while the Conservatives sat glumly silent. In an attempt to clarify the unfortunate phrase, he turned to his supporters and said with emphasis 'a truly liberal policy' whereupon the Conservatives cheered loudly and the Liberals laughed.

It was a shaky start to a stormy and unpleasant session in which Gladstone was to seize and keep the initiative. Ireland, always a dangerous question, was to be the subject of the session, which Disraeli approached with extreme caution, planning to defer controversy by referring the difficult issues of Irish Education and Land to Royal Commissions. He had been hoping against hope that the thorny question of the Disestablishment of the Irish Church might also be postponed until after an election which might give him a majority. He had, however, reckoned without Gladstone, now sole leader of the Liberal party since Russell's retirement, and in messianic mood. Gladstone had, he told Lord Granville, 'been watching the sky with a strong sense of the obligation to act with the first streak of dawn'.[16] Now, as 1868 opened, he thought that he had seen it, detecting in the public a desire to see the Irish question settled. It was to be the beginning of his 'mission to pacify Ireland', and the first step would be the disestablishment of the Anglican Church in Ireland – once described by Disraeli himself as 'that alien church in a hostile land' – and to which Gladstone had referred as 'a hideous blot'.

Gladstone allowed Disraeli only three weeks' grace before he threw down the gauntlet on 16 March in a great speech declaring that the time had come when the Church of Ireland as a Church supported by the State must cease to exist and announcing that he would put forward a resolution to that effect. Gladstone's declaration against the Irish Church had at one stroke wrested from Disraeli the Catholic vote that he had so carefully cultivated, and forced him into a die-hard position. A week later, Gladstone, described as 'in full feather and lively as a lark' put forward his proposal. Disraeli wrote apprehensively to the Queen that 'we are embarking on stormy waters and ... a very serious political session is setting in'.

The political waters were indeed rough, with Disraeli's enemies Lowe and Cranborne constantly attacking him, Cranborne being, said Hardy, 'venomous and remorseless against Disraeli'. Disraeli fought back against them, particularly Lowe, in his best manner, comparing him with a baying hound joining in Cranborne's chorus:

> When the bark is heard on this side, the right hon. member for Calne emerges, I will not say from his cave, but perhaps from a more cynical habitation. He joins immediately in the chorus of reciprocal malignity, and 'hails with horrid melody the moon' ... The right hon. member for Calne is a very remarkable man ... but what is more remarkable than his learning and logic is that power for spontaneous aversion which particularises him. There is nothing that he likes, and almost everything that he hates. He hates the working classes of England. He hates the Roman Catholics of Ireland. He hates her Majesty's Ministers. And until the right hon. gentleman the member for South Lancashire [Gladstone] placed his hand upon the ark, he almost seemed to hate the right hon. gentleman.

Disraeli was defeated on 4 April by a majority of 48, but deftly evaded the issue by adjourning the House for the Easter recess. Conservative faith in his parliamentary dexterity remained unbounded, for as one fox-hunting squire remarked, 'Depend upon it, however successfully you may think you have stopped the earth, this cunning fox knows some hole unstopped'.[17]

The 'cunning fox' had indeed laid his plans. Foreseeing another defeat in the renewed debate on the question scheduled for 28 April, he had determined that he would not be pushed out of office by Gladstone and would not resign. In the event of defeat he would make a dramatic dash down to Osborne and return with the royal assent to dissolution. It was all to be concerted beforehand with the Queen, who was by now very pro-Disraeli and very anti-Gladstone. Four days before the debate, Disraeli wrote to tell her of his plan, flattering her with a view of her position which was hardly constitutional: 'On great political occasions, it is wise, that the visible influence, as it were, of the Sovereign should be felt and recognised by the nation, and that Parliament should practically comprehend, that the course of a Ministry depends on the will of the Queen.'[18] On the morning of 1 May, as he had foreseen, Disraeli was again defeated on Gladstone's Resolutions, but by an increased majority of 65; he adjourned Parliament and went down to Osborne as planned.

Speculation as to what Disraeli would do was intense; Cranborne, now 3rd Marquess of Salisbury, wrote to his ally, Sandford, that he thought 'the Jew' would not dissolve but effect a sham resignation, withdrawing it at the earnest entreaty of the Queen. 'Matters seem very critical', he wrote, ' – a woman on the throne, & a Jew adventurer who [has] found out the secret of getting round her'.[19] Salisbury's language set the tone of the debates of the first week in May, generally known as 'Passion Week', intense heat being generated by Opposition suspicions, not unfounded, that Disraeli had prejudiced the Queen's mind against them, and was using her to maintain his position.

Disraeli's speech explaining his intention of eventual dissolution in preference to immediate resignation was one of his best, cleverly designed to cool the temperature; but tempers quickly rose to fever pitch when Bright delivered a stinging attack on the Prime Minister to a crowded and shouting House on 7 May. Referring to Disraeli's original opinion of the Irish Church as 'alien', he implied that Disraeli had not been frank with the Queen and was unjustifiably using her:

> The right hon. gentleman the other night, in a manner at once pompous and servile, talked at large of interviews which he had with his Sovereign. I venture to say that a Minister who deceives his Sovereign is as guilty as a conspirator who would dethrone her ... if he has not changed the opinion which he held twenty-five years ago, and which he has said in the main was right, then I fear that he has not stated all that it was his duty to state in the interview which he had with his Sovereign. Let me tell hon. gentlemen opposite, and the right hon. gentleman in particular, that any man who puts the Sovereign in the front of a great struggle like this into which we may be about to enter – who points to the Irish people, and says from the floor of this House, 'your Queen holds the flag under which we, the enemies of religious equality and justice to Ireland, are marshalled', – I say that the Minister who does that is guilty of a very high crime and a great misdemeanour against his country.[20]

Bright had cut Disraeli to the quick; he rose 'pale with anger' and, according to one witness 'spoke as perhaps he had never spoken before, and as he most certainly never spoke afterwards – with no sparkling epigrams, or fanciful turns, or picked phrases; but with unwonted emphasis and abundance of natural gesture, and amazing vehemence of emotion'.[21] Bright described the debate as 'rough', the end of 'our ancient alliance and understanding'; he can hardly have been surprised that his speech, impugning Disraeli's honour as it did, had caused mortal offence. Bright, indeed, came to hate Disraeli, remaining unforgiving even at his death and refusing to vote for a monument to him. Despite all the sound and fury, however, Disraeli's first session as Prime Minister ended relatively tamely; with the Election in prospect, nothing was resolved on the Irish Church Question. For Disraeli it had not been a successful début; he had succeeded in denying Gladstone the pleasure of forcing him to resign, but only by fighting a constant rearguard action, and Gladstone had emerged the undoubted victor of the session.

In only one area had he been outstandingly successful; he had succeeded in captivating the Queen and making her as pro-Conservative as she had formerly been pro-Liberal. The Queen relished his daily letters, written, Lady Augusta Bruce retailed, 'in his best novel style, telling her every scrap of political news dressed up to serve his own purpose, & every scrap of social gossip cooked to amuse her. She declares she never had such letters in her life . . . and she never before knew everything'.[22] She was grateful for his consideration for her nerves and illnesses and for his gracious compliments on her *Leaves from a Journal of our Life in the Highlands* which she sent him in January; and flattered when Disraeli, the story goes, prefaced his remarks with the phrase 'We authors, Ma'am'. Having once heard Disraeli say 'he was so fond of May and all those lovely spring flowers', she began sending him primroses, a custom she was to continue until the day of his funeral when a simple bunch of primroses with the inscription 'his favourite flower' was to be laid on the coffin. Whether they were indeed his favourites is uncertain; Gladstone once snorted that he had never heard him express any such preference and thought lilies would have been more suitable. But the royal spring bouquets were greeted with effusions such as this which, although written by Mary Anne, is so Disraelian in style as to have been almost certainly dictated by her husband: 'Mr. Disraeli is passionately fond of flowers, and their lustre and perfume were enhanced by the condescending hand which had showered upon him all the treasures of spring'.[23]

He was not always to be successful in managing the Queen; there were frequent disagreements over Church appointments which the Queen insisted should be decided on grounds of merit and doctrine, but which Disraeli persisted in regarding in the light of political rewards. Disraeli did not give in easily, but the Queen usually had her way. He received a stern royal rebuff over his proposal that the Prince of Wales should acquire a residence in Ireland so that he could combine hunting with representing the British Crown, which would, he wrote in a mistaken effort to make the suggestion palatable, 'combine the fulfilment of public duty with pastime, a combination which befits a princely life'.[24] The Queen, who considered that 'Bertie' had far too much fun already, delivered an epistolary box on the ear to her Prime Minister: 'she *entirely* objects to the latter part of Mr. Disraeli's letter ... in the Prince of Wales's case, *any encouragement* of his constant love of running about, and not keeping at home, or near the Queen is most *earnestly* ... to be deprecated'.[25] Disraeli never ventured to raise the subject again. In the late summer of 1868 the Court went to Switzerland for the Queen's health, with Victoria travelling incognito as 'the Countess of Kent', passing through Paris *en route*. There was, Disraeli reported in an amusing letter to Lord Chancellor Cairns, a Fenian incident at Paris, but, 'I fear, between ourselves, the greater outrage was that our dear Peeress [Victoria] did not return the visit of the Empress. This is to be deplored, particularly as they named a Boulevard after her, and she went to see it!'[26] The Queen did not respond to Disraeli's tactful plea to put things right by some graceful gesture on her return journey beyond sending the Empress a note saying that she hoped to see her at some future time. Victoria was stubborn and even Disraeli, adept as he quickly became at managing her, could not always, in Salisbury's phrase, 'get round her'.

On the Queen's return from Switzerland in September, Disraeli was summoned to his sojourn of attendance at Balmoral, a duty which ministers dreaded. The atmosphere at Balmoral, according to Sir Henry Ponsonby, the Queen's Private Secretary who succeeded General Grey, was curiously like a school; there were no homely comforts, hideous tartan decoration and, as the Queen hated fires, the house was extremely cold. The Household, following the Queen's example, communicated with one another by letter, and in the atmosphere of unrelieved tedium there were constant petty rows which were almost looked forward to. Discipline was very strict, the presence of the Queen, even when unseen, was felt in the remotest recesses of the castle, and she ruled her Household with a rod of iron. No one was allowed to leave the house until the Queen had gone out; the Maids of Honour were not permitted to accompany the Gentlemen without a chaperon, and ponies for riding were divided into five strict categories, each being allocated to a particular person. Conversation at the Queen's table depended entirely upon her mood; public affairs were not to be discussed and speaking in a loud voice or the introduction of a subject by anyone other than the Queen was frowned upon. The principal amusements at Balmoral were deer-stalking which, on great occasions, ended in a torchlight dance round the carcasses while the gillies got drunk on whisky; the annual celebration to Prince Albert's memory at the cairn erected to him; the Braemar Gathering; and the Queen's favourite amusement, which was particularly dreaded by visiting ministers and the Household, the gillies' ball, organized by her personal servant, John Brown. Brown's influence with the Queen was unparalleled; he was, said Ponsonby, the only person who could 'fight and make the Queen do what she did not wish', and with his rough, overbearing manners he was detested by the Royal Highnesses, the Household, servants and gillies alike. Disraeli was almost alone in getting on well with Brown who loathed Gladstone, regarding him as no better than a 'Papist'.

The Queen did her best to make Disraeli feel at home at Balmoral, inviting him to dine with her in the library and commissioning the ladies to amuse him by showing him the falls of Garrawalt and Braemar Castle, but she also gave him a great deal of work to do. He missed Mary Anne and was suffering from one of his usual bilious attacks, which was hardly surprising since he regarded copious doses of sherry as a remedy. 'Although all goes on well here,' he told Mary Anne, 'I am extremely nervous, my health being very unsatisfactory ... I have never tasted one of your dear peaches, which I much wished to do for your sake, and have drunk nothing but sherry'.[27] The Queen, however, was convinced his visit had been a great success, confiding to her journal on the day of his departure that he 'seemed delighted with his visit & made himself most agreeable'.

Disraeli's idyll with the Queen was cut short by his defeat at the General Election in November. His twin hopes that the newly-enfranchised electorate would prove their gratitude to the Conservatives and that a strong appeal to Protestantism from his electoral platform would win votes proved equally illusory. The Liberals almost doubled their previous majority by gaining 112 seats, and almost the only crumb of comfort was Gladstone's defeat in South Lancashire. Disraeli was returned unopposed for Aylesbury, where he got his own back upon the Irish Question which had precipitated his defeat by declaring that the main problem with the Irish was that they were bored and that it was their own fault. It was a curiously superficial view which illustrates how little understanding and indeed interest Disraeli showed towards the Irish question. It would, however, be only fair to point out that, as head of a minority Government and leader of a party pledged to the defence of the established Church, he had been in a very awkward position, and one which Gladstone had well known how to exploit.

Disraeli resigned, taking his defeat, as General Grey said, in a 'proper and manly' spirit. He made only one request which, however, the Queen and Grey agreed was 'very embarrassing', that the Queen should confer a peerage on Mary Anne. Grey wrote to the Queen that it 'would not be a kindness to Mrs. Disraeli to subject her to what would be made a subject of endless ridicule', but neither he nor Victoria thought it could be decently refused. On 24 November the Queen wrote Disraeli a gracious letter conferring on Mary Anne the title of Viscountess Beaconsfield: 'The Queen,' she wrote, 'can truly sympathise with his devotion to Mrs. Disraeli, who in her turn is so deeply attached to him'. The new Viscountess was overjoyed; coronets rapidly appeared on her carriage doors, her furniture, her cushions, and, of course, her writing paper; from now on even her letters to Disraeli were to be signed no longer 'Mary Anne' but 'Beaconsfield'. London society and the Radical press made what Disraeli's biographer Buckle described as 'ill-mannered comments', but Disraeli ignored them; it was his defiant gesture of gratitude to the woman who had helped to make him Prime Minister.

A month later, just as Disraeli and Mary Anne were preparing to leave London to spend Christmas with Lord Beauchamp at Madresfield, James D'Israeli, inconvenient to the last, died suddenly, aged fifty-seven. Disraeli, to his chagrin, found that he was his brother's executor; 'the death was sudden', he wrote to Beauchamp, 'everything so unprepared, everybody away, I finding myself executor without having had the slightest hint of such an office devolving on me, & having to give orders about everything, & things wh: I least understood & most dislike – that I am really half distracted'.[28] There were disagreeable discoveries to be made about James's private life; as executor Disraeli was responsible for paying off Mrs Bassett, his brother's housekeeper-mistress, although there is no evidence to show whether he knew of the existence of James's illegitimate daughter, then aged eleven. Ten years later, the daughter, Annie, was to write to him that she had only discovered in the past year that James was her father, having previously thought her name was Bassett. She had apparently been brought up at Richmond, probably under the care, though not in the house, of Sarah D'Israeli, and James used to visit her there. She had, she said, according to her father's wish, been educated 'as a young lady' at a school in Lewisham. She had a sister (who may or may not have been James's child) and at the time she wrote to Disraeli, the two young women were living in London, penniless, according to Annie, who complained that she had twice asked Disraeli for an interview without receiving a reply.[29] There is no evidence as to whether Disraeli ever saw his illegitimate niece, or did anything for her; James's 'low ties' had been a source of annoyance to him all his life. James, however, had redeemed himself in later years; Disraeli described him to Corry as 'a man of vigorous and original mind and great taste', and had become a collector of French eighteenth-century paintings and *objets d'art*, contemporary drawings and fine wines.

Having paid off Mrs Bassett to the tune of £6,000, Disraeli was his brother's residuary legatee, receiving £5,300. Ralph was not mentioned in the will, and wrote a resentful letter in reply to the invitation to James's funeral at Hughenden where he was to be buried in the vault beside Mrs Brydges Willyams. Indeed Disraeli's relations with Ralph over the past eighteen months had been delicate; in the spring of 1867 Ralph's wife, the former Kate Trevor, a relation by marriage of Disraeli's aunt, Olivia Basevi, had given birth to Coningsby, the only Disraeli male heir. Ralph had asked Disraeli to stand as godfather to the boy, and Disraeli had at first willingly agreed: 'I congratulate you: & shall be happy to comply with your request: in person if I can, & if I be alive, wh: is rather doubtful if the present struggle goes on', he wrote from 11 Downing Street on 30 March 1867.[30] Once again, however, Mary Anne's feelings came between the brothers; there seems to have been some discussion between them as to the possibility of Disraeli making Coningsby his heir, but Disraeli felt that Mary Anne, being childless and naturally sensitive on the subject, might find such a formal acknowledgement of her failure to bear a child hard to accept. 'Having thought over "our matter"', he wrote to Ralph on 15 April:

I feel that for the sake of the future, it is highly expedient that nothing should be done without the knowledge & approbation of Mary Anne, & I have never yet had the opportunity of speaking to her on a subject wh: cannot be done hurriedly.

> I think, therefore, that it will be best for you not to postpone the ceremony. I shall, of course, be gratified, tho' not present, in being a sponsor, & I trust my god-child may prove a credit to the family.[31]

Clearly, for the sake of domestic peace, Disraeli thought it wiser not to attend his god-child's christening, and it is doubtful whether he ever summoned up the courage to broach to Mary Anne, the question of making Ralph's son his heir the fact that she was suffering from cancer of the womb making the question doubly sensitive. On Disraeli's death Hughenden, but not the Beaconsfield title, was to pass to Coningsby.

Amidst all these domestic annoyances, there was the by now almost traditional unpleasantness on handing over Downing Street to Gladstone who succeeded Disraeli as Prime Minister. This time it was not Disraeli's fault, and was highly embarrassing to him. It was discovered that the Royal Bounty and Special Service Fund, a privy purse at the disposal of the Prime Minister, was, at the time of Disraeli's resignation, overdrawn by £1,600, some of it accounted for by payments to his private secretaries. 'I can truly say that nothing in my public life has ever vexed me more', Disraeli wrote angrily to Corry, blaming his other secretary Charles Fremantle for the contretemps. Nonetheless, he treated Fremantle with a forbearance which goes far to explain why he was loved by his employees. 'Dear Diz has behaved like an angel', Fremantle wrote to Corry, describing his chief as 'disgusted but not cross'. He realized only too acutely Disraeli's mortification at being thus put in the wrong *vis-à-vis* Gladstone; 'If it was not Gladstone and Diz it would not matter in the least', he told Corry, 'but as it is, it is a bore'.[32] The 'bore' was smoothed over; Gladstone, firmly installed in the seat of power with his 'mission to pacify Ireland' in the forefront of his mind, was disposed to be generous.

Disraeli, for the time being, was prepared to leave the field to Gladstone. He had achieved his supreme goal, the premiership, however briefly, and in the circumstances, with his rival in command of a large majority, there was very little he could do. 'I think on our part there should be, at the present moment, the utmost reserve and quietness', he told Stanley early in the New Year. For once his sights were set on a goal other than politics; after more than twenty years of creative inactivity he had begun work on a new novel, *Lothair*.

19 Success and Sorrow

Disraeli, at sixty-four, had achieved the goal of his political life; within just under two years he had achieved a second pinnacle of achievement as the author of a best-selling novel.

Lothair, written in secret during 1869 and published on 2 May 1870, was an instant popular success. Within less than a week of publication the first print run of 5,000 copies had been sold out and the publishers, Longman's, were in a state of siege. Eight English editions were printed in that same year while in America 80,000 copies were sold in five months; by the end of 1876 *Lothair* had earned its author over £10,000, a very considerable sum in contemporary terms. *Lothair* had all the qualifications for a best-seller, with an author who was an international celebrity, and all the ingredients for popular success – topicality, high life, and the international secret societies which were the Victorian equivalent of the twentieth-century espionage–terrorism *genre*.

Lothair was a thriller. Based on the sensation of 1868, the conversion of the fabulously wealthy young nobleman, the Marquess of Bute, to the Church of Rome, it derived its excitement from contemporary fears of revolution organized by the secret societies and the insidious aggression of the Roman Catholic Church. Lothair, young, fantastically rich, aristocratic, and portrayed in the mould of Disraeli's previous heroes, is torn between three parties anxious to gain his name and wealth for their cause – the Church of England, the Church of Rome and the revolutionary societies, represented respectively by three beautiful women, Lady Corisande, Clare Arundell and Theodora Campion. After many vicissitudes, including fighting for the Garibaldian cause in Italy and falling into the clutches of predatory cardinals at Rome, Lothair, as befits the hero of a novel written by the champion of the Established Church of England, ends up safely in the arms of Lady Corisande and the Anglican Establishment.

It is difficult for a modern reader to take a deep interest in the spiritual pilgrimage of the dull and priggish Lothair, as it is hard to enter into the paranoid sense of danger which a generation shocked by papal aggression and the conversions first of Newman and then of Bute experienced *vis-à-vis* the Roman Catholic

Church. There are, however, parallels to be drawn between the mid-nineteenth-century nationalist revolutionary societies depicted in *Lothair* and their modern equivalents, the ideological terrorist movements. Disraeli's idea of the oldest secret society in the world, the *Madre Natura*, at war with Christianity (which he terms 'the Semitic revelation'), in its fight to restore classical, pagan ideals, may have been fanciful in the extreme, as was his depiction of the international revolutionary brotherhood which he touchingly called the '*Mary-Anne*'; but he had had first-hand knowledge of the workings of the Fenian brotherhood and their international contacts from the winter of 1867-8, and his description of the exiles' café behind Leicester Square where *émigré* plots were hatched had an authentic touch.

J.A. Froude, in his biography of Disraeli, thought that the true value of the book lay in its:

> perfect representation of patrician society in England ... the full appreciation of all that was good and noble in it; yet the recognition, also, that it was a society without a purpose, and with no claim to endurance. It was then in its most brilliant period, like the full bloom of a flower which opens only to fade.[1]

One may wonder if Disraeli, consciously or subconsciously, felt this; whether this portrait of aristocratic society in final full bloom was some kind of act of contrition for the part he himself had played in raising the sluices of democracy which would eventually sweep it away. *Lothair* was to be the last book in which he portrayed contemporary aristocratic society; ten years later in *Endymion* he would hark back to the world of the 1850s, feeling perhaps that it represented the golden age of a self-confident aristocracy unthreatened by Carlyle's democratic 'Niagara'.

Lothair represents also the dichotomy in Disraeli's attitude towards the aristocratic world in which he had chosen to live; his appreciation of the physical beauty of its material existence coupled with a keen realization of the accompanying mental void. The English aristocracy is described as 'excelling in athletic sports, speaking no other language than their own, and never reading', a heartfelt phrase contrasting with the lovingly detailed portrayals of the grand life – the croquet match at ducal Brentham, 'a marvellous lawn, the Duchess's Turkish tent with its rich hangings, and the players themselves ... with their coquettish hats, and their half-veiled and half-revealed under-raiment scarlet and silver, or blue and gold'. There is more than a touch of Marie Antoinette about the Duchess's new dairy 'a pretty sight ... with its flooring of fanciful tiles, and its cool and shrouded chambers, its stained windows and its marble slabs, and porcelain pans of cream, and plenteous platters of fantastically formed butter'. Another passage reveals Disraeli's sheer delight in the excitement of the opening of the London season:

> Town was beginning to blaze. Broughams whirled and bright barouches glanced, troops of social cavalry cantered and caracolled [sic] in morning rides, and the bells of prancing ponies, lashed by delicate hands, gingled [sic] in the laughing air. There were stoppages in Bond Street, which seems to cap the climax of civilisation, after crowded clubs and swarming parks.[2]

Disraeli must have enjoyed writing *Lothair*, using portraits drawn from life which were easily recognizable to contemporaries, with gentle digs at the amiable, vain Duke of Abercorn and subtly malicious pen-portraits of men who had crossed him, like Cardinal Manning and Bishop Wilberforce. He dug freely into his own past and into the *Reminiscences* he had jotted down in the sixties; the Austens, discarded patrons of his youth, featured as the lawyer Mr Putney Giles and his talented social-climbing wife, Apollonia; while Lothair, like the young Disraeli, cruised the Mediterranean on a yacht, visiting Malta, Gibraltar and Palestine and reproducing Disraeli's own reveries in the Holy Land forty years before. The pages are liberally sprinkled with his own likes and dislikes – good-looking young men, and 'infernal' Sundays in country houses, and favourite phrases – 'I live only for climate and the affections'.

It was perhaps, stylistically, his best book; largely free from the extravagant phraseology of which he was normally all too fond. In *Lothair* Disraeli seems to be a forerunner of Oscar Wilde and 'Saki'; Wildean epigrams sparkle and his gilded young men, Hugo Bohun and the Duke of St Aldegonde are precursors of Reginald and Clovis. 'I hate anecdotes', Hugo Bohun declares, 'and I always get away when conversation falls into ... its anecdotage', and, 'My idea of an agreeable person is a person who agrees with me.' St Aldegonde, handsome, languid and rich, was a republican duke 'of the reddest dye ... opposed to all privilege, and indeed to all orders of men, except dukes, who were a necessity ... strongly in favour of the equal division of all property except land'. St Aldegonde, in constant dread of being 'bored to extinction', escaped it only in the company of Mr Pinto, a mysterious, humorous Portuguese, whose irony had a strong echo of George Smythe; 'English', said Mr Pinto to St Aldegonde, 'is an expressive language, but not difficult to master ... It consists, as far as I can observe, of four words: "nice", "jolly", "charming" and "bore".'

The critics, stigmatized in advance by Disraeli, as 'the men who have failed in literature and art', hated the book as much as the public loved it. Trollope denounced it as his worst book to date with 'that flavour of hair-oil, that feeling of false jewels ... the very bathos of story-telling'.[3] Abraham Hayward, the Whig littérateur, one of the men whom Disraeli truly detested, delivered a bitter attack in the *Quarterly* and Dicky Monckton Milnes a powerful broadside in the *Edinburgh*. Considering that *Lothair* was outside the mainstream of English literature which, over the past twenty years, had seen the publication of great novels by Mrs Gaskell, Charlotte and Emily Brontë, Thackeray, Dickens, George Eliot and Trollope himself, there was considerable justification for their attack. Disraeli, however, chose to see their hostility as motivated, which to some degree it was, by personal jealousy of his outstanding public and literary success; he hit back at Hayward and Milnes in the General Preface to the collected edition of his novels later that year:

> There are critics, who, abstractedly, do not approve of successful books, particularly if they have failed in the same style; social acquaintances also of lettered taste, and especially contemporaries whose public life has not exactly realised the vain dreams of

their fussy existence ... would seize the accustomed opportunity of welcoming with affected discrimination about nothing, and elaborate controversy about trifles, the production of a friend.

It was the old battle between Disraeli and the literary establishment, but this time Disraeli, from the point of view of commercial success if not of merit, had the upper hand. With satisfaction he jotted down a list of testimonials to *Lothair's* popularity: a street, a perfume, two ships, two songs, a waltz and a *galoppe*, even a racehorse were named after Lothair, while Baron Meyer de Rothschild's star filly, winner of the Cesarewitch, was named 'Corisande'.[4]

But while Disraeli enjoyed his popular success, the usual discontent was growing among his political followers. The sight of their leader returning to his novel-writing displeased many of them, while the reissue by Longman of his novels, including the suspect *Vivian Grey*, revived all the old feelings that Disraeli was not a gentleman, still less a serious statesman. Many of the upper echelons of the party had not forgiven him for the Reform Bill, especially since the 'surrender' of Conservative principles in 1867 had not brought compensating electoral gains in 1868. Salisbury, still his bitter enemy, continued to campaign against him with another savage article in the *Quarterly* of October 1869.

Salisbury was not the only threat to Disraeli's leadership. In October 1869, Derby died at Knowsley, managing a last aristocratic joke on his deathbed. On being asked how he felt, he replied, 'bored to extinction'. Stanley, aged forty-three, became fifteenth Earl of Derby, and as such was seen by many as a more fitting leader for the Conservative Party than a sixty-five-year-old Jewish novelist. They did not yet know the new Lord Derby well; Disraeli did. He knew the indecision of mind that lay beneath Derby's cold and passionless exterior, the diffidence and caution which, among other things, made him unfitted to take the lead. Moreover, he was an uneasy Conservative, torn between the intellectual attractions of liberalism and the conservative traditions inherited from his father. But although these qualities in Derby, coupled with a lack of personal ambition, ensured that he would not actively rival Disraeli for the leadership, they also negated his value as a supporter against Salisbury. When Cairns resigned the Conservative leadership of the House of Lords in the winter of 1869, Disraeli earnestly pressed Derby to take over from him and thus keep out Salisbury who was the second-choice candidate. Derby, however, for all his friendship for Disraeli, declined; fortunately for Disraeli, Salisbury decided it would be impossible to act in tandem with the hated Dizzy, and the Duke of Richmond was prevailed upon to take the uncoveted post.

The real danger to Disraeli, however, was to come from a growing conviction among the responsible members of the late Government that Disraeli was 'past it' as a leader, an impression reinforced by his apathetic opposition to Gladstone. Disraeli believed that Gladstone, given enough rope, would eventually hang himself, and contented himself with stinging his rival into a fury in the House of Commons while avoiding major confrontations in which he was bound to be beaten. Indeed, within a year of his accession, Gladstone was already showing signs of strain as pressure of work and the responsibility of leading a government pledged to a major legislative programme told upon his explosive temperament. Derby noted that his temper was 'visible and audible' whenever he rose to speak and that 'the mixture of anger and contempt in his voice [was] almost painful to witness'.[5] Disraeli, said Derby, was quite aware of the advantage he possessed in his 'natural calmness', and took every opportunity to make the contrast noticeable.

By December 1870 both Cairns and Malmesbury reported that the Liberals expected Gladstone 'either to die or break down', rumours which were reinforced by titillating gossip concerning Gladstone's latest escapade in pursuit of his penchant for reforming 'fallen women'. 'Strange story', Derby noted in his diary, 'of Gladstone frequenting the company of a Mrs. Thistlethwaite, a kept woman in her youth, who induced a foolish person with a large fortune to marry her. She has since her marriage taken to religion, and preaches or lectures. This, with her beauty is the attraction to G.'. He added that he could hardly believe the report that Gladstone intended to spend a week with the Thistlethwaites at their country house – 'she not being visited or received in society'.[6] But Gladstone, quite indifferent to scandal, did go. 'We were all in a state of respectable frenzy at Cranborne', Salisbury reported to his crony, Sandford, 'She is our next neighbour there'.[7]

Events in Europe during that autumn and winter of 1870 gave Disraeli a chance to score off Gladstone. In September, Napoleon III, now a shadow of his former self, racked by disease and bullied by his intransigent Empress, had been swept from his throne in the cataclysm of the Franco-Prussian war. Disraeli thought that the Emperor had only himself to blame: 'This collapse of France has all come from the Emperor's policy of nationality', he wrote to Derby. 'That has created Italy and Germany wh: destroyed the French monopoly of Continental compactness'.[8] He perceived that the triumph of Prussia had changed the face of Europe and altered the old balance of power which had existed since the Congress of Vienna. 'This war,' he told the House of Commons, 'represents the German revolution, a greater political event than the French revolution of the last century ... Not a single principle in the management of our foreign affairs, accepted by all statesmen for guidance up to six months ago, any longer exists'.[9] Gladstone appeared unable to control events, as he was also unable to exercise any influence over Bismarck, who referred to him contemptuously as 'Professor Gladstone', or indeed over Russia, which chose this moment of confusion to repudiate the clause of the Treaty of Paris guaranteeing neutralization of the Black Sea. A conference called in London had no alternative but to endorse Russia's action and, when Gladstone tried to justify himself in the Commons, he laid himself open to a biting attack from Disraeli. 'The Premier was like a cat on hot bricks', an observer recorded, 'and presented a striking contrast to Disraeli; for Disraeli cuts up a Minister with as much *sang-froid* as an anatomist cuts up a frog ... when Gladstone rose, you could see that every stroke of Disraeli's had gone home. He was in a white passion, and almost choked with words'.[10]

1870 was a bad year for the English Royal Family also; in February the Prince of Wales had been involved, albeit innocently, in the unsavoury Mordaunt divorce case. The Prince was subpoenaed to appear in court, and two letters of his to Lady Mordaunt, who was by then in a lunatic asylum, were read out. The Prince's letters were perfectly innocuous, but in an era when divorce was regarded as the ultimate social disgrace the Prince's connection with the case confirmed the general impression that he was a scandalous good-for-nothing who thought only of fast horses and fast women. The Queen was not popular and rarely seen, and her pro-German sympathies during the Franco-Prussian war ran counter to her subjects' sympathy with France as the underdog. At a Republican meeting in October 1870, the Court was publicly referred to as 'a pack of Germans'. The events of the Paris Commune in 1871 inspired what appeared to be a rising tide of republicanism in England, fifty republican clubs being founded in that year alone. Gladstone was distressed: 'In rude and general terms,' he told Granville, 'the Queen is invisible, and the Prince of Wales is not respected.'[11] His solution to what he termed 'the Royalty Question' was that the Queen should be forced out of her seclusion and the Prince of Wales set to work. A fierce running battle between Queen and Prime Minister ensued, with the Queen complaining pathetically that she was ill and that her Ministers were trying to kill her with overwork, while Gladstone attributed this to female self-will which must be overborne.

Disraeli must have agreed with Gladstone's aims, if not his methods; as early as 1869 he told Stanley at dinner that he thought the monarchy was in danger from gradual loss of prestige: 'The queen has thrown away her chances [and] people find out that they can do as well without a court', he said.[12] But, naturally, he kept out of the war between Gladstone and the Queen, doing his best to keep on good terms with her by sending graceful letters, such as this one on the engagement of the Princess Louise to the Marquis of Lorne: 'You will miss her, Madam, only like the stars: that return in their constant season and with all their brightness'.[13] When, in the autumn of 1871, the Queen was really seriously ill, he made a speech in her defence at the Hughenden harvest festival which was widely reported and particularly unfortunate. Disraeli, the press reported with malicious glee, in using the phrase 'morally and physically incapacitated' had declared the Queen mentally unfit for her work. Victoria was deeply offended, and Disraeli hastened to write an anxious letter of explanation to her doctor, Sir William Jenner. A few months later the Prince of Wales nearly died of typhoid contracted at a grand house party. Lord Chesterfield, who was also a guest, died of the disease, a proof that even the great were not safe from the perils of Victorian sanitation, and for days the Prince's life was despaired of. Then suddenly, on 14 December, the anniversary of his father's death from the same disease, he recovered, and royal short-comings were forgotten in a wave of loyal relief which swept the country.

Disraeli and Mary Anne were at Grosvenor Gate during the Prince's illness, driven from Hughenden by the 'severe and savage weather' which, Disraeli told Monty 'quite sickened' Mary Anne who was prevented from her favourite occupation of marking and planting trees: 'Now she sighs for Park Lane, and twilight talk and tea'.[14] Disraeli had other reasons for wishing to be 'at headquarters', as he put it, as the New Year opened. He saw signs of a Conservative revival as Gladstone's popularity plummeted. Gladstone's reforms had offended many powerful interests, notably the brewers and victuallers and the army; his handling of foreign policy was seen as ineffective and contributory to the decline of Britain's prestige abroad; while he had also committed recent high-handed blunders that had offended politicians on both sides.

Other leading Conservatives also read the signs; dissatisfied with Disraeli's apathetic leadership over the past two years, they determined that, with office in view, Disraeli should be replaced by Derby. On 3 February 1872 a meeting of high-ranking Conservatives took place at Lord Exeter's house, Burghley, attended by Cairns, Pakington, Ward Hunt, John Manners, Stafford Northcote, Gathorne-Hardy, the party whip, Gerard Noel, and Monty's father, Henry Corry. The Brutus of the conspiracy, it appears from Hardy's diary account of the meeting, was Cairns, one of Disraeli's most valued and respected colleagues – in itself significant of the seriousness of the dissatisfaction with Disraeli's leadership. It was Cairns who broached the subject of Derby's taking the lead; only Manners objected, while Noel said that Derby's name as leader would favourably affect 40 or 50 seats. Hardy, for his part, did not think much of Derby, but, he wrote, 'I cannot but admit that Disraeli, as far as appears, has not the position in House and country to enable him to do what others might.'[15] None of the conspirators, however, had the courage to tell Disraeli, and within a few weeks it was to be strikingly demonstrated how wrong they had been in their estimation of Disraeli's popularity in the country.

On 27 February a service of thanksgiving for the recovery of the Prince of Wales was held at St Paul's; as the procession wound its way back from the cathedral, Gladstone was received with silence and the occasional catcall, Disraeli with what Fraser described as 'an overpowering ovation' which continued all the way from the City via Waterloo Place and Regent Street to Grosvenor Gate (where Mary Anne descended) and from thence to the Carlton. The cheers which greeted him from all classes, Fraser said, convinced him that, for the day at least, a more popular man did not exist in England. The effect upon Disraeli was electrical; Fraser, seeing him just after his arrival at the Carlton, was struck by an expression on his face which he had never seen before:

> I have heard it said by one who spoke to Napoleon 1 at Orange in France, that his face was as that of one who looks into another world: that is the only description I can give of Disraeli's look ... He seemed more like a statue than a human being ... He was thinking that he will be Prime Minister again![16]

It must indeed have been an overwhelming sensation for Disraeli to find himself, at sixty-seven, a popular hero for the first time. For the last twenty years he had been famous, or rather, notorious; his wax image stood in Madame Tussaud's and scarcely a week went by without his appearing in some periodical, usually in the form of a satirical cartoon. Now, at long last, he was not only famous, but popular. At that moment all the years of struggle, of patient acceptance of hatred and insults, public and private derision, must have been compensated for by this great wave of popular feeling. Dorothy Nevill said that the reason why he was easily depressed by political matters going against him was because he entertained 'a settled conviction' that he was unpopular, and that opposition to his views arose from this cause alone. More than once when his Government was arousing hostile criticism he had told her, 'Ah, it is not my Government they dislike: I tell you it is me they dislike'. 'I do not think' Lady Dorothy recorded in her *Reminiscences*, 'that quite till the end of his life he could divest himself of the idea that the great mass of the people of England were prejudiced against him. His early experiences of the House of Commons and the hostile reception of his first speech had made a deep and long-abiding impression on his mind'. It was only, she said, 'when he had reached the highest pinnacle to which political ambition in England can aspire that he became convinced that his unpopularity was a thing of the past. I remember congratulating him, and his reply: "It is all well and good now – I feel my position assured." '[17]

Why, one wonders, was there this sudden upsurge in public feeling in Disraeli's favour? Popularity, and its timing, is often largely inexplicable. In Disraeli's case his widely reported victories over Gladstone at the time of the Reform Bill may have had something to do with it, as also the fame of his best-selling *Lothair*; and the sense, perhaps, that in Queen Victoria's words, he was 'a man risen from the people'. Gladstone's unpopularity undoubtedly caused a reaction in Disraeli's favour, but hardly to such an extent. Disraeli was undoubtedly a celebrity; he was now almost a public pet, universally known as 'Dizzy' – as if the English public had come to recognize that he was an extraordinary being, quite unlike anyone else, liking him for what he was rather than what he did. It was a feeling expressed to Fraser by Mr Pell, one of the Tory county members: 'In spite of it all, damn the fellow! One cannot help loving him!'

The demonstration of 27 February was followed by another popular triumph at Manchester at Easter, brilliantly stage-managed by John Gorst, recently appointed by Disraeli as party manager to head the newly-founded Conservative Central Office. Disraeli and Mary Anne were greeted on Easter Monday by a cheering crowd of workers who insisted on forming a human team to draw their carriage, and on the following day several hundred Conservative Associations from the county of Lancashire paraded in front of the Disraelis with banners flying; but the highlight of the visit was a sensational speech by Disraeli on Wednesday at the Free Trade Hall. Disraeli was inexperienced as a demagogue, and was determined to fortify himself for the occasion. Mindful of the time during one of the Reform debates when he was accused of being drunk after having been seen to down a huge tumbler containing two-thirds brandy to one of water, he made sure that nothing in the colour of what he would drink should betray him to his enemies again. Monty Corry was sent out to scour the liquor shops of Manchester in search of white brandy which would be indistinguishable from the water with which it was mixed. Fortified by the brandy, of which apparently he drank two bottles in ever stronger doses, Disraeli made a fiery speech, keeping up the pace for three and a quarter hours.[18]

He presented the Conservatives as the patriotic party, leaders of a united country, contrasting their ideal with the divisive and dangerous tendencies of Gladstonian Liberalism which had attacked every interest and class and was tainted with Republicanism and Home Rule. For the first time he proclaimed what was to be the platform of the new Conservative party: social welfare and the preservation of the Empire, two themes which were to dominate his last Government, but which, unfortunately, were to prove incompatible. Resorting to a ghastly pun, '*Sanitas sanitatum, omnia sanitas*', he declared that 'the first consideration of a Minister should be the health of the people', and ended with a rallying call to England as a powerful, united country with an imperial destiny:

> ... it is not merely our fleets and armies, our powerful artillery, our accumulated capital, and our unlimited credit on which I so much depend, as upon that unbroken spirit of her people, which I believe was never prouder of the Imperial country to which they belong.[19]

He was to follow up the Manchester meeting with another great image-making speech at the Crystal Palace on 24 June, when he again put forward the ideology of the Conservative party of the future as having three main objectives, 'to maintain our institutions, to uphold the Empire, and to elevate the condition of the people'.

Perhaps the most quoted and remembered passage of the Manchester speech was, however, his metaphor for Gladstone's great reforming Ministry:

> As I sat opposite the Treasury Bench the Ministers reminded me of one of those marine landscapes not very unusual on the coasts of South America. You behold a range of exhausted volcanoes. Not a flame flickers on a single pallid crest. But the situation is still dangerous. There are occasional earthquakes, and ever and anon the dark rumbling of the sea.

Even Gladstone's biographer, Lord Morley, was forced to admit that this was perhaps Disraeli's finest hour as a party leader; for he, and not Gladstone, had succeeded in divining the spirit of the times:

> Disraeli's genius, at once brooding over conceptions and penetrating in discernment of fact, had shown him vast Tory reserves that his household suffrage of 1867 would rally to his flag. The same genius again scanning the skies read aright the signs and characteristics of the time ... National pride ... was silently but deeply stirred; the steady splendour of the economic era for a season paled in uncalculating minds. This coming mood the Tory leader, with his rare faculty of wide and sweeping forecast, confidently divined, and he found for it the oracle of a party cry about Empire and Social Reform.[20]

Disraeli for the first time had given the Conservative party an ideology, with goals more concrete than the vaguely defined idealistic paternalism of Young England, transforming what had been a 'confused mass' of reactionary squires into a party which the new electorate and aspiring young politicians could accept.

For Disraeli too this speech marked the transformation of the opportunist adventurer into the statesman, as the eighty-year-old Mary Anne recognized when, like a young girl, she ran to meet him after the Manchester speech, throwing herself into his arms crying, 'Oh! Dizzy, Dizzy it is the greatest night of all. This pays for all!'[21]

It was to be their last public triumph; when they returned to London Mary Anne collapsed, and this time they must both have known that she would not recover. She was suffering from terminal cancer, in pain and almost unable to eat. Brandy, excitement and concern about Mary Anne took their toll of Disraeli also, who was confined to the house by their doctor, Leggatt, who reassured him that one of his bronchial tubes was clogged but there was nothing organically wrong. Disraeli wrote sad little bulletins on Mary Anne's condition to Monty Corry, who was absent, also ill – 'My poor dear wife just the same ...'. Indomitably social, Mary Anne went to an evening party at Lady Waldegrave's on 6 May, but was obliged to come home almost immediately. 'But', Disraeli reported to Monty, 'as she boastfully says, her illness was not found out'. Despite her age and illness, she had delighted Lady Waldegrave's fourth husband, Chichester Fortescue, by telling him that she had heard him very much praised. 'He pressed her very much when & where', Disraeli retailed. 'She replied "It was in bed." ' 'Sir William gives a good account of her today' he went on,' & seems to think he has remedied the pain wh: is all we can hope for, & has sanctioned, even advised, her to go to Court – but I don't think he allows enough for her extreme weakness.'[22] The visit to Court, as Disraeli had feared, was not a success:

> She was suffering as we went, & was taken so unwell there, that we had to retreat precipitately ... the attack was accounted for by the horrible remedy wh: they had given her, & its only substantial evil is that she will have no further recourse to that remedy, wh: had at least, freed her from pain & given her sleep.[23]

The only good news Disraeli had to give Monty was of his triumphant reception at the dinner of the Literary Fund, which, he said, was 'equal to Manchester! The mob consisting of Princes, ambassadors, wits, artists – & critics!' He wrote of his pain at watching Mary Anne gradually dying:

> To see her every day weaker & weaker is heartrending. I have had, like all of us, some sorrows of this kind: but in every case, the fatal illness had been apparently sudden, and comparatively short. The shock is great under such circumstances no doubt, but there is a rebound in the nature of things. But to witness this gradual death of one, who has shared so long, and so completely, my life, entirely unmans me.[24]

Bravely Mary Anne, encouraged by her doctor, still made attempts to go out in society, but she could endure very little. A visit to Hughenden did not improve her condition; she suffered greatly, moving with difficulty, and was unable to endure the slightest roughness in the paths of the German Forest, although pushed gently along in a perambulator by their servant, Antonelli.

Mary Anne returned from Hughenden determined to resume her former life; social as she was, she could not bear the seclusion of an invalid, nor, with a kind of desperate pride, did she want society to know that she was seriously ill, although the signs must have been written on her face. She went to her last party at Lady Loudoun's on 17 July, but collapsed and had to be taken home. This time her condition could not be concealed, and the hostess and guests, now aware of the seriousness of her illness, were amazed at the heroism with which she bore it. Disraeli now never left her side unless an important parliamentary division demanded his presence. Even then he wrote to her from the House:

> I have nothing to tell you except that I love you, which, I fear, you will think rather dull. Natty [Nathaniel de Rothschild] was very affectionate about you, and wanted me to come home and dine with him ... but I told him that you were the only person now, whom I could dine with; and only relinquished you to-night for my country. My country, I fear, will be very late; but I hope to find you in a sweet sleep.[25]

The next day Mary Anne, alone at Grosvenor Gate, wrote what was probably her last note to him: 'My own Dearest, I miss you sadly. I feel so grateful for your constant tender love and kindness ... Your own devoted Beaconsfield.'

As August came and London emptied of society the Disraelis remained at Grosvenor Gate, Mary Anne being too ill to attempt the journey to Hughenden. At least, as Disraeli told Cairns, they had the advantage of looking out upon the trees and grass of Hyde Park, 'we try to forget, that the Park is called Hyde, and that the bowers are the bowers of Kensington.' To pass the time they went on long drives through London and its suburbs, surprised to find how vastly the city had expanded during their lifetime. From 1 August to the end of September, Disraeli calculated that they travelled some 220 miles in their carriage past miles of new brick villas, recently-built Gothic churches and what Disraeli termed 'gorgeous palaces of Geneva' [public houses]. One day, Disraeli wrote, they came upon 'a real feudal castle, with a donjon keep high in the air. It turned out to be the new City prison in Camden Road, but it deserves a visit; I mean externally.'[26] But beneath their cheerfully assumed enjoyment, both were suffering, as Disraeli wrote to Gathorne-Hardy, 'Her condition occasions me the greatest disquietude, tho' they tell me there is some improvement. Her illness ... is a total inability to take any sustenance, and it is to me perfectly marvellous how she exists, and shows even great buoyancy of life.'[27]

In the last week of September, there was a remission of the disease; Mary Anne was well enough to go down to Hughenden and even experienced a renewal of appetite. Monty Corry, on a fishing cruise with friends off the west coast of Ireland, seems to have had little apprehension of danger, resuming his shooting-parties when he returned to England and even contemplating arrangements for Disraeli to visit Glasgow for his installation as Rector later that year. But in mid-October there was a crisis, and another early in November. Leggatt, hastily summoned by Disraeli, reassured him that there was no immediate danger if only she could be persuaded to eat. 'But how to manage that?' Disraeli wrote despairingly to Monty. 'The truth is, she never even tasted any of the dishes, that the Rothschilds used to send her in London, and anxious as she was to partake of the delicacies you so kindly provided for her, and which touched her much, it has ended with them as with the feats of Lionel's [de Rothschild's] chef'.[28]

There was another remission in mid-November; the pain ceased and Mary Anne, although still unable to eat much, could at least enjoy life. On 23 November, they held their last house-party at Hughenden, the guests being Lord and Lady John Manners, Disraeli's Liberal friend, the witty Sir William Harcourt, and Lord Ronald Gower, son of the Duke of Sutherland, a much-travelled amateur painter and sculptor of some talent, who was exactly the kind of young man whom Disraeli liked. Gower and Harcourt found their host on their arrival looking 'quite boyish', lively, and anxious for the latest gossip from town, but Mary Anne's appearance shocked Lord Ronald:

> ... she poor old soul sadly altered since London in looks. Shrunk & more like an anointed corpse than ever, but dressed in her usual gorgeous mode, a black velvet sort of cushion on her poor old wig, with a huge star on one side banded with a circlet of gold, her poor old shoulders covered with a gaudy crimson velvet & tinselled shawl.[29]

Sitting beside Mary Anne at dinner, Lord Ronald noted that she ate nothing and drank only seltzer water, while conversation was spoilt by Disraeli's obvious concern about her health. 'Although occasionally flashing out into conversation', Lord Ronald recorded, 'with all his curious action of arms & shrugging of shoulders [he was] evidently very much depressed at her state'. His attentions to her were touching; Mary Anne was constantly appealed to and, 'he often caresses her before the servants', Lord Ronald noted in amazement. After dinner was even more tedious – 'one having to sit by & hear much of the poor old lady's twaddle & little of Mr. D's talk'.

On Sunday, after a walk on the terrace accompanied by Disraeli in his favourite brigand-like hat, the guests ate a hearty breakfast of sausages and cold meat while their host breakfasted with Mary Anne. Later he appeared to escort them to church, dressed in his long brown Spencer overcoat, and, said Lord Ronald, looking quite the lord of the manor as he crossed the churchyard, 'returning the greetings of the people & patting the children quite à la Sir Roger de Coverley style on the head'. Disraeli proudly showed them monuments to the de Montforts in the church, and complained that the vicar, Mr Blagden, was too High Church for his taste, and very much given to intoning against his patron's instructions. Nevertheless, Lord Ronald thought the singing excellent and the sermon tolerable, Mr Blagden having chosen the Old Testament lesson upon old age and death – 'the great and inevitable change' – as his text. 'Very appropriate with that poor vain old lady we had left at the "Manor",' Lord Ronald commented, '& this must have crossed Mr. D's mind.'

'The poor old lady' put in an appearance at luncheon and afterwards led the way in a pony chair as they walked through the German Forest which, Disraeli said romantically, reminded him of views of Bohemia. Anxious to show his guests a farm of which he was very proud, Disraeli lost his way out of the wood and led them floundering over muddy fields to the farm so that it was nearly five o'clock and getting dark before they got back to Hughenden. 'The pride of an English landlord comes out very strong on Sunday afternoons in showing his possessions', Disraeli said to Harcourt. Dinner that evening was more lively than the previous night, with Disraeli in better conversational form, but afterwards, alone with the men, he did not conceal his misery about Mary Anne. 'She suffers so much at times', he said. 'We have been married thirty-three years & she has never given me a dull moment.' Mary Anne had a bad night which distressed Disraeli, but bravely came down to breakfast with her guests and was 'wonderfully brisk'. The guests left at mid-day, the morning being miserably wet, which, in Lord Ronald's words, 'seemed to add to the melancholy feeling of seeing the last of the poor old lady who with all her faults & oddities is certainly a most kind & devoted wife.'

Just over a week after the visitors left Hughenden, the final crisis came. Disraeli wrote incoherently to Corry on 5 December, 'Things have taken a bad turn here – I am most distressed. Leggatt is here & has been here for ten days, it was impossible & is impossible to write anything to guide you ... Last night very bad – but this afternoon better – a hope – there is congestion on the lungs'.[30] The following day she was worse. 'Affairs are most dark here', Disraeli wrote desperately to Philip Rose. 'I tremble for the result, and even an immediate one ... I entirely trust to your coming to me, if anything happens. *I am totally unable to meet the catastrophe*'.[31] Monty hastened down to Hughenden to support his chief who scarcely left his dying wife's bedside. Mary Anne had double pneumonia and was frequently delirious. One note from Disraeli to Corry reads, 'She says she must see you. Calm, but the delusions stronger than ever. She will not let me go out to fetch you. Come. D.'[32] In her lucid moments, her thoughts dwelt on her admiration for her husband; the clergyman, she told Monty, had exhorted her to turn her thoughts to Jesus Christ. 'But I couldn't' she said, 'You know *Dizzy* is my J.C.' But, tragically, in her worst delirium she turned against him, raving bitterly to Corry, her ravings heard by Disraeli listening in tears outside the door.

Mary Anne died at noon on Sunday 15 December 1872. Typically she faced death with courage; refusing to go to bed, she sat in her chair fighting to the last. Typically also she had concealed her real age to the end, even from Disraeli; her death certificate gave her age as seventy-six – she was in fact eighty. Despite occasional storms, her life, as she once said, had been 'such a happy one. I have had so much affection, and no troubles – no contradictions', adding rather pathetically, ' that is what has kept me so young and well'.[33]

Over sixteen years before, in June 1856, she had, somewhat dramatically, written Disraeli a last letter:

If I should depart this life before you, leave orders that we may be buried in the same

grave at whatever distance you may die from England. And now, God bless you, my
kindest, dearest! You have been a perfect husband to me ... And now, farewell, my dear
Dizzy. Do not live alone, dearest. Some one I earnestly hope you may find as attached
to you as your own devoted Mary Anne.[34]

She was buried on 20 December in the churchyard vault in the east wall where
Mrs Brydges Willyams and James D'Israeli had been buried before her and where
Disraeli would eventually join her. A dark, wet winter day added gloom to the
simple funeral as Mary Anne's coffin, carried by the Hughenden tenants, and
followed by Disraeli with Monty Corry, Philip Rose and Dr Leggatt, was borne
down the hill from the house to the church. Disraeli stood for ten minutes looking
down on his wife's coffin after it was laid in the vault, then walked slowly back to
the house.

Tributes and condolences poured in; *The Times* called their marriage 'an
historical event', while the Queen wrote that she 'knew and admired as well as
appreciated the unbounded devotion and affection which united him to the dear
partner of his life, whose only thought was him'. She could not resist adding,
'*Yesterday* was the anniversary of her great loss', nor, with her morbid fascination
with death, could she refrain from inquiring of Monty Corry, through Lady Ely,
details of Mary Anne's last hours. Gladstone wrote somewhat stiffly but with real
emotion:

> You and I were, as I believe, married in the same year. It has been permitted to both of
> us to enjoy a priceless boon through a third of a century. Spared myself the blow which
> has fallen on you, I can form some conception of what it must have been and be ... I
> offer only the assurance which all who know you, all who knew Lady Beaconsfield, and
> especially those ... who like myself enjoyed for a length of time her marked though
> unmerited regard ... the assurance that in this trying hour they feel deeply for you, and
> with you.[35]

'I am much touched by your kind words in my great sorrow', Disraeli replied.
'Marriage is the greatest earthly happiness, when founded on complete sympathy.
That hallowed lot was mine, and for a moiety of my existence; and I know it is
yours ...'.[36] It was to be their last friendly exchange.

Replying to letters of condolence, Disraeli described Mary Anne's death as 'the
supreme sorrow of my life'. A year later he talked about his marriage to the young
Constance de Rothschild. Taking her aside at a dinner party, he described at
length his lost happiness and the great qualities indispensable to a happy married
life: '"Sympathy" he said, and repeated it over and over again. "Sympathy goes
before beauty or talent. Sympathy – and that is what I have had!"'[37] At last he
commissioned the portrait of Mary Anne which, as he told Lord Ronald Gower
in the month before her death, he had long planned. It was a romanticized
portrayal of Mary Anne as she may have looked when he first knew her. He could
hardly have hung such a portrait upon the walls of Hughenden while Mary Anne
was still alive without exciting ridicule, as the contrast between the blooming
thirty-year-old woman and the painted, dying idol would have been too painful.

Disraeli, with his refusal to grow old and his disgust at the physical deterioration which it imposed, did not care to face reality. Mary Anne was to appear to posterity and to himself as they had both liked to picture her, youthful, desirable, gracious. Disraeli was pleased with the portrait; the artist, Middleton, he told Monty, 'has succeeded in giving to the countenance an expression of sweet gravity, wh: is characteristic'. In accordance with convention he ordered notepaper and envelopes edged with black; like the Queen, he retained it to the end of his life, as if to abandon this outward sign of mourning would be to consign Mary Anne to oblivion. As he was to explain to Lady Bradford two years later:

> It is strange, but I always used to think that the Queen persisting in these emblems of woe, indulged in a morbid sentiment. And yet it has become my lot and seemingly an irresistible one. I lost one who was literally devoted to me . . . and when I have been on the point sometimes of terminating this emblem of my bereavement, the thought that there was no longer any being in the world to whom I was an object of concentrated feeling overcame me and the sign remained.[38]

Disraeli lost not only Mary Anne, but Grosvenor Gate, his home for more than thirty years, and Mary Anne's £5,000 a year which reverted to the Wyndham Lewis estate. The indispensable Monty found him rooms at Edward's Hotel in George Street off Hanover Square. Their only virtue in Disraeli's eyes was that they had once been Lady Palmerston's, where, as Lady Cowper, she had flirted passionately with the youthful Palmerston; otherwise, as he told friends, lonely rooms in an hotel were a 'cave of despair'.

Mary Anne's death and the loss of his London home were traumatic events for Disraeli, but they did not weaken his interest in politics. Gladstone's reputation and parliamentary force were deteriorating, and the prospect of a fresh confrontation with his old enemy gave Disraeli strength in his sorrow. Less than ten days after Mary Anne's funeral the message came from Hughenden to his principal colleagues via Monty Corry, assuring them of 'Disraeli's continued interest in politics, and . . . his intention to be in his place in the beginning of the Session'.[39] Cairns and Hardy visited him at Hughenden on 20 January to discuss parliamentary business, and early in February he came up to London to hold meetings at Edward's Hotel to concert tactics for the session. Hardy, calling there on 6 February found him, despite his mourning, arrayed in one of his exotic Oriental dressing-gowns, in good spirits, and with his parliamentary plans arranged.

Prospects looked promising; the main measure of the session, the Irish University Bill proposing to unite the Anglican Trinity College in Dublin with Newman's Catholic University and the various 'godless' colleges founded by Peel in 1845, was bound to arouse opposition. Indeed, events moved quickly to a surprise defeat for Gladstone on the bill on 12 March, when Conservatives and Irish Catholics combined to put the Government in a minority of 3. A parliamentary poker game then ensued between Gladstone and Disraeli. Gladstone, angry and weary of power, hoped by resigning to force Disraeli into taking office as a minority Government while he led a majority Opposition. But Disraeli had no intention of playing Gladstone's game; encouraged by the popular demonstration the previous year, the obvious unpopularity of the Government, and the fact that the Liberals had lost thirteen by-elections over the past two years and gained none, he looked to a dissolution and an election which might give the Conservatives a majority for the first time since 1846.

Gladstone resigned on 15 March and the Queen sent for Disraeli, who met with 'a more than gracious reception' at Buckingham Palace, but nonetheless declined. An unseemly wrangle between the two men ensued, with Gladstone angry and Disraeli amused, telling Ponsonby frankly that the Conservatives were gaining in popularity but that two months in office with a hostile majority would ruin them. Gladstone fired off a long letter to the Queen abusive of Disraeli, accusing him of behaving in an unconstitutional manner in refusing to take office after he had caused the defeat of the Government; Disraeli did the same, in a missive almost equally long, refuting Gladstone's charges. Gladstone was forced to resume office.

The Speaker, Henry Brand, an acute judge of politics, assessed Disraeli's tactics shrewdly: 'He desires to drive Gladstone to a dissolution, when he will make the most of Gladstone's mistakes, while he will denounce a policy of destruction and confiscation'.[40] In the event, that is exactly what Disraeli did. At the end of the session Gladstone, beset by scandals and resignations, acted as most Prime Ministers do in difficult circumstances; he re-shuffled his administration. Disraeli did not think this would help him: 'I hear he is deeply mortified by the utter destruction of the prestige of his Administration', he wrote to John Manners on 28 August, 'and that his only thought now is to ... rehabilitate it, before it disappears. He will find this a hard task.'[41] The time had come, he considered, for him to come out fighting and to pummel Gladstone publicly with some hard-hitting words. On 3 October he issued an open letter to Lord Grey de Wilton, Conservative candidate in the by-election at Bath:

> For nearly five years the present Ministers have harassed every trade, worried every profession, and assailed or menaced every class, institution, and species of property in the country. Occasionally they have varied this state of civil warfare by perpetrating some job [partisan appointment] which has outraged public opinion, or by stumbling into mistakes which have always been discreditable, and sometimes ruinous. All this they call a policy, and seem quite proud of it; but the country has, I think, made up its mind to close this career of plundering and blundering.[42]

The 'Bath' letter was in Disraeli's best hustings style, provoking what Disraeli described as 'a hypocritical howl' from the Liberal press. It was, after all, as he pointed out to the Conservative agent Major Keith-Falconer, only the same language he had used on previous occasions in the House of Commons, and he went on to defend it in his speech of installation as Rector of Glasgow University the following month.[43] Glasgow was a popular triumph, as Disraeli told Rose, 'the greatest reception ever offered to a public man, far beyond Lancashire even!' As at Oxford twenty years before, the undergraduates responded ecstatically to Disraeli's style, his personality and his appeal to youth. Perhaps carried away by the enthusiasm, he made it quite clear that he intended to remain undisputed leader of his party, denying rumours that the Conservatives were anxious to 'get rid of my services'. It would seem that this claim was principally aimed at Derby, who was now married to the ambitious and neurotic Lady Salisbury, and definitely in the running for the leadership, as is evident from a letter from Monty reporting the Duke of Richmond's reaction to Disraeli's remarks:

> He told me that none of your words at Glasgow had afforded him so much pleasure as your remarks on the leadership, which he thought well-timed and in excellent taste. He hopes the mouths may now be shut of those who, 'whenever Lord Derby goes about starring at Mechanics' Institutes, etc.,' cry out 'Here is *the* man!'[44]

In the end Gladstone played into his hands with a *coup* that he had long been meditating. In August 1873 Disraeli had predicted to Manners that Gladstone would not go without 'attempting something' to restore the prestige of his discredited Government, while at the same time Gladstone was writing to Bright of his inclination to go to the country with 'a *positive* force to carry us onward as a body'. Preparing for the session of 1874, Gladstone, encouraged by a budget surplus of five million pounds, resolved to stake his all on one striking measure – the abolition of the income tax. Faced with inevitable opposition from the spending departments whose budgets would be severely cut, Gladstone saw dissolution and a fresh mandate from the country as the only solution. For the Liberal Government it must be kill or cure, and the more Gladstone meditated this plan, the more he liked it, particularly the surprise element; '... the enemy will be furious', he wrote gleefully to Herbert Gladstone on 24 January, the day after the Cabinet had agreed to dissolve.

Gladstone's principal enemy had arrived in London quite by chance and earlier than expected to attend a meeting of the British Museum Trustees on Friday 23 January, the very day the decision had been taken. Lying in bed in his room at Edward's Hotel on Saturday morning, he opened his copy of *The Times* and was stunned to read not only the news of the impending dissolution, but Gladstone's election manifesto, boasting of the five-million surplus and promising to abolish the income tax. Far from being 'furious', Disraeli was happily galvanized into immediate action, telegraphing for Monty, Derby, Cairns, Hardy and Northcote, and setting to work on his own manifesto to be published in Monday's papers.

Disraeli's biographer, Buckle, described the Conservative manifesto as 'rather of a negative character', but that, perhaps, in the eyes of the public, was a virtue rather than otherwise. Five years of a dynamically reforming Government had been enough, and Disraeli's manifesto, like his public speeches, was designed to appeal to imperial pride but also to the fear of the revolutionary and iconoclastic tendencies of Gladstone's Radical and Irish allies. Gladstone had hoped that his lightning move would take his opponents by surprise, but in the event it was the Liberals themselves who were found unprepared. Disraeli had envisaged the possibility of a dissolution since the Irish University vote, and the Conservative political machine was better funded and better organized than that of the Liberals.

Largely due to his initiative, the Conservative Central Office had been created with the National Union and local associations under its control, and two able men, John Gorst and Keith Falconer, at its head.

Parliament was formally dissolved on 26 January 1874 and the country went to the polls in the last week of the month. Gorst's pre-election predictions to Disraeli had been modest – 'Con[servative]s. 328 ... Radicals [Liberals], 325'. In the event it was a landslide victory for the Conservatives, not only in the counties, but in the boroughs, normally Liberal territory, where the Conservative gains of over 30 seats justified Disraeli's prediction in 1867 that the lower the franchise went the greater gain there would be to the Tories. Disraeli, who was faced with a contested election in Buckinghamshire, came top of the poll, while at Greenwich Gladstone, to his great mortification, came second to a Mr Boord, a member of the brewing and victualling trade, alienated by his Licensing Act. In the circumstances it was perhaps understandable that he should write to his brother, 'We have been borne down in a torrent of gin and beer', while Bright opined that in Lancashire publicans and Irishmen had joined together to defeat the Liberals, 'the one for delirium tremens, and the other for religious education'. In Ireland itself, which Gladstone's measures had failed to pacify, 57 Home Rulers were elected, pledged to act independently from the Liberals, while in Great Britain as a whole the figures were Conservatives 350, Liberals 245. Monty Corry in London reported 'bitterness and despair' at Brook's, while at the Carlton, Disraeli's former critics – 'all the dear "old lot" whom we know so well – all the *frondeurs* and the cynics, professors, now, of a common faith – cry for "the Chief", as young hounds bay for the huntsman the day after the frost is broken up'.[45]

For Disraeli indeed the frost had broken up in the election of 1874. The Conservative party now enjoyed the first majority it had had since the days of Peel; Disraeli had broken up Peel's party, but he had successfully reconstructed it, giving it both an organization and an ideology, and attracting to its ranks young men of talent without whom no party could have a future. Indeed the efficiency of the Conservative machine under John Gorst and Major Keith-Falconer at the Central Office was as potent a factor in the party's success in 1874 as the decay of that organization was to be in the Conservative defeat six years later. A part of his electoral success was also due, as so often, to the desire of the electorate for a change; part of it too to Gladstone's mismanagement and bad luck, and the scandals which often herald the break-up of a government. But Disraeli had been the first to diagnose that desire for change, to attack Gladstone on the very points which had created unease in the country, and to stir up national pride in favour of his party by pointing out the humiliations inflicted upon it by Gladstone's ineffective foreign policy – providing a Conservative alternative with clarion calls to patriotism.

For an anxious period it seemed as if Gladstone, despite his great defeat, would not resign; during the first and second week of February he seriously considered meeting Parliament and was only dissuaded from doing so by Granville and the more influential Liberals. He would have preferred to have been able to dispose of his precious five million pound surplus as he wished before his rival could lay hands upon it. 'Is it not disgusting', Mrs Gladstone wrote to their son Herbert, 'after all Papa's labour and patriotism and years of work to think of handing over his nest-egg to that Jew?.⁴⁶ The Queen could not wait for him to resign and wrote to Granville on 13 February telling him so. Her son, Alfred, Duke of Edinburgh, and his bride, the Grand Duchess Marie of Russia, were due to arrive shortly, and 'she could not *physically* go through the *work* and *fatigue* necessitated by a change of Government at the same *time* as the arrival of the young couple takes place', she told Granville peremptorily.⁴⁷

Privately the Queen was delighted with the Conservative victory: 'Mr G. has contrived to alienate and frighten the country', she wrote to the Crown Princess on 10 February. 'Since '46 under the great, good and wise Sir Robert Peel – there has not been a Conservative majority!! It shows a healthy state of the country'.⁴⁸ The Queen, subjective as she was, was persistently unfair to Gladstone, who failed to understand that she needed to be handled with persuasion, tact and flattery. She complained that he spoke to her 'as if he were addressing a public meeting' and his lectures made her both obstinate and suspicious. Recalling that Palmerston had told her that Gladstone was 'a very dangerous man', she launched into a diatribe against him, 'And so very arrogant, tyrannical and obstinate, with no knowledge of the world or human nature ... a fanatic in religion. All this and much want of regard towards my feelings ... led to make him a very dangerous and unsatisfactory Premier', she told the Crown Princess on 24 February.⁴⁹ She was, however kind to Gladstone when he came down to Windsor to resign on 17 February, refraining from telling him, as she noted in a private memorandum at the time, that his defeat 'was greatly owing to his own unpopularity and to the want of confidence people had in him'. Immediately Gladstone had left, she despatched Ponsonby to London to summon Disraeli.

Ponsonby found Disraeli installed in no. 2 Whitehall Gardens, a handsome house which he had rented from the Duchess of Northumberland; he was 'open and joyous' and not concealing his delight at his astonishing majority. On 18 February he went down to Windsor for a happy reunion with his 'Faery' (as he habitually referred to the Queen). Apart from their mutual dislike of Gladstone, bereavement had created an additional bond of sympathy between the widowed Queen and her Minister. Romantically, the sixty-nine-year-old Disraeli knelt and kissed her hand, saying, 'I plight my troth to the kindest of Mistresses'. It was a great moment for Disraeli, not only undisputed leader of a powerful and united party but Prime Minister for the second time.

20 Power and the Affections

'Threescore and ten ... is the period of romantic passions', Disraeli wrote in *Lothair*. Within less than a year of Mary Anne's death Disraeli, on the verge of seventy, was to fall passionately in love.

Lonely in his 'cave of despair' at Edward's Hotel after Mary Anne's death, and without the companionship and protection of Monty who was attending his dying father, Disraeli missed that female sympathy on which he had so much depended. There was, however, more than one society woman willing to take Mary Anne's place, one of them being Angela Burdett-Coutts, philanthropist, friend of Dickens and, as the Coutts heiress, the richest woman in England; but the first in the field was the outrageous Countess of Cardigan. Born in 1824, she was, at 50, almost exactly twenty years younger than Disraeli, having been in her prime at the time of the Crimean campaign when, as the dashing Adeline de Horsey, she had shocked London society by living openly with her lover, Lord Cardigan, even before his wife's death. Cardigan subsequently married her; she was now a rich widow, a countess and mistress of the Brudenell home, Deene Park, but still looked upon as not quite respectable, a view which she did nothing to counteract by her eccentric behaviour.

Disraeli dined with her alone on 18 February, by which time he was already referring wryly to her in his letters to Monty as 'my Countess'; he was soon in a state of siege. Lady Cardigan pursued him relentlessly, twice proposing herself as his private secretary and finally as his wife. 'I have had 12 offers of marriage since Lord Cardigan's death', she informed him, but she was now convinced that a union between 'the greatest man we have in genius & intellect with the wealthiest relict of the staunchest Conservative Peer that ever lived' would bring her the greatest comfort and happiness.[1] Disraeli, apparently, remained unconvinced of the benefits of such a marriage; only a draft letter he wrote to her has survived and its tone is distinctly cautious – 'I wd. fain hope you will not misinterpret my suggestion that at present it wd. be better that we shd. not meet'.[2]

Later that year, Lady Cardigan married a Portuguese nobleman, the Conde de Lencastre, but she continued to press Disraeli for favours; she was particularly anxious that Queen Victoria who disliked her, should receive her at court. She never forgave Disraeli his rejection of her, and later was to give a vicious account of the affair in her *Recollections*, claiming that Disraeli had proposed to her and she had refused him on the advice of the Prince of Wales whom she met hunting at Belvoir:

> I was riding my famous horse 'Dandy' ... and that morning I was much exercised in my mind about a proposal of marriage I had just received from Disraeli. My uncle, Admiral Rous, had said to me, 'My dear, you can't marry that d-d old Jew', but I had known Disraeli all my life & I liked him very well. He had, however, one drawback as far as I was concerned, and that was his breath ... I was wondering whether I could possibly put up with this unfortunate attribute in a great man, when I met the King [then the Prince of Wales] who was graciously pleased to ride with me. In the course of our conversation I told him about Disraeli's proposal and asked him whether he would advise me to accept it, but the King said he did not think the marriage would be a very happy one.[3]

By the time the book was published Disraeli was dead and could not defend himself, while Edward VII stated that she had seriously misrepresented the conversation. Lady Cardigan's remarks about Disraeli in her *Recollections* bear every sign of a woman scorned, nor did she forbear to strike back at the woman he had preferred to her, Selina, Countess of Bradford.

Selina Bradford was fifty-four when Disraeli fell in love with her in the late summer of 1873, but she was still attractive, fashionably dressed, charming and reasonably intelligent. She was a 'great lady' in aristocratic society, grand-daughter of the 4th Duke of Rutland, daughter of the Shropshire magnate, Lord Forester, and wife of the 3rd Earl of Bradford. She and her elder sister, Anne, Countess of Chesterfield, had been beauties in their day and in the thirties when Disraeli first met them, they and their sporting husbands had been members of the 'ton', the exclusive hunting-racing set of which d'Orsay had been an honorary member but from which Disraeli had definitely been excluded. Both women by birth and by marriage belonged to those aristocratic circles which had always regarded Disraeli with distrust and dislike; '... somehow he is a man I cannot respect', Selina Bradford had written of Disraeli early in 1849. In the late seventies when Anne Chesterfield was heard to wonder why she and her sister had not known Disraeli well in the early days, Dorothy Nevill commented, 'Many people fought shy of him and later on many disliked his wife'. Anne Chesterfield was to become one of Disraeli's dearest friends; he proposed marriage to her but she refused, partly because her daughter Lady Carnarvon was against it, partly, one suspects, because all the family knew that Disraeli's object in marrying Anne would be to be near Selina.

Disraeli, now a celebrity and no longer hampered by Mary Anne's absurdities, had won the entrée to the aristocratic inner circle. As an experienced social climber he was well aware of the distinction between what he liked to call 'real society' and the crowd of obscure titles who swarmed on its fringes; and indeed his letters to Selina were somewhat pathetically larded with snobbish comment. He often warned her not to mix with nonentities – 'You are too great a lady'.

Disraeli's crucial encounter with Selina, which was to lead to such a passionate attachment, took place on 26 July 1873 at a dinner party given by Mr and Lady Augusta Sturt, later Lord and Lady Alington. He wrote a careful note to her the next day ('Dear Lady Bradford'), asking for an interview; within a month she had become 'Dearest Lady Bradford' and by the end of the year he was deeply in love. The pattern of his love for Selina mirrored his pursuit of Mary Anne over thirty years before; beginning with a gallant friendship it developed into a *grande passion* with all its attendant delights and miseries – ecstatic joy at the prospect of seeing his beloved, wretchedness at their separations, happy tenderness when things were going well, angry hurt when Selina did not share the intensity of his feelings. There was, however, one major difference; Selina was married and respectable, and his passion was requited only with friendship.

There is no concrete evidence of Selina's feelings for Disraeli; only a few innocuous social notes from her to him have been found, and in all probability her letters were destroyed or returned to her for destruction by Monty Corry on Disraeli's death. The documentary proof of Disraeli's love for Selina lay at the Bradford family seat, Weston Park, in Shropshire, in a trunk containing over 1,000 letters to her and some 500 to Anne Chesterfield. He poured out his life to her, writing sometimes as often as twice a day; even in the busiest moments in his second term as Prime Minister he thought of her, wrote to her, tried to snatch an hour to visit her in her house in Belgrave Square. His life centred on the prospect of seeing her, invitations to dinners and country houses were accepted and declined according to the chances of Selina's being there, and he was frequently hurt when she, amid the social commitments of her marriageable daughters and the sporting life of her racing husband, disappointed him. Sometimes too, the ardour of his passion, his demands, and the frequency of his visits irritated and embarrassed her and then he was in despair.

Selina, alarmed by the effect which the openness with which he wrote and visited her might have upon her reputation, asked him to send his letters to her without his signature, the official frank, upon the envelopes. Disraeli could only assure her that to despatch his letters without the frank would seem odd to the officials who posted them from Downing Street or Whitehall Gardens and 'would attract all the attention we wish to avoid'.[4] She complained too that the sight of his distinctive brougham standing daily outside her door would cause gossip; two years later Disraeli was to rejoice that her inquisitive neighbour, the Duchess of Montrose, was to marry a Mr Crawford and give up her house in Belgrave Square and would therefore no longer be able to pass on news of his visits, which her friend, the witty, gossiping Bernal Osborne, then retailed to London society.[5]

Selina's family profited by her connection with the Prime Minister. In July 1874, Disraeli obtained a vacant canonry at York for one of her relations, the Rev. Orlando Forester. Indulgently the Queen approved it, 'as Mr. Disraeli is very anxious for it, and he is a good man', warning however that she hoped that in future Disraeli would try and select only those whose merits rather than their birth entitled them to promotion. At the outset of his term of office he took the greatest pleasure in obtaining the coveted Household post of Master of the Horse for Lord Bradford, writing delightedly to Anne Chesterfield, 'Selina will ride in royal carriages, break the line even in the entrée and gallop all over her Majesty's lieges'. Less than a year later he offered him the Lord Lieutenancy of his county, Shropshire. Selina's advice was always asked when there were honours or posts to be awarded and mutual friends, like the Sturts, obtained coronets.

Nonetheless her family understandably found the seventy-year-old Disraeli's passion for Selina faintly ridiculous and sometimes irritating, as would appear from occasional nervous remarks in his letters. Once, Disraeli's German valet, Mr Baum, thinking to please, forwarded primroses sent by the Queen to Disraeli on to Selina. Their reception at Belgrave Square evoked an apology from Disraeli for Baum's 'officiousness' and he referred sadly to 'those innocent visits of mine, at which your family looks so much askance'.[6] On another occasion, having sent Selina an oriental talisman which he had had made for him in Cairo in 1831, he wrote of her husband's reaction, 'Bradford was even cordial', a curious remark which suggests that cordiality was often lacking. It may well have been that Disraeli, playing his role of romantic lover, liked to imagine Bradford as jealous in order to give piquancy to the affair, although it is hardly likely that he should have seriously been so. Bradford, a sporting peer in the tradition of the late Lord Derby, was not at all Disraeli's type and beyond Conservative politics and the asthma from which they both suffered, they can have had little in common. Although Bradford seems to have liked Disraeli well enough he was probably bored by the visits to Hughenden which loyalty impelled him to make, particularly if they interfered with the racing calendar.

One wonders if Bradford saw all Disraeli's letters to his wife, or hers in return. Outwardly Selina's manner to Disraeli was discouraging. 'I don't think she likes me to hang about her much in public', he wrote to her sister, but there is evidence that her private attitude to him was warmer. Disraeli wrote of the 'contrast between your letters and your general demeanour to me' in February 1875, and two months later, comforting himself for a temporary rebuff by reading Selina's letters of a year ago, he directly quoted a phrase from one: 'Have confidence in me, believe in me, believe that I am true – oh, how true'.[7] These were perhaps warmer words than Selina thought proper to be seen by anyone but Disraeli; and that she was nervous about them is evident from a letter which Disraeli wrote to her in August 1874 reassuring her on that point: 'How could you suppose even for an instant, that any mortal eye should with my cognisance see anything you have ever written to me! I guard your letters as an Egyptian Priest would the sacred writings of his creed.'[8] Two letters written by Disraeli to Selina in February 1875 which bear the signs of subsequent deletion and mutilation, would seem to indicate that she had expressed fears that some passages of her letters might be seen, or, in the event of his death, that they might be returned to her family:

'I do not like you even in jest to speak of your departure from this world before myself', he wrote on 2 February, 'I shall precede you by many years & I hope *delete* [? any compromising passages] . . .'.[9] On 18 February he told her how much pleasure her letters had given him, adding, '& even under the circumstances which you referred to the other day they would not be returned. Rest assured of that.'[10]

Love rejuvenated Disraeli in the earlier months of his relationship with Selina in 1873. After a gloomy August spent at Hughenden arranging Mary Anne's papers – 'she died for me 100 times in the heartrending, but absolutely inevitable process' he told Monty – he looked forward to visiting Selina at Weston and Anne Chesterfied at Bretby at the end of September. Full of youthful ardour at Weston, and perhaps remembering the far-off days of his passion for Henrietta when he went hunting on her Arab mare, Disraeli went cub-hunting. It was not a success; after three or four hours in the saddle he was so exhausted he could scarcely stand. But Selina, occupied with her other guests, could not give him her exclusive attention, as he grumbled crossly to Henry Lennox on 2 October, 'The fact is, visiting does not suit me . . . I linger on here, boring and bored, notwithstanding a charming hostess on whom I feel myself a tax.' In retrospect, however, things seemed better and when Selina sent him the cuckoo clock she had promised him at Weston he wrote, 'When shall I ever pass another week like that? amid a scene so fair and with a companion so full of sympathy and bright intelligence?'[11] Even as, in the first week of February 1874, the election results flooded in and it became obvious that he had won a famous victory, his thoughts were full of Selina and his longing to see her, 'I am very well, but sigh for moonlight,' he wrote romantically, 'I think I could live and love in that light for ever.'[12]

Sometimes, however, even he was aware of the disparity between his youthful feelings and his ageing body. 'There is no greater misfortune for a man than to have a heart which never grows old', he wrote sadly to Anne Chesterfield. 'Some think it has its compensations: I do not see them'.[13] As his feelings for Selina waxed stronger during the spring and summer of 1874, their relationship became stormy and his private feelings in the midst of his busy public life were always in turmoil. 'If we have to govern a great country, we ought not to be distrait & feel the restlessness of love',[14] he told Selina who, irritated or perhaps prudent in the face of his increasing ardour, returned a cooling letter. Disraeli was hurt but unrepentant; all the passionate feelings of his youth had returned and he was determined to express them. 'Your view of correspondence, apparently, is that it should be confined to facts & not admit feelings. Mine is the reverse', he replied on 17 March. She may have wondered, he said, that amidst all his work and cares he found time to write to her – 'it was because my feelings impel me to write to you. It was my duty & my delight: the duty of my heart & the delight of my life'. She had told him that she found his demands upon her unreasonable, but – 'I have never asked anything from you but your society. When I have that I am content . . . When we were separated, the loneliness of my life found relief in what might have been a too fond idolatry'. Selina, apparently, had threatened to cease seeing him: 'The menace of perpetual estrangement seemed a severe punishment for what might have been a weakness, but scarcely an unpardonable one'. In his hurt pride he reverted to a phrase very similar to one which he had used in his ultimatum to Mary Anne thirty-five years before, 'I awake from a dream of baffled sympathy and pour forth my feelings, however precious, like water from a golden goblet on the sand'.[15]

Selina may have blown hot and then cold upon her admirer's ardour, but both of them must have known that the threat of 'perpetual estrangement' was an empty one. Selina, who was out of town, responded to Disraeli's wounded appeal with a cautious suggestion that he should call on her daughter-in-law, Ida, Lady Newport, who was staying at Belgrave Square. Disraeli hurried round thinking, he told Selina, that all was over between them, 'I wished to show you ... that there was not bitterness in my heart, but deep grief.' Ida Newport, whom Disraeli was wont to call 'the dear little ortolan', was out, but Disraeli, in his relief at the proffered olive branch, wrote Selina a wily letter, delicately reminding her of the greatness of his present position. The Prince of Wales had been with him all morning to discuss 'difficult and delicate affairs', then there had been the question of settling the Address to the Queen, and a long Cabinet, followed by his official banquet: 'Mine was most successful ... I gave Gunter *carte blanche*, & he deserved it ... Baroness Rothschild sent me six large baskets of English strawberries, 200 head of gigantic Parisian *asperges*, and the largest & finest Strasburg *foie gras* that ever was seen'.

Skilfully he changed his tone, inserting a romantic element, 'I thought at dinner how much I should like to give a certain person a banquet in this room, which is a fine room built, I believe by Sir Christopher Wren, and then I thought perhaps I shall never see her again, or worse than never seeing her, meeting with alienated glance'.[16] Arriving home late, he received his reward, 'I found a letter which took a load off my heart, and I pressed it often to my lips.' Meetings of reconciliation were then in prospect; Anne Chesterfield asked him to spend Easter at Bretby with the Bradfords among the party and, more delightful still, Bradford accepted his invitation to spend Whitsun at Hughenden. Disraeli was ecstatic; 'Lord and Lady Bradford will be the nucleus of the party wh: must not be a large one. There ought to be at least one dame for you, & also to amuse my lord ... the next should be agreeable men – I thought of Pembroke, Ronald Gower, Orford'.[17] One may wonder if Disraeli remembered his unkind comment upon another elder statesman in a similiar situation – 'I have seen Metternich in love ... I thought it absurd'.[18]

'I live for power and the affections', Disraeli wrote to Selina.[19] For the first time opposition to his leadership within the party was generally stilled; even Salisbury, reported by Carnarvon as softening towards him, joined the Cabinet. He now also enjoyed a following among the younger MPs, men in their twenties like Lord George Hamilton, son of the Duke of Abercorn, an able young man upon whom Disraeli came to rely both as an official and a friend. The younger men, Hamilton recorded, were attracted to Disraeli because, old as he was, he seemed to have 'a juvenility and expansion in his ideas and policy' which held out more hope for the future than the narrow beliefs of the middle-aged 'ultra-Tories'. Disraeli, he said, would encourage the young men of the party to talk to him in the lobby during divisions as he stood with his back to the fire chatting and eagerly picking up gossip.[20]

Disraeli enjoyed the trappings of power, the delights of patronage in particular, as he wrote to Selina:

> After all, it is affectation to talk of the bore and bother of patronage and all that. The sense of power is delightful. It is amusing to receive the letters I do ... I had no idea I was the object of so much esteem; and as nobody in the world, were I to die tomorrow, would give up even a dinner party, one is sensible of the form of life.[21]

He relished bestowing high-sounding posts in the Royal Household upon historic names, as he wrote to the Queen in a phrase which might have been taken from *Coningsby*; 'Mr. Disraeli thinks it of importance that the high nobility should be encouraged to cluster round the throne.' He had even created his own duke, Abercorn, whom he appointed Lord Lieutenant of Ireland. He wrote to Selina of Abercorn:

> No one amuses me so much, such simplicity & winning naturalness of manner, blended with such absorbing vanity. He has one master idea – good-looking people, & of all good-looking people has no doubt who is pre-eminent. He came to me yesterday to talk over the government of Ireland: I soon found the only idea in his head was his own triumphal entry into Dublin and his fear lest Punchestown races might mar its effect.

He recalled with glee how Abercorn had said to Lord Mayo, 'What a wonderful fellow Dissy is! . . . he arranges his hair so well'.[22]

His Cabinet was an able one, and contained one middle-class politician, Richard Cross, a portent for the future. The list was as follows:

Disraeli	First Lord of the Treasury
Lord Cairns	Lord Chancellor
Duke of Richmond	Lord President and Leader of the House of Lords
Lord Derby	Foreign Office
Lord Salisbury	India Office
Lord Carnarvon	Colonial Office
Lord Malmesbury	Lord Privy Seal
Sir Stafford Northcote	Chancellor of the Exchequer
Gathorne-Hardy	War Office
Richard Cross	Home Office
Lord John Manners	Postmaster-General

'Dear Henry' Lennox, Disraeli's constant companion in the absence of Monty, was offered and accepted the Board of Works but, deeply offended at not being in the Cabinet, went round the clubs saying venomous things about his 'dear Dis'. The Queen, however, was pleased, writing somewhat defensively to the Crown Princess: 'Instead of being a Government of Dukes as you imagined it will contain only one, and he a very sensible, honest and highly respected one. The others are all distinguished and able men – not at any rate retrograde, but still not bent on changing everything which was most alarming and had alarmed the country.'[23]

Disraeli agreed with the Queen; indeed, having come into office he seemed to have little idea what should be done beyond rewarding his supporters and 'not alarming the country'. Richard Cross, the middle-class administrator, was appalled by the Prime Minister's apparent lack of interest in formulating legislation and its attendant detail:

> When the Cabinet came to discuss the Queen's speech, I was, I confess, disappointed at the want of originality shown by the Prime Minister. From all his speeches, I had quite expected that his mind was full of legislative schemes, but such did not prove to be the case; on the contrary, he had to entirely rely on the various suggestions of his colleagues, and as they themselves had only just come into office, and that suddenly, there was some difficulty in framing the Queen's Speech.[24]

Given Disraeli's lack of a programme beyond a vague desire to soothe the country, the main legislation of the 1874 session was cautiously designed to please. The Budget, hastily put together by Stafford Northcote with Disraeli's approval, included the repeal of the sugar duties which, in Disraeli's opinion would 'satisfy the free traders and the democracy', although only a penny was taken off the income tax as a gesture to the middle class, despite Disraeli's election pledge to abolish it. Bills shortening the hours of work in factories and lengthening the hours of drinking pleased the working class and the licensing and victualling trade which had opposed Gladstone.

The only controversial measure of the session, the Public Worship Regulation Bill, was foisted upon Disraeli by the Archbishop of Canterbury, supported by the Queen. Designed to curb the ritualist excesses of the High Church party, and to enable the hierarchy to discipline unorthodox clergy, it caused the usual bitter religious explosion or 'ecclesiastical mess' as Derby termed it. The Bill cut across party lines, with both Gladstone and Salisbury opposing it; and while the Liberal Sir William Harcourt bitterly attacked his leader, Disraeli turned on his colleague Salisbury, describing him as 'a master of jibes and flouts and jeers'. Disraeli, disliking High Church ritualism as much as he did Low Church attitudes, would have preferred not to legislate on so controversial a subject, but was driven on by the Queen who pestered him with telegrams. 'Pray show that you are in earnest and determined to pass this Bill and not to be deterred by threats of delay', she ordered from Windsor on 13 July. Disraeli persevered, despite thunderous intervention from Gladstone and stinging speeches by Salisbury, and the Bill finally passed into law at the end of the session.

The Queen's support, undoubtedly a source of strength to Disraeli, was thus not without its difficulties. Indeed she gave him a great deal of trouble. Encouraged by his deference to her wishes, she became increasingly demanding, bombarding him daily with letters and telegrams on any subject which happened to possess her mind at the moment, from the Public Worship Bill to protests against vivisection and the culling of young seals. Two of her ladies had jewellery stolen, and the Queen took it as a personal affront. 'Two of my ladies!' she exploded to Disraeli. 'The police must be very inefficient. It is a disgrace to the Country!'[25] Disraeli found it endearing and the Queen's mode of expression delightfully artless, but it was also time-consuming. 'The Court is a department in itself', he complained to Selina.[26]

As Prime Minister he became increasingly involved in the often troubled relationship between the Queen and the Prince of Wales, acting as mediator between the Palace and Marlborough House. Disraeli liked the genial 'Prince Hal' as he and his colleagues were wont to refer to him, but he trusted neither his judgement nor his discretion and disapproved of his intimates, describing them as 'the Prince's parasites' or 'the Marlborough club banditti'. There were awkwardnesses between Prince and Prime Minister when 'Hal' who was unable to refuse anybody anything, personally passed on requests from his cronies for official positions for which they were utterly unfit. Disraeli, embarrassed, felt obliged to refuse, complaining to Selina on 23 May 1875: 'It is a curious thing but there has not been a place ... in my gift that HRH has not asked me for one of his friends – and always the most unqualified candidates. But because the Prince is good-natured, I must not be silly.'[27]

The Prince's inability to refuse his friends favours was, in Disraeli's eyes, less serious than his lack of discretion. Ponsonby thought Disraeli, always secretive and wary, overestimated the danger and was 'rather too much afraid of imaginary bogies at Marlborough House'; and the Prince was offended by the Prime Minister's refusal to let him see the most sensitive papers, particularly those relating to foreign affairs. Disraeli defended himself to the Queen on the grounds that the Prince 'lets them out and talks to his friends about them', but the Prince was frequently mortified to find that he only learned about important developments in British foreign policy when he read of them in the newspapers. In the following year, 1875, the Prince was justifiably furious when Disraeli, for fear of the gossips at Marlborough House, neglected to inform him in advance of the controversial Royal Titles Bill. The Prince was on his travels at the time, and Disraeli's excuse in reply to his remonstrance 'that he did not know his address', was transparently ingenuous.

Disraeli's passion for Selina continued its turbulent way; a cold look at a ball or a reproving letter was enough to throw him into a paroxysm of despair, and rows were followed by promises of calmer behaviour, usually quickly broken. His public life, in contrast, was glittering and relatively serene. The session of 1874, the Public Worship battles apart, had been a relatively easy one for the Government. The Liberal party were in disarray after their crushing defeat, and Gladstone was sulking, while the party's most formidable speaker in the Commons, the brilliant, caustic Harcourt, was antagonistic towards his chief and amiable towards his friend Dizzy.

The Queen too was relatively amenable; Disraeli scored a personal triumph in persuading her to postpone her departure for Osborne in order to welcome the Tsar in May. 'My head is still on my shoulders' he boasted to Selina on 5 May. 'Everybody had failed even the Prince of Wales . . . Salisbury says I have averted an Afghan war.'[28] He attended all the festivities in honour of the Russian Emperor and had a personal interview with him at Buckingham Palace on 15 May, when he was struck by the sadness of the Emperor's expression: 'Whether it is satiety, or the loneliness of despotism, or the fear of violent death, I know not', he told Anne Chesterfield. The season was exceptionally brilliant and costume balls the rage. The Prince of Wales gave a 'gorgeous, brilliant, fantastic' costume ball at which only Disraeli, with the Prince's special permission, and the Commander-in-Chief, the Duke of Cambridge, were allowed to appear in official as opposed to fancy dress. 'Really I don't think Commanders-in-Chief and Prime Ministers ought to figure in Charles the 2nd wigs and false mustachios', Disraeli commented. In June he took the initiative in arranging Government funds for the National Gallery to buy the celebrated Barker collection of Old Master paintings, visiting Christie's to view the pictures and holding secret meetings with Burton, the Gallery's director. 'We must be very silent until Saturday, as I don't want any one to know the Government is a purchaser', he told Selina, adding in mock-dramatic manner that he believed it would end in the Commons repudiating his purchase – 'I shall have to appeal to Rothschild, Lord Bradford and some other great friends to take the treasures off my hands and relieve me by a raffle, from my aesthetical embarrassments'.[29] The Commons did not object to the purchase and the National Gallery acquired twelve of the Barker Old Masters, including two Botticellis, three Pinturicchios and the Piero della Francesca *Nativity* for a total of 10,670 guineas.

The close of the parliamentary session kept Disraeli in London until the end of the first week in August. The town was emptying, and Ladies Bradford and Chesterfield had retired to their country houses. Tired, lonely and dispirited, his habitual melancholy came to the fore. 'My mind is greatly disturbed and dissatisfied', he wrote wretchedly to Selina. 'I require perfect solitude or perfect sympathy. My present life gives me neither of these ineffable blessings. It may be brilliant but it is too fragmentary . . . It gives me neither the highest development of the intellect or the heart. Neither Poetry nor Love'.[30] He was dreaming of writing again, of continuing his last novel, *Endymion*, which was already half-finished, living in his imagination with Selina at Hughenden as he had lived with Mary Anne – 'writing in the early hours of morn, passing my day in wood rambles with you or drives to ancient heaths – & in the evening reading to you my mature labours, & profiting by the criticism of your quick wit & taste. Dreams of impossible . . . yet ineffable bliss!'[31]

Disraeli, however, had no time for writing; August and September were to be taken up with visits to the Queen and to the great country houses. At Osborne the 'Faery' received him with such affectionate delight that he thought she was going to embrace him; wreathed in smiles, she glided about the room 'like a bird' as she talked. As a signal mark of favour she insisted on his taking a chair, 'Only think of that!' Disraeli told Selina proudly on 7 August. 'I remember Lord Derby, after one of his illnesses, had an audience of her Majesty, and he mentioned it to me as proof of the Queen's favor, that her Majesty had remarked to him how sorry she was she could not ask him to be seated, the etiquette was so severe.'[32] During his brief visit to the Isle of Wight Disraeli saw the beautiful, ill-starred Empress Elizabeth of Austria, but, despite her wonderful hair and statuesque figure, he was not altogether impressed, writing unkindly to Selina that she had very bad teeth. She was, he said, so painfully conscious of this defect that she scarcely opened her mouth when speaking which, he said, she rarely did 'either from want of ideas in which she certainly does not abound, or for fear of compromising her reputation for beauty by the physical revelations attending her conversation'. He was much struck by her extreme superstitiousness; if a hair of her head fell to the floor while it was being combed, she regarded it as an evil omen and would retire from society for a day or longer. In short, Disraeli commented, she was very like her mad cousin Ludwig of Bavaria.[33]

From Osborne, he went on to stay with Lord Bath at Longleat, an invitation which he had accepted long ago in the hope of seeing Selina there, but she could not come and he fell into deep gloom. 'I am wearied to extinction and profoundly unhappy', he wrote. As usual when he found nothing to interest him, he was himself uninteresting; Lord Bath, never prejudiced in Disraeli's favour, said he was the dullest guest who had ever stayed at Longleat.[34] His only amusement there was to watch Lords Bath and Malmesbury competing for the favours of the seductive Walburga, Lady Paget, the German wife of the diplomat Sir Augustus Paget, and a great favourite at Court where she was known as 'Wally'. 'Wally' Paget tried her charms on Disraeli also; he described to Selina 'her matchless conversation, consisting of high art and Court scandal [which] receives additional lustre from her undulating figure, the profusion of her cinque-cent jewels, her renaissance hands and her Luini-like eyes'. Lord Bath, he wrote on 11 August, was completely besotted by her and had quite cut out the wretched Malmesbury, while the long-suffering Lady Bath, the only person at Longleat whom Disraeli liked, sat every morning for her portrait to 'Lady P[aget]'.[35] Escaping from Longleat, he went to Fonthill, stopping on his way in the little village of Hindon, which had been briefly the centre of his parliamentary hopes over forty years before. In 1830 before the Reform Bill, he told Selina, the hamlet had returned two MPs and he had hoped to secure the nomination to one of the seats at a cost of £1,000 a year. 'I was so disgusted I went abroad', he told her, recalling the vivid pangs of disappointment he had felt at 'not representing these Cottages in the House of Commons'.[36]

Back in London on 14 August, *en route* for Anne Chesterfield's house, Bretby,

Disraeli was at his most melancholy. 'Fortune, fashion, fame even power may increase & do heighten happiness but they cannot create it. Happiness can only spring from the affections', he told Selina. 'It is a terrible lot, almost intolerable. Nothing but the pressure of public affairs keeps me straight'.[37] He felt calmer in radiant weather at Bretby, but bored with the monotony of country house life and the routine of walks with his hostess in the mornings, drives in the afternoon and endless cards in the evenings when he was apt to commit the social crime of revoking at whist. His mercurial feelings were, however, restored by a brief visit to the Bradfords' house at St Catherine's on Lake Windermere, strengthening him for his official visit to Balmoral.

At Balmoral, the 'Faery' was more than kind, opening her heart to him on all subjects and showing him her most secret and interesting correspondence, but within three days of his arrival he was ill, confined to bed with a mustard poultice on his back. Jenner seemed optimistic, but Derby, who came over from his house at Abergeldie to see Disraeli, told him he had been overdoing things and must at all costs cancel a visit to Ireland projected by Abercorn. Derby was right; a ferocious attack of gout when he returned to Bretby on 19 September put paid to any idea of visiting Ireland. Disraeli dosed himself with colchicum and the remedies which his man, Baum, always carried with him, but the attack was severe; at dinner he thought he was going to fall from his chair from weakness and had to be carried upstairs.

In fact Disraeli's health had broken down under the strains of office and social life combined. When someone congratulated him on his success in becoming Premier, he replied sadly, 'Yes, but it has come too late'. He was right; Disraeli in 1874, despite his indomitable spirit, was no longer physically the man he had been when last in office. He suffered from gout, bronchitis, asthma and later on kidney disease, and his bouts of ill-health affected his capacity to operate as Prime Minister.

In London that November he was frequently so unwell that the Cabinet meetings had to be held at his house, and rumour had it that his health was so bad he would soon retire. 'I fear the great Dizzy is very shaky and that his illness has been very serious', Harcourt wrote to Sir Charles Dilke on 4 November. 'I doubt if we shall see or hear much more of him'.[38] Nonetheless the Cabinets went smoothly, so that Disraeli could write proudly, 'I never knew a body of men more united and better drilled.' Although Cross may have complained of the Prime Minister's neglect of detail, Carnarvon wrote admiringly in his journal of Disraeli's breadth of vision and ability to see straight to the core of a question. 'He never worries or intrigues unnecessarily', he added.[39] Nonetheless, Carnarvon reported, beneath the united surface of the Cabinet there was an undercurrent of intrigue, born of the supposition that Disraeli's days as leader were numbered.[40] Derby as usual was the prime candidate for leader; as early as February Salisbury had reported that Derby and his wife had by no means given up thoughts of the leadership, and Disraeli's protracted illness must have inspired them with fresh hope. If Disraeli was aware of this he made no mention of it in his correspondence; his only reference to Derby in his letters to Selina being to report that he had a heavy cold and never ceased blowing his nose during Cabinets, 'literally snorting like a hippopotamus'.

When the Cabinets were over, at the instigation of the Queen and Jenner he retreated to newly-fashionable Bournemouth to take the sea air. He occupied a suite of rooms on the first floor of the Bath Hotel, but although the staff made every effort to make him comfortable, he was bored and cross, his letters to Selina a string of complaints. 'I detest this place, it is a large overgrown watering-place, almost as bad as Torquay', he wrote on 6 December, grumbling about the 'total absence of all comfort and convenience in my hotel, and the frightful food they furnish'.[41] He might just as well have stayed in London but for the fogs, he said, as he took very little of the Bournemouth air, walking on the cliffs in the morning, leaning on Monty's arm and then retiring to bed. Friends did what they could to alleviate his life, besieging him with recommendations for local doctors – 'I thought I had come here to get rid of Doctors', Disraeli wrote tartly, 'or at least we might have them down from London, as we do our fish.' Lord Cairns offered him his newly-built mansion but Disraeli, driving past it, found it apparently unfinished: 'What an Irish invitation', he sniffed. Angela Burdett-Coutts, created a Baroness by the Queen for her philanthropic activity, wrote inviting him to stay with her in her new house at Torquay. 'Being nursed by the Baroness and Mrs Brown [her companion] would, I think turn my head' he commented.[42] He liked to tease Selina by reporting approaches made to him by the 'romantic Baroness', and even, in one letter hinted that he might have married her – 'perhaps I wouldn't have been so unhappy as I am now'. Friends sent him delicacies, pheasants came from the Prince of Wales and a weekly hamper from the Gunnersbury Rothschilds. When the Queen who 'writes me the prettiest notes' despatched Ponsonby from Osborne in her yacht to reconnoitre her Prime Minister's health, Disraeli and Monty were thus able to give him a good dinner – 'soups & quenelles, & a Foie-gras pie from Rothschild, fat pheasant from the Duke of Richmond, teal & widgeon from Malmesbury, and golden grapes from Bretby.'[43]

The monotony of his Bournemouth life was disturbed by minor irritations; Harry Lennox was causing trouble again. Disraeli wrote to Selina that he had had to address a 'terrible Dispatch' to him and that he 'terribly distresses me.' Two days later it was still not settled, 'He is an eel, but I do not think he will escape my grasp, which can be firm'.[44] The Henry Lennox affair or 'scrape' as Disraeli described it, dragged on into the early months of 1875. Disraeli it seems lost patience and intended to sack him from his job as Commissioner of Works, but kind-hearted and loyal as he was, found himself moved by 'dear Henry's' pleas: 'He threw himself on his knees & went into hysterics! What can I do with such a man if he be one?'[45]

There were also small satisfactions; the Queen bestowed a pension of £50 a year on the D'Israelis' former cook, the widow of Tita, whom Disraeli proudly described to Selina as 'Lord Byron's faithful servant & once mine.' And, with his contempt for literary men, it must have given him a wry amusement to offer, at Lady Derby's suggestion, a baronetcy to Tennyson and a GCB and pension to Carlyle. Both refused the honours but Carlyle was momentarily embarrassed at receiving such an offer from the man he habitually and bitterly abused. 'He is the only man I almost never spoke of except with contempt', he told John Carlyle, '... and yet here he comes with a pan of hot coals for my guilty head'. His guilt was short-lived; a few years later he reverted to his old habits, referring to Disraeli as 'a cursed old Jew, not worth his weight in cold bacon'. Disraeli, with his long experience of the hatred of the literary establishment, was no doubt not in the least surprised.

Despite ill-health and emotional turmoil, the first year of his Premiership had been, as he told Selina, a 'wondrous 12 months'. 'I have at least had my dream,' he wrote, '& if my shattered energies never rally ... I have, at any rate, reached the pinnacle of power & gauged the sweetest & deepest affections of ye heart.'[46]

21 *To the Elysian Fields*

As the new year of 1875 opened, Disraeli recovered health and spirits. He antici-pated with pleasure the new session for which the Government had prepared a major programme of social legislation, a pleasure heightened by Gladstone's announcement, on the eve of the session, of his decision to retire from the Liberal leadership.

Disraeli was delighted: 'Never was a man in a prouder position than myself', he wrote to Selina on 2 February. 'Only those who are acquainted with the malignity of Gladstone through a rivalship of five and twenty years, can under-stand this'.[1] Moreover, the new Liberal leader, the Marquess of Hartington, heir to the Duke of Devonshire, was, although intelligent and capable, hardly of Gladstone's political calibre. Familiarly known as 'Harty-Tarty', he was devoted to racing and cards, and was the assiduous lover of the glamorous Louise, Duchess of Manchester, the intimate friend of the Prince of Wales and an arbiter of London society. Disraeli liked Hartington and sympathized with his love for Louise, but he could not refrain from reporting gleefully to Selina a conversation between the new Liberal leader and the Austrian ambassador. ' "I said to Hartington", the ambassador reported, "what with whist, the turf, &, what I delicately called 'morning visits' [to the Duchess], I wonder how you can find time for politics". "I wonder too," replied Harty.'[2]

The Government's programme of social reform was the most far-reaching yet undertaken by any government during the nineteenth century. Eight major Bills were to be put forward designed to satisfy the needs and demands of the working class. The legislation was the responsibility of the Home Secretary, Richard Cross, encouraged and protected by Disraeli who, by his own account, was the only member of Cabinet who had supported Cross's proposed labour laws, which went beyond the recommendations of the Royal Commission appointed the previous year. The two Bills, the Employers and Workmen Bill and the Conspiracy and Protection of Property Bill, by removing the threat of prosecution for breach of contract against workmen who went on strike, represented a major advance in trade union freedom.[3] Disraeli was fully conscious of their importance as far as the party was concerned; he described the labour law as 'one of those measures which root and consolidate a party', although he was somewhat over-optimistic in his claims that the legislation would 'gain and retain for the Tories the lasting affection of the working classes'.[4]

Disraeli had always stressed the importance of improving working-class housing; the previous year he had attended the inauguration of Shaftesbury Park, a working class estate in Lambeth, the brainchild of Lord Shaftesbury, and found it 'an astonishing spectacle' which, he thought 'may change England more than all the Reform Bills – change it always for the better.'[5] For him, therefore, the chief measure of the session was the Artizans Dwelling Bill which empowered municipal authorities to designate for improvement areas where conditions were certified as unhealthy by a health official and to buy the land for the provision of working-class housing with cheap loans provided by the Public Works Loan Commissioners.

Other welfare measures of the session were the Pollution of Rivers Bill, which was defeated, the Sale of Food and Drugs Bill, a Bill for the regulation of the Friendly Societies, and lastly, the controversial Merchant Shipping Bill, which brought the Government into confrontation with the seamen's hero, Samuel Plimsoll. The Government Bill, drawn up by the President of the Board of Trade, C.F. Adderley, on the advice of the permanent officials, was mismanaged by him in the Commons and its provisions offended both seamen and shipowners alike. It had a rough passage through Parliament until Disraeli, on Northcote's advice, announced its postponement, provoking an outburst from Plimsoll who shouted that he would unmask the villains who sent seamen to their graves, shook his fist at Disraeli and, defying the Speaker, charged out of the House. Public feeling ran high and was not assuaged by a compromise Bill introduced by the incompetent Adderley which eventually passed in August, after considerable Government concessions. Disraeli was forced to admit to Anne Chesterfield that it had been very much touch and go, and that if the Opposition had realized the weakness of his support, they could have substituted a bill of their own.

Indeed, *The Times*, the Opposition and some of his own followers considered that Disraeli had been less than competent in his conduct of parliamentary business. Questions of privilege concerning Dr Kenealy, the counsel for the Tichborne claimant and John Mitchel, an Irish felon, had disrupted business, while a mass Tory desertion to Ascot in June cost the Government a division on a Liberal resolution on compulsory education. Disraeli, characteristically, attributed all the difficulties to a concerted plan on the part of the Opposition – 'not Harty-Tarty – but then he is always at Newmarket, or somewhere,' – to waste time, hold up the Government measures and then blame them for getting nothing done.[6] It is difficult to say whether Opposition charges against Disraeli of parliamentary incompetence had any foundation; he was certainly seized by bouts of illness during the spring and summer, to the extent that, according to Carnarvon, there were renewed secret discussions speculating on his retirement and replacement by Derby in July. Any government, however, which succeeds in passing the quantity of major legislation which Disraeli's did in the summer of 1875 can hardly be said to have been failing.

The social reform legislation of 1875 was to be Disraeli's last real attempt to redeem his pledges to the working class given at Manchester and the Crystal Palace in 1872, but it represented a not inconsiderable achievement. He had not been responsible for putting forward the specific measures as is all too evident from his vague remark to Salisbury in November 1874, 'I believe the Secretary [Cross] is working on a Dwelling Bill', but if he was not concerned with the detail of the legislation he was sympathetic to its spirit. His earlier speeches had provided the climate in which such legislation could be put forward and he had used his authority as Prime Minister to support it. Although limited in scope and pragmatic in its motivation, the reform legislation of 1875 could at least provide some concrete justification for the 'one nation' ideal which was to inspire high-minded Conservative politicians in the future. It was Disraeli's last blow in his long-running battle with the political economists, a battle that he had waged, with lessening vigour it must be admitted, since *Popanilla* in 1828. After 1875 Disraeli's imagination, which was both his strength and his driving force, was to be increasingly directed away from the condition of the people towards foreign and imperial politics.

Disraeli made his first essay into European politics in the early summer of 1875. He was determined to play a Palmerstonian, interventionist role and to reassert England's influence abroad. He was faced with two major difficulties: firstly, that since the Gladstone era, Britain was isolated and the affairs of Europe were regulated by the *Dreikaiserbund*, the alliance of Germany, Russia and Austria; and secondly, he was saddled with the over-cautious Derby who has been described by A.J.P. Taylor as 'the most isolationist Foreign Secretary Great Britain has ever known'. Much of his time was spent prodding Derby into action on the one hand, and making excuses for him with the fiercely interventionist Queen on the other. Nonetheless in May 1875 he scored his first success, co-operating with Russia to force Bismarck to back down over what had threatened to be a German attack on France. Bismarck, putting a brave face on the affair, sent a congratulatory message, 'thanking us for our interference, and glad to see England taking an interest in continental affairs again', as Disraeli proudly told Selina. 'I believe,' he added, 'since Pam, we have never been so energetic, and in a year's time we shall be more.'[7]

While Bismarck disturbed the peace of Europe by, in Disraeli's words, 'playing the old Bonaparte', at home the 'Court department' was giving more than its usual share of trouble. The Prince of Wales had set his heart on a visit to India at Government expense, a project to which his mother strenuously objected. The Prince with considerable cunning and some bending of the truth succeeded in obtaining the Queen's reluctant assent by representing to her that his scheme had ministerial approval. Disraeli, summoned to Windsor after Easter, found himself the man in the middle, greatly bothered by the Princess of Wales who was determined to accompany her husband, and the Queen who was equally determined she should not. 'Court wearies one', Disraeli complained to Selina, 'so many persons wanting something & so many contrary objects – & all come to me', adding, in a revealing phrase, 'Naturally one must pay for being a Grand Vizier'.[8]

The Prince's project involved endless complications; a compromise was eventually reached over the question of the Princess of Wales who was to be allowed to visit her parents in Denmark while her husband was away, but the financing of the Prince's trip was not so easily settled. 'Where is the money to come from?' Disraeli wrote despairingly to Salisbury on his return from Windsor. 'He has not a shilling: she will not give him one.'[9] The Queen expected Disraeli to manage the affair and induce Parliament to vote enough money to enable her son to visit India 'on an imperial scale', no easy task.

The Prince suspected the Government of parsimony for which he blamed Disraeli, saying in public to Monty Corry after he had enjoyed a winning week at Ascot, 'Tell the Prime Minister I have had a good week of it, & it will not be necessary, this session, to come down for a vote to pay for the Prince of Wales'. 'This quite loud before all the servants', Disraeli commented.[10] Disraeli obtained a vote of expenses for the Prince, but was thoroughly disgusted by the behaviour of the Prince's 'thoughtless parasites' among whom he included the Marquess of Blandford and his brother, Lord Randolph Churchill, who in a letter to *The Times* put forward a more grandiose and expensive itinerary than that agreed upon by the Government, and accused Disraeli of treating the Prince shabbily over the matter. The Duke of Sutherland, another Marlborough House crony, attempted to stir up trouble by saying to the Prince, ' "What a shabby concern this vote is! If I were you, Sir, I would not take it. I would borrow the money off some friends at five per cent". "Well, will you lend it me?" said the Prince, who shut the Duke up', Disraeli reported gleefully on 19 July.[11]

There was even more difficulty over the Prince's companions on the trip. The Government suspected that the primary object of 'Hal's' Indian odyssey was amusement, and tiger-shooting in particular, an assumption confirmed by the Prince's choice of companions for the expedition. They included such boon companions as Charley Carrington, Charley Beresford, and 'Sporting Joe' Aylesford whose after-dinner speciality was crawling around the room on all fours while the Prince and his guests whacked him boisterously on the behind. The Queen, naturally and understandably, objected and the Prince expected Disraeli to persuade her. Prince and Prime Minister had a stormy interview at Downing Street on the subject; the Prince, probably prompted by his cronies, was resentful and suspicious of Disraeli, offended that the Queen had ordered all questions concerning the trip to be referred first to Salisbury and Disraeli instead of being directly discussed with her, and probably a little jealous of Disraeli's influence with his mother. This was unfair; Disraeli, probably against his better judgement, succeeded in persuading the Queen to consent to the Prince's choice of companions, 'The Faery had yielded – even to Charley Beresford. Salisbury said to-day he thought it the greatest of my triumphs', he boasted to Selina on 12 June. In fact Disraeli did his best to smooth the Prince's path even at the risk of incurring the Queen's displeasure. When the Queen adamantly refused to allow the Prince to hold an investiture of the Star of India while there, Disraeli again had to intervene. The Queen replied, 'As you recommend me to do it, I consent, but I don't like it.' 'This is not pleasant', Disraeli commented.

As a gesture of reconciliation the Prince, 'the most amiable of mortals' as Disraeli described him to Anne Chesterfield, invited him to Sandringham in October for a last visit before his departure later that month. Dutifully but gloomily, Disraeli accepted. 'It is a dull house – for me', he told Selina. He disliked the boisterous horseplay which was the rule in the Prince's household and the company was not to his taste. There were very few ladies, and, apart from the ageing wits, Quin and Bernal Osborne, he grumbled, 'a strong brigade of the dark sex: buffoons & butts & parasites & swash-bucklers ... & Sykes & Co., & nameless toadies in the shape of mysterious Polish Counts picked up at Roulette Baths'.[12] The mysterious Polish Count was a good-looking young man named Miecislas Jaraczewski whom the Prince had met on the Riviera; nicknamed 'Sherry and Whisker', he was a favourite at Marlborough House until in March 1881 he committed suicide to avoid arrest for debt. Chief among the 'buffoons & butts' was Christopher Sykes who was later to bankrupt himself amusing 'Hal'; the royal children were encouraged to crawl under the damask-covered table during luncheon and pinch his legs, and on one occasion to Disraeli's pained surprise, mistook his legs for Sykes's.

Disraeli was in critical mood, his temper not improved by discovering how the public money for the Prince's expenses was being spent. He had a low opinion of Sir Bartle Frere, Master of the Prince's Household, a man who was to cause him a great deal of embarrassment in the latter years of his administration. Frere, he complained, was a most incompetent adviser in money matters and had allowed the Prince to allot no less than £300 to each member of his suite, including the phenomenally rich Duke of Sutherland, to buy themselves cotton underclothes for India. Lord Alfred Paget had immediately spent his 'lingerie' allowance on an expensive dressing-case, saying delightedly, Disraeli recorded with disgust, that 'it was the first dressing case he had ever had in his life!' Paget, Disraeli said, had only been invited because he had bored the Prince into asking him. 'He cannot say "No" – or as I would put it Bo – to a goose!' Disraeli lamented. 'This is the weak part of a character, not by any means deficient in intelligence or knowledge of men'.[13] Perhaps the Prince, who was sensitive in personal relations, felt Disraeli's disapproval; he seems to have found it easier to get on with Gladstone, always eager to promote him in public affairs and who, not being favoured by the Queen, could, in contrast to Disraeli, be considered to be on the Prince's side.

On 11 October the Prince took a sad farewell of his wife whom, as Disraeli said, 'he truly loves' and embarked on the Indian expedition. It was to prove a spectacular success in terms of loyal demonstrations, gifts of jewels to the Crown and bags of dead elephants and tigers but, within less than six months, it was to give rise to one of the most difficult social scandals to confront Disraeli in his term of office.

A further royal imbroglio disturbed the peace of Disraeli's autumn retreat to Hughenden. On 18 August the Royal yacht *Alberta*, *en route* from Osborne to Portsmouth with the Queen, Prince Leopold and Princess Beatrice aboard, collided with a private yacht, the *Mistletoe*, which sank within minutes with the loss of two lives. The Queen, naturally upset by the disaster, was furious when, following the coroner's report, the Admiralty censured Captain Welch, commanding officer of the *Alberta*. Disraeli had to soothe her and to explain the realities of the situation. 'She cannot understand that Captain Welsh [sic] is not merely her servant, but also an officer in the British Navy who receives his pay and appointments from the House of Commons', he told Selina. 'Although you say I spoil her, it has fallen to my lot to tell her these grave truths; but how they will be borne I do not know. Very badly I suspect.'[14]

At Hughenden that autumn he passed his time arranging the portraits of his friends, 'the history of my life' as he called them. He always got up at 7.30 am, checked through his correspondence, then, if it was a fine day, after dressing walked on the terrace reviewing his peacocks, and then worked in his study on his correspondence until one o'clock. After half an hour for a light lunch, he worked on his official boxes in his favourite room, the library, enjoying the sunbeams playing on the bindings of his books. Since Mary Anne's death he had become a collector of rare books, chiefly of the Renaissance, which he bought through Bernard Quaritch. The pride of his collection was Francesco Colonna's *Hypnerotomachia* which he referred to as the *Somnium Poliphili*, describing it to Selina as 'one of the most beautiful volumes in the world'. He also kept a set of Aldine editions locked in a black wooden cabinet decorated with nineteenth-century Dresden plaques, much admired by the Queen when she visited Hughenden the following year. Disraeli was particularly attracted to the Renaissance which he called 'the sacred time'; one of his treasures was a volume with a binding stamped with the arms of the Medici Pope, Clement vii, which he liked to think had been taken in the sack of Rome by the Constable of Bourbon.

The chief event that autumn at Hughenden was the reconsecration of the church which had been rebuilt at Disraeli's expense. Fearing that the vicar, Mr Blagden, and the Bishop of Oxford, a High Church appointment of Gladstone's, would make it into an occasion of excessive ritual, he appealed to his friend, Harcourt, for support. 'I hear there is to be a procession of stoled priests, of great length', he told him. 'I must have some of the reformed faith present to keep me countenance'.[15] Harcourt replied in a letter of the most affectionate friendship that he would be ready and willing 'to do battle by your side in the good cause, and if need be to shy a stool at the mass-mongers'. True to his word, he was there on 28 September to help Disraeli confront what he described as a 'tremendous sacerdotal procession of nearer 100 than 50 clergymen in surplices and parti-coloured scarves.' Defiantly Disraeli made a very Protestant speech by way of protest.

Further from home, events during the late summer and autumn of 1875 turned Disraeli's attention to the East, a direction in which it was almost exclusively to remain for the remainder of his premiership. In July revolt broke out in the Turkish province of Bosnia, a small and apparently insignificant spark which was to re-ignite the century-old Eastern Question, the issue of the Turkish Empire in Europe. Disraeli's first reaction was dismissive. It was, he wrote to Selina on 20 August, nothing serious, merely something got up by the newspapers to compensate for the dearth of news in the Parliamentary vacation. But the revolt rumbled on amid the usual reports of Turkish atrocities against rebellious Christians, while in October the Sultan's government, the Porte, complicated the situation by repudiating its financial obligations. In his speech at the Lord Mayor's Banquet at the Guildhall in November, Disraeli made it clear that the British Government intended to play an active role in the Eastern Question. 'I really believe "the Eastern Question" that has haunted Europe for a century, and wh: I thought the Crimean War had adjourned for half another, will fall to my lot to encounter – dare I say to settle', he wrote to Selina on 23 November.

As the shadow of Russia hovered over Constantinople where the Tsar's Machiavellian ambassador, General Ignatiev, played a complex game of intrigue against the British envoy, Sir Henry Elliot, Disraeli and Salisbury also became increasingly concerned over Russian ambitions in Central Asia. There the strategic prize was the establishment of a sphere of influence in Afghanistan, regarded as the key to India. India, with the glamour of its ancient civilizations, had always fascinated Disraeli, and he was outraged by the Prince of Wales's reports of the attitude of British officials towards the Indians. 'Nothing is more disgusting', he wrote to Salisbury forwarding the Prince's comments, 'than the habit of our officers speaking always of the inhabitants of India – many of them descended from the great races – as "niggers" ... We ought to do something'.[16]

India was, indeed, very much on his mind in the autumn and winter of 1875; apart from anxieties about the Russians and Afghanistan, and the Prince's arrival there on 8 November, he had in October to appoint a successor to the Viceroy, Lord Northbrook, who had indicated his wish to resign. To his chagrin he experienced considerable difficulty in finding a suitable candidate for what he liked to describe as 'the superb but awful post'. First Lord Powis and then John Manners declined it. Disraeli was particularly disgusted by the refusal of Manners, once the romantic Young Englander, to contemplate the task of holding the gorgeous East in fee. 'The fact is he is corpulent & uxorious', he wrote unkindly of his old friend to Selina, '& he destroyed a fine intelligence & finer spirit with an indulgence in middle class vices + eating & drinking & marrying vulgar women'.[17] Carnarvon, whose wife had died in January, also declined and the search con tinued with the Queen cunningly putting forward Derby's name in the hope of ridding herself of the Foreign Secretary. Salisbury was amused by her Majesty's manoeuvre, describing it to Disraeli as 'a charming touch of nature ... [which] reveals a world of untold suffering – and desperate hope.'[18] Finally Disraeli's choice fell upon Bulwer Lytton's son, then British Minister at Lisbon. In appointing the second Lord Lytton for the quality which he most prized, imagination, Disraeli overlooked the fact that the son had inherited the principal sin of the father, vanity; it was a choice he was later to regret.

It was the Middle East, however, which provided Disraeli with his most sensational *coup*: the purchase by the British Government of the Suez Canal shares in November 1875.[19] The Suez Canal, built over four years from 1865 by the brilliant but unscrupulous French engineer, Ferdinand de Lesseps, was owned and managed by the *Compagnie Universelle du Canal Maritime de Suez*, of which the major shareholders were de Lesseps and other French interests, and the Khedive of Egypt, vassal of the Turkish Sultan. Britain, blind to the potential of the Canal, had refused to take up the shares allotted to her, a mistake which quickly became apparent. As the importance of the Canal as the sea route to India increased, de Lesseps, greedy and resentful of the British for their treatment of him, continually made trouble by raising the dues to British shipping contrary to the terms of the canal company's constitution. Disraeli, determined to assert British interests in the East, had already attempted in the early summer of 1875 to rectify the situation by negotiating secretly with de Lesseps through the medium of the London Rothschilds for the purchase of his shares in the company, a proposal which de Lesseps rejected.

On 15 November Disraeli learned through his friend Baron Lionel de Rothschild of an opportunity to acquire the coveted shares. The extravagance of the Khedive of Egypt, Ismail Pasha, had led him into such financial straits that, faced with the prospect of having to raise between three and four million pounds by 30 November, he had on 13 November commenced negotiations to sell his Canal shares to two French banks. Two days, therefore, had elapsed before Disraeli was told of the negotiations on 15 November; on the same day Frederick Greenwood, editor of the *Pall Mall Gazette*, informed Derby, who telegraphed to General Stanton, British Consul General at Cairo to investigate the rumour. On receiving a cable from Stanton that the Khedive would prefer to sell his shares to Britain, Disraeli went into immediate action. Overriding Derby's characteristically negative reaction, he put the matter to the Cabinet at a meeting on 17 November. 'The thing must be done', he told the Queen in a breathlessly excited letter. ' 'Tis an affair of millions; about four, at least'. Typically he exaggerated the case, saying in one sentence that possession of the Khedive's share would give Britain an immense influence in the management of the Canal, which was reasonably true, while implying in the next that the Canal would then 'belong to England' which was not.

Disraeli master-minded the affair with considerable skill. Even before the first

Cabinet meeting on 17 November he had most probably concocted with Baron Lionel de Rothschild the plan which was eventually agreed to by the Cabinet on 24 November, after five meetings – that Rothschilds should advance the British Government the money to buy the Khedive's shares. On the day of the crucial Cabinet meeting, the twenty-fourth, a love-sick Monty Corry, who had an assignation with a lady, was kept waiting outside the Cabinet room to be despatched to Baron Lionel with the news that the Cabinet had given the go-ahead. 'I think the time may come when you may hear something of these days of travail', Disraeli wrote cryptically to Selina. His letter to the Queen on the same day was flamboyantly explicit: 'It is just settled: you have it Madam ... Four millions sterling! and almost immediately. There was only one firm that cd. do it – Rothschilds ... the entire interest of the Khedive is now yours, Madam.'[20]

The next day he gave Selina twenty-four hours advance notice of the *coup* in a letter of pure melodrama: 'We have had all the gamblers, capitalists, financiers of the world, organised and platooned in bands of plunderers, arrayed against us, and secret emissaries in every corner, and have baffled them all, and have never been suspected.'[21]

Disraeli may be forgiven if he 'wrote up' his *coup* in the same terms he might have used to describe a financial operation by Sidonia. The success of the affair was due to his own daring and decision and to the trust and friendship between himself and Rothschild. Derby and Stafford Northcote, two of the most influential members of the Cabinet, had been opposed to the purchase of the shares by Britain, preferring to see the management of the Canal in the hands of an International Commission, but Disraeli's firmness had overruled them. Speed had been essential since negotiations between the Khedive and the French banks, encouraged by their Government, had already begun two days before he got wind of it. Any other Prime Minister would have had recourse to the Bank of England, a procedure that would necessarily have taken some time, while it was by no means certain that the Bank would have agreed. Disraeli was probably right in saying that only Rothschilds could have done it and, although they charged $2\frac{1}{2}\%$ commission, they had to take the risk that Disraeli would not fail to persuade Parliament to repay their loan to the Government. The London Rothschilds had to take Disraeli's word for it and, as he told the Queen, they behaved with admirable discretion and loyalty, even breaking with family tradition by withholding the news from the Paris Rothschilds, until the negotiations were completed.[22]

Public opinion as a whole saw the Suez Canal Share purchase in the light in which Disraeli presented it, as a daring and dramatic assertion of British interests, a victory over scheming foreigners. Disraeli certainly saw it as a personal triumph, telling Selina after an ecstatic interview with the Queen, 'I believe the whole country will be with me. The Faery thinks so'. Derby attempted to adjust the balance in favour of realism by telling an Edinburgh audience that all the Government had done was to secure the passage to India and to prevent the

Canal, three-quarters of whose traffic was British, from being 'exclusively in the hands of the foreign shareholders of a foreign company'. Such mundane explanations did not please a public which preferred to cheer Disraeli's *coup* as a national triumph, and the Queen was particularly indignant: 'Lord Derby tried to pour as much cold water as he could on the great success of the affair of the Suez Canal', she told Disraeli. Congratulations poured in from abroad; even the young future Kaiser Wilhelm II wrote to his mother, the Crown Princess of Prussia, 'I know you will be so delighted that England has bought the Suez Canal. How jolly!'

The Liberal Opposition, headed by Gladstone, Granville and Disraeli's enemy, Robert Lowe, thought the affair far from 'jolly' and prepared for 'war to the knife', as Disraeli put it, when the question of voting the four millions was discussed at the opening of the session of 1876. Despite their attacks, the Commons voted the money without a division, the debate ending with a magisterial speech by Disraeli justifying the Government's action on the ground that the assertion of one's rights by peaceful means was far preferable to the use of force. Although the Liberals voiced the fear that the Canal purchase would be the prelude to further imperial expansion by Britain in the area – expansion which eventually came about – this played no part in Disraeli's thinking at the time. His object was to guarantee Britain's interest in the Suez Canal and the results of his action were immediately beneficial. With the previous obstacles to British shipping through the Canal removed, the volume of traffic increased and, with it the value of the shares and their yield. Strategically and financially Britain did extremely well out of the Canal until the advent of Colonel Nasser and the disastrous expedition of 1956 ended its era of prosperity. Ironically when the British Government's Canal shares were finally sold in 1979 they fetched some £22 million, a little over £3 million in terms of 1875 monetary value.[23]

His public exertions over for the year, Disraeli embarked on a round of visits: to Longleat, Windsor, to the Alingtons at Crichel where Selina was a fellow guest, and finally to Hatfield, his first visit there for nine years. His relations with the Salisburys, later to become cordial, were not entirely easy and Disraeli, comparing the present with the past regime at Hatfield, was inclined to be critical. Although he admired improvements to the house which included the long armoury, now lit by figures in suits of mail with gas lanterns on their heads, he found the company less exclusive than in the days of Mary Salisbury (now Lady Derby). At dinner there were 'country neighbours who, in old days, were not permitted to enter Hat-House except for County balls', he sniffed. He cut short his visit, 'This would not do after the delicate circles of Longleat, & Crichel, & Ashridge'.[24]

He spent Christmas at Hughenden with Monty and, as the year ended, found himself overwhelmed with business and annoyed by Monty's lightning comings and goings to various country houses. 'He is like one of those short-time soldiers we hear of so often now who enlist several times in the course of a year & desert as often,' he grumbled to Selina. 'But I cannot scold him, for he is the only person in the world except one who has never offended my taste'.[25]

He had reason to look back on the year 1875 with satisfaction. Domestically, with the passage of the social reform programme, it had been a year of achievement. The Cabinet had been united and Parliament and the country relatively serene. 'You have made England dreadfully dull', Harcourt teased Disraeli, 'which I suppose is the test of *national* success'.[26] But the calm was to be short-lived.

Early in the New Year of 1876, Disraeli basked in the Queen's favour. On 26 February she presented him with her portrait by von Angeli for his collection at Hughenden; Disraeli dropped to his knees, saying, 'I think I may claim, Madam, the privilege of gratitude.' The Queen, Disraeli told Selina, gave him her hand to kiss 'which I did three times very rapidly, and she actually gave me a squeeze'. The Queen was particularly pleased with her 'Primo' since he had agreed to include in his programme for the forthcoming session a Royal Titles Bill, by which she should be styled not only Queen of England but also Empress of India. Ponsonby recorded that the idea of the Bill was the Queen's, which she forced upon Disraeli despite his secret dislike of it. In order to demonstrate her support for the Prime Minister, the Queen opened Parliament in person. Disraeli was almost knocked down and trampled by the mob of members of the Commons crowding to the House of Lords to see the Queen. 'This shall never happen again', he was heard to mutter angrily; it was a prophetic remark.

Perhaps because of his lack of enthusiasm for the Titles Bill, Disraeli was singularly inept in his management of it. He neglected to consult the Opposition leaders beforehand, which he should have done in such a matter and which might have avoided trouble. Then he was mysteriously vague as to the precise nature of the contemplated change, giving rise to unnecessary fears about it; and lastly in neglecting to inform the Prince of Wales he committed a gross breach of etiquette. In the event the Bill aroused an outcry, with *The Times* and London society sneering at the idea and all sections of the Opposition united in a ferocious attack upon it. Ponsonby opined that the real reason for the intensity of the opposition to the Bill was the fear that the Queen intended to substitute the title of Empress for that of Queen, and that many people blamed Disraeli for not making it sufficiently clear from the outset that this was not the case. Others were simply using the furore as a means of attacking the Government; this was, understandably, the explanation which Disraeli gave the Queen.

Victoria was outraged at what she termed the 'disgraceful' conduct of the Opposition, writing to Albert's biographer Theodore Martin that it was 'a *mere* attempt to injure Mr. Disraeli, but which is *most disrespectful* & indecorous'. Endearingly, her chief concern was for Disraeli, to whom she wrote regretfully, 'the worry & annoyance to which Mr. Disraeli is exposed by this unfortunate & most harmless Titles Bill, grieves the Queen deeply as she fears she is the cause of it'.[27] She never forgave the language used by some members of the House of Lords against the bill, notably Lord Granville, a former favourite. The protracted parliamentary struggles over the Bill imposed considerable strain upon Disraeli who had suffered bouts of severe ill-health both before and during the session, but he took a defiant pride in his success at forcing it through, telling Selina on 21 March, 'I look upon the Titles Bill to have proved more than anything the strength of the Ministry. I see no rocks ahead now; and I am going down to the House for the first time this Session, without that tension of the nervous system, wh. I have had since Parlt. met.'[28]

The affair of the Titles Bill provided him with one personal satisfaction – that of publicly crushing his enemy, Robert Lowe. Lowe made an unwise speech at Thetford in April claiming that at least two Prime Ministers had refused the Queen over the imperial title, adding with a hit at Disraeli, 'More pliant persons have now been found and I have no doubt the thing will be done'. It was an echo of Bright's 'servile' speech in 1868, and Disraeli took the utmost pleasure in humiliating Lowe in the House, where, in a speech of brilliant invective he dramatically revealed that he had the Queen's authority to deny that she had ever made any such approaches to previous Prime Ministers. Lowe had no alternative but to make an abject apology; his credibility as a politician, shaken by his performance in Gladstone's administration, received the *coup de grâce* at the hands of Disraeli.

The battle over the Titles Bill was not the last of Disraeli's royal troubles for the year; social scandal erupted in the Prince of Wales' intimate circle which was to cause him endless trouble until the end of the year. On 26 February, 'Sporting Joe' Aylesford, in India with the Prince, received a letter from his wife informing him that she intended to elope with the Marquess of Blandford, another of the Prince's intimates. Aylesford sped back to England, threatening to divorce his wife which would have meant certain social ruin for the guilty couple and an open scandal which would damage the Prince himself.

It was not long before rumours of the affair began to spread beyond the confines of high society. 'The Blandford–Aylesford scandal, or rather catastrophe ... is getting into the mouths of the vulgar', a worried Disraeli told Selina. 'I understand the lady insisted on going off with the Marquess – so patching-up is impossible. They say that our friend Ld. Alington has been trying his hand in this way, & has most indiscreetly, & fruitlessly entrapped – of all persons in the world – the Pss. of Wales into the business'.[29]

The villain of the piece was not, however, Disraeli's and Selina's friend, Lord Alington, but Blandford's younger brother, Lord Randolph Churchill. In an attempt to save his brother from social ruin he had hit upon an extremely distasteful method of bringing pressure on the Prince of Wales to force Aylesford to drop the idea of divorce. Lady Aylesford had given her lover, Blandford, a packet of innocently flirtatious letters written to her by the Prince which Blandford passed on to Lord Randolph. Boasting that he had the Crown of England in his pocket and dragging with him the unfortunate Alington, Churchill called at Marlborough House where he told the Princess of Wales that her husband should advise Aylesford to drop the divorce case. He threatened her that he would use every means in his power to prevent the case, including the letters which, he cruelly told the Princess, were of 'the most compromising character'. He warned her that if the case were to come on the Prince would be subpoenaed to give evidence, and that if his letters to Lady Aylesford were published they would ensure that the Prince of Wales 'would never sit upon the Throne of England'. Furious at the insult and pain caused his wife by Lord Randolph's threats, the Prince, who was in Egypt on his way home, sent Charles Beresford to see Churchill. He was to give Churchill a challenge to a duel with the Prince as soon as he arrived in England; to this Churchill returned an insolent refusal.

At this point Disraeli was obliged to intervene. On 14 March he sent for Alington and Churchill and advised them to apologize to the Prince; Alington was terrified and repentant, Churchill obdurate. Meanwhile he pressed Lord Hardwicke to persuade Aylesford to drop the case, which reluctantly and after a great deal of pressure he agreed to do in favour of a private separation. Public scandal was thus averted but the Prince, stoutly supported by the Queen, remained coldly furious with the Churchills. London society disapproved; Lord Randolph only avoided ostracism by retiring to America with his wife, the former Jennie Jerome. His parents, the Duke and Duchess of Marlborough, were tactfully sent by Disraeli as Viceroys to Dublin to escape the awkward social atmosphere, while the Queen appealed to Disraeli to help mediate between the Prince and Lord Randolph. The affair dragged on almost to Christmas and, although the Prince finally formally accepted an apology drawn up by the mediators, Disraeli, Cairns and Hartington, he did not forgive Churchill until after Disraeli's death. Disraeli, complaining to Selina that the Prince's affairs were almost as troublesome as the Balkan crisis, did however derive a certain cynical amusement in observing the recently-ennobled Alington, who had fallen ill from worry that the Prince might ostracize him too. Disraeli wrote to Selina:

> His illness is entirely P of W and ... if the Prince had not spoken a few gracious words to him at a party, his life might have been in danger. He has only one thought, feeling & aim – Position + & after all his struggles & success, he cannot endure the consciousness that he has destroyed the house of cards in a moment![30]

Constant ill-health made these troubles increasingly hard to bear. The east wind of which he constantly complained brought on bronchitis and he suffered several severe attacks of gout. A new doctor, Sir William Gull, 'tinkered' with him, advising him to drink port, which he had not allowed himself for the past ten years. Disraeli was delighted at first as he had a fondness for vintage port and was tired, he said, of drinking 'plebeian wines', but the regime made him worse than ever. Early in June he indicated to the Queen that he would like to retire from the gruelling routine of the leadership of the House of Commons, if not from public life. The Queen responded by offering him a peerage; she would not contemplate his retirement, she said, because of his immense importance to the throne and to the country, but the Upper House would be far less fatiguing and from there he would be able to '*direct* everything'. In his weariness he contemplated giving up the premiership to Derby who, faced with the actual prospect of power, drew back, declining the offer and saying firmly that he would refuse to serve under anyone but Disraeli. Disraeli, therefore, had no alternative but to accept the offer, to remain Prime Minister, and to join the Lords as Earl of Beaconsfield and Viscount Hughenden of Hughenden.

On Friday 11 August 1876 Disraeli made his last speech as a member of the House of Commons. As he did so, Derby's younger brother, Frederick Stanley, who was amongst the few Members aware of the secret, saw with compassion that he had tears in his eyes, but otherwise nothing in his manner indicated that anything was different. The speech, in answer to an attack by Harcourt on the Government's reaction to the Bulgarian Atrocities, was not particularly striking, but its conclusion contained a phrase which was to be the keynote of his remaining years, 'our duty is at this critical moment ... to maintain the Empire of England'. At the close of the debate Disraeli walked slowly down the House to the Bar to take a long last look at the place that had been the centre of his life for nearly forty years; then he retraced his steps and went out behind the Speaker's Chair. In the lobby he stood leaning on Monty Corry's arm, shaking hands with those of his colleagues and members who knew the significance of the occasion. He was carefully dressed in his favourite long white summer overcoat and lavender kid gloves, but otherwise it was a deliberately low-key departure from the stage which he had so long dominated.

In the House of Commons there was a general sense of loss, not unmixed in some Opposition quarters with relief; while his friend Harcourt wrote, 'The House of Commons will be devilish dull without the great Dizzy', another Liberal, Henry James, commented with satisfaction, 'They will never manage in the House without him. How relieved we shall all be at feeling he is not there to pitch into us'.[31] Disraeli was a great Parliamentarian. He attached great importance to attendance in Parl-i-ament, as he carefully pronounced it, lecturing even his senior colleagues if they failed in this respect, and to parliamentary rules and etiquette. Although his delivery as a speaker was generally reported as somewhat monotonous, the Liberal MP Fawcett, who, being blind was particularly sensitive, told George Hamilton that Disraeli had the most beautiful voice he ever heard, clear and carrying, and that his diction was perfect. He could be tedious as a speaker, and at times, particularly when unsure of his ground, laboured and over-elaborate, but his 'hits', carefully orchestrated and delivered with perfect timing, were always worth waiting for. Above all his sarcasm made him feared, his keen perception of human character giving his phrases their sting, as, for instance, when he described Gladstone as coming down to the House 'with countenance carefully arranged for the occasion'. As long as he was there members were careful not to expose themselves to his ridicule; George Hamilton thought that, had he not left the Commons, he might have given even the obstructionist Irish Home Rulers pause, 'as they love epigrams and hate being laughed at'. Gladstone, he said, had never dared attempt a joke as long as Disraeli was in the Commons but, as soon as he retired to the Lords 'blossomed out, if not as a humourist, at least as one who could not only understand a joke but occasionally make one'.[32] Indeed, the apparent retirement of Gladstone from the Liberal leadership had entered into Disraeli's calculations; with Gladstone quiescent, he later told Hamilton, he had thought that he could safely leave the leadership of the party in the Commons in the hands of Hardy and Northcote. It was a serious miscalculation for, within a few months, Gladstone would once again, like Achilles, emerge wrathful from his tent.

Disraeli's peerage was made public on 12 August. Congratulations poured in from all sides, but some people regarded his ennoblement as unworthy of him. 'This creation of the Earl of Beaconsfield reads like the conclusion of a novel', Bernal Osborne wrote from Carlsbad to Dorothy Nevill. 'Of course health is the excuse for the transformation. With all his genius, Dizzy loves tinsel! I cannot help looking upon this elevation as a *fall* to such a man!'[33] It was indeed like the conclusion of one of Disraeli's novels, if less predictable; the despised Jewish novelist and distrusted adventurer, hooted down by his fellow members on his first appearance in Parliament had become not only twice Prime Minister of England, but a belted Earl. (Not even Disraeli dared become a Duke.) Disraeli's own reaction when asked after his introduction to the House of Lords how he felt in his new surroundings was: 'I am dead; dead but in the Elysian fields.'

22 The Road to Berlin

Disraeli now saw his role as that of elder statesman playing his part on the world stage. 'After rates and taxes and shipping bills, *la haute politique* is refreshing; worth living for', he told Anne Chesterfield in June. Over the next two years his mind was to be entirely occupied with the settlement of the Eastern Question raised by the rebellion in the Turkish Balkan provinces. His principal objects would be to break the diplomatic cartel of the *Dreikaiserbund* by asserting Britain's right to play a major role in any settlement and to curb the Russian threat to the Turkish Empire and to British interests in the East. Already that summer he had made his position clear by refusing to join in the Berlin Memorandum, an attempt by the Powers to impose an armistice between the Turks and the rebel provinces, on the grounds that Britain had not been consulted in its preparation, and, following the murder of the French and German consuls at Salonika in May, he had despatched the British fleet to Besika Bay at the mouth of the Dardanelles. He was pleased with the results of his assertiveness, boasting to Anne Chesterfield on 9 July that 'all the Great Powers ... now seem anxious to defer to England and something like the old days of our authority appear to have returned.'

Unfortunately for the peaceful prosecution of his '*haute politique*' events in Bulgaria, where a revolt against the Turks had broken out in May, were to provide Gladstone with an opportunity to arouse a tide of public passion against his old enemy. On 23 June 1876 a report appeared in the *Daily News* of atrocities committed in Bulgaria by the Bashi-Bazouks, irregular troops employed by the Turkish Government to suppress the revolt. A further report on 8 July alleged that in one province alone 25,000 people had been slaughtered, sixty villages burned, Bulgarian girls and children sold as slaves and, in one instance, forty girls had been seized, violated and subsequently burned alive in a straw-loft. The Bashi-Bazouks, it was reported, were to be seen parading cartloads of severed heads.

Public opinion was outraged, with the Queen, always sensitive in cases of cruelty and oppression, taking the lead. 'The Bashi-Bazouks shd. really *not* be allowed to *outrage* the feelings of Europe', she expostulated, pressing Derby and Disraeli to remonstrate with the Turkish Government. Questions on the atrocities were asked in Parliament, and in the first debate on 10 July Disraeli, who had been given no accurate information as to the veracity of the atrocity reports and tended to discount them, was betrayed into an unfortunate phrase. He doubted, he said, whether torture had actually been practised by the Turks, 'an Oriental people who seldom, I believe, resort to torture, but generally terminate their connection with culprits in a more expeditious manner'. The House took it as a joke and laughed. 'What is there to laugh at?' Disraeli was heard to mutter angrily. There was indeed nothing to laugh about; later reports confirmed that atrocities, although greatly exaggerated, had certainly been committed and Disraeli's remark was widely seen as a cynical jest at the expense of suffering humanity, and Christian humanity at that. An anti-atrocity movement sprang up which quickly took on the character of a crusade to protect the Balkan Christians against the barbarous infidel Turks, with Disraeli in the villain's role as supporting the oppressors. Gladstone gave the movement a powerful impetus by publishing on 6 September a voluminous pamphlet entitled *The Bulgarian Horrors and the Eastern Question* which sold 40,000 copies in the first few days.

Disraeli, at Hughenden in the first week of September, received in quick succession two characteristically different presents from the leaders of the Liberal party; the first a brace of grouse from Harty-Tarty, the second, far less welcome, was Gladstone's pamphlet. Disraeli indignantly denounced the pamphlet as 'passionate, . . . vindictive, and ill-written – that of course. Indeed in that resepct, of all the Bulgarian horrors, perhaps the greatest.' Ill-written or not, Gladstone's pamphlet had touched a chord of public opinion; while the anti-atrocity movement had its fair share of fanatical clergymen and Dizzy-haters, many fair-minded people were repelled by the horror stories, and the movement's promoters included W. T. Stead, Lords Shaftesbury and Bath and the Duke of Westminster. Some of the reports were absurd; two clergymen friends of Gladstone asserted that they had seen Christians crucified by the Turks on the banks of the Danube when what they had actually seen was only the cross-stakes used by the local fishermen for hanging out their nets. But an official report by the Government's emissary testified that he had seen several villages razed to the ground and heaps of bodies lying unburied, testimony that did not help Disraeli's position.

Gladstone kept the public temperature running high, pillorying Disraeli in his public speeches; indeed the Bulgarian Atrocities ushered in a new phase of personal bitterness between the two men. Gladstone's niece, Lady Frederick Cavendish, recorded in her diary that he was motivated not only by a love of justice and mercy but by 'an utter disbelief in Dizzy'. Disraeli, in private, exploded into a fit of savage anger against Gladstone: 'There may be more infamous men but I don't believe there is anyone more wicked', he wrote to Selina on 19 September. 'And millions believe he is a virtuous, moral, even transcendent being! Abandoned in his private life, *criblé des* [sic] *dettes* & the willing votary of every delusion that may bring him favor!'[1] Some of Gladstone's followers in the anti-atrocity movement were openly anti-Semitic in their attacks, the historian Freeman habitually referring to Disraeli as 'that lying Jew' and Hughenden as 'the ghetto'. Gladstone himself suspected that Disraeli's 'crypto-Judaism' made him indifferent to the fate of the Christians. As he was to write later to his friend Arthur Gordon:

> I have watched very closely his strange & inexplicable proceedings on this Eastern Question and I believe their fountainhead to be race antipathy, that aversion which the Jews, with a few honourable exceptions, are showing so vindictively towards the Eastern Christians. Though he has been baptised, his Jew feelings are the most radical & the most real, & so far respectable, portion of his profoundly falsified nature.[2]

Was Gladstone correct in his reading of Disraeli's motivation or was he being grossly unfair when he publicly quoted passages from *Tancred* as proof of Disraeli's anti-Christian feelings? Gladstone's judgement, though undoubtedly sincere, tended to be clouded – like Disraeli's – by personal dislike. If Stanley is to be believed, Disraeli, while stoutly defending the Established Church as an institution of England, privately scoffed at all religions, and he certainly does not seem to have been moved by any feeling that the Balkan Christians were of his religion. There is no evidence, however, that he felt racial antipathy towards them as Gladstone thought. His attitudes had been fixed by the experience of his Eastern Tour, when he wrote flippantly to Austen of the delights of dining with the ferocious Bey in Albania who had been 'daily decapitating half the province'. His experiences in the East had coloured his attitude towards the Turks, a people whom he liked and admired, but as was to become apparent at the Congress of Berlin he was not prepared to sacrifice English interests out of sentiment for the Turks. His interest in the settlement of the Eastern Question was political, not emotional, and, as he wrote of the anti-atrocity agitation to Derby on 6 September, 'All this tumult is on a false assumption, that we have been or are, upholding Turkey. All the Turks may be in the Propontis as far as I am concerned'.

His primary concern was that Russia should not seize the opportunity raised by the nationalist revolts in the Balkans, which her pan-Slav Ambassador at Constantinople, General Ignatiev, had been secretly working to promote, as a pretext for coming to the aid of her fellow Christians and Slavs. Indeed Disraeli's chief fear was that Russia might gain a foothold in the Mediterranean or even Constantinople and thus threaten Britain's sea communications with India. He was deeply concerned lest Russia should interpret the anti-Turk agitation in England as meaning that England would not oppose Russian attempts to coerce Turkey. To disabuse Russia of this idea and in response to a threatening message from the Russian Chancellor Gortchakov, he made a bellicose speech at the Guildhall on 9 November. The Tsar's response was to repeat in a public speech Gortchakov's threat that Russia might be forced to resort to arms if her terms for the settlement of the Serbo–Turkish war were not met at the forthcoming conference of the Powers at Constantinople.

It was an inauspicious prologue to the peace conference which assembled at Constantinople on 11 December 1876. In order to calm domestic fears that his Government might be over-committed to Turkey, Disraeli made the skilful choice of Salisbury, whose pro-Christian views were well known, as British plenipoten-tiary. At Constantinople Salisbury soon made his anti-Turkish proclivities evident, entering into close relations with Ignatiev, while not concealing his contempt both for the Sultan's Government and the pro-Turk British Ambassa-dor, Sir Henry Elliot. The Embassy and the British delegation were soon hardly on speaking terms, while the Ignatievs, a clever, handsome and charming couple, overwhelmed the Salisburys with flattery both social and sexual. Witnesses re-ported that Ignatiev acted as if enthralled by Lady Salisbury, while his wife attempted to seduce the virtuous Salisbury. Disraeli became extremely worried, complaining to Derby on 30 December, 'Sal. seems most prejudiced, and not to be aware, that his principal object, in being sent to Const., is to keep the Russians out of Turkey, not to create an ideal existence for Turkish Xtians'.[3] Nothing, however, was to come of the conference; on 18 January the Turks refused the terms put to them by the Powers and the meeting broke up.

Meanwhile the anti-atrocity agitation in England continued to rage, princi-pally directed against Disraeli as the supposed supporter of Turkish barbarity and in favour of Russia as the protector of the Balkan Christians. The Queen, now fiercely anti-Russian, was particularly enraged with Gladstone, who had been one of the protagonists of a meeting held at St James's Hall on 8 December. Gladstone's opposition to the Government seemed to her positively treasonable; she thought that the Attorney General 'ought to be set at these men', she ex-claimed to Disraeli. At Windsor she and Disraeli exchanged titillating gossip about Gladstone who had not only publicly offered his arm to Ignatiev's ally, the pan-Slav temptress, Olga Novikov, at the conclusion of the St James's meeting but, careless of appearances as usual, had dined afterwards with the notorious Mrs Thistlethwaite. 'The Faery was charming to me. She knows all about Mrs. Thistelthwayte [sic]!', Disraeli wrote gleefully to Selina. 'She really thinks G. mad!'[4]

The Faery's indulgence towards Disraeli did not, however, extend to permitting him to leave Downing Street during the conference crisis to spend Christmas as he had hoped with the Bradfords at Weston. He dined alone at Whitehall Gardens on Christmas Day, consoling himself with the contemplation of 'ruby mitts' knitted for him by Selina, and a large Christmas card from the Queen, signing herself for the first time 'V.R. et I.' On New Year's Day 1877 'our poetical Viceroy' as Disraeli described Lytton, was to proclaim her Empress of India, and she celebrated the occasion with a dinner at Windsor where she startled her guests, who included Disraeli and George Hamilton, by appearing loaded down with a mass of Oriental jewellery. The jewels were mostly very large pearls and uncut stones, gifts from the Princes of India; few of them, Lord George recorded, were perfect in shape or without some flaw and, although they made a handsome blaze of colour they did not suit her Majesty's small and homely figure.

Disraeli celebrated his own New Year at Whitehall Gardens by changing the pictures in his bedroom, ordering the Duchess of Northumberland's portraits of bishops and archbishops out of the room in favour of 'Gussie' Alington, Princess Beatrice and, of course, Selina. Physically he was constantly unwell from the beginning of the year, but emotionally a new calm had entered into his relations with Selina. Petulant outbursts of offended passion were now rare; his letters were amusingly gossipy or filled with Eastern news. He was still not above trying to make Selina jealous, boosting his ego by pointing out to her that other ladies were still in romantic pursuit of him. He had received a graceful letter from Angela Burdett-Coutts – 'I fancy she is not indisposed to recur to her ancient feelings', he surmised. Recently he had been under renewed siege by an unidentified lady who had insinuated herself into his life as Mary Anne was dying, and to whom, at the time of the Glasgow meeting in November 1873, he had been almost on the point of proposing. The lady had taken fright and failed to keep the Glasgow rendez-vous, whereupon Disraeli, finding his feelings towards her suddenly changed, cut off the relationship, leaving Monty Corry the task of answering her letters. 'I thought it was entirely dead', he told Selina on 27 March, 'when, this autumn just past, a violent attack was made, but I formed a square, like the Duke at Waterloo'.[5]

Less than two months after the break-up of the Constantinople Conference, the Eastern Question re-emerged; indeed, in the course of that year it was to enter its most critical phase. Early in March Russia took the initiative by proposing a new protocol containing deceptively mild terms for peace in the Balkans. On 2 March Ignatiev left Moscow for the West bearing with him the protocol for signature, visiting first Berlin and then Paris. He then intended, Disraeli was aghast to learn, to avail himself of an informal invitation to visit England issued by Salisbury. Both he, the Queen and the Russian Ambassador in London, Shuvalov, strongly opposed to Ignatiev's belligerent pan-Slav policies, were alarmed at the prospect of the intriguing General in their midst. 'The Ignatieff arrival is a thunderbolt', he told Selina. 'Absolute dismay at [royal] headquarters about the visit'. The Queen warned Derby that the protocol was a trap laid by Russia and Bismarck to lure England into coercing Turkey, but Disraeli's view was that trap or no, Britain must at all costs not be left out of the settlement.

Shuvalov and Ignatiev were the bitterest of rivals, not only because the former was anxious for peace and the latter for war, but because both hoped to take over the direction of Russian foreign policy when the aged Chancellor Gortchakov should disappear from the stage. Shuvalov, a man of charm and high spirits, a great drinker and seducer of women, was extremely popular in London society which, on Ignatiev's arrival, divided into pro-Shuvalov or pro-Ignatiev camps. Disraeli enjoyed the social cold war to which the Russian rivalry gave rise, delightedly describing to Selina the banquet he gave in honour of the General and Madame Ignatiev. Prince 'Hal', who had appointed himself head of the Shuvalov faction, offered his arm to Madame Ignatiev to take her into dinner for form's sake, but then ostentatiously ignored her, talking to Lady Londonderry who sat on his other side or to the Duchess of Manchester across the table. Monty, sitting on Madame Ignatiev's other side, took advantage of the Prince's neglect and got on excellently with her, except when he offered her mineral water. 'Not the custom of Russian ladies,' she replied, and drank eagerly of whatever wine was offered her. 'But [she] is very calm & collected & must have had, therefore, an early training at it', Disraeli commented. The great ladies of London society, having heard that Madame Ignatiev gave herself airs, were determined to outdo her. Louise Manchester was covered with diamonds from head to foot, indeed Disraeli reported that they were 'stuck in every part of her costume'; while Lady Londonderry 'staggered under the jewels of the 3 united families of Stewart & Vane & Londonderry ... Madame Ignatiev had many diamonds & a fine costume, but paled before this'.[6]

Britain signed the Protocol on 31 March 1877 after much wrangling in Cabinet where Disraeli pressed for firmness over Russian demobilization of their troops on the Turkish frontier. Being, as he told the Queen, more afraid of the two pro-Christian peers in the Cabinet, Lords Salisbury and Carnarvon, than of Count Shuvalov or General Ignatiev, he put it bluntly to the Cabinet that they were faced with two conflicting policies – 'the Imperial Policy of England, & the Policy of Crusade'. He succeeded in persuading the Cabinet to adopt his policy of firmness but the settlement came to nothing; the Turks rejected the Protocol as humiliating and it became clear that a Russo-Turkish war was imminent.

Meanwhile at Constantinople the British Ambassador, Sir Henry Elliot, had been persuaded to resign and replaced by Sir Henry Layard, the discoverer of Nineveh. Layard, an able man whom Disraeli trusted, had two special connections with Disraeli's past. He was the nephew of Sara Austen, while his wife was the daughter of the former Lady Charlotte Bertie whom Disraeli had once considered marrying and who had acted as decoy in the early days of his affair with Henrietta Sykes. Layard arrived at Constantinople on 20 April and made urgent attempts to preserve peace by persuading the Sultan to compromise, but it was too late. On 24 April Russia declared war on Turkey.

The Russian declaration provoked a split within the British Cabinet which, for Disraeli, represented a threat to the conduct of his foreign policy almost as great as the Russian aggression towards Constantinople. Lords Salisbury and Carnarvon, in sympathy with the Christian subjects of the Turkish Empire in Europe, were inclined to side with Russia as their protector. 'Lord Salisbury seems to think that the progress of Russia is the progress of religion & civilisation', Disraeli complained to the Queen. Moreover, the question of whether Britain should or should not take up a belligerent stance towards the Russian aggression precipitated the struggle which had long been brewing between the non-interventionist Derby and the imperialist Disraeli, backed by a rabidly anti-Russian Queen. The situation was complicated further for Disraeli by the intrigues of Lady Derby, who, regarding herself as an unofficial channel of communications between Britain and Russia, leaked information about the Cabinet discussions – and dissensions – to Shuvalov who passed them on to the Russian Government.

There was only one crumb of comfort for Disraeli in his difficulties: the Opposition, split along more or less the same lines as the Cabinet, were unable to take advantage of the Government's disunity. The rift in the Liberal leadership was made apparent when on 14 May Hartington refused to support a motion put by Gladstone that Britain should withdraw all moral and material support from Turkey unless the Sultan reformed his administration, and the Government gained a majority of 131. As usual, when thwarted in Parliament, Gladstone, excited by what he himself described as 'a kind of idolising (popular) sentiment' towards him, sought to express his opposition through demagogic channels. Animated by a strong personal feeling against Disraeli whom he considered to be the 'master and mainspring on the other side', he told a meeting of some 30,000 people at Birmingham that the Government was 'turning its course directly to the old sense of virtual assistance to the Turk, like the dog returning to his vomit, or the sow to wallowing in the mire', and that it was therefore the people's responsibility to influence foreign policy not only against the executive Government but also against the House of Commons. Unfortunately for Gladstone British public opinion, so strongly with him the previous autumn was now, seeing Turkey as the underdog, turning against Russia.

Mutual suspicion between Disraeli and Derby ran high, with Disraeli telling the Queen that Derby seemed for peace at any price, while Derby for his part thought that the Queen was pushing Disraeli into war. His friend Shuvalov wrote contemptuously to his Government of 'this conspiracy of a half-mad woman with a minister who had once had genius but has degenerated into a political clown'.[7] Although the Queen was recklessly aggressive, showering her Prime Minister with passionately anti-Russian letters and telegrams, Disraeli was not, as Shuvalov suspected, conspiring with her to declare war, but making use of her to push the Cabinet in the direction of firmness *vis-à-vis* Russia. Even Derby admitted that Disraeli's object was not war, but to place Britain in 'a commanding position'. He did, however, believe that this forward policy could lead to war, while Disraeli for his part repeatedly told Northcote that he feared Derby's inaction would have the same result.

From the moment of the Russian declaration through the summer of 1877 the gulf between the two men widened, with Disraeli increasingly resorting to secret methods and going behind his Foreign Secretary's back. On 6 June, he wrote to Ambassador Layard (without informing Derby) directing him to obtain the Sultan's permission to occupy the Gallipoli peninsula to protect the Dardanelles. A few days later, he attempted to forward an approach from Austria over which Derby was dragging his feet, by negotiating himself with Andrassy through Monty and a chargé at the Austrian Embassy. Meanwhile he warned Derby not to inform Shuvalov of the Austrian negotiation, advice which the Foreign Secretary ignored. In August, while Derby drafted the cautious official reply to a tentative peace plan transmitted from the Tsar through the British military attaché, Colonel Wellesley, Disraeli, with the Queen's approval, sent a private message via Wellesley warning that if the war was not soon terminated and if Russia began a second campaign in the spring of 1878, 'England must take her place as a belligerent'. Derby meanwhile was understandably becoming increasingly suspicious and resentful of interference and pressure from Disraeli and the Queen. In July Disraeli reported him to Victoria as being 'savage & sullen' at being forced to send Layard a telegram requesting him to sound out the Sultan about inviting the British fleet to Constantinople. He considered nonetheless that even if war was declared, Derby would not resign. The Queen longed for his departure; furious at the Derbys' communications with Shuvalov and the impression they conveyed that Britain would not intervene, she raged about him to Disraeli. 'Ld. Derby & his wife *most likely* say the *reverse right & left & Russia goes on!* It maddens the Queen to feel that all our efforts are being destroyed by the minister who ought to carry them out. The Queen must say she *can't* stand it!'[8] Disraeli however, was not yet prepared to press for Derby's resignation. On 30 July 1877 the Turks under Osman Pasha inflicted a second defeat on the Russians at Plevna and, with the end of the parliamentary session, the Eastern crisis was temporarily in abeyance.

Worn out by the effort of restraining the Queen and outflanking Derby and Shuvalov, Disraeli was again ill that summer. Doctors Gull and Jenner competed with each other to recommend conflicting cures. 'Gull is all froth and words', Disraeli grumbled to Selina on 1 July. 'They are all alike. First they throw it on the weather then there must be a change of scene. So Sir W. Jenner after blundering and plundering in the usual way sent me to Bournemouth, and Gull wants to send me to Ems. I should like to send them both to Jericho'.[9] Still in London in mid-August, he was incapable of walking upstairs: 'Gout & bronchitis have ended in asthma, the horrors of which I have never contemplated or conceived', he told a friend, Mrs de Burgh.

He had been annoyed briefly in July by what he termed the 'impertinent' Pigott affair, when he had been unjustly accused of appointing the son of a former vicar of Hughenden to a civil post in return for electoral favours. He had been able, however, to trump his enemies' cards by pointing out that far from owing the Rev. Mr Pigott a favour, the man had actually voted against him and that he did not even know the son by sight. There had, however, been lighter moments that summer. On 13 June he met the sensation of the season, Lily Langtry, although the light, with his poor eyesight, was too bad for him to scrutinize her satisfactorily, while the next day the De la Warrs took him to the latest fashionable rage, the Alhambra music-hall. There were moments of nostalgia; 'Gussie' Alington invited him to dinner on the Sunday before Goodwood, the exact anniversary of the occasion four years ago when he had begun his romance with Selina. 'Four years ago!' he wrote to her on 28 July. 'It makes one very sad. I gave you feelings you could not return. It was not your fault; my fate & my misfortune'.[10] Two days later there was another, more satisfactory occasion for nostalgia; a visit to the House of Commons for the first time since he had left it almost a year before. 'My first visit' he told Selina, 'after I had sate there nearly forty years and had led – on one side or the other – more than a quarter of a century. When they recognised me in the gallery both sides gave me a cheer!'[11]

Disraeli, always depressed by the approach of autumn, 'dreading the fall of the leaf', was unusually melancholy this year. Although enjoying the unwise regime of vintage port recommended by his doctors – 'I find in old port perpetual youth' he told Selina – he was often alone. Monty, upon whom he so much depended for companionship was in love with a daughter of the Earl of Ilchester and always 'running away' to Melbury in Dorset, or, when he was at Hughenden, presenting a picture of resigned misery, sighing between the intervals of taking a letter. Disraeli complained to Selina of being too weak to walk any distance and of hating country drives. 'I am quite alone & unless I had the companionship of those I love wh: I never shall have, alone I wish to remain.' Even the prospect of Monty's return failed to cheer him; he predicted that his secretary would be dull for a day or two and sigh between courses at dinner, he told Selina, adding plaintively, 'I used to do these things myself, but have lived long enough to have nobody to sigh about'. In October his doctors recommended Brighton as a cure, but Monty had deserted him again, pleading illness, and his complaints about his secretary's gallivanting grew louder. 'When he has been ill for a few days it ends in a shooting party in Dorset', he wrote acidly to Selina from Brighton on 11 October.

> When more prolonged, he is oblig'd to go to Ireland to pay a visit to the Dartreys. It is quite curious how these two visits are ever coincident with his severest attacks ... he had no desk work at Hughenden during 2 months, he had his horse & rode every day, then his sister [to stay] & drives every day, & after that generally playing Lawn Tennis with a variety of young ladies he manag'd to pick up – yet he is still so very ill that he is oblig'd to consult Lady Ilchester & her Mariana.[12]

He was waiting anxiously for news from the East, hoping that the Turks would succeed in checking the Russian advance. At first the news was encouraging and he rejoiced prematurely, telling Selina that 'at any rate the Turks have proved their vigour & resources & that they have a right to be regarded among the Sovereign Powers of the World', and gleefully retailing reports of heavy Russian losses. The Turkish position, however, soon deteriorated and on 10 December 1877 Osman Pasha, besieged by the Russians at Plevna, capitulated with his entire army of some 30,000 men. Disraeli's Cabinet, which for the past six weeks had been wrangling over proposals for mediation, were faced with the undeniable fact that Turkey's resistance was at an end. For Russia the road to Constantinople was open.

And so as the year 1878 opened the need for a decisive British reaction to the Russian advance became immediate, revealing the continuing dissension within the Cabinet. Derby and Carnarvon were adamantly for non-belligerence; Salisbury, Carnarvon's former ally, as yet equivocal. Disraeli was in an unpleasant position. The Queen was hot for war, 'Oh, if the Queen were a man, she would like to go and give those Russians ... such a beating!' she wrote furiously from

Osborne on 10 January. Ponsonby said that she regarded the question as a struggle for supremacy between herself and the Tsar and that Disraeli had led her to take this view; nonetheless he could not help feeling some sympathy for Disraeli under ceaseless fire from the Queen, which he said, Disraeli had resented and resisted, refusing to commit the Government to war.[13]

Derby, however, thought differently; suspecting that Disraeli was contemplating military preparations, a warlike speech and armed intervention such as the occupation of Constantinople, he appealed to Salisbury for support. Such measures, he told Salisbury, would be the slippery slope to war; he then used a curiously revealing phrase about Disraeli: 'He believes thoroughly in "prestige" *as all foreigners do* [my italics], and would think it ... in the interests of the country to spend 200 millions on a war if the result was to make foreign States think more highly of us as a military power.'[14] Disraeli also attempted to enlist Salisbury's help; given that every Cabinet decision was retailed through Lady Derby via Shuvalov to the Russian Government, he wrote, it was of the utmost importance that the Russians should be given the impression of a firm and united Cabinet which could be achieved if he and Salisbury acted together.[15]

Salisbury held the key to the balance of power within the Cabinet, and at a series of stormy Cabinet meetings on 21 and 22 January 1878, it appeared that he was now prepared to support Disraeli. Disraeli succeeded in obtaining a majority agreement to summon Parliament to obtain a £6 million vote of credit, to negotiate for an alliance with Austria, and to send a fleet through the Dardanelles. Derby, his suspicions confirmed, at once resigned and with him Carnarvon, to the Queen's 'immense satisfaction'. As a gesture of support she offered Disraeli the Garter, which he declined; 'As Lord Melbourne said,' he told Selina, '"I don't want to bribe myself"'. News then arrived of a Russo-Turkish agreement and the order to send the fleet was countermanded. Derby was persuaded to stay and the Queen to accept him, which she agreed to do very reluctantly, yielding to Disraeli's argument that Derby's departure would lose the party his great electoral influence in Lancashire.

Derby returned, but his relations with his chief were distant and strained. He did not take his usual seat in Cabinet next to Disraeli, but sat in Carnarvon's vacant chair. 'This was very marked', Disraeli told the Queen. 'He is evidently in a dark temper, but all must be borne at this moment.' Derby appeared to be in a comatose state, perhaps due to his reported heavy drinking,[16] passively accepting that control of foreign policy had passed to Disraeli, Salisbury and Cairns. The ex-Minister Carnarvon behaved badly, making what Disraeli described as 'an ungentlemanlike speech' justifying his conduct 'with details which ought never to have been mentioned', and leaking Derby's resignation, which Disraeli had hoped to keep secret, to the *Daily News*. Amidst all these difficulties Monty Corry collapsed with a nervous breakdown and Gladstone reopened his anti-Dizzy campaign with a speech at Oxford in which he claimed openly that for the past eighteen months he had been working night and day to 'counterwork as well as I could what I believe to be the purpose of Lord Beaconsfield'. 'The mask has fallen', Disraeli wrote to Selina on 1 February, '... instead of a pious Xtian, we find a vindictive fiend, who confesses he has, for a year and a half, been dodging and manoeuvring against an individual – because he was a successful rival.'[17]

Disraeli was, however, now in a stronger position, strengthened in Cabinet by the support of Salisbury and the emasculation of Derby, and backed by opinion in the country at large. As the Russians advanced steadily towards Constantinople and the harsh terms of their peace proposals became known, Britain was gripped by anti-Russian fever and 'jingoism' entered the English language with the music-hall refrain: 'We don't want to fight, but, by Jingo if we do, We've got the ships, we've got the men, we've got the money too'.

But although Cabinet and country were united behind Disraeli, it was difficult to know what to do; preparations were made for an expedition to Gallipoli and Britain appeared to be playing a dangerous game of poker with Russia, not always effectively. Orders for the fleet to be sent up to Constantinople were given and countermanded three times in three weeks during February, prompting Ponsonby to compare the British squadron at the mouth of the Dardanelles to a terrier sniffing at a hole hoping to find a rabbit but fearing that a badger might be at the bottom of it. Fortunately for the Government's credibility patriotic fever raged to such an extent that their confusion passed unnoticed, and the Opposition, with the exception of Gladstone who had his windows broken for his pains, judged it prudent to refrain from pointing it out. On 3 March the signing of the peace treaty at San Stefano between Russia and Turkey brought the uncertainty to an end, ushering in a new phase of the Eastern Question.

When the terms of the treaty reached London on 23 March, three weeks after the signing at San Stefano, Disraeli found them unacceptable. The treaty postulated the complete extinction of Turkey in Europe, with independence for Rumania, Serbia and Montenegro, and autonomy for Bosnia-Herzegovina. While these clauses might have been accepted by Britain and Austria, neither country was prepared to contemplate the proposed creation of a big Bulgaria stretching from the Black Sea to the Aegean, which, with a prince selected by Russia and its administration and garrisons in Russian hands, would be no more than a Russian puppet state. Disraeli, always sensitive to Russian designs on Constantinople and the Dardanelles, also objected to a clause providing the cession by Turkey to Russia of a fifty-mile stretch of territory on the Asian shore of the Black Sea. The Russians announced that they would submit the treaty for consideration by the Powers at a Congress to be held at Berlin, but while allowing the other Powers 'the liberty of raising questions' at the Congress, Russia would reserve the right to accept or refuse the discussion of such questions.

After months of confusion and shilly-shallying, the critical point had arrived. Disraeli was determined that firm action should immediately be taken to avoid a situation in which Britain might be forced to go to war. 'If we are bold and determined,' he told Hardy, 'We shall secure peace, and dictate its conditions to

Europe ... We have to maintain the Empire and secure peace; I think we can do both.'[18] On 27 March the Cabinet agreed to Disraeli's proposals to call out the reserves and send troops from India to occupy Cyprus and Alexandretta.

As expected, Derby resigned, but this time there was to be no going back. The Queen termed his resignation 'an unmixed blessing' and the sense of relief at the termination of an impossible situation was general, not least to Derby himself. Stress had made him ill, and for the past months he had been subjected to a stream of vituperation from the war faction at the Carlton. The most scurrilous stories were being circulated by his enemies about both himself and his wife; Derby, they said, had become a drunkard and had even, it was whispered, raped a teenage girl at Liverpool,[19] while Lady Derby was the mistress of Count Shuvalov.

For Disraeli relief was mixed with sadness. He felt a personal loyalty to the Stanley family. Despite differences, he had owed much to the late Lord Derby, while his friendship with Derby himself went back nearly thirty years. At first the parting was cordial but, as so often in such cases, recent experiences had left a legacy of touchiness and suspicion on both sides which soon resulted in permanent estrangement. Derby was angry that Disraeli should have taken his younger brother, Frederick Stanley, whom he disliked, into the Cabinet in an obvious attempt to retain some of the Stanley electoral interest, and by tactless references which Disraeli made in a speech to Derby's position early in the year. Wounded, Derby revealed more than he ought of Cabinet proceedings in a speech which Disraeli described to the Queen as 'disagreeable and unauthorised', compounding his sin by further revelations in July relating to the proposal to send Indian troops to seize Cyprus. As the Treaty of Berlin had by then been signed, Derby felt himself free to reveal what had really happened, but his disclosures evoked a stinging reply from Salisbury and a strong rebuke from the Queen. Derby suspected, unfairly, that Disraeli had instigated the Queen's letter and bitterly resented it; it was the final nail in the coffin of their old friendship. Two years later Derby was to join Gladstone.

Derby was replaced by Salisbury who soon demonstrated his ability as a strong and determined Foreign Secretary. On 1 April he issued a circular defining the British position on the Treaty of San Stefano and making it clear that Russia should not be allowed to reserve any questions from consideration by the forthcoming Congress. As a sign of further pressure upon Russia, Indian troops were sent to Malta, while preparatory negotiations were begun with the Sultan, Austria and Russia. On 4 June an agreement was made with the Sultan, by which Turkey ceded Cyprus in return for British protection. Disraeli saw Cyprus not only as a strategic position in the Eastern Mediterranean but as a security for the sea route to India. By 3 May two agreements had been reached with Russia whereby the projected bigger Bulgaria was reduced in size and removed from the Aegean, while the other European Powers as well as Russia were to have a voice in the administrative organization of the remaining Turkish provinces in Europe. On 6

June the issues to be discussed were agreed with Austria and the way was open for the Congress to be held in Berlin in the second week of June. Disraeli and Salisbury were to attend as the British plenipotentiaries.

At first the Queen, anxious that the strain of attending a conference at so distant a place might prove too much for Disraeli's frail health, resisted his going. The Prince of Wales argued with her, pointing out that Disraeli was 'the only man ... as he would show Russia and the other Powers that we were really in earnest'. The Queen objected: 'You know that Lord Beaconfield is 72 and $\frac{1}{2}$ [he was $73\frac{1}{2}$], [and] is far from strong', she told the Prince, 'and that he is the firm & wise head & hand, that rules the Government, & who is my great support & comfort, for you cannot think how kind he is to me, how attached! His health and life are of immense value to me & the country, & should on no account be risked. Berlin is decidedly too far.'[20] Disraeli himself was determined that the Queen's solicitude should not prevent him from playing the part he had always dreamed of as a principle actor on the European stage. Skilfully using the Queen's fear and distrust of Bismarck, he intimated that he, the Prime Minister, was the only one capable of dealing with him as an equal. He assured her he would take care of his health:

> Lord Beaconsfield will travel to Berlin by himself & with his personal suite, & he will take four days for this operation, so that he will arrive quite fresh. Then he will have interviews with all the chief statesmen, so that there will be no mistake as to the designs, and the determination, of this country.[21]

In fact Disraeli was now in better health than at any time since he became Prime Minister. He was being treated by a celebrated homeopath, Dr Kidd, for whom he had conceived an admiration and trust quite unlike his usual contempt for the medical profession. Kidd had diagnosed that he was suffering from a disease of the kidneys, Bright's disease, also bronchitis, asthma and gout, and that previous doctors' treatments had only worsened his condition. Under the regimes of Doctors Leggatt, Gull and Jenner, Disraeli had been prescribed ipecacuanha for his asthma which made him feel sick, and port and iron-based medicines which had aggravated his gout. Dr Kidd substituted potassium iodide for the ipecacuanha and the 'finest Château Lafite' for the iron medicines and port, recommending 'a mild course of arsenic' for the bronchitis and a light dinner without pastry, pudding or fruit. Disraeli was to have vapour baths to encourage perspiration before he went to bed and help him to sleep. He had devised his own method of avoiding indigestion by arranging with his cook that there should be a ten-minute period between each course during which he would read the classical authors while allowing his food to settle.[22] Whatever may have been the real merits of Dr Kidd's treatment, Disraeli felt that it did him good and at least avoided the sleepless nights which took such a toll on his capacity for work. He therefore felt physically able to face the strain ahead, the more so because Monty (of whom he had written despairingly in May that he feared his career was over), was once more at his side.

Disraeli left England on 8 June accompanied by Monty and his 'personal suite'. He must have embarked on the journey to Berlin with a sense of adventure; it was twenty years since he had been abroad, on his last visit to Paris with Mary Anne, and more than half a century since he had visited Germany with his father and William Meredith, sailing down the romantic Rhine and determining that he would never be a lawyer. Now, as if he were a character out of one of his own novels, he was travelling towards Berlin to meet the statesmen of Europe upon equal terms and to settle the affairs of Europe and Asia. Much has been made of his lack of qualifications for the role he was to play. His knowledge of geography was vague in the extreme and his interest in it minimal. He was no linguist, speaking only bad French, 'grocer's French' as most people described it, and was therefore hardly intelligible in the *lingua franca* of European diplomacy. He was uninterested in detail; as he said somewhat grandly to the Queen, he proposed to attend the Congress 'and exhibit his full powers' and then leave Lord Salisbury to 'complete all the details of which he is consummate master'. Moreover, his memory sometimes failed him and at Constantinople Salisbury had to remind his chief of points already agreed upon. Yet what Disraeli shared with European statesmen on the grand scale – with Metternich, Churchill and de Gaulle – was a deep sense of history, of the consequences of the past and of the bearing of the present upon the future. He had, moreover, an understanding of human nature and a supreme skill in what he had always liked to describe as 'the management of men'. Berlin would be the test of Disraeli's long-held vision of himself.

Impressed with the historical importance of the scene in which he was about to play his part, he kept a journal, something he had not done since his late twenties.[23] In its pages the proceedings of the Congress and the round of assemblies, balls and banquets which were the glittering front to secret horse-trading in private rooms, unrolled like a gorgeous pantomime round the principal actors. The key figure was undoubtedly Prince Bismarck, creator and virtual ruler of Germany, the man who had changed the face of nineteenth-century Europe, humbling Austria, destroying the empire of Napoleon III and elevating the King of Prussia into Emperor of a united Germany. Bismarck was a giant of a man, six foot two, with a puffy red face adorned with imposing white mustachios. He had a gigantic appetite; as Disraeli had once reported delightedly to Selina, his idea of a strict diet being only five courses – pickled salmon, smoked herrings, oysters, caviare and potato salad, accompanied by his favourite beverages, ale and champagne, which he swigged alternately. Despite all this and an appearance of careless affability, Bismarck was a man with a tortuous, Machiavellian mind, suspicious to the point of paranoia, vindictive, and with a profound contempt for humanity. His voice, Disraeli said, in contrast to his 'ogre-like form' was sweet and gentle and his conversation when not on strict business, 'recklessly frank'. He indulged in what Disraeli described as 'Rabelaisian monologues' and 'endless revelations of things he ought not to mention', even to the extent of telling Disraeli that his recent illness had been brought on by 'the horrible conduct of his Sovereign'. His characterizations of people, Disraeli, no mean judge himself, found 'extremely piquant'.

The two men met for the first time for a private conversation on 11 June only two hours after Disraeli's arrival in Berlin where he lodged at the Kaiserhof hotel. Both were sufficiently wary of each other to regard this meeting as an opportunity to assess each other's character and abilities, their previous impressions being not entirely favourable. Disraeli regarded Bismarck as a consummate liar and intriguer, while Bismarck, according to a colleague, had a strong prejudice against Disraeli whom he described as the 'romantic-oratorical Semite', and, while acknowledging his genius and political resourcefulness, thought him 'not ... sufficiently honourable and reliable'.[24] Moreover the German Ambassador in London, Count Münster, had sent in an unfavourable pre-Congress report on Disraeli to Bismarck, warning Bismarck that he would find it very difficult to carry on a really serious conversation with him as 'he is very vain and also enfeebled by age. It is true that illuminating and brilliant ideas are often produced,' Münster continued, 'but the higher conception, the moral groundwork, is lacking.' In the event Disraeli succeeded in winning Bismarck's respect, for at the end of the Congress the Prince paid tribute to his abilities, 'In spite of his fantastic novel-writing, he is a capable statesman,' he told Radowitz. 'It was easy to transact business with him: in a quarter of an hour you knew exactly how you stood with him, the limits to which he was prepared to go were exactly defined, and a rapid summary soon put a point upon matters.'[25]

Bismarck is reported to have said of Disraeli at the Congress, 'The old Jew, that is the man', and, as far as public interest went, Disraeli was certainly the central figure, a European celebrity. Crowds followed him as he walked out with Monty and within days of the opening of the Congress all his novels were sold out and emergency orders placed by the Berlin booksellers and circulating libraries for further supplies from England. The two British plenipotentiaries Disraeli and Salisbury made an ill-assorted pair; the frail Prime Minister with his dyed black curls and lined Semitic countenance, accompanied by the great English aristocrat, an imposing figure with what Werner, the painter of the Congress, described as his 'fine apostle's head'. There may have been a residue of jealousy or perhaps exasperation on the part of Salisbury against Disraeli; a week after the Congress opened he was to complain to his wife: 'What with deafness, ignorance of French and Bismarck's extraordinary mode of speech, Beaconsfield has the dimmest idea of what is going on, understands everything crossways and imagines a perpetual conspiracy'.[26] Nonetheless they worked well together, with Disraeli playing the warlike part against Russia counterbalanced by Salisbury's known pro-Christian and anti-Turkish sentiments.

The other principal figures at Berlin were the Russian plenipotentiaries, Shuvalov, and the aged Chancellor Gortchakov, now in his eightieth year and determined to end his career in a blaze of diplomatic splendour. Described by Disraeli as 'that old coxcomb', he was vain, jealous of his abler younger colleague, anxious to win kudos for any Russian successes and equally to offload upon Shuvalov the onus of any concessions. The principal Austrian plenipotentiary, Count Andrassy, was a man of imagination, strong will and some suppleness, but dismissed by Disraeli, not always as good a judge of character as he liked to think, as 'a picturesque-looking person, but apparently wanting in calm'; while he described the French representative, Georges Waddington, to the Queen as having the appearance and intelligence of a grocer. Disraeli was wrong too in his estimate of the Turkish plenipotentiary, Carathéodory, who appeared to him as 'good-looking, full of finesse, and yet calm and plausible: a man of decided ability'. Salisbury, advised by Layard, thought him a 'poor, weak, frightened creature, and when not frightened, not wholly trustworthy'. Carathéodory, frightened of his master the Sultan and of Layard who threatened to break his neck if he found him playing false, was to be the victim of the Congress.

The Congress was to be opened officially on 13 June. The night before, so the story goes, the British delegation, fearing that Disraeli's appalling French would make a ludicrous impression, implored the British Ambassador at Berlin, Lord Odo Russell, to persuade him to make his opening speech in English. Russell caught Disraeli as he was about to go to bed and told him what a disappointment it would be to the delegates were he to address them in French. 'They know that they have here in you the greatest living master of English oratory', he said, 'and are looking forward to your speech in English as the intellectual treat of their lives'. Whether Disraeli took this flattery as a hint or a compliment Lord Odo never knew, but on the following day and throughout the Congress he spoke in English.

The Congress, presided over by Bismarck, met in the huge ballroom of the Radziwill Palace, a glittering scene of gold-laced uniforms and jewelled orders. Disraeli was delighted by a ridiculous incident that took place during the morning's session which he retailed to the Queen:

> P[rince] Gortchakoff, a shrivelled old man, was leaning on the arm of his gigantic rival, and P[rince] Bismarck being seized with a sudden fit of rheumatism, both fell to the ground. Unhappily P. Bismarck's dog, seeing his master apparently struggling with an opponent, sprang to the rescue. It is said that P. Gortchakoff was not maimed or bitten thro' the energetic efforts of his companion.

Disraeli thoroughly enjoyed the heady mixture of high diplomacy and high society at Berlin. At Vienna, in Metternich's famous phrase, the delegates had danced; at Berlin, according to Disraeli, they ate. Banquet succeeded banquet; he was amazed at the appetite of the pretty Hungarian Countess Karolyi who told him at a dinner that she never refused a dish. 'I watched her and it was literally true,' Disraeli told the Queen. 'I watched her with amazement, that so delicate and pretty a mouth could perform such awful feats'. At the Turkish Embassy there was a mountain of splendid pilaff which tempted the 'grocer' Waddington to two helpings. But perhaps the banquet which interested him most was given by Bismarck's Jewish banker, Bleichröder, in the new palace he had built of 'every species of rare marble, and, where it is not marble, it is gold.' Disraeli gave the Queen a graphic picture of the great banker's humble wife:

> After dinner we were promenaded thro' the splendid saloons & picture galleries, & a ball-room fit for a fairy tale, & sitting alone on a sofa was a very mean-looking little woman, covered with pearls & diamonds, who was Madame Bleichröder ... whom he had married very early in life when he was penniless.

The Congress met in plenary session from two to five, but it was largely a formality, as Disraeli told Selina: 'All questions are publicly introduced, and then privately settled'. Disraeli's major victory over Russia came on the first question on the agenda, that of Bulgaria. He set out to frighten Shuvalov by telling him that the Russian proposal that the Sultan should not be allowed to garrison the frontier of that part of Bulgaria south of the Balkans which was to remain under his administration was 'outrageous', and a 'gross insult to England'. 'Lord B. spoke thunder about it. It will be given up by St Petersburg', Disraeli told the Queen confidently on 14 June. He kept up the pressure on Shuvalov, letting it be known through a conversation with the Italian representative, Count Corti, that if the Russians would not accept the British position he would break up the Congress. Days passed with no word from St. Petersburg, but Disraeli remained confident that the Russians would yield and he would achieve his principal objective, as he wrote on 20 June, 'Russia will be again entirely excluded from the Mediterranean, the object of the last, and all their wars'.

The next day he took a step towards fulfilling his threat to break up the Congress, ordering Monty Corry to arrange a special train for the departure of the British delegation, knowing that the news would soon spread round Berlin. Corry recorded that Disraeli was not bluffing and that he really intended to return to London, consult the Queen and advise a declaration of war on Russia. Bismarck took the threat seriously, hurrying round to see Disraeli. 'Am I to understand it is an ultimatum?' he asked. 'Yes, my Prince, it is,' Disraeli replied. That evening, sending his excuses to the British Embassy where he had an engagement, Disraeli dined instead with Bismarck *en famille*. At dinner Bismarck made no allusion to politics, 'tho' he ate & drank a great deal, [and] talked more', but after dinner the two men retired for a private discussion. Bismarck smoked a cigar and Disraeli, sacrificing health for intimacy, followed his example. 'I believe I gave the last blow to my shattered constitution' he wrote, 'but I felt it absolutely necessary.' After an hour and a half of conversation on high politics of which Disraeli unfortunately kept no record, Bismarck was convinced that the ultimatum was no sham and, Disraeli wrote, 'before I went to bed, I had the satisfaction of knowing that St. Petersburg had surrendered'. It was a deserved victory for Disraeli who had not had the advantage of knowing, as Bismarck did, that the Russian delegates had the Tsar's orders to give in rather than risk war. His firmness had carried the day.

In forcing the Russians to back down over Bulgaria, Disraeli's object had been not so much to help the Sultan, but, as he said, to keep the Russians out of the

Mediterranean, and in subsequent negotiations he showed little regard for Turkish interests. Austria, who had supported Britain in the struggle over Bulgaria received her reward in the second phase of the conference when Salisbury proposed that she should have the mandate to occupy Bosnia-Herzegovina. First Bismarck, then Disraeli, bludgeoned the helpless Turks into submission and the provinces were handed over to Austria with a sublime disregard for the claims of Turkish imperialism and Slav nationalism alike.

There remained the claims of Russia to the Turkish territories on the Asian shore of the Black Sea including Kars and Batum. At first Disraeli had considered this to be a question of vital importance to Britain, now, with the Cyprus agreement settled, he was disposed to compromise. There were farcical scenes as Gortchakov insisted upon settling the question alone. Salisbury exclaimed, 'But Lord Beaconsfield can't negotiate: he has never seen a map of Asia Minor'.[27] Indeed the two septuagenarians got into a tremendous muddle over their respective maps of the area; Colonel Wellesley opined that being both rather blind and confused, they had in fact 'inadvertently exchanged their most secret maps' prepared for them by their respective military staffs. In the end Disraeli and Salisbury were satisfied with a mild compromise by which Batum was made a free port and a portion of the territory restored to the Sultan.

In the mean time news of the Cyprus Convention leaked out. Although the Convention had been signed on 4 June, the Sultan had delayed issuing the *firman* for the cession of the island until the last moment, when, browbeaten by Layard with threats of concessions over Thessaly, Epirus and Crete, he caved in. Disraeli regarded it as a great triumph and the key to British influence in the East; he had even gone so far as to tell the Cabinet on 5 June that with the possession of Cyprus he was 'convinced that the virtual administration of the East by England was the only hope for the prosperity of those Countries and peoples'. Bismarck, who approved of territorial annexations, congratulated Disraeli, 'You have done a wise thing', he told him. 'This is progress. It will be popular: a nation likes progress'. 'His idea of progress was evidently seizing something', Disraeli commented to the Queen.

Disraeli dined privately for the last time with Bismarck and his family on 5 July, when as before the two men sat together afterwards – smoking cigars and talking politics. He enjoyed the Prince's extravagant conversation, retailing the more piquant passages to the Queen. Bismarck was obsessed with the Socialist threat and had conceived the odd idea that England's main bulwark against the advance of Socialism was the national passion for the turf. 'Here', the Prussian autocrat grumbled, 'a gentleman cannot ride down the street without twenty persons saying to themselves ... "Why has that fellow a horse, and I have not one?" In England the more horses a nobleman has, the more popular he is. So long as the English are devoted to racing, Socialism has no chance with you.' 'This will give you a slight idea of the style of his conversation', Disraeli told the Queen.[28]

But smoking with Bismarck, banqueting with Bleichröder and negotiating with

Gortchakov was having its effect upon his health. On 8 July Corry found his chief feeling so unwell that he telegraphed for Dr Kidd, who arrived post-haste two days later to find his patient suffering in the chest and gouty, but succeeded in patching him up for the signature of the treaty on 13 July. Disraeli was too weak to attend the final celebratory banquet but, as he told the Queen in a letter announcing the signature of the treaty, consoled himself with the thought that he had 'assisted in bringing about a settlement which will probably secure the peace of Europe for a long time', concluding, 'He cannot very well guide his pen, but yet will try to say how deeply & finely he feels the privilege of being the trusted servant of a Sovereign whom he adores!'[29]

Disraeli had reason to be content; from the signing of San Stefano to the conclusion of the Berlin Congress, he had, ably supported by Salisbury, fought with skill and determination for British interests as he saw them and, upon every point which he regarded as important, he had won. After fifteen years of comparative isolation, Disraeli had broken into the cartel of the *Dreikaiserbund* and Britain was once more among the Powers of Europe. This time the victory over Russia had been achieved without the loss of a single British life. The Congress of Berlin was the apotheosis of Disraeli's career; he was now recognized as a statesman of world rank, and, more than that, as the quintessence of English patriotism. As the *Journal des Débats* wrote in tribute, 'The traditions of England are not quite lost, they survive in the hearts of a woman and of an aged statesman.'

23 The Last Defeat

On his return to London Disraeli was received as a conquering hero. Arriving at Charing Cross leaning on the arm of Lord Salisbury and looking pale and worn but in good spirits, he was greeted by red carpets, cheering crowds and 'thrilling ladies', the 'romantic Baroness' among them. At Downing Street Ponsonby welcomed him with a bouquet of flowers and an enthusiastic letter from the Queen, and from the window, with Salisbury at his side, Disraeli proudly proclaimed to the waiting crowds that he had brought back 'Peace with Honour'.

Most thought Disraeli's claim justified, although the 'jingos' were disappointed that Russia had not been trounced and thought that Turkey had been shabbily treated, while the extreme liberals disliked the annexation of Cyprus. 'High and low are delighted', the Queen wrote, 'excepting Mr Gladstone, who is frantic'.[1]

The Faery was ecstatic; nothing was too much for her triumphant Prime Minister. She insisted on his taking the Garter and wanted to make him a Duke or a Marquess and Ralph D'Israeli – and hence Coningsby – his heir, a Baron or a Viscount. Disraeli accepted the Garter while insisting it should be bestowed also upon Lord Salisbury, but he refused a dukedom for himself and hereditary honours for Ralph. With his strict ideas as to qualifications for the peerage, he no doubt did not consider that Ralph's fortune or his talents merited the honour. He had always refused to use his position to help his family beyond what he considered to be their deserts, and indeed, since he had become Prime Minister, had frequently turned down Ralph's requests to advance him socially by putting him on the official lists for receptions at Marlborough House. Disraeli was right in refusing honours for Ralph which were quite unjustified and would only have given rise to ridicule; but Ralph, always touchy where his successful brother was concerned, must, if he knew of the Queen's offer, have been deeply chagrined.

In the midst of his triumph the conquering hero was too unwell even to see his beloved sovereign, having to conserve his strength to make his official statement in the House of Lords two days after his arrival. On 18 July he made a long speech to the Lords defending the terms of the Treaty of Berlin and the Cyprus Convention. Russia, he said, had been told that as far as Turkey and the Mediterranean were concerned it was 'Thus far, and no farther', and all this had been achieved 'without shedding the blood of a single Englishman'. He closed his statement on a high imperialist note; the possession of Cyprus, he declared, was necessary for the preservation of English influence in Asia, and, playing on a theme calculated to appeal to the missionary qualities of Victorian England, he talked of England's presence in Asia as a 'civilising agent'. The best defence for our Empire, he told the Lords, was 'the consciousness that in the Eastern nations there is confidence in this country, and that, while they know we can enforce our policy, at the same time they know that our Empire is an Empire of liberty, of truth, and of justice.'

Such imperialist notions were anathema to Gladstone; he was later to describe them as 'all brag ... prestige ... jingo'. Three days later in a speech at Southwark he referred to the Cyprus agreement as an 'insane covenant ... an act of duplicity not surpassed and rarely equalled in the history of nations'. As far as Gladstone was concerned anything Disraeli did reeked of duplicity; Disraeli should have been used to this, but he hit back publicly at Gladstone at a banquet in his honour at the Knightsbridge Riding School on 27 July. He asked his audience:

> Which do you believe most likely to enter an insane convention, a body of English gentlemen honoured by the favour of their Sovereign and the confidence of their fellow-subjects, managing your affairs for five years, I hope with prudence, and not altogether without success, or a sophistical rhetorician, inebriated with the exuberance of his own verbosity, and gifted with an egotistical imagination that can at all times command an interminable and inconsistent series of arguments to malign an opponent and glorify himself?

The usual public squabble between the two rivals ensued, with Disraeli complaining without grounds in the House of Lords that Gladstone had described him as 'devilish', and Gladstone writing to Disraeli for particulars of personal attacks Disraeli alleged him to have made upon him. Disraeli replied in the third person that he was really too busy to research all the instances of the past two and a half years, but in the end could not resist coming up with some choice epithets which Gladstone had recently flung at him. It was all childish and far from edifying in two political leaders, one a septuagenarian and the other verging on seventy, but, as Lord Granville later explained to the Queen:

> Lord Beaconsfield and Mr. Gladstone are men of extraordinary ability; they dislike each other more than is common among public men. Of no other politician would Lord Beaconsfield have said in public that his conduct was worse than the Bulgarian atrocities. He has a power of saying in two words that which drives a person of Mr Gladstone's peculiar temperament into a great state of excitement.[2]

Gladstone, biding his time, retired growling to the comfort of his family, who wished that the Queen would make Disraeli Duke of Jericho and send him there. It was emphatically Disraeli's hour of glory. On 3 August, breathless from asthma and with incipient bronchitis, he drove through cheering crowds to the Guildhall to receive the freedom of the City of London. Three days later seven hundred deputies representing nearly a thousand Conservative Associations waited upon him and Salisbury at the Foreign Office; not only did he have to shake hands with each one as they filed past, but to address them afterwards. Nonetheless that same night he went with Monty to see his first Gilbert and Sullivan opera. He was apprehensive: 'Some nonsense which everybody is going to see', he told Selina on 6 August. 'Parasol or Pinafore – a burlesque – a sort of thing I hate'.³ He did hate it: 'Except at Wycombe Fair in my youth,' he wrote two days later, 'I have never seen anything so bad as *Pinafore*'. Then there were grand dinners given by Louise Manchester, Cabinets to settle the Queen's speech, and the prospect of attendance on the Faery at Osborne. Disraeli was tired to death: 'I want to go to bed for a week', he told Selina, 'or lie on the summer grass if it would not rain.'⁴

But it did rain, and the weather was thundery, a portent of things to come. On the face of it Disraeli's government, with the Eastern crisis successfully concluded, looked set fair for the remaining years of their office. The Cabinet, re-shuffled since Derby's departure, contained some new men of ability; Sir Michael Hicks-Beach in place of Carnarvon at the Colonial Office; W.H. Smith as First Lord of the Admiralty; Frederick Stanley at the War Office and Lord Sandon as President of the Board of Trade. The 'new boy' Lord Sandon, invited by Disraeli to join the Cabinet in May, was, he recorded in his diary, 'much struck with the evident unanimity of the Cabinet, their business-like manner and thorough knowledge of their own departments. I felt that one could hardly be associated with a more high-minded and efficient body of men.'⁵

Even before the Cabinet had parted for the vacation in mid-August, however, the storm signals of economic depression and imperial adventure that were to destroy the Government had already arisen. After years of surplus the revenue was in deficit to the tune of £2.6 million and in Cabinet on 10 August Salisbury, Cairns and Cross warned that the future would be one in which the question of economy would be 'one of life and death to the Party and the Government'.⁶ A week before, the Viceroy of India, Lytton, had telegraphed news of the arrival of a Russian mission at Kabul, and his own proposal that a forceful demand should be made of the Emir of Afghanistan for the reception of an English representative there – a situation fraught with the possibilities of a Russo-English confrontation in Afghanistan on India's north-west frontier.

At Hughenden that autumn Disraeli seems to have felt an instinctive intimation of a coming storm which he might or might not survive, for on 15 October he and Corry ceremoniously placed the unfinished manuscript of *Endymion* in the newly-built strong-room. Disraeli did not tell Monty that with the manuscript he had enclosed a letter instructing him how the novel should be finished, leaving it to Monty to add the hundred pages still unwritten and to publish it in Disraeli's name.

Meanwhile in India Lytton was playing the 'great game' of countering Russia on the north-west frontier with Kiplingesque fervour. Without waiting for a definite go-ahead from the British Government and unaware of their negotiations with Russia over Central Asia, he sent a mission up the Khyber, to the Afghan frontier where the Emir, Sher Ali, refused it entry. Disraeli was alarmed and annoyed, writing crossly to Selina of 'distant and headstrong counsels', but he should not have been surprised. Evidence of the Viceroy's 'forward' policy and of his obsession with the intrigues of Russia and Sher Ali at Kabul had been given two years before when Lytton took over Baluchistan and sent a force to garrison Quetta on the southern flank of Afghanistan. Moreover, Disraeli was well aware of Lytton's character and admired it, writing to Salisbury at the time, 'we wanted a man of ambition, imagination, some vanity, & much will – & we have got him'. Nor can he have been unaware of the *folie de grandeur* with which the Viceroy had become increasingly infected, writing to the Queen in the first person as if addressing a fellow sovereign, and complaining to Cranbrook (the former Gat-horne-Hardy) of the shabby and ill-assorted dress of the officials who attended the viceregal court. Disraeli, sympathizing with Lytton's view of the importance of maintaining British prestige in Indian eyes, had made little effort to restrain him, and even now, faced with the dangers of the forward policy which he had tacitly approved, vacillated in his reactions.

Lytton's characteristic reaction to the snub delivered by the Emir was to ask the home Government's permission to declare war. At a Cabinet meeting held on 25 October, opinions were divided, with Cairns, Salisbury and Cross arguing that there was no *casus belli* to justify taking such a step. Salisbury in particular was very bitter against Lytton who, he said, was 'forcing the hand of the Government' as he had been doing since he first arrived in India and was compromising their European policy by his aggressive attitude towards Russia. Cranbrook, won over by voluminous reports written in the most elegantly persuasive style by the Viceroy, supported Lytton. Disraeli chose what was perhaps the worst course, compromise. An ultimatum was to be sent to the Emir demanding an apology and a promise to receive the British Mission at Kabul, while a British force was to cross the frontier and occupy certain points as 'a material guarantee'. He then strengthened the impression that the Government intended some warlike move on the frontier with some injudicious and misleading remarks at the Lord Mayor's Banquet in November, in which he referred to the frontier as 'haphazard and not ... scientific' and to the Government's intention to rectify it. Disraeli himself was pleased with his speech: 'The party is on its legs again, and jingoism triumphant!' he boasted to Selina. But it was precisely by encouraging such attitudes that he was preparing the way for disaster; on 21 November, no answer to Lytton's ultimatum having been received from the Emir, Roberts crossed the frontier at the head of an invading force and, for the second time in the century, Britain was militarily involved in Afghanistan.

Gladstone and Granville, watching on the sidelines, thought that the potent combination of the two literary imperialists, Disraeli and Lytton, could produce an explosive situation for the Government. Gladstone thought that it was a ploy to distract attention from the growing domestic distress: 'The position of the

Government is bad – and Dizzy, to whom I give credit for abundance of Parliamentary pluck and political daring, is just the man to play double or quits without limit', he wrote to Granville on 17 September. 'He may cover his deficit and every think [sic] else in a great Asiatic feat'.[7] Granville replied with bad reports of Lytton, that he would listen to no one who disagreed with his views, had no judgement and 'has taken to eat and *drink* much more than is good for him'.[8] 'The pot is beginning to boil ... My belief has been pretty firm since the Anglo-Turkish Convention that the Tory party is travelling towards a great smash', Gladstone wrote happily from Hawarden in November.[9] 'I do not see how he [Disraeli] is to shake off the financial difficulty', Granville replied on 14 November.[10]

The pot may have been beginning to boil; but when Parliament met early in December to discuss the Afghan situation, Disraeli was unrepentant and ultimately triumphant. Throwing all the blame upon the Emir, who, he said, far from being bullied by the British, had been 'treated like a spoiled child', he denied that it was in any way a move against Russia, or that annexation of Afghanistan was intended, merely a 'scientific rectification' of the frontier. In a speech which was strong in what Gladstone would have dubbed prestige and jingo he told the Lords it was not merely a local question but one which 'concerns the character and influence of England in Europe', following up this somewhat questionable statement with an appeal to the Lords to condemn the 'deleterious dogmas' of the peace at any price party.

The lack of news from India was a relief to Disraeli, and during November he was in relatively good spirits. Monty's house in South Audley Street was his headquarters for the November Cabinets; he had given up 'Eleanor of Northumberland's' house in Whitehall Gardens because the stairs were too much for him to manage and Downing Street was being redecorated. He took considerable enjoyment in observing the complications of Monty's love life. Melbury was being neglected in favour of an unnamed lady with a castle in Scotland whom Monty had met the previous year in Venice where they had 'glided together in gondolas', Disraeli informed Selina. 'I know from old experience, that's very dangerous & was quite prepared for the important change in his life.'[11] By mid-November the affair had progressed considerably; although Monty still visited the Ilchesters, Disraeli reported that 'his liaison with his new flame seems very *intime*, & there has been an exchange of "love tokens". I think this rather unprincipled; however he is amused & pretty well', he added indulgently.[12] The gay deceiver planned to spend Christmas at Melbury, 'though he writes to another lady every day & calls upon a third every day without exception. What a Don Juan!' Disraeli wrote.[13] Monty's active love life interfered with his efficiency as a secretary and this, coupled with his passion for shooting, made him somewhat unreliable. But Disraeli could forgive him anything. 'He has so many admirable qualities that we can only regret the state of his nervous system, which requires constant air, exercise & the company of charming women', he told Selina.

Monty accompanied his chief on a visit to Sandringham in November. Disraeli felt bound to make the trip as he had thrown over the Prince in favour of Selina the previous year and had been found out. The party at Sandringham was more 'agreeable' to Disraeli than usual as the Manchesters, Salisburys and other 'superior' friends were there, but still he complained that they were counterbalanced by an equal number of 'permanent or temporary parasites' who greatly marred the occasion. 'There scarcely can be any conversation with such ruffians as Oliver Montagu, writing all dinner time idiotic remarks on bits of paper, making fun of the Menu & jokes of silly slang,' he grumbled.[14]

The year closed gloomily. On 14 December, the anniversary of her father's death, Princess Alice of Hesse, the Prince of Wales's favourite sister, died of diphtheria contracted from her children, one of whom also died. 'She was the pearl of the family', Disraeli told Selina. He made a speech on the vote of condolence to the Queen referring melodramatically to the mother receiving 'the kiss of death' from her son. 'Inconceivable bathos', commented one observer; 'beautiful' thought the Queen. Despite tidings of British successes in Afghanistan early in December, Disraeli, arriving back in London from Windsor a week before Christmas in a black fog, found darker news awaiting him, of financial disasters and bank failures – 'another black Friday', he commented. Windsor, that 'Palace of the Winds' as he called it, had made his asthma worse and he was too ill to make the journey to Weston he had planned. He did, however, manage to get down to Hughenden for Christmas in thick snow. Warmed by the central heating which he had had installed after Mary Anne's death he wrote a Christmas letter to Selina which, despite the usual complaints about his chest, ended on an optimistic note: 'Everything, they say, comes too late. It is something if it comes. However, I won't complain of life. I have had a good innings & cannot at all agree with the Great King that all is Vanity.'[15]

It was to be only a brief moment of content; snow gave way to hard frost, the bitter weather only serving to accentuate the economic problems which had already been looming large when Parliament met before Christmas. Disraeli was helpless in the face of a general industrial and agricultural depression which was not his Government's fault and with which it was ill-equipped to deal. Gladstone's cherished 'nest-egg', the £5-million surplus in 1874, had been transformed into a series of deficits – £2.6 million in 1877–8, £2.3 million in 1878–9, and would worsen in 1879–80 to £3.3 million. The deficits were the result not of imperial ventures but of the depression of British industry as foreign competition, protected by tariff walls, made increasing inroads upon British markets. Profits and prices fell, output declined and unemployment rose, and the industrialists' reaction was to reduce wages in line with the falling prices and profits. In agriculture things were still worse; a run of bad harvests was accompanied not by a rise in the price of wheat but by an actual fall because of competition from the American wheatlands.

The severe winter of 1878–9 caused great hardship among the working class and the Government, as Disraeli had admitted in the Queen's Speech on 5

December 1878, simply did not know what to do and had prepared no measures to deal with the distress. Large-scale manipulation of the economy was not part of the political thinking of the time and even the Opposition, while they might be expected to make capital out of the situation, did not want the Government to take such measures, considering, as Granville told the Lords, that such action 'would be in violation of those principles of political economy in which I am a sincere believer'.[16] Disraeli's bewilderment and distress as he contemplated the suffering of the people after Christmas that year were patent in a letter he wrote Selina on 27 December:

> There are so many plans, so many schemes, and so many reasons why there should be neither plans nor schemes.
>
> What I fear is that the Opposition, who will stick at nothing, may take up the theme for party purposes. If we then don't support them, we shall be stigmatised as unpatriotic; if we do they will carry all the glory. And yet – what is the cause of the distress? And if permanent, is there to be a permanent Committee of Relief? And the property of the nation to support the numbers of unemployed labor? Worse than Socialism ... There are 1,000 things to be said (on both sides) – but after all Starvation has no answer.[17]

He believed, as many others did, that the distress was all part of a cycle which would naturally be followed by a recovery. But for his Government it was a question of how long the cycle of depression would last and early in 1879 there were signs that Disraeli's luck was running out.

As the New Year dawned the bitter weather had its usual effect upon his health; he was suffering from 'bronchitis, asthma & all the grisly crew', and, as he told Selina on New Year's Day, people were dying of bronchitis every day – 'I don't see why I don't.' By 19 January, however, he was well enough to go up to London by a specially-heated salon carriage which had been kept warming up for him at Wycombe for a week. He attended the pre-session Cabinets early in February in newly-decorated Downing Street, then spent a few days resting at Hatfield. Somewhat revived by the rest and the weather which had turned wet and warm, he travelled up to London on 10 February in a contented and optimistic mood, totally unprepared for the shattering news he was to receive the following day.

Three weeks before, on 22 January 1879, a British force of 800 white soldiers and 500 Africans was surrounded and overwhelmed by Cetewayo and his Zulus at Isandhlwana. It was the worst blow to British military prestige within living memory; Disraeli reeled under the shock, well aware of the effect it would have upon the reputation of his Government. 'The terrible disaster has shaken me to the centre', he told Anne Chesterfield on 13 February, 'and what increases the grief is that I have not only to endure it, but to sustain others and to keep a bold front before an unscrupulous enemy.'[18]

The blow was a particularly bitter one for Disraeli, as it was the result of a policy with which he had little sympathy in a part of the world in which he took minimal interest. Since 1874 until his resignation in 1877 Southern Africa had been under the energetic control of Carnarvon, whose policy of consolidation and expansion had brought him first into conflict with the Boers of the Transvaal and then with the only powerful black leader in the region, Cetewayo, king of the Zulus. The confrontation had not been of Cetewayo's choosing but that of Sir Bartle Frere who was convinced that there would be no security for the area until the Zulu power was broken for ever. Frere, a Carnarvon appointee of whose abilities Disraeli had a low opinion, was an empire-builder *par excellence*, a man whose soft voice and manners belied a spirit of action and expansion; whose object, contrary to any instruction from the home Government, was to see the British sphere of influence extended to the borders of the Portuguese Empire to the north. There was no telegraphic communication between London and South Africa, a situation which allowed ample scope for independent action by such a man as Frere. Hicks-Beach, who had replaced Carnarvon at the Colonial Office, was unfamiliar with the situation and could not, as he told Disraeli, control Frere without a telegraph system, admitting ruefully 'I don't know that I could, with one'. In December Frere had presented Cetewayo with an ultimatum which he knew the king could not accept and in January 1879 the Zulu War had begun with Lord Chelmsford in command. Over-confident and underestimating the fighting qualities of the Zulus, Chelmsford had advanced with dilatoriness and lack of caution – Isandhlwana had been the result.

Disraeli, although defending their conduct in Parliament, remained furious with both Frere and Chelmsford, regarding the former as dangerously self-opinionated and the latter as weak and incompetent. 'Sir Bartle Frere, who ought to be impeached, writes always as if he were quite unconscious of having done anything wrong!' he exploded to Anne Chesterfield.[19] Chelmsford, he complained, 'does nothing with the 15,000 troops he has ... [and] seems cowed & confused'.[20] Feeling as he did, he ought perhaps to have recalled them, but he did not. He demonstrated his disapproval by sending an official despatch censuring Frere for declaring war without authorization, and he appointed Sir Garnet Wolseley as High Commissioner and Commander-in-Chief for Natal, Transvaal and adjacent territories, including Zululand. Wolseley, therefore, was to have supreme civil and military power within that area; the dangerous Frere was to be confined to the Cape; and the suspect Chelmsford demoted to second-in-command under Frere. The appointment of Wolseley came up against furious opposition from the Queen who, approving of Frere's forward policy, feared it might 'discourage poor Sir Bartle', and from the Horse Guards where Wolseley was very unpopular. Disraeli stood out against them all, including the Prince of Wales who supported Frere. 'The Horse Guards are furious, the Princes are raging, and every mediocrity as jealous as if we had prevented him from conquering the world', he told Anne Chesterfield on 28 May.[21] Wolseley had his faults, he admitted, but so did most successful men of action. 'It is quite true that Wolseley is an egotist & a braggart. So was Nelson', he wrote to the Queen. So might he himself have been, he added wryly, had he not had 'the immense advantage ... of being vilified & decried for upwards of forty years ... which has taught him self-control, patience, & some circumspection.'[22]

Isandhlwana was not the last tragedy of the Zulu War; on 1 June 1879 the Prince Imperial, only son and heir of Napoleon III and Eugénie, was killed in an ambush in circumstances that gave another bad impression of British military skill *vis-à-vis* the Zulus. In the confusion the Prince's companions rode off not realising that he was not with them; his saddle had given way and he was unable to remount his frightened horse before being caught and speared to death. Again it was hardly Disraeli's fault; he had done his best to stop the Prince going but the Queen and the Empress had insisted, and, as he said afterwards to Lord Redesdale, 'What can you do against two obstinate women?' He was angry about the whole incident, not least with the Queen who personally attended the funeral at Chislehurst among a panoply of Bonaparte exiles. 'The Queen seems highly pleased at all that occurred at Chislehurst this morning', he grumbled to Anne Chesterfield on 12 July. 'I hope the French Government will be as joyful. In my mind nothing cd. be more injudicious than the whole affair.'

Resentment against Frere and Chelmsford for the embarrassment they had caused him led to a rare row between Disraeli and the Queen. When Chelmsford returned to England as a conquering hero after having finally defeated the Zulus at Ulundi on 4 July, Disraeli absolutely refused to obey the Queen's appeal to receive him at Hughenden, sending her a 'tremendous indictment' of Chelmsford by way of explanation. 'He mixes up Lord Chelmsford in no small degree with the policy of the unhappily precipitate Zulu War, the evil consequences of which to this country have been incalculable', Disraeli wrote furiously, proceeding to blame both the General and the war for everything that had gone wrong in foreign affairs that summer.

> He charges Lord Chelmsford with having invaded Zululand '*avec un coeur léger*', with no adequate knowledge of the country he was attacking, & no precaution or preparation. A dreadful disaster occurred in consequence, & then Lord Chelmsford became panic-struck; appealed to yr. Majesty's Govt. practically for reinforcements, & found himself at the head of 20,000 of yr. Majesty's troops in order to reduce a country not larger than Yorkshire.

He would not even allow Chelmsford credit for his final victory: 'Had he not been furtively apprised by telegraph that he was about to be superseded, Lord Chelmsford would probably never have advanced to Ulundi'.[23] The Queen was 'grieved & astonished' at Disraeli's attitude, but he would not give in, although he attempted to soothe her Majesty by sending loving messages via his partisan, her lady in waiting, Lady Ely, known, for obvious reasons, as 'whispering Jane'. 'I love the Queen – perhaps the only person in this world left to me that I do love,' he wrote.[24] The Queen received Chelmsford at Balmoral and was fascinated by the huge Zulu warrior's shield with which he presented her while with touching humanitarianism she worried in case Cetewayo and his wives might be humiliated by being forced to wear European dress. Disraeli, sick of both Cetewayo and Chelmsford, would do no more than grant the General a few formal minutes at Downing Street.

Disraeli's behaviour over the Zulu War and his treatment of Frere and Chelmsford exhibited a pettishness and lack of objectivity that was quite out of character, contrasting strangely with his forbearance towards Lytton who had, after all, committed a similar sin of disobedience which was eventually to result in an almost equally embarrassing disaster. Ill-health, bad weather to which he was always sensitive, and feelings of frustration in the face of what appeared to be a run of increasingly bad luck may have contributed to his testy reaction. But personal dislike no doubt fuelled his resentment, as Ponsonby commented, 'He can't bear either Frere or Chelmsford'.

His differences with the Queen over the issue revealed a fundamental divergence in their attitudes to Empire. The Queen was very expansionist over 'her' Empire, as she felt moved to urge him in September 1879: 'Our keeping these countries in India & elsewhere *is* (& always will be) because the *Native* Sovereigns CANNOT maintain *their authority*. It is not for *aggrandisement*, but to *prevent war &* *bloodshed* that we *must* do this.' He must never, she told him, say 'we shall keep nothing'.[25] Earlier, at the time of their differences over Chelmsford, she had felt obliged to tell him that he should never let the army and navy down: 'If we are to maintain our position as a *first-rate* Power ... we must ... be prepared for *attacks* & *wars, somewhere* or *other*, CONTINUALLY'.[26]

Disraeli disliked colonial wars and was opposed to annexation wherever possible. He was, as both Gladstone and Derby had noted, principally interested in Britain's international prestige of which he saw her glamorous Indian possessions as an essential part. Lytton's forward policy could be forgiven because it was a part of the global 'great game' which Britain played with Russia; provocation of Zulus and Boers which necessitated the despatch of costly expeditionary forces was not. Moreover he was deeply and justifiably concerned that such expenditure would upset the policy of economy to which he and the Government had committed themselves as 'a matter of life and death'. He was interested in glamour, prestige and '*haute politique*', but in no way shared the Victorian colonialist ethic of 'the white man's burden', 'the Bible and the Sword' attitude, which inspired imperial heroes like Gordon of Khartoum, and which he would have regarded as dreadfully middle class. In international affairs he modelled himself upon Metternich and Pitt and, to a lesser extent, Palmerston.

Thus it was singularly ironic that colonial disasters should have dominated what was to be the last year of his premiership. The final Cabinets of the summer session of 1879 were occupied in battles over how to finance the expenses incurred by military forces in India, Africa and the Mediterranean. Disraeli was furious with Northcote who, true to the traditions of his former mentor, Gladstone, was opposed to deficit financing and proposed a tax on the country's most cherished commodity, tea. 'Insane pedantry' was the reaction of Disraeli who had never seen anything wrong in being in debt. Pitt, he said, would not have hesitated to leave the whole debt to posterity, 'But alas! there are no longer Mr Pitts', he wrote to the Queen on 24 July, 'but a leader of the House of Commons [Northcote], who, tho' one of the most amiable & gifted of men, thinks more of an austere smile from Mr. Gladstone, ... than the applause & confidence of a great historic party.'[27]

By the end of the session of 1879, however, Disraeli might have been forgiven for thinking that his imperial troubles were over. The Zulus had been defeated, while in Afghanistan after a successful campaign by Roberts and the replacement of Sher Ali by his son, Yakub Khan, a British mission headed by Sir Louis Cavagnari was installed at Kabul. On 14 August Disraeli wrote to Lytton congratulating him on the achievement of 'a scientific & adequate frontier for our Indian Empire' which was, he said, largely due to Lytton's 'energy & foresight'. But, even before Disraeli's letter reached India the murder of Cavagnari and the entire mission by mutinous Afghan troops at Kabul threw the whole situation into confusion. 'This is a shaker', Disraeli wrote to Salisbury. Roberts's subsequent campaign was swift and successful but the Opposition were able to present the murder of Cavagnari as the logical consequence of the Government's rash and unjustified forward policy in India.

'The Stars in their courses have fought against me', Disraeli quoted in a letter to Lytton on 14 August.[28] It had been a terrible summer, with ceaseless rain, thunder, and lightning heralding the worst harvest of the century, the colonial disasters and a difficult session in Parliament where Parnell and the Irish members had begun a campaign of obstruction. 'I have had to struggle against four bad harvests & four wars ... with a failing Exchequer', Disraeli complained to Lytton. There had been personal sadness too, with the sudden death of Lionel de Rothschild in June. As if all this were not enough, the signs of disaster were all around him as he spent a wet late August at Hughenden. It rained night and day and, a sure sign of deepening agricultural depression, his tenants were threatening not to renew their tenancies. 'I think the agricultural bankruptcy must finish us', he wrote gloomily to Selina on 25 August.

Gladstone, whose keen political instinct sensed the possibility of victory, was already working out his plan of attack. He thought the Government would like to remain quiet and allow the memories of past disasters to fade. This he was determined they should not be allowed to do. 'In my view ... they will not supply any new matter of such severe condemnation as what they have already furnished', he wrote to Granville on 6 August. 'Therefore, my idea is, we should keep the old alive & warm.'[29] At Balmoral in September the Queen was also contemplating the possibility of a defeat for the Government. Taking her customary extreme view of her constitutional powers, she took the step, through Ponsonby, of warning the Liberal Opposition (or rather the moderate Whig section of it, Hartington and Granville) against the policies and Ministers she would not be prepared to accept from them. There was to be no pandering to Russia or 'letting down our Empire in India & the Colonies', while 'she never could take' either Gladstone – 'violent, mischievous & dangerous' – Lowe, or the republican Sir Charles Dilke as Ministers.

As Gladstone had predicted, Disraeli's intention that autumn was to avoid controversy and his speech at the Guildhall in November caused general disappointment, being confined to comments, but not remedies, on the economic distress and vague appeals to '*Imperium et Libertas*'. His speech was to pale into insignificance beside the brilliant popular oratory of Gladstone in his first Midlothian campaign later that month. Gladstone prophesied that Disraeli would dissolve Parliament in the spring of the following year, 1880, and therefore intended, as he had told Granville in August, to carry on a continuous process of 'stirring the country' against the Government in good time for the election. As usual with Gladstone, a political campaign became a moral crusade; however, his niece Lady Frederick Cavendish recorded that he put himself up for Midlothian which would offer him a perfect platform for public speaking, 'simply and solely because he was told on good authority that his winning that seat would best promote the cause which to him was the cause of right and morality, viz., the turning out of Dissy's Government.'[30]

The Midlothian campaign of the last week of November 1879 was Gladstone's finest hour as a popular orator and politician. Disraeli called it disparagingly 'a pilgrimage of passion'; Gladstone himself 'a festival of freedom'. Speaking to huge audiences of working-class Scots men and women, he denounced the Government's record in a torrent of passionate, emotive words, accusing the Conservatives of financial profligacy in the pursuit of 'phantoms of glory', of rampant aggression and immoral disregard for the rights of native peoples. 'Remember the rights of the savage,' he told them. 'Remember that the happiness of his humble home, remember that the sanctity of life in the hill villages of Afghanistan, among the winter snows, is as inviolable in the eyes of Almighty God as can be your own'. In a direct hit at Disraelian oratory he implored his wildly cheering audience never 'to suffer appeals to national pride to blind you to the dictates of justice'. Disraeli's foreign policy, he said, had violated every canon of morality, inflicted great injuries upon his country, endangered the peace of the world and 'all the most fundamental interests of Christian society'. He painted pathetic pictures of Afghan mothers and children driven from their homes to perish in the snow and, as for the Zulus, ten thousand of their innocent people had been slaughtered 'for no other offence than their attempt to defend against your artillery with their naked bodies, their hearths and homes, their wives and families'. He appealed to his audience to reject the Disraelian road to 'suffering, discredit and dishonour' and to take that 'which slowly, perhaps, but surely, leads a free and high-minded people towards the blessed ends of prosperity and justice, of liberty and peace'.

Disraeli, the object of these tirades, refused to read a word of the 'drenching rhetoric' uttered by the 'Impetuous Hypocrite'. 'What a waste of powder & shot,' he wrote to Selina on 28 November, 'all ... planned on the wild assumption that Parlt. was going to be dissolved', assuring her that there was no intention of going to the country before 1881.[31] Perhaps he would have done better to meditate upon Gladstone's Midlothian themes for this was one of the occasions when his rival's political instinct was surer than his own, and Gladstone's impassioned speeches were sounding the death knell of Disraeli's Government. He had brilliantly turned the tables on Disraeli, presenting the Conservative leader's imperial theme as a synonym for immoral aggression and skilfully implying that the distress of the country was the direct result of his reckless pursuit of 'phantoms of glory'. It was not difficult for the working class suffering unemployment, reduced wages and hardship in some of the bitterest weather of the century, to follow Gladstone's argument that only a change of Government could make things better. Moreover, Disraeli's failure to answer Gladstone's charges led the public to conclude that he had no reply to make.

In contrast to his energetic rival Disraeli felt 'terribly knocked down' by the fogs and frosts of this harsh November that early in December gave way to thick snow. Gladstone, elated by his triumphs, retired to Hawarden in December to write messianic passages in his journal. It was the eve of his seventy-first birthday and he looked back on the years of his retirement from the Liberal leadership as a developing process guided by a divine hand:

> For the past three and a half years I have been passing through a political experience which is, I believe, without example in our parliamentary history. I profess to believe it has been an occasion when the battle to be fought was a battle of justice, humanity, freedom, law, all in their first elements from the very root, and all on a gigantic scale. The word spoken was a word for millions, and for millions who for themselves cannot speak. If I really believe this, then I should regard my having been morally forced into this work as a great and high election of God.[32]

Had Disraeli read this passage, he would doubtless have agreed with Henry Labouchere who said that he did not mind Gladstone's seeming always to have an ace up his sleeve, but he did object to his implying that God had put it there.

The year 1879 closed with the news of the Tay Bridge disaster on the night of 28 December. A great storm brought down the bridge while a train was crossing it and all aboard were drowned. 'So ends the year', Cranbrook wrote in his diary, 'a calamitous one for the public', and, he might have added, for Disraeli's Government.

The Prince of Wales paid a visit to Hughenden early in the New Year. It was, perhaps, a conciliatory exercise, for Disraeli had certainly suspected in November that the Prince did not favour his Government, complaining angrily to Selina that the Prince had 'never been of the slightest use to the Government & never gained us a single vote, tho' he was always asking for something for himself or his friends'.[33] However all passed off well at Hughenden, with the Prince at his most amiable, praising the house, the pictures and the dinner and considerately refraining from keeping his frail host up after midnight.

Disraeli travelled up to London for the pre-session Cabinet meetings in January only to find most of the principal Ministers ill and unable to attend. Grand dinners in honour of the Princess Louise, late hours and 'poisonous claret' at Stafford House combined with the strain of daily Cabinets and working on the Queen's

Speech soon sapped what strength he had. As he wrote half-humorously to Selina on 29 January:

> I am unable to move, Salisbury is confined to his room at Hatfield & must do no work, the Lord Chancellor attacked by asthma for the first time was so frightened that he rushed to Bournemouth, where he found the fog blacker than here. The Chancellor of the Exchequer is in bed with influenza. Sandon is at Liverpool. Where John Manners's broken bones are I hardly know – but if there had been a Cabinet today *six* would have been absent.[34]

He was stricken with gout and although he managed to hold the traditional eve of session dinner he was incapable of carrying the sword of state at the opening of Parliament on 5 February. As he told Selina, he had not yet been able to put on a boot and was as shaky as a man can be who has been shut up for two weeks. He struggled to his place in the Lords for the evening's debate but Cranbrook observed that he was physically feeble and evidently feeling his gout, and by his own account he had great difficulty in speaking 'and what I did say, I said badly'. It was an ill-omened beginning for what was to be Disraeli's last parliamentary session as Prime Minister.

It was unlikely to be an easy one. Distress in Ireland had occupied much of the attention of the winter Cabinets and obstruction by the Irish Home Rulers in the Commons would ensure that the Government had difficulty getting business done. Charles Stewart Parnell was the virtual, although not yet nominal leader of the Irish group; stern, inflexible, with no sense of humour and little imagination, he was a formidable figure. Although the number of Home Rulers was small, parliamentary rules of the day were quite inadequate to deal with the concerted obstruction he directed. There was no closure, no power of finishing a debate or of checking perpetual motions for adjournment, with the result that the few Irish members could hold up the whole executive and legislative work of the Government, and indeed on one occasion between five and seven Irishmen kept the House sitting continuously for twenty-six hours. Moreover, while Disraeli, had he still been Leader of the House might just possibly, as George Hamilton thought, have been able to deal with the Irish, his successor, Sir Stafford Northcote was not. With the first week of the session of 1880 it became clear that Parnell would, and could, obstruct the measures for Ireland which the Government put forward, even though they included bills for the relief of distress. More importantly in view of the activities of the Land League in Ireland, the Coercion Act or, as it was now termed, the Prevention of Crime Act, was due to expire and any attempt to renew it would inevitably draw the concentrated fire of Parnell and his followers.

By the second week of the session the Government, faced with the prospect of Irish obstruction and of an embarrassing struggle over the minor but potentially dangerous issue of the Metropolitan Water Company, was beginning to exhibit signs of war-weariness. 'The general bias is now to an early election,' Cranbrook wrote in his diary on 9 February. 'I have always doubted whether we could keep things going this session'. The Queen offered her own somewhat over-simple

solution to keep her Government going: 'Ought you not to come to some agreement with some of the sensible & reasonable & not violent men on the other side',
she asked Disraeli on 12 February, 'to put a stop to what clearly is a determination
to force the disruption of the British Empire?'[35] Disraeli disillusioned her: 'There
are no "sensible & reasonable, & really not violent men" in the ranks of the
Opposition', he replied on 13 February. 'The nominal leaders [Granville and
Hartington] have no authority; & the mass, chiefly under the guidance & authority, or rather inspiration, of Mr. Gladstone, who avoids the responsibility of his
position, are animated by an avidity for office, such as Lord Beaconsfield, after
more than forty years' experience, cannot recall.'[36] The Queen sent him a Valentine to cheer him up, to which he replied in suitably flowery language: 'He
wishes he could repose on a sunny bank, like young Valentine in the pretty picture
that fell from a rosy cloud this morn ... [but] Lord Beaconsfield, no longer in the
sunset, but the twilight of existence, must encounter a life of anxiety & toil.'[37]

Dissolution was discussed in Cabinet on St Valentine's Day but Disraeli, despite
an encouraging by-election result at Southwark where the Conservatives gained
a seat from the Liberals, still considered an autumn election preferable. Most of
his colleagues disagreed, as Cranbrook recorded on 19 February: 'Northcote
seems to apprehend a state of things which will in all probability bring this
Parliament to a close. I fancy almost all wish for it.' At some point within the next
two weeks Disraeli changed his mind; possibly because he feared that the discontent of the farmers, normally a bastion of Tory strength, would undoubtedly grow
worse by the autumn; possibly he was misled by the rosy predictions of the party's
electoral managers, encouraged by the Liverpool and Southwark results. Dissolution was agreed upon in Cabinet on 6 March and formally announced two days
later; Parliament was to be dissolved on 24 March and the election would follow.

If Disraeli hoped that the election would be fought on his terms he was much
mistaken. Beaconsfield the statesman seemed to have lost the sure touch of Disraeli
the politician. His election manifesto, issued on 9 March in the form of an open
letter to the Duke of Marlborough, attempted to put the integrity of Great Britain
and the Empire as the major issue to be decided by the electorate. It raised the
spectre of Home Rule and an independent Ireland, and fell back upon the old
argument of accusing Gladstone and the Liberals of attempting to disrupt that
integrity. 'There are some who challenge the expediency of the imperial character
of this realm', he declared. 'Having attempted, and failed, to enfeeble our colonies
by their policy of decomposition, they may perhaps now recognise in the disinte-
gration of the United Kingdom, a mode which will not only accomplish but
precipitate their purpose.' His second plank was an active foreign policy; peace,
he said, could not be obtained by the passive principle of non-intervention. 'Peace
rests on the presence, not to say the ascendancy, of England in the councils of
Europe.'

Disraeli had rightly foreseen that the problems of Ireland would occupy the
centre stage of British politics in the near future. Public opinion, however, was

not with him, tending to agree with the Opposition who accused him of raising the question to distract attention from the grave economic problems at home. For the majority hardship at home was the major issue, and they had little time for the problems of Ireland or the Empire, or for Britain's ascendancy in the councils of Europe. Gladstone took care to hammer home the point that their suffering was the direct result of 'Beaconsfieldism'. Fulfilling his promise to Granville of keeping the old issues 'alive and warm', he embarked on a second Midlothian campaign on 16 March, carrying on his fierce moral denunciations of Disraeli and his Government over the critical electoral period at Easter. Like Disraeli in 1872 he appealed to the nation, and, following his own populist traditions of 1866 he launched his appeal over the heads of the aristocratic establishment. The electorate, he told his audiences, were the jury in a great State Trial which was now proceeding on the acts of Disraeli and the late Government, and he urged them to bring in a verdict of 'Guilty'. In answer to this populist rhetoric, the Tory speakers had singularly little to say for themselves. The leading speakers on the Conservative side – Disraeli, Salisbury and Cranbrook – were as peers barred from taking part in elections and in general little attempt was made by the Tory party to appeal to the working class on the basis of their past record of social legislation. '*Sanitas sanitatum*' had been superseded by '*Imperium et Libertas*', a cry which raised no response in the hearts of people who believed, as Gladstone told them, that their suffering was the price that had been paid for the massacre of innocent Afghans and Zulus. They believed it too when Gladstone pointed to one man as the cause of it all – Disraeli.

The object of all this hatred spent the electoral period at Hatfield, Salisbury having gone abroad with his wife to recuperate. Disraeli's health was feeble; George Hamilton, who saw him before the election campaign started, found him very weak after an attack of gouty asthma. He asked Hamilton to give him his arm as he wished to see if he could walk and, when Hamilton expressed concern at his weakness, replied, 'Yes, I am far from well, but I have a clever doctor who cooks me up when I have anything public to do. I then manage to crawl to the Treasury Bench, and when I get there to look as fierce as I can.' It was impossible, Hamilton recorded, not to admire 'the dauntless spirit of this old man, contrasted with the frail body in which it was enshrined'. Nor could he help contrasting the bitter hostility with which Disraeli was now regarded in his own country with his immense reputation in Europe.[38]

At that critical moment, however, it was the opinion of England not of Europe which counted. Hamilton warned Disraeli that the party might lose the election as the forces operating against them were so widespread in origin and so plausibly utilized by the Opposition. Out of touch with the urban electorate and misled by the Southwark and Liverpool by-elections Disraeli would not believe him, although he admitted to Cranbrook that he had his doubts about the counties. In fact the party managers totally misread the situation, Sir George Russell of the Central Office telling Cranbrook on 29 March that failure to secure a substantial majority would be 'contrary to reasonable expectations'.

The two rivals passed their time waiting for the results of the polls in characteristically different ways. Gladstone energetically indulged his passion for hewing down trees on the Scottish estate of his host, Lord Rosebery, while Disraeli at Hatfield wrapped in furs against the cold wind, took cautious walks in the grounds and sipped Château Margaux 1870 provided for him by special order of Lord Salisbury. 'At this awful pause', he told Selina on polling day, 31 March, 'my mind is a blank.'

Within twenty-four hours it was obvious that the Conservatives were facing a defeat of landslide proportions; on the final count they had lost over 100 seats to the Liberals, being returned with a strength of only 237 against 353 Liberals and 62 Irish members. The working class vote against Disraeli and his policies was particularly significant; in the large boroughs the Conservatives actually did worse than they had in 1868, and lost what they had gained in 1874. By 2 April Disraeli admitted defeat, correctly attributing it (although characteristically not taking into account the skill of the Opposition campaign) to the economic depression. 'Never was so great a discomfiture with a cause so inadequate', he wrote bitterly to Selina. ' "Hard Times" was the cry against us. The suffering want a change; no matter what, they are sick of waiting.'[39] Although he put a brave face upon his defeat, he felt it deeply. When one of Salisbury's sons at Hatfield tried to console him by saying, 'It will all turn out all right some day', he replied, 'It is all very well for you to consider this lightly; but with me it is the end of my career.'[40]

It was indeed a bitter defeat; he was seventy-five and it was therefore unlikely that he would ever be Prime Minister again. The election result represented a personal defeat for him and a personal triumph for Gladstone, who had, almost single-handedly, mobilized the electorate against Disraeli and 'Beaconsfieldism' in a brilliant campaign. For Disraeli the election of 1880 must have been something like that of 1945 for Churchill; after a long political career and apotheosis as a popular hero and symbol of England, he was decisively rejected by a huge working-class vote. But for Disraeli, unlike Churchill, this was, as he said, the end of his career.

Gladstone, although expecting a victory, was 'stunned' at its magnitude. 'The downfall of Beaconsfieldism', he wrote to the Duke of Argyll on 12 April, 'is like the vanishing of some vast magnificent castle in an Italian romance.' The Queen, at Baden in Germany, was equally stunned; on receiving Disraeli's telegram forecasting certain defeat, she could hardly bring herself to believe it. 'This is a terrible telegram', she wrote to Ponsonby, '& surely *how* can he yet be *sure* of *this*?' Two days later as the dreadful truth was brought home to her, her thoughts flew to Gladstone: 'The Queen ... would sooner *abdicate* than send for or have any *communication* with that *half-mad firebrand* who wd. soon ruin everything & be a *Dictator*', she wrote hysterically to Ponsonby. 'Others but herself *may submit* to his democratic rule, but *not the Queen*.'[41]

When Ponsonby tried to soothe her by presenting Gladstone as loyal and devoted to herself she indignantly rejected the idea. Loving Disraeli as she did she could feel nothing but repulsion for the man who had brought him down. Gladstone, she wrote fiercely, 'showed a most unpardonable & personal hatred to Ld. B. who had restored England to the position she had lost under Mr. G's Govt.'.[42]

There was a touching exchange of letters between the Queen and Disraeli as they contemplated the prospect of parting. The Queen wrote: 'The grief to her ... at having to part with the kindest & most devoted as well as one of the wisest Ministers the Queen ever had, is not to be told', adding hopefully that she felt sure it would only be for a very short time.[43] Disraeli admitted to her that his defeat 'costs him a pang', but that 'his separation from your Majesty is almost overwhelming. His relations with your Majesty were his chief, he might almost say, his only happiness & interest in this world. They came to him when he was alone, and they have inspired & sustained him in his isolation'.[44] The Queen replied emotionally, thanking him for his 'most kind letter, which affected me much', and conferring on him the rare privilege of corresponding with her in the first person. The use of the third person, she said, was 'too formal; & when we correspond, which I hope we shall on many a *private* subject & without anyone being astonished or offended, & even more without anyone knowing about it – I hope it will be in this more easy form. You can be of such use to me about my family & other things & about great public questions'. 'You must not think it is a real parting', she continued, 'I shall always let you know how I am & what I am doing, & you must promise me to let me hear from & about you'.[45] Once again, in order that his cherished name should be perpetuated, she offered to bestow a barony on his nephew Coningsby; once again Disraeli refused.

There was, however, one man far closer to Disraeli than his immediate family – Monty Corry. Disraeli was determined to do his best for Monty before power should slip from his hands. Two days after his defeat he told Lord Barrington that he 'chiefly deplored his fall from power, on account of M. Corry, who in his opinion was fitted to fill any *Cabinet* office'. He had already in March 1875 offered Monty a permanent quasi-sinecure as Clerk of the Parliaments, while in the autumn of 1878 the Queen had been prepared to make him Keeper of the Privy Purse on the death of the previous holder of the office, Sir Thomas Biddulph. Corry had declined both honours. Disraeli doted on Monty, now aged forty, as if he were the son he had never had; he once complained to Ronald Gower that von Angeli's portrait of Corry had not 'given the gold light in Monty's hair', which light, Lord Ronald commented dryly, 'I had never seen, nor had Angeli, it seemed'. As the Queen wrote after Disraeli's death, 'Such unselfish devotion & affection on the one side & such love & confidence on the other are rare & beautiful to see'. Disraeli was determined to lay plans to ensure Monty's future.

On 7 April he wrote to Monty's rich, childless aunt, Lady Charlotte Lyster, telling her that he planned to ask the Queen for a peerage for her nephew and that the whole scheme depended upon Lady Charlotte's making Monty her heir and thus fulfilling the conditions of income and property necessary for a peerage.

The next day he wrote to the Queen, gently reminding her that whereas his predecessor, Gladstone, had asked her to create 37 peers in five years, he, in six years, had only asked for half that number. When the Queen responded with the offer of a barony for Coningsby, Disraeli, jumping the gun as far as Monty's legacy was concerned and with a disregard for the exact truth, asked her to make Monty Baron Rowton of Rowton Castle in Shropshire, telling her that he had come into possession of Rowton Castle with an estate of 7,000 acres and an income of £10,000 a year. In fact Monty was not to come into full possession of his aunt's estate until her death nine years later and the income of the estate was not ten thousand a year, but five. The Queen hesitated; the ennoblement of private secretaries was an unprecedented step and liable to give rise to malicious gossip, but she liked Monty and could not refuse Disraeli anything. And so Monty became Baron Rowton, to a chorus of Liberal jokes about Caligula's horse. He was far from being a mere man about town, as his enemies liked to represent him; indeed his abilities and energy were such that Richard Cross at the outset of Disraeli's premiership had been moved to note: 'M. Corry is in fact Prime Minister'. He had his serious side, founding the charitable Rowton Houses later in life, but he was personally unambitious; after Disraeli's death he did not attempt a political career and, although he intended to write the authorized life of his chief, never did so.

Disraeli had returned from Hatfield on 3 April to face what he described as 'the most painful passage in political life, the transition from power to obscurity'.[46] He was besieged by requests for places and honours from Conservatives who would soon be in the political wilderness. 'A most dreary life & labor mine!' Disraeli exclaimed to Selina. 'Winding up a Government is as hard work as forming one without any of its excitement.' His ante-room was filled with what he described as 'pesterers of the 11th hour', 'beggars mournful and indignant', and his desk was 'covered with letters like a snowstorm'. 'It is the last & least glorious exercise of power', he commented bitterly, '& will be followed, wh: is the only compensation, by utter neglect & isolation'.[47] He was disgusted by the greed of his petitioners, 'a rapacious crew', with their avidity for money and titles. 'How is the Opposition to be carried on if all those, who have had the advantage of official experience, desire to leave the House of Commons?' he pointedly asked one such petitioner.[48] Friends and loyal supporters were a different case; the brewing trade which had vehemently backed the Conservatives was rewarded with the first member of the 'beerage', a Guinness. Northcote, Cross and John Manners, sole survivor of the Derby Cabinets, were given the GCB, while another former Young Englander, Alexander Baillie-Cochrane, at long last and after much pressure was promoted as Lord Lamington. He tried to do his best for the impecunious and importunate Henry Lennox, now a friend again and still a nuisance, refusing posts he considered not good enough and pursuing heiresses, even one who advertised for a husband in a French newspaper. Disraeli proposed to make 'dear Henry' Chief Civil Service Commissioner with a salary of £1,500 a year but his more prudent Cabinet colleagues warned him that Parliament would certainly denounce the appointment as a 'job' and persuaded him to give up the idea.

Disraeli's final task was to advise the anxious Queen as to whom she should invite to form the next Government. Like Victoria he could not bring himself to contemplate Gladstone as his successor, refusing to recognize the fact that Gladstone, although no longer formally leader of the Liberal Party, had won the election for them and that the country wished and expected him to take the lead. And so he recommended Hartington, whom he described as 'in his heart a conservative, a gentleman, & very straightforward in his conduct', and who in fact had gone out of his way during the late election to counteract Gladstone's denunciations by publicly praising Disraeli's patriotism. Disraeli misled the Queen either deliberately or because he was ignorant of the actual state of the Liberal party, overemphasizing the strength of the Old Whig section. He advised her that they numbered some 200 and that if she appointed Hartington, the moderate Whigs could rally round him and combine with the Conservatives to render the Radicals 'harmless'.

To his chagrin, however, and that of the Queen, Granville and Hartington, well aware that they could not carry on without Gladstone who had refused to serve in any position but that of Premier, were unable to follow the Disraelian formula and, on 23 April the Queen was forced to accept Gladstone as her new Prime Minister. It was a bitter pill for her to swallow, as she wrote to Disraeli immediately afterwards, 'Her trial is great'. She consoled herself by reporting that Gladstone looked 'very ill, very old & haggard', and that his voice was feeble. She clung to his having said twice during the interview that he did not think he would be long in office, 'as it was too much for him, & being Leader & Chancellor of the Exchequer as well as Prime Minister is utterly too much for a man of 70!'[49] In fact Gladstone was to be her Prime Minister for the next five years and again, for the last time, at the age of eighty-two.

Disraeli accepted defeat gracefully; unlike Gladstone in 1874 he neither sulked nor blamed his colleagues, maintaining a calm and cheerful public face. The last Cabinet before his resignation on 21 April was held in an undramatic even conversational atmosphere. Disraeli simply thanked them for the cordiality and harmony with which they had worked with him, while Salisbury wished to record ' that there had never been a cloud between him and the Prime Minister through all their arduous work'. 'All assented heartily to the expressions of good feeling', Cranbrook wrote in his diary, 'and I can record without hesitation my belief that a more united Cabinet than the one that has now been dissolved has never sat.' On 25 April he left 10 Downing Street for the last time. Two days later he had a final farewell audience with the Queen at which she presented him with statuettes of herself, John Brown, the royal pony and the dog 'Sharp', with which he tactfully expressed himself 'much delighted'. He no longer had a home in London and so, after staying with the Beauchamps in Belgrave Square, he went to Hughenden in the first week of May. He was, as he wrote to Anne Chesterfield with a tinge of sadness, 'no longer *responsible* in any sense'.

Disraeli's last premiership had ended in a calm acceptance of a total and personal defeat for which he can hardly be held responsible, and, indeed, it is significant that his party did not hold him to blame for it. He had had his faults as Prime Minister; the failure to grasp detail or to initiate legislative programmes for which Cross had criticized him, and he had lacked the necessary ruthlessness to get rid of failures like Adderley or dissidents like Derby. As leader of the Cabinet, however, he had amply demonstrated that he had not lost his skill in the 'management of men', even succeeding in converting Salisbury from an inveterate enemy into an admirer and friend. He could also be blamed for allowing his interest in foreign affairs to lead him to neglect domestic policy and to substitute 'Beaconsfieldism' with its emphasis on Empire and international prestige for Disraelian Conservatism with its 'one nation' theme. But, as a recent authority, Dr Paul Smith, has pointed out, he was the leader and thus to some extent the prisoner, of a party which had never been sympathetic towards the claims of the urban working classes, and which, after his death, was to become still less so.[50] Disraeli had pointed the party briefly, but not ineffectively, in the direction of social reform; he could do no more. He should perhaps have been aware that the Conservative electoral machine which he himself had done so much to make effective had, with the resignation of his appointee John Gorst in 1877, fallen into such disarray that it could not compete with the efficiency of the Liberal organization, and in particular with the caucus system initiated at Birmingham by Joseph Chamberlain. Strictly speaking, however, party organization should have been the responsibility of the Leader in the Commons, Sir Stafford Northcote, and of the Chief Whip, Sir William Hart-Dyke.

Ill-luck, economic depression, the polemical skills of Gladstone in turning his own weapons against him and the traditional desire of the British electorate for a change, had been responsible for his defeat rather than any sins of omission or commission on his part. Disraeli was not far from the truth when he wrote to Lytton from his retirement at Hughenden on 31 May:

> Whatever philosophers may say, there is such a thing as luck & fortune – & the reverse – & that it should have fallen to my lot to govern England for a series of years with a decaying commerce & the soil stricken with sterility presents an issue which, I believe, no calculation could have foreseen or baffled.
>
> The distress of this country is the cause & the sole cause of the fall of the government over wh: I presided.[51]

As usual, he refused to give any credit to Gladstone.

24 *The Twilight of Existence*

But it was Gladstone who kept Disraeli's interest in politics alive during his last year. From Hughenden in the early summer of 1880 Disraeli watched with growing anger and despair the activities of the 'A[rch] V[illain]', as he was now wont to term his rival. 'Vindictive' was an epithet he frequently applied to Gladstone, and he was convinced that his party and his policies would be the first victims of the new Prime Minister's vengeful nature. Gladstone indeed felt himself morally bound to complete the destruction of 'the vast magnificent castle of Beaconsfieldism', above all in foreign policy; while on the domestic front a major part of his proposed legislation was cleverly designed to drive a wedge between landlords and farmers, thus depriving the Conservative party of its traditional support.

Disraeli regarded himself as the guardian not only of the Conservative party but of the established order of England, both of which he felt were menaced by Gladstone's vindictive and revolutionary intentions. At the first public meeting of the party since the election held at Bridgewater House on 19 May and attended by some 500 peers and members of the House of Commons, Disraeli told them that their role was to be watchdogs for the Empire and the constitution, warning them that 'the first step towards any organic change must be a revolution in the tenure of land – in other words the pulling down of the aristocracy, which was the first object of the revolutionary party'. Announcing that he would continue to lead the party 'in the hour of failure' he sat down to a storm of cheers after speaking for an hour and forty minutes.

For once the Conservatives in defeat neither blamed nor wished to shake off their leader. Disraeli was regarded as the party oracle and a stream of anxious politicians made the journey down to Hughenden to consult him. 'Every train brought some ex-Cabinet Minister', he grumbled to Ronald Gower, 'Lord Cairns or Mr. W.H., or is it H.W. Smith? I never know which it is, or Mr. Secretary Cross, whom I always forget to call Sir Richard . . .'.[1]

Indeed the party leadership had every reason for anxiety; not only were they numerically weak in the Commons but their front bench was quite unable to stand up to the thundering oratory of Gladstone or the aggressive debating skills of Harcourt on the Government side. Stafford Northcote, who had once been Gladstone's private secretary, quailed before the eagle glare of his former chief; indeed it was remarked of him that he was like an old and trusty retriever who could not resist coming to heel at the whistle of the poacher who had first broken him. Overborne by Gladstone, he was also unable to control the bright young men of his own party, John Gorst, Harry Drummond Wolff, Salisbury's nephew, Arthur Balfour and Lord Randolph Churchill, recently returned from his strategic retreat to Ireland as his father's private secretary in the wake of the Aylesford scandal. Dubbed the 'Fourth Party', the group were contemptuous of Northcote, whom they nicknamed 'the Goat' for his excessively hairy face, and led their own independent parliamentary forays. They looked to Disraeli for inspiration and encouragement, and he, reminded of his Young England days, found it hard not to sympathize even if he could not, as leader, support them against Northcote. 'I fully appreciate your feelings and those of your friends', he told Drummond Wolff, 'but you must stick to Northcote. He represents the respectability of the party. I wholly sympathise with you all, because I was never respectable myself.'[2] Gorst interpreted this to mean that they should treat 'the Goat' with respect and avoid an open breach with him, 'But, just at present we need not be too scrupulous about obeying our leader', he wrote to Randolph Churchill. Disraeli, though, also tried to reassure Northcote, promising, 'I will assist you, as much as I possibly can, in looking after the Fourth Party.'

If Northcote found his position as leader uncomfortable, Gladstone, to his surprise and mortification, faced the most turbulent Parliament he had known. He expected it, he told a friend on 10 May, 'to act on well-tried and established lines, and do much for the people and little to disquiet my growing years'.[3] Within a short time of the opening of the session, however, a major parliamentary row developed over the case of Charles Bradlaugh, newly-elected MP for Northampton. Bradlaugh, an avowed atheist, reputed republican and advocate of contraception, claimed the right to take the Oath of Allegiance by affirmation since the words 'so help me God' in the prescribed form had no meaning for him. The majority of the House was outraged and a Select Committee rejected his claim, whereupon Gladstone, who sincerely believed the House should not refuse to accept an elected representative of the people, put forward another Committee to inquire whether the House had the right to do so. When that Committee also decided against Bradlaugh on the grounds of his atheism, Gladstone proposed a motion allowing him to affirm. After excited debates in which Randolph Churchill wittily represented the unfortunate Gladstone as an advocate of atheism and contraception, the Government motion was defeated by 275 votes to 230.

Disraeli watching from the sidelines must have enjoyed Churchill's gadfly tormenting of Gladstone, but he was deeply concerned at what he saw as the Prime Minister's deliberate attack on the landed classes. Gladstone's Budget proposed the repeal of the Malt Tax, a long-standing aim of the farmers, and a measure which Disraeli glumly described as 'another attempt to divert and separate the farmers from the gentlemen [which] will be successful'.[4] More dangerous still from Disraeli's point of view was a Game Bill, which touched upon the sorest point between farmers and their sporting landlords and aroused feudal passions on the Tory side. Under Gladstone's proposals farmers were to be allowed to exterminate hares and rabbits on their land, a measure certain to provoke an agricultural class war. 'I think the Game Bill, with this view, the most devilish of the A.V's schemes', Disraeli wrote to Selina. 'In time the farmers will find out that the Repeal of the Malt Tax will do them no good, but they will stick to the hares & rabbits, and there will be a chronic cause of warfare.'[5] He made the most strenuous efforts to restrain the Tory Lords from, as he put it, cutting their own throats by throwing out the bill, and came up to London in August for a week of private lobbying. The strain brought on a severe attack of asthma but he succeeded, as he told Anne Chesterfield, in preventing them from rejecting the bill and thus losing the support of 'the only classes on wh. we once thought we cd. rely – the landed interest in all its divisions.'[6]

Disraeli was indeed obsessed with Gladstone's revolutionary intentions. 'Gladstone ... will never rest till he has destroyed the landed interest', he repeated to Selina on 18 July. To Anne Chesterfield he was even more gloomy in his predictions as to the implications of the proposed Irish Compensation for Eviction Bill. 'If the Eviction Bill passes, there will not be many more seasons. It is a revolutionary age, and the chances are that you & I may live to see the final extinction of the great London season, wh. was the wonder & admiration of our youth.'[7] The bill, which provided for compensation in the case of eviction for non-payment of rent, was regarded by the landed interest – both Whig-Liberal and Conservative – as the extinction of the last right remaining to the Irish landlord. Its principal political effect was to accelerate a movement which Disraeli had long envisaged, a recognition of common class interest between Whig and Tory landlords. Disraeli's strategy against the bill was to let the Whigs make the running and not to embarrass them by letting them be seen to be playing the Tory game. Although the Whigs in the Commons were too weak to carry the vote with the Conservatives against the combined Radical, Liberal and Irish strength, his strategy was successful in the Lords where the Whig peers Grey and Lansdowne, who had resigned from the Government in protest against the bill, master–minded its rejection. It was a small victory but an encouraging sign for the future.

The Queen certainly thought so; like Disraeli she saw the only hope of resisting Gladstone and the Radicals in joint action between moderate Whigs and Conservatives. She was ecstatic about the Lords' vote: 'Do *you* EVER remember *so many* voting against the Government to whose party they belong? *I* do *not*', she wrote to Disraeli from Osborne on 5 August. Indeed after Disraeli's departure, Victoria regarded herself as the principal defender of Crown, Constitution and Empire, and was genuinely alarmed by what she saw as the revolutionary tendencies of the new Parliament. Distrusting Gladstone she corresponded principally with

Granville, the leader of the party in the Lords, and on 8 August wrote him a heavily underlined, almost hysterical letter of advice which she instructed him to show to the Cabinet:

> She is *seriously* alarmed at the *extreme Radicals* being at all cajoled by the present Government, and she must tell Lord Granville that she thinks the moderate Members of the Government *ought* to do *all* to obtain the *support* of their *moderate Whig* supporters *instead* of courting the support of the *extreme* Party. She *knows* that the Opposition would give them *every support*, in resisting any policy which *strikes* at the *root & existence* of the Constitution & Monarchy. The Queen herself can *never* have any *confidence* in the men who encourage *reform* for the *sake of alteration & pulling down what exists* & what is essential to the *stability* of a Constitutional Monarchy. *A Democratic Monarchy* she will not *consent to belong to. Others* must be found *if* that is to be.[8]

Granville showed this royal outpouring to Gladstone, who was ill; it can hardly have improved his state of mind. He was deeply wounded by the Queen's hostility and the difficulties of dealing with her added considerably to the strains of office. He suspected Disraeli of continuing to set the Queen against him; indeed Disraeli stayed twice with the Queen at Windsor in May and July and there is little doubt that their conversation must have included mutual condemnation of the Arch-Villain. The letter that Disraeli wrote to Anne Chesterfield on his return from his second visit probably echoed their conversation: 'As to politics, Gladstone will be as fatal to the aristocracy as the weather; & if he were younger the Crown would not be safe'.[9] The Queen assured him that she was on the alert as far as the Government was concerned, writing to him on 9 May, 'I think you may be quite easy about Foreign Affairs. Lord Granville manages them entirely, & the PM never even names them to me, & I watch very carefully.' She corresponded with Disraeli privately, bypassing her Liberal private secretary, Ponsonby, asking his advice and assuring him of her affection. 'I often think of you – indeed constantly', she wrote on 4 May, telling him that she found reassurance in contemplating his portrait, '& rejoice to see you looking down from the *wall* after dinner'. At their first reunion since his resignation she almost managed to forget that he was no longer her Prime Minister. 'I feel so happy', she told him, 'that I think what has happened is only a horrid dream.'[10] But the reality was inescapable; 'Oh, if only I had you, my kind friend & wise councillor & strong arm to help & lean on!' she wrote pathetically to him in October, 'I have *no one*'.[11]

Meanwhile in the three months since his resignation Disraeli had been secretly working on completing the manuscript of *Endymion*. Only Monty knew of its existence and it was he who negotiated with the publisher, Longman, who offered the enormous sum of £10,000 advance for the novel without even seeing it. Disraeli was astounded and delighted: 'I confess I accepted it with a scruple', he wrote later to Selina, 'such a sum never having before been given for a work of fiction. I fear it will prove rather the skill of Monty's diplomacy than Mr. Longman's acumen.'[12]

When Longman visited Hughenden on 13 September to hand over the cheque for the advance and take delivery of the manuscript, Disraeli went to inordinate lengths to prevent even his valet, the taciturn Mr Baum, from learning of the novel's existence. Longman recorded the scene in a memorandum so characteristic of Disraeli's passion for secrecy that it is worth quoting at length:

Knowing I had to leave rather early the next morning, I ventured to suggest that it might be convenient for us to do our little business before dinner. The business *I* alluded to was connected with our bankers, but it is certain Ld. B's idea of the business was the formal delivery of the MS. to me. 'Oh yes, certainly', was the reply to my suggestion. 'Of course, much better to get our business done, the sooner the better. Ah, let me see, how shall we manage it?' I confess I did not quite understand his lordship's meaning, because everything seemed to me simple enough, so I said nothing, and waited for another cue, as it was clear to me Ld. B. was a little fidgety and rather excited. The formal delivery of his precious child appeared to be too much for him. 'Well, Mr. Longman', continued the author in a somewhat low tone of voice, 'shall I ring for Mr. Baum, and have my study lighted?' Of course I agreed ... but to my surprise his lordship turned to me and said, 'No, no, Mr. Longman, stop a minute, Mr. Baum knows nothing of this and we must not excite his suspicion. We must light the candles ourselves.'[13]

... I followed him upstairs to his own apartment. He is very shortsighted, and I had to render him a great deal of assistance in finding and lighting the candles. 'We must light ALL the candles, M. Longman; I can't get on without plenty of light!' said Ld. B. and continued; 'but we must have your room lighted also. But Mr. Baum can do that'. So Mr. B. was summoned and instructed to light my room. No sooner had Mr. Baum left us and the door been closed with special care than the distinguished author proceeded to lay open three red despatch boxes. Each volume was carefully tied up in red tape, and each in its own box. These ... being emptied, I felt a little anxious to know what was to come next. After a moment's pause he turned to me and said, 'Are you ready?' 'Oh yes', I replied 'I am quite ready, are you?' What was going to happen? ... The air was full of mystery. 'Can you carry two?' he continued. 'Yes' I replied, not saying one word more than was absolutely necessary. The door being opened – slowly, solemnly, carefully, mysteriously I followed the ex-Premier as he trod lightly along the passage, to my apartment! Having arrived safely, and closing the door with extra precaution, he remarked, 'I am most anxious none of my servants should know anything of this; that is why I am so careful'.

Another comic scene ensued as the two men searched for Longman's portmanteau in which to deposit the manuscript. Not daring to ask Baum where he had put it they searched the room, under the bed, in the wardrobe and in every corner until it was eventually located in the dressing-room and the volumes hidden within it. This done, they returned to Disraeli's study where Longman handed over the cheque and took Disraeli's receipt. Disraeli was as excited as any young author might have been with the huge cheque from Longman. 'I know of no magic of the Middle Ages equal to it!' he wrote delightedly to Monty. 'And you are the Magician, best and dearest of friends!'[14] The first proofs arrived for Disraeli's correction within a week, completion was scheduled for the end of October, and on 26 November *Endymion* was published.

Endymion is perhaps Disraeli's most readable book and shows him at his best as a political novelist. The background is a skilful précis of political events between the death of Canning in 1827 and the fall of the Coalition in 1855, and its theme is the powerful influence of women upon a young man's career. In that sense it is autobiographical, although Disraeli took pains to make the hero, Endymion Ferrars, as unlike himself as possible. As a result Endymion, like most of Disraeli's heroes, is a dull young man, and indeed it is difficult to see why a succession of powerful women should have taken such an interest in him. Disraeli admitted to a friend that Endymion was a 'plodder',[15] and the only quality he allowed his hero to share with himself was a driving ambition for political power.

'I owe everything to woman' was a favourite remark of Disraeli's, and the book is a tribute to the two women who devoted themselves to him, Sarah and Mary Anne. Both are unrecognizable in the characters drawn by Disraeli. Only a few phrases link the real Sarah to Endymion's sister, Myra, and Mary Anne to his wife, Berengaria, Countess of Montfort. Myra is Endymion's twin sister, cold, proud, the most beautiful woman of her day. She marries first Lord Roehampton (Palmerston), and then King Florestan (Napoleon III) – not bad, as Lord Blake remarks, for a penniless girl. However, she, like Sarah, is utterly devoted to her brother and 'ever willing to be his slave', she had confidence in his 'star' and tells him, 'My only joy in life is seeing you', while the book ends with Disraeli's last tribute to his beloved Sa, in a scene in which Myra, now Queen, embraces Endymion, now Prime Minister, in the house in which they were brought up as children.

Berengaria, Countess of Montfort, who marries Endymion as her second husband, has on the face of it very little in common with Mary Anne. Referred to as 'the Queen of Whiggism', she is aristocratic and sophisticated with men at her feet in scores. Disraeli himself told the Queen that he had drawn upon 'features of Lady Palmerston in her youth' for his character of Berengaria, '& some traits of devotion drawn from someone else', by which he intended Mary Anne. Berengaria's first husband, the fabulously rich, eccentric Earl of Montfort, like Wyndham Lewis, conveniently dies, leaving the field free for Endymion to marry the widow. She with her thirty thousand a year, a house in London and a mansion in the country, uses her wealth, position and influence to make him Prime Minister. While Berengaria outwardly resembles Lady Palmerston far more closely than she does the humbler Mary Anne, certain phrases point out the similarities. Montfort said of Berengaria, as Disraeli of Mary Anne, that he never had a dull moment in her company; Berengaria, like Mary Anne, while married to her older first husband, restlessly sought male admiration, and, like Mary Anne, finds emotional and, one assumes, sexual satisfaction with her young second husband: 'Feelings of affection, long mortified and pent up, were now lavished and concentrated on a husband of her heart and adoration, and she was proud that his success and greatness might be avowed as the objects of her life.'

As if the assistance of these two dazzling ladies were not enough, Endymion receives a seat in Parliament through the influence of the beautiful Countess of

Beaumaris, a dressmaker's daughter who captures a Tory Earl, and £20,000 in consols from an anonymous female donor who turns out to be Adriana Neuchatel, daughter of a fabulously rich Swiss banker.

Writing at the end of his career Disraeli took this opportunity to reward old friends and pursue old hatreds. George Smythe figures largely as Waldershare in a characterization that brings him superbly to life, and the title of the book itself may have been taken from a Cavalier ancestor of Smythe's, Endymion Porter. Palmerston, whom Disraeli had always liked and admired, appears in sympathetic guise as the powerful attractive Foreign Secretary, Lord Roehampton, whom Myra marries; the Rothschilds are the Neuchatels. Adrian Neuchatel, the head of the house, shrewd and generous, entertaining lavishly at Hainault House (Gunnersbury), is probably a portrait of Disraeli's friend Baron Lionel. Disraeli's former patroness, Lady Jersey, is given a brief but flattering part as Zenobia, Queen of the Tory party; and Bismarck as the redoubtable Count Ferroll talks of uniting his country by 'blood and iron'; while Metternich puts in a brief appearance to lecture Endymion on Disraeli's theories of race. Generously, since Napoleon III had neither liked nor appreciated him, Disraeli gives him a central role as the romantic Prince Florestan, with a sympathetic résumé of his real-life adventures before becoming Emperor, ending with his fairy-tale marriage to Myra. Manning, who had fallen out with Gladstone and made his peace with Disraeli since the publication of *Lothair*, here appears in a more sympathetic light, and the Cobden–Bright figure, Job Thornberry, is also fairly treated, although Disraeli wickedly gives him a son who sympathizes with Young England.

If Disraeli's political opponents are let off lightly, or not mentioned at all, one old literary foe – Thackeray – is savagely attacked in the character of St Barbe. Many people thought it in questionable taste to attack a man lately dead who could not defend himself, but Disraeli had clearly never forgotten or forgiven the derision heaped upon him by Thackeray and his friends. In *Endymion* he pays him back in full, depicting him as an envious, conceited, untrustworthy snob, jealous of anyone's success and particularly of Dickens, here called 'Gushy'. 'I am as much robbed by that fellow Gushy as men are on the highway', St Barbe complains. 'He is appropriating my income and the income of thousands of honest fellows. And then he pretends he is writing for the people! The people? Annals of the New Cut and Saffron Hill. He thinks he will frighten some lord who will ask him to dinner.' In fact the passages portraying St Barbe are very funny, accurately-recorded dialogue, and Disraeli dilutes the bitterness by epitomizing him as the 'vainest, most envious and most amusing of men'. Nonetheless, Disraeli's treatment of Thackeray in *Endymion* is a piquant illustration of a heart-felt remark which he makes later in the book on 'the envy and hatred which all literary men really feel for each other'.

Disraeli himself is mentioned only once, briefly and not by name, as a member of the Who-Who Ministry – 'a gentleman without any official experience whatever who was not only placed in cabinet, but was absolutely required to become the

Leader of the House of Commons, which had never occurred before, except in the instance of Mr. Pitt in 1782'. The strangest omission of all is the absence of any characterization of Peel in the story; perhaps he felt he had already done it well enough in *Lord George Bentinck*, possibly too he preferred to gloss over this not altogether creditable passage in his past. Certainly he does not refer to the part he played in Peel's defeat in 1846, and it is notable that Endymion 'never opened his lips during the whole session'.

Like all Disraeli's novels, *Endymion* is a quarry for biographical clues, past experiences, remembered phrases and personal credos. There are evocative descriptions of Bradenham and of the London of his youth, while Lord Roehampton echoes Disraeli's own lament on having 'the feelings of youth and the frame of age'. Lady Montfort talks of the importance of personal acquaintance with European statesmen, and of 'real politics: foreign affairs, maintaining our power in Europe'. One wonders whether Disraeli was thinking of his own experience when he wrote of England, 'an insular country subject to fogs, and with a powerful middle class, requires grave statesmen'.

Endymion can hardly have added gravity to Disraeli's reputation; it is a light-hearted, cynical résumé of the closed-circle politics of Disraeli's earlier political experience. There is not one single political principle to be found in it, and, if it is anything, it is a celebration of the power of personal ambition; the moral, if any, is that money is the key to success. One can hardly blame Archbishop Tait for putting down the book 'with a painful feeling that the writer considers all political life as mere play and gambling'.[16] Disraeli was fond of remarking 'there is no gambling like politics', and he looked upon the practice of politics as a game of skill. He enjoyed all aspects of the game, the power struggle, sometimes great and sometimes petty, waged in Parliament, the drawing-rooms and the clubs over the heads of the masses without. Indeed the masses scarcely make an appearance in the book; the curtain is briefly drawn back to reveal a necessary industrial backdrop, but although the period covered includes the years which produced *Coningsby* and *Sybil*, there is not even a passing reference to the 'one nation' ideal which he had once so ringingly proclaimed. The scene is the gilded world that Disraeli loved and yet saw through, and his treatment of it, half-romantic, half-cynical, illustrates his own attitude to the aristocratic society in which he had chosen to live.

Endymion differs from all his previous novels in one significant respect; it contains no element of personal pilgrimage, no quest for self-fulfilment. Endymion Ferrars is self-seeking, not self-searching. Despite the fairy-tale aura necessary to veil what is essentially a tale of sordid self-interest, Disraeli turned his back upon his earliest and most powerful influence, Goethe. His personal quest for recognition, self-fulfilment and identity was over; at seventy-five, twice Prime Minister, fêted throughout Europe and cherished by his sovereign and his party, even regarded as the symbol of England, he had arrived. 'Power and power alone should be your absorbing object', Myra tells Endymion; for Disraeli, supreme power meant self-fulfilment.

Disraeli's burst of creative energy did not end with *Endymion*. He immediately began another novel in which the chief character was based upon the man who obsessed him, Gladstone. One can imagine how much Disraeli must have enjoyed the sharp pen strokes with which he filled in his portrait of Joseph Toplady Falconet, alias Gladstone. Falconet suffered from 'a complete deficiency in the sense of humour'.

> His memory was vigorous, ready and retentive; but his chief peculiarity was his disputatious temper, and the flow of language which ... was ever at his command to express his arguments ... Though of an eager and earnest temper, his imagination was limited, and quite conscious of his powers, being, indeed, somewhat arrogant and peremptory, he aspired only to devote them to accomplishing those objects which ... he had been taught were the greatest ... Firm in his faith in an age of dissolving creeds, he wished to believe that he was the man ordained to vindicate the sublime cause of religious truth.

While all this was not essentially unfair, Disraeli could not resist making a sharper dig at the Arch-Villain: 'He was essentially a prig, & among prigs there is a freemasonry which never fails. All the prigs spoke of him as the coming man'.[17]

One may speculate that the novel which Disraeli did not have time to complete before he died would have taken its title from the name of its hero, Falconet, as had been the case with all his previous books. The name Falconet may have been inspired by Gladstone's appearance; to admirers he resembled an eagle, to Disraeli, perhaps, a bird of prey. Nihilism features largely in the book, inspired probably by the Nihilists' attempt to assassinate the Tsar earlier that year, and it is tempting to speculate whether Disraeli, convinced of Gladstone's destructive tendencies, might have converted the fanatically religious Falconet into a politically fanatical Nihilist. Sadly, we shall never have a book by Disraeli on Gladstone.

Disraeli remained obsessed with Gladstone, his letters of the autumn and winter of 1880 abounding in alarmist comment. 'What a state of affairs!' he exploded to Selina on 17 September, 'I am really alarmed for the country, governed by a vindictive lunatic!'[18] There were grounds for alarm: Ireland, where the Land League was becoming daily more powerful, was in a state of eruption. On 25 September a Galway landlord, Lord Mountnorres, was murdered, while the new system of intimidation, known as 'boycotting' after the agent of Lord Erne against whom it was first practised, was widespread. In the Transvaal the Boers, disappointed by Gladstone's failure to give them a constitution, were in revolt; there was continuing trouble in Afghanistan; and the Government made ineffective threatening gestures against Turkey. Disraeli felt tempted to say, 'I told you so', but politically he was helpless in the face of Gladstone's huge majority. 'What is the use of cutting up the A.V. into thousands?' he wrote bitterly to Selina on 2 November. 'He carries all before him, & all his foreign scrapes count for nothing, while he has detached farmers & clergy, one of the two prime elements of the Tory party, entirely from us. I see no chances of salvation unless he really goes mad, but he is such a hypocrite, that I shall never believe that till he is in Bedlam'.[19] In the circumstances, it is hardly surprising that he should have attempted to retire from the leadership of the House of Lords in favour of Salisbury, with a view to making him his eventual successor as leader of the party, but Salisbury declined.

His health seriously worsened during the winter of 1880; he had a severe attack of both gout and asthma in October, and in November a fit of gout so ferocious that it reminded him of 'poor Lord Derby'. Kidney disease weakened and depressed him as his body filled with toxins that his kidneys were increasingly unable to eliminate. He had no Monty to comfort and console him, for that dutiful brother had been ordered by the doctors to take his ailing sister abroad. In mid-November, after more than five weeks' imprisonment in his room at Hughenden, too weak even to walk downstairs, he struggled to London, partly to see Dr Kidd, for, as he told Selina, 'If he continued his visits to Hughenden, I shd. have to execute a mortgage on my estate', and partly to negotiate with Lord Tankerville for the purchase of his house in Curzon Street, to be financed by the money from *Endymion*.

Lord Ronald Gower, visiting him at Hughenden in November, had found him looking older and weaker. On an earlier visit Disraeli had not concealed his bitterness at his defeat and his sense of personal failure. 'I am the unluckiest of mortals', he told Lord Ronald, 'six bad harvests in succession, one worse than the former, this has been the cause of my overthrow; like Napoleon, I have been beaten by the elements!' He mused upon what might have been had he still been in power, 'Bismarck and I were perfectly *d'accord*,' he said. 'Had the late Government lasted we would have kept the democrats of Europe in check; but now all is over!' He talked a good deal of Bismarck, whom he told Lord Ronald, he had much admired and personally liked. 'He is one of the few men', he said, 'that at my age I have been able to feel real attachment for; but all that is now over, and were he to come to England I should not ask to see him; there is no such thing as sympathy or sentiment between statesmen. I have failed, and he would not care to see me, nor I him'. Typically, Disraeli's last words to Lord Ronald on his first visit were a jibe at Gladstone. As the two men were standing in the porch at Hughenden *The Times* arrived containing Gladstone's letter to the public thanking them for their sympathy during his illness. 'Did you ever hear anything like that?' Disraeli exclaimed. 'It reminds one of the Pope blessing all the world from the balcony of St. Peter's'.[20]

In November Lord Ronald found Disraeli, although physically weaker, in a more relaxed and contemplative mood, sunning himself in a long fur coat among the peacocks on the south veranda. After luncheon they sat in the library before a blazing fire, talking of love, life and death. Disraeli reminisced about the beautiful Sheridans, and Helen Blackwood in particular; it was on this occasion that, as he spoke of her, he gazed nostalgically into the fire murmuring, 'Dreams! Dreams! Dreams!' His comments on life and death had the flavour of his novels. Life, he told Lord Ronald, was either an anxiety or a bore – the self-made man worries whether he may lose what he has gained while the nobleman has nothing to strive for; as Lord Ronald pointed out, he had left out three-quarters of the population who fitted into neither category. As to a life after death, Disraeli said, 'My idea of a happy future state is one of those long midsummer days, when one dines at nine o'clock ...'.[21]

Disraeli spent Christmas alone at Hughenden in deep gloom. Monty was still abroad in attendance on his sister. 'Sisters shd. marry & not require such sacrifices', Disraeli wrote acidly to Selina. He had temporarily appointed George Barrington, once the late Lord Derby's private secretary, in his place, but he too was away and so Disraeli was alone, contemplating the bad news pouring in from every quarter. 'Old England seems to be tumbling to pieces', he wrote to Anne Chesterfield on 22 December. 'Ireland in revolution, S. Africa in rebellion, & the Radicals & Jacobins in England so intent on the destruction of the landed interest, wh: is the backbone of the State.' He thought that the farmers, once solidly Conservative, were now secretly in sympathy with the Irish revolt against the landlords, consoling himself with the prediction that, despite his recent defeat, the Tory working man would rise again: 'The only portion of the Constituencies', he wrote to John Manners on Christmas Eve, '... who may be depended upon when affairs are riper, are the English working-classes.'[22]

But his indomitable spirit would not allow him to remain an old man by a fireside, maundering over the past and decrying the present. He determined to go up to London at the end of the year to rally the landed interest for a last battle against the 'Radicals and Jacobins', and to go into society again. Disraeli remained young in his appetite for society, never grumbling as old men are apt to do about deterioration in people and morals since the days of his youth and maturity. In fact, as he had written in *Endymion*, the London of his youth had been a dull place compared with the capital in the eighties. Although the gaming-houses were closed and the convivial chop-houses almost extinct, theatre life was no longer confined to Covent Garden and Drury Lane. In the summer of 1879 Sarah Bernhardt took London by storm and in November 1880 Disraeli saw Irving for the first time, although he did not think much of him – 'third-rate & never will improve'. And, although Disraeli may have been bored by the buffooneries of the Marlborough House 'parasites', the Prince of Wales set the pace for a luxury-loving hedonistic society.

Disraeli was the centre of attraction wherever he went, almost an object of awe when he appeared 'like a black sphinx' to quote Lady Randolph Churchill, at dinner parties, balls and banquets.[23] He could be intimidating; sometimes he was 'rather cross' Lady Randolph said, and if bored or irritated did not hesitate to let people know it. He would make a cutting remark or take refuge in silent melancholy; sometimes, when tackled by bores like Sir William Fraser, he would appear lethargic and almost on the point of death until roused by something which interested him. He could put people down either cruelly or delicately, as when an eager Tory lady sitting beside him at a dinner party urged him to political action, 'Lord Beaconsfield, what are you waiting for?' 'At this moment, for the potatoes, madam.' He hated all-male dinners and, according to Fraser, only shone in conversation when women were present, although someone who had been a guest at Hughenden said that when he spoke to them directly his conversation was laboured and his elaborate compliments clumsy. If this was so, it was certainly not noticed by Lady Randolph, a favourite of his; her only criticism being of his fondness for dragging in French words, which, she said, he spoke with a weird accent so ludicrous that she could hardly keep from laughing.

Disraeli moved up to London on the last day of 1880 to begin his social and political campaign. He was the guest of Alfred de Rothschild at 1 Seamore Place; his new house, 19 Curzon Street, which he had bought with a nine-year lease to run – enough, he said, to see him into the Elysian fields – would not be ready for him until 15 January. He was now considered by the Rothschilds almost an honorary member of the family. At the wedding of Hannah Meyer, heiress of Mentmore, to Lord Rosebery two years before, he had given the bride away, and at another Rothschild wedding in January that year, of Alfred's son, Leopold, to Miss Perugia, although the snowy weather was too severe for him to attend the service, he was the star of the reception afterwards. 'I have always been of opinion that there cannot be too many Rothschilds', he had written gracefully to Leopold congratulating him on his engagement, and at the reception he was, as Anthony de Rothschild's daughter Constance put it 'quite playful and elated'.

The weather was bitter, with thick snow – 'a white world', Disraeli wrote to Selina on 12 January. Three days later a frosty fog enveloped the frozen city and the cabmen thumped their chests to keep warm as they drove, the carriage wheels silent on the snow. Nevertheless Monty was back, and the two of them struggled out to dinner party after dinner party, to Louise Manchester's, and to the Alfred de Rothschilds' for endless wedding festivities. At the Rothschilds', Disraeli sat by the beautiful Lady Dudley which pleased him, and was enchanted by the unusual spectacle of the garden illuminated by electric light; 'magical', he told Selina.

Despite a bout of asthma he braved the weather to speak in the debate on the Address in the House of Lords on 7 January, denouncing Gladstone's policy of reversing what the previous Government had done as responsible for the troubles in which the country now found itself. He particularly accused Gladstone of blindness to the dangerous situation in Ireland, a charge which Gladstone later admitted to be not without foundation. 'I frankly admit', he was to tell an audience at Edinburgh three years later, 'I had much on my hands connected with the doings of the Beaconsfield government in almost every quarter of the world, and I did not know ... the severity of the crisis that was already swelling upon the horizon.'[24] Ireland was to be the subject of the session and here Gladstone reaped the whirlwind of his failure to deal urgently with the question in the previous year's session. His policy was that of the stick and the carrot: a ferocious Coercion Bill, which practically enabled the Viceroy to imprison anyone he chose and to detain them for as long as he pleased, followed by a Land Bill, known as the 'three Fs' – fair rents, fixity of tenure and right of free sale. Parnell, who with other leaders of the Land League had been brought to trial without result in Dublin in December, immediately launched a campaign of obstruction without precedent which, in Disraeli's words, made the English House of Commons 'the laughing-stock of Europe'. Disraeli may have enjoyed Gladstone's discomfiture but, as far as the Coercion Bill was concerned, there was no alternative but to support the Government.

He was determined, however, to fight his old enemy on another issue, Kandahar, which Gladstone proposed to abandon. In what was to be his penultimate speech he used the famous phrase 'the key of India is in London', which he had apparently characteristically appropriated from the conversation of the Russian Ambassador the previous day. He argued that a policy of containment, the possession of strategic fortifications, was the only alternative to annexation. Sadly, in view of the past, he could not resist a hit at his former friend, Derby, who had made what he termed a 'very animated' speech advocating evacuation of Kandahar. 'I do not know', Disraeli said, 'that there is anything that would excite enthusiasm in him except when he contemplates the surrender of some national possession.' This was the old Disraeli, demonstrating that despite his age and health he still had the capacity to wound. He was indeed already a very sick man; Granville later testified that he had drugged himself in order to be able to make this final challenge to Gladstone on the question of Empire. The blind MP Fawcett said to George Hamilton after hearing Disraeli speak, 'I was very sorry to hear how ill Lord Beaconsfield is'; when Hamilton asked him how he knew this he replied, 'Oh, through his voice: it is the voice of a sick man'.[25] On Tuesday 15 March Disraeli made a speech in the Lords supporting the Vote of Condolence to the Queen on the assassination of the Tsar by the Nihilists two days before; it was his last appearance in Parliament.

'I am very unwell', he wrote the following morning in what was to be his last letter to Selina, 'but have a great diplomatic banquet to-day, wh: will finish me'.[26] It did not finish him, but another guest at the party, Mrs Goschen, noted that he had lost his old spirit and seemed very aged. 'I only live for climate and I never get it', he told her. 'I want you', he wrote pathetically to Monty who was once again with his sister in Algiers. 'My health has been very bad, & I have really been fit for nothing, but perhaps the spring, wh: commences in a week, may perhaps help me.' But spring did not come in time to save him; on what was, by his doctor's account, one of the worst nights in March, the 22nd, he went out to dinner and on returning home 'was caught for a minute by the deadly blast of the north-east wind laden with sleet'. On the following morning he developed bronchitis with, according to Dr Kidd, 'distressing asthma, loss of appetite, fever, and congestion of the kidneys'.[27] During the first week of his illness it seemed that this attack was no worse than the others; only Kidd and Disraeli himself knew how weak were the resources of strength remaining to him. He was nursed by Baum and Mrs Baum and visited three times a day by Kidd, who decided that the small stuffy bedroom with its flock wallpaper and heavy curtains was making his asthma worse and had his bed moved into the airy drawing-room. Laid up in bed and breathing with difficulty, Disraeli had still not given up the fight against Gladstone. On 26 March he summoned Cairns, Cranbrook, and the Marquess of Ailesbury to concert the attack in the Lords upon the Government's South African policy which had led to the disaster at Majuba Hill. Rose, visiting him on 1 April, found him delighted with the progress of the debate and a great speech by Cairns. 'Capital' he told Rose. 'But this is all my arrangment. I settled it all. I felt that the eyes of the country ought to be opened, and that there was no one who could do it like Cairns.'[28] Sir Charles Dilke, whom Barrington brought in to see him, found him 'still the old Disraeli', full of pleasant but unabated spitefulness about Gladstone. To George Hamilton and Sir William Hart-Dyke he gave a short but very succinct account of the perils ahead and how they could be dealt with, then, according to Hamilton 'he bitterly criticised the vanity of the one man who, in his judgement, was the primary cause of our encircling difficulties'.

Despite the brave face that he presented to fellow politicians, Disraeli felt he was dying, telling his old friend Philip Rose on 29 March, 'Dear friend, I shall never survive this attack. I feel it is quite impossible ... I feel this is the last of it.' Two days later when Rose visited him again, he said in the most clear and distinct tones, 'I feel I am dying. Whatever the doctors may tell you, I do not believe I shall get well.' Yet he remained, as Dilke said, 'still the old Disraeli', taking pains to correct the proofs of his last speech for Hansard – 'I will not go down to posterity talking bad grammar.'[29] The Queen bombarded Barrington with anxious telegrams and by 5 April, the date of her last letter to Disraeli, 'dear Lord Beaconsfield' had become 'dearest Lord Beaconsfield'. She saw to it that his room was filled with primroses from Osborne and hinted that she would like to visit him. Disraeli's reaction was characteristic: 'No, it is better not. She would only ask me to take a message to Albert'.

For three days he felt himself unable to face the emotional strain of seeing Monty who had hurried back from Algiers on 7 April. 'He still shrinks from seeing me!' an agonized Monty wrote to Selina, at Weston nursing her asthmatic husband. He sneaked in to look at his old friend while he was sleeping and, a day or two later, took his courage in his hands and simply walked into the room and sat down by the bed to read Disraeli a Parliamentary report for which he had asked.

Disraeli's case was now serious enough to require extra medical attendance and special nursing. The official medical profession, not recognizing homeopathy, was reluctant to be associated with Dr Kidd but, under pressure from Barrington and Rose backed by the Queen, two leading chest specialists, Doctors Richard Quain and Mitchell Bruce from the Brompton Hospital, agreed to attend with day and night nurses. Bruce and Kidd took it in turns to sit up at night with the patient, Quain visited daily; even the haughty Sir William Jenner, driven by the Queen to overcome his prejudice against homeopaths, made three visits. An adjustable 'fracture couch' with special soft padding was provided in place of Disraeli's own bed, which made him more comfortable, but his asthmatic fits and dry coughing with inability to bring up the mucus clogging his chest, left him exhausted and in pain. With a grim reference to the torture methods of the Tsarist police he said wryly: 'I have suffered much. Had I been a Nihilist, I should have confessed all'.

'I had rather live, but I am not afraid to die', he said. He was afraid that the doctors were concealing the truth from him and begged them to tell him the worst 'if it is to be'. He watched them closely for tell-tale signs, saying with a smile, 'You have given a good report, but your face looks anxious', and studying the bulletins which they wrote out every night at eleven for the morning papers. Kidd admitted later that they did their utmost not to alarm him. 'It was very difficult steering to give a true idea of the gravity of his illness without causing anxiety to him on reading it.' Disraeli, however, was not deceived; reading through one bulletin, 'Lord Beaconsfield's strength is maintained', he commented, 'I presume the physicians are conscious of that. It is more than I am'. Both Rose and Cairns wanted to call a clergyman but the doctors refused on the grounds that if the patient realized his case was hopeless he would turn his face to the wall and die. Kidd, in his memoir of Disraeli's last illness, was at pains to point out that Disraeli had twice spoken to him on spiritual subjects, as he somewhat defensively put it, 'in a manner indicating his appreciation of Christ and the redemption', but Disraeli himself did not ask to see a clergyman. Never having held a high opinion of the clergy during his lifetime, he did not change his mind at the end.

On 18 April, Easter Monday, there was a sudden change for the worse and it became obvious that he was near death. In the medical language of Dr Kidd, there was 'increased restlessness, loss of strength, incoherence of speech, occasional delusion, restlessness alternating with the heavy sleep of coma, increased frequency of pulse, and of respiration'. Monty, who never left his side during the last days, described his experience in a moving letter to Selina:

> Day and night I was with him trying to help him over all his pains and troubles, as each arose, or to dispel some of the confusions which came over his poor tired brain. It was weary work that sitting, with my hand in his, in the night watches, trying to guide that mighty mind, as a child's had to be led – that trying to be cheerful, when I could scarcely help weeping![30]

The last piece of information Monty was able to give his dying friend was the cheering news that Longman's were at last making a profit from the sales of *Endymion*. Disraeli, he said, who had anxiously offered to refund the advance, heard the intelligence with 'extreme satisfaction'. Perhaps too he was cheered by a telegram recorded by Kidd: 'Don't die yet; we can't do without you. A British Workman.'

Both Monty and the doctors testified to the courage with which Disraeli bore his illness, and to the gentleness and consideration whith which he treated them. 'He often said he had no chance, & seemed to wish almost that the doctors would tell him so', Monty wrote broken-heartedly to Selina:

> But they did not know – or would not tell him, & so he glided on till the ship of his life

got among the clouds & the breakers, & he began to sink without knowing where he was. And so it came that he had not the opportunity of sending a word to some, to whom, as I thought I could see, he would have sent a loving message had he known what was so near. I never doubted what the end must be. I knew too well, how little of reserve force for long past was left in him'[31]

At midnight on 18 April it became clear that Disraeli was dying, passing into the sleep that precedes death. Monty, Kidd and Bruce, who had been watching all night, at one o'clock summoned Quain, Barrington and Rose. Monty and Barrington held the dying man's right hand, Dr Kidd his left. At 4.15 on the morning of the nineteenth Disraeli made his last, characteristic, movement, half-raising himself from the bed and stretching himself out 'as his wont was when rising to reply in debate'. His lips moved, but no words came. Fifteen minutes later, at 4.30 am, in a calm and peaceful sleep, Benjamin Disraeli died.

Epilogue

Disraeli's death evoked a great wave of public emotion, the outpourings in the press exceeding even the eulogies bestowed upon Palmerston and Peel. The secret of this 'electric and universal posthumous popularity', wrote the editor of the *Illustrated London News*, was not so much what he had done, as what he was as a man.[1]

At Osborne the Queen wrote out the death notice for the Court Circular in her own hand, as a last duty to the man who had been her friend as well as her favourite Prime Minister. 'And she did love him', Monty, summoned to give the Queen every detail of Disraeli's last hours, told Selina; while the Queen herself wrote broken-heartedly to Barrington, 'Words are too weak to say what the Queen feels; how overwhelmed she is with this terrible irreparable loss ... all is silent now & still; & the terrible void makes the heart sick.'[2] There is no record of how Selina Bradford, far away at Weston, felt at the death of the old man who had loved her with such youthful ardour. Although she could not go to the funeral, she made a sentimental pilgrimage to Hughenden in May and sent the Queen a touching letter describing it. The Queen responded through Jane Ely, showing that she was not, as Disraeli would have put it, 'jeal.[ous]' of Selina. 'She said', Lady Ely wrote, 'I was to tell you how deeply & truly she felt all you said about Hughenden & how much she regrets & thinks of her dear friend now gone. I do not think the Queen's spirits have been the same since, she always had him to turn to. Her Majesty knows how great & true was the friendship that existed between you & Him'.[3] The Queen too made her pilgrimage to Hughenden the day after the funeral to lay a wreath of china flowers on Disraeli's coffin (the vault having been opened for her) and to take tea in the library as she had on her last visit to him there in December 1877.

For Gladstone, Disraeli's death presented an acute moral problem; it would be his duty to deliver the eulogy of the man whom he had regarded as a political Antichrist. He managed to write an honest but graceful letter of condolence to the Queen and offered a state funeral but, when it was discovered that Disraeli had specified his wish for a private burial at Hughenden, he regarded it as the final piece of show and sham on his old enemy's part. 'As he lived, so he died – all display, without reality or genuineness', he told his secretary, Edward Hamilton. He could not bring himself to attend the funeral, excusing himself on the grounds of pressure of work, and the prospect of pronouncing the parliamentary eulogy on Disraeli brought on a sharp attack of diarrhoea. Nor could he bring himself to put forward the motion for a national memorial to Disraeli to be erected in Westminster Abbey, deputing Lord Richard Grosvenor to do it in his place. However, after much heart-searching and praying for guidance, his speech on Disraeli on 9 May was a masterpiece of dignity and tact. He praised him for his unique career, his loyalty to his race, his devotion to his wife, and his absence of rancour, and for the qualities which he had genuinely admired his rival. Disraeli had possessed, he said, 'in a degree undoubtedly extraordinary', strength of will, long-sighted consistency of purpose, remarkable power of self-government; 'and last, but not least, ... great parliamentary courage – a quality which I, who have been associated in the course of my life with some scores of Ministers, have, I think, never known but two whom I could pronounce his equal.'

Gladstone later said that the eulogy of Disraeli was one of the most difficult things he had ever had to do in his life.

Disraeli's body was taken secretly out of 19 Curzon Street at one o'clock in the morning of Sunday 27 April, to avoid the huge crowds that had been waiting outside the previous day. Attended only by Mr Baum, who followed in a hansom cab, it was taken to Paddington and placed on a special train for High Wycombe. At Hughenden, Monty and Disraeli's two other executors, Philip Rose and Lionel de Rothschild's only son, Nathaniel, waited to receive it and at four o'clock in the morning it was placed in the drawing-room in preparation for the funeral on Tuesday afternoon.

On the day of the funeral, 29 April, all the shops in Wycombe were closed and the old red lion which Disraeli had used as a prop in his rousing election speech in 1832 had a piece of black crape tied round its neck. The mourners, as Disraeli would have liked, were royal and highly aristocratic; there were three princes of the blood – the Prince of Wales, the Duke of Connaught and Prince Leopold who represented the Queen; the French, Russian, German and Turkish Ambassadors; six dukes – Richmond, Norfolk, Somerset, Beaufort, Portland and Marlborough; and a galaxy of marquesses, earls and other peers including Beauchamp, Bradford, Salisbury, Lytton, Cairns, and, in spite of all, Derby.

The coffin, covered with scented white flowers and a wreath of wild primroses inscribed by the Queen in her own hand, 'His favourite flowers; from Osborne, a tribute of affection and regret from Queen Victoria,' was wheeled down the hill from the house to the churchyard vault by Disraeli's tenants. It was preceded by Mr Baum carrying a crimson velvet cushion with the Earl's coronet and insignia and followed by the chief mourners, Ralph D'Israeli and his son Coningsby, now a Charterhouse schoolboy of fourteen, Monty, Barrington, Nathaniel de Rothschild and Philip Rose. After them walked the princes, ambassadors and other mourners, past the dark-green-clad ranks of the Buckinghamshire Volunteers and rows of local people and tenants, overlooked by men and boys who had climbed trees for a better view.

Disraeli's coffin was wheeled down into the churchyard vault to lie between Mrs Brydges Willyams and Mary Anne. The vault was closed and the mourners walked back up to the house for a pious tour conducted by Monty and to hear the reading of the will. At 5.30 they all departed by special train for London, leaving Hughenden empty but for Disraeli's servants.

Disraeli's wish to be buried simply at Hughenden was his last identification with the country gentlemen of England. He died, like the hero of one of his novels, rich, full of honours, twice Prime Minister, celebrated throughout Europe, an Earl and a Knight of the Garter. There was, however, to be no Disraeli dynasty; Coningsby, who inherited Hughenden, had an undistinguished career as an MP from 1892 to 1906, and died childless in 1936. Perhaps it was better so. Disraeli remained unique.

Notes

The following abbreviations are used for sources referred to repeatedly in the text:

HP Hughenden Papers
DL Disraeli Letters
M&B Moneypenny, W.F., and Buckle, G.E., *The Life of Benjamin Disraeli, Earl of Beacons-field* (new and revised edition, 2 vols, 1929)
Blake Blake R., *Disraeli*

1 The Byronic Youth

1. Article by Barrington in *Notes and Queries*, 6th series, x, 458, 1884
2. *Contarini Fleming*, Pt. I, ch. ii
3. Memoir preface to 14th edition of *Curiosities of Literature*, 1849
4. *ibid.*
5. Edward Koch, *Leaves from the Diary of a Literary Amateur*, 1911
6. Bodleian MS. Douce d 33, ff. 26-7
7. HP/A/I/Misc, Letter by Rev. Edward Jones in *Standard*, 28 April 1884
8. M&B, I, iii, p. 28
9. HP/A/III/Diary, June 1820
10. *Contarini Fleming*, Pt. II, ch. ii
11. Anne Dundas of Arniston, quoted by J.I. Brash, *Disraeli Newsletter*, Vol. 5, no.1, Spring 1980
12. *ibid.*
13. Blake, p. 19
14. DL 12, Disraeli to Sarah D'Israeli [6 Aug. 1824]
15. DL 14, same to same [19 Aug. 1824]
16. HP/A/IV/12/B/12, Isaac D'Israeli to Maria and Sarah D'Israeli [29 Aug. 1824]
17. Mutilated Diary, 1 Sept. 1833, DL I, App. III

2 The First Fall

1. *Vivian Grey*, Bk. I, ch. vii
2. DL 84, Disraeli to Thomas Mullett Evans, 9 May 1830
3. Lockhart Letters, MS 931 (Nat. Lib. Scot.), J. Murray to J.G. Lockhart, 25 Sept. 1825
4. DL 20, Disraeli to J. Murray [? April 1825]
5. DL 21, Disraeli to Robert Messer [? April 1825]
6. DL 28, Disraeli to J. Murray, 21 Sept. 1825
7. *see* Lang, A., *Life and Letters of J.G. Lockhart*, 2 vols, 1897, I, p. 368
8. Smiles, S., *Memoir of John Murray*, 2 vols, 1891, II, p. 199
9. Grierson, H.J.C., ed., *The Letters of Sir Walter Scott*, 12 vols, 1932-7, IX, p. 303
10. DL 41, Disraeli to J. Lockhart [?24] Nov. 1825
11. Douglas, D., ed., *Familiar Letters of Sir Walter Scott*, 2 vols, 1890, Appendix III
12. DL 38, Disraeli to J. Lockhart [?22 Nov. 1825]
13. DL 36, Disraeli to J. Lockhart [?12] Nov. 1825

14. *ibid.*
15. Pinney, T., ed., *The Letters of Thomas Babington Macaulay*, Vol. I, 1974, p. 207
16. *Vivian Grey*, Bk. IV, ch. ii
17. Grierson, *op. cit.*, p. 413 n2
18. Fraser, Sir W., *Disraeli and his Day*, 1891, p. 1
19. HP/A/IV/D/4 Sara Austen to Disraeli, n.d.
20. *Vivian Grey*, Bk. I, ch. vii
21. Phipps, Hon. E., *Memoir of Plumer Ward*, 2 vols, 1850, pp. 147-9
22. *Contarini Fleming*, Pt. II, ch. xv
23. Murray Papers, n.d., [21 May 1826], *cit.* Blake, p. 45
24. Murray Papers, 16 Oct. 1826, *cit.* Blake, p. 47
25. *Contarini Fleming*, Pt. I, ch. xi

3 Eastern Odyssey
1. HP/A/IV/12/C/3, Sara Austen to Disraeli, n.d. [1826]
2. HP/AI/V/12/C, Sara Austen to Sarah D'Israeli
3. HP/A/IV/12/C, Sarah D'Israeli to Disraeli, 26 Aug. 1826
4. DL 51, Disraeli to Isaac D'Israeli, 21 Aug. 1826
5. M&B, I, viii, p. 120
6. HP/B/XXI/T/216, Disraeli to Sharon Turner (copy), March 1828
7. DL 74, Disraeli to Benjamin Austen, 8 Dec. 1829
8. *ibid.*
9. *The Young Duke*, ed. Lucien Wolf, 1904-5, ch. xviii
10. *ibid.*
11. HP/B/XX/Ly/108, Edward Lytton Bulwer to Disraeli, 10 April 1830
12. DL 86, Disraeli to John Murray, 27 May 1830
13. Diary of William Meredith, *cit.* Blake, pp. 58-9
14. DL 81, Disraeli to Benjamin Austen, 13 April 1830
15. DL 84, Disraeli to Thomas Mullett Evans, 9 May 1830
16. DL 92, Disraeli to Isaac D'Israeli, 14 July 1830
17. DL 90, same to same, 1 July [1830]
18. *ibid.*
19. DL 91, Disraeli to Isaac D'Israeli, 1 July 1830
20. *ibid.*
21. DL 92
22. HP/A/IV/E/7, Sarah D'Israeli to Disraeli, 28 July 1830
23. DL 94, Disraeli to Maria D'Israeli, 1 Aug. 1830
24. *ibid.*
25. M&B, I, ix, pp. 152-3
26. DL 97, Disraeli to Isaac D'Israeli, 25 Aug. 1830
27. Gregory, Sir W., *An Autobiography*, 1894, p. 96
28. DL 99, Disraeli to Ralph D'Israeli, [1]7 Sept. [1830]
29. *ibid.*
30. *ibid.*
31. DL 101, Disraeli to Isaac D'Israeli, 25 Oct. 1830
32. DL 103, Disraeli to Benjamin Austen, 18 Nov. 1830
33. DL 101
34. DL 104, Disraeli to Isaac D'Israeli, 23 Dec. 1830
35. DL 107, Disraeli to Edward Lytton Bulwer, 27 Dec. 1830
36. DL 110, Disraeli to Sarah D'Israeli, 20 March 1831
37. DL 111, same to same, 28 May 1831
38. HP/A/IV/F/1, Paul Emile Botta to Disraeli, 3 Dec. 1831
39. HP/A/IV/F/2, same to same, July 1832. He refers to a form of female circumcision in which the vagina is artificially closed until the wedding night when it is opened with a knife.
40. DL 113, Disraeli to Isaac D'Israeli, 20 July 1831
41. DL 114, Disraeli to Sarah D'Israeli, 20 July 1831
42. DL 118, Disraeli to Isaac D'Israeli, 17 Oct. 1831
43. HP/B/XXI/240, James Clay to Disraeli, 21 Dec. 1831
44. DL 118

4 The First Steps
1. HP/B/XXI/240, James Clay to Disraeli, 21 Dec. 1831

2. DL 124, Disraeli to Sarah D'Israeli, [12 Nov. 1831]
3. DL 126, Disraeli to Sarah D'Israeli, 14 Nov. 1831
4. HP/B/XX/Ly/9, Edward Lytton Bulwer to Disraeli, n.d., [1831]
5. HP/A/IV/G/3, Clara Bolton to Disraeli, n.d., [1832]
6. DL 160, Disraeli to Sarah D'Israeli, [28 March 1832]
7. DL 209, same to same, [4 Aug. 1832]
8. DL 192, Disraeli to Sarah D'Israeli, 24 March [1832]
9. Fraser, *op. cit.*, p. 187
10. DL 195, Disraeli to Sarah D'Israeli [29 May 1832]
11. HP/A/IV/G/13, Clara Bolton to Disraeli, n.d. [1832]
12. DL 142, Disraeli to Sarah D'Israeli [24 Feb. 1832]
13. HP/A/IV/G/2, Clara Bolton to Disraeli, n.d. [1832]
14. HP/A/I/B/416, Isaac D'Israeli to Disraeli, n.d., [?26 Feb. 1832]
15. DL 144, Disraeli to Sarah D'Israeli, [27 Feb. 1832]
16. HP/A/IV/G/9, Clara Bolton to Disraeli, n.d.
17. DL 169, Disraeli to Sarah D'Israeli, 2 April 1832
18. Devey, L., *Life of Rosina, Lady Lytton*, 1887, p. 412
19. Mutilated Diary, *op.cit.*, 1834
20. DL 140, Disraeli to Sarah D'Israeli, [20 Feb. 1832]
21. HP/A/I/B/426, Sarah D'Israeli to Disraeli, 11 May 1832
22. *ibid.*
23. HP/A/IV/G/2, Clara Bolton to Disraeli, n.d.
24. DL 201, Disraeli to Sara Austen, 10 June 1832

5 Dreams of Fair Women

1. Zetland, Marquess of, ed., *The Letters of Disraeli to Lady Bradford and Lady Chesterfield*, 2 vols, 1929, II, p. 9
2. DL 234, Disraeli to Sarah D'Israeli, [14 Feb. 1833]
3. DL 240, Disraeli to Helen Selina Blackwood, [?23 Feb. 1833]
4. DL 255, same to same, [? 18 March 1833]
5. Dufferin Papers, D1071F/A4/2, Helen Blackwood to Disraeli, n.d., [? May 1833]
6. DL 265, Disraeli to Helen Blackwood, [?17 April 1833]
7. Mutilated Diary, *op. cit.*
8. Gower, Lord Ronald, *My Reminiscences*, 2 vols, 1883, II, p. 359
9. HP/A/I/B/459, Sarah and James D'Israeli to Disraeli, 29 March 1832
10. Dufferin Papers, D1071F/A4/2, Helen Blackwood to Disraeli, n.d., [1833]
11. Dufferin Papers, D1071B/3/9B, Isaac D'Israeli to Helen Blackwood (written in Disraeli's hand), n.d., [? March 1833]
12. HP/A/I/B/479, Sarah D'Israeli to Disraeli, 23 May 1833
13. HP/A/I/B/480, Sarah D'Israeli to Disraeli, 31 May 1833
14. DL 276, Disraeli to Sarah D'Israeli, [5 June 1833]
15. HP/A/I/B/480, Sarah D'Israeli to Disraeli, [? March 1833]
16. HP/A/IV/H/46, Henrietta Sykes to Disraeli, n.d., [? July 1833]
17. HP/A/IV/H/1, same to same, 16 Aug. 1833
18. HP/A/IV/H/82, same to same, n.d.
19. HP/A/IV/H/14, same to same, [?20] Aug. 1833
20. HP/A/IV/H/88, same to same, n.d., [?22/23 Aug. 1833]
21. HP/A/IV/H/8, same to same, 11 Oct. 1833
22. HP/A/IV/9, same to same, 20 Oct. 1833
23. *ibid.*
24. HP/A/I/B/500, Sarah D'Israeli to Disraeli, 13 Nov. 1833
25. HP/A/I/C/46, Isaac D'Israeli to Disraeli, 25 Sept. 1833
26. HP/A/IV/H/13, Henrietta Sykes to Disraeli, 24 Dec. 1833
27. BL Add. MSS. 49508, Benjamin Austen to Disraeli, 1 Dec. 1833
28. DL 299, Disraeli to Benjamin Austen, 7 Dec. [1833]

29. HP/A/IV/H/13, Henrietta Sykes to Disraeli, 24 Dec. 1833
30. Layard, Sir H., 'The Early Life of Lord Beaconsfield', *Quarterly Review*, no. 335, 1889, pp. 1-42
31. Willis, N.P., *Pencillings by the Way*, 1852
32. Gronow, Capt., *Reminiscences*, 2 vols, 1900
33. *see* Sadleir, M., *Blessington-d'Orsay, a Masquerade*, 1933, pp. 307-8
34. Blake, p.114
35. DL 331, Disraeli to Sarah D'Israeli, [19 June 1834]

6 Roundabouts and Swings

1. Swartz, M.H., and M., eds, *Disraeli's Reminiscences*, 1975, p. 119
2. HP/A/IV/H/23, Henrietta Sykes to Disraeli, 25 Sept. 1834
3. HP/A/IV/20, same to same, 8 Sept. 1834
4. HP/A/IV/85, same to same, [? Oct. 1834]
5. Memorandum by Disraeli, DL ii, p. 426
6. Greville, *Memoirs*, ed. Lytton Strachey and Roger Fulford, 8 vols, 1938, III, p. 118
7. M&B, I, xiii, pp. 285-6
8. Thompson, F.M.L., *English Landed Society in the Nineteenth Century*, 1963
9. HP/B/XXI/B/101, Thomas Barnes to Disraeli, 4 May 1836
10. DL 408, Disraeli to Sarah D'Israeli, 27 June 1835
11. Londonderry, Edith Marchioness of, and Hyde, H.M., *More Letters from Martha Wilmot*, 1935, pp. 108-9
12. DL 410, Disraeli to Sarah D'Israeli, [3 July 1835]
13. DL 522, Disraeli to Sarah D'Israeli, [20 Aug. 1836]
14. DL 515, Disraeli to William Pyne, [21 July 1836]
15. DL 505, same to same, [31 May 1836]
16. HP/A/I/C/58, Isaac D'Israeli to Disraeli, 14 Dec. 1835
17. HP/A/I/C/65, same to same, 21 Feb. 1836
18. DL 538, Disraeli to William Pyne, 5 Dec. [1836]
19. DL 542, Disraeli to d'Orsay, [18 Dec. 1836]
20. DL 547, Disraeli to Pyne, 28 Dec. [1836]
21. HP/B/XXI/580, Marguerite Blessington to Disraeli, 26 Dec. 1836
22. DL 545, Disraeli to d'Orsay, [?23 Dec. 1836]
23. DL 659, same to same, [?31 Aug. 1837]
24. HP/A/IV/H/48 Henrietta Sykes to Disraeli, n.d., [? Aug. 1837]
25. *see* Sadleir, *op. cit.*, pp. 258-9
27. *Henrietta Temple*, Bk. VI, ch. xiii
28. DL 588, Disraeli to d'Orsay, [13 March 1837]
29. HP/B/XXI/296, d'Orsay to Disraeli, n.d. [? March 1837]
30. DL 591, Disraeli to Pyne, [23 March 1837]
31. Gramont Papers, VI, Disraeli to d'Orsay 'Friday 24', [? 1837]
32. *Venetia*, ch. xviii
33. M&B, I, xvi, 380, Mary Anne Wyndham Lewis to John Viney Evans, 29 July 1837

7 Mary Anne

1. Escott, T.H.S., *Club Makers and Club Members*, 1914, pp. 62-3
2. HP/A/I/C/72, Isaac D'Israeli to Disraeli, Dec. 1837
3. Fraser, *op. cit.*, p. 231
4. Rothschild, C. de, *Reminiscences*, 1922, p. 229
5. *ibid.*, p. 233
6. M&B, 5, vi, p. 570
7. Hardwick, M., *Mrs. Dizzy*, 1972, p. 72
8. HP/A/I/A/24, Disraeli to Mary Anne Wyndham Lewis, 17 April, 1838
9. HP/A/I/A/558, Mary Anne Wyndham Lewis to Disraeli, n.d. [?20 May 1838]
10. *See* Disraeli, R, ed., *Lord Beaconsfield's Correspondence with his Sister*, 1886, p. 106
11. HP/A/I/A/30, Disraeli to Mary Anne Wyndham Lewis, 20 Aug. 1838

12. HP/A/I/A/35, same to same, 7 Oct. 1838
13. HP/A/I/A/39, same to same, 18 Oct. 1838
14. HP/B/XXI/299, d'Orsay to Disraeli, 25 Dec. 1838
15. HP/B/XXI/300, same to same, [?31 Dec. 1838]
16. HP/A/I/A/57, Disraeli to Mary Anne Wyndham Lewis, 23 Dec. 1838
17. HP/A/I/A/60, Disraeli to Mary Anne Wyndham Lewis, 30 Dec. 1838
18. HP/A/I/A/61, same to same, 31 Dec. 1838
19. HP/B/XXI/301, d'Orsay to Disraeli, n.d. [1839]
20. HP/A/I/A/89, Disraeli to Mary Anne Wyndham Lewis, 7 Feb, 1839
21. HP/A/I/A/445, Mary Anne Wyndham Lewis to Disraeli, n.d., [?8 Feb. 1839]
22. Macready, W.C., *The Journal*, 1832–51, ed. J.C. Trewin, p. 135
23. HP/A/I/B/183, Disraeli to Sarah D'Israeli, n.d., [summer 1839]
24. Hardwick, *op. cit.*, p. 108
25. HP/A/I/A/97, Disraeli to Mary Anne Wyndham Lewis, 8 July 1839

8 A Rising Talent

1. HP/B/IB
2. HP/B/I/B/29
3. HP/B/I/B/30
4. HP/B/I/B/31
5. de Gramont Papers, n.d. [29 June 1841]
6. M&B, 2, iv, p. 516
7. *ibid.*, pp. 516–7
8. *ibid.*, p. 518
9. *ibid.*, p. 518
10. HP/A/I/B/256, Disraeli to Sarah D'Israeli, 6 Sept. 1841
11. HP/A/I/A/165, Disraeli to Mary Anne Disraeli, 16 Feb. 1842
12. HP/A/I/A/180, same to same, 8 March 1842
13. HP/A/V/D/2, Indenture between Disraeli and George Samuel Ford, 18 March 1842
14. HP/XXI/329–44, Exmouth–Disraeli correspondence, and section A/V/C for financial documents relative to Exmouth
15. HP/A/I/C/9, Disraeli to Isaac D'Israeli, 13 Aug. 1842
16. Fonblanque, E.B. de, *Lives of the Lords Strangford*, 1877, p. 238
17. Whibley, C., *Lord John Manners and his Friends*, 2 vols, 1925, I, p. 140
18. *Endymion*, ch. lxxi
19. HP/B/II/108, Disraeli to General Baudrand, 15 Nov. 1842
20. M&B. 2, xii, Appendix, p. 807
21. *Coningsby*, Bk. V, ch. viii
22. Whibley, *op. cit.*, I, i, p. 141
23. *ibid.*, pp. 142–3
24. *ibid.*, p. 146
25. *ibid.*
26. *ibid.*, p. 149
27. *ibid.*, p. 146

9 Young England

1. Hansard, 3rd series, lxviii, 1028
2. *Times* Archive, Walter Papers, C.M. Walter to Edward Walter, Aug. 1843
3. Whibley, *op. cit.*, I, p. 153
4. Broadlands Papers, Shaftesbury MSS., SHA/PD3
5. Hansard, lxxi, 460
6. *ibid.*, 841
7. Jennings, L.J., *The Croker Papers . . .*, 3 vols, 1884, III, p. 9
8. Parker, C.S., ed., *Sir Robert Peel from his Private Papers*, 3 vols, 1891–9, III, pp. 424–5
9. *Coningsby*, Bk. II, ch. v
10. *ibid.*, Bk. VIII, ch. iii
11. *Sybil*, Bk. II, ch. v
12. *ibid.*, Bk. I, ch. v
13. *ibid.*, Bk. IV, ch xiii
14. M&B, 2, vi, pp. 583–4
15. *ibid.*, p. 585
16. Hansard, lxxiii, 1419
17. Broughton, Lord, *Recollections of a Long Life*, 6 vols, 1909–11, VI, p. 115
18. Hansard, lxxv, 1029
19. Broughton, *op. cit.*, VI, p. 118
20. *ibid.*
21. Fonblanque, E. B. de, *Lives of the Viscounts Strangford*, 1878, pp. 224–5

22. HP/B/XX/M/7, Lord John Manners to Disraeli, 17 Nov. 1844
23. M&B, 2, viii, p. 647
24. M&B, 2, viii, p. 640*n*
25. Greville, *op. cit.*, V, p. 213
26. Hansard, lxxvii, 998
27. *ibid.*, 154-5
28. Hansard, lxxviii, 1028
29. Reid, T.W. (ed), *The Life ... of Richard Monckton Milnes ...*, 2 vols, 1890, I, p. 352
30. Hansard, lxxix, 565-6
31. Greville, *op. cit.*, V, pp. 224-5

10 Peel's Adversary

1. Broadlands Papers, Palmerston MSS, GC/BE/406/3, Disraeli to Palmerston, 14 Dec. 1845
2. *ibid.*, GC/BE/406/1, Beauvale to Palmerston, 19 Dec. 1845
3. Morley, J., *The Life of William Ewart Gladstone*, 3 vols, 1903, I, p. 283
4. Parker, *op. cit.*, III, p. 74
5. Whibley, *op. cit.*, I
6. Broadlands Papers SHA/PD/4, 19 June 1846
7. Wemyss, *op. cit.*, I, p. 352
8. *Lord George Bentinck, a Political Biography*, 1852, ch. iii
9. *ibid.*
10. Hansard, 3rd series, lxxxiii, 95
11. *ibid.*, 120
12. *ibid.*, 126
13. *Bentinck*, ch. iv
14. Greville, *op. cit.*, V, p. 303
15. Greville, *op. cit.*, V, p. 310
16. Reid, T.W., *op. cit.*, I, p. 371
17. Broughton, *op. cit.*, vi, 170
18. Hansard, lxxxvi, 675
19. *ibid.*, 689
20. *ibid.*, 689-90
21. Broadlands Papers SHA/PD/4, 18 May 1846
22. Greville, *op. cit.*, V, p. 328
23. Broadlands Papers SHA/PD/4, 26 June 1846
24. Hansard, lxxxvii, p. 1055
25. Greville, *op. cit.*, V, pp. 329-30
26. Kitson, C.G., 'Hunger and Politics in 1842', *Journal of Modern History*, Dec. 1953, p. 374

27. Broadlands Papers SHA/PD/4, 22 May 1846
28. HP/A/I/A/205aa, Disraeli to Mary Anne Disraeli, 29 June 1846

11 Emotional Undercurrents

1. Whibley, *op. cit.*, I, p. 185
2. Vincent, J.R., ed., *Disraeli, Derby and the Conservative Party, the Political Journals of Lord Stanley, 1848-69*, 1978, p. 33
3. Fitzwilliam MSS., A 26, Disraeli to Sarah D'Israeli, n.d., [Feb. 1840]
4. Fitz., A30, same to same, n.d., [Aug. 1840]
5. Fitz., A28, same to same, 21 Aug. 1840
6. HP/A/I/A/165, Disraeli to Mary Anne Disraeli, 16 Feb. 1842
7. HP/A/I/A/173, same to same, 25 Feb. 1842
8. HP/A/I/B/288, Disraeli to Sarah D'Israeli, 19 July 1845
9. James, R.R., *Rosebery*, 1963, p. 43
10. HP/A/I/B/267, Disraeli to Sarah D'Israeli, n.d., [? July 1845]
11. HP/A/I/B/290, same to same, 6 Sept. 1845
12. *ibid.*
13. Cohen, L., *Lady de Rothschild and her Daughters, 1821-1931*, 1935, pp. 47-9
14. Carnarvon Papers, BL Add. MSS. 60900, 6 Feb. 1868
15. HP/B/XX/Lx/57, Henry Lennox to Disraeli, 4 Feb. 1855
16. HP/A/I/D/10, James D'Israeli to Disraeli, '½ past 2 o'clock,' n.d., [21 April 1847]
17. M&B, 3, VI, p. 958
18. HP/R/I/A/6, Disraeli to Philip Rose, 24 March 1847
19. HP/A/I/B/317, Disraeli to Sarah D'Israeli, 2 May 1849
20. BL Add, MSS. 59887, same to same, 30 April 1849
21. *ibid.*, same to same, 18 July 1849
22. Cohen, *op. cit.*, p. 46
23. BL Add. MSS. 59887, Disraeli to Sarah D'Israeli, 7 Sept. 1849
24. HP/A/I/B/322, same to same, 16 Sept. 1849

25. HP/A/I/B/639, Sarah D'Israeli to Disraeli, 10 Aug. 1849
26. HP/A/I/B/653, same to same, 27 March 1850
27. HP/A/I/B/361, Disraeli to Sarah D'Israeli, 8 Oct [1849], incorrectly dated as 1852
28. HP/A/I/B/324, same to same, 4 Nov. 1849
29. HP/R/I/A/52, Disraeli to Rose, 4 Nov. 1849
30. BL Add. MSS. 59887, Disraeli to Sarah D'Israeli, 10 Feb. 1850
31. HP/A/I/B/344, same to same, 1 Aug. 1851
32. HP/A/I/B/345, same to same, 23 Aug. 1851
33. HP/A/I/B/351, same to same, 14 Oct. 1851
34. HP/A/I/B/353, same to same, 7 Nov. 1851
35. Kebbel, T.E., *Lord Beaconsfield and other Tory Memories*, 1907, p. 40
36. Gregory, *op. cit.*, p. 94
37. Rothschild, *op. cit.*, pp. 235–6
38. Fraser, *op cit.*, p. 79

12 The Mystery Man

1. Nevill, R., ed., *The Reminiscences of Lady Dorothy Nevill*, 1906, p. 200
2. Broughton, *op. cit.*, VI, p. 228
3. *Tancred*, Bk. II, ch. xi
4. *ibid.*, Bk. VI, ch. ii
5. *ibid.*, Bk. III, ch vii
6. Whibley, *op. cit.*, II, p. 283
7. Hansard, 3rd series, xcv, 1263
8. *ibid.*, 1278
9. *ibid.*, 1323–1331
10. Hansard, cxiii, p. 795
11. Cohen, *op. cit.*, p. 42
12. Rothschild Archive, cited, A. Gillam, in *Disraeli Newsletter*, Vol. 5, no. 1, Spring 1980
13. Rothschild, *op. cit.*, p. 232
14. Vincent, *op. cit.*, p. 32
15. Cohen, *op. cit.*, p. 47
16. *ibid.*, p. 46
17. HP/A/I/B/344, Disraeli to Sarah D'Israeli, 1 Aug. 1851

13 The Jew and the Jockey

1. Whibley, *op. cit.*, I, p. 291
2. Greville, *op. cit.*, VI, p. 13
3. Malmesbury, Earl of, *Memoirs of an ex-Minister*, 2 vols, 1884, Vol I, 10 Feb. 1848
4. Derby MSS. 132, Bentinck to Stanley, 9 Feb. 1848, *cit.* Blake, p. 261
5. Whibley, *op. cit.*, I, p. 305
6. *ibid.*
7. Greville, *op. cit.*, VI, p. 121
8. *ibid.*, pp. 290–1
9. M&B, 3, v, p. 938
10. *ibid.*
11. Vincent, *op. cit.*, p. 1
12. Bentinck to Stanley, 4 Feb. 1848, *in* Stewart, R.W., *The Politics of Protection*, 1971, p. 132*n*
13. Londonderry, Marchioness of, ed., *The Letters of Benjamin Disraeli to Frances Anne, Marchioness of Londonderry*, 1938, p. 25
14. Nevill, Ralph, ed., *Leaves from the Note-Books of Lady Dorothy Nevill*, 1907, p. 75
15. Whibley, *op. cit.*, I, p. 310
16. M&B, 3, vii, p. 1005
17. M&B, 3, viii, p. 1035
18. BL Add. MSS. 59887
19. Vincent, *op. cit.*, p. 25
20. *ibid.*, pp. 23–4
21. Swartz, *Reminiscences*, p. 23
22. Vincent, *op cit.*, p. 47
23. *ibid.*, p. 49
24. Swartz, *op cit.*, pp. 46–7
25. Vincent, *op cit.*, p. 51
26. *ibid.* p. 50
27. Benson, A.C., and Viscount Esher, eds., *The Letters of Queen Victoria*, 3 vols, 1907, II, p. 417
28. Malmesbury, *op cit.*, I, 21 February 1852
29. HP/B/XXl/325, d'Orsay to Disraeli, 7 Jan. 1850

14 Public Affairs and Private Friendships

1. Benson and Esher, *op cit.*, II, p. 450
2. Broadlands Papers, SHA/PD6, 23 Feb. 1852

3. HP/B/XX/S/54, Derby to Disraeli, 30 April 1852
4. Greville, *op cit.*, VI, p. 342
5. Vincent, *op cit.*, p. 72
6. *ibid.*
7. HP/B/XX/Lx/16, Lord Henry Lennox to Disraeli, [20 Oct. 1852]
8. HP/B/XX/Lx/13, Lennox to Disraeli, 15 Sept. [1852]
9. Hansard, 3rd series, cxxiii, 603 & 612
10. M&B, 3, xii, p. 1239
11. Memorandum by Prince Albert in Benson and Esher, *op. cit.*, II, p. 491
12. Bailey, J., ed., *Diary of Lady Frederick Cavendish*, 2 vols, 1927, 21 June 1859
13. Broadlands Papers, GC/DI/139, 24 Nov. 1852
14. Vincent, *op cit.*, p. 88
15. Bassett, A.T., ed., *Gladstone to his Wife*, 1936, 6. Dec. 1852
16. M&B., 3, xii, p. 1256
17. Trevelyan, G.M., *The Life of John Bright*, 1913, p. 207
18. Bassett, *op. cit.*, 17 Dec. 1852
19. Hansard, 3rd series, cxxiii, 1666
20. Vincent, *op cit.*, p. 90
21. Bassett, *op. cit.*, 18 Dec. 1852
22. *The Times*, 18 Dec. 1852
23. Vincent, *op. cit.*, pp. 90–1
24. Benson and Esher, *op cit.*, II, p. 506
25. Kebbel, T.E., *op. cit.*, p. 92
26. Vincent, *op. cit.*, p. 362
27. HP/B/XX/Lx/5, Lennox to Disraeli, n.d. [15 July 1852]
28. M&B, 3, xii, p. 1200
29. HP/B/XX/Lx/11, Lennox to Disraeli, 25 Aug. 1852
30. M&B, 3, xii, p. 1203
31. Whibley, *op. cit.*, II, pp. 57–8
32. Vincent, *op. cit.*, p. 361
33. HP/B/XX/Lx/29, Lennox to Disraeli, n.d.
34. HP/B/XX/Lx/130, same to same, 23 Sept. 1858
35. HP/B/XX/Lx/31, same to same [20 Oct. 1853]
36. Vincent, *op. cit.*, p. 177
37. HP/XX/M/106/75, Manners to Disraeli, 21 March 1851
38. Disraeli to G.M.W. Peacocke, 20 Oct. 1857, MS. sold Sotheby's, 21 July 1980

39. HP/XXI/S/652, Smythe to Disraeli, 2 July 1852
40. *Endymion*, ch. xxii
41. HP/A/I/B/349, Disraeli to Sarah D'Israeli, 1 Aug. 1851
42. M&B, 3, xiii, p. 1269
43. *ibid.*, pp. 1271–2
44. *ibid.*, p. 1276
45. *ibid.*, p. 1279, 3 Oct. 1861

15 The Restless Fifties

1. Trevelyan, *op. cit.*, p. 207
2. Vincent, *op. cit.*, p. 104
3. HP/B/XX/S/585, Stanley to Disraeli, 20 Jan. 1853
4. HP/B/XX/S/118, Derby to Disraeli, 20 June 1853
5. Greville, *op. cit.*, VI, p. 404
6. M&B, 3, xiv, p. 1309
7. Vincent, *op. cit.*, p. 102
8. Kebbel, *op. cit.*, pp. 3–4
9. HP/B/XXI/L/376, Samuel Lucas to Disraeli, 5 May 1853
10. HP/B/XX/Lx, n.d., [Sept/Oct, 1857]
11. Londonderry, *op. cit.*, p. 130
12. Vincent, *op. cit.*, p. 114
13. *ibid.*, p. 121
14. Londonderry, *op. cit.*, pp. 145–6
15. *ibid.*
16. Malmesbury, *op. cit.*, II, 15 Dec. 1856
17. Private Collection
18. M&B, 4, iii, p. 1454
19. Swartz, *op. cit.*, p. 66
20. HP/B/XX/E/5, 5 Feb. 1857
21. HP/B/XX/Lx/86, 7 Jan. 1857
22. Londonderry, *op. cit.*, p. 130
23. Greville, *op. cit.*, VII, p. 195
24. Malmesbury, *op. cit.*, II, 15 Dec. 1856
25. Vincent, *op. cit.*, p. 148
26. Malmesbury, *op. cit.*, ii, 3 Feb. 1857
27. M&B, 4, iv, p. 1501, 23 Nov. 1857
28. Greville, *op. cit.*, vii, p. 337
29. Vincent, *op. cit.*, p. 156
30. M&B, 4, v, pp. 1557–8
31. *ibid.*, 1563
32. HP/B/XX/E/89, Ralph Earle to Disraeli, n.d., [Dec. 1858]
33. M&B, 4, vi, p. 1618
34. M&B, 4, vi, p. 1623
35. *ibid.*, 1591

36. Derby MSS., 145/6, Disraeli to Derby, 3 April 1859
37. M&B, 4, vii, pp. 1635-6
38. Kebbel, *op. cit.*, p. 18
39. Vitzthum von Eckstaedt, C.F., *St Petersburg and London, 1852-64*, 2 vols, 1887, I, pp. 355-6
40. Kebbel, *op. cit.*, p. 20

16 A Time for Reflection
1. BL Add. MSS. 59887, Disraeli to Ralph D'Israeli, [1]9 Dec. 1859
2. Blake, p. 425
3. HP/R/I/C/39, Sarah D'Israeli to Disraeli, 27 Feb. 1852
4. *Endymion*, ch. ci
5. Swartz, *op. cit.*, p. 67
6. Kebbel, *op. cit.*, p. 4
7. Swartz, *op. cit.*, p. 148
8. Vincent, *op. cit.*, p. 33
9. Londonderry, *op. cit.*, p. 164
10. Swartz, *op. cit.*, p. 74
11. HP/R/I/A/153, Disraeli to Philip Rose, 7 Dec. 1862
12. HP/R/I/A/168, same to same, 17 Nov. 1863
13. HP/B/XX/R/18, Philip Rose to Disraeli, 16 Nov. 1863
14. HP/R/I/A/169, Disraeli to Philip Rose, 1 Dec. 1863
15. BL Add. MSS. 59887
16. Vincent, *op. cit.*, p. 346
17. Beauchamp MSS., Disraeli to 'dearest Elmley' (Beauchamp), 28 Sept. 1863, sold Sotheby's, 15 Dec. 1980
18. Kebbel, *op. cit.*, p. 36
19. Vitzthum, *op. cit.*, II, p. 176
20. Swartz, *op. cit.*, p. 77
21. *ibid.*, p. 82
22. *ibid.*, p. 84
23. M&B, 4, xi, p. 128
24. Blake, p. 491
25. M&B, 4, xi, p. 132
26. Swartz, *op. cit.*, p. 87
27. Greville, *op. cit.* vii, p. 460
28. M&B, 4, ix, p. 59
29. Vincent, *op cit.*, p. 213
30. *ibid.*, p. 179
31. *ibid.*, p. 31

32. *ibid.*, p. 227
33. Magnus, Sir P., *Gladstone*, 1954, p. 142
34. *ibid.*, p. 143
35. Vincent, *op. cit.*, p. 234
36. Trevelyan, *op. cit.*, p. 333
37. Vincent, *op. cit*, p. 216
38. *ibid.*, p. 215
39. Ridley, J., *Lord Palmerston*, 1972, p. 774
40. Swartz, *op. cit.*, p. 136
41. HP/B/XX/S/335, Derby to Disraeli, 4 Aug. 1865
42. HP/B/XX/S/336, same to same, 12 Aug. 1865
43. Vincent, *op. cit.*, p. 227
44. *ibid.*, p. 237

17 Disraeli v Gladstone
1. Vincent, *op. cit.*, p. 114
2. *ibid.*, p. 251
3. BL Add. MSS. 50,063A, in Blake, p. 439
4. Magnus, *op. cit.*, pp. 179-80
5. Vincent, *op. cit.*, p. 252
6. Disraeli to Henry Liddell, 15 June 1866; MS sold Christie's 20 July 1977
7. M&B, 4, xiii, p. 174
8. Carnarvon Papers, BL Add. MSS. 60899, 1 Aug. 1867
9. HP/B/XX/E/373, Ralph Earle to Disraeli, 1 July 1866
10. M&B, 4, xiii, 187, 29 July 1866
11. Carnarvon Papers, BL Add. MSS. 60899, 25 Feb. 1867
12. see Cowling, M., *1867: Disraeli, Gladstone and Revolution*, 1967, p. 196
13. Beauchamp MSS, 18 April 1867, sold Sotheby's 15 Dec. 1980
14. M&B, 4, xv, 268
15. White, W., *The Inner Life of the House of Commons*, 2 vols, 1897, II, p. 67
16. Magnus, *op. cit.*, p. 188
17. White, *op. cit.*, II, pp. 77-8
18. see Maxwell, Sir H., ed., *The Life and Letters of George William Frederick, Fourth Earl of Clarendon*, 2 vols, 1913, II, pp. 333-4
19. M&B, 4, xv, p. 291
20. Cowling, *op. cit.*, p. 338

18 The Top of the Greasy Pole

1. Burghclere, Lady, ed., *A Great Lady's Friendships*, 1933, p. 174
2. Buckle, G.E., ed., *The Letters of Queen Victoria*, 3 vols, 1926, I, pp. 451–4
3. M&B, 4, xv, p. 304
4. *ibid.*, p. 306
5. HP/A/I/A/509, Mary Anne Disraeli to Disraeli, n.d., [Nov./Dec. 1868]
6. HP/A/I/A/546, same to same, n.d., [Nov./Dec. 1868]
7. HP/A/I, unnumbered note, same to same, n.d., [Nov./Dec. 1868]
8. Maxwell, *op. cit.*, II, p. 338
9. M&B, 4, xvi, p. 319
10. HP/R/I/B/102aa, Philip Rose to Disraeli, 13 Jan. 1866
11. Vincent, *op. cit.*, p. 331
12. M&B, 4, xvi, p. 325
13. Blake, p. 490
14. *ibid.*, p. 487
15. Maxwell, *op. cit.*, II, p. 342
16. Morley, *op. cit.*, II, p. 240
17. White, *op. cit.*, II, p. 92–3
18. Buckle, *op. cit.*, I, p. 526
19. Hatfield MSS. 3M/DD, Salisbury to G.M. Sandford (Peacocke), 1 May 1868
20. Trevelyan, *op. cit.*, p. 392
21. *ibid.*
22. Maxwell, *op. cit.*, II, p. 346
23. M&B, 5, i, p. 388
24. Longford, E., *Victoria R.I.*, 1964, pp. 365–6
25. *ibid.*
26. M&B, 5, i, p. 390
27. HP/A/I/A/377, Disraeli to Mary Anne Disraeli, 26 Sept. 1868
28. Beauchamp MSS., 24 Dec. 1868, sold Sotheby's 15 Dec. 1980
29. HP/A/D/38, Annie Bassett to Disraeli, n.d., [post Aug. 1876]
30. BL Add. MSS. 59887, Disraeli to Ralph D'Israeli, 30 March 1867
31. BL Add. MSS. 59887, same to same, 15 April 1867
32. HP/B/XX/D/131, C. Fremantle to M. Corry, 31 Dec. 1868

19 Success and Sorrow

1. Froude, J.A. *Lord Beaconsfield*, 1890, p. 231

2. *Lothair*, ch. xxi
3. Trollope, A., *An Autobiography*, U. of Cal. Press, 1947, p. 217
4. M&B, 5, iv, p. 505
5. Vincent, *op. cit.*, p. 341
6. *ibid.*, p. 346
7. Hatfield MSS. 3M/DD, Salisbury to Sandford, 20 Dec. 1869
8. M&B 5, iii
9. *ibid.*, p. 473
10. *ibid.*, pp. 475–6
11. Magnus, *op. cit.* p. 207
12. Vincent, *op. cit.*, p. 340
13. M&B, 5, iii, 469
14. *ibid.*, p. 486
15. Gathorne-Hardy, A.E., ed., *Gathorne-Hardy, First Earl of Cranbrook: A Memoir*, 2 vols, 1910, I, p. 305
16. Fraser, *op. cit.*, p. 376
17. Nevill, *op. cit.*, p. 201
18. Hamilton, Lord George, *Parliamentary Reminiscences and Reflections, 1868–85*, 2 vols, 1916–22, II, pp. 57–8
19. M&B, 5, v, p. 532
20. Morley, *op. cit.*, II, p. 392
21. Hardwick, *op. cit.*, p. 183
22. M&B, 5, vi, p. 562
23. *ibid.*
24. *ibid.*
25. *ibid.*, p. 563
26. *ibid.*, p. 565
27. *ibid.*
28. *ibid.*
29. BL Add. MSS. 59887
30. HP/B/XX/D/189, Disraeli to Corry, 5 Dec. 1872
31. M&B, 5, vi, p. 567
32. HP/B/XX/D/190, Disraeli to Corry, n.d. [Dec. 1872]
33. M&B, 5, vi, p. 564
34. *ibid.*, p. 572
35. *ibid.*, p. 570
36. *ibid.*
37. Cohen, *op. cit.*, p. 49
38. Zetland, Marquess of, ed., *The Letters of Disraeli to Lady Bradford and Lady Chesterfield*, 2 vols, 1929, I, p. 286
39. M&B, 5, v, p. 532
40. Morley, *op. cit.*, II, p. 456
41. Whibley, *op. cit.*, II, pp. 163–4
42. M&B, 5, vii, p. 602
43. Disraeli to Keith Falconer, 10 Oct.

1873, MS. sold at Sotheby's 21 July 1980

44. M&B, 5, vii, p. 608
45. *ibid.*, viii, p. 620
46. Battiscombe, G., *Mrs Gladstone*, 1956, p. 158
47. Buckle, *op. cit.*, I, pp. 315–16
48. Fulford, R. ed., *Darling Child, Private Correspondence of Queen Victoria and the Crown Princess of Prussia, 1871–8*, 1976, p. 128
49. *ibid.*, p. 131

20 Power and the Affections
1. HP/A/IV/K/24, n.d., June 1873 according to Blake, p. 531
2. HP/A/IV/K/24a, *see* Blake, p. 530n
3. Cardigan and Lencastre, Countess of, *My Recollections*, 1909
4. Bradford MSS., 13 April 1874
5. Bradford MSS., 24 Jan. 1876
6. *ibid.*, 19 April 1875
7. *ibid.*, July 1875
8. *ibid.*, 16 Aug. 1874
9. *ibid.*, 2 Feb. 1875
10. *ibid.*, 18 Feb. 1875
11. Zetland, I, p. 32
12. *ibid.*, p. 52
13. *ibid.*, p. 57
14. *ibid.*, p. 57
15. *ibid.*, p. 59
16. *ibid.*, p. 60
17. Bradford MSS., 19 March 1874
18. Fraser, *op. cit.*, p. 17
19. Zetland, *op. cit.*, I, p. 73
20. Hamilton, *op cit.*, pp. 54–5
21. Zetland, *op cit.*, p. 297
22. Bradford MSS, 1 March 1874 and n.d. [*c.* 4 March 1874]
23. Fulford, *op. cit.*, pp. 129–30
24. Cross, Viscount, 'A Political History', in Smith, P., *Disraelian Conservatism and Social Reform*, 1967, p. 199
25. Zetland, *op. cit.*, I, p. 242
26. *ibid.*
27. *ibid.*, p. 246
28. *ibid.*, p. 80
29. *ibid.*, p. 97
30. Bradford MSS., 3 Aug. 1874
31. Bradford MSS., 28 July 1874

32. Zetland, *op. cit.*, I, p. 129
33. Bradford MSS., 7 Aug. 1874
34. M&B, 5, ix, p. 679
35. Zetland, *op. cit.*, I, pp. 133–4
36. *ibid.*, p. 135
37. Bradford MSS., 14 Aug. 1874
38. Gardiner, A.G., *Life of Sir William Harcourt*, 2 vols, 1923, I p. 281
39. Carnarvon Papers, BL Add. MSS. 60907, 15 Nov. 1874
40. *ibid.*, 30 Nov. 1874
41. Zetland, *op. cit.*, I, pp. 178–9
42. Bradford MSS., 17 Dec. 1874
43. *ibid.*, 28 Dec. 1874
44. Zetland, *op cit.*, p. 184
45. Bradford MSS., [? 12 March] 1875
46. Zetland, *op. cit.*, p. 151

21 To the Elysian Fields
1. Zetland, *op. cit.*, I, p. 196
2. Bradford MSS., 8 Aug. 1875
3. *see* Smith, *op. cit.*, p. 217
4. Zetland, *op. cit.*, I, p. 260
5. *ibid.*, p. 124
6. *ibid.*, p. 250
7. *ibid.*
8. Bradford MSS., 29 March 1875
9. Magnus, P., *Edward VII*, 1964, p. 132
10. Bradford MSS., 12 June 1875
11. Zetland, *op. cit.*, I, p. 262
12. Bradford MSS., 4 Oct. 1875
13. *ibid.*
14. Zetland, *op. cit.*, II, p. 34
15. Gardiner, *op. cit.*, I, pp. 291–2
16. M&B, 5, xi, p. 772
17. Bradford MSS, 4 Nov. 1875
18. M&B, 5, xi, p. 776
19. *see* Rothschild, Lord, '*You Have it, Madam*', 1980, for the most recent and detailed account of the Suez Canal Share Purchase
20. *ibid.*, p. 20
21. Zetland, *op. cit.*, p. 306
22. Rothschild, *op. cit.*, p. 27
23. *ibid.*, p. 49
24. Bradford MSS., 20 Dec. 1875
25. Zetland, *op. cit.*, I, p. 312
26. Gardiner, *op. cit.*, I, p. 292
27. M&B, 5, xii, p. 809
28. Zetland, *op. cit.*, II, pp. 26–7

29. Bradford MSS., 5 March 1876
30. *ibid.*, 2 Aug. 1876
31. Gardiner, *op. cit*, II, pp. 304–5
32. Hamilton, *op. cit.*, I, p. 144
33. Nevill, *op. cit.*, p. 115

22 The Road to Berlin

1. Bradford MSS, 19 Sept. 1876
2. Gladstone to A. Gordon, Sept. 1876 and cf. Morley, *op. cit.*, II, p. 552
3. M&B., 6, iii, p. 983
4. Bradford MSS., 20 Dec. 1876
5. Bradford MSS., 27 March 1877
6. Zetland, *op. cit.*, II, p. 109
7. Seton-Watson, R.W., *Disraeli, Gladstone and the Eastern Question*, 1935, p. 293
8. Millman, R., *Britain and the Eastern Question 1875–1878*, 1979, p. 316
9. Zetland, *op cit.*, II, p. 125
10. *ibid.*, p. 126
11. *ibid.*, p. 127
12. Bradford MSS., 20 21 27 Aug., 11 Oct. 1877
13. Ponsonby, A. *Henry Ponsonby, His Life from his Letters*, 1942, p. 167
14. Blake, p. 636
15. *ibid.*, pp. 636–7
16. Millman, *op cit*, pp. 9–10
17. Zetland, *op. cit.*, II, p. 158
18. Hardy, *op cit*, II, p. 36
19. Millman, *op cit*, p. 476 *n*15
20. M&B, 6, viii, p. 1178
21. *ibid.*
22. Kidd, J. 'The Last Illness of Lord Beaconsfield', *Nineteenth Century*, 26 July 1889
23. Cecil, Lady G., *Life of Robert, Marquis of Salisbury*, 4 vols, 1921, ii, p. 287
24. M&B, 6, viii, p. 1188 *et seq.*
25. Seton-Watson, *op. cit.*, p. 438
26. *ibid.*, p. 439
27. *ibid.*, p. 437
28. *ibid.*, p. 454
29. M&B, 6, ix, pp. 1204–5
30. *ibid.*, p. 1216

23 The Last Defeat

1. M&B, 6, ix, p. 1218

2. Magnus, *op. cit.*, p. 253
3. Zetland, *op. cit.*, II, p. 180
4. *ibid.*, p. 181
5. Howard, C., and Gordon, P., 'The Cabinet Journal of Dudley Ryder, Viscount Sandon, 11 May–10 August 1878', *Bulletin of the Institute of Historical Research*, Nov. 1974, p. 4
6. *ibid.*, p. 51
7. Ramm, A. ed., *The Political Correspondence of Mr Gladstone and Lord Granville*, I, 1962, p. 77
8. *ibid.*, p. 83
9. *ibid.*, p. 85
10. *ibid.*, p. 86
11. Bradford MSS., 26 Aug. 1878
12. *ibid.*, 13 Nov. 1878
13. Zetland, *op. cit.*, II, p. 198
14. Bradford MSS., 19 Nov. 1878
15. Zetland, *op cit.*, II, p. 200
16. Smith, *op. cit.*, p. 301
17. Zetland, *op. cit.*, II, p. 200
18. *ibid.*, p. 208
19. M&B, 6, xi, p. 1310
20. *ibid.*, p. 1301
21. *ibid.*, pp. 1305–6
22. *ibid.*, p. 1307
23. Blake, p. 673
24. M&B, 6, xii, p. 1334
25. Buckle, *op. cit.*, III, p. 43
26. *ibid.*, p. 37
27. M&B, 6, xi, p. 1320
28. M&B, 6, xiii, p. 1347
29. Ramm, *op cit.*, I, p. 99
30. *Diary of Lady F. Cavendish*, *op. cit.*, p. 249
31. Zetland, *op. cit.*, II, p. 250
32. Morley, *op. cit.*, II, p. 597, 28 Dec 1879
33. Bradford MSS, 11 Nov. 1878
34. Zetland, *op. cit.*, II, p. 261
35. M&B, 6, xiv, p. 1383
36. *ibid.*
37. Buckle, *op cit*, III, p. 71
38. Hamilton, *op. cit.*, pp. 168–9
39. Zetland, *op. cit.*, II, p. 266
40. Wolff, Sir H. D. *Rambling Recollections*, 2 vols, 1908, II, p. 248
41. Ponsonby, *op. cit.*, p. 184
42. *ibid.*, p. 188
43. M&B, 6, xiv, p. 1398
44. *ibid.*, p. 1399

45. *ibid.*, pp. 1399–1400
46. Zetland, *op cit.*, II, p. 267
47. *ibid.*
48. M&B., 6, xiv, p. 1403
49. *ibid.*, p. 1411
50. Smith, *op. cit.*, p. 322
51. Blake, p. 721

24 The Twilight of Existence
1. Gower, *op. cit.*, II, p. 336
2. M&B., 6, xvi, p. 1461
3. Morley, *op. cit.*, II, p. 631
4. Zetland, *op. cit.*, II, p. 278
5. *ibid.*
6. M&B., 6, xvi, p. 1462
7. *ibid.*, p. 1453
8. Buckle, *op. cit.*, III, pp. 130–1
9. Zetland, *op. cit.*, II, p. 282
10. M&B, 6, xiv, p. 1415
11. *ibid.*, p. 1416
12. Zetland, *op. cit.*, II, p. 300
13. M&B., 6, xv, pp. 1424-26
14. *ibid.*, p. 1424
15. BL Add. MSS., 59887, 15 Dec. 1880

16. M&B, 6, xv, p. 1440
17. M&B, Appendix, p. 521 *et seq.*
18. Bradford MSS., 17 Sept. 1880
19. *ibid.*, 2 Nov. 1880
20. Gower, *op. cit.*, II, pp. 334–5, 355, 357
21. *ibid.*, p. 359
22. Whibley, *op. cit.*, II, pp. 203–4
23. Churchill, Lady R. *Reminiscences*, 1908, p. 55
24. Morley, *op. cit.*, III, p. 48; speech at Edinburgh, 1 Sept. 1884
25. Hamilton, I, pp. 197–8
26. Zetland, *op cit.*, II, p. 313
27. Kidd, *op. cit.*, p. 69
28. M&B, 6, xvi, p. 1484
29. *ibid.*
30. Zetland, *op. cit.*, II, p. 316
31. *ibid.*

Epilogue
1. 30 April 1881
2. M&B, 6, xvi, p. 1491
3. Bradford MSS., 1 June 1881

Manuscript Sources

Bradford Papers, Staffordshire County Record Office.
British Library Add. MSS. 32425, 37502 & 59887.
Broadlands Papers, Shaftesbury and Palmerston Papers, Public Record Office.
Carnarvon Papers, British Library.
Disraeli Papers, Fitzwilliam Museum, Cambridge.
Dufferin Papers, Public Record Office of Northern Ireland.
de Gramont Papers, Paris.
Hatfield House MSS.
Hughenden Papers, Bodleian Library.
Walter Papers, Archives of *The Times*.

Bibliography

Argyll, George Douglas, Eighth Duke of, *Autobiography and Memoirs*, ed. the Dowager Duchess of Argyll, 2 vols, 1906

Ashley, E., *The Life of Henry John Temple, Viscount Palmerston, 1846–65*, 2 vols, 1876

Bagehot, Walter, 'Why Mr Disraeli has succeeded', in *Bagehot's Historical Essays*, ed. Norman St John-Stevas, New York, 1965

Bassett, A. Tilney (ed), *Gladstone to his Wife*, 1936

Benson, A.C. and Viscount Esher (eds), *The Letters of Queen Victoria, 1837–66*, 3 vols, 1907

Berlin, Isaiah, *Against the Current, Essays in the History of Ideas*, 1979

Bermant, Chaim, *The Cousinhood, the Anglo-Jewish Gentry*, 1971

Blake, Robert, 'The Dating of *Endymion*', *Review of English Studies*, n.s. 17 (1966), 177–82

Briggs, Asa, *Victorian People*, 1954
  Chartist Studies, 1959

Broughton, Lord (J.C. Hobhouse), *Recollections of a Long Life*, 6 vols, 1909–11

Buckingham and Chandos, Duke of, *Memoirs of the Courts and Cabinets of William IV and Victoria*, 2 vols, 1861

Buckle, G.E. (ed), *The Letters of Queen Victoria*, Second Series, *1862–86*, 3 vols, 1926

Burn, W.L., *The Age of Equipoise*, 1964

Cardigan and Lencastre, Countess of, *My Recollections*, 1909

Carlisle, H.E., (ed), *A Selection from the Correspondence of Abraham Hayward, from 1834 to 1884*, 2 vols, 1886

Cartwright, Julia, (ed), *The Journals of Lady Knightley of Fawsley, 1856–1884*, 1915

Cavendish, Lady Frederick, *Diary*, ed. J. Bailey, 2 vols, 1927

Cecil, Lady Gwendolen, *Life of Robert, Marquis of Salisbury*, 4 vols, 1921

Churchill, Lady Randolph, *Reminiscences*, 1908

Churchill, W.S., *Lord Randolph Churchill*, 1951

Cohen, Lucy, *Lady de Rothschild and her Daughters, 1821–1931*, 1935

Cowles, Virginia, *The Rothschilds, a Family of Fortune*, 1973

Cowling, Maurice, *1867: Disraeli, Gladstone and Revolution*, 1967

Cross, Richard Assheton (Viscount), *A Political History*, 1903

Dasent, A.I., *John Thadeus Delane Editor of 'The Times', his Life and Correspondence*, 2 vols, 1908

Devey, Louisa, *Life of Rosina, Lady Lytton*, 1887

Disraeli, Benjamin, *Lord George Bentinck, a Political Biography*, 1852
  Hughenden edition of the Novels and Tales, 11 volumes, 1881
  Letters, 1815–1837, ed. J.A.W. Gunn, J. Matthews, D.M. Schurman, and M.G. Wiebe, 2 vols, 1982

D'Israeli, Ralph, ed., *Home Letters*, 1830–31, 1885
  Lord Beaconsfield's Correspondence with his Sister, 1886

Ellis, S.M. (ed), *Unpublished Letters by Lady Bulwer Lytton to A.C. Chalon*, 1914

Feuchtwanger, E.J., *Disraeli, Democracy and the Tory Party*, 1968

Fonblanque, E.B. de, *Lives of the Lords Strangford*, 1878

Foster, R.L., *Lord Randolph Churchill, a Political Life*, 1981

Fraser, Sir William, *Disraeli and His Day*, 1891

Froude, J.A., *Lord Beaconsfield*, 1890

Fulford, Sir Roger (ed), *Darling Child, Private Correspondence of Queen Victoria and the Crown Princess of Prussia, 1871–1878*, 1976

Gardiner, A.G., *Life of Sir William Harcourt*, 2 vols, 1923

Gash, Norman, *Politics in the Age of Peel*, 1953
  Sir Robert Peel, The Life of Sir Robert Peel after 1830, 1972

Gathorne-Hardy, A. E. (ed), *Gathorne-Hardy, First Earl of Cranbrook: A Memoir*, 2 vols, 1910

Gladstone, William, *Diaries*, ed. M.R.D. Foot and H.C.G. Matthew, 6 vols, 1968–78

Gower, Lord Ronald, *My Reminiscences*, 2 vols, 1883

Gregory, Sir William, *An Autobiography*, ed. Lady Gregory, 1894

Greville, C.F., *The Greville Memoirs, 1814–1860*, ed. Roger Fulford and Lytton Strachey, 8 vols, 1938

Halévy, Elie, *The Age of Peel and Cobden*, 1948

Hall, S.C., *Retrospect of a Long Life, from 1815 to 1883*, 2 vols, 1883

Hamilton, Lord George, *Parliamentary Reminiscences and Reflections, 1868–85*, 2 vols, 1916–22

Hardwick, Mollie, *Mrs Dizzy, The Life of Mary Anne Disraeli, Viscountess Beaconsfield*, 1972

Heine, Heinrich, *English Fragments*, 1880

Henderson, G.B., 'Ralph Anstruther Earle', *English Historical Review*, 58 (1943), 172–89

James, R.R., *Rosebery*, 1963

Jennings, L.J., *The Croker Papers, The Correspondence and Diaries of the Late Rt. Hon. J.W. Croker*, 3 vols, 1884

Jerdan, William, *Autobiography*, 4 vols, 1852–3

Jerman, B.R., *The Young Disraeli*, Princeton, 1960

Kebbel, T.E., *Lord Beaconsfield*, 1888

  Lord Beaconsfield and other Tory Memories, 1907

  (ed), *Selected Speeches of the Late Earl of Beaconsfield*, 2 vols, 1882

Kennedy, A.L. (ed), *My Dear Duchess: Social and Political Letters to the Duchess of Manchester, 1858-69*, 1956

Kidd, Joseph, 'The Last Illness of Lord Beaconsfield', *Nineteenth Century*, 26 (1889), 65-71

Kitson Clark, G., 'Hunger and Politics in 1842', *Journal of Modern History*, 25 (1953), 355-74

  The Making of Victorian England, 1962

  An Expanding Society: Britain, 1830-1900, 1967

Koss, Stephen, *The Rise and Fall of the Political Press in Britain*, Vol. I, 1981

Lang, Andrew, *Life, Letters and Diaries of Sir Stafford Northcote, First Earl of Iddesleigh*, 2 vols, 1890

  Life and Letters of J.G. Lockhart, 2 vols, 1896

Layard, Sir A.H., *Autobiography and Letters*, 1903

  'The Early Life of Lord Beaconsfield', *Quarterly Review*, February 1889

Londonderry, Marchioness of, (ed), *The Letters of Benjamin Disraeli to Frances Anne, Marchioness of Londonderry*, 1938

  The Russian Journal of Lady Londonderry, 1836-7, ed. W.A.L. Seaman and J.R. Sewell, 1973

Longford, Elizabeth, *Victoria, R.I.*, 1964

Lucy, H.W.A., *Men and Manners in Parliament*, 1874

Lytton, Earl of, *The Life of Edward Bulwer, First Lord Lytton*, 2 vols, 1913

Macaulay, R.T.B., *Letters*, ed. T. Pinney, vols I-IV, 1974-7

Macready, W.C., *The Journal, 1832-1851*, ed. J.C. Trewin, 1967

Magnus, Sir Philip, *Gladstone: a Biography*, 1954

  King Edward the Seventh, 1964

Mallock, W.H. (ed), *Letters, Remains and Memoirs of Edward Adolphus Seymour, Twelfth Duke of Somerset*, 1893

Malmesbury, Earl of, *Memoirs of an ex-Minister*, 2 vols, 1884

Maxwell, Sir H.E. (ed), *The Life and Letters of George William Frederick, Fourth Earl of Clarendon*, 2 vols, 1913

Meynell, Wilfrid, *The Man Disraeli*, 1927

Millman, Richard, *Britain and the Eastern Question, 1875-1878*, 1979

Moneypenny, W.F., and Buckle, G.E., *The Life of Benjamin Disraeli, Earl of Beaconsfield*, revised ed., 2 vols, 1929

Morgan, Lady S., *Memoirs*, 2 vols, 1862

Morley, John, *Life of William Ewart Gladstone*, 3 vols, 1903

Nevill, Ralph (ed), *The Reminiscences of Lady Dorothy Nevill*, 1906

  Leaves from the Note-Books of Lady Dorothy Nevill, 1907

  My Own Times, by Lady Dorothy Nevill, 1912

Ogden, James, *Isaac D'Israeli*, 1969

Phipps, Edmund, *Memoir of the Political and Literary Life of Robert Plumer Ward*, 2 vols, 1850

Ponsonby, Arthur, *Henry Ponsonby, his Life from his Letters* (1942)

Raikes, St-J. (ed), *The Life and Letters of H. C. Raikes*, 1898

Ramm, Agatha (ed), *The Political Correspondence of Mr Gladstone and Lord Granville*, Vol. 1, 1962

Read, Donald, *Cobden and Bright, A Victorian Political Partnership*, 1967

Redding, Cyrus, *Fifty Years Recollections*, 3 vols, 1858

Reid, T. Wemyss (ed), *The Life, Letters and Friendships of Richard Monckton Milnes, First Lord Houghton*, 2 vols, 1890

Ridley, Jasper, *Lord Palmerston*, 1970

Robson, R. (ed), *Ideas and Institutions of Victorian Britain*, 1967

Rose, Michael E., *The English Poor Law, 1780–1930*, 1971

Rosenbaum, B., and Pamela White, *Index of English Literary Manuscripts*, Vol. IV, Pt 1, Benjamin Disraeli, First Earl of Beaconsfield, 1982

Rothschild, Constance de, *Reminiscences*, 1922

Rothschild, Lord, '*You Have it Madam*', *The Purchase, in 1875, of Suez Canal shares by Disraeli and Baron Lionel de Rothschild*, 1980

Russell, G.W.E., *Collections and Recollections*, 1904

Portraits of the Seventies, 1916

Russell, Lord John, *The Later Correspondence, 1840–1878*, ed. G.P. Gooch, 2 vols, 1925

Sadleir, Michael, *Bulwer and his Wife: a Panorama, 1803–36*, 1931

Blessington–d'Orsay, a Masquerade, 1933

Salisbury, Mary, Marchioness of, *A Great Lady's Friendship, Letters to Mary, Marchioness of Salisbury, 1830–52*, ed. Lady Burghclere, 1933

Sandon, Viscount, *The Cabinet Journal of Dudley Ryder, Viscount Sandon, 11 May–10 August 1878*, ed. C. Howard and P. Gordon, *Bulletin of the Institute of Historical Research*, (1974) Special Supplement No. 10

The First Balmoral Journal of Dudley Ryder, Viscount Sandon . . . 6–14 November 1879, ibid., (1977), pp. 82–109

Schreiber, Lady Charlotte, *Lady Charlotte Schreiber, Extracts from her Journal, 1853–1891*, ed. Earl of Bessborough, 1952

Schwarz, Daniel R., *Disraeli's Fiction*, 1979

Scott, Sir Walter, *Familiar Letters*, ed. David Douglas, 2 vols, 1894

The Letters, ed. H.J.C. Grierson, 12 vols, 1932–7

Seton-Watson, R.W., *Disraeli, Gladstone and the Eastern Question*, 1935

Smiles, Samuel, *Memoir and Correspondence of the late John Murray*, 2 vols, 1891

Smith, Paul, *Disraelian Conservatism and Social Reform*, 1967

(ed), *Lord Salisbury and Politics*, 1972

Stanley, Lady Augusta, *Later Letters, 1864–76*, 1929

Stern, Fritz, *Gold and Iron*, 1977

Stewart, Robert, 'The Ten Hours and Sugar Crises of 1844: Government and the

House of Commons in the Age of Reform', *Historical Journal*, 12 (1969), pp. 35–57

The Politics of Protection, Lord Derby and the Protectionist Party, 1841–1852, 1971

The Foundation of the Conservative Party, 1830–1867, 1978

Stewart, R.W. *Benjamin Disraeli*, Scarecrow Author Bibliographies, 7, Metuchen, N.J., 1972

Sultana, Donald, *Benjamin Disraeli in Spain, Malta and Albania, 1830–32*, 1976

Swartz, H.M. and M. (eds), *Disraeli's Reminiscences*, 1975

Sykes, James, *Mary Anne Disraeli, The Story of Viscountess Beaconsfield*, 1928

Taylor, A.J.P., *The Struggle for the Mastery in Europe, 1848–1918*, 1954

Thompson, F.M.L., *English Landed Society in the Nineteenth Century*, 1963

Thompson, G.C., *Public Opinion and Lord Beaconsfield, 1876–80*, 1886

Thompson, J.M., *Louis Napoleon and the Second Empire*, 1954

The History of the Times, Vol. 1, '*The Thunderer*' *in the Making, 1785–1841*, 1935

Vol. 2, *The Tradition Established, 1841–85*, 1939

Trevelyan, G.M., *The Life of John Bright*, 1913

van Thal, Herbert (ed), *The Prime Ministers*, vol 2, 1975

Vincent, John, *Disraeli, Derby and the Conservative Party, Journals and Memoirs of Edward Henry, Lord Stanley, 1849–1869*, 1978

Vitzthum von Eckstaedt, C.F., *St Petersburg and London, 1852–64*, 2 vols, 1887

Walling, R.A.J. (ed), *The Diaries of John Bright*, 1930

Walpole, Sir Spencer, *The History of Twenty-Five Years, 1856–70*, 2 vols, 1904

Whibley, Charles, *Lord John Manners and his Friends*, 2 vols, 1925

White, William, *The Inner Life of the House of Commons*, 2 vols, 1897

Willis, N.P., *Pencillings by the Way*, New York, 1852

Wolff, Sir H. Drummond, *Rambling Recollections*, 2 vols, 1908

Woodward, E.L., *The Age of Reform, 1815–70*, 1962

Zetland, Marquess of (ed), *The Letters of Disraeli to Lady Bradford and Lady Chesterfield*, 2 vols, 1929

Ziegler, Philip, *Melbourne*, 1976

Index

Abercorn, James Hamilton, 1st Duke of, 289, 312, 317
Aberdeen, George Hamilton Gordon, 4th Earl of, 160, 195, 200–201, 217, 224, 226, 229
Adams (Bradenham cook), 62
Adderley, Sir Charles F., 321, 374
'Adullamites' ('the Cave'), 260–62, 267, 270–71
Afghanistan, 326, 356–9, 364, 383
Age, The, 52, 69
Ailesbury, Ernest Augustus Charles Brudenell-Bruce, 3rd Marquess of, 388
Albania, 39
Albert, Prince Consort: relations with BD, 141, 207, 214, 245; hostility to Protectionists, 201; and Palmerston, 204; influencence on Queen, 207; recommends Gladstone, 210; mistrusts BD, 213–14, 249; death, 248–9; memorial, 251; BD eulogizes, 251–2; and Victoria's widowhood, 274
Alberta (Royal yacht), 325
Albion club, London, 46
Alexander II, Tsar, 226, 315, 337, 387
Alexandra, Princess of Wales (*later* Queen), 249–50, 323, 331–2
Alice, Princess of Hesse, 359
Alington, H.G. Sturt, 1st Baron and Augusta, Lady, 308–9, 329, 331–2, 342
Almack's (London), 74
Alroy (BD), 30, 41, 59–61, 92, 179, 243
Althorp, John Charles Spencer, (*later* 3rd Earl Spencer), 78
Andrassy, Julius, Count, 341, 350
Angeli, Heinrich von, 330, 371
Angerstein, Captain, 47, 49, 57
Anglo-Mexican Mining Company, 14–15
Annual Register, 21
Anson, George, Baron, 245
Anti-Corn Law League, 111, 117, 122, 128, 130
Arbuthnot, Dr, 29
Arbuthnot, George, 115
Argyll, George Campbell, 8th Duke of, 241, 370

Arrow (ship), 234
Arthur, Prince, *see* Connaught, Arthur Duke of
Artizans Dwelling Bill (1875), 321
Ashburton, Lady, 231
Ashley, Lord, *see* Shaftesbury, Anthony Ashley Cooper, 7th Earl of
Athenaeum club, London, 46, 252
Austen, Benjamin, 12, 22; trip to Italy, 27–8; and BD's parliamentary ambitions, 30, 55; and BD's Eastern trip, 31–3, 39–40, 337; BD drops, 62; lends money to BD, 70–71, 87; in *Lothair*, 289
Austen, Sara: relations with BD, 22–4, 29; and *Star Chamber*, 25; trip to Italy with BD, 27; and BD's nervous illness, 29; and *The Young Duke*, 32; letters from BD on Eastern trip, 40; and BD's political aspirations, 56; and *Revolutionary Epick*, 70; praises *Venetia*, 93; in *Lothair*, 289; and Layard, 340
Austin (lawyer), 102–3
Austria, 238–41, 322
Aylesbury (Buckinghamshire), 58
Aylesford, Lady, 331–2
Aylesford, 'Sporting Joe', 323, 331–2
Aylmer Papillon (BD, unpublished), 30
Azeglio, d', 240

Bagehot, Walter, 272
Baillie, Henry, 119, 121, 126, 131
Baillie-Cochrane, Alexander, 1st Baron Lamington ('Kok'), 122, 126–7, 129, 131, 134, 138, 372
Balfour, Arthur James, 376
Balmoral, 283–4
Balzac, Honoré de, 246
Baring, Alexander, 14
Baring, Sir Thomas, 55–6, 223
Barker collection (paintings), 315
Barnes, Thomas, 16, 84–5, 130
Barrington, George, 7th Viscount, 371, 385, 388, 390–92

Barrow, Sir John, 18
Barry, Sir Charles, 95
Basevi family, 1
Basevi, George, 15, 18
Basevi, Napthali, 5
Basevi, Nathaniel, 12
Bashi-Bazouks, 335
Bassett, Mrs (James D'Israeli's mistress), 285
Bassett, Annie (daughter of above), 285
Bath, Frances Isabella Catherine, Marchioness of, 316
Bath, John Thynne, 4th Marquess of, 316, 336
Baudrand General, 124, 129-30
Baum (BD's valet), 309, 317, 379, 387, 392
Baum, Mrs, 387
Beauchamp, 4th Earl of, *see* Elmley, Henry Lygon, Viscount
Beauchamp, Frederick Lygon, 6th Earl, 248, 269, 272, 284-5
Beauclerk, George, 100, 106
Beauvale, Frederick James Lamb, Baron (*later* 3rd Viscount Melbourne), 147
'Bedchamber Crisis', 107
Bedford, William Russell, 8th Duke of, 191, 245
Bell's Weekly Messenger, 7
Bellamy (of House of Commons dining room), 96
Bentham, Jeremy, 83
Bentinck, George P. ('Big Ben'), 252-3, 266
Bentinck, Lord George: refuses help to BD, 79; supports BD on Corn Laws, 149-50, 152-4, 156, 160; friendship with BD, 153, 160, 190-91; and Irish Coercion, 157; lends money to BD, 167; BD's biography of, 172, 174, 191, 203; bust, 176; supports Jewish Disabilities Bill, 182, 184; resigns leadership, 189; death, 189-92; on BD's candidacy for leadership, 190, 194; on Conservative Party, 195
Bentinck, Lord Henry, 192-3
Bentley, Richard, 32
Beresford, Lord Charles, 323-4
Beresford, William, 153, 189, 195, 198-200, 202, 208, 332
Berkeley, Augustus Fitzhardinge, 100, 102, 106
Berlin, Congress of: and Russo-Turkish treaty, 345-7; Treaty signed, 346; BD attends, 347-9; opening and conduct, 350-3; terms, 354
Berlin Memorandum, 335
Bernhardt, Sarah, 385
Bertie, Lady Charlotte, *see* Guest, Lady Charlotte
Biddulph, Sir Thomas, 371
Bingley (Yorkshire), 140-41
Bismarck, Otto von, Prince, 244, 291, 322, 348-52, 381, 384
Blackwood, Helen (*neé* Sheridan), *see* Dufferin, Helen, Marchioness of
Blackwood's Magazine, 17, 19, 24

Blagden, Rev. Henry, 298, 325
Blake, Robert, Lord, 183, 380
Blandford, George Charles Spencer-Churchill, Marquess of (*later* 8th Duke of Marlborough), 323, 331
Bleichröder, Herr and Mme, 350-52
Blessington, Charles Gardiner, 1st Earl of, 73
Blessington, Marguerite, Countess of, 72-3, 75, 90-91, 204
Boers, 383
Bolingbroke, Henry St John, Viscount, 83
Bolton, Clara, 47, 48-50, 56-7, 65-7, 69, 71-2
Bolton, Dr George Buckley, 47, 69, 72, 120
Bonham (Tory election manager), 80, 112, 115, 142-3, 195
Book of Beauty, The, 73
Boord, Thomas William (Greenwich MP), 304
Bosnia, 326
Botta, Paul Emile, 42-3
Bournemouth, 318
Bradenham (house), 5, 7, 30, 62, 168-9
Bradford, Orlando George Charles Bridgeman, 7th Earl of, 309, 311
Bradford, Selina, Countess of: and BD's aristocracy principles, 197, 308; BD's strong feelings for, 218, 243, 307-11, 317, 339, 359; and BD's mourning for Mary Anne, 301; letters and confidences from BD, 311-12, 314-15, 318-20, 322, 324-6, 328, 332, 336, 338-9, 342-5, 348, 351, 355-8, 364-5, 367, 370, 372; letters from Corry, 388-9, 391; and BD's death, 391
Bradlaugh, Charles, 376
Brand, Henry, 302
Bright, John: opposes Peel, 158; Conservative Party opposition to, 196; and BD's approaches over 1852 budget, 211; on BD's ambitions, 222; and India Bill, 223; *The Press* on, 225; combines with BD, 230, 234; opposes Palmerston, 234-6; opposes 1858 Derby government, 237; attacks BD's Reform proposals, 239; and Italian cause, 240; and BD's finances, 246; and paper duties, 253; and Gladstone, 255-6, 260-61, 268; and Reform, 264, 267-8; on BD's succession, 279; attacks BD on Irish Church, 281-2; on 1874 Election results, 304; in *Endymion*, 381
British Museum, 251-2
Brougham, Henry Peter, Baron Brougham and Vaux, 55, 236
Broughton de Gyfford, Baron, *see* Hobhouse, John Cam
Brown, John, 249, 274, 283, 373
Bruce, Lady Augusta, 282
Bruce, Dr Richard, 388, 390
Brunet (huntsman), 34-5
Bryce (publisher), 224
Brydges-Willyams, Mrs Sarah (*née* da Costa);

relations with BD, 220-21, 243, 245, 249,
251; letters and confidences from BD, 229,
235; death, legacy and burial, 247, 285, 300,
393
Buckingham, Richard Grenville, 2nd Duke of
formerly Marquis of Chandos), 57, 79, 81, 91,
115, 141-2
Buckingham, Richard Campbell Grenville, 3rd
Duke of, 279
Buckinghamshire: BD MP for, 167
Buckle, G.E., 251, 284, 303; see also
Monypenny, W.F. and Buckle, G.E.
Bulgaria: attrocities, 40, 123, 333, 335-6; and
Congress of Berlin, 351
Bulgarian Horrors (The) and the Eastern Question
(Gladstone), 336
Buller, Charles, 84
Buller, Sir John Yarde, 195
Bulwer, Edward Lytton see Lytton, Bulwer
Bulwer, Henry (i.e William Henry Lytton,
Baron Dalling and Bulwer), 109, 124, 208
Burdett, Sir Francis, 93
Burdett-Coutts, Angela, Baroness, 93, 162, 306,
318, 339
Burton, Sir Frederic William, 315
Bute, John Crichton-Stuart, 3rd Marquess of,
287
Byron, George Gordon, Lord: and Murray, 10,
14; in Switzerland, 27-8; self-exile, 30; and
The Young Duke, 31; death, 38; travels, 38-9;
dual nature, 53; notoriety, 59; influence on
BD, 88, 178-9; in *Venetia*, 91-3

Cairns, Hugh McCalmont, 1st Earl, 283;
resignation, 290; and party leadership, 293;
and Mary Anne's illness, 297; and BD's 1874
parliamentary tactics, 301; in BD's 1874
Cabinet, 312; offers home to BD, 318; and
Aylesford scandal, 332; and foreign policy,
344; on national economy, 356; visits BD,
375, 388; on South Africa, 388; and dying
BD, 389
Calimani, Simon, 3
Cambridge, George, 2nd Duke of, 315
Canning, George, 16, 55, 143
Canterbury, Archbishop of, see Tait, A.C.
Carathéodory, Alexander, Pasha, 350
Cardigan, Adeline, Countess of (*formerly* de
Horsey), 305-6
Carlton Chronicle, 87
Carlton Club, London, 85, 93, 115, 129, 139,
153, 268
Carlyle, Jane Welsh, 51, 74
Carlyle, John, 319
Carlyle, Thomas, 74, 138, 272, 288, 319
Carnarvon, Henry Herbert, 4th Earl of, 262;
opposes Reform, 265-6; resignation, 266; in
BD's 1874 Cabinet, 312, 317; and BD's

illness, 321; declines Indian Viceroyalty, 326;
and Eastern question, 340, 343, resigns, 344;
and South Africa, 360
Carnarvon, Countess of, 307
Carrington, Charles, 323
Carrington, Robert Smith, 1st Baron, 76, 79
Castellane, Comtesse de, 124
Castlereagh, Frederick Stewart, Viscount, 85
Cavagnari, Sir Louis, 364
'Cave, the ', see 'Adullamites'
Cavendish, Lady Frederick, 261, 336, 364
Cavour, Camilo, Count, 238-9
Cecil, Lord Robert, see Salisbury, Robert Cecil,
3rd Marquess of
Central Agricultural Protection Society, 149
Cetewayo, 360-62
Chamberlain, Joseph, 374
Chandos, Marquess of, *see* Buckingham,
Richard Grenville, 2nd Duke of
Charles I, King of England, 9
Charles X, King of France, 47, 54
Charleville, Lady, 61
Chartism (People's Charter), 107-8, 111-12,
117, 140; national petition, 119, 196;
increasing bitterness, 122, 128; decline, 197
Chelmsford, Frederick Thesiger, 1st Baron,
279
Chelmsford, Frederick Thesiger, 2nd Baron,
361-3
Chesterfield, Anne, Countess of: as BD's
confidante, 243, 315, 321, 324, 335, 360-62,
373, 377-78, 383, 385-7; BD's devotion to,
307-11
Chesterfield, George Philip Cecil Arthur
Stanhope, 7th Earl of, 292
Chesterfield, George Stanhope, 6th Earl of, 101
Chetwodes, 172
Chubbe (Vicar at Hughenden), 247
Church of England, 254-5, 287
Church of Ireland, 280
Churchill, Jenny (Lady Randolph Churchill),
332, 385, 386
Churchill, Lord Randolph, 323, 331-2, 376
Churchill, Sir Winston, 370
Cicogna, Count, 28
Clanricarde, Ulick John de Burgh, 1st Marquess
of, 235-6
Clarendon, George Villiers, 4th Earl of, 166,
234-5, 255-6, 272, 277, 279
Clark, Sir George, 153
Clay, James, 37-9, 41-3, 45, 57, 120
Cobden, Richard: and Corn Laws, 111, 117,
123, 128, 144, 148, 157-9; BD attacks, 130,
190; on working hours, 138; and Peel, 142,
157-8; Conservative Party opposition to, 196;
BD proposes office for, 211; attacks
Palmerston government, 234-5; in *Endymion*,
381

Cogan's, Dr (school), 8
Colburn, Henry: publishes Plumer Ward, 22–3; publishes BD, 23–4, 28–9, 31–2, 41, 88, 93, 106; publishes *New Monthly Magazine*, 52; publishes Sarah's novels, 164
Coleridge, J.T., 19
Collins (creditor), 92
Colonna, Francesco: *Hypnerotomachia*, 325
Columbian Mining Association, 14–15
Committee of Three, 195
Compagnie Universelle du Canal Maritime de Suez, 327
Compensation for Eviction Bill, Ireland (1880), 377
Coningsby (BD): Lockhart attacks, 82; and aristocracy, 82; characters, 119, 121, 134–5, 137; on monarchy, 126; political theme, 134–6, 141, 160; published, 137–8; writing, 163; Lennox reads, 216
Connaught, Arthur, Duke of, 275, 392
Conservative Central Office, 303–4
Conspiracy and Protection of Property Bill (1875), 320
Conspiracy Bill (1858), 236
Constantinople, 40–41; peace conference (1876), 337–9
Contarini Fleming (BD): on Jewishness, 2; fathers in, 6; on criticism, 24, 26; writing, 30, 44; Jerusalem in, 41; Botta in, 42; published 53; on foreign policy, 123
Cookesley, W.G., 135
Copley, John Singleton, 77
Cork and Orrery, Isabella Henrietta, Countess of, 61, 64, 76, 78
Corn Laws, 57–8, 111–12, 117, 123, 128–9; BD on, 130; Peel converted to repeal of, 144, 147–54, 158–9; Bill passed, 153–9; agitation for reintroduction, 198–9
Corry, Henry, 201, 293
Corry, Montague, Lowry (*later* 1st Baron Rowton): friendship with BD, 218, 263–4, 268–9, 329, 347; as BD's private secretary, 263, 286, 295; on Reform, 265–6; and BD's illness, 275; and BD as Prime Minister, 277; and Fremantle, 286; and Mary Anne's illness and death, 296–301, 310; and BD's leadership, 303; and 1874 Election, 303–4; destroys some BD papers, 308; and Prince of Wales's Indian trip, 323; and Suez Canal, 328; and Mme Ignatiev, 340; and Russo-Turkish war, 341; love-life, 343, 358; nervous breakdown, 344; attends Congress of Berlin, 347, 349, 351; and *Endymion*, 356, 378–9; peerage, 371–2; abroad with sister, 384–5, 387; in BD's old age, 386, 388, and BD's death and funeral, 389–90, 392
Corti, Count L., 351
Coulton, D.T., 226

Coventry Club, London, 75
Cowley, Henry Wellesley, 1st Baron, 124
Cowley, Henry Richard Charles Wellesley, 1st Earl of, 232, 234, 269
Cranborne, Viscount, *see* Salisbury, Robert Cecil, 3rd Marquess of
Cranbrook, Gathorne Gathorne-Hardy, 1st Earl of, 228; in 1866 government, 262; on Earle, 268; appointed Home Secretary, 270; and BD's tactics against Gladstone, 271; and Fenians, 275; on Cranborne, 280; and BD's leadership, 293; and parliamentary tactics, 301; and 1874 Election, 303; in 1874 Cabinet, 312; in Commons, 334; and Russo-Turkish treaty, 345; supports Lytton, 357, pessimism, 366–8; and 1880 Election, 369; and BD's resignation, 373; visits declining BD, 388
Craufurd, Madame, 73
Crimean War, 225, 229–30, 233
Crisis Examined, The (BD), 79
Crockford's (gaming house), London, 74–5
Croker, John Wilson, 10, 18–19, 53, 55, 133, 135
Cross, Sir Richard Assheton (*later* 1st Viscount): in 1874 Cabinet, 312–13, 317, 374; social reform programme, 320, 322; on national economy, 356; on Corry, 372; GCB, 372; visits BD, 375
Cyprus Convention, 352, 354–5

Daily News, 344
Dalhousie, James Ramsay, 1st Marquess of, 272
Darwin, Charles (and Darwinism), 179, 246, 254–5
Davis (creditor), 92
Dawson, Mrs (Peel's sister), 137
De Burgh, Mrs, 342
Delane, John Thadeus, 130, 194, 238
Derby, Edward George Stanley, 14th Earl of: and brother's disgrace, 46; Melbourne on, 75, 95; resigns, 78; in Commons, 95, 192; and Peel, 115–16; BD requests help for brother, 134, 173; and BD's anti-Peel campaign, 139; and Peel's resignation, 147; and Corn Laws, 153, 156; hostility to BD as leader, 189–90, 192–4; career, 192–3; described, 192–3; and nature of Conservative Party, 195–6; and BD's agricultural proposals, 198–9; and Gladstone's overtures, 200; abortive 1851 administration, 201–2; and Palmerston, 204; forms 1852 government, 204, 206–8, 210, 213; on BD's 1852 Budget, 207, 211; defeated, 212–13; attitude to BD, 213, 222–4, 257–8, 277; and son, 215; translates *Iliad*, 223; opposes *The Press*, 224–5; and fall of Aberdeen coalition, 229–30; Lennox intrigues against, 232–3; attacks Palmerston, 234; forms 1858 government, 236; 1859 Election, 239; accent,

245; anti-monarchism, 249; and paper duties, 253; and 1865 Election, 257; forms 1866 government, 262–4; and Reform, 264–6, 271; decline, 274, 277; retirement, 277–8; death, 290

Derby, Edward Henry Stanley, 15th Earl of: on BD's marriage, 161; on BD and Peel's death, 199; on Protectionism, 200; and father's 1851 administration, 202–3; in 1852 government, 206–8; on Albert's view of BD, 214; relations with BD, 214–15, 218, 237, 275, 346; character, 214; and India Bill, 223; supports *The Press*, 224–5; and Reform Bill, 228–9; and BD's frustrations, 230, 233; in 1858 government, 236–7; and BD's later interests and ideas, 245, 254–5; and Garibaldi, 254; on Gladstone, 256; and Palmerston's death, 258; and Reform, 259; as potential party leader, 260, 262, 290, 293, 303, 317–18, 322, 332; and Gladstone's Reform Bill, 261; as Foreign Secretary, 262, 274–5, 322; Queen and, 274–5; succeeds to earldom, 290; on Gladstone's eccentricities, 291; marriage, 303; and 1874 Election, 312, and BD's illness, 317; and Suez Canal, 327–9; on BD's irreligion, 337; and Russians in Eastern question, 339, 341; and Russo-Turkish war, 341, 342–4; apathy, 344–5; resignation, 346; and BD's imperialist views, 363; BD retains, 374; and Kandahar, 387; at BD's funeral, 392

Derby, Mary, Countess of (*formerly* Salisbury), 303, 329, 340, 344, 346

Devonshire, 8th Duke of *see* Hartington, Spencer Compton Cavendish, Marquess of

Dick, Quintin, 126

Dickens, Charles, 108, 245, 246

Dilke, Sir Charles, 317, 364, 388

D'Israeli, Benjamin (grandfather), 2–4

Disraeli, Benjamin, 1st Earl of Beaconsfield and Viscount Hughenden of Hughenden: birth and family, 1–3, 6–7; Jewishness, 1–2, 59, 179, 187–8, 255; relations with parents, 5–6, 9; fondness for women, 5–6, schooling and tutoring, 7–9; baptised, 7–8; appearance, 8, 10; pugnacity, 9; early reading, 9; law studies, 11–12; first trip abroad, 11–12; stock market speculations, 13–17, 21; and English aristocracy, 16, 82–3, 197, 288; visits Lockhart and Scott, 16–20; appetite for revenge, 22; in own novels, 24, 135; nervous illnesses, 27, 29, 91; to Italy with Austens, 27–8; travels to East, 30–31, 33–44; fear of blindness, 35–6; unpopular behaviour, 37–8; sexual initiation and VD, 41, 43; first political aspirations, 44, 54–7, 67–8, 80; move to London, 45–8; clubs, 46, 75, 85, 252; marriage prospects, 49–50, 63–4; affectation and dress, 51, 57, 59, 71, 177–8; in Rosina

Lytton novel, 51; political vacillations, 55–8, 79; prose style, 59–60; supports Jewish emancipation, 60, 182–8; and Sheridan sisters, 60–61; affair with Henrietta Sykes, 64–72, 77–8, 90; 'mutilated diary', 67–8, 179; debts and financial problems, 70–71, 87–8, 91–2, 113, 120–21, 167, 169, 219–20, 246; eloquence, 75–6, 178; social successes, 76, 85, 252; extravagance, 77; fights Taunton by-election, 80; on Conservative Party and democracy, 82; 'Runnymede' letters, 84–5; breaks with Henrietta, 86–90; appointed JP, 88; elected MP for Maidstone, 90, 94; Commons maiden speech, 97–9, 101–7; at Victoria's coronation, 101; and Austin's bribery charge, 102–3; ultimatum letter to Mary Anne, 105–6; on condition of England ('two nations'), 109, 111, 119, 136, 141; marriage and domestic life, 109, 161–5, 169–75, 300; wins Shrewsbury seat, 112–14; attacks Palmerston, 118, 233–4; on foreign policy, 118, 122–4, 129; dispassionate views and manner, 122–3, 178–9; poor French, 123, 386; and French alliance, 124–6 129, 147, 231; on Corn Laws, 130, 148–54, 198–9; and Young England, 131, 140–41, 160; campaign against Peel, 132–3, 137–40, 142–6, 148–51, 154, 157, 160, 209; on Peel's resignation, 159; elected MP for Buckinghamshire, 167; inheritance, 168; supposed infidelity, 170; trouble with gums, 171; love of books, 176; described, 177–9; candidacy for party leadership, 190–95; and party policy and aims, 196–7, 222–5, 272, 295–6; and Protectionism, 198–201; boredom with country house visits, 199; and Derby's 1851 administration, 202–3; on racial purity, 203; as Chancellor in 1852 government, 204, 206–8, 210–13; Catholic scheme, 208; Wellington eulogy, 209; Peelites attack, 209–10; on coalitions, 212; government defeated, 212–13; and Chancellors robe, 213; honorary Oxford DCL, 214; popularity with young, 214, 227, 302; and younger men, 214–19, 232, 263; and *The Press*, 224–6; MacKnights' biography of, 227; Phillips attacks, 227; in 1858 Derby government, 236; and Reform, 239, 241; and Italian liberation and Piedmont crisis, 239–41; dress and appearance in later life, 244; biographical jottings, 244; reading, 246; party discontent with leadership, 252–4, 290, 293; increasing Conservatism, 254–5; and religious controversies, 254–5; and Palmerston's death, 258; succeeds with Reform Bill, 259–61, 264–73; Chancellor in 1866 government, 262; unpopularity, 267; parliamentary tactics, 270–71, 280–81; recurrent illnesses (gout/

Index

Disraeli, Benjamin - *cont.*
asthma), 275-6, 317-19, 332, 342, 347, 352-3, 359-60, 367, 369, 384, 387-9; succeeds Derby as Prime Minister, 278-80; and Irish Church, 280-82; 1868 Election defeat, 284; popular acclaim for, 293-5, 355-6; and Mary Anne's illness and death, 296-301; moves London home, 301; declines to form government, 302; harasses Gladstone, 302; 1874 Election manifesto and victory, 303-4; relish for power, 312; Cabinet work, 313, 317-18; 1875 social and labour reform legislation, 320-22, 330; foreign and imperial affairs, 322, 326; collects rare books, 325; and Eastern question, 326, 335-41, 343-5; peerage, 332-4; leaves Commons, 332-3; parliamentary style and manner, 333; religious feelings, 337; at Congress of Berlin, 347-53; made Knight of Garter, 354; and national economy, 356, 359-60, 364, 366, 369; and Afghanistan, 357; and Zulu War, 360-63; imperialist policy, 363, 365-6, 369, 374, 387; 1880 Election defeat, 368-70; resignation, 372-3; leadership assessed, 374; opposition to Gladstone's administration, 375-7, 383, 386-8; social life in old age, 385-6; death, 390; tributes and memorial, 391-2; funeral and burial, 247, 392-3

D'Israeli, Coningsby (nephew), 285-6, 354, 371-2, 392

D'Israeli, Isaac (father): family life and marriage, 1, 5-6; literary interests, 1, 4-5; character, 3-5; influence on son, 5, 9, 11, 198; has children baptised, 7-8; conflict with synagogue, 7-8; and BD's education, 9; and Byron, 10; and BD's career, 11-12, 88; and Lockhart, 17; in *Vivian Grey*, 24; and John Murray, 25; nervous illness, 29; moves to Bradenham, 30; and BD's Eastern trip, 35-6; and sons' marriages, 49, 63; buys Hambledon farm, 54; and Henrietta Sykes, 70; and BD's debts, 88, 92, 167; on BD's maiden speech, 97; illness, 100; approves BD's marriage, 109; loses sight, 110; wife's death, 166-7; death, 168; memorial, 248; *Commentaries on ... Charles I*, 41; *The Curiosities of Literature*, 4, 6, 10, 168, 220; *Despotism*, 4; *Flim-Flams*, 4; *Vaurien*, 4

D'Israeli, Isabella (*née* Cave), 173

D'Israeli, James (brother): appearance, 6; relations with BD, 6-7, 169, 173-4; education, 8; and Sarah, 27, 168; at Bradenham, 62; rescues BD from debt writ, 92; BD seeks posts for, 134, 155, 173-4; and Mary Anne, 163, 172; and mother's death, 166; and father's death, 168-9; private life, 173-4; Treasureship, 206; promoted to Commissioner of Excise, 238; death 284-5, 300; illegitimate daughter, 285

D'Israeli, Kate (*née* Trevor; Ralph's wife), 285

D'Israeli, Maria (mother), 1, 5-6, 8, 25, 33, 56; death, 166-7

Disraeli, Mary Anne (*formerly* Mrs Wyndham Lewis), 51, 63; on BD's future, 94, 100; courtship by BD, 97-9, 101-7; background, 98-100, 175; BD's ultimatum letter to, 105-6, 311; marriage and domestic relations, 109, 161, 169-75, 218, 243, 277, 300; helps BD in electioneering, 112-14; pleads for BD with Peel, 115-16; and BD on Corn Laws, 117-18; and BD's finances, 120-21, 219, 247; in Paris, 124; and BD on Peel, 129; *Sybil* dedicated to, 136, 161; introduced to Queen, 141-2; temperament and emotionalism, 161, 165-6; jealousy of Sarah, 161-3, 166, 169-73, 219; will, 165-6; bequest from Isaac, 168; and Rothschilds, 186-7; and BD's candidacy for leadership, 194; and country house visits, 199; and BD's young men, 219; and Sarah's death, 242; burial, 247, 393; portraits, 248, 300-301; at Hughenden, 248, 293, 298-9; at Prince of Wales's wedding, 249-50; illness, 275-6, 296-9; and Gladstone, 276-7; made Viscountess, 284; death, 299-300; and *Endymion*, 380

D'Israeli, Napthali (brother), 6

D'Israeli, Ralph (brother): appearance, 6; relations with BD, 6, 285; education, 8, 37; and Sarah, 27, 168; letters from BD in Malta, 38; and marriage, 49; in Duke Street, 68; and Victoria's coronation, 101; at father's death, 168-9, edits BD's letters, 169-70; and Mary Anne, 172; on death of Bentinck, 190; and Sarah's death, 242; and James's death, 285; son, 285-6; BD declines honours for, 354; at BD's funeral, 392

D'Israeli, Sarah (*née* Shiprut de Gabay; grandmother), 3

D'Israeli Sarah (sister): attachment to BD, 6, 27, 68-70, 85, 161-4, 168-71, 219, 242-3; and Meredith, 11, 34, 42-3, 45; and BD abroad, 12, 27, 35-6, 41; and Angerstein, 49; and BD's Wycombe seat, 55; in BD's novels, 60, 243; and Austens, 62; and BD's marriage prospects, 63; and Henrietta Sykes, 64, 86-7; on Clara Bolton, 65; co-authors *A Year at Hartlebury*, 68; and Eyton, 88; and BD's marriage, 109; relations with Mary Anne, 161-6, 169-73, 219; and death of parents, 166-8; in Hastings, 168, 171; moves to Twickenham, 172; and brother James, 173-4; and BD's party leadership, 195; death, 242-3; and Annie Bassett, 285; and *Endymion*, 380

Don, Sir George, 34

Don Pacifico, 234

d'Orsay, Alfred, Count, 7; BD meets, 51; and Lady Blessington, 72-3, 75; life and background, 73-4; style, 74, 88; rescues BD

financially, 87; letter from BD, 89; and Henrietta Sykes, 90; friendship with BD, 91, 103, 218; in *Henrietta Temple*, 91; and BD's debts, 92, 105, 113, 120; coronation party, 101; and Mary Anne, 103-4; flight to Paris, 120; bust of Bentinck, 176; death 204-5, 218
d'Orsay, Harriet, 73
Drage, Dr, 257
Dreikaiserbund, 322, 335, 353
Drummond, Edward, 128
Dudley, Georgiana Elizabeth, Countess of, 386
Dufferin, Helen, Marchioness of (*née* Sheridan, *then* Mrs Price Blackwood), 60-64, 384
Duncombe, Tom, 119, 123, 142-3
Dunkellin, Ulick Canning de Burgh, Lord, 261
Du Pré, Caledon, 167
Durham, John George Lambton, 1st Earl of, 75-6, 79

Earle, Ralph Anstruther: friendship with BD, 218, 232, 238, 263; intrigues against Palmerston, 232-4; as BD's private secretary, 237; mission to Napoleon III, 238; and papal court, 254; and Liberal leadership, 260; political appointmentments, 262-3; breach with BD, 268-9; death, 269
East India Company, 235
Eastern question, 326, 335-9, 343-5; *see also* Russia; Turkey
Ecclesiastical Titles Bill (1851), 201, 208
Eden, Emily, 255
Edinburgh Review, 53, 272, 289
Edward, Prince of Wales (*later* King Edward VII): marriage, 249, 252; relations with BD, 250, 314, 318, 323-4, 366; BD proposes residence in Ireland, 282-3; and Mordaunt divorce, 292; typhoid, 292-3; and Lady Cardigan, 307; and Royal Titles Bill, 314, 330; social life, 315, 385; visit to India, 322-6; relations with Gladstone, 324; and Aylesford scandal, 331-2; and BD at Congress of Berlin, 347; at BD's funeral, 392
Egerton, Lord Francis, 101, 106
Egypt, 41-2
Eldon, John Scott, 1st Earl of, 14-15
'Elector', Shrewsbury, 119
Eliot, Lord (Edward Granville Eliot, *later* Earl of Saint Germans), 48, 83, 118
Eliot, George, 246
Elizabeth, Empress of Austria, 316
Ellenborough, Edward Law, 1st Earl of, 237
Elliot, Sir Henry, 326, 338, 340
Elliot, Mrs William, 20
Elmley, Henry Lygon, Viscount (*later* 4th Earl of Beauchamp), 218
Ely, Jane, Lady, 300, 362, 391
Employers and Workmen Bill (1875), 320
Endymion (BD): Smythe in, 121, 219, 381; on

foreign policy, 123; Sarah in, 243, anecdote on Derby, 245; Corry in, 263; aristocracy in, 288; writing, 315, 356, 378; published, 379, 389, described, 380-83; on social life, 385
England and France (BD), 54
Enquiry into ... the American Mining Companies, An (BD), 14
Esher, William Balliol Brett, Viscount, 200
Espinasse, Francis, 244
Eton College, 38, 135-6
Eugénie, Empress of France, 362
Evans, John, 98
Evans, John Viney (Mary Anne's brother), 94, 98, 100, 107
Evans, Thomas Mullett, 13, 33
Exeter, Brownlow Cecil, 3rd Marquess of, 194, 199, 293
Exmouth, Edward Pellew, 3rd Viscount, 120, 167, 191
Eyton, John, 88

Falcieri, Giovanni Battista ('Tita'), 38-9, 41, 59, 62, 168, 318-19
Fawcett, Henry, 333, 387
Fector, J. M. (Maidstone MP), 102
Feilding, Colonel, 275
Fenians, Fenianism, 275, 288
Ferrand, Walter Busfield, 128, 130-31, 138-40, 246
Ford, H.S., 120
Forester of Willey Park, John George Weld-Forester, 2nd Baron, 112
Forester, Rev. Orlando, 308
Fortescue, Chichester, 296
Francis, George Henry, 177-8
Franco-Prussian War, 291-2
Fraser's Magazine, 52, 59, 177
Fraser, Sir William, 134, 167; on BD's house, 175; on Stanley, 192; and BD's country house visits, 199; and Smythe's gift to BD, 219; and Earle, 269; on BD's popularity, 293-4; and BD in old age, 385-6
Fremantle, Charles, 286
Fremantle, Sir Thomas, 114
Frere, Sir Bartle, 324, 361-3
Friendly Societies Bill (1875), 321
Froude, J.A., 288

Gaettani, Dr, 42
Game Bill (1880), 377
Garibaldi, Giuseppe, 254
Gash, Norman, 155
George IV, King of England, 35
Germany, 322
Gibraltar, 34, 37
Gibson, Thomas Milner-, 236, 241
Gilbert and Sullivan, 356
Gladstone, Herbert, 303, 305

Gladstone, William Ewart: on Bulgarian
massacres, 40, 335-7; in Commons, 95; and
Peel, 138, 160, 210; resigns over Maynooth
Bill, 145; and Corn Laws, 148; supports
Jewish Disabilities Bills, 184-5, and Peel's
death, 199-200; and Protectionism, 200;
mutual mistrust of BD, 201; and Derby's 1851
administration, 201; on BD as Chancellor,
206, 211-12; proposed as alternative to BD,
210; parliamentary rivalry with BD, 212-13,
227, 229, 253, 258-61, 265, 269-71, 281-2,
290-92, 294, 301, 336, 355; as coalition
Chancellor, 213, 227; Derby seeks support of,
229; and Palmerston government, 230;
attacks Palmerston, 234; opposes 1858 Derby
government, 237; as Ionian Islands
Commissioner, 237-8; supports Italian cause,
240; in Palmerston's 1859 government, 241;
increasing radicalism, 255-6; Emily Eden on,
255; and party leadership, 257, 260-62; loses
Oxford seat, 257; and Reform, 259-61, 264-
5, 267-71, 294; excitability, 260-61, 265, 290;
Whig fear of, 267-8, 270; on Mary Anne's
illness, 276; as sole party leader, 280; on Irish
Church, 280; loses 1868 Election seat, 284;
1869 administration, 286, 290-91; and reform
of 'fallen women', 291; and foreign policy,
291, 293; and Queen, 292, 305, 364, 370-71,
377, 378; unpopularity, 292-3; defeated on
Irish Universities, 301; 1873 resignation and
resumption, 302-3; and budget surplus, 303,
359; and 1874 Election, 303-4; in opposition,
313-15; announces retirement from
leadership, 320; relations with Prince of
Wales, 324; opposes Suez Canal purchase,
329; BD describes 333; and BD's elevation to
Lords, 333-4; increasing vindictiveness to
BD, 336, 344-5, 354-5, 375; and Russo-
Turkish war, 341; and BD's imperialist views,
355, 357-8, 363-4, 369; campaigns against
BD's administration, 364-6, 369; and
Northcote, 363-4; 1880 Election victory, 368-
70, 374; premiership and legislation, 373,
375-7, 383; and Bradlaugh, 376; in
unfinished BD novel, 383; BD denounces,
386-8; and Ireland, 386; and BD's death,
391-2
Gladstone, Mrs W.E. (Catherine), 305
Glasgow, 302
Globe, The, 84, 209
Godwin, William, 50
Goethe, J.W. von, 28, 53, 382
Goldsmith, Miss (*later* Lady Lyndhurst), 90
Goldsmith, Lewis, 124
Gordon, Arthur, 337
Gordon, General Charles George, 363
Gordon, Sir Robert, 40
Gore, Catherine, 51

Gore, Charles, 47
Gorst, John, 294, 304, 374, 376
Gortchakov, Prince, 337, 339, 349-50, 352
Goschen, Mrs, 387
Gough, John, Jr., 112
Goulbourn, Henry, 212
Gower, Lord Ronald, 174, 247-8, 298, 300, 311,
371, 375, 384-5
Graham, Sir James: resignation, 78; fears social
revolution, 123; seeks BD's removal from
party, 133, 137; BD seeks aid for brother, 134,
173; and BD's anti-Peel campaign, 139, 145;
and fall of Peel, 160; on BD's indispensability,
200; BD criticises in budget speech, 212
Gramont, Ida, Duchesse de, 74, 124
Granby, Charles Cecil John Manners,
Marquess of (*later* 6th Duke of Rutland), 189-
90, 193-5
Granville, Granville George Leveson-Gower,
2nd Earl: in Palmerston government, 241; on
Gladstone's resignation, 255; and Gladstone's
Irish Church views, 280; and Gladstone's
views on royal family, 292; and Gladstone's
reluctance to resign, 304; opposes Suez Canal
purchase, 329; Queen's disapproval of, 330,
378; on Gladstone-BD dispute, 355; and
Afghanistan, 357-8; and national economy,
360; and Gladstone in opposition, 364-5, 368;
and Liberal premiership, 373; on BD in old
age, 387
Greece, 40
Greenwood, Frederick, 327
Gregory, Sir William, 37, 121, 174-5
Greville, Charles Fulke: on BD's politics, 79; on
Maidstone, 94; on BD's anti-Peel campaign,
145-6, 150-51, 153-5, 157; Bentinck quarrels
with, 149; on Peel and repeal of Corn Laws,
152-5, 158; on Conservative leadership, 189;
obituary of Bentinck, 191; on Stanley, 192-3,
215; on 1848 revolutionary petition, 196; on
protectionists, 198; on BD's life of Bentinck,
203; on BD's budgets, 207, 211; and Lennox,
217; and *The Press*, 226; and BD's frustrations
and intrigues, 233; and Palmerston's secret
treaty, 234; on Gladstone-BD conflict, 253;
on Gladstone, 255
Grey, Charles, 2nd Earl, 55-6, 77-8, 84
Grey, General Charles, 56-7, 80, 277, 284
Grey, George, 145
Grey, Henry George, 3rd Earl, 377
Grillion's club, 252
Gronow, Captain Rees Howell, 74
Grosvenor, Lord Richard, 392
Guest, Lady Charlotte (*née* Bertie), 63, 65,
340
Guest, Sir Josiah John, 63
Guizot, F.P.G., 149
Gull, Sir William, 275, 332, 342, 347

HMS Pinafore (Gilbert and Sullivan), 356
Haber, Baron de, 47-8, 54, 65, 87
Halifax, Charles Wood, 1st Viscount, 212, 235, 272
Hall, Peter, 25
Hall, S.C., 21
Halse, James, 86
Hamilton, Lord George, 311, 333-4, 338, 367, 369, 387-8
Hamilton, Princess Marie Amelie Elizabeth Caroline, Duchess of, 231
Hamilton, Edward, 392
Harcourt (Aylesbury Tory candidate), 91
Harcourt, Sir William, 289-9, 313, 315, 317, 325, 330, 333, 376
Hardinge, Sir Henry, 148
Hardwicke, Charles Philip Yorke, 5th Earl of, 332
Hart-Dyke, Sir William, 374, 388
Hartington, Spencer Compton Cavendish, Marquess of (*later* 8th Duke of Devonshire; 'Harty Tarty'): as Liberal Leader, 320-1; and Aylesford scandal, 332; relations with BD, 336; and Eastern question, 341; and Queen, 364; in opposition, 368; BD recommends as Prime Minister, 373
Hatfield House, 329
Haussez, Baron d', 54
Hayward, Abraham, 289
Heathcote, Sir William, 152
Helps, Arthur, 252
Henley, J.W., 202, 206
Henrietta Temple (BD), 62, 78, 87-8, 91
Henry, Prince (Hal), 339-40
Herald, The, 224
Herbert, Sidney, 144, 160, 209, 229-30
Herries, E.H., 193-5, 202, 206, 223
Hertford, Francis Charles Seymour-Conway, 3rd Marquess, 76, 135
Hicks-Beach, Sir Michael, 356, 361
High Wycombe (Buckinghamshire), 44, 54-8, 277
Hill, Marcus, 47
Hirsch, Baron, 269
Hobhouse, John Cam (*later* 1st Baron Broughton de Gyfford), 14, 79, 138-9, 145, 155-6, 178, 219-20
Hodgkinson, G., 270-71
Hodgson brothers, 126
Holland, Elizabeth, Lady, 62, 217
Hood, Thomas: 'Song of the Shirt', 117
Hope, Beresford, 127
Hope, Henry, 127, 131, 134, 161, 224
Horton, Wilmot, 17
Houghton, Richard Monckton Milnes, 1st Baron: and Young England, 131; on BD's anti-Peel campaign, 145, 149; loses confidence in Peel, 154; in Venice, 162; on

BD and Bentinck, 190; entertains BD, 220; BD describes, 245; on Gladstone and BD, 271; criticises *Lothair*, 289
Houlditch (creditor), 92, 168
Huffam (Wycombe political agent), 55
Hughenden: BD purchases, 167; style, 175-6, mortgages, 246-7; improvements, 247-8; passes to Coningsby, 286; church reconsecrated, 325
Hume (creditor), 168
Hume, Joseph, 56, 84, 133
Hunt, George Ward, 279, 293
Hyde Park Riots (1866), 264

Ignatiev, General, 326, 337-40
Ignatiev, Mme, 338-40
Ilchester, Mariana, 343, 358
Illustrted London News, 391
India Bill (1852), 223; (1858), 235, 237
Indian Mutiny (1857-8), 235
Inglis, Sir Robert, 138, 182
Ionian Islands, 237
Irish Arms Bill (1843), 132
Irish Coercion Bill (1834), 78; (1846), 156-8; (1881), 386-7
Irish Land Bill (1881), 386
Irish University Bill (1873), 301, 303
Irving, Sir Henry, 385
Irving Washington, 10
Isandhlwana, 360-61
Ismail Pasha, Khedive of Egypt, 327-8
Israeli, Isaac (great grandfather), 2
Italy, 27; liberation movement, 238-41, 254

Jamaica, 107
James, Henry (MP), 333
Jameson, D.D., 141
Jaraczewski, Miecislas, 324
Jaucourt, Comte de, 240
Jenner, Sir William, 274, 292, 296, 317-18, 342, 347, 388
Jerdan, William, 24
Jersey, Sarah Sophia, Viscountess, 99, 164
Jerusalem, 41, 180
Jews: emancipation, 60, 179, 182-9, 203; in *Tancred,* 134, 166, 179-82, 203
Jones, Thomas, 13, 169
Journal des Débats, 353
Jowett, Benjamin, 254

Kabul, 364; *see also* Afghanistan
Kandahar, 387
Karolyi, Countess, 350
Kebbel, T.E., 226, 240, 248
Keith-Falconer, Major Charles, 302, 304
Kenealy, Dr Edward, 224, 321
Kidd, Dr Joseph, 347, 352, 384, 387-90
Kinnaird, Douglas, 30-31
Knatchbull-Hugessen, Sir Edward, 129

Labouchere, Henry, 80, 366
Lamb, Lady Caroline, 38, 50, 91
Lamb, E.B., 247
Land League (Ireland), 367, 383, 387
Landon, Letitia Elizabeth (L.E.L.), 51, 99
Langtry, Lily, 342
Lansdowne, Henry Charles Keith Petty-Fitzmaurice, 5th Marquess of, 377
Lansdowne, Henry Thomas Petty-Fitzmaurice, 4th Marquess of, 235
Layard, Sir Henry Austen, 71, 340–41, 350, 352
Lefevre, Shaw, 115
Leggatt, Dr, 296, 298, 300, 347
Legh, John, 112
Leigh, Augusta, 10, 50, 173
Lencastre, Conde de, 306
Lennox, Lord Alexander, 217
Lennox, Lord Henry Charles: in 1852 government, 206, 215; and Catholic scheme, 208; on Stanley, 214; in relations with BD, 215–19; 239; marriage prospects, 217; on BD and *The Press*, 226; and Napoleon III, 231; and Earle, 232, 238; intrigues against Derby, 232–3; in 1858 government, 237; quarrel with BD, 238; on Gladstone's unpopularity, 260; and BD's hunting with Lady Bradford, 310; disgruntlement in the 1874 government, 312, 318; and BD's resignation honours, 372–3
Lennox, Lord William, 79
Leopold I, King of the Belgians, 142, 204, 206–7
Leopold, Prince, 392
Lesseps, Ferdinand de, 327
Letters of Runnymede (BD), 84–5, 226
Lewis, Wyndham, 94, 97–100
Liddell, George, 38
Liddell, Henry, 261
Life of Lord George Bentinck (BD), 172, 174, 191, 200, 203, 382
Lincoln, Henry Pelham Clinton, Earl of (*later* 5th Duke of Newcastle), 156, 160
Lindo family, 1
Lindo, Benjamin, 33
Literary Gazette, The, 23–4
Lockhart, John Gibson: BD negotiates with for Murray, 14, 16–20; and *Quarterly Review*, 18–19; hostility to BD, 21, 32, 52–3; on Lytton, 32, 52
Londonderry, Frances Anne, Marchioness of: BD meets, 85; BD confides in, 99–101, 228, 230, 233, 243, 245–6; reads *Sybil*, 164; and 1848 revolutions, 196; and Sarah's death, 242; and Mme Ignatiev, 339–40
Long, Colonel, 46
Longman's (publishers), 287, 290, 378–9, 389
Lonsdale, Augusta, Countess of, 76
Lorne, John Douglas Sutherland Campbell, Marquess of (*later* 9th Duke of Argyll), 292
Lothair (BD), 245, 275, 287–9

Loudoun, Edith Maude, Countess of, 297
Louis Napoleon, *see* Prince Imperial
Louis Philippe, King of France, 55, 124–7, 147, 203–5, 208, 244–5
Louise, Princess, 292, 366
Lovell, William, 120
Lowe, Robert (*later* 1st Viscount Sherbrooke), 260, 280, 329, 331, 364
Lowther, Jem, 266
Lucas, Samuel, 225–6
Ludwig, King of Bavaria, 109, 316
Lyell, Sir Charles, 246
Lygon, Henry, *see* Elmley, Henry Lygon, Viscount
Lyndhurst, John Singleton Copley, 1st Baron: Toryism, 55, 77, 81–2, 115; BD meets, 76; background and career, 77; and Henrietta Sykes, 77–8, 86–7, 90, 101; in 1834 Peel government, 79; aids and encourages BD, 81, 84–5, 88, 115; and Municipal Corporations Bill, 82; marriage, 90; *Venetia* dedicated to, 92; and Queen, 93; at coronation, 101; best man at BD's wedding, 109; on BD out of office, 214
Lyster, Lady Charlotte, 371
Lyttelton, George William, 4th Baron, 121, 136
Lyttelton, Lucy, 241
Lytton, Bulwer (i.e. Edward George Earle Lytton Bulwer, 1st Baron); and *The Young Duke*, 32; letters from BD in East, 34, 40; and *Athenaeum*, 46; relations with BD, 50, 72, 91, 121, 218; marriage, 50–51, 72; aids BD in political aims, 55, 57; on BD and Henrietta Sykes, 86, 90; separation from Rosina, 91; Mary Anne and, 104, 121; writes for *The Press*, 225; as Colonial Secretary, 236–7; and Gladstone, 237; and Dickens, 245; *England and the English*, 52; *Pelham*, 32
Lytton, Edward Robert Bulwer, 1st Earl of, 327, 338, 356–8, 363–4, 374
Lytton, Rosina Lady (Bulwer Lytton's wife), 50–51, 72, 91; *Very Successful*, 51

Macaulay, Henry, 21
Macaulay, Thomas Babington, Lord, 21
McCarthy, C.J., 145, 154
Mackarness, John Fielder, Bishop of Oxford, 325
MacKnight, T., 227
Maclise, Daniel, 30, 58, 89–90
Macready, William Charles, 106
Maginn, William, 20–21, 52, 59
Maidstone, 90, 94
Majuba Hill, 388
Malmesbury, James Howard Harris, 3rd Earl of: on BD's candidacy for party leadership, 190–91, 204; on Derby as sportsman, 192; on Herries and Henley, 202; as Foreign

Secretary, 206; on BD's ambitions, 222; and Derby's attitude to BD, 223, 230; on *The Press*, 225; and Crimean War, 229; and Napoleon III, 231, 239; Lennox intrigues against, 233; and Palmerston's 'secret treaty', 234; and 1859 defeat, 240; as Lord Privy Seal, 262; and BD's leadership, 279; in 1874 Cabinet, 312; and Lady Paget, 316

Malt Tax, 376-7

Malta, 37-8

Manchester: BD's 1872 speech, 294-6, 322

Manchester Athenaeum, 140

Manchester, Louise, Duchess of, 249, 320, 332-40, 356, 386

Mann, Sir Horace, 3

Manners, Lord John, friendship with BD, 121-2, 214, 218, 298; and Young England, 121, 126-7, 129, 131, 140-41; in *Coningsby*, 134, 141; on working hours, 138; breaks with BD, 141-2, 146; and Peel's resignation, 147; and Isaac D'Israeli's death, 168; and Jewish emancipation, 182, 189; and BD's leadership, 195-7, 293; on BD's biography of Bentinck, 203; in 1852 government, 206; marriages, 218; in 1858 government, 237; in 1866 government, 262; and BD's succession, 279; and Gladstone's reorganized administration, 302-3; in 1874 Cabinet, 312; offered Viceroyalty of India, 326; GCB, 372; and BD's views on working class, 385

Manning, Henry Edward, Cardinal, 289

Manvers, Charles Herbert Pierrepont, 2nd Earl, 190

Maples, Frederick, 11-12

March, Earl of, *see* Richmond, Charles Henry Gordon-Lennox, 6th Duke of

Marlay, Catherine, 218

Marlborough, John Winston Spencer Churchill, 7th Duke of, 279, 332, 368

Marlborough, Duchess of, 249, 332

Martin, Theodore, 330

Marylebone, *see* St Marylebone

Mash, Thomas, 56, 87-8

Maurice (Byron's boatman), 28

Mayne, Sir Richard, 264, 275

Maynooth Bill, (1845), 140, 145-6

Mayo, Richard Southwell Bourne, 6th Earl of, 279

Melbourne, William Lamb, 2nd Viscount: and BD's political ambitions, 75; 1834 administration, 78, 80-81; BD attacks, 82, 84; depends on O'Connell, 96, 107; at coronation, 101; resigns, 107, 114; and Corn Laws, 112, 149

Meredith, Ellen, 49-50, 63-4, 105

Meredith, Georgina, 49-50

Meredith, William: travels with BD, 11, 34-5, 37-9, 41-2, 348; and Sarah, 11, 34, 42-3, 45;

and *Star Chamber*, 25; and BD's nervous illness, 29; and BD's dress, 32; death, 42-3, 161

Merimée, Prosper, 231

Merivale, John Herman, 5

Messer, Robert, 13, 15, 33, 169

Metropolitan Water Company, 367

Metternich, Clemens W.N. Lothar, Prince von, 197-8, 254, 311, 362, 381

Middleton, J.G., 248, 300

Miles, Sir William, 144, 152-3, 195, 252

Milman, Henry Hart, 52

Mistletoe (yacht), 325

Mitchel, John, 321

Montagu, Andrew, 246-7

Montagu, Oliver, 359

Montrose, Caroline Agness, Duchess of, 308

Monypenny, W.F., 105, 115; and Buckle, G.E., 216, 238, 269

Moore, Thomas, 50

Mordaunt divorce case (1870), 292

Morgan, Sydney, Lady, 50-51

Morley, John Viscount, 295

Morning Chronicle, 133, 193

Morning Herald, 108, 189-90

Morning Post, 81

Municipal Corporations Bill (1835), 81

Münster, Count, 349

Murray, Anne (*née* Elliot, Mrs John II), 10

Murray, John I, 10

Murray, John II; social circle, 10; relations with BD, 14, 21, 25, 232, 244, 269; and BD's mining speculations, 15-16; newspaper project (*Representative*), 16-22, 25; and editorship of *Quarterley Review*, 18-19; in *Vivian Grey*, 22-3, 25; BD repays Powles' debt to, 28; and *The Young Duke*, 32; and *Contarini Fleming*, 53-4; publishes *England and France*, 54-5

Murray, Sophia (Mrs John II), 22

Nana Sahib, 235

Napoleon III, Emperor of the French, 226, 231-2, 236-40, 291, 362, 380-81

Nash (political agent), 57

Nasser, Colonel Gamal Abdel, 329

National Association for the Protection of British Industry and Capital, 198

National Club, London, 194

National Gallery, London, 315

National Petition of the Chartist Convention, 119

Neil, Captain, 102, 106

Neville, Lady Dororothy, 178-9, 196, 275, 279, 294, 307, 334

New Monthly Magazine, 23, 52

Newcastle, Henry Pelham Clinton, 4th Duke of, 192, 210, 241

Newcastle, Henry Pelham Clinton, 5th Duke of, *see* Lincoln, H.P. Clinton, Earl of
Newdegate, Charles, 153, 189, 226
Newman, John Henry, Cardinal, 287
Newport, Ida, Lady, 311
Noel, Gerrard, 293
Normanby, Constantine Henry Phipps, 1st Marquess of, 204
Norris, 'Daddy', 167, 248
Northbrook, Thomas, George Baring, 1st Earl of, 326
Northcote, Sir Stafford: unimpressed by BD's oratory, 228; letter from BD on Gladstone and Stanley, 260; as President of Board of Trade, 262, 264; and BD's leadership, 293; and 1874 Election, 303; as Chancellor in 1874 government, 312–13; and Shipping Bill, 321; and Suez Canal, 328; in Commons, 334; and Russo-Turkish war, 341; financial policy, 363; and Parnell's obstructionism, 367; and dissolution, 368; GCB, 372; and party organization, 374; leadership, 376
Northumberland, Algernon Percy, 4th Duke of, 224, 252
Northumberland, Eleanor, Duchess of, 305, 338, 358
Norton, Caroline, (*née* Sheridan), 51, 60–61, 75, 84
Norton, George, 60
Novikov, Olga, 338
Nugent, George Nugent Grenville, 1st Baron, 57

O'Brien, Augustus Stafford, 131, 152–3, 195
O'Brien, William Smith, 157
O'Connell, Daniel: at Wycombe, 55, 84; defeats Grey, 78; BD attacks, 80–82, 84; in Commons, 96; Melbourne's dependence on, 96, 107; and repeal of Reform Acts, 128; Peel subdues, 137
O'Connell, Morgan, 81
Orford, Earl, 311
Orsini, Felice, 236
Osborne, Bernal, 74, 308, 324, 334
Osman Pasha, 342–3
Oxford Movement, 122, 131, 146
Oxford, Bishop of, *see* Mackarness, J.F.; Wilberforce, S.

Paget, Lord Alfred, 324
Paget, Sir Augustus and Walburga, Lady, 316
Paine, Thomas, 256
Pakington, Sir John (*later* 1st Baron Hampton), 206, 223, 262, 293
Palmerston, Emily Mary, Viscountess, 164, 235–6, 301, 380
Palmerston, Henry John Temple, 3rd Viscount: BD lampoons, 84; in Commons, 95; BD's attacks on, 118, 123, 129; supports Young England, 133; and BD's anti-Peel campaign, 145, 147; and Corn Laws, 156; BD intrigues for, 196, 210, 222, 228–9, 239; as champion of Establishment, 197; approves of Louis Napoleon's *coup*, 204 dismissed, 204; and Peelites' attack on BD, 210; Lennox and, 217, 232–3; and Crimean War, 225, 233; 1855 government, 230; and Napoleon III, 231, 236, 239–40; BD campaigns against, 233–4; foreign interventions, 234–5; 1857 Election victory, 235; fall, 235–6; in opposition, 237; 1859 government, 241; and Queen, 251; and paper duties, 253; Italian policy, 254; and Gladstone, 255–6, unpopularity in north, 256; health, 257; on Gladstone, 257; death, 258–9; influence on BD, 363; in *Endymion*, 380–81
Paper Duties Bill (1860), 253
Paris Commune, (1871), 292
Parkes, Joseph, 81
Parnell, Charles Stewart, 364, 367
Parry, Sir Love, 113
Peel, Jonathan, 154, 262, 265–6
Peel, Sir Robert: BD meets, 48; Toryism, 55, 81; 1834 administration, 79; BD flatters, 85; BD's 1846 speech attacking, 90; in Commons, 95, 112, 129, 152; and BD's maiden speech, 97; 1839 administration and resignation, 107–8; and class interests, 112; 1841 victory, 114–15; relations with BD, 115–16, 118–19, 132, 134, 142, 155, 200; and social unrest, 117, 128–9; and relations with France, 125; party opposition to, 129, 157–8; and Young England, 131; BD's campaign against, 132, 137–40, 142–6, 148–54, 157, 160, 209; in *Coningsby*, 135; supports repeal of Corn Laws, 144, 147–59, 209; 1845 resignation and reinstatement, 147; 1846 resignation, 158–9; and Jewish emancipation, 179; and BD's candidacy for leadership, 194; and party organization, 195; as leader, 196–7; death, 199–200; Cecil invokes, 253; Emily Eden on, 255, Queen on, 305; omitted from *Endymion*, 382
Pell, Mr, 294
Pembroke, George Robert Charles Herbert, 13th Earl of, 311
Persigny, Duc de, 240
Pery, Edward, 38
Phillips, Samuel, 189–90, 192–5, 215, 227
Piedmont, 238–41
Pigott, Sir Digby, 342
Pitt, William, 96, 213, 363
Pius IX, Pope, 254
Plimsoll, Samuel, 321
Ponsonby, Sir Frederick and Lady, 38
Ponsonby, Sir Henry, 283, 302, 305, 314, 318, 330, 344–5, 364, 370, 378
Ponsonby, John Ponsonby, 1st Viscount, 154

Poor Law (1834), 108, 111, 117, 128, 130
Poor Law Commissioners, 119
Popanilla, see *Voyage of Captain Popanilla, The*
Portland, William John Cavendish Bentinck-Scott, 5th Duke of (*formerly* Marquess of Titchfield), 192, 246
Potticary, Rev. John, 7
Powis, Edward James Herbert, 8th Earl of, 326
Powles, J.D., 13-16, 21, 28, 54
Press, The, 217, 224-6, 229
Prevention of Crime Act (Ireland), 367
Prince Imperial (Louis Napoleon), 362
Prussia, 291
Public Works Loan Commissioners, 321
Public Worship Regulations Bill (1874), 313-14
Pusey, Edward Bouverie, 122
Pyne, William, 87-8, 91-2, 113, 119, 162

Quain, Dr Richard, 388, 390
Quaritch, Bernard, 325
Quarterly Review: Murray publishes, 10, 16; Lockhart and, 18-19; and *Representative*, 21; and *Vivian Grey*, 25; attacks BD, 52; Cecil attacks BD in, 253-4, 290; and BD's Reform Bill, 272; on *Lothair*, 289
Quin, Dr Frederic Hervey Foster, 324

Radowitz, H. von, 349
Redding, Cyrus, 23
Redesdale, John Thomas Freeman-Mitford, 1st Earl of, 362
Redistribution Bill (1867), 271
Reform Bill (1832), 44-5, 259; (1854), 228-9; (1859), 54-6, 80, 84, 111; (1859), 239, 253, 265; (1867), 174, 259, 265-72, 290, 294
Reform League, 264
Reform Union, 270
Reminiscences (BD), 227, 245, 255, 289
Representative, The, 21-3, 25, 52, 224
Reschid Pasha, 39-40
Revolution of 1848, 196-7
Revolutionary Epick (BD), 70-72, 102, 245
Richmond, Charles Gordon Lennox, 5th Duke of, 149, 194, 208
Richmond, Charles Henry Gordon Lennox, 6th Duke of, (*formerly* Earl of March), 238, 279, 290, 303, 312
Rickett, Louisa, 33
Ridley, Sir Matthew White, 268
Roberts, Field-Marshal Frederick Sleigh, 1st Earl, 357, 364
Roebuck, John Arthur, 229
Rogers, Samuel, 5, 51-3
Roper, Miss (school), 7
Rose, Sir Philip: on Clara Bolton, 47; and BD's finances, 167, 219-20, 246-7; and *The Press*, 226; on Sarah, 243; Earle complains to, 268; and BD's leadership, 278; and Mary Anne's

death, 299-300; and BD in Glasgow, 302; and BD's death and funeral, 388-90, 392
Rose, William Stewart, 17, 52
Rosebery, Archibald John Primrose, 4th Earl of, 164, 175, 219
Rosebery, Archibald Philip Primrose, 5th Earl of, 155, 370
Rosebery, Hannah Meyer, Countess of (*née* Rothschild), 386
Ross, Sir William Charles, 248
Rothschild family: rise, 2; and Mary Anne, 98; and Jewish emancipation, 185; friendship with BD, 186-8, 386; European intelligence, 275; and BD's illness, 318; and Suez Canal, 327-8
Rothschild, Alfred de, 188, 386
Rothschild, Alice de, 188
Rothschild, Sir Anthony de, 187-8, 217, 386
Rothschild, Constance de, 175, 186, 300, 386
Rothschild, Evelina de, 165
Rothschild, Ferdinand James de, 188
Rothschild, Hannah Meyer, see Rosebery, Hannah Meyer, Countess of
Rothschild, Leopold de, 188, 386
Rothschild, Lady de (*née* Montefiore), 187
Rothschild, Lionel de, Baron, 138, 182, 185-7, 246-7, 364, 381
Rothschild, Baroness Lionel de, 165-6, 170, 185-6, 327-8
Rothschild, Meyer Amschel de, 169-70, 186-8, 290
Rothschild, Baroness Meyer de, 275
Rothschild, Nathaniel de, 188, 297, 392
Routledge (publishers), 278
Rowton House, 372
Rowton, 1st Baron, *see* Corry, Montague Lowry
Royal Bounty and Special Service Fund, 286
Royal Titles Bill (1875), 314, 330-31
Runnymede, Letters of, see *Letters of Runnymede*
Russell, Sir George, 369
Russell, Lord John (*later* 1st Earl): and Irish Church revenues, 78; in Commons, 95; BD chides, 111; supports free trade, 112; loses seat, 114; at Rothschild party, 138-9; and BD's anti-Peel speeches, 145, 154; and Peel's resignation, 147; and Corn Laws, 148, 150, 154, 156; opposes Irish Coercion, 157; premiership, 158; and Jewish Disabilities Bill, 182, 185; 1848 administration, 190; party opposition to, 196; reformism, 197; 1851 resignation, 201; dismisses Palmerston, 204; and Catholic vote, 208; in opposition, 208, 237, 239; *The Press* on, 225; Reform Bill, 228-9; in 1859 government, 241; and Tory attacks on BD's leadership, 253; succeeds Palmerston, 259; resignation, 280
Russell, Lord Odo (1st Baron Ampthill), 350
Russell, William Howard, 229

Index

Russia: and Crimean War, 229; and Black Sea, 291; alliance with Austria and Germany, 322; and Eastern question, 326, 337-40, 346; war with Turkey, 340-45; at Berlin Congress, 349-52, 354-5; mission to Kabul, 356; and 'Great Game' in Central Asia, 356-8
Rutland, John Henry Manners, 5th Duke of, 140, 199

St Marylebone, 58, 61
Sale of Food and Drugs Bill (1875), 321
Salisbury, Georgina Charlotte, Marchioness of, 338
Salisbury, Mary Catherine, Marchioness of, 164, 260, 279
Salisbury, Robert Arthur Talbot Gascoyne-Cecil, 3rd Marquess of (Lord Robert Cecil; then Viscount Cranbourne): attacks BD, 253-4, 272, 280-81, 290; as Secretary of State for India, 262; opposes Reform, 265-6, 272; resignation, 266; on BD and Queen, 281; on Gladstone and Mrs Thistlethwaite, 291; in BD's 1874 Cabinet, 312; opposes Public Worship Bill, 313; and succession to BD, 317; and Prince of Wales's India visit, 323; and Eastern question, 326, 340; relations with BD, 329, 345, 373; at Constantinople peace conference, 338; and Russo-Turkish war, 340, 343-4; as Foreign Secretary, 346; at Berlin Congress, 347-53; Garter, 354; acclaimed, 356; on national economy, 356; and 1880 Election, 369-70; and BD's resignation, 373; declines party leadership, 384
Salmon, Thomas, 64
San Stefano, Treaty of (1877), 345-6
Sand, George, 246
Sandford, Francis Richard John, 1st Baron, 281, 291
Sandon, Dudley Ryder, Viscount (later 2nd Earl of Harrowby), 133, 356
Saqui, Moses, 7
Scott, John, 223
Scott, Sir Walter, 14, 16-19
Scrope, William, 107, 109
Serbo-Turkish War, 337
Seymour, Georgiana, Lady, see Somerset, Georgiana, Duchess of
Shaftesbury Park (Lambeth), 321
Shaftesbury, Anthony Ashley Cooper, 7th Earl of (styled Lord Ashley until 1851), 117, 119; on Peel's unpopularity, 131-2; Ten Hour Amendment, 138, 140, 159; and BD's anti-Peel campaign, 148-9; on Peel and repeal of Corn Laws, 156; and Peel's defeat, 158-9; opposes Jewish Disabilities Bill, 183; on BD as Chancellor, 206; on Palmerston's election victory, 235; and Indian Mutiny, 235; and

Gladstone, 257; and social reform, 320; and Bulgarian atrocities, 336
Sheil, Richard Lalor, 97
Shelley, Percy Byssche, 91-3
Sher Ali, Emir of Afghanistan, 357-8, 364
Sheridan sisters, see Dufferin, Helen, Marchioness of; Norton, Caroline; Somerset, Georgiana, Duchess of
Sheridan, Mrs Caroline H., 60-61; Carwell, 60
Shipping Bill (1875), 321
Shiprut, Esther (great grandmother), 4
Short Time Committee, 117, 159
Shrewsbury, 112-14
Shropshire Conservative, 113-14
Shuvalov, Count, 339-42, 344, 346, 349, 351
Sibthorpe, Colonel Charles de Laet Waldo, 138, 151
Sidney, Sir Philip, 252
Smith, Adam, 111
Smith, Paul, 374
Smith, Robert, 55, 57, 80
Smith, Rev. Sydney, 45
Smith, W.H., 356, 375
Smythe, George Sydney (later 7th Viscount Strangford): friendship with BD, 119, 214, 218-19; and Young England, 121-2, 126-7, 129, 131, 140; in BD's novels, 121, 134, 137, 180, 219, 245, 289, 381; opposes Peel's leadership, 132-3; break with BD, 142, 146; on BD's marriage, 161, 174; and BD's 'infidelity', 170; on BD and Lennox, 216-17; death, 218-19; and industrial England, 246
Somerset, Georgiana, Duchess of (née Sheridan; then Lady Seymour), 60, 170
South Africa, 360-61, 385, 388
Southey, Robert, 4, 30
Spain, 35-7
Spectator, 260
Spencer, John Poyntz Spencer, 5th Earl, 269
Standard, The, 152, 224
Stanley, Edward George, see Derby, Edward George Stanley, 14th Earl of
Stanley, Edward Henry, see Derby, Edward Henry Stanley, 15th Earl of
Stanley, Emily, 245
Stanley, Frederick, 333, 346, 356
Stanley, Henry, 45-6, 75, 186
Stanton, General, 327
Stapleton, (Mary Anne's suitor), 102
Star Chamber, The, 25
Stead, W.T., 336
Stone, Lowndes, 172
Strangford, Percy Clinton Sydney Smythe, 6th Viscount, 119, 140
Strangford, 7th Viscount, see Smythe, George Sydney
Suez Canal: share purchase, 187, 327-9
Sugar Duties, 138

Sutherland, George Granville William Leveson-Gower, 3rd Duke of, 323-4
Swain, Stevens, Maples, Pearse and Hunt (solicitors), 11, 13-14
Sybil (BD), 93, 134, 136, 141, 146, 164, 246
Sykes, Christopher, 324
Sykes, Sir Francis, 64-72, 78, 86-8, 90
Sykes, Henrietta, Lady, affair with BD, 64-72, 77-8, 101, 310, 340; and Lyndhurst, 77, 80, 84, 86-7, 101; extravagance, 77-8, 86; BD breaks with, 86-90; affair with Maclise, 88-90; death, 90; in *Venetia*, 93

Tait, Archibald Campbell, Archbishop of Canterbury, 313, 382
Tamworth Manifesto (1835), 81, 135, 196
Tancred (BD): Jerusalem in, 41, 180; on debts, 88; Smythe in, 121; themes, 134, 179-81; on race and Jews, 134, 166, 179-80, 186, 203, 220, 237; writing, 166; on private reserve, 179; reception, 181; Sarah in 243; publication, 245
Tankerville, Charles Bennet, 6th Earl of, 384
Tankerville, Olivia, Countess of, 74, 77
Taunton (Somerset), 80
Tavistock, Lady, 76
Tay Bridge disaster (1879), 366
Taylor, A.J.P., 322
'Tea-Room Revolt', 268
Ten Hour Amendment, 138, 140
Tennyson, Alfred, Lord, 319
Thackeray, William Makepeace, 52, 53, 138, 182, 381
Thiers, Louis Adolphe, 124, 209
Thistlethwaite, Mrs, 291, 338
Thompson, Colonel Perronet, 94
Times, The: BD attacks Whigs in, 84; BD's letter on Austin, 102-3; BD's 'Laelius' letters to Queen, 108; on 1841 Conservative victory, 114; BD's 'Psittacus' letters on Peel, 115; ownership, 130; supports Young England, 130-31, 133; and BD's anti-Peel campaign, 145; on *Tancred*, 181-2, 187; on BD and Jewish emancipation, 185, 187; defends BD's Wellington eulogy, 209; on Gladstone-BD budget debate, 213; supports Aberdeen coalition, 224; and *The Press*, 225; Phillips attacks BD in, 227; on BD and Gladstone, 227-8; on Crimean War, 229; defends BD against party criticism, 253; opposes Gladstone, 257; on Mary Anne's death, 300; and Gladstone's 1874 Election manifesto, 303; criticises BD's parliamentary competence, 321; on Royal Titles Bill, 330
Titchfield, William John Cavendish, Bentinck-Scott, Marquess of, *see* Portland, W.J.C. Bentinck Scott, 5th Duke of
Tragedy of Count Alarcos, The (BD), 102, 104, 106

Trevor, Olivia, (*née* Basevi), 62, 285
Trollope, Anthony, 289
Trotter, Margaret, 49-50
Turkey, Turks: BD's admiration for, 39-40, 55, 337; and Eastern question, 326, 335-8, 340; war with Russia, 340-45; and Congress of Berlin, 350-52, 354
Turner, Sharon, 7, 25, 29

Ulundi, 362
Utilitarianism, 83

Venetia (BD), 88, 91-3
Victoria, Queen: accession, 93; relations with BD, 95, 201, 214, 243, 249-51, 263, 274, 278-9, 281-3, 292, 305, 313-14, 316-17, 330, 356, 368, 371, 378; coronation, 101; and 'Bedchamber Crisis', 107-8; BD's *Times* letter to, 108; BD introduced to, 141; hostility to Protectionism, 210; and Palmerston, 204; on Derby's 1852 government, 206-7; on BD as Chancellor, 207; and Albert's death, 249, 251-2; and John Brown, 249, 274, 283; personal interview with BD, 250-51; unpopularity, 274, 292; and BD's succession to Derby, 278-9, 316; travels abroad, 283; household and home life, 283; and Gladstone, 292, 305, 364, 370-71; illness, 292; and Mary Anne's death, 300; and 1874 Conservative victory, 305; supports Public Worship Bill, 313-14; and BD's ill-health, 318; and Prince of Wales's India visit, 322-4; and Royal Yacht accident, 325; and Suez Canal, 327-9; and Royal Titles Bill, 330; on Bulgarian atrocities, 335; anti-Russian views, 338-41, 343; proclaimed Empress of India, 338; and Russo-Turkish war, 340-42; and Derby's resignation, 346; and Congress of Berlin, 347-8, 350-54; and Zulu War, 361-3; imperialism, 363; policy warning to Liberals, 374, and 1880 Liberal victory, 370; ennobles Corry, 372; and Gladstone as Prime Minister, 373, 377-8; and dying BD, 388; and BD's death and funeral, 391-2; *Leaves from a Journal in the Highlands*, 282
Vigny, Alfred de, 244
Villarcal family, 3
Villiers, Charles Pelham, 117, 209-10, 241
Villiers, Clementina, 233
Vindication of the English Constitution, A (BD), 82-4, 134, 197
Viney, Eleanor, *see* Yate, Eleanor
Vitzthum, Eckstaedt von, Count, 227, 236, 240, 249
Vivian Grey (BD), 4, 6, 8, 13, 22-5, 31, 53, 290; part 2: 28
Voyage of Captain Popanilla, The (BD), 29-30, 83, 255, 322

Waddington, Georges, 350
Wakley, Thomas, 112
Waldegrave, Frances Elizabeth Anne, Countess of, 296
Wales, Prince of, *see* Edward, Prince of Wales
Walewski, Count, 204, 234
Waller, Charles, 120
Wallpole, Spencer, 206, 262, 270
Walter, Catherine, 131
Walter, John II, 127, 130-31, 133
Ward, Robert, Plumer, 30, 63; *Tremaine*, 22-4
Ward, Thomas, 120
Warren, Samuel, 71
Washington Treaty, 129
Welch, Captain (of Royal Yacht), 325
Wellesley, Colonel, 341, 352
Wellington, Arthur Wellesley, 1st Duke of, 79, 107, 147, 152, 202, 206, 208-9
Werner, Anton Alexander von, 349
Westmacott, Charles Molloy, 52, 69
Westminster, Hugh Lupus Grosvenor, 1st Duke of, 336
Whigs and Whiggism (BD), 85
White, William, 256, 270-71
Wilberforce, Samuel, Bishop of Oxford, 192, 255, 271, 289
Wilhelm II, Kaiser, 329
Wilkinson, Sir Gardner, 41
William IV, King of Great Britain, 78, 93
Willis, N.P., 73, 75, 178
Wilson, John, 17

Winchester College, 8
Wiseman, Nicholas Patrick Stephen, Cardinal, 254
Wolff, Harry Drummond, 376
Wolseley, Field-Marshal Sir Garnet (*later* Viscount), 36
Wood, Charles, *see* Halifax, Charles Wood, 1st Viscount
Wright, William, 17-18, 141
Württemberg, Duke of, 73
Wycombe, *see* High Wycombe

Yakub Khan, Emir of Afghanistan, 364
Yardley, William, 119
Yate, Eleanor (*formerly* Viney; Mary Anne's mother), 98, 107
Yate, Thomas, 98
Year at Hartlebury, A (BD and Sarah), 68, 167
Young Duke, The (BD), 31, 52-3, 252
Young England: formation, 118-19; 121; composition, 121; BD and, 122-4, 126-7, 163-4; publicity, 130; opposition to Peel, 131-4, 137, 142, 159-60; in *Coningsby*, 134-5, 137-8, 141, 160; break-up, 140-41, 146; and *Sybil*, 146; in *Endymion*, 381
Young, G.F., 198
Young, John, 156

Zionism, 60, 186, 224
Zulu War, 360-64